22만 6천 ...명의 선택

김영편입
영어

독해

워크북 **2** 단계

김앤북
KIM&BOOK

22만 6천 편입합격생의 선택

김영편입 영어
독해
워크북 2단계

PREFACE

당신이 탑을 높이 쌓고 있다고 상상해 보시길 바랍니다. 무턱대고 탑을 쌓다보면 탑은 얼마 안 되어 금방 무너져 버릴 것입니다. "무엇이 잘못되었을까요?" 탑을 받치는 아랫부분이 넓고 튼튼했어야 했는데, 그러지 못해서 탑을 위로 높이 쌓아 올릴 수 없었던 것입니다.

지금 이 책을 보는 편입 수험생의 경우도 마찬가지입니다. 목표는 저 위에 있어서 실력을 쌓으려고 하는데, 자신의 실력이 어느 정도인지, 내가 무엇을 잘하고 무엇을 못하는지 알지 못한 채 무턱대고 책상에 앉아 공부만 한다면, 우리가 상상해봤던 탑처럼, 금방 무너져 버려 중도하차해 버리고 싶은 마음이 들 수도 있습니다.

그래서 공부는 탑을 쌓는 마음으로 해야 합니다. 탑을 쌓을 때처럼 기초 실력이 탄탄하다면, 그 실력을 바탕으로 더 높이 목표에 도달할 수 있을 것입니다.

바로 이것이 "워크북 2단계"가 나오게 된 이유입니다. "기출 2단계"에서 어려운 기출문제를 풀면서 고급 문제를 내 것으로 소화했다면, "워크북 2단계"에서는 이미 학습한 기출문제의 출제 포인트를 기출문제를 토대로 출제한 예상문제로 다시 한 번 숙지하고 반복학습을 해서 실력을 한층 더 강화하는 데 목표를 두었습니다.

"김영편입 워크북 시리즈"는 "김영편입 기출 시리즈"와 동일한 구성으로 단계별 학습이 가능하도록 만든 책입니다. 따라서 "기출 2단계"를 풀고 나서 "기출문제 해설집"으로 바로 넘어가도 좋지만, "기출문제 해설집"으로 가기에는 실력이 아직 부족하다면, "기출 2단계"와 동일한 난이도의 "워크북 2단계"로 실력을 보강한 다음 "기출문제 해설집"을 학습하시기 바랍니다.

"워크북 2단계"는 편입시험의 대표 유형인 문법, 논리, 독해의 3종으로 구성되어 있습니다. 문법과 논리의 경우, 기출 1단계와 워크북 1단계에서 핵심 이론을 학습하고 이론을 문제에 적용하는 연습을 했다면, 워크북 2단계에서는 기출 2단계와 마찬가지로 다양한 유형의 문제를 학습하여 응용력을 심화시킬 수 있도록 했습니다. 그리고 독해의 경우, 기출 1단계와 워크북 1단계에서 유형별 학습을 하는 데 초점을 맞췄다면, 워크북 2단계에서는 기출 2단계와 마찬가지로 분야별 학습을 하는 데 중점을 두어 다양한 주제의 지문으로 실전 문제풀이 능력을 향상시킬 수 있도록 구성했습니다.

문제는 많이 풀수록 나의 실력이 됩니다. '스스로 학습할 수 있도록 제작된 책'이라는 워크북(workbook)의 사전적 의미처럼, "워크북 2단계"를 통해 어떤 어려운 문제라도 자신 있게 풀어낼 수 있는 능력을 만들 수 있기를 기원합니다.

김영편입 컨텐츠평가연구소

HOW TO STUDY

출제자의 관점으로 문제를 바라보자!

한번쯤은 출제자의 입장이 되어 볼 필요가 있습니다. '이 문제에서는 무엇을 물어볼까?', '여기쯤에 함정을 파놓으면 어떨까?' 이렇게 출제자의 관점에서 문제를 바라보면, 모든 문제가 완전히 새롭게 보일 수 있습니다.

문제의 난이도를 몸으로 익혀보자!

강물의 깊이를 알면 더 빠르고 안전하게 건널 수 있듯이, 문제의 난이도가 어느 정도인지 파악하게 되면, 문제를 더 노련하게 접근해 풀 수 있습니다. 그리고 난이도를 몸으로 익힐 수 있는 지름길은 없습니다. 다양한 난이도의 문제를 가능한 많이 풀어보는 것이 유일한 방법입니다.

제한시간을 설정하자!

실전에 대비할 수 있는 가장 좋은 방법은 실전과 똑같은 환경에서 훈련하는 것입니다. 문제를 풀 때는 반드시 제한시간을 설정하여 학습하시길 바랍니다. 실전에서와 같은 압박감과 긴장감을 조성하기에 가장 좋은 방법입니다.

오답에서 배우자!

편입시험은 정답만 기억하면 되는 OX 퀴즈가 아닙니다. 문제를 풀고 난 후엔 맞힌 문제보다 틀린 문제에 주목해야 합니다. 어째서 정답을 맞히지 못했는지 일련의 사고 과정을 면밀히 되짚어봐야만 틀린 문제를 다시 틀리지 않을 수 있습니다.

문법, 논리, 독해는 원래 한 몸이다!

본 시리즈는 문법, 논리, 독해라는 세 가지 영역을 나눠서 각각을 한 권의 책으로 구성했지만, 영역 구분에 지나치게 신경 쓰며 학습하는 것은 좋지 않습니다. 오히려 독해문제에서 중요 어휘와 문법구문을 정리하는 방식처럼 서로 영역을 통합해 학습하게 되면 더 큰 시너지를 일으킬 수 있습니다.

실전 문제 TEST

○ 시험에 자주 출제되는 13가지 분야로 구성했으며, 최신 기출문제를 토대로 출제된 총 200개의 중·장문 독해 지문 200개를 수록하였습니다.

○ 출제 빈도에 따라 각 분야별 지문수를 다르게 구성하여, 출제 가능성이 높은 분야를 집중적으로 학습하고 배경지식을 쌓을 수 있게 했습니다.

정답과 해설 ANSWERS & TRANSLATION

○ 각 문제에 대한 유형을 표시하여 『김영편입 영어 독해 워크북 1단계』에서 익힌 내용을 중·장문 지문에서 다시 한 번 확인하고 심화 학습을 할 수 있도록 했습니다.

○ 각 지문을 통해 분야별로 익힐 수 있는 필수 어휘를 꼼꼼히 정리하였으며, 상세한 분석과 오답에 대한 TIP을 수록하여 혼자서도 학습이 가능하도록 했습니다.

CONTENTS

해설편

 교재의 내용에 오류가 있나요?

www.**kimyoung**.co.kr ➡ 온라인 서점 ➡ 정오표 게시판

정오표에 반영되지 않은 새로운 오류가 있을 때에는 교재 오류신고
게시판에 글을 남겨주세요. 정성껏 답변해 드리겠습니다.

22만 6천 편입합격생의 선택

**김영편입 영어
독해**

워크북 **2** 단계

01

역사·인물

01 역사·인물

01

The Black Death was catastrophic. Historians still disagree over the timing of the plague — but 1348-51 and 1361-2 were peaks for much of Europe. About a third of the European population perished. Historians have clashed over the plague's economic effects. Usually, people focus on the plight of peasants during and after the plague. There was a massive decline in the supply of labour. And basic economic theory suggests that as worker numbers declined, their wages and conditions would increase.

Medieval governments were certainly concerned about the growing power of labour after the first wave of deaths. In England, the Statute of Labourers, first proposed about a year after the arrival of the Black Death in 1348, fixed wages at their 1345 level. A French statute passed in 1351 tried much the same thing. And after a workers' uprising in 1381, English employers clamoured for even more restrictive legislation. The upper strata of 14th-century society were concerned that the surviving workers were exploiting their privileged position.

1 Why does the author refer to basic economic theory?

① To reconstruct the circumstances of the outbreak of the Black Death

② To show that real wages did not return to pre-Black Death levels

③ To point out that the theory cannot explain the situation during the plague

④ To demonstrate factual evidence to prove the economic theory

2 Which of the following is NOT true according to the passage?

① Real wages could not increase despite huge falls in the labour supply.

② The beginning of the Black Death might start in Europe in 1345.

③ Prohibiting a wage increase was a cause of subsequent workers' revolt.

④ The Statue of Labourers was designed to suppress the labor force.

02

Marcus Tullius Cicero was a Roman statesman and philosopher in the final years of the Republic and remains one of the greatest and most influential orators in Western history. Among his many famous tracts and speeches, one of the most remarkable remains the first Catilinarian Oration, a condemnation of the senator Lucius Sergius Catiline for his role in a conspiracy against the Republic. Enraged at having lost the election for consulship the previous year to Cicero, his political rival, Cataline wove a plot to assassinate Cicero and several other senators to ensure his victory in the election of 63 BCE. When the plot was uncovered and foiled, the election was postponed, and the Senate meeting moved to a more secure location the following day to discuss the conspiracy.

Cataline arrived at the Senate, shocking the entire Senate, but Cicero quickly recovered and delivered the first Catilinarian Oration, a masterpiece of oratory skill, which prompted the rest of the Senate to denounce Cataline as a traitor. Cataline fled the city with his conspirators and was killed a year later in a battle with Republican soldiers.

1 What is the topic of this passage?

① The works of Marcus Tullius Cicero
② The effects of the first Catilinarian Oraiton
③ The Catilinarian conspiracy
④ The first Catilinarian Oration
⑤ Famous orations

2 From what is stated or implied in the passage, which of the following is true?

① Catilinarian Oration was against a condemnation of Catiline.
② Cataline put his plot into action.
③ Cicero delivered two or more Catilinarian Orations.
④ Cataline was elected as a consul.
⑤ The Senate denounced Cicero.

03

Francis Bacon's importance today is that he was able to distance himself from his misfortunes, and analyze the problems of ambition with a lucidity that has a universal relevance. He was not ashamed to admit that he had not been able to follow the principles of virtue and honesty that he preached. He had lived Ⓐtwo separate lives, he said, and his ideals had been defeated by unforeseen temptations: "My soul has been a stranger in the course of my pilgrimage." The rewards of ambition had not been what he had expected. Only too late did he realize that he had unthinkingly been trapped by a strange desire to seek power and to lose liberty, or to seek power over others and to lose power over himself. He could not explain it, nor why so many others suffered from that strange desire. High office, to his surprise, had reduced him to the status of a servant of the routines of administration. The process of achieving power was sometimes base; retaining it was slippery, and losing it is a melancholy thing because when a man feels that he is no longer what he was, he loses all his interest in life. Success comes at too high a price: By indignities men rise to dignities. His hunger for power had indeed made him master of the art of Ⓑlicking the boots of the influential, of making promises and betraying those who were once friends but were no longer useful. He concluded that power had isolated him from other humans; he was the first to find fault with others but the last to recognize his own faults.

1 Which of the following is the major topic of the passage?

① Universality of Francis Bacon's life

② Supremacy of Francis Bacon's life

③ Multiplicity of Francis Bacon's life

④ Hypocrisy of Francis Bacon's life

2 Which of the following is closest to what Ⓐ refers to?

① having ideals and defeating temptations

② preaching virtues and seeking ambitions

③ living as a stranger and as a pilgrim

④ seeking power and regretting his follies

3 Which of the following is implied by Ⓑ?

① flattering those he is abhorrent of

② giving his workers the cold shoulder

③ courting his boss's good graces

④ enduring the humiliating treatment

04

The formal restoration of the English ⓐmonarchy, after a temporary period when the royal family was eliminated, took place when King Charles II was restored to the throne on May 8, 1660. Ⓐ<u>The reason it was unoccupied</u> was due to events dating back to the early 1640s, when civil war first broke out against the monarchy. Later in that decade, a second uprising occurred, and it was during this, in 1649, that a death warrant for King Charles I was signed and Ⓑ<u>he was deposed and beheaded</u>. The Puritan general Oliver Cromwell filled the void as the head of the new Puritan Commonwealth. Cromwell's new state aimed to uphold religious ideals and do away with the repression of the monarchical system, although Ⓒ<u>it only saw uneven success</u>. When his son, Richard, took over after his death, it became clear that he was not adequately forceful to continue in his father's footsteps. He promptly lost control of the army and was removed from power.

After the removal of Richard, there was gradual progress toward the return of the king, Ⓓ<u>which was expedited</u> by the resistance of some of Cromwell's remaining governors. The English legislature, or Parliament, was at first only partially restored by the army; this was famously termed the "Rump Parliament" because of its size and ineffectiveness. Soon, however, Parliament was fully restored, and on April 25, 1660, it met again for the first time in twelve years; by May 8th, its members had announced that during the entire span of the Commonwealth and Protectorate, Charles II, son of Charles I, had in fact been the rightful ruler of the country. Charles, who was in exile, accepted Parliament's invitation to return and came back to the throne on May 29, 1660.

1 위 글에서 논지의 흐름상 가장 적합하지 <u>않은</u> 것을 고르시오.

① Ⓐ
② Ⓑ
③ Ⓒ
④ Ⓓ

2 According to the passage, which of the following is true?

① After being deported, King Charles I was decapitated.
② Oliver Cromwell decollated and uprooted the royal family.
③ The restoration of the monarchy proceeded without a hitch.
④ A blue-blooded person ascended to the gaddi after Richard.

3 What does the underlined ⓐ"<u>monarchy</u>" refer to?

① a political system governed by a few heavyweights
② a state where the supreme power is lodged in a potentate
③ a government that is administered primarily by bureaus
④ a social status conferred by a system based on class

05

Dr. Joseph Ignace Guillotin did not invent the execution machine that bears his name. However, it was Dr. Guillotin who on October the 10th, 1789 proposed to the Constituent Assembly that all condemned criminals should be beheaded on the grounds of humanity and equality.

A Beheading requires a skilled executioner with a lot of strength, a very steady hand and a good eye, if it is to sever the criminal's head with a single stroke. Sanson proved to be right, as during the Terror, the rate of executions reached Ⓐstaggering proportions, well beyond the capacity of the few skilled headsmen to carry out.

B It was clear that some sort of machine was required and after consultation with Dr. Antoine Louis, the Secretary of the Academy of Surgery, such a machine was devised and built.

C The Constituent Assembly duly passed a decree making beheading the only form of execution on the 25th of March 1791, and this came into law on the 25th of March 1792. But there was a small problem to this, as was indicated by the then official executioner, Sanson, who pointed out the impracticality of executing all condemned persons by the sword.

D Beheading was seen as by far the most humane method of execution at the time and was allowed to people of noble birth in many countries. Ordinary prisoners were slowly hanged, broken on the wheel (an horrendously cruel form of execution) or burnt at the stake. The idea of a standardized, quick and humane death was much more in line with revolutionary thinking.

It was initially known as the louisson or louisette, but no doubt, much to the relief of the good surgeon took on the name of its proposer and became known as the guillotine.

1 윗글의 원활한 흐름을 위해 A-D의 가장 적절한 배열은?

① A — B — C — D
② B — A — D — C
③ C — D — B — A
④ D — C — A — B

2 다음 중 Ⓐstaggering과 가장 가까운 의미는?

① enormous
② insignificant
③ religious
④ interesting

3 윗글의 내용과 일치하지 <u>않는</u> 것은?

① The guillotine is a device for beheading the condemned.

② The guillotine was not created by Dr. Guillotin.

③ The guillotine replaced far more gruesome methods of death.

④ The guillotine was used only for the executions of commoners.

06

The Declaration of Independence announced to the world the unanimous decision of the Continental Congress of the thirteen American colonies to separate themselves from Great Britain. But its true revolutionary significance — then as well as now — is the declaration of a new basis of political legitimacy in the sovereignty of the people. The Americans' final appeal was not to any man-made decree or evolving spirit but to rights Ⓐ_____ possessed by all men. These rights are found in eternal "Laws of Nature and of Nature's God." Ⓑ_____, the Declaration's meaning transcends the particulars of time and circumstances.

The circumstances of the Declaration's writing make us appreciate its exceptionalist claims even more. The war against Britain had been raging for more than two years when the Continental Congress, following a resolution of Richard Henry Lee on June 7, 1776, appointed a committee to explore the independence of the colonies from Great Britain. John Adams, Benjamin Franklin, Roger Sherman, and Robert Livingston turned to their colleague Thomas Jefferson to draft a formal declaration which they then submitted, with few corrections, to Congress. On July 2 Congress voted for independence and proceeded to debate the wording of the Declaration, which was, with the notable deletion of Jefferson's vehement condemnation of slavery, Ⓒ_____ approved on the evening of July 4.

1 **Which pair best fits Ⓐ and Ⓑ?**

① inherently — As such

② factitiously — On the come

③ indigenously — Au contraire

④ fastidiously — On that account

⑤ ingeniously — A posteriori

2 **Which best fits Ⓒ?**

① without a blink ② with reservations

③ without preamble ④ with rancor

⑤ without dissent

3 Which of the following is true about the passage above?

① Congress unanimously approved the declaration drafted by Thomas Jefferson without any correction.

② Shortly after the 13 colonies declared independence from Great Britain, they were acknowledged as a sovereign nation.

③ The Declaration of Independence approved by the Continental Congress is revolutionary in that people have sovereignty.

④ Benjamin Franklin and Robert Livingston had informally objected to the Declaration drafted by Thomas Jefferson.

⑤ The significance of the Declaration varies according to the attribute of time and circumstances.

07

Albert Einstein was a German-born theoretical physicist who developed the general theory of relativity, one of the two pillars of modern physics in company with quantum mechanics. While best known for his mass-energy equivalence formula $E=mc^2$ (which has been dubbed "the world's most famous equation"), he received the 1921 Nobel Prize in Physics "for his services to theoretical physics, and especially for his discovery of the law of the photoelectric effect." The latter was pivotal in establishing quantum theory.

Near the Ⓐinception of his career, Einstein thought that Newtonian mechanics was no longer enough to reconcile the laws of classical mechanics with the laws of the electromagnetic field. This led to the development of his special theory of relativity. He realized, however, that the principle of relativity could also be extended to gravitational fields, and with his subsequent theory of gravitation in 1916, he published a paper on the general theory of relativity. He continued to deal with problems of statistical mechanics and quantum theory, which led to his explanations of particle theory and the motion of molecules. He also investigated the thermal properties of light which laid the foundation of the photon theory of light. In 1917, Einstein applied the general theory of relativity to model the large-scale structure of the universe.

1 According to the passage, which of the following did Einstein unearth?

① the laws of the electromagnetic field
② the thermal properties of light
③ the law of photoelectric effect
④ the photon theory of light

2 According to the passage, which of the following is true of the general theory of relativity?

① Einstein explained particle theory and the motion of molecules contrary to it.
② Einstein scooped up money for it, laying the foundation for developing the special theory of relativity in modern physics.
③ It stemmed from Einstein's discontent with existing theories and he applied it to other fields.
④ It has no inextricable relation with the special theory of relativity except in name.

3 According to the passage, which of the following was indispensable to quantum theory?

① the general theory of relativity

② the mass-energy equivalence formula

③ the special theory of relativity

④ the law of the photoelectric effect

4 According to the passage, which of the following is closest in meaning to the underlined Ⓐ?

① beginning

② apex

③ summit

④ nadir

08

During the Holocaust, "Muselmann," sometimes called "Moslem," was a slang term that referred to a prisoner in a Nazi concentration camp that was in very poor physical condition and had given up the will to live. A Muselmann was seen as the "walking dead" or a "wandering corpse" whose remaining time on Earth was very short.

[A] These poor conditions plus long hours of forced labor caused prisoners to burn essential calories just to regulate body temperature. Weight loss occurred rapidly and the metabolic systems of many prisoners were not strong enough to sustain a body on such limited caloric intake.

[B] Additionally, daily humiliations and torture transformed even the banalest tasks into difficult chores. Shaving had to be done with a piece of glass. Shoelaces broke and were not replaced. A lack of toilet paper, no winter clothes to wear in the snow, and no water to clean oneself were just a few of the everyday hygiene problems suffered by camp inmates.

[C] It was not difficult for concentration camp prisoners to slip into this condition. Rations in even the harshest labor camps were very limited and clothing did not adequately protect prisoners from the elements.

[D] Just as important as these harsh conditions was the lack of hope. Concentration camp prisoners had no idea how long their ordeal would last. Since each day felt like a week, the years felt like decades. For many, the lack of hope destroyed their will to live.

It was when a prisoner was ill, starving, and without hope that they would fall into the Muselmann state. This condition was both physical and psychological, making a Muselmann lose all desire to live.

1 **Choose the best order of** [A], [B], [C], **and** [D] **in the passage.**

① [A] — [C] — [B] — [D]

② [B] — [A] — [D] — [C]

③ [C] — [A] — [B] — [D]

④ [D] — [C] — [A] — [B]

2 **What is the best title of the passage?**

① How a Prisoner Became a Muselmann

② Where the Muselmann Term Came from

③ How Camp Prisoners Died during the Holocaust

④ How the Nazi Concentration Camps Worked

3 Which of the following is <u>not</u> true according to the passage?

① Concentration camp prisoners needed to have a strong desire to avoid slipping into a Muselmann.

② In spite of what happened in a concentration camp, Muselmanns never lost their will to live.

③ The Muselmann prisoners exhibited an apathetic listlessness regarding their own fate.

④ Once a camp prisoner was labelled "Muselmann", one was likely to die shortly thereafter.

09

In his historical *Essay on the Principle of Population*, Robert Malthus hypothesized that poverty and famine would become a global epidemic if populations continued to go unregulated. Malthus based his theory on the idea that plants and animals always produce more offspring than can survive. He also believed that humans, namely the lower class, were no different, and that checks needed to be in place in order to prevent the destruction of the human race. According to Malthus, in a balanced population the population growth was controlled by "positive checks" such as disease, and "preventative checks" such as the postponement of marriage.

As a political economist, Malthus was concerned about the direction society seemed to be heading towards in the 19th-century England. According to Malthus, living conditions were steadily declining as a result of a high birthrate, an inadequate supply of resources, and the irresponsible working class. Malthus suggested that population might be controlled if the lower class took it upon themselves to only have as many children as they could financially support. He also felt that if the lower class just got a taste of luxury they might be more likely to start families later, and therefore have fewer children. While Malthus' controversial paper made him a celebrity, many people, especially the working class, Ⓐ_____ his pessimism and went as far as to call him a "prophet of doom." Charles Darwin read Malthus' essay and was inspired to develop his own theory of Natural Selection. Darwin considered overpopulation to be a necessity, in that with more offspring than food, siblings were forced to become more competitive. From this came Darwin's theory on the survival of the fittest.

1 **Which of the following is given as an example of a "preventative check" on population growth?**

① dying from an illness

② being consumed by pollution

③ delaying marriage

④ getting hit by an earthquake

2 **According to the passage, what did Malthus specifically blame the lower class for?**

① Having more children than they could support

② Not putting in enough hours of labor

③ Destroying the air quality in cities like London

④ Wanting too many luxury items

3 Why does the author mention Charles Darwin?

① To show that Malthus wasn't taken as seriously as Darwin

② To illustrate the difference between two well-respected theorists

③ To explain how Malthus' work inspired another important theory

④ To introduce a political economist from another century

4 Which of the following is most appropriate for the blank Ⓐ?

① deplored   ② conceded

③ fathomed   ④ tolerated

10

The post-World War II era marked a period of unprecedented energy against the second-class citizenship accorded to African Americans in many parts of the nation. Resistance to racial segregation and discrimination with strategies like civil disobedience, nonviolent resistance, marches, protests, boycotts, and rallies received national attention as newspaper, radio, and television reporters and cameramen documented the struggle to end racial inequality. When Rosa Parks refused to give up her seat to a white person in Montgomery, Alabama, and was arrested in December 1955, she set off a train of events that generated a momentum the civil rights movement had never before experienced. Deciding to boycott the buses, the African-American community soon formed a new organization to supervise the boycott. The boycott, more successful than anyone hoped, led to a 1956 Supreme Court decision banning segregated buses.

In 1960, four black freshmen from North Carolina Agricultural and Technical College in Greensboro strolled into the F. W. Woolworth store and quietly sat down at the lunch counter. They were not served, but they stayed until closing time. The next morning they came with twenty-five more students. Two weeks later similar demonstrations had spread to several cities, within a year similar Ⓐ_____ demonstrations took place in over a hundred cities North and South. The August 28, 1963, March on Washington riveted the nation's attention. Rather than the anticipated hundred thousand marchers, more than twice that number appeared, astonishing even its organizers. Blacks and whites, side by side, called on President John F. Kennedy and the Congress to provide equal access to public facilities, quality education, adequate employment, and decent housing for African Americans. During the assembly at the Lincoln Memorial, the young preacher who had led the successful Montgomery, Alabama, bus boycott, Reverend Dr. Martin Luther King, Jr. delivered a stirring message with the refrain, "I Have a Dream."

1 Which would be the best title for this passage?

① The Big Accomplishment of the Civil Rights Movement: the Right to Vote

② The Unparalleled Leader of the Civil Rights Movement: Martin Luther King, Jr

③ The First Victory in the Civil Rights Movement: Banning Segregated Buses

④ African American Odyssey: the Civil Rights Movement after the World War II

⑤ The Hidden Hero of the Civil Rights Movement: Rosa Parks

2   Which statement <u>cannot</u> be inferred from the passage above?

① Before World War Ⅱ, African Americans were treated as the second-class citizen.

② One of the ways to resist racial segregation and discrimination was nonviolent resistance.

③ Boycotting segregated buses, Rosa Parks became an icon of the civil rights movement.

④ The March on Washington was one of the largest civil rights rallies in US history.

⑤ Because Martin Luther King, Jr. obeyed government demands, he led March on Washington nonviolently.

3   Which expression best fits Ⓐ?

① violent   ② inanimate

③ peaceful   ④ imprudent

⑤ sensational

심리·교육

02

심리·교육

▶▶▶ **ANSWERS** P.324

01

'Helena got a pay rise. I'm not surprised, the way she flirts with the boss,' grumbles a colleague who'd like to be promoted herself. 'That skinny minnie? I'm sure she's anorexic,' replies her friend.

Ah, the comfort of gossip. A few spiteful words shared in confidence can give us such a boost. With friends, colleagues or family, saying bad things about other people feels good.

However much we may disapprove in theory, it's very common behaviour, says social psychologist Laurent Bègue. 'About 60 per cent of conversations between adults are about someone who isn't present,' he says. 'And most of these are passing judgement.'

We all know it's wrong to gossip, and no one wants to seem malicious. So why do we indulge in Ⓐthis guilty pleasure? Gossip builds social bonds because shared dislikes create stronger bonds than shared positives. Two people who don't know each other will feel closer if they share something mean about a third person than if they say nice things about them. It's a way of demonstrating their shared values and sense of humour. Add to that the thrill of transgression, since we're supposed to be nice and positive.

1 According to the passage, what is the best title?

① What to Earn and What to Lose during Gossip
② Pent-up Feelings: Are We Supposed to Be Nice?
③ The Reason Why We Covertly Lapse into Gossip
④ Giving Gossip Disapprovers an Active Endorsement

2 According to the passage, which of the following is <u>not</u> similar to the underlined Ⓐ?

① exchanging opinions about a rumor without foundation
② taking selfies to feel satisfied in a room where nobody stays
③ slandering ex-girlfriends on social media behind their backs
④ talking about celebrities' private lives featured in the tabloids

02

The hedgehog's dilemma, sometimes called the porcupine dilemma, is an analogy about Ⓐthe challenges of human intimacy. It describes a situation in which a group of hedgehogs all seek to become close to one another in order to share heat during cold weather. They must remain apart, however, as they cannot avoid hurting one another with their sharp spines. Though they all share the intention of a close reciprocal relationship, this may not occur for reasons they cannot avoid.

Both Arthur Schopenhauer and Sigmund Freud have used this situation to describe what they feel is the state of individual in relation to others in society. The hedgehog's dilemma suggests that despite good will, human intimacy cannot occur without substantial mutual harm, and what results is cautious behavior and weak relationships. With the hedgehog's dilemma, one is recommended to use moderation in affairs with others because of self-interest as well as out of consideration for others. The hedgehog's dilemma is used to justify or explain Ⓑ_____.

1 Which of the following is NOT true according to the passage?

① Hedgehogs and porcupines are gregarious animals with poisonous spines on the back.
② The hedgehog's dilemma exhibits a universal situation of human beings as social beings.
③ The hedgehog's dilemma can be a subject of philosophical or psychological studies.
④ The human good will cannot prevent humans from falling into the hedgehog's dilemma.
⑤ The hedgehog's dilemma is likely to lead us to keep the middle path when we socialize.

2 Which of the following proverbs best reflects the underlined Ⓐ?

① There is safety in numbers.
② A leopard can't change its spots.
③ Don't bite the hand that feeds you.
④ Every cloud has a silver lining.
⑤ Familarity breeds contempt.

3 Which of the following is most suitable for the blank Ⓑ?

① cooperation and collectivism
② introversion and isolationism
③ solidarity and philanthropy
④ selfishness and intervention
⑤ extroversion and estrangement

03

When children's interests and abilities are different from what society expects, they're often subjected to discrimination and bullying. It is natural for parents to want their children to be accepted socially. ⒜ But if children's strengths don't always conform to society's or your own expectations, it's important to help them fulfill their own unique potential rather than force them into the mold of current or traditional gender behavior. ⒝ That is, some children who are gender nonconforming in early childhood grow up to become transgender adults (persistently identifying with a gender different from their assigned sex at birth), and others don't. ⒞ The causes for this are likely both biological and social; there is no evidence of a link to parenting or experiencing childhood trauma. There is no way to predict how children will identify later in life. ⒟ This Ⓐ_____ is one of the hardest things about parenting a gender-nonconforming child. It is important for parents to make their home a place where their children feel safe, loved unconditionally, and accepted for Ⓑ_____. Research suggests that gender is something we are born with; it can't be changed by any interventions.

1 Choose the best words for blanks Ⓐ and Ⓑ.

① variability — who they should be

② ambivalence — who they want to be

③ uncertainty — who they are

④ inevitability — who they can be

2 Choose the best location for the following statement.

"For some young children, identifying as another gender may be temporary; for others it isn't."

① Ⓐ   ② Ⓑ

③ Ⓒ   ④ Ⓓ

04

Generally speaking, an introvert is someone for whom human interaction can be physically and/or mentally exhausting, and so they seek out a certain measure of solitude in order to "recharge." Extroverts, on the other hand, are energized by being around other people, and so seek out forms of social interaction on a regular basis. Ⓐ_____ it's helpful to think of introversion-extroversion as two ends of a scale, or a continuum, rather than a Ⓑdichotomy. Very few people are either purely introverted or purely extroverted. As such, most people are considered "ambiverts," or displaying a mix of introverted and extroverted traits — thereby being your "introverted extrovert" or "extroverted introvert." So what you might find with an "introverted extrovert" is a person who enjoys being around others, going out for a social event, or is otherwise very comfortable around other people, but who might also make an effort to enjoy time alone once in a while. For the "extroverted introvert," you might have a person who values group interactions, even if she's not the most talkative type, and shows willingness for being in social settings; but if given the choice, she would rather Ⓒhave a night in than go out on the town.

1 Which best fits into the blank Ⓐ?

① So   ② But
③ In fact   ④ While

2 Which is closest in meaning to the underlined Ⓑdichotomy?

① similarity   ② split
③ convergence   ④ diffusion

3 Which is closest in meaning to the underlined Ⓒhave a night in than go out on the town?

① have moments of solitude than social gathering
② try to avoid spending time alone
③ enjoy a night in the town than out of the town
④ go to a town to spend a night

4 Which is NOT true according to the passage?

① An introvert is hard pressed to deal with people.
② An extrovert is a man of social disposition.
③ An introverted extrovert is scared of time alone.
④ An extroverted introvert is able to enjoy his time in isolation.

05

Studies on creative people have consistently demonstrated that creativity is associated with openness to new ideas, risk-tasking, and being inner-directed. However, many creative students find that they are at odds with the education system and people that they are surrounded by. Creative students are generally Ⓐ_____ thinkers, and many public school settings do not encourage or help these students further develop these latent creative skills.

In public education, left brain tactics still tend to dominate as they have for generations. Schools throughout history churned out graduates who were good at storing facts, but lacked problem-solving skills. Students were taught to conform rather than challenge authority, so they were unable to think in fresh, inventive ways. This style of teaching which seems to persist even today, gives the greatest benefits to students that are more analytical and less creative. However, these overly structured school environments are not challenging for students with strong creative sides. They are often labeled below average, since they score lower on objective tests and this leaves these students with feelings of frustration and damaged self-esteem. This may give some insight as to why creative children often have trouble in school: their Ⓑ_____ minds wander while their teachers attempt to make them memorize information. This traditional teaching style was fine during the days when students were not overstimulated, but the creative children of today instinctively see this memory-focused learning as irrelevant or trivial compared to understanding the "big picture" in life. The problem is that students of today are fundamentally different from the ones of previous years.

1 Why have public schools NOT provided creative education?

   ① Both public schools and teachers believe that memorization is a key part of education.

   ② In public schools, teachers are not allowed to cultivate the creativity of students.

   ③ It is a new concept and public schools have been very traditional through the years.

   ④ Students in previous generations denounced the use of creative approach in public education.

2 Which of the following best fits into the blank Ⓐ and Ⓑ?

   ① right-brain — left-brain

   ② left-brain — right-brain

   ③ right-brain — right-brain

   ④ left-brain — left-brain

06

Confirmation biases impact how people gather information, but they also influence how people interpret and recall information. Consider the debate over gun control. Sally is in support of gun control. She seeks out news stories and opinion pieces that reaffirm the need for limitations on gun ownership. When she hears stories about shootings in the media, she interprets them in a way that supports her existing beliefs. Henry, on the other hand, is adamantly opposed to gun control. He seeks out news sources that are aligned with his position, and when he comes across news stories about shootings, he interprets them in a way that supports his current point of view. A number of experiments demonstrate that people have a tendency to seek information that confirms their existing beliefs. Unfortunately, this type of bias can prevent us from looking at situations objectively, can influence the decisions we make, and can lead to poor or faulty choices. During an election season, for example, people tend to seek out positive information that paints their favored candidates in a good light while looking for information that casts the opposing candidate in a negative light. By not seeking out objective facts, interpreting information in a way that only supports their existing beliefs, and only remembering details that uphold these beliefs, people often _____ that might have otherwise influenced their decision on which candidate to support.

1 Choose the one that best fills in the blank.

    ① give up their initial position   ② stay pleased with their grasp

    ③ miss important information   ④ try to outsource new ideas

2 Which of the following CANNOT be inferred about "Sally" and "Henry" if they both are confirmation-biased?

    ① Sally will weigh pros against cons in order to prove her argument that guns be regulated.

    ② Henry will join a club whose position is that everyone is responsible for his own safety.

    ③ If a shooting accident occurs, Sally may interview the victim, avoiding the culprit.

    ④ Henry may deliberately ignore news stories about shooting accidents from the outset.

3 What is the purpose of the passage?

    ① to warn people against relying too much on their existing beliefs

    ② to stress the importance of making unbiased decisions and choices

    ③ to analyze the influence of prejudice on the details of our daily life

    ④ to clarify a particular tendency of our mind by providing examples

07

There are two distinct theories about the nature and cause of aggression: Instinct and social learning theories. Aggression, as many theories allege, is a basic and natural human instinct. The instinct theory holds that aggression is biological. According to Sigmund Freud, aggression was a consequence of a more primary instinct he named Thanatos (the death instinct), an innate drive toward disintegration that was directed against the self. Given that he is right, why is it that we all don't commit suicide? It is partly because, luckily, Eros mostly wins the struggle between Thanatos and Eros (our instinctive force toward life). However, it is also because displacement outwardly diverts our self-destructive energies. Instead of aggressing against ourselves, we aggress against others, and this process is called displacement. How, then, do people control their extreme violence against one another? According to Freud, catharsis is the answer: as we watch violent events or get involved in minor displays of anger, the aggressive urge dwindles and our emotions are purified and calmed. Aggression, as this instinctive theory claims, builds up regardless of outside provocation until aggressive behavior breaks out with little or no outside provocation. The supporters of this theory base it on the study of the behaviors of animals in their natural habitats. According to the aggression as instinct theory, this instinct is shared by people and animals.

1 Which of the following is most likely to follow the passage?
   ① aggression in social learning theories
   ② aggression in instinct theories
   ③ displacement theories
   ④ controlling aggression and catharsis

2 Which of the following is true of displacement?
   ① Displacement occurs when Thanatos overwhelms Eros.
   ② Displacement is usually directed inwardly.
   ③ Displacement is based on the idea that aggression is biological.
   ④ Displacement accompanies self-disintegration.

08

The next time your little boy is roughhousing, rather than scold him, you might want to encourage him. Some educators and researchers claim that banning violent play from classrooms can be harmful to boys, LiveScience reports. And the moms and teachers who try to put a stop to playing "superhero" or cops and robbers are misguided, experts say. "ⒶThey have a belief — call it an urban myth — that if boys play this way it will desensitize them to violence and they will grow up to be more violent. But it is a misunderstanding of what makes adults violent," Michael Thompson, a psychologist who co-wrote "Raising Cain: Protecting the Emotional Life of Boys" said.

Ⓐ In fact, suppressing the normal instinct boys have to play rough may only make Ⓑthem more violent. "When you try to oppress it, it comes out in sneaky ways," said Jane Katch, author of "Under Deadman's Skin: Discovering the Meaning of Children's Violent Play."

Ⓑ "Boys are innately wired for dominance and that is going to affect the kinds of stories they like and the kind of games they play," he added. In fact, playing games with "bad guys" can help boys develop, said Mary Ellin Logue of the University of Maine, who conducted a survey of 98 female teachers who work with 4-year-old boys.

Ⓒ "They are also working on impulse control, Ⓒthey are trying really hard to be good, but it's really hard to be good," she said. "These bad guys give Ⓓthem a way to externalize that part of them that they are trying to conquer."

1 Among Ⓐ, Ⓑ, Ⓒ and Ⓓ, which one has a DIFFERENT meaning?

① Ⓐ   ② Ⓑ

③ Ⓒ   ④ Ⓓ

2 Choose the best order of the paragraphs Ⓐ, Ⓑ and Ⓒ.

① Ⓐ — Ⓑ — Ⓒ   ② Ⓐ — Ⓒ — Ⓑ

③ Ⓑ — Ⓒ — Ⓐ   ④ Ⓒ — Ⓑ — Ⓐ

3 Which of the following CANNOT be inferred from the passage?

① Parents should recognize what their sons need emotionally.

② A little rough play doesn't hurt ordinary little boys.

③ Violent boys will be better off if they are better understood.

④ Rough fantasy play should be shut out in school.

09

Sorting anything from furniture to animals to concepts into different folders inside our brains is something that happens automatically, and it helps us function. In fact, categorization has an evolutionary purpose: assuming that all mushrooms are poisonous and that all lions want to eat you is a very effective way of coping with your surroundings. Forget being nuanced about nonpoisonous mushrooms and occasionally nonhungry lions — certitude keeps you safe.

But a particular way of categorizing can be inaccurate, and those false categories can lead to prejudice and stereotyping. Much psychological research into bias has focused on how people essentialize certain categories, which boils down to assuming that these categories have an underlying nature that is tied to inherent and immutable qualities.

Like other human attributes such as gender, age and sexual orientation, race tends to be strongly — and inaccurately — essentialized. This means that when you think of people in that category, you rapidly or even automatically come up with assumptions about their characteristics. Common stereotypes with the category 'African Americans', for example, include 'loud', 'good dancers' and 'good at sports'. Essentialism about any group of people is dubious — aged people are not inherently feebleminded, women are not innately gentle — and when it comes to race, the idea of deep and fundamental differences has been roundly debunked by scientists.

1 위 글의 요지(main idea)를 다음과 같이 나타냈을 때 빈칸에 들어갈 가장 적절한 것은?

Wrong categorization leads to stereotyping, which in turn results in _____.

① rapid and automatic categorization
② inherent and immutable qualities
③ scientifically disproved essentialism
④ fully justified racial discriminations

2 위 글의 내용과 일치하지 <u>않는</u> 것은?

① Categorization can have both positive and negative effects.
② Overgeneralization can sometimes make our life more secure.
③ Characteristics that a category has can be acquired and changed.
④ Essentialism can explain strong-willed older people and violent women.

10

The kind of world that produces anxiety is actually a world of relative safety, a world in which no one feels that he himself is facing sudden death. Possibly sudden death may strike a certain number of unidentified other people, but not him. The anxiety exists as an uneasy state of mind, in which one has a feeling that something unspecified and undeterminable may go wrong. If the world seems to be going well, this produces anxiety, for good times may end. If the world is going badly, it may get worse. Anxiety tends to be without focus; the anxious person doesn't know whether to blame himself or other people. He isn't sure whether it is the current year or the Administration or a change in climate or the atom bomb that is to blame for this undefined sense of unease.

It is clear that we have developed a society which depends on _____ to make it work. Psychiatrists have been heard to say, "He didn't have enough anxiety to get well," indicating that, while we agree that too much anxiety is inimical to mental health, we have come to rely on anxiety to push and prod us into seeing a doctor about a symptom which may indicate cancer, into checking up on that old life-insurance policy which may have out-of-date clauses in it, into having a conference with Billy's teacher even though his report card looks all right. On balance, our age of anxiety represents a large advance over savage and peasant cultures.

1 **Choose the one that best fills in the blank.**

① anxiety overriding other emotions
② warding off anxiety with humor
③ overcoming anxiety in proper ways
④ having the right amount of anxiety

2 **What is the best title for the passage?**

① Waiting for Anxiety-Free Society
② One Vote for This Age of Anxiety
③ Rethinking the Safety in Daily Life
④ An Insight into the Roots of Anxiety

3 **Which of the following CANNOT be inferred about "anxiety"?**

① It is not a barometer for the instability of our society.
② It usually arises from unidentifiable and unspecific sources.
③ It has diminished with the transition from primitive to civilized society.
④ It is like a necessary evil which we don't like but need for our life.

11

Scientific knowledge, humanized and well taught, is the key to achieving a lasting balance in our lives. The more biologists learn about the biosphere in its full richness, the more rewarding the image. Ⓐ_____, the more psychologists learn of the development of the human mind, the more they understand the gravitational pull of the natural world on our spirit, and on our souls.

We have a long way to go to make peace with this planet, and with each other. We took a wrong turn when we launched the Neolithic revolution. We have been trying ever since to ascend from Nature instead of to Nature. It is not too late for us to come around, without losing the quality of life already gained, in order to receive the deeply fulfilling beneficence of humanity's natural heritage.

Part of the dilemma is that while most people around the world care about the natural environment, they don't know why they care, or why they should feel responsible for it. By and large they have been unable to articulate what the stewardship of Nature means to them personally. This confusion is a great problem for contemporary society as well as for future generations. It is linked to another great difficulty, the inadequacy of science education, everywhere in the world. <u>Both</u> arise in part from the explosive growth and complexity of modern biology. Even the best scientists have trouble keeping up with more than a small part of what has emerged as the most important science for the twenty-first century.

1   Which of the following CANNOT be inferred from the passage?

① Every educated person should know something about Nature and humanity.
② Living Nature has long opened a broad pathway to the service for humanity.
③ The breath of our life and our spirit depends upon the survival of Nature.
④ Because we are part of Nature, we cannot avoid being dominated by Nature.

2   Which of the following is most suitable for the blank Ⓐ?

① Similarly   ② Contrarily
③ Surprisingly   ④ Consequently

3   Which of the following is referred to by <u>Both</u>?

① care about natural environment and stewardship of Nature
② problems for contemporary society and for future generations
③ ignorance of natural environment and inadequate science education
④ irresponsibility for and confusion about natural environment

4 According to the passage, which of the following is true?

① The human mind has no influence on Nature, nor is it influenced by Nature.

② Humans had been more in harmony with Nature before the Neolithic Revolution.

③ We cannot benefit from our natural heritage without losing the quality of life.

④ Only in the 21st century can scientists keep up with the scientific development.

12

Socratic argument is not undemocratic. Nor is it subversive of the just claims of excluded people. In fact, as Socrates knew, it is essential to a strong democracy and to any lasting pursuit of justice. In order to foster a democracy that is reflective and deliberative, rather than simply a marketplace of competing interest groups, a democracy that genuinely takes thought for the common good, we must produce citizens who have the Socratic capacity to reason about their beliefs. It is not good for democracy when people vote on the basis of sentiments they have absorbed from talk-radio and have never questioned. This failure to think critically produces a democracy in which people talk at one another but never have a genuine dialogue. In such an atmosphere bad arguments pass for good arguments, and prejudice can all too easily Ⓐ_____ as reason. To unmask prejudice and to secure justice, we need argument, an essential tool of civic freedom. Liberal education in our colleges and universities is, and should be, Socratic, committed to the activation of each student's independent mind and to the production of a community that can genuinely reason together about a problem, not simply trade claims and counterclaims. Despite our allegiances to families and traditions, despite our diverse interests in correcting injustices to groups within our nation, we can and should reason together in a Socratic way, and our campuses should prepare us to do so. By looking at this goal of a community of reason as it emerges in the thought of Socrates and the Greek Stoics, we can show its dignity and its importance for democratic self-government. Connecting this idea to the teaching of philosophy in undergraduate courses of many sorts, we shall see that it is not Socratic education, but its Ⓑ_____, that would be fatal to the health of our society.

1 **Which of the following would be best for this title?**

① Liberal Education in a Socratic Way

② The Enemy of Democracy

③ The Removal of Prejudices by Socrates

④ Who Opposes Socrates' Education?

2 **According to the passage, which of the following is true?**

① Those who reason in a Socratic way hold positions of power and influence in our community.

② The Socratic emphasis on reason seems not only subversive but also democratic.

③ The Socratic capacity fosters a democracy that is conducive to competing marketplace.

④ Socratic education is helpful for developing the ability to think critically and communicate effectively.

3　Which of the following fits best in the blanks Ⓐ and Ⓑ?

①　masquerade — absence

②　abbreviate — abundance

③　depreciate — practice

④　accord — ontology

13

The Stockdale Paradox is named after admiral James Stockdale, who was a United States military officer held captive for eight years during the Vietnam War. Stockdale was tortured more than twenty times by his captors, and never had much reason to believe he would survive the prison camp and someday get to see his wife again. And yet he never lost faith during his ordeal: "I never doubted not only that I would get out, but also that I would prevail in the end and turn the experience into the defining event of my life, which, in retrospect, I would not trade."

Then comes the paradox: While Stockdale had remarkable faith in the unknowable, he noted that it was always the most optimistic of his prisonmates who failed to make it out of there alive. "They were the ones who said, 'We're going to be out by Christmas.' And Christmas would come, and Christmas would go. Then they'd say, 'We're going to be out by Easter.' And Easter would come, and Easter would go. And then Thanksgiving, and then it would be Christmas again. And they died of a broken heart."

What the optimists failed to do was confront the reality of their situation. They preferred the ostrich approach. That self-delusion might have made it easier on them in the short-term, but when they were eventually forced to face reality, it had become too much and they couldn't handle it. Stockdale approached adversity with a very different mindset. He accepted the reality of his situation. He knew he was in hell, but, rather than bury his head in the sand, he stepped up and did everything he could to lift the morale and prolong the lives of his fellow prisoners.

1 Which of the following is the difference between James Stockdale and his optimistic prisonmates?

① James Stockdale ignored the problem rather than attempting to solve it.

② James Stockdale hypnotized himself to be released from prison anytime soon.

③ James Stockdale combined the optimism with brutal reality and a willingness to take action.

④ James Stockdale had never doubted that he could achieve his aims no matter how noble they might be.

2 According to the passage, the Stockdale Paradox reveals why _____.

① people live resolutely without losing hope

② things develops the way people do

③ it is easy to confuse hopeful thinking with grim reality

④ hope is not the fundamental solution under all circumstances

3 Which one best describes the underlined term "<u>ostrich approach</u>" according to the passage?

① refusing to face reality and hoping for the difficulties to go away

② making progress by pursuing a bold but sensible approach

③ transcending the most horrific situations

④ defying the unprecedented pessimism

14

Morality may be a hard concept to grasp, but we acquire it fast. Marc Hauser, professor of psychology at Harvard University believes that all of us carry what he calls a sense of moral grammar — the ethical Ⓐ_____ of the basic grasp of speech that most linguists believe is with us from birth. However, merely being equipped with moral programming does not mean we Ⓑ_____ moral behavior. Something still has to boot up that software and configure it properly. ©Just as syntax is nothing until words are built upon it, so too is a sense of right and wrong useless until someone teaches you how to apply it. It's the people around us who do that teaching. Our species has a very conflicted sense of when we ought to help someone else and when we ought not, and the general rule is: "Help those close to home and ignore those far away." That's in part because the plight of a person you can see will always feel more real than the problems of someone whose suffering is merely described to you. But part of it is also rooted in you from a time when the welfare of your tribe was essential for your survival but the welfare of an opposing tribe was not. One of the most powerful tools for enforcing group morals is the practice of shunning. If membership in a tribe is the way you ensure yourself food, family and protection from predators, being Ⓓblackballed can be a terrifying thing. Clubs, social groups and fraternities expel undesirable members, and the U.S. military retains the threat of discharge as a disciplinary tool, even grading the punishment as "dishonorable," darkening the mark a former service person must carry for life. Human beings were small, defenseless and vulnerable to predators. Avoiding banishment would be important to us.

1 Which of the following is best suitable for the blanks Ⓐ, Ⓑ?

① consistency — exercise 　② equivalent — practice

③ precedent — retain 　④ disposition — alter

2 Which of the following best describes the underlined sentence ©?

① Nothing is complete unless you put it in final shape.

② Many a little makes a mickle.

③ A stitch in time saves nine.

④ Actions should go hand in hand with words.

3 Which of the following best replaces the underlined word Ⓓblackballed?

① harassed 　② excluded

③ threatened 　④ suspected

4 According to the passage, morality functions _____.

① as a symbol of humanity

② as a criterion of performance

③ as a means of security

④ as a way of obtaining success in life

15

The educational process feels more than ever like a race, one that starts in pre-preschool and doesn't end until your child is admitted to the perfect college. There is a lot of advice out there on how best to help our kids thrive, but what we don't think about enough is how to help our children build their character. Ⓐ Recent research by a team of psychologists led by Mark Seery of the University at Buffalo, State University of New York, found that adults who had experienced little or no adversity growing up were actually less happy and confident than those who had experienced a few significant setbacks in childhood. Ⓑ Overcoming obstacles, the researchers hypothesized, "could teach effective coping skills, help engage social support networks, create a sense of mastery over past adversity, and foster beliefs in the ability to cope successfully in the future." Ⓒ When we protect our children from every possible adversity — when we call their teachers to get an extension on a paper; when we intervene in the sandbox to make sure everyone is sharing their toys; when we urge them to choose only those subjects they're good at — we are denying them those same character-building experiences. Ⓓ As the psychologists Madeline Levine and Dan Kindlon have written, that can lead to difficulties in adolescence and young adulthood, when overprotected young people finally confront real problems on their own and don't know how to overcome them. Ⓔ In the classroom and outside of it, parents need to encourage children to take chances, to challenge themselves. Paradoxically enough, _____ may be one of the best ways we can help them succeed.

1 When the above passage can be divided into three paragraphs, which would be the best boundaries?

① Ⓐ and Ⓑ   ② Ⓐ and Ⓔ

③ Ⓑ and Ⓒ   ④ Ⓒ and Ⓓ

⑤ Ⓒ and Ⓔ

2 Which of the following is most appropriate for the blank?

① lessening creative activities

② helping our kids minimize challenges

③ giving our kids room to fail

④ establishing meticulous school schedules

⑤ exposing our kids to praise

3 According to the passage, which of the following is true?

① Real challenges do not often come during childhood.

② Parents overprotecting their kids may hold them back from developing self-assurance.

③ Parents are overwhelmed with the flood of information on helping their kids develop social skills.

④ Children are vulnerable to traumatic adverse experiences.

⑤ Young adults are more open to experiencing adversity than kids.

16

A basic assumption of game theory is that every decision maker acts in his or her own self-interest. People seek to maximize their own benefit, and the welfare of others is secondary. In such a situation, individual interests often conflict with the interests of the group as a whole. This is well expressed in a famous hypothetical situation known as the prisoner's dilemma.

In the prisoner's dilemma, two prisoners, prisoner A and prisoner B, are being questioned by the police in separate rooms. Each prisoner has two choices: either remains silent, or betrays the other prisoner by talking to the police. There are three possible outcomes. If both prisoners remain silent, they will go to jail for six months. If prisoner A remains silent and prisoner B betrays him, prisoner A will go to jail for 10 years but prisoner B will go free. The reverse will happen if prisoner B remains silent and prisoner A betrays him. If both prisoners betray each other, they will go to jail for 2 years. In this situation, the best possible choice for the prisoners would be to remain silent. This, however, requires a large measure of trust. If one prisoner remains silent and the other prisoner betrays him, he will receive the worst possible outcome. Since neither prisoner is 100% sure he can trust the other, the most logical choice is for both prisoners to betray the other.

This is the basic principle at work in many decisions that may at first seem illogical. For example, it is entirely possible for a nation to eliminate or at least largely reduce its pollution, but its economy would suffer because it would have to create less energy or use more expensive technologies that cause less pollution. Again, the best possible choice for the Earth as a whole would be for every nation to make Ⓐthis choice. However, if one nation chooses to stop polluting but other nations do not, then that nation suffers the effects of pollution, since most pollution affects the world as a whole and not just the nations producing it. Therefore, the most logical choice for each nation is to Ⓑ_____, even though that will lead to a more negative outcome for the world as a whole.

1 Which of the following would be best for this title?

① Game Theory Explaining Seemingly Illogical Decisions
② The Use of Game Theory throughout History
③ The Application of Game Theory to the Pollution Issues
④ Game Theory as a Solution to the Prisoner's Dilemma

2 Which of the following is NOT true according to the passage?

① Individuals usually make decisions based on their own self-interests.
② Game theory can be applied to many political situations and the decisions of various groups.
③ People often make choices which harm them slightly to minimize their risk.
④ Game theory prevents the prisoners from picking a solution mutually beneficial to them.

3 According to the passage, what does the underlined Ⓐ refer to?

① continue polluting

② betray other nations

③ stop polluting

④ stop waging war

4 Which of the following best fits in the blank Ⓑ?

① develop alternative energy sources

② continue polluting the Earth

③ take the initiative in protecting the environment

④ sign a treaty pledging to reduce greenhouse gases

17

The bandwagon effect is a well-documented form of group-think in behavioral science and has many applications. The general rule is that conduct or beliefs spread among people, with the probability of any individual adopting it increasing with the proportion of those who have already done so. As more people come to believe in something, others also <u>hop on the bandwagon</u> regardless of the underlying evidence. The tendency to follow the actions or beliefs of others can occur because individuals directly prefer to conform, or because individuals derive information from others.

The bandwagon effect occurs in voting: some people vote for those candidates or parties who are likely to succeed or are proclaimed as such by the media, hoping to be on the winner's side in the end. And it has been applied to situations involving majority opinion where people alter their opinions to the majority view. Such a shift in opinion can occur because individuals draw inference from the decisions of others.

Because of time zones, election results are broadcast in the eastern parts of the United States while polls are still open in the west. This difference has led to research on how the behavior of voters in western United States are influenced by news about the decisions of voters in other time zones. In 1980, NBC News declared Ronald Reagan to be the winner of the presidential race on the basis of the exit polls several hours before the voting booths closed in the west.

It is also said to be important in the American Presidential Primary elections. States all vote at different times, spread over some months, rather than all on one day. Some states (Iowa, New Hampshire) have special precedence to go early while other have to wait until a certain date. This is often said to give undue influence to these states, and a win in these early states is said to give the candidate a big momentum and propel him to win the nomination.

1 **Choose the one closest in meaning to the underlined "<u>hop on the bandwagon</u>."**

① follow what most people do or think

② join the mainstream of a given society

③ rely on someone else's accomplishment

④ climb up the ladder of success in life

2 Which of the following CANNOT be inferred from the passage?

① People tend to go along with what a majority of people do without considering whether it is right.

② The likelihood of a bandwagon effect increases as more and more people adopt an idea or behavior.

③ The bandwagon effect shows that the creative few do more to change the world than the ordinary many.

④ In 1980, Ronald Reagan may have owed his success in the Presidential election to the bandwagon effect.

3 Which of the following does NOT exemplify "the bandwagon effect"?

① A few people promote hateful racial generalizations, which spread to the rest of the community, leading to racism.

② Most of the classmates join the same social networking site and enjoy listening to the same musical group.

③ Independents decide to vote for the Republican candidate when the Republican is expected to win the election.

④ A person claims to purchase a designer garment because of its threading technique, longevity, and fabric.

4 What is the author's attitude toward "the bandwagon effect"?

① affirmative   ② neutral

③ incoherent   ④ critical

18

DVDs and educational programs on TV have a growing place in helping young children to learn. But there's new evidence that they may not be as effective as Ⓐold-fashioned conversation.

Even before birth, children hear sounds and words and can babble a variety of noises that will eventually Ⓑ_____ into language. "Before nine months of age, a baby produces a babble made up of hundreds of phonemes from hundreds of languages," Elisabeth Cros, a speech therapist with the Ecole Internationale de New York told *TIME* in April. "Parents will react to the phonemes they recognize from their native tongues, which reinforces the baby's use of those selected ones."

It's that dynamic interaction between the infant and her caregiver — a back-and-forth that Ⓒ_____ videos and television programs can't provide — that is critical for efficient language learning. And a group of researchers from the University of Washington, Temple University and the University of Delaware explain why.

The scientists studied 36 two-year-olds who were randomly assigned to learn verbs in three different ways. A third of the group trained with a live person, another third learned through video chat technology like Skype, and the final third learned by watching a pre-recorded video of a language lesson from the same person.

Their results, published in the journal *Child Development*, showed that kids learned well in person and in the live video chat, likely because both scenarios allowed for an interaction between the child and the teacher, allowing the youngsters to be more responsive and therefore retain more from their experience. The children using the recorded videos, by contrast, did not learn new vocabulary words by the end of the 10 minute learning and testing task.

1   **What is the best title according to the passage?**

① The Interaction between the Baby and the Caregiver
② Why Effective Ways to Learn Change as Time Passes
③ The Various Scenarios Being Conducive to Learning
④ Why Videos Aren't the Best Way for Kids to Learn

2 According to the passage, which of the following is the most likely example of the underlined Ⓐ?

① You can improve your toddler's speech by saying words to him or her and reacting to his or her saying.

② I remember watching Sesame Street and many other educational programs on TV dubbed in my own language.

③ Most people don't watch educational programs on TV when entertaining programs are available.

④ Some educational programs on TV can actually augment children's linguistic development.

3 Which of the following best fits in the blanks Ⓑ and Ⓒ?

① coalesce — static

② acquiesce — aesthetic

③ convalesce — kinetic

④ adolesce — anesthetic

4 Which of the following is NOT true according to the passage?

① Learning a new language may start even before delivery.

② For children learning a language, language acquisition is influenced by their parents.

③ Learning a language may be based on imitation and repetition.

④ For children learning a language, using a single learning mechanism is a prerequisite to language acquisition.

19

Here is a diagnosis of a certain malady in our body politic: the "both sides have a point" reflex. It stems from a desire for fairness and from the recognition that real issues are more complex than their advocates often allow, but Ⓐleads to a pathological bypass of healthy brain function. Sometimes it also appears as the "the truth is somewhere in between" reflex or the "See? I am balanced" reflex.

"Both sides have a point," as a habitual thought, often leads people into the illusion that they are above having an opinion on a subject (since people with definite opinions, by the "both sides have a point" logic, fail to recognize the truth in those opinions they disagree with). This leads to an avoidance of the meat of the questions at issue. People with this malady often fail to discover those points of specific difference in matters of fact and philosophy, because they think there is no point in exploring the debate themselves, relying on others to form definite opinions, which to them merely add up to a tableau to look at. They think their role is to "let people make up their own minds," forgetting that they count, too.

Sometimes it is true that both sides of an argument have a strong basis in reality. Perhaps it is even true most of the time. Recognizing the complexity of an issue results in complex opinions once you think things out. But it is never true a priori that "the truth is somewhere in between"; that is, when it's true that both sides have a point you can only know it by paying close attention to what both sides are saying and thinking about it. "Let's hear both sides" — that's a salutary thought. But a presumption in advance that both sides are equally right, that's just lazy, and, unfortunately, common.

Part of the cause of this kind of thinking is that journalists have turned to it as a way of avoiding criticism from bellicose right wingers who write letters to advertisers when the newspapers publish analyses that they disagree with, or facts that they want to suppress. Instead of just telling the truth in articles about hot topics, journalists now mostly provide a platform for "both sides," regardless of how bogus one side's statements actually are. Many in the public follow suit, thinking that this kind of "balance" equals objectivity. It doesn't. That's what's so cancerous about this habit of thought. Objectivity can draw conclusions. A priori "balance" cannot. In the absence of a public that's engaged enough to draw conclusions, who leads?

1 **Choose the one closest in meaning to the underlined Ⓐ.**

① lowers people's intelligence chronically

② makes people reluctant to think thoroughly

③ distracts people's mind from health problems

④ spreads mental illness among people

2 Which of the following can be associated with the "both sides have a point" reflex?

① excuse for lack of thought   ② absoluteness of truth

③ black and white logic   ④ religious fundamentalism

3 Which of the following can be inferred from the passage?

① Those who think that the truth is somewhere in between have a fair and balanced mind.

② The truth can be attained by congregating the definite opinions of both parties concerned.

③ Journalists should take the initiative to tell the truth and draw conclusions on the basis of objectivity.

④ Complex opinions about a complex issue can get in the way of reaching any conclusions.

4 Which of the following statements would the author of the passage most probably agree with?

① If President Obama said that the earth was flat, the best headline of the news article would be "Opinions Differ on Shape of the Earth."

② I think so much about the world is relative, and thus, we should embrace the notion of cultural pluralism.

③ Journalists have to present two sides of the "climate change" issue, despite the scientific consensus on the matter.

④ I can't understand how they can disagree with the Burka and at the same time defend a woman's right to wear it.

5 What is the main idea of the passage?

① We should try to decide between the two sides by probing into both of them.

② It is required that we avoid proclaiming our subjective opinions in any debate.

③ Many people use the "both sides have a point" logic to avoid the responsibility.

④ Journalists are forced to take a neutral attitude under the pressure from right wingers.

20

The animal man becomes a civilized man only through a fundamental change of his nature, transforming not only the instinctual aims but also the instinctual values — that is, the principles that govern the attainment of the aims.

Freud described this change as the transformation of the pleasure principle into the reality principle. The interpretation of the mental apparatus in terms of these two principles is basic to Freud's theory. It corresponds largely (but not entirely) to the distinction between unconscious and conscious processes. The unconscious, ruled by the pleasure principle, comprises the older primary processes. They strive for nothing but gaining pleasure; from any operation which might arouse unpleasantness (pain), mental activity draws back.

But the unrestrained pleasure principle comes into conflict with the natural and human environment. The individual comes to the traumatic realization that full and painless gratification of his needs is impossible. And after this experience of disappointment, a new principle of mental functioning gains ascendancy. The reality principle supersedes the pleasure principle: man learns to give up momentary, uncertain and destructive pleasure for delayed, restrained, but assured pleasure.

With the establishment of the reality principle, the human being which, under the pleasure principle, has been hardly more than a bundle of animal drives, has become an organized ego. It strives for what is useful and what can be obtained without damage to itself and to its vital environment. Under the reality principle, the human being develops the function of reason: it learns to test the reality, to distinguish between good and bad, true and false, useful and harmful. Man acquires the faculties of attention, memory, and judgment. He becomes a conscious, thinking subject, geared to a rationality which is imposed upon him from outside.

The function of motor discharge, which, under the supremacy of the pleasure principle, had served to unburden the mental apparatus of accretions of stimuli, is now employed in the appropriate alteration of reality.

The scope of man's desires and the instrumentalities for their gratification are thus immeasurably increased, and his ability to alter reality consciously in accordance with what is useful seems to promise a gradual removal of extraneous barriers to his gratification. However, neither his desires nor his alteration of reality are henceforth his own: they are now organized by his society. And this organization represses and transmutes his original instinctual needs.

1 Which of the following best represents the main idea of this passage?

① Man cannot satisfy all his instinctual needs without restraint regardless of reality.

② Man's reason and mental abilities are dormant as long as the pleasure principle dominates.

③ Human beings are civilized through the change of their instinctual aims and values.

④ The pleasure principle and the reality principle are central concepts of Freud's theory.

2 Which of the following is NOT associated with the unconscious process?

① limitless gratification of needs

② damage to human environment

③ indifference to good and bad

④ appropriate alteration of needs

3 Which of the following can be inferred from the passage?

① An animal man need not make conscious efforts to gain pleasure.

② A civilized man also faces obstacles to gratification of his needs.

③ Disappointment plays the greatest role in developing human societies.

④ The reality principle reduces man's desires and ability to satisfy them.

4 Which of the following is true of an organized ego?

① It is ruled by the pleasure principle.

② It accepts self-sacrifice as a valuable virtue.

③ It is an intelligent, rational and contemplative being.

④ It disregards extrinsic and environmental factors.

5 According to the passage, the function of motor discharge becomes more _____ under the reality principle.

① productive   ② primitive

③ passive   ④ prohibitive

6 According to the passage, the change in the human value system can be said to be that from absence of repression to _____.

① indulgence   ② security

③ liberation   ④ fantasy

22만 6천 편입합격생의 선택

김영편입 영어
독해

워크북 **2**단계

03

문화·예술

03

문화·예술

▶▶▶ ANSWERS P.340

01

In *The Greening of America*, a much-debated 1970 Ⓐpaean to the dawning of a utopian new age, Charles A. Reich hailed blue jeans as a symbol of the liberating spirit of Consciousness III, the new generation that was going to lead America into an anti-materialist, community-minded, freedom-loving era of love, peace and hope. He wrote that the clothes worn by certified members of Consciousness III were basically machine-made, and that there was no attempt to hide that fact, no shame attached to mass-produced goods, no social points lost for wearing something that sold at $4.99 from coast to coast and had its measurements printed on the outside for all to read.

Needless to say, Mr. Reich's predictions — about blue jeans and just about everything else — have failed to come true. As James Sullivan notes in his pedestrian new cultural history, blue jeans have become a designer staple that routinely fetch $100 to $200 at places like Barneys and Fred Segal, and rare vintage ones can go for tens of thousands of dollars. Far from being utilitarian garments signifying egalitarianism and the common man, jeans have become status symbols, relentlessly updated, redesigned and embellished, and even more aggressively marketed.

1 Choose the one closest in meaning to the underlined Ⓐ"paean".

① eulogy
③ lament

② paradox
④ nostrum

2 Which of the following is NOT true according to the passage?

① Reich predicted that Consciousness III would become the zeitgeist of America's new era.

② Reich thought wearing cheap blue jeans did not matter to the members of Consciousness III.

③ Sullivan's accounts falsify Reich's prediction that blue jeans would be typical garments of the general public.

④ Barneys and Fred Segal are specialty stores exclusively for high quality blue jeans fans.

3 What is the purpose of the passage?

① To explain how Consciousness Ⅲ came into being and how it has changed

② To claim blue jeans are no longer a symbol of the spirit of Consciousness Ⅲ

③ To contrast the two authors' viewpoints of the recent American public culture

④ To suggest that blue jeans be designed to meet the tastes of ordinary people

02

Up to about 1915, movies were short and programs were made of several works. Then, D. W. Griffith and others began to make full-length films which provided the same powerful emotional appeal as did melodrama and presented spectacles far beyond what the theatre could offer. Consequently, after World War Ⅰ increasing numbers of spectators deserted the theatre for the movies. This trend was accelerated in the late 1920's as a result of two new elements: In 1927, sound was added to the previously silent film, and thus one of the theatre's principal claims to superiority vanished. In 1929, a serious economic depression began. Since audience could go to the movies for a fraction of what it cost to see a play, theatregoing became a luxury which a few could afford, especially as the depression deepened. By the end of World War Ⅱ, the American theatre had been reduced to about thirty theatres in New York City and a small number of touring companies originating there.

1 **Up to the 1920's one objection to films was that _____.**

① they were silent

② they were too short

③ they were too expensive

④ they did not tell a complete story

2 **One thing that made people choose the movies over the theatre was _____.**

① World War Ⅰ

② a depression

③ the fact that films were silent

④ the fact that films were shorter

3 **By the end of World War Ⅱ, _____.**

① the theatre was no longer considered a luxury

② theatre had become entertainment for the masses

③ there were no theatrical performances outside of New York City

④ professional theatrical performances were confined mainly to New York City

03

Neoclassicism was a widespread and influential movement in painting and the other visual arts that began in the 1760s, reached its height in the 1780s and '90s, and lasted until the 1840s and '50s. Ⓐ<u>In painting, neoclassicism generally took the form of an emphasis on austere linear design in the depiction of classical themes and subject matter, using archaeologically correct settings and costumes.</u> Neoclassicism arose partly as a reaction against the sensuous and frivolously decorative Rococo style that had dominated European art from the 1720s on. Ⓑ<u>Neoclassicism sought to revive the ideals of ancient Greek and Roman art.</u> Neoclassic artists used classical forms to express their ideas about courage, sacrifice, and love of country. Ⓒ<u>The Rococo is sometimes considered a final phase of the Baroque period.</u>

Although the movement spread throughout Western Europe, France and England were the countries that used the style most frequently in their arts and architecture. Ⓓ<u>The movement was inspired by the discovery of ancient Italian artifacts at the ruins of Herculaneum and Pompeii.</u> Neoclassicism emphasized rationality and the resurgence of tradition. Ⓔ<u>Neoclassical artists incorporated classical styles and subjects, including columns, pediments, friezes, and other ornamental schemes in their work.</u>

1 Choose the one that is <u>inappropriate</u> for the whole context.

① Ⓐ   ② Ⓑ

③ Ⓒ   ④ Ⓓ

⑤ Ⓔ

2 Which of the following best describes "neoclassicism"?

① It emphasized color, light and atmosphere over line quality.

② It used the classical elements to express traditional ideas.

③ It tried to depict settings and costumes in modernized forms.

④ It sought to revive the showy decorations of ancient arts.

⑤ It thought highly of arts showing transcendental religious faith.

04

The horror of World War I caused tremendous disillusionment. One expression of this was the birth of a movement called "dada." (Considerable debate exists about when and how the word "dada" — it is French for "hobby-horse" — came to be chosen. The dadaists themselves accepted it as two nonsense syllables, like one of a baby's first words.) During the years 1915-1916, many artists gathered in neutral capitals in Europe to express their disgust at the direction western societies were taking. Dada was thus a political protest, and, in many places, the dadaists produced more left-wing propaganda than art.

By 1916, a few works of art began to appear, many of them found objects and experiments in which Ⓐ_____ played an important role. For example, Jean Arp produced collages that he made by dropping haphazardly cut pieces of paper onto a surface and pasting them down the way they fell. Max Ernst juxtaposed strange, unrelated items to produce unexplainable phenomena. This use of conventional items placed in circumstances that alter their traditional meanings is characteristic of dadaist art. Irrationality, meaninglessness, and harsh, mechanical images are typical effects as shown in *Woman, Old Man, and Flower*. This is a nonsensical world in which pseudo-human forms with their bizarre features and proportions suggest a malevolent unreality.

1 **Choose the one that best fills in the blank Ⓐ.**

① chance   ② scheme

③ motive   ④ outcome

2 **According to the passage, how is the origin of the word dada?**

① dual   ② mythical

③ unequivocal   ④ controversial

3 **According to the passage, what is true about "dada"?**

① It began as an escape from the disillusionment after World War I.

② It advocated art for art's sake in reaction to the Western civilization.

③ It expressed new machines and scientific experiments in artistic ways.

④ It ignored traditional aesthetics, and prized nonsense and illogicality.

05

Many 20th-century composers turned away from harmonic methods that had been used in music for the past 150 years. The Frenchman Claude Debussy (1862-1918) rejected the rules of 19th-century harmony as they were taught in the Paris Conservatoire, instead infusing his practice with harmonic techniques from East Asia and Russia. With Debussy, we enter the "Modern" era of Western art music, an era which presumably continues to the present day. For Debussy, music developed organically from many varieties of rhythms, harmonies, textures and colours. He was not a didactic revolutionary in the mould of Stravinsky or Schoenberg. His works create the impression of having been conceived in a flash of inspiration, though many pieces he sent for publication took months or even years to complete. Debussy's later music was perceived as sharing certain characteristics with the Impressionist painters, Monet, especially. The composer did not approve of the comparison, _____ it is hard to avoid noticing the striking correspondences between the Impressionists' tendency towards softening structural outlines and their fascination with light and colour, and the musical brushwork of Debussy's *Préludes* for piano, and his orchestral pieces *Images* and *La mer*.

1 It appears that later music of Debussy seemed colored by _____.

① the rules of 19th-century harmony

② the music of Stravinsky

③ the pictures of East Asia

④ Russian literature

⑤ Impressionists' paintings

2 The most appropriate expression for the blank would be _____.

① therefore   ② yet

③ finally   ④ so

⑤ meanwhile

Sitting down to an elegant dinner in tie and tails are a room full of distinguished men each seeming bent on out-shining the next in terms of breeding and class. Ⓐ As one reaches across the table to retrieve the dish of butter, his arm hits the salt cellar, which wobbles once or twice, and then falls. The crystals of salt have barely scattered on to the silk table cloth when the gentleman reaches forward, picks up a few grains in a pinch, and then tosses them over his left shoulder. ⒶThis display of the superstitions about spilling salt passes uncommented upon as the dinner continues. Ⓑ It is considered bad luck to spill salt, but the superstition most associated with this activity is not the act of spilling, but what comes next. In order to prevent the bad luck from settling on the salt spiller, the person who did the spilling is required to toss some of the spilled salt over his left shoulder. This very specific action is supposed to act as a shield, but must be done immediately for its benefits to take hold. This very interesting superstition has been around for a very long time, although its exact origins are obscured in history. Ⓒ The origins of the spilling salt superstitions may lie in the fact that spilling salt was considered bad form long before it was considered bad luck. In ancient times salt was an expensive commodity, and one that had many useful purposes. Ⓓ Wasting salt, therefore, was frowned upon, and so some suggest that the admonition of spilling salt being "bad luck" came about as a way to stop the careless from wasting a precious spice.

1 Which of the following is the best title for the passage?

① How to Deal with the Lapse of Dinner Etiquette

② A Superstitious Practice and its Provenance

③ The Irreplaceable Value of Salt in a Daily Life

④ Why the Myth about Spilling Salt Emerges

2 According to the passage, which of the following is the purpose of the underlined Ⓐ?

① to apologize to diners for his reckless conduct

② to put the scattered salt back into the cellar

③ to boast himself that he is a man of culture

④ to provide a shield to forestall misfortune

3 When the passage is divided into three paragraphs, which would be most appropriate boundary?

① Ⓐ and Ⓒ   ② Ⓑ and Ⓒ

③ Ⓑ and Ⓓ   ④ Ⓒ and Ⓓ

07

"Light," wrote Cezanne in one of his letters, "does not exist for the painter." By this paradoxical statement he meant to imply that light can and usually does distort the actual form of an object. Its general effect is to fall Ⓐ_____ on those prominent points that it meets and from which it is reflected, and to throw into insignificant shade all parts of an object that lie outside the immediate area of impact. The resulting chiaroscuro can, of course, be exploited as an end in itself, and it was the chief delight of the Mannerist painters of the seventeenth and eighteenth centuries. Cezanne, striving to realize the cubic volume and tactile surfaces of the objects he painted, was rightly horrified by such rhetorical devices. He did his best to render colors in their purity, that is to say, with the precise tone values they possess in an evenly distributed light, and he believed that the real form of the object then emerged. "When color has attained richness, form has reached its plenitude. If this evasion of arbitrary light effects is essential for the painter in his rendering of three-dimensional form on the two-dimensional surface of his canvas, it is obviously still more important for the sculptor who is striving to create three-dimensional forms of direct sensational appeal," he said.

1 Choose the one that best fills in the blank Ⓐ.

① with obliterating force
② in a flickering manner
③ with reviving power
④ by supernatural means

2 Which of the following is NOT true about Cezanne?

① He rejected the intense contrasts of light and shadow in his painting.
② Unlike the Mannerist painters, he was extremely antipathetic to chiaroscuro.
③ He viewed the real form as attainable through colors not distorted by light.
④ He thought painting to be more vulnerable to light effects than sculpture.

3 What is the best title for the passage?

① Cezanne's Style of Painting
② Cezanne and the Effect of Light
③ How Cezanne Differs from His Predecessors
④ Cezanne as a Magician of Light and Color

08

The turn of the 20th century was a generally _____ era, as life in Europe and the United States underwent some dramatic shifts. Industrialism was on the rise, many nations participated in the First World War, and society was rapidly changing. As the rules of life shifted underfoot, some dancers began to feel that the formal rules of classical ballet were too restricting, and they began to develop their own style of free-flowing dance, which came to be known as "modern" dance, to differentiate it from classical ballet.

Modern dance is now more closely mingled with other disciplines like jazz dance, ballet, and tap, and some dancers work in both modern and classical dance styles, drawing techniques from both. In a modern dance performance, the dancer is often barefoot, or wearing soft shoes. He or she moves in a free, almost improvisational style, and it is common to see controlled falls and other interesting interplays of body weight and gravity. Unlike ballet, which reaches for the stars with leaps and high kicks, modern dance often lingers near the ground, especially in a piece heavily influenced by psychology and intense emotional states.

1 Choose the one that best fills in the blank.

① frivolous   ② hedonistic

③ treacherous   ④ iconoclastic

2 According to the passage, what does NOT characterize "modern dance"?

① performing impromptu

② following the rigid rules

③ combining various elements

④ staying low to the floor

3 Which of the following CANNOT be inferred about "modern dance"?

① In an era of nonconformism, it was born to break boundaries.

② It uses body weight and center of gravity to embellish movements.

③ It places emphasis on the serious expression of inner emotions.

④ It was hailed as an answer to social maladies in the twentieth century.

09

No maker of chisels would say to his employer, "You wish me to make sharp chisels. I, on the other hand, can only express myself to the full by making blunt chisels." The artist, like the maker of chisels, serves a master but in doing so he gives his master Ⓐsomething he never bargained for. When Rembrandt painted *The Night Watch*, he was ostensibly painting the portraits of a certain Captain Banning Cocq and the members of his shooting company. Presumably something corresponding to a group photograph of the school hockey team would have satisfied the club, but Rembrandt had things to say that had nothing to do with the likenesses of the captain and his friends — things about how light falls in dark places, and how it strikes hard here and gently caresses there — and he insisted on saying them. In doing so he began to lose sight of the original purpose of his picture. Banning Cocq and his friends became mere excuses for an essay in chiaroscuro. The club was offended; certain members of it complained that their faces had been plunged into semidarkness; they were more interested in themselves than in chiaroscuro. We, on the other hand, are delighted. We have lost interest in seventeenth-century shooting clubs, but what Rembrandt had to say about the play of light on flesh is as Ⓑ_____ today as it was in 1642.

1 In Rembrandt's case, what is referred to by the underlined Ⓐ?

① the portraits of a shooting club
② something like a group photograph
③ things about how light plays
④ the original purpose of his picture

2 According to the passage, which of the following distinguishes an artist from an artisan like a chisel maker?

① Part of an artist's work goes beyond meeting what his master wants.
② An artist feels free to say anything about what his master expects of him.
③ What an artist has to do is create something that only a few can appreciate.
④ An artist makes it his goal to paint a picture much like a photograph.

3 Choose the one that best fills in the blank Ⓑ.

① confusing
② fascinating
③ irritating
④ encouraging

10

Cubism was a truly revolutionary style of modern art developed by Pablo Picasso and Georges Braque. It was the first style of abstract art which evolved at the beginning of the 20th century in response to a world that was changing with unprecedented speed. Cubism was an attempt by artists to Ⓐrevitalize the tired traditions of Western art which they believed had run their course. The Cubists Ⓑchallenged conventional forms of representation, such as perspective, which had been the rule since the Renaissance. Their aim was to develop a new way of seeing which reflected the modern age. In the four decades from 1870-1910, western society witnessed more technological progress than in the previous four centuries. During this period, inventions such as photography, cinematography, sound recording, the telephone, the motor car and the airplane heralded the dawn of a new age.

The problem for artists at this time was how to reflect Ⓒthe modernity of the era using the tired and trusted traditions that had served art for the last four centuries. Photography had begun to replace painting as the tool for documenting the age and for artists to sit illustrating cars, planes and images of the new technologies was not exactly rising to the challenge. Artists needed a more Ⓓconservative approach — a 'new way of seeing' that expanded the possibilities of art in the same way that technology was extending the boundaries of communication and travel. This new way of seeing was called Cubism — the first abstract style of modern art. Picasso and Braque developed their ideas on Cubism around 1907 in Paris and their starting point was a common interest in the later paintings of Paul Cézanne.

1 위 글의 제목으로 가장 적합한 것을 고르시오.

① The Father of Cubism: Picasso
② Various Facets Experimented with by Cubists
③ The Contradictory Relationship of Cubism and Modern Abstraction
④ The Historical Background Giving Rise to Cubism

2 위 글에서 논지의 흐름상 가장 적합하지 <u>않은</u> 것을 고르시오.

① Ⓐ   ② Ⓑ
③ Ⓒ   ④ Ⓓ

11

When Marcel Duchamp's 1912 painting *Nude Descending a Staircase, No. 2* debuted, it sparked one of the greatest uproars the art world has ever known. But after facing scads of rejection, mockery, and even a presidential put-down, this provocative piece rose to the ranks of masterpiece. *Nude Descending a Staircase, No. 2* reimagines the human form through a mechanized and monochromatic lens in keeping with Cubism, and in the century since its completion, it has repeatedly been displayed in Cubist art exhibits. However, Duchamp's use of 20 different static positions created a sense of motion and visual violence that Cubists claimed made this piece more Futurist than a true example of their avant-garde art movement.

The French artist had hoped to debut the painting in the Salon des Indépendants's spring exhibition of Cubist works. However, the tantalizing title *Nude Descending a Staircase, No. 2* was roundly rejected by the hanging committee, which included Duchamp's brothers Jacques Villon and Raymond Duchamp-Villon. The pair visited the painter in his Neuilly-sur-Seine studio, where they entreated him to either withdraw the work, or change/paint over its title. The Salon committee agreed with Duchamp's brothers, insisting, "A nude never descends the stairs — a nude reclines."

Despite his brothers's reservations, Marcel Duchamp flat out refused to change his piece. He later recounted, "I said nothing to my brothers. But I went immediately to the show and took my painting home in a taxi. It was really a turning point in my life, I can assure you. I saw that I would not be very much interested in groups after that." _____, the Salon d'Or (a group of Cubist artists which included Duchamp's brothers) accepted the unchanged *Nude Descending a Staircase, No. 2* for its fall exhibition. But the Duchamp brothers' bond was forever fractured.

1 Which of the following is <u>not</u> true about *Nude Descending a Staircase, No. 2*?

① It was too raunchy for anyone except Cubists to understand.
② Duchamp's Cubist contemporaries did not accept it as a piece of Cubism.
③ Duchamp's brothers thought it was unsuitable for exhibition and wanted it changed.
④ It made the Duchamp's brothers spark a family rift.

2 Choose the one most suitable to fill in the blank.

① As a result   ② Furthermore
③ Nonetheless   ④ Likewise

12

The importance of the Surrealist movement to Magritte must be emphasized. Certainly, none of the other isms of his time suited him, though fin de siecle Symbolism, which had cast its spell over Belgian art, left its mark. Surrealism offered him a base sympathetic to his forays into the irrational and insoluble. _____, Magritte didn't always share the Surrealists' central concerns. In particular, the unconscious was a key notion for them. It's impossible to imagine Dali's work of the late 1920s and the 1930s without Freud's ideas about the expression of unconscious desire in dreams. The founding fathers of Surrealism, including Andre Breton and the poet Paul Eluard, were devoted to techniques of free association, like automatic writing and drawing, that were intended to bypass the rational mind and dredge up material directly from the unconscious. However, Magritte plotted out his pictures meticulously and had no interest in automatic anything. What Magritte did share with the Surrealists was a sense of revolutionary mission, the idea that art could set people free. He once called his paintings "material tokens of the freedom of thought." In *On the Threshold of Liberty*, from 1937, a cannon takes aim at images representing some of the conventional sign systems that beguile us every day — sex, the sky, nature — as well as a few, like horses' bells and doily-cut paper patterns, that were among Magritte's odd recurrent motifs. <u>What will happen when the cannon fires? Then again, what will happen if it doesn't?</u>

1 Choose the one that best fills in the blank.

① As a result   ② All the same
③ In addition   ④ For instance

2 Which of the following is associated with the last two underlined sentences?

① unconscious desire   ② free association
③ automatic drawing   ④ freedom of thought

3 Which of the following can be inferred about "Magritte"?

① He was a Belgian surrealist artist very distinct from other surrealists.
② He shared more things in common with Dali than with other surrealists.
③ He was mainly concerned with ordinary art easily understood by people.
④ He kept himself in his own conscious, reasonable and conventional world.

13

George Bryan "Beau" Brummell, described as the most famous and influential man in early 19th-century London, was the center of a revolution. He sparked change not with rhetoric or military might, but with innovations in masculine sartorial style and manner. Men copied what he wore, his mannerisms, and even his daily grooming routine.

Today he is remembered as the world's first dandy, but although his name became synonymous with the label, he didn't inspire its creation. The *Oxford English Dictionary*, defining the term as one "who studies above everything to dress elegantly and fashionably," traces its origins to 1780, just two years after Brummell's birth. Nevertheless, Brummell became a symbol of a new masculine style, one that still dictates the way people dress today.

Brummell's fashion mantra urged "the maximum of luxury in the service of minimal ostentation." Or as people might say today, "less is more." Elegance was about cut and quality rather than color and decoration. He warned that "If people turn to look at you in the street, you are not well dressed, but either too stiff, too tight, or too fashionable."

Brummell also advocated innovations in _____. Just as clothes should look polished and clean-cut, so too should one's person. He replaced a reliance on perfume and hair powder with the concept of a daily bath. For his contemporaries, bathing often meant washing only face, hands, and arms in cool water; sweating was believed to rid the body of toxins. Brummell's suggestion of a daily soak in hot water was nothing short of revolutionary.

1 According to the passage, which of the following is not true about George Bryan "Beau" Brummell?

① He was rich enough to buy clothes then in vogue, but he developed his own style.
② His contemporaries believed that a daily bath was not good for their health.
③ He valued refining the cut of his clothes above clothes with prints and decoration.
④ He invented masculine sartorial style and manner that men still follow today.

2 What is implied by the underlined phrase "less is more"?

① Clothes with details lead the fashion.
② Simple outfits look elegant and polished.
③ Having fewer clothes makes one's life easier.
④ Minimalism in fashion is no longer in style.

3 Which of the following is most appropriate for the blank?

① fashion design ② synthetic detergent
③ personal hygiene ④ fragrant materials

14

The concept of avant-garde refers primarily to artists, writers, composers and thinkers Ⓐ_____ and often has a trenchant social or political edge. Many writers, critics and theorists made assertions about vanguard culture during the formative years of modernism. Vanguard culture has historically been opposed to "high" or "dominant" culture, and it has also rejected the artificially synthesized mass culture that has been produced by industrialization. Each of these media is a direct product of Capitalism — they are all now substantial industries — and as such they are driven by the same Ⓑ_____ of other sectors of manufacturing, not the ideals of Ⓒ_____. For avant-garde artists, these forms were therefore kitsch: phony, faked or mechanical culture, which often pretended to be more than they were by using formal devices stolen from vanguard culture. For instance, during the 1930s the advertising industry was quick to take visual mannerisms from surrealism, but this does not mean that 1930s advertising photographs are truly surreal. On the contrary, they express a style without underlying substance. In this sense avant-garde artists carefully Ⓓ_____ true avant-garde creativity from the market-driven fashion change and superficial stylistic innovation that are sometimes used to claim privileged status for these manufactured forms of the new consumer culture.

1 Choose the best phrase for the blank Ⓐ above.

  ① whose work is in favor of mainstream cultural values

  ② whose work is in pursuit of the art-for-art principle

  ③ whose work is opposed to mainstream cultural values

  ④ whose work thinks lightly of the art-for-art principle

2 Choose the best phrase for the blanks Ⓑ and Ⓒ above.

  ① profit-fixated motives — true art

  ② art-oriented motives — fake art

  ③ ideology-based motives — revolutionary idea

  ④ family-oriented motives — family value

3 Choose the best word for the blank Ⓓ above.

  ① repudiated   ② distinguished

  ③ identified   ④ embraced

4 Which statement CANNOT be inferred from the passage?

① The mass culture is the product of the development of industry on an extensive scale.

② The artists going along with avant-garde lodges an objection against pop culture.

③ Avant-garde artists lose spirit of resistance in the face of consumerism culture.

④ Avant-garde artists refute the artistic value of highbrow culture.

15

Some people have compared music to verbal language, with which different signs and meanings are delivered to the audience. According to this theory, composers are formulating "non-lingual stories" about different experiences of their own and expressing them in their musical compositions. Music is communication, it has been compared to the sacred text, which contains untold stories, quiet whispers and shouts about mental pictures, memories, meanings and things, which are linked to the psychic processes during the creative process of composing. These expressions Ⓐ_____ composers' highly subjective and inner worlds of the mind and its reality.

Understanding that reality requires an emphatic listener, who is constantly trying to understand music by catching the similar structures (mental pictures, memories, emotions etc.) presented in a musical composition from his or her own subjective mental world. The subject who is creating, performing or receiving music can thus use meaningful musical structures to build his or her own world into a meaningful and harmonious entirety. In the process of creating or sketching music, the external performance of a composer/musician coincides with an internal working process of shaping his or her own internal world, through which the external product of sounds then acquires its final configuration.

1 **What does the author mainly talk about in the passage?**

① the value of music

② the process of musical communication

③ the role of a composer and a listener

④ the analogy between music and language

⑤ how to fully appreciate music

2 **According to the passage, why have people compared music to verbal language?**

① Because verbal language delivers different signs and meanings to the audience.

② Because music is connected with a composer's psychic process during composition.

③ Because music expresses a musician's own experiences explicitly.

④ Because a composer shapes a story about his or her own experiences and reveals it in his or her musical composition.

⑤ Because music contains untold stories, quiet whispers and shouts about mental pictures, memories, meanings and things.

3 Which is most appropriate for the blank Ⓐ?

① are deeply anchored to

② are completely detached from

③ give rise to

④ efficiently capitalize on

⑤ stiffly compete with

16

Perhaps the most striking difference between 1990s hip-hop and more modern tracks is the lyrics. In general, hip-hop in the previous decade had a relatively narrow focus. Songs were less about an artist's success and more about his or her rise to it; even the most financially successful rappers wrote about violence, crime, and living in poverty. According to Rauly Ramirez, manager of Billboard's Hip-Hop chart, '90s rappers "would create this persona," portraying themselves as thugs and gangsters because that was "the character [they] had to be to succeed." The necessity for an artist to create and maintain this character led to a common theme among rap songs in the '90s. Rap was the story of the ghetto life and the anthem of gangsters, which prevented hip-hop from joining pop and rock in the mainstream.

While, a decade later, rap lyrics still tell an artist's story, each rapper has a different one; artists no longer need to write about the "ghetto life" to be signed by a major record label. The definition of who a rapper can be, and what stories hip-hop can tell, has broadened indefinitely since the mid-2000s. Ramirez pinpoints the origins of this _____ to the release of Kanye West's 2004 debut album, "The College Dropout." Rather than focusing on drug dealing or violence or living on the streets, the album addressed religion, West's pursuit of music, and as he says on the track "Breathe In Breathe Out," his desire to "say something significant." In the years following the release of Kanye's first album, more and more rappers moved away from "gangsta rap" and towards developing their individuality as artists. Today's most successful hip-hop artists rap about everything from thrift shopping to the sheer excess of their lifestyles.

1 **The best title of the above passage would be _____.**

① The Noticeable Features of 1990s Hip-hop
② The Most Influential Hip-hop Artists in Our Age
③ The History of Hip-hop Music
④ The Future of Hip-hop Music
⑤ The Dissimilarity of Hip-hop between 1990s and 2000s

2 **Which of the following is NOT the characteristic of 1990s hip-hop?**

① The favorite themes of the lyrics were far from being colorful.
② Some rappers considered the process as being more important than the result.
③ Living in poverty was rappers' regular material for writing a rap.
④ Some rappers became a gangster to be a real rapper admired by other rappers.
⑤ Rap songs were not considered as a mainstream form of music.

3 Which of the following would be best for the blank?

① transition   ② stagnation

③ regression   ④ cognition

⑤ prejudice

17

The development of French Impressionism was one of the most important <u>watersheds</u> in art history. The Impressionists revolutionized art by pioneering new painting practices, all the while influencing numerous other areas of the artistic process and setting the stage for the rejection of previous art standards that emphasized tradition and realism. When Claude Monet showed his piece entitled, *Impression: Sunrise*, during an exhibition in 1872, a French art critic dismissed his work and that of several other artists as merely a sketchy "impression" of a scene, not a finished work of art. Thus, the group of painters at this exhibition came to be known as Impressionists.

The subjects and style of Impressionism were unique. Artists painted many subjects considered inappropriate for fine art, such as the everyday lives of maidservants, peasants, and washwomen. In doing so, it may be argued that painters began to "democratize" their work, shifting their focus to the tastes of a broadening audience. Several critics derided the Impressionists and resented them for their popularity. On many occasions, they were not considered mainstream or talented enough to exhibit at the national art show of France, the Salon, but a few Impressionists experienced some success there. As a whole, though, the traditional art world viewed Impressionist artists as rebellious. Undaunted by their critics, they staged their own exhibits and limited their ties to the Salon.

The Impressionists, as their name suggests, wanted to portray only an impression of an image, instead of a clearly defined picture. They preferred short brushstrokes and dabbing the art canvas with their paintbrush, instead of applying perfectly uniform coats of paint. The Impressionists' technique achieved a soft, blurry, almost dream-like quality.

1 **Which of the following can be inferred about Impressionism?**

① Its area of influence was primarily limited to France.
② Natural forms are represented in geometric shapes in it.
③ It was not wholeheartedly embraced by the art community at first.
④ It was the first artistic genre to emphasize the portrayal of natural scenes.

2 **Which of the following statements is NOT true about the majority of works of art exhibited in the Salon?**

① They were more realistic compared to Impressionist pieces.
② They provided a more detailed portrayal than Impressionist works.
③ They did not focus on various scenes of lower class or everyday life.
④ They are more valued today than the Impressionist paintings.

3 The author of the passage implies that the term "Impressionist" _____.

① failed to capture the spirit of the new movement

② offended the painters to whom it was applied

③ was limited to use in newspapers or magazines

④ eventually lost its negative overtones

4 Choose the word which is closest in meaning to <u>watersheds</u>.

① junctures   ② elicitations

③ overtures   ④ avocations

18

Verbatim theatre tells true stories through the words of those involved in accidents or disasters. The lines are spoken by actors, but they come directly from the transcripts of interviews with ordinary people who happened to find themselves in extraordinary situations (sometimes with the addition of public testimony from sources such as the Commission of Inquiry). Generally the sets are abstractly minimal — there is no attempt to recreate the events being described. The power is all in the words being spoken. Unlike the _____ dialogue of traditional theatre, verbatim plays include the *ums* and *ahs* and unfinished sentences that characterize real speech. The effect can be electrifying. The accident experiencers who saw these plays say, "I had my hands in my face when the play first started, but it was amazing. Just sensational."

People who are unfamiliar with verbatim theatre sometimes get worried that it is going to exploit someone's heartache and personal drama for entertainment. But theatre is a great medium for talking about things and to some extent healing. We can address something head-on by verbatim theatre and feel that the community is supporting and embracing the people in that story. Another common misconception is that the playscript is just a cut-and-paste job, where all the work is done by the interviewees. For that matter, it is useful to compare this with the process of making a documentary film, where the writer's role is to decide who will be interviewed and what they'll be asked about, and then decide which sections of which interviews will be used, and weave it all together to tell a cohesive story.

1 Choose the one that best fills in the blank.

① dragging and vexing

② clipped and polished

③ artless and undesigning

④ unsettled and responsive

2 Choose the closest in meaning to the underlined "address something head-on."

① deal with something in a direct manner

② call the public's attention to something

③ speak straightforwardly about something

④ put something onto the table of debate

3 Which of the following CANNOT be inferred about "verbatim theatre"?

① It can bring to the stage the voices that might otherwise be hidden.

② It can pose an ethical issue with regard to the infringement of privacy.

③ It is not its flaw that its script is made by interviewees, not playwrights.

④ It is being blamed for hurting the survivors by reproducing the disaster.

4 What is the purpose of the passage?

① to warn against making plays of unfortunate events

② to compare a popular theater with a similar film

③ to give information about a reality-based form of play

④ to point out misunderstandings about a real-life drama

19

This "freedom" of art from the institutional constraints of religion and collective life has allowed it to play a much more critical social role. To the average viewer, much contemporary art may not appear "spiritual" at all; rather, it may appear self-analytical and highly critical of contemporary society and the human condition. Even though contemporary art may not seem spiritual, this critical function is an extension of art's assumption of the traditional role of religion. Art becomes the new arbiter of morality, though this often involves the inversion of moral codes rather than an affirmation of conventional morality. As Barzun has argued, in the early twentieth century the strategy of the Symbolists and other early Modernists was to represent art as the core of reality by which all other things were shown to be false and artificial and, therefore, subject to doubt. Art became the true measure of vitality; all other values were overturned or suspected in what Nietzsche called the _____.

This _____ of the spiritual and material continues to motivate influential late-twentieth-and twenty-first-century artists. In a famous performance piece, *Coyote: I Like America and America Likes Me* (Rene Block Gallery, New York, 1974), the artist Joseph Beuys wrapped himself in a felt blanket and stayed for a week in a room with a coyote. One of the few props in the room was a copy of the *Wall Street Journal*. For Beuys, the *Wall Street Journal* upon which the coyote had so persistently urinated epitomized the "ultimate rigor mortis" afflicting thinking about life today: economic capital is the only "substance" revered by a culture that is prepared to sacrifice everything in its name. What Beuys meant by "substance" (or capital) was utterly different, growing out of a shamanic perception of art (capital) as creative, animistic energy and imagination: the ultimate root of any possibility of growth towards <u>a non-totalitarian world of social and cosmic totality</u>. Beuys' political artwork exemplifies the way that "spiritual" art served a critical role in contemporary culture in the late twentieth century, extending a tendency that began more than one hundred years ago with the birth of the avant-garde.

1 다음 글의 제목으로 가장 적절한 것은?

① Increasing Secularity of Art

② The Critical Role of Art

③ Artists as Shamans

④ Symbols and the Collective Meaning of Art

⑤ Art and Religion in Intercultural Contexts

2 빈칸에 공동으로 들어갈 가장 적절한 것은?

① reconciliation   ② immortality

③ opposition   ④ transcendence

⑤ aesthetics

3 밑줄 친 "<u>a non-totalitarian world of social and cosmic totality</u>"의 의미로 가장 적절한 것은?

① an extremely stable society like a postmortem rigid body

② a society dominated by rationality that has overcome shamanistic superstitions

③ a society that ended totalitarian rule through a free market economy

④ a society that honors a variety of spiritual and cultural values

⑤ a pure spiritual society that overthrew everything materialistic

4 윗글의 내용과 가장 가까운 것은?

① Religion has come to perform the social critical functions that art has held.

② Symbolists and other modernists saw modern art as an epitome of fallacy and artificiality.

③ In the Beuys' work, the coyote symbolizes the evils of environmental destruction caused by capitalism.

④ Beuys' political artwork was completely separated from the path that the avant-gard had suggested.

⑤ Contrary to the outward impression, "spiritual" elements can be found in some modern political art.

20

To explain the reasons clothes were first worn, the modesty theory holds that our primitive ancestors wore clothes to avoid feelings of guilt and shame resulting from exposure of particular parts of the body. The idea that a sense of modesty underlies all original motives for clothing the body may be a popular belief, but it is neither generally accepted by scholars in the field nor borne out by observable facts.

The first reason for rejecting the modesty theory as a major explanation for wearing clothes is the wide variety of ideas people have about what constitutes modesty and nakedness. Most people in the world do use dress to conceal parts of the body but the parts it conceals vary from culture to culture. The women in the Suya tribe in the Amazon jungle wear large cylindrical wooden plugs in their earlobes and disks in their lower lips. They are not ashamed of their naked bodies, but they are terribly embarrassed if outsiders see them without their disks in place. The women on the island of Yap in the South Pacific hold to a very strict tradition of modesty, but what must never be exposed are the thighs, not the breasts.

Another reason for rejecting the modesty theory is that there is now evidence that indicates that modesty is not an instinct, but a culturally induced habit that varies depending on the time and place. A sense of modesty is completely lacking in young children of our own society, who at the age of three may well undress on the front lawn and visit the neighbors in no clothes.

Additionally, the concept of modesty changes with age. Pictures of naked babies appear in magazines and in family albums. Not only is photographing naked babies acceptable, but it is often encouraged, much to the embarrassment of children looking at their baby pictures in later years. A baby or small child may be undressed in public, for example, at the beach, and a baby's diaper may be changed there. However, at some older age, this practice becomes indecent exposure and is strictly punishable by laws in most countries.

In conclusion, many people in today's society wear clothes for the reason of modesty, but it is probably not of primary importance and it cannot account for the origin of clothes.

1 **What is the best title for the passage?**

① Social Practices of Modesty and Nakedness

② The Variety of Wardrobe Among Tribes

③ A Theory on the Original Function of Clothing

④ The Impact of the Modesty Theory on Fashion

2 Which of the following is NOT a reason that the modesty theory is untenable?

① The things people think about modesty are not the same.

② Expressions of modesty are habits set by the society we live in.

③ The sense of modesty developed only after mankind was civilized.

④ As people get older, their concept of modesty changes.

3 Which of the following is true of the modesty theory?

① We can find much evidence of its validity around us.

② It may agree with the common sense of ordinary people.

③ It is mainly applied to the women in primitive societies.

④ It holds that the need to adorn made humans wear clothes.

4 Which of the following, if true, would probably support the modesty theory?

① Adam and Eve covered themselves with fig leaves, ashamed of their naked bodies.

② Some women wear clothing in such a way that it calls attention to sensual parts of their bodies.

③ The earliest article of clothing was an animal's skin draped around the body for warmth.

④ Some intelligent animals such as apes attempt to decorate themselves with bits of string or cloth.

5 Which of the following CANNOT be inferred from the passage?

① Whether a child's naked body is indecent depends on its age.

② Suya women are ashamed of their exposed lower lips.

③ People in different cultures may think differently about bodily exposure.

④ According to the modesty theory, clothing is the cause of modesty.

6 What would the paragraph following the passage most probably discuss?

① some arguments for the modesty theory

② what types of clothes have been worn

③ another theory on the origin of clothes

④ the historical change of clothing styles

언어·문학

04 언어·문학

01

Saussure's two key ideas provide new answers to the questions 'What is the object of linguistic investigation?' and 'What is the relationship between words and things?' He makes a fundamental distinction between langue and parole — between the language system, which pre-exists actual examples of language, and the individual utterance. Langue is the _____ aspect of language: it is the shared system which we (unconsciously) draw upon as speakers. Parole is the individual realization of the system in actual instances of language. This distinction is essential to all later structuralist theories. The proper object of linguistic study is the system which underlies any particular human signifying practice, not the individual utterance. This means that, if we examine specific poems or myths or economic practices, we do so in order to discover what system of rules — what grammar — is being used. After all, human beings use speech quite differently from parrots: the former evidently have a grasp of a system of rules which enable them to produce an infinite number of well-formed sentences; parrots do not.

1 Choose the one that best fills in the blank.

① cognitive   ② social

③ acoustic   ④ historical

2 Which of the following is true about "langue" and "parole"?

① Langue is the original form of language from which parole derives.

② Not langue but parole is what Saussure thinks linguists should investigate.

③ Langue is the linguistic equivalent of the grammar governing economic practices.

④ Parole is an aspect distinguishing human language from animal communication.

02

Theater of the Absurd is a term used to identify a body of plays written primarily in France from the mid-1940s through the 1950s. These works usually employ illogical situations, unconventional dialogue, and minimal plots to express the apparent absurdity of human existence. French thinkers such as Albert Camus and Jean-Paul Sartre used the term absurd in the 1940s in recognition of their inability to find any rational explanation for human life. The term described what they understood as the fundamentally meaningless situation of humans in a confusing, hostile, and indifferent world.

Samuel Beckett and Eugene Ionesco reacted against traditional Western theatrical conventions, rejecting assumptions about logic, characterization, language, and plot. For example, Beckett's *Waiting for Godot* (1954) portrays two tramps waiting for a character named Godot. They are not sure who Godot is, whether he will show up to meet them, and indeed whether he actually exists, but they spend each day waiting for him and trying to understand the world in which they live. Beckett often reduced character, plot and dialogue to a minimum to highlight fundamental questions of human existence.

1 **What makes Samuel Beckett's *Waiting for Godot* an absurd drama?**

① The characters in the play use less conversation.
② Samuel Beckett often uses elements of comedy in various ways.
③ The characters are waiting for Godot who may or may not exist.
④ The characters in the play detest Godot and the meaning of a drama.

2 **What is true of the *Theater of the Absurd*?**

① The *Theater of the Absurd* is closely related with logical situations.
② The term "absurd" came from writers such as J.P. Sartre and A. Camus.
③ In *Waiting for Godot* Samuel Beckett describes his autobiographical life.
④ Albert Camus asserts that he can explain the affirmative value of human lives.

03

The Sapir-Whorf hypothesis explores the nature of the relationship between language and thought. According to the teachings of Sapir and Whorf, languages that require different patterns of speech will cause the people who employ them to emulate these patterns in their thoughts, and ultimately to adopt different behaviors than speakers of other tongues. Thus, if the theory is valid, a person who is raised speaking one language can be expected to think and act differently than a person who is raised speaking another language.

Although the theory is undoubtedly provocative, the Sapir-Whorf hypothesis is, in fact, somewhat overstated. Considering the great variety of stimuli that humans encounter each day, language cannot be the only factor that determines thought. However, it is also unlikely that language has no influence whatsoever on mental processes. Instead, the majority of modern scholars agree that language can indeed affect thought and behavior, but only to a limited and non-comprehensive extent. Current studies are occupied with determining the precise degree of language's influence. The Sapir-Whorf hypothesis may need to be modified according to the most modern scholars, but the underlying idea that human thought is affected by speech and language remains a central one in linguistics.

1 Which of the following is true of the Sapir-Whorf hypothesis?

① It relates the way humans speak to the way they act.
② It claims that the way people think affects the way they speak.
③ It states that knowledge of grammar determines personality.
④ It posits that all languages affect thought in generally similar ways.

2 Which of the following is true of most modern scholars?

① They agree with most of the assertions of the Sapir-Whorf hypothesis.
② They believe that the Sapir-Whorf hypothesis should be modified.
③ They cannot determine whether there is any merit to the Sapir-Whorf hypothesis.
④ They are conducting research to decide whether the Sapir-Whorf hypothesis is valid.

04

J. D. Salinger's *The Catcher in the Rye* has become, since its publication, an enduring classic of American literature. The novel is a favorite because of its humor, its mordant criticism of American middle-class society and its values, and the skill with which Salinger captures colloquial speech and vocabulary. *The Catcher in the Rye*, ironically enough, has received some criticism over the years because of its rough language, which Holden Caulfield cites to denounce. The novel's story is told in retrospect by the main character, Holden, apparently while staying in a psychiatric hospital in California. What Holden tells is the story of his disenchantment with his life and the direction it is taking him. Throughout the novel, Holden speaks of his loneliness and depression; the story of a few days in his life indicates how sad and lonely his search for moral values is in a society in which he finds them sorely lacking. As the novel begins, Holden has been expelled, immediately before Christmas, from an exclusive preparatory school in Pennsylvania. He knows his parents will be angry with him, so he decides to spend a few days in New York City before going home. In New York, Holden endures several adventures before explaining to his only real friend, his sister, Phoebe, just what it is he believes in. This discovery of some moral identity does not, however, save Holden from hospitalization.

1 According to the passage, *The Catcher in the Rye* _____.

① was published by J. D. Salinger
② has enjoyed worldwide popularity except America
③ praises the middle-class values of America
④ has a formal style which is full of literary expressions
⑤ has been subject to some criticism for its coarse language

2 According to the passage, which of the following is NOT true about Holden Caulfield?

① He is a typical model student.
② He remains on the right side of his sister, Phoebe.
③ He is in a state of loneliness throughout the novel.
④ He has been dismissed from school before Christmas.
⑤ He wanders from place to place in New York before going home.

05

So what's the difference between acquiring a language and learning it? For one thing, learning a language requires ongoing social interaction, and that assumption forms the basis of Bruner's theory of the 'language acquisition support system', or LASS, for short. According to Bruner, some type of LAD(Language Acquisition Device) may exist, but parents and siblings also play a key role in a child's language development. By involving young children in routine behaviors like saying 'hello' and 'goodbye' and daily rituals like meal times and bath times. So it's probably no surprise that the expression 'mother tongue' evolved. After all, we all remember listening to the familiar sounds and repetitive phrases our mothers used when we were young. In fact, a researcher named Moerk nicknamed this type of language modeling as 'motherese.' The second assumption of Bruner's theory is that language learning is developmental. In other words, parents or siblings create a learning environment that supports the child as he or she builds language skills. So in the beginning, they are quite vocal and the child is rather passive. But as children develop the language skills, they become more active. From this perspective, language learning is more a process of discovery, and children learn to construct new ideas by linking it with previous knowledge and experiences. Therefore, it's evident that Bruner's theory strongly supports the notion that nurture is as essential as nature in language development.

1 **Why does the author mention the expressions "mother tongue" and "motherese"?**

① To prove that mothers are better language role models than fathers

② To illustrate how parents provide a support system for language learning

③ To compare normal speech patterns with the baby talk that parents use

④ To argue that second language learning is more difficult for adults

2 **What can be inferred about the relationship between nurture and language acquisition?**

① Preschooler's interaction with adults has no effect on their communication skills.

② Toddlers are unable to communicate because they haven't learned the rules of grammar yet.

③ Babies should be exposed to situations where language is modeled so that they can learn to use it.

④ Children who imitate sounds or words are not really communicating meaning.

06

Although best known by many modern readers for his short stories and poems involving the macabre and the fantastic, Edgar Allan Poe's contributions to literature extend to criticism as well as the detective story and science fiction. In fact, there is a wide range of genres and writers that directly and indirectly owe much to Poe's work.

A Interestingly, many of his stories would have been read as science fiction by his original readers, not as horror, which is how they are read today. At the core of science fiction, there is an attempt to explore how new technology will affect society. B So, when Poe was writing about the South Pole, as he did in *The Narrative of Arthur Gordon Pym*, or hypnosis, he was writing about the ideas that were new to the general public at the time. For example, in one story a man is put into a trance just before he dies. At the end of the story, when the trance is broken, he finally passes away. C Today, it reads more like a ghost story. Like Mary Shelley, the author of *Frankenstein*, Poe popularized stories in which human discovery leads to shocking results. D Intellectual descendents of this style of story can be seen in everything from movies with giant ants created through radiation to violent aliens attacking Earth. H.G. Wells, whose works are considered classics of science fiction, wrote that Poe showed what a writer of that genre must do: he must show what an intelligent mind can imagine.

1 Which of the following can be inferred about the Edgar Allan Poe's works?

① Future generation will understand them differently.
② They will gain more popularity as time goes on.
③ Only the horror stories will continue to be famous.
④ People will read them instead of Mary Shelly's stories.

2 Choose the most appropriate place for the sentence below.

Readers in Poe's time would have understood this to be a frightening application of a new science.

① A   ② B
③ C   ④ D

3 What is the H.G. Wells' attitude toward Edgar Allan Poe?

① admiring   ② obsessive
③ sneering   ④ neutral

07

Nineteen-Eighty-Four is a novel published by George Orwell in 1949. It was his last work, written shortly before his death from a tubercular haemorrhage in 1950. It presents a dystopian view of a world which has been taken over by totalitarianism. The novel's main protagonist, Winston Smith, briefly attempts small forms of resistance against the Party, which rules with the figurehead of Big Brother.

Indeed due to its vast popularity, Orwell scholars such as Bernard Crick have complained of its widespread misinterpretation; it should, Crick suggested, be read as a satire in the vein of Jonathan Swift. Such an interpretation explains the coexistence of moments of humour with an unremitting Ⓐ_____ of tone; we are left with a vision of the future as 'a boot, stamping on a human face — for ever'. Yet this is intended as a warning, rather than a prophecy.

Much of the novel's phraseology and many of its ideas have passed into general use. These include 'Newspeak', a form of language which enforces certain types of thought; the 'Doublethink' which can produce phrases such as 'War is Peace, Ⓑ_____', and '2+2=5'. Independent thinking, by contrast, is characterised as 'thoughtcrime', and punished brutally by the Thought Police. The much-abused adjective 'Orwellian' stems from the total surveillance established by the Party, partly through 'telescreens' which both show propaganda and allow the authorities to watch their audiences through cameras. This has produced the now-ubiquitous phrase 'Big Brother is watching you'.

1 **Which is the most appropriate for the blank Ⓐ?**

① foresight   ② bleakness

③ buzz   ④ diversion

2 **Which does not fit in the blank Ⓑ?**

① Freedom is Slavery

② Ignorance is Strength

③ Hate is Love

④ Surveillance is Restriction

3 **According to the passage, which of the following cannot be inferred?**

① Big Brother in *1984* is merely a symbolic head that suits the goals of the Party.

② The whole aim of Doublethink is to expand the range of thoughts.

③ We live in a surveillance society that George Orwell warned against.

④ People in *1984* are only permitted to think what the Party tells them to think.

08

Many people today feel that historically women have not been treated as well as men in most cultures. In the Western world, as recently as Ⓐ<u>a hundred years ago</u>, they were not allowed to vote in elections and were excluded from most professions. The attitude of favoring one sex over another (in this case, favoring the male) is called *sexism*, which is thought Ⓑ<u>by many to present</u> in ⓐ_____. For example, the verb *to mother*, used in the latter part of the article, generally means "to care for, protect" (for example, "that teacher mothers all her students."); whereas the verb *to father* usually means simply "to engender or originate" (for example, "He fathered three sons."). Here the idea that women, not men, should take care of children Ⓒ<u>is locked into</u> our everyday speech.

Feminists claim that there are examples of sexism in the vocabulary and even in the grammar of the English language. A common example is the use of the word *man* or *mankind* to refer to the whole human species: "*Man* is the only tool-using animal.... The achievements of *mankind* after the agricultural era began..." Certain critics of the feminists have argued that this usage doesn't really matter because everyone knows that the words *man* and *mankind* also Ⓓ<u>refer to women</u>. Feminists, however, generally believe that this manner of speaking has created the idea that men have been ⓑ_____ in history — working, building, exploring, inventing — while women have sat quietly on the sidelines, helping them.

Some people favor language reform and think that the words *people* or *humanity* should be used in these contexts. Others say, "Well, let's be honest! Men have been the active ones throughout history."

1 문맥상 빈칸 ⓐ에 들어갈 어구로 적당한 것은?

① the very language we speak   ② the culture we live in

③ the education systems   ④ the few specific societies

2 문맥상 빈칸 ⓑ에 들어갈 어구로 적당한 것은?

① the insolent participants   ② the suppressed participants

③ the intimidated participants   ④ the active participants

3 밑줄 친 부분 중 문맥을 고려했을 때 어법상 옳지 <u>않은</u> 것은?

① Ⓐ   ② Ⓑ

③ Ⓒ   ④ Ⓓ

09

Linguistics is the scientific study of language. It endeavors to answer the question — what is language and how is it represented in the mind? Linguists focus on describing and explaining language and are not concerned with the prescriptive rules of the language, ie. do not split infinitives. Linguists are not required to know many languages and linguists are not interpreters.

The underlying goal of the linguist is to try to discover Ⓐ_____. That is, what are the common elements of all languages. The linguist then tries to place these elements in a theoretical framework that will describe all languages and also predict what can not occur in a language. Linguistics is a social science that shares common ground with other social sciences such as psychology, anthropology, sociology and archaeology. It also may influence other disciplines such as communication studies and computer science. Linguistics for the most part though can be considered a cognitive science. Along with psychology, philosophy and computer science, linguistics is ultimately concerned with how the human brain functions.

This science comprises several different disciplines. The fields of phonetics, phonology, morphology, syntax, semantics and language acquisition are considered the core fields of study and a firm knowledge of each is necessary in order to tackle more advanced subjects.

1 Which of the following is the major theme of the passage?

① Linguistics as a social science
② The goals of linguists
③ The applied fields of linguistics
④ An introduction to linguistics
⑤ The contribution of linguistics to modern education

2 According to the context, which of the following best fits into Ⓐ?

① the universals concerning language
② the features of individual languages
③ the relations between linguistics and other studies
④ the practical functions of languages
⑤ the methods to analyze a given language

3 Which of the following is NOT stated or implied in the passage?

① Linguists do not necessarily need to know many languages.

② It is safe to say that linguistics is a kind of cognitive science.

③ The main concern of linguistics is to elaborate general mechanism of language.

④ Linguistics has common ground or concerns with not only psychology but computer science as well.

⑤ Studying advanced subjects of linguistics doesn't require a thorough understanding of its sub-fields.

10

New ideas often provoke Ⓐphilistine and anti-intellectual reactions, and this has been especially true of the reception accorded the theories which go under the name of structuralism. Structuralist approaches to literature challenge some of the most cherished beliefs of the ordinary reader. The literary work, we have long felt, is the child of an author's creative life, and expresses the author's essential self. The text is the place where we enter into a spiritual or humanistic communion with an author's thoughts and feelings. Another fundamental assumption which readers often make is that a good book tells the truth about human life — that novels and plays try to tell us how things are. However, structuralists have tried to persuade us that the author is 'dead' and that literary discourse has no truth function. In a review of a book by Jonathan Culler, John Bayley spoke for the anti-structuralists when he declared 'but the sin of semiotics is to attempt to destroy our sense of truth in fiction. ⋯ In a good story, truth precedes fiction and remains separable from it.' In a 1968 essay, Roland Barthes put the structuralist view very powerfully, and argued that writers only have the power to mix already existing writings, to reassemble or redeploy them; writers cannot use writing to express themselves, but only to draw upon that immense dictionary of language and culture which is 'always already written' (to use a favorite Barthean phrase). It would not be misleading to use the term 'anti-humanist' to describe the spirit of structuralism. Indeed the word has been used by structuralists themselves to emphasize their opposition to all forms of literary criticism in which the human subject is the source and origin of literary meaning.

1 **Choose the one closest in meaning to the underlined Ⓐ"philistine".**

① unrestricted   ② offensive

③ uncultured   ④ ruthless

2 **Which of the following CANNOT be inferred about "structuralism"?**

① It elicited harsh criticism in the existing literary world when it first emerged.

② It argues that literary works should be hard for ordinary people to understand.

③ It gives the cold shoulder to the truth waiting to be found in the literary work.

④ It asserts the decisive influence of language and culture on a writer's writing.

3 According to the passage, which of the following is LEAST relevant to "structuralism"?

① the cult of the author

② the rejection of humanism

③ semiotic analysis

④ Roland Barthes' essay

4 What is the main idea of the passage?

① New ideas are subject to strong resistance, scepticism, or criticism at first.

② Literary works reflect how authors live and what they value most highly in life.

③ Structuralists stand against all forms of literary criticism focusing on humans.

④ Structuralists make assertions contradicting the public's view of literature.

11

Words have meaning only in the context of a game. Whilst watching a soccer match, this philosophical idea occurred to Wittgenstein. If a person with no prior knowledge of soccer is watching a game, to him it will seem very random and meaningless. A For it to take meaning, he must first understand the rules of the game: there are two opposing sides, each has eleven players, each is trying to score against the other by putting the ball in the opposite net. Once he understands the overall context of the game then the men running around chasing a ball no longer seem mad but have meaning in the game.

B If one does not understand the context of the language and the rules that are imposed upon the specific discourse, then essentially, one cannot understand the words in their truest form. He acknowledged that people who understand the rules of one game (i.e. football) can find similarities in other games (i.e. Rugby) but essentially, these games are inherently different and thus to understand fully, one must understand the specific rules of that game and its differences from other games.

What Wittgenstein was saying was that language only has meaning in its specific context. C When taken out of that context and put into a different one, it may not mean the same thing. Wittgenstein was warning us against prescriptivism and being too stuck in one way of thinking. D Wittgenstein thought that one could not stand outside a game and legislate about it or attempt to impose the rules of another game — Ⓐ_____! So too, he said that a player of one game could not criticize the player of another, without first learning the rules and entering into the game.

1　For Wittgenstein, it can be inferred that _____.

① people cannot criticize others' use of language without first understanding their full context and intended meaning

② people who speak certain languages fluently can understand the context of conversations under any circumstances

③ people who don't know the rules of the game can fully enjoy the atmosphere of the event

④ people should do something that their opponents respect during the match

2　Which of the following best fits in Ⓐ?

① rugby players can be drafted in to play football

② football is commonly known as soccer

③ you cannot play basketball as if it's football

④ you can set rules in an effort to play fair

3 Which of the following is the best place for the sentence below?

So too, concluded Wittgenstein, is it with language.

① Ⓐ ② Ⓑ

③ Ⓒ ④ Ⓓ

12

Walden emphasizes the importance of solitude, contemplation, and closeness to nature in transcending the "desperate" existence that is the lot of most people. The book is not a traditional autobiography, but combines autobiography with a social critique of contemporary Western culture's consumerist and materialist attitudes and its distance from and destruction of nature. That the book is not simply a criticism of society, but also an attempt to engage creatively with the better aspects of contemporary culture, is suggested both by Thoreau's proximity to Concord society and by his admiration for classical literature. Ⓐ_____ for three reasons: First, it was written in an older prose, which uses surgically precise language, extended, allegorical metaphors, long and complex paragraphs and sentences, and vivid, detailed, and insightful descriptions. Thoreau does not hesitate to use metaphors, allusions, understatement, hyperbole, personification, irony, satire, metonymy, synecdoche, and oxymorons, and he can Ⓑ_____ a scientific to a transcendental point of view in mid-sentence. Second, its logic is based on a different understanding of life, quite Ⓒ_____ what most people would call common sense. Ironically, this logic is based on what most people say they believe. Thoreau, recognizing this, fills *Walden* with sarcasm, paradoxes, and double entendres. He likes to tease, challenge, and even fool his readers. And third, quite often any words would be inadequate at expressing many of Thoreau's non-verbal Ⓓ_____ into truth. Thoreau must use non-literal language to express these notions, and the reader must reach out to understand.

1 Choose the best phrase for the blank Ⓐ above.

① *Walden* is an intriguing book to read

② *Walden* is a difficult book to read

③ *Walden* is an emotionally powerful book to read

④ *Walden* is a readable book to read

2 Choose the best blank for the Ⓑ and Ⓒ above.

① adhere to — because of

② interfere with — according to

③ shift from — contrary to

④ result in — in spite of

3 Choose the best word for the blank Ⓓ above.

① insights   ② illusions

③ subjectivities   ④ identities

4   Which statement CANNOT be inferred about *Walden*?

① It shows us ways to be free from our desperate destiny.

② It combines various genres of writings in creative ways.

③ It makes use of diversified rhetorical figures quite freely.

④ It intends to subvert all the important values of the United States.

13

In Old English, *you* was originally not even a subject pronoun. It was the objective form of *ye*, the second-person plural pronoun. In other words, it could be a direct object, indirect object or the object of a preposition, but not a subject. From one 15th-century citation in the Oxford English Dictionary(OED): "I in you, and ye in me." It could also be used Ⓐ_____, as in "get you home" (ie, "get yourselves home".)

You then crept into subject position. The first OED citations come from the 14th century, and are flagged as potential copying errors. By the 15th century, the usage was clear: *you* was being used alongside *ye*. Both appear in the King James Bible, 1611: *Ye shall not surely die.* (Genesis 3:4) *Why will you goe with mee?* (Ruth 1:11)

Ye, originally plural, had also begun to be used as a formal way to address one person, under the influence of the French *vous*. As *you* encroached on *ye*'s territory, it did so on both fronts, being used for the plural and formal singular.

The informal singular was still *thou*, in those centuries in which English maintained the informal/formal pronoun distinction that many modern European languages still have: *tu-vous, du-Sie, tú-usted*, etc. But Ⓑsocial change sealed *you*'s triumph by piecemeal.

Using a plural to address a single person was once reserved for the very highborn, but made its way down the social ladder until any social superior was to be addressed with *you*. It didn't stop there, though, as *vous* and *Sie* did. Instead, having once crowded out *ye*, *you* now edged out *thou* in the early modern period.

To Ⓒ_____: *you* began as an objective, then became usable in subject position too. Then it went from plural only to singular too. Then it went from formal use to informal use too. *Ye, thou* and *thee* (the objective form of *thou*) were all left behind in the history books. Quite the conquering pronoun. Good job, *you*.

1 Which of the following best fits in the blanks Ⓐ and Ⓒ?

① quixotically — abridge

② reflexively — recap

③ recursively — recant

④ dichotomously — abrade

2 What is the best title according to the passage?

① The Kaleidoscopic Conjunction of Old English

② The Classic Example of Versification Using *You*

③ The Reason Why *You* Never Fail to Burgeon

④ The Vicissitude of Second-person Pronouns

3   **What does the underlined ⑧ mean according to the passage?**

① The society used *you* instead of *thou* in referring to the coroneted, which was conventionally cemented in a flash.

② *Thou* was put on the backburner by a fluke with the society also preferring *you* to *thou* as the informal singular.

③ The society used *you* instead of *thou* in referring to the coroneted, which was conventionally cemented by ill-fortune.

④ *Thou* was put on the backburner by stages with the society also preferring *you* to *thou* as the informal singular.

4   **What is the tone of the passage about *you*?**

① panegyrical   ② ignominious

③ stupefacient   ④ mordacious

14

Much as they may deplore the fact, historians have no monopoly on the past and no franchise as its privileged interpreters to the public. It may have been different once, but there can no longer be any doubt about the relegation of the historian to a back seat. Far surpassing works of history, as measured by the size of their public and the influence they exert, are the novel, works for the stage, the screen, and television. It is mainly from these sources that millions who never open a history book derive such conceptions, interpretations, convictions, or fantasies as they have about the past. Whatever gives shape to popular conceptions of the past is of concern to historians, and this surely includes fiction. Ⓐ

Broadly speaking, two types of fiction deal with the past — historical fiction and fictional history. The more common of the two is historical fiction, which places fictional characters and events in a more or less authentic historical background. Examples range from *War and Peace* to *Gone With the Wind*. Since all but a few novelists must place their fictional characters in some period, nearly all fiction can be thought of as in some degree historical. Ⓑ Fictional history, on the other hand, portrays and focuses attention upon real historical figures and events, but with the license of the novelist to imagine and invent. It has yet to produce anything approaching Tolstoy's masterpiece. Ⓒ Some fictional history makes use of invented characters and events, and historical fiction at times mixes up fictional and nonfictional characters. Ⓓ As a result the two genres overlap sometimes, but not often enough to make the distinction unimportant.

Of the two, it is fictional history that is the greater source of mischief, for it is here that fabrication and fact, fiction and nonfiction, are most likely to be mixed and confused. Ⓔ Of course historians themselves sometimes mix fact with fancy, but it is a rare one who does it consciously or deliberately, and he knows very well that if discovered he stands convicted of betraying his calling. The writer of fictional history, on the other hand, does this as a matter of course, and with no Ⓐ_____ whatever.

1 Which of the following CANNOT be inferred from the passage?

① Historical fiction and fictional history are based on the real historical events.

② Writers of historical fiction must thoroughly research and attempt to understand the time period they are writing about.

③ A historical event presented as a TV series is likely to be accepted as truth by many people.

④ Fictional history has succeeded because readers are interested in the historical backgrounds.

⑤ Professional historians understand that they should not mix fact and fiction in their works.

2 Which of the following is mentioned as a characteristic of historical fiction in paragraph 2?

① imaginary characters or events from the past
② dramatized characters in authentic historical settings
③ ancient stories that deal with gods and heroes
④ novels dealing with sentimentalized characters
⑤ a series of ridiculously unlikely turns of events

3 The following sentence could be added to the passage. Where would the sentence best fit?

But the term is applied as a rule only to novels in which historical events figure prominently.

① A   ② B
③ C   ④ D
⑤ E

4 Choose the word that can best fill in the blank Ⓐ.

① avarice   ② intimacy
③ homage   ④ concoction
⑤ compunction

15

A 39-year-old Manhattan hedge fund manager named Anthony Chiasson was slapped with a six-and-a-half year prison term and a $5 million fine for crimes connected to insider trading. The defendant had been "fabulously wealthy" — making $10 to $23 million a year — at the time he used tech-stock tips to make $68 million for his hedge fund, Level Global.

But are Chiasson's actions all that incomprehensible? Is it so hard to understand that a wealthy man might want to be wealthier; or that a person might be tempted to push his luck too far? The subject has not defied the imaginations of the world's great authors.

Whole libraries could be filled with books and stories devoted to the subject of men and women with unwholesome attitudes toward money. In 1906, Leo Tolstoy wrote a cautionary tale about Pahom very much like Chiasson who had much, but wanted more, and whose covetousness and cleverness betrayed him.

What pushes a fortunate man like Pahom, or Chiasson, to risk all in the hope of more? D. H. Lawrence wrestled with the discontent of well-off people in his dark fable, "The Rocking-Horse Winner." Published in 1926, three years before the stock market crash, the story tells of a boy growing up in torment despite his comfortable surroundings, plagued by his mother's financial aspirations. Luck, the mother tells the boy, is "what causes you to have money," and her husband doesn't have any. Her son resolves to be lucky, whatever it takes. He discovers that if he maniacally rides a rocking horse in the nursery, the names of winning ponies at the races will come to him as epiphany. The results are profitable; the end catastrophic.

While the rocking-horse winner's tips were supernatural, Chiasson's were illegal. But both speculators relied too much on luck. The judge who sentenced Chiasson chided him that "anyone who engages in this kind of conduct for this kind of money" ought to realize "what to expect if you get caught."

There's no excuse for Chiasson's unethical behavior at Level Global. But it's not hard, it turns out, to imagine why he did it; and why he might have thought he'd get away with it. The explanations already exist in literature — prefigured and pre-explained by writers whose life's work was not to <u>dispense</u> justice, but to show the contradictions of human nature. The way we live now, wrong and right, echoes the way we lived once and long ago; it's all recorded in the literature of the past, where today's headlines live in the pages of yesterday's fiction.

1 The underlined word <u>dispense</u> is meaning closest to _____.

① apply
② withstand
③ laud
④ agonize
⑤ exonerate

110 김영편입 영어 독해 워크북 2단계

2   What is the passage mainly about?

① The novels help create the ethos that embodies economic equality.

② The craze for money has led lots of people into all manner of reprehensible activities.

③ The world's great authors have taught us about self-destruction by greed.

④ Through Chiasson's case investors change their attitude toward money in a positive way.

⑤ The rich take it for granted that they are lucky and never get caught.

3   According to the passage, which of the following statements about *The Rocking-Horse Winner* is NOT true?

① The boy's clairvoyance brings about misfortune in the end.

② The boy can predict what horse is going to win with riding a rocking horse.

③ The mother is dissatisfied with her marriage because her husband is not lucky.

④ Its writer anticipated the aftermath of the stock market crash.

⑤ The boy's ability to name winning ponies makes money.

4   According to the passage, the judge who sentenced Chiasson intends to _____.

① exercise the judicial power

② reserve the sentencing proceedings

③ fight to retain his post

④ discourage others from engaging in financial crimes

⑤ affix a jail sentence to the defendant

05

철학·종교

05

철학·종교

01

Humanism carried within it the idea of progress and was in turn borne along by it. Since the time of Condorcet, progress had been treated as a law that human history must obey. It seemed as though moral progress inevitably went along with reason, democracy, and progress in science, technology and economics. This belief originated in the West, and in spite of the terrible evidence to the contrary provided by the 20th century's totalitarianism and world wars, the West maintained and spread the belief throughout the world. In the 1960s the West promised a harmonious future, the East a radiant one. Both these futures collapsed shortly before the century's end, and were replaced by uncertainty and anxiety; faith in progress became more a matter of possibility than promises. Now we need a regenerated humanism. The previous form of humanism did not include the concrete interdependence between all humans in a single community of destiny, which has been created and is constantly being extended by globalisation.

1 Which of the following is NOT stated or implied in the passage?

① The idea of progress had an influence on humanism.

② Progress was regarded as the categorical imperative that human history should follow.

③ In the 1960s, both the West and the East foresaw a rosy future.

④ The support for progressive faith disappears completely in the 21st century.

2 According to the passage, the idea of progress _____.

① was invented by Condorcet in the 19th century

② has ignored the importance of progress in science and technology

③ will be taken place of by a regenerated humanism in the near future

④ has played a decisive role in creating modern world

114 김영편입 영어 독해 워크북 2단계

02

Why have materialist views been so dominant? Part of the answer is that it is far from clear that dualist views, at least those that go much beyond the bare denial of materialism, are in any better shape. But it must be insisted that the inadequacies of dualism do not in themselves constitute a strong case for materialism: arguments by elimination are always dubious in philosophy, and never more so than here, where the central phenomenon in question (that is, consciousness) is arguably something of which we still have little, if any, real understanding. Ⓐ_____, materialism seems to be one of those unfortunate intellectual bandwagons to which philosophy, along with many other disciplines, is so susceptible — on a par with logical behaviorism, phenomenalism, the insistence that all philosophical issues pertain to language, and so many other views that were once widely held and now seem merely foolish. Ⓑ_____, such a comparison is misleading in one important respect: it understates the fervency with which materialist views are often held. In this respect, materialism often more closely resembles a religious conviction — and indeed, as I will suggest further in a couple of places below, defenses of materialism and especially replies to objections often have a distinctively scholastic or theological flavor.

1 **Which of the following is most appropriate for the blanks Ⓐ and Ⓑ?**

① Therefore — In addition
② Thus — Indeed
③ Instead — However
④ Nevertheless — Rather

2 **Which of the following can be inferred from the passage?**

① Materialism seems to have originated from religious and theological views.
② The author regards the insistence that all philosophical issues pertain to language as appropriate.
③ In philosophy, arguments by elimination are trustworthy.
④ It seems that the author deals with some issues like consciousness.

03

Modern skepticism is of a wholly different order from that of the intellectuals of the ancient world. It has attacked and destroyed not merely the outward forms of the religious spirit, its particularized dogmas, but the very essence of that spirit itself, belief in a meaningful and purposeful world. For the founding of a new religion a new Jesus Christ or Buddha would have to appear, in itself a most unlikely event and one for which in any case we cannot afford to sit and wait. But even if a new prophet and a new religion did appear, we may predict that they would fail in the modern world. No one for long would believe in them, for modern men have lost the vision, basic to all religion, of an ordered plan and purpose of the world. They have before their minds the picture of a purposeless universe, and such a world-picture must be fatal to any religion at all, not merely to Christianity.

We must not be misled by occasional appearances of a revival of the religious spirit. Men, we are told, in their disgust and disillusionment at the emptiness of their lives, are turning once more to religion, or are searching for a new message. It may be so. We must expect such wistful yearnings of the spirit. We must expect men to wish back again the light that is gone, and to try to bring it back. But however they may wish and try, the light will not shine again, not at least in the civilization to which we belong.

1 **Which of the following most distinguishes modern skepticism from ancient according to the passage?**
① its meaningless purpose
② the class of its proponents
③ the target of its attack
④ its scientific argumentation

2 **Which of the following can be inferred from the passage?**
① The religious spirit is outward and general, but the dogma inward and specific.
② New religions will fail because people have believed in previous ones too long.
③ We should rely on religious reform to regain a meaningful and purposeful life.
④ Today's human spirit tends to seek in vain after the light of a new message.

3 **What is the tone of the passage?**
① hopeful   ② pessimistic
③ detached   ④ expectant

04

The famous statement "God is dead" occurs in several of Nietzsche's works (notably in "The Gay Science" of 1882), and has led most commentators to regard Nietzsche as an Atheist. He argued that modern science and the increasing secularization of European society had effectively "killed" the Christian God, who had served as the basis for meaning and value in the West for more than thousand years. He claimed that this would eventually lead to the loss of any universal perspective on things and any coherent sense of objective truth, leaving only our own multiple, diverse and fluid perspectives, a view known as Perspectivism, a type of Epistemological Relativism. (Among his other well-known quotes of a relativistic nature are: "There are no facts, only interpretations"). At the heart of many of Nietzsche's ideas lies his belief that in order to achieve anything worthwhile, whether it be scaling a mountain to take in the views or living a good life, hardship and effort are necessary. He went so far as to say that everyone cared about a life of suffering, sickness and serious reversals in life, so that he or she could experience the advantage of overcoming such setbacks. His was the original "no pain, no gain" philosophy, and he believed that in order to harvest great happiness in life, it was necessary to live dangerously and take risks. For Nietzsche, therefore, sorrows and troubles were not to be denied or escaped (he particularly despised people who turned to drink or to religion), but to be welcomed and cultivated and thereby turned to one's advantage.

1 The best title of the above passage would be _____.

① The Secret Private Life of Nietzsche
② The Brief Overview of Nietzsche's Idea
③ Nietzsche and the Christian God
④ What is Perspectivism
⑤ The Portrait of Young Nietzsche

2 According to the passage, which of the following is NOT an idea of Nietzsche?

① Atheism   ② Perspectivism
③ Relativism   ④ You can't get something for nothing.
⑤ Theism

3 According to the passage, Nietzsche's attitude toward life is _____.

① pessimistic   ② optimistic
③ bleak   ④ naive
⑤ inconsistent

05

One of the key arguments about freedom was presented by the 19th century philosopher J.S. Mill in his book *On Liberty*. He argued that, in all conduct that is 'self-regarding' (in other words, whatever concerns yourself alone), there should be absolute liberty. The only limitation on liberty was what he termed the 'harm' principle, namely that you should do nothing that causes harm to another person. And, of course, it follows that you should allow everyone else the same degree of freedom that you seek for yourself.

The implication of this is that, if whatever you do concerns only yourself (or other consenting adults) you should be free to do it, even if you _____ in the process. The only point at which the law should step in, or you should be criticized morally, is if your actions — or words, or thoughts — cause harm to others.

The context of Mill's argument was that he wanted everyone to be able to develop themselves to their maximum potential, and not be stunted by having to conform to the norms of others. He saw freedom as <u>an essential requirement for that</u>.

---

1 **Choose the one that best fills in the blank.**

① harm yourself   ② harm others

③ benefit yourself   ④ benefit others

2 **Choose the one closest in meaning to the underlined "an essential requirement for that."**

① an essence of his philosophical theory

② a prerequisite for full self-development

③ an obstacle requiring much self-sacrifice

④ a tool for conforming to social norms

3 **Which of the following arguments would J.S. Mill NOT support?**

① We should be able to seek after our own interest in a society where freedom is reciprocally allowed.

② A citizen can do anything in so far as it does not do harm to others and the whole society.

③ One should be allowed to do whatever is right though it may infringe someone else's freedom.

④ A society will flourish when its members each have freedom and allow freedom to the others.

06

Greek and Roman society was built on the conception of the subordination of the individual to the community, of the citizen to the state; it set the safety of the commonwealth, as the supreme aim of conduct, above the safety of the individual whether in this world or in a world to come. Trained from infancy in this unselfish ideal, the citizens devoted their lives to the public service and were ready to lay them down for the common good; or, if they shrank from the supreme sacrifice, it never occurred to them that they acted otherwise than basely in preferring their personal existence to the interests of their country. All this was changed by the spread of Oriental religions which inculcated the communion of the soul with God and its eternal salvation as the only objects worth living for, objects in comparison with which Ⓐ_____. The inevitable result of this selfish and immoral doctrine was to withdraw the devotee more and more to concentrate his thoughts on his own spiritual emotions, and to breed in him a contempt for the present life, which he regarded merely as a probation for a better and eternal. The saint and the recluse, disdainful of earth and rapt in ecstatic contemplation of heaven, became in popular opinion the highest ideal of humanity, displacing the old ideal of the patriot and hero who, forgetful of self, lives and is ready to die for the good of his country. The earthly city seemed poor and contemptible to men whose eyes beheld the City of God coming in the clouds of heaven. Thus the centre of gravity, so to say, was shifted from the present to a future life, and, however much the other world may have gained, there can be little doubt that this one lost heavily by the change. A general disintegration of the body politic set in. The ties of the state and the family were loosened: the structure of society tended to resolve itself into its individual elements and thereby to relapse into barbarism; for civilization is only possible through the active co-operation of the citizens and their willingness to subordinate their private interests to the common good.

1 **Which of the following best fits the blank Ⓐ?**

① the earthly religions aligned with the state were hostile to Oriental religions
② the prosperity and even the existence of the state sank into insignificance
③ the nobles were in cahoots with Oriental religions trying to keep their privilege
④ human self-interest is the basic motive for politics and religion

2 **According to the passage, which of the following is NOT true?**

① The contempt for the earthly city and the wish for the City of God are indicative of religious committment.
② The religious devotee tends to exclusively concentrate on being in communion with God.
③ Greek and Roman society put the state before the individual interests.
④ The alliance between religion and state was enriched and increased to the extent that no one would have thought possible.

The ancient Greeks were members of one of history's first societies to claim that nature could be understood through reason alone, without recourse to superstition or religion. Before the sixth century BC, Greek thinkers had often turned to myths to make sense of the world. When, for instance, they tried to explain how fire originated, they told the story of Prometheus, who in defiance of the god Zeus stole fire from Mount Olympus, the home of the gods. Beginning with the philosopher Thales of Miletus, however, Greeks began to speculate on the nature of the physical world, proposing theories about the nature of reality based on reason alone. Although their understanding of science was limited — largely because they failed to carry out experiments to test their ideas — the ancient Greek philosophers set the stage for a systematic, scientific view of reality treasured to this day.

One key difference between the thinkers before and after Thales can be found in their underlying assumptions about the characteristics of reality. Most authors before Thales believed that nature was unpredictable, Ⓐ_____. Thales broke from tradition by suggesting that beneath the seeming chaos of nature was an underlying order that could be uncovered through careful thought. Perhaps because of its importance to life, its ability to transform from a gaseous into a liquid and solid state, and its presence in a variety of substances, water was held by Thales to be the basic component of all matter. In scientific terms, Thales's achievement was to advance a concrete hypothesis, or a possible systematic explanation for a given phenomenon.

1 **Which of the following is true about the passage above?**

① Thales of Miletus theorized that nature represented a series of hierarchies.
② Thales of Miletus wasn't able to advance his ideas enough because of lack of scientific knowledge.
③ The logic Greek philosophers developed no longer is used in branches of rational inquiry.
④ Thales of Miletus suggested that matter was a mixture of multiple substances.
⑤ Greek philosophers before Thales tried to expand Greek culture into foreign lands.

2 **Which example would best fit Ⓐ?**

① a source of inspiration for all learning
② best understood with reason
③ purely materialistic and open to examination
④ governed by the whims of the gods
⑤ growing toward a state of perfection

08

The simulacrum has long been of interest to philosophers. In his *Sophist*, Plato speaks of two kinds of image making. The first is a faithful reproduction, attempted to copy precisely the original. The second is intentionally distorted in order to make the copy appear correct to viewers. He gives the example of Greek statuary, which was crafted larger on the top than on the bottom so that viewers on the ground would see it correctly. If they could view it in scale, they would realize it was malformed. This example from the visual arts serves as a metaphor for the philosophical arts and the tendency of some philosophers to distort truth so that it appears accurate unless viewed from the proper angle. Nietzsche addresses the concept of simulacrum (but does not use the term) in the *Twilight of the Idols*, suggesting that most philosophers, by ignoring the reliable input of their senses and resorting to the constructs of language and reason, arrive at a distorted copy of reality. Postmodernist French social theorist Jean Baudrillard argues that a simulacrum is not a copy of the real, but becomes truth in its own right: the hyperreal. Where Plato saw two types of representation — faithful and intentionally distorted (simulacrum) — Baudrillard sees four: basic reflection of reality; perversion of reality; pretence of reality (where there is no model); and simulacrum, which "bears no relation to any reality whatsoever". In Baudrillard's concept, like Nietzsche's, simulacra are perceived as negative, but another modern philosopher who addressed the topic, Gilles Deleuze, takes a different view, seeing simulacra as the avenue by which an accepted ideal or "privileged position" could be "challenged and overturned". Deleuze defines simulacra as "those systems in which different relates to different by means of difference itself. What is essential is that we find in these systems no prior identity, no internal resemblance".

1 Which of the following is the best title of the passage?

① The Various Origins of Simulacrum

② The Different Meanings of Simulacrum

③ The Diverse Applications of Simulacrum

④ The Improper Use of Simulacrum

2 Which of the following is NOT implied or stated in the passage?

① Plato explained his own meaning of simulacrum through Greek statuary.

② Nietzsche considered simulacrum as a distorted copy of reality.

③ As for Jean Baudrillard, simulacrum is closely related with reality.

④ Gilles Deleuze see simulacrum as a way to challenge a privileged position.

Anarchism is the political philosophy which rejects (and supports the elimination of) compulsory government or compulsory rule, and holds that society can (and should) be organized without a coercive state. This may, or may not, involve the rejection of any authority at all. Ⓐ<u>Anarchists believe that government is both harmful and unnecessary</u>. Philosophical Anarchism contends that the State lacks moral legitimacy, that there is no individual obligation or duty to obey the State and, conversely, that the State has no right to command individuals. However, it does not actively advocate revolution to eliminate the State, but calls for a gradual change to free the individual from the oppressive laws and social constraints of the modern state. Ⓑ<u>The term "anarchy" is derived from the Greek "anarchos" ("without ruler")</u>. Up until the 19th Century, the term was generally used in a positive manner, to describe a coherent political belief, and it was only later that it became used pejoratively (to mean something akin to chaos).

Ⓒ<u>Anarchism is related to Libertarianism (which advocates maximizing individual rights and free will, and minimizing the role of the state)</u> and, in particular, to Libertarian Socialism (which advocates a worker-oriented system that attempts to maximize the liberty of individuals and minimize the concentration of power or authority), with which it is all but synonymous. Ⓓ<u>Conflicts between anarchist and Marxist movements have emerged in terms of theory, strategy, practice and immediate political goals</u>. There is no single defining position that all Anarchists hold, beyond their rejection of compulsory government or "the State", and proponents may support anything from extreme individualism (the political outlook that stresses human independence and the importance of individual self-reliance and liberty) to complete collectivism (the political outlook that stresses human interdependence and the importance of the collective).

1 글의 흐름상 적합하지 <u>않은</u> 것을 고르시오.

① Ⓐ   ② Ⓑ

③ Ⓒ   ④ Ⓓ

2 위 글의 제목으로 적합한 것을 고르시오.

① How to Research the History of Anarchism

② How to Predict the Future of Anarchism

③ How to Explain the Characteristics of Anarchism

④ How to Apply the Theory of Anarchism to Practice

3 위 글을 통해 추론할 수 <u>없는</u> 것으로 적합한 것을 고르시오.

① Anarchists refuse the idea that a coercive state can be the ultimate authority.

② Some anarchists consider a violent revolution as the only way to refuse statism.

③ The meaning of the term "anarchy" has changed in the course of history.

④ Anarchist schools of thought can differ, supporting anything from individualism to collectivism.

10

A The Pope is the Bishop of Rome and the leader of the worldwide Catholic Church. The importance of the Roman bishop is largely derived from his role as the traditional successor to Saint Peter, to whom Jesus gave the keys of Heaven and the powers of "binding and loosing," naming him as the "rock" upon which the church would be built. The current pope is Francis, who was elected on 13 March 2013, succeeding Benedict XVI.

B The office of the Pope is the papacy. His ecclesiastical jurisdiction is often called the "Holy See", or the "Apostolic See" based upon the Church tradition that the Apostles Saint Peter and Saint Paul were martyred in Rome. The pope is also head of state of Vatican City, a sovereign city-state entirely enclaved within the Italian capital city of Rome.

C The popes in ancient times helped in the spread of Christianity and the resolution of various doctrinal disputes. In the Middle Ages they played a role of secular importance in Western Europe, often acting as arbitrators between Christian monarchs. Currently, in addition to the expansion of the Christian faith and doctrine, the popes Ⓐ_____ in ecumenism and interfaith dialog, charitable work, and the defense of human rights.

D Popes, who originally had no temporal powers, in some periods of history Ⓑ_____ wide powers similar to those of temporal rulers. In recent centuries, popes were gradually forced to give up temporal power, and papal authority is now once again almost exclusively restricted to matters of religion.

1 Choose the most appropriate place for the sentence below.

The papacy is one of the most enduring institutions in the world and has had a prominent part in world history.

① A   ② B
③ C   ④ D

2 According to the passage, which of the following is most appropriate for the blank Ⓐ and Ⓑ?

① engage — accrued
② liquidate — waived
③ dissolve — amassed
④ participate — forfeited

3 According to the passage, which of the following is NOT true?

① The Apostles Saint Peter and Saint Paul suffered death as the penalty for refusing to renounce the faith.
② The first pontiff was Saint Peter, to whom Jesus gave the keys to the kingdom of Heaven.
③ The Vatican is an independent nation enclosed by the Italian capital city.
④ The mundane authority the Bishop of Rome now retains has never been stronger.

4 According to the passage, which of the following is NOT mentioned about the Pope?

① the location of the Holy See
② the propagation of Christianity
③ the hierarchy of the papal office
④ the disciples of Jesus Christ

11

The crux of Althusser's argument is the structure and functioning of "ideology". Althusser explains the structure and functioning of ideology by presenting two theses. Firstly, he posits that ideology represents the imaginary relationship of individuals to their real conditions of existence. This Ⓐ_____ of reality is caused by material alienation and by the active imagination of oppressive individuals who base their domination and exploitation on the falsified representations of the world in order to enslave the relatively passive minds of the oppressed. Secondly, he posits that ideology always has a material existence in the form of Ⓑ_____ entities or apparatuses (ISAs: Ideological State Apparatuses). Hence, an individual's belief in various ideologies (imaginary realities) is derived from the ideas of the individual who is a subject endowed with a consciousness that is defined by the ISAs. This (false) consciousness inspires and instigates the subject to behave in certain ways, adopt certain attitudes and participate in certain regular practices which conform to the ideology within which he recognizes himself as a subject.

Althusser's central thesis states that ideology transforms individuals as subjects by a process of interpellation or hailing. The Family ISA(Ideological State Apparatuses) is at work even before a child is born because it predetermines the identity of the child before its birth. Hence, ©an individual is always-already a subject. An individual is subjected to various levels of ideological subjection and each level of subjection or each ISA that subjects the individual influences the individual's day to day activities and thereby determines his real conditions of existence. Further, Althusser demonstrates that the recognition of oneself as a 'free' subject within an ideology is only a misrecognition because the notion of a 'free' subject in ideology is only an illusion. In reality, the subject is always subjugated, limited, restricted and controlled by ideology. Due to this misrecognition the subject acts and practices rituals steeped in the dominant ideology that are detrimental to his/her own welfare.

1 윗글의 제목으로 가장 적합한 것을 고르시오.

① The Controversy Surrounding Althusser's Theory of Ideology
② What Is Althusser's Theory of Ideology
③ The Dark Side of Althusser's Theory of Ideology
④ How to Apply Althusser's Theory of Ideology to Practice

2 윗글의 흐름상 빈칸 Ⓐ와 Ⓑ에 들어갈 말로 가장 적절한 것은?

① perfection — abstract
② distortion — concrete
③ portrayal — transcendental
④ affirmation — profane

3 윗글의 흐름상 ⓒ의 밑줄 친 부분의 의미와 가장 가까운 것을 고르시오.

① In spite of ISA(Ideological State Apparatuses), an individual can be a free subject.

② In any case, an individual is unable to escape the restriction of ideology.

③ An individual can be a free subject with the help of ISA(Ideological State Apparatuses).

④ An individual can transgress the barrier of ideology to be a subject who can decide his/her fate.

12

Over two millennia after it first came to prominence, stoicism is having a moment. It's on the internet, of course: the stoicism subreddit, the largest meeting place for stoics online, has over 28,000 subscribers, many times the number of erstwhile rival Epicureanism (around 4,000). But it is also infiltrating real life, even in its toughest forms. The Navy Seals teach stoic insights to new recruits; throughout the NFL, players and coaches are devouring Ryan Holiday's guide to stoicism, "The Obstacle Is the Way".

Even in antiquity, stoicism was noted for its Ⓐ_____. Ancient Greek and Roman stoics wrote about theology, logic and metaphysics, but their focus was on the "hic et nunc", the here and now. "Stoicism tells you what in life is worth having and gives you a way to get there," says William Irvine, the author of the stoic handbook, "A Guide to the Good Life". The key is learning to be satisfied with what you've got. "Some things are up to us and others are not," taught Epictetus. "Up to us are opinion, impulse, desire... Not up to us are body, property, reputation, office, in a word, whatever is not our own action." This indifference to everyday comforts has left stoicism with a reputation for coldness. In reality, its defenders argue, it is simply a rational approach to managing expectations. The central insight of stoicism is that life is tough and changeable, so prepare for difficulty.

Many modern stoics argue that this doctrine has already been partially revived in the form of cognitive behavioural therapy (CBT), the "problem-focused" therapy now widely seen as psychology's best weapon against depression, anxiety and every kind of unhelpful thinking. Like stoicism, CBT encourages practitioners to distinguish between events and perceptions, and nearly every CBT textbook contains some version of Epictetus's dictum: Ⓑ"Men are disturbed not by things, but the views they take of them." Yet although the founders of CBT openly acknowledged the influence of stoicism, they tended to adopt the techniques without reference to the wider moral framework. "Stoicism transcends most modern self-help and therapy by offering the view that much of our emotional suffering is caused by false values, such as egotism, materialism or hedonism," says Donald Robertson, a cognitive-behavioural psychotherapist who is one of the organisers of Stoic Week.

1 According to the passage, the stoic idea is that _____.

① facing up to the reality and getting better at dealing with it would make one feel stable in life

② physical gratification is superior to the mental satisfaction offered by expectation management

③ devising a plan with grand ambitions allows you to prepare for hardships

④ bringing forward subconscious thoughts changes one's underlying beliefs and values

2 Which of the following best fits in Ⓐ?

① indulgence   ② redemption

③ practicality   ④ moderation

3 What is the meaning of the underlined part Ⓑ?

① People suffer not mentally, but physically from every kind of unhelpful thinking.

② People look into the problem from different angles, not theirs.

③ People have their own views not to avoid the issue but to confront it.

④ People are affected not by events but by their attitudes toward them.

13

Religions are belief systems, so they are in fact a kind of ideology. But they are set apart from other ideologies by their origin in divine inspiration. This makes them so different from other ideologies that it is only in a technical sense that we would call them "ideologies." Their divine core makes them more difficult to argue about, because one either does, or does not, believe in the divine basis of a religion. Two who share that belief may argue about important differences of interpretations within the religion, but Ⓐa believer and a nonbeliever just have to agree to disagree. This is a very different discourse than what we usually think of as ideological argument.

How much religious discourse differs from other ideological discourse depends in part on how fundamentalist the believer is. Fundamentalist believers take it that every word of the God-given scripture, be it the Bible or the Qu'ran, is true because it came from God. Less fundamentalist believers, noting that in every religious book there are inevitable contradictions and ambiguities, see the documents of their faith as having a central core of principles, but as being interpretable as to exact prescriptions. These more interpretive believers may not compromise on the Golden Rule, for instance, but may consider God's words on homosexuality Ⓑ_____. Interpretive belief often leaves a good deal of room for blending with elements from other ideologies like liberalism, socialism, or conservatism, and so discourse about such belief is in the end somewhat more like other ideological discussion than is discussion based on fundamentalist belief. But to the extent that understandings of God's truth are part of the discussion, any religious discourse always has a special character.

1 Choose the one closest in meaning to the underlined Ⓐ.

① A believer must argue against atheism.

② Differences in belief can be eliminated.

③ Opposing ideas are tolerated in religion.

④ Religious creeds are beyond argument.

2 Choose the one that best fills in the blank Ⓑ.

① more open to discussion

② much to the point

③ out of the question

④ less disprovable

3 **Which of the following CANNOT be inferred from the passage?**

① What religions have in common is that they are based on belief in deities.

② Like religions, nonreligious ideologies are belief systems of some kind.

③ Interpretive belief is closer to secular ideology than to fundamentalist belief.

④ Even interpretive believers regard the Golden Rule as core of their faith.

4 **What is the best title for the passage?**

① The Origin of Religion as an Ideology

② The Nature of Religious Discourse

③ The Intolerance of Religious Fundamentalism

④ The Ideological Arguments in Religion

14

That postmodernism is indefinable is a truism. However, it can be described as a set of critical, strategic and rhetorical practices employing concepts such as difference, repetition, the trace, the simulacrum, and hyperreality to <u>destabilize</u> other concepts such as presence, identity, historical progress, epistemic certainty, and the univocity of meaning. The term "postmodernism" first entered the philosophical lexicon in 1979, with the publication of *The Postmodern Condition* by Jean-François Lyotard. An economy of selection dictated the choice of other figures for this entry. I have selected only those most commonly cited in discussions of philosophical postmodernism, five French and two Italian, although individually they may resist common affiliation. Ordering them by nationality might duplicate a modernist schema they would question, but there are strong differences among them, and these tend to divide along linguistic and cultural lines.

The French, for example, work with concepts developed during the structuralist revolution in Paris in the 1950s and early 1960s, including structuralist readings of Marx and Freud. For this reason they are often called "poststructuralists." They also cite the events of May 1968 as a watershed moment for modern thought and its institutions, especially the universities.

The Italians, by contrast, draw upon a tradition of aesthetics and rhetoric including figures such as Giambattista Vico and Benedetto Croce. Their emphasis is strongly historical, and they exhibit no fascination with a revolutionary moment. Instead, they emphasize continuity, narrative, and difference within continuity, rather than counter-strategies and discursive gaps. Neither side, however, suggests that postmodernism is an attack upon modernity or a complete departure from it. Rather, its differences lie within modernity itself, and postmodernism is a _____ of modern thinking in another mode.

1 **What is the main purpose of the passage?**

① To criticize the core concepts of postmodernism

② To prospect the future of postmodernism

③ To explain the salient features of postmodernism

④ To describe the controversy over postmodernism

2 **Choose the one that best fills in the blank.**

① severance   ② continuation

③ betrayal   ④ subordination

3 Choose the closest in meaning to the underlined "<u>destabilize</u>" in the context.

① deconstruct   ② approve

③ progress   ④ promise

4 Which of the following can be inferred from the passage?

① The advocate of postmodernism might believe in the progress in history.

② It is needless to say about the difficulty of defining the meaning of postmodernism.

③ The French postmodern philosophers are utterly indifferent to structuralist revolution.

④ Postmodernism and modernism in Europe are currently at odds over the issue of truth.

15

Emptiness is a challenging concept: slippery in definition and elastic in meaning. It implies a total lack of content: people, buildings, objects or markings on a map. In the abstract, emptiness equals nothingness, a perfect void. Yet when one thinks of places on the globe that one might associate with being empty — the Gobi or Sahara deserts, the depths of the Pacific ocean — it is quickly evident that none is truly devoid of everything. The most cursory survey of these two expanses would reveal an array of contents: mineral deposits, complex eco-systems, transitory forms of life, migrants and long-standing patterns of circulation and movement. Even the ultimate vacuum — the cosmos — is full of planets, stars, asteroids, debris and space junk. Yet these contents do not necessarily contradict a palpable identification of emptiness. In this sense, emptiness is inherently relational, defined as much by what does not fill or is expected to fill a space as by what is in fact there.

Emptiness is therefore less the result of site-specific quantitative assessment and more something perceived through comparison with other places. Empty sites appear emptier than elsewhere, containing fewer people, fewer signs of life, fewer traces of human activity. Ⓐ As a state, emptiness necessarily invokes what is not present; it is in some ways a condition of absence. It thus follows that as emptiness is a matter of perception, it is a highly subjective phenomenon, dependent to a large extent on who is doing the observing and what the subject expects to find. What is devoid of objects or meaning to one person or group might very well be 'full' to another. Ⓑ With this in mind, emptiness cannot be accepted at face value; it is by no means an objective state. Absences — literally blank spaces on early modern European maps — must be subject to historical investigation and critical analysis.

This examination of emptiness can be situated within a long trend towards the study of spatial history. While there is a tendency to speak of a twenty-first century 'spatial turn' in history, spatial history finds its roots in a much deeper past. Cumulatively, these efforts have radically altered an older, Cartesian conception of space which first placed emphasis on the stability and timelessness of places and landscapes and then in the nineteenth century subordinated space to time in contemporary thought. Ⓒ The gradual re-evaluation of space as a critical concept in understanding the world around us began in the late nineteenth and early twentieth centuries, when scholars around the globe contributed to the growing field of human geography, studying the effects of geography and environment on culture. They tied concepts from the hard sciences, like biomes and ecosystems, to cultural phenomena, but still thought of spaces as bounded and stable. Ⓓ It was only from the late 1970s and 1980s onwards that historians and geographers, influenced by discourse analysis and studies in postmodernism, began to think of spaces as social constructs in constant transformation.

1 아래의 문장이 들어갈 위치로 가장 적합한 곳을 고르시오.

Taking this one step further, emptiness is thus deeply rooted in how places are imagined and, a potent tool in the articulation of power between individuals and collectives.

① A ② B

③ C ④ D

2 위 글을 통해 추론할 수 <u>없는</u> 것으로 가장 적합한 것을 고르시오.

① The emptiness is not an absolute absence, but a result of the relational recognition of spaces by those who have a relationship with them.

② Descartes posited the concept of transcendental space by focusing on the stability and eternity of space.

③ Nineteenth-century thinking tends to emphasize the integration of the two in relation to time and space.

④ Influenced by postmodernism and discourse analysis, a view of space as a constantly changing social construct has emerged.

사회·정치

01

Are the terms American Indian and Native American essentially synonyms, in the same way that the terms black and African American are often used interchangeably? Or is using the term American Indian instead of Native American the equivalent of using Negro instead of black — offensive and anachronistic? Is the insistence on using Native American to the exclusion of all other terms a sign of being doctrinaire? While these were once raging questions in the culture wars, they have now happily sorted themselves out. Over the years, the people whom these words are meant to represent have made their preference clear: the majority of American Indians/Native Americans believe it is acceptable to use either term, or both. Many have also suggested leaving such general terms behind in favor of specific tribal designations. As the editor of *The Navajo Times* puts it, "I would rather be known as a member of the Navajo tribe, instead of a Native American or American Indian. This gives an authentic description of my heritage, rather than Ⓐ_____ me into a whole race of people."

1 Which of the following best fits into Ⓐ?

① severing   ② distorting

③ lumping   ④ correcting

2 Which of the following is true of the passage?

① A number of Indians living in America set tribal identity above ethnic identity.

② The term African American is regarded as offensive to many Americans.

③ Most Indians living in America prefer Native American to American Indian.

④ Both African American and American Indian are likely to belittle their heritage.

02

On the one hand, there were a lot of thoughts that war had been effectively ended by progress, diplomacy, globalization, and economic and scientific development. $\boxed{\text{A}}$ At the same time, each nation's culture was Ⓐ<u>shot through</u> with strong currents pushing for war: armaments races, belligerent rivalries and a struggle for resources. $\boxed{\text{B}}$ Millions of men went through the military via conscription, producing a substantial portion of the population who had experienced military indoctrination. Nationalism, elitism, racism and other belligerent thoughts were widespread, thanks to greater access to education than before, but an education that was fiercely biased. $\boxed{\text{C}}$ Violence for political ends was common and had spread from Russian socialists to British women's rights campaigners. $\boxed{\text{D}}$ Violence for your country was increasingly justified, artists rebelled and sought new modes of expression, new urban cultures were challenging the existing social Ⓑ<u>order</u>. Europe was essentially primed for people in 1914 to welcome war as a way to recreate their world through destruction.

1 Which is closest in meaning to the underlined Ⓐ<u>shot through</u>?

① stagnant
② filled
③ volatile
④ insufficient

2 Which is closest in meaning to the underlined Ⓑ<u>order</u>?

① rule
② class
③ command
④ request

3 Which is the best place for the following?

No sane person would risk war and ruin the economic interdependence of the globalizing world.

① $\boxed{\text{A}}$
② $\boxed{\text{B}}$
③ $\boxed{\text{C}}$
④ $\boxed{\text{D}}$

03

There are many people on earth who live in detestable condition. Between international war, civil war, starvation, disease, ethnic cleansing, illiteracy, and poverty, many people of earth face many hardships. Though the tribulations people of the Third World face are unfortunate, the United States of America and other countries do not have the right to rid the world of its bane. Politicians who have the ability to venture in foreign affairs should ask themselves before undertaking any endeavor: Does the action I support serve the just interest of my people? In many situations the action simply does not, for foreigners are not the constituents of any politician. Politicians should only concern themselves with the national interests.

Genocide is one of the most despicable Ⓐ_____ that a people can embark upon. Although it is a curse for humanity, the United States and other countries do not have a moral obligation to strive for it to be ended. If a state did not start a problem, that same state does not have a moral obligation to end it — even if it has the ability to do so. Tony Lake, the National Security Advisor in President Clinton's administration, once stated that "the possession of such power does not bring with it the automatic responsibility to use it." The United States must decide carefully what needs to be done to Ⓑ_____ its own national interests and deviate away from all other initiatives.

1　**Which of the following best expresses the author's position?**

　① The US should not intervene in other countries problems unless it serves its national interests.

　② The US should focus on humanitarian aid for the Third World as its priority.

　③ The US should consider its own interests as well as resuming humanitarian aid to the Third World.

　④ The tribulations the Third World faces are inevitable, so nobody can help it.

2　**Choose the words that best fill in the blanks Ⓐ and Ⓑ.**

　① dexterities — forward

　② truculences — impede

　③ atrocities — further

　④ prowesses — advance

04

Ethnomethodology, as founded by sociologist Harold Garfinkel, is a theory that looks at how we make sense of everyday situations. Though we may view a situation differently from those around us, our backgrounds provide us with some basic assumptions about everyday life. Ethnomethodology studies what those background assumptions are, how we arrive at them, and how they influence our perceptions of reality. In order to understand these assumptions, students of ethnomethodology are often taught to violate or challenge the taken-for-granted assumptions we have about everyday life. In the United States, one background assumption is that emergency personnel, such as police officers, wear identifiable uniforms when on duty. An officer at an accident scene who is wearing everyday clothes might find that crowds won't obey someone who claims to be a police officer but is without a uniform. The officer might have difficulty Ⓐ_____ or redirecting traffic away from the scene. When the background assumption is not fulfilled, members of the public will not respond as respectfully as they would if the officer were in uniform, and the officer will have a hard time performing required duties.

1 Which of the following best fits into Ⓐ?

① writing the accident report
② keeping onlookers at bay
③ collecting evidence on the scene
④ giving first aid to the injured

2 According to the passage, ethnomethodology can be defined as the study of _____.

① the ways in which people understand the world around them
② human social and cultural worlds in comparison with each other
③ the relationships between humans and their patterns of social life
④ the traditions, customs, and stories that are passed along by word

3 Which of the following is NOT true about background assumptions?

① They are some basic assumptions about how the world and people interact.
② In our daily life, we unconsciously think and do in a way that satisfies them.
③ To better our daily life, we should question them, not take them for granted.
④ When they are violated, it causes us to have difficulty doing our daily duties.

05

The American dream has always been Ⓐ_____. In 1931, when the historian James Truslow Adams first introduced the concept, he credited the dream with having "lured tens of millions of all nations to our shores." Yet in recent years, a troubling gap has developed between this original dream and a new one that speaks far less eloquently to the rest of the world. The original dream has three strands. The first is about Ⓑ_____: the classic saga of penniless strivers working hard to lift their families into the middle class. An integral part of this saga is continuity between generations — with parents sacrificing so their children can succeed, and successful children never forgetting "where they came from." Needless to say, this dream of hard work and intergenerational mobility is shared by the 95 percent of humanity who are not American. But it is called the American dream because the United States was the first nation in history where it actually came true for large numbers of people.

The United States is also the nation where the deliberate exclusion of any individual or group from the dream came to be condemned. This points to the second and third strands: democracy and freedom. For the dream to function properly, the basic rights of individuals must be respected. On this point Adams is clear: "It is not a dream of motor cars and high wages merely, but a dream of social order in which each man and each woman shall be able to attain to the fullest stature of which they are innately capable."

1 윗글의 목적으로 가장 알맞은 것은?

① to criticize the abuse of American dream

② to propose an alternative to American dream

③ to describe the true meaning of American dream

④ to prospect the future of American dream

2 다음 빈칸 Ⓐ와 Ⓑ에 들어갈 가장 알맞은 것은?

① municipal — liberty

② national — equality

③ regional — philanthropy

④ global — prosperity

06

We can defend political authority by asking the reader to imagine life in society without it — with the police, the army, the legal system, the civil service, and the other branches of the state all taken away. What would happen then? Perhaps the most famous thought-experiment along these lines can be found in Thomas Hobbes's *Leviathan*, published in 1651. Hobbes had experienced the partial breakdown of political authority brought about by the English Civil War, and the picture he painted of life in its absence was unremittingly bleak. He described the 'natural condition of mankind' without political rule _____ for the necessities of life, leaving people in constant fear in case they should be robbed or attacked, and constantly inclined, therefore, to strike at others first. It is sometimes said that Hobbes reaches this pessimistic conclusion because of a belief that people are naturally selfish or greedy, and will therefore try to grab as much for themselves as they can when unrestrained by political authority. But this misses Hobbes's real point, which is that cooperation between people is impossible in the absence of trust, and that trust will be lacking when there is no superior power to enforce the law. Those things that Hobbes describes as missing in the 'natural condition' are above all things that require numbers of people to work together in the expectation that others will do their part, and in the absence of political authority it is not safe to have any such expectation.

1 윗글의 내용과 가장 가까운 것은?

① Those who imagine the absence of the political systems tend to be politically idealistic.
② Hobbes maintains that the first aim of political authority is to control our selfish greed detrimental to society.
③ According to Hobbes, humans in natural condition seek to survive by competing and compromising.
④ According to Hobbes, political authority begets trust among citizens, which in turn enables civic cooperation.
⑤ Hobbes's thought-experiment reveals that war is a result of the violent political authority.

2 빈칸에 들어갈 가장 적절한 것은?

① as one of ferocious competition
② one of ferocious competition
③ as one of ferocious competitions
④ one of ferocious competitions
⑤ as one of the ferocious competitions

07

After the horrific shooting in Las Vegas, the impulse of politicians is to lower flags, offer moments of silence, and lead somber tributes. But what we need most of all isn't Ⓐ_____, but action to lower the Ⓑ_____ of guns in America. We needn't simply acquiesce in this kind of slaughter. When Australia suffered a mass shooting in 1996, the country united behind tougher laws on firearms. The result is that the gun homicide rate was almost halved, and the gun suicide rate dropped by half, according to *The Journal of Public Health Policy*. America's gun homicide rate is now about 20 times Australia's.

Skeptics will say that there are no magic wands, and they're right. But it is unconscionable for politicians to continue to empower killers at this scale. Since 1970, more Americans have died from guns (including suicides, murders and accidents) than the sum total of all the Americans who died in all the wars in American history, back to the American Revolution. Every day, some 92 Americans die from guns, and American kids are 14 times as likely to die from guns as children in other developed countries, according to David Hemenway of Harvard. But we're not helpless and we should take order to make a difference.

1 According to the passage, which pair best fits Ⓐ and Ⓑ?

① mourning — toll
② ingratitude — fare
③ magnanimity — casualties
④ lamentation — regulation

2 According to the passage, which of the following can be inferred?

① The author doesn't agree with the skeptical view of the silver bullet regarding a mass shooting.
② We don't have to present our condolences to bereaved family members of a mass shooting.
③ The author believes we shouldn't sit idle in coping with the gun crime and instead do something to forestall it.
④ We should fix the blame on politicians because they have connived at the horrific shooting.

3 According to the passage, what is most likely to be discussed following the passage?

① suspending all the firearms manufacture in the United States
② figuring out the relationship between illegal immigrants and crime
③ coming up with statistics on the gun homicide and suicide
④ taking proactive measures to prevent mass shootings beforehand

08

The leisure class is in great measure sheltered from the stress of those economic exigencies which prevail in any modern, highly organized industrial community. The exigencies of the struggle for the means of life are Ⓐ_____ exacting for this class than for any other; and as a consequence of this privileged position we should expect to find it one of the Ⓑ_____ responsive of the classes of society to the demands which the situation makes for a further growth of institutions and a readjustment to an altered industrial situation. The exigencies of the general economic situation of the community do not freely or directly impinge upon the members of this class. They are not required under penalty of forfeiture to change their habits of life and their theoretical views of the external world to suit the demands of an altered industrial technique, since they are not in the full sense an organic part of the industrial community. Therefore these exigencies do not readily produce, in the members of this class, that degree of uneasiness with the existing order which alone can lead those of any other class to give up views and methods of life that have become habitual to them. The office of the leisure class in social evolution is to retard the movement and to conserve what is obsolescent. This proposition is by no means novel; it has long been one of the commonplaces of popular opinion.

1   What is the author's attitude toward "the leisure class" in the passage?

① indifferent   ② supportive
③ critical   ④ ambivalent

2   Which of the following can be inferred about "the leisure class" from the passage?

① It is likely to be more conservative than other classes in our society.
② It keeps a strong tie with other classes in the same community.
③ It is very susceptible to the alteration of economic situations.
④ In recent years, it has tried to change its reputation among the public.

3   Choose the one that best fills in the blanks Ⓐ and Ⓑ.

① more — most   ② more — least
③ less — most   ④ less — least

4   Which of the following best describes "the leisure class"?

① socially-conscious   ② change-resistant
③ poverty-stricken   ④ self-sustaining

09

In cases of war, what one group tries to do to another group is what happens to individuals in cases of murder. The soldiers involved in a war are responsible for acts of violence against "the enemy," in the sense that the violence would not have occurred if the soldiers had refused to act. The Nuremberg trials after World War II attempted to establish that individual soldiers are responsible morally and legally too, but this attempt overlooked the extent to which the institutionalization of violence changes its moral dimension. On the one hand, an individual soldier is not acting on his own initiative and responsibility, and with the enormous difficulty in obtaining reliable information and making a timely confrontation of government claims, not even U.S. Senators, let alone soldiers and private citizens, are in a good position to make the necessary judgments about the justice of a military engagement. On the other hand, a group does not have a soul and cannot act except through the agency of individual men. Thus there is a real difficulty in assigning responsibility for such institutional violence. The other side of the violence, its object, is equally ambiguous, for "the enemy" are being attacked as an organized political force rather than as individuals, and yet since a group does not have a body any more than it has a soul "the enemy" is attacked by attacking the bodies of individual men.

1 Choose the one closest in meaning to the underlined sentence.

    ① War is no less an act of violence than murder.

    ② An individual's murder leads to war between groups.

    ③ War as well as murder is an act of humans.

    ④ Individuals commit murder and groups wage war.

2 Which of the following can be inferred from the passage?

    ① Soldiers are different from civilians in that their killing other people is not murder.

    ② The Nuremberg trials attempted to deal with those who refused to follow an unlawful order.

    ③ The responsibility for war is easier to place on the defeated state than on its soldiers.

    ④ The fact that war is institutional violence makes it questionable to punish war criminals.

3 What is the purpose of the passage?

    ① to argue that every soldier should disobey the order to kill the enemy

    ② to point out that the Nuremberg trials were appropriate in many respects

    ③ to explain in what respects a state's war differs from an individual's murder

    ④ to stress that an act of violence should be banned, be it war or murder

10

American sociology reveals, in general, exactly opposite characteristics to Marxist sociology. American sociologists, in my own experience, never talk about laws of history, first of all because they are not acquainted with them, and next because they do not believe in their existence. Because they are men of intelligence, they would prefer to say that these laws have not been established with any certainty; but if they were to express their real thoughts, they would probably say that what the Soviets regard as laws of history have no scientific validity and that there is no justification for deriving such laws either from recurrent patterns through the ages or from evolutionary tendencies sufficiently obvious to permit the accurate prediction of the future from the present.

American sociology is fundamentally _____; it proposes to examine the way of life of individuals in the societies with which we are familiar. Its energetic research is aimed at determining the thoughts and reactions of students in a classroom, professors in or outside their universities, workers in a factory, voters on election day, and so forth. American sociology prefers to explain institutions and structures in terms of the behaviour of individuals and of the goals, mental states, and motives which determine the behaviour of members of the various social groups.

1　It can be inferred from the passage that Marxist sociology _____.

① assumes that sociology can't always hold on to scientific approaches
② tries to suggest historical laws derived from long repetitive patterns
③ has been preferred by unintelligent scholars
④ gives laws of history no scientific approval
⑤ aims at clarifying social institutions in light of individual behaviors and their motives

2　Which of the following is most appropriate in the blank?

① synthetic and historical　　　　② progressive as well as determinist
③ synthetic and meticulous　　　　④ analytical and empirical
⑤ individual and logical

3　Which of the following is the most accurate description of the organization of the second paragraph?

① A sequence of observations leading to a prediction
② A list of inferences drawn from facts stated at the beginning of the passage
③ A series of assertions related to one general subject
④ A statement of the major idea, followed by specific reasons for the idea
⑤ A succession of ideas moving from specific to general

11

Kemalism, also known as Atatürkism, or the Six Arrows, is the founding ideology of the Republic of Turkey. Kemalism, as it was implemented by Mustafa Kemal Atatürk, was defined by sweeping political, social, cultural and religious reforms designed to separate the new Turkish state from its Ottoman predecessor and embrace a Westernized way of living, including the establishment of democracy, secularism, state support of the sciences and free education, many of which were first introduced to Turkey during Atatürk's presidency in his reforms.

Kemalism turned Turkey too secular too soon to sustain for generations. Thus, the resurgence of political Islam in Turkey indicates the country is preparing itself for a departure from Kemalism. One's not sure as to how this seesaw is going to affect Turkish society and politics in the future. I think the following are Turkey's nemeses, which we need to understand as to what might happen to the country now: Kemalism; the Kurdish problem; Turkey's neighbours; and Turkey's relationship with America.

Turkey is very unique from its European and Muslim neighbours. Being straddled on two continents, this Muslim-majority country is officially secular in the strictest sense. It's not just another postcolonial country in the Muslim World, it's rather a former colonial power, the centre of the mighty Ottoman Empire, which once ruled parts of Eastern Europe, West Asia, and North Africa for several centuries up to the end of World War I. Turkey's Ottoman legacy of ruthless subjugation of European nations — including forcible conversions of Christians into Muslims, and the infamous Armenian Genocide — is still a factor behind its exclusion from the EU by European nations.

1   **Which of the following best describes the main idea of Kemalism?**

① It is designed to create a secular Turkish state out of a portion of the Ottoman empire.

② It is a political movement stressing the traditional and established doctrine of Islam.

③ It is characterized by equality of individual wealth and by freedom of people to participate in politics.

④ It takes the responsibility of providing the social security for the population.

2   **According to the passage, which of the following is not true?**

① Atatürk moved to erase the legacy of dominance long held by religion and tradition.

② The EU turns a blind eye to Turkey's maintaining control over the religious sphere of Islam.

③ Anti-Kemalists may insist Turkey should have an ideology based on Islamism rather than a secularism.

④ European nations still have bitter feelings about Turkey which colonized Eastern Europe in the Ottoman days.

12

In many situations related to war or internal strife, people are forced to flee their homes to escape anticipated or realized violence, often leaving behind all of their possessions. These groups are referred to as forced migrants. Where these migrants end up gives them further categorization, which significantly affects how international organizations are able to assist them.

If forced migrants are able to leave their country to seek asylum abroad, they become refugees. When this happens, the host country generally provides them, as a group, with basic life needs. More important, international response agencies are granted access to them and are able to offer them food, shelter, and medical assistance. Refugees are also defended by a set of universally accepted laws that offer them a considerable degree of protection. Eventually, following the end of whatever conflict forced them from their homes, they are given assistance in returning to their former lives as best as possible. The United Nations High Commissioner for Refugees (UNHCR) estimates that there are more than 10 million refugees throughout the world today.

When forced migrants are unable or unwilling to cross the borders of their country, they become internally displaced persons(IDPs). There are many reasons why IDPs do not leave their country, including war in neighboring countries, little ability to travel long distances, and impassable border regions. IDPs have very little physical protection, and often face severe shortages of food, water, and other basic life necessities. They are afforded little protection under international law, and widely recognized agreements like the Geneva Convention are often difficult to apply. Mere recognition of IDP crises can be difficult and, once identified, access by international response and relief agencies can be both cumbersome and dangerous. The domestic government, which may view the uprooted people as "enemies of the state," _____. UNHCR estimates that there are currently over 25 million internally displaced people in at least 50 countries throughout the world.

1 위 글에서 빈칸에 들어가기에 가장 적합한 것을 고르시오.

① joins the family of nations for truce

② provides relief for internally displaced persons

③ retains ultimate control over their fate

④ takes emergency measures designed to recover order

2 위 글의 내용과 일치하지 <u>않는</u> 것을 고르시오.

① It is estimated that there are more IDPs than refugees throughout the world today.

② Even if conflict ceases which compelled them to leave their homes, refugees can never return to their former lives.

③ Many IDPs are suffering from want of food and water.

④ How forced migrants could be classified depends on where they stay.

13

Conservatism was a strong force throughout Europe in the nineteenth and early twentieth centuries. With the massive changes brought by World War II and its aftermath, European conservatism changed. ⒶThe nobility were generally destroyed or discredited, the church was in ferment, and most countries had introduced a sweeping expansion of taxation and social services, the "welfare state," to make people more equal. ⒷAfter the huge destruction of the war, it was not always clear that there was a social order for conservatism to defend. ⒸConservatives' traditional emphasis on the responsibility of the powerful to help the poor and weak, together with a willingness (in contrast to the position of liberals) to see power concentrated, made it fairly easy for conservatives to accept the welfare state. ⒹAlso, conservatism welcomes active encouragement of religion by the state, whereas liberalism is suspicious of it; large numbers of Europeans after the war felt a need for a stability of values offered by religion, although among recent generations religious practice has now dropped off sharply. ⒺWhile liberalism declined in Europe throughout the twentieth century, conservatism has lived on healthily. Its adherents accepted the welfare state but urged that it be built in ways that were consistent with traditional moral values and that it should not lead to a leveling of society. In other words, conservatives felt that _____.

1 Which of the following best fits in the blank?

① the shortcomings of liberalism would make the public eager for an alternative
② some structure should remain by which one part of society can lead the rest
③ their objectives could be achieved without going as far as outright meritocracy
④ the time had come for everyone to participate equally in all fields of society
⑤ their creeds were ignored by the youth and under attack in the culture at large

2 Which of the following is the best place for the sentence given below?

However, conservatism adapted fairly rapidly to these changed circumstances.

① Ⓐ   ② Ⓑ
③ Ⓒ   ④ Ⓓ
⑤ Ⓔ

3   Which of the following best describes the main idea of the passage?

① Conservatism has both vied and banded with liberalism since World War II.

② Their noblesse oblige enabled the conservatives to accept the "welfare state."

③ Unlike liberalism, conservatism successfully got its message across to the public.

④ Welfare states should preserve traditional values but should not be standardized.

⑤ Conservatism has thrived on despite the upheaval after the second world war.

14

Economists examined life satisfaction scores provided by 2.3 million Americans state by state, and compared these with state suicide rates. Utah, for example, ranks highest in life satisfaction — but also has the ninth highest suicide rate in the U.S. New York, in contrast, comes in 45th in life satisfaction but has America's lowest suicide rate.

Both happiness and crime rates tend to be tied to rankings of economic inequality in states as well as countries — the larger the gap between rich and poor, the less happiness there is and the more crime. Overall life expectancy also tracks with inequality, with a bigger wage gap meaning shorter lives and worse health — for both rich and poor, though the poor are hit much harder.

Researchers suspect that this gradient is linked to stress caused by our place in the social hierarchy: Stanford's Robert Sapolsky, for example, has found that even in baboons, lower ranked animals have higher levels of stress hormones and worse health. But when status conflicts are reduced, producing a more Ⓐ_____, these differences are also reduced. Studies of British civil servants have also found that stress-related health problems — like heart disease, obesity and stroke — are directly linked with hierarchy, increasing as a person moves lower down the totem pole.

So why doesn't suicide follow this same gradient? The current study doesn't provide the whole answer but author Stephen Wu said that comparisons with others — comparisons of relative happiness in this case, rather than status — may play a role: "Perhaps for those at the bottom end, in a way their situation may seem worse in relative terms, when compared with people who are close to them or their neighbors. For someone who is quite unhappy, the relative comparison may lead to more unhappiness and depression."

Sadly, this may mean that increasing happiness by reducing economic inequality could paradoxically produce more suicides as a "side effect." But this is one problem we are unlikely to have, as economic inequality is high and rising in the U.S.

1 What is the best title for the passage?

① The Requirements for Our Long and Healthy Life
② A Side Effect of the Social Hierarchy
③ Why the Happy States Have High Suicide Rates
④ A Great Harmful Influence of Economic Inequality

2 Which of the following CANNOT be inferred from the passage?

① Increasing happiness does not always lead to positive results.
② Social hierarchy has been found to have substantial effect on stress.
③ People holding higher positions on the social ladder tend to have a longer lifespan.
④ Developed countries tend to have a higher suicide rate than developing countries.

3 Choose the one that best fills in the blank Ⓐ.

① egalitarian situation
② racial discrimination
③ tactical fight
④ ruling hierarchy

15

What ever happened to civility in politics? That lament is getting louder these days. Hobbesian campaign ads — nasty, brutish and short — are making the airwaves toxic. Professional polemicists are infecting the culture with outrageous claims and slanders. Yet for all this, the notion that we need a more civil politics is only half right — and the half that's wrong is dangerously wrong. Civility is hot right now. Organizations across the U.S. are springing up to promote more civil discourse. To be sure, civility and politeness are preferable to coarseness and snarkiness, and a conversation is nicer than a screaming match. It's certainly possible to have fierce disagreements in a respectful tone. That's what we teach our children, and it seems our political leaders should be held to at least that standard. The problem is, focusing on civility makes us pay disproportionate attention to the part of politics that's rational. Which is tiny. Democracy is not just about dialogue and deliberation; it's also — in fact, primarily — about blood and guts. That's certainly been the case with the grassroots segment of the Tea Party and the shorter-lived Occupy movement. If war is "politics by other means," as Prussian military strategist Carl von Clausewitz famously put it, then these two half-articulate expressions of populist anger remind us that politics is war by other means. Humans by nature fight over privilege, status and power. We engage in battles that challenge identities and threaten interests — and thus excite passions. It's right to want to convert that combative instinct into nonviolent expressions like legislative action. But it's wrong to imagine that the instinct itself can be legislated out of existence. The Constitution our framers gave us did not ask that we be mild or moderate; it anticipated and channeled our immoderation.

1　**The best title of the passage would be _____.**

① Combative Politics as a Compelling Trait

② Extreme Examples of People Participating in Politics

③ The Political Role of Politeness as Conflict-Avoidance

④ Warning Against a Fierce Political Debate

⑤ Decreasing Demands for Civil Attitude in Politics

2　**According to the passage, the author views civility in politics as _____.**

① efficient strategy

② an exemplary manner

③ overrated virtue

④ personality indication

⑤ an outdated standard

3   The author argues that _____.

① courtesy creates respect that can overcome disagreements

② democracy is on the verge of collapse due to the lack of participation

③ emotional conflicts should not get in the way of a constructive debate

④ a hostile attitude is embedded in humans participating in politics

⑤ politicians attempt to persuade citizens by asserting superficial arguments

16

Is terrorism justifiable? The Proposition is expected to defend violent behaviour towards civilians, at least in some cases; however, the Opposition cannot necessarily expect blowing up kindergartens to be defended.

The Proposition believes that sometimes minorities under oppressive regimes have no other means of expression, as they are denied access to media, political system or the outside world, as were the ANC in South Africa under apartheid. Ⓐ<u>As a last resort</u> it may be defensible to resort to violence.

Also, Ⓑ_____; it may be that the eventual outcome of a terrorist campaign is beneficial and this outweighs the harm done in achieving it. History will be the judge, as when terrorism in East Pakistan helped to bring about the creation of Bangladesh, or the Jews forced the British out of Palestine and led to the creation of Israel.

However, the Opposition says that having no other means of expression is no justification for harm done to innocent civilians. Gandhi and others showed the potential success of peaceful protest. A noble cause is devalued if it is fought through violence.

They also argue that there are very few cases of terrorism actually working. In some cases the satisfactory outcome is only achieved once the terrorists are forced to renounce violence, but in most cases the fighting continues and Ⓒ_____. The IRA won no concessions from the British government in seventy years of violent campaigning, and the PLO was forced to renounce terrorism before negotiations began.

1 밑줄 친 Ⓐ의 의미에 가장 가까운 것은?

① to take radical strategies to negotiate

② to use something that is bad in order to succeed

③ to propose solutions to end the conflict

④ to adopt a final expedient to settle a difficulty

2 빈칸 Ⓑ에 들어갈 가장 적절한 표현을 고르시오.

① Will is power

② The end justifies the means

③ Other times, other manners

④ Add fuel to the fire

3 위 글의 내용과 일치하지 <u>않는</u> 것은?

① Appealing to violence probably helped East Pakistan build up Bangladesh.

② Britain ended its mandate over Palestine and the Jews declared the establishment of Israel.

③ The Irish applauded IRA's decision to formally end its armed campaign.

④ South Africa's apartheid regime must have regarded members of the ANC as dissidents.

4 문맥상 빈칸 ⓒ에 들어갈 어구로 적당한 것은?

① nothing is achieved

② international pressure mounts

③ truce talks proceed apace

④ they gain more power in negotiation

17

There is one great exception to <u>this rule</u> in modern history: the United States. America has risen to global might, and yet it has not produced the kind of opposition that many would have predicted. In fact, today it is in the astonishing position of being the world's dominant power while many of the world's next most powerful nations — Britain, France, Germany, Japan — are all allied with it. This is the exception that needs to be explained.

The reason surely has something to do with the nature of American hegemony. The U.S. does not seek colonies or conquest. After World War II, it helped revive and rebuild its enemies and turned them into allies. For all the carping, people around the world do see the U.S. as different from other, older empires.

But it also has something to do with the way that the U.S. has exercised power:_____. Historically, America was not eager to jump into the global arena. It entered World War I at the tail end of the war, late enough to avoid the worst bloodshed but still tipping the balance in favor of Britain and France. It entered World War II only after Japan attacked Pearl Harbor. It contained Soviet aggression in Europe but was careful not to push too far in other places. And when it did, as in Vietnam, it paid a price.

There is a long and distinguished school of American statesmen — from Dwight Eisenhower to Henry Kissinger to Robert Gates — who believe that America helps enlarge the scope of freedom around the world by staying strong; husbanding its power; creating a stable, liberal order; and encouraging economic and political reform. It is central to this mission that America is disciplined about its military interventions.

1 **Which of the following agrees with the underlined "this rule"?**

① If a country finds itself weaker than its enemy, it resorts to the help of all its allies.

② A country keeps aloof from the war between others unless its own interests are threatened.

③ As a country becomes powerful and asserts itself, others gang up to bring it down.

④ If two countries have a common enemy, they can work with each other to advance their common goals.

2 **Choose the one that best fills in the blank.**

① stealthily   ② reluctantly

③ preemptively   ④ boastfully

3 Which of the following CANNOT be inferred about the American foreign policy?

① It has so far kept its basic principle "No intervention, no enemy."

② Its proponents believe it morally superior to those of other countries.

③ The Vietnam War was a case where it went too far with much damage.

④ Some believe it is playing a vital role in making the world freer and better.

4 What is the main idea of the passage?

① America is an exceptional empire to which no other world powers can be antagonistic.

② America owes its current status as a dominant global power to its successful foreign aid.

③ America has a long legacy left by patriotic statesmen who have given advice at every crucial time.

④ America has become a different kind of global power by being smartly involved overseas.

18

Ironically, in the United States — a country of immigrants — prejudice and discrimination continue to be serious problems. There was often tension between each established group of immigrants and each succeeding group. As each group became more financially successful and more powerful, they excluded newcomers from full participation in the society. Prejudice and discrimination are part of our history; however, this prejudicial treatment of different groups is nowhere more unjust than with black Americans.

Blacks had distinct disadvantages. For the most part, they came to the "land of opportunity" as slaves and they were not free to keep their heritage and cultural traditions. They could not mix easily with the established society, either, because of their skin color. It was difficult for them to adapt to the American culture. Even after they became free people, they still experienced discrimination in employment, housing, education, and even in public facilities, such as restrooms.

Until the twentieth century, the majority of the black population lived in the southern part of the United States. Then there was a population shift to the large cities in the North. Prejudice against blacks is often associated with the South. Slavery was usually more common there and discrimination was blatant; Water fountains, restrooms, and restaurants were often designated "white only."

In the 1950s and 1960s, blacks fought to gain fair treatment, and they now have legal protection in housing, education, and employment. Because their neighborhoods are segregated, many blacks feel that educational opportunities are not adequate for their children.

One attempt to equalize employment and educational opportunities for blacks and other minorities is "affirmative action." Affirmative action means that those in charge of businesses, organizations, and institutions should take affirmative action to find minorities to fill jobs. Many whites are angry about this regulation, because very qualified people sometimes do not get jobs when they are filled by people from a certain minority. People call this practice "reverse discrimination."

The situation of blacks is better today than it was in the 1950s, but racial tension persists. Time will be the real solution to the problem of race.

1 **According to the author, when will there be a solution to racial problems?**

① since affirmative action

② in the future

③ after the Civil War

④ since the 1950s

2 According to the passage, the author thinks that prejudice and discrimination _____ in the United States.

① are natural by nature

② are temporary for the same for all groups

③ form part of history

④ are indispensable to national solidarity

3 The author thinks that prejudice is ironic here _____.

① because the United States is the world's biggest, richest economy

② in that the United States has the most powerful effects on the world economy

③ because the United States is a country of immigrants

④ because the United States makes established groups unjust

19

Today's politicians seem more comfortable invoking God and religion than they do presenting facts or numbers. Of course, everyone is entitled to his or her own religious beliefs. But when science and reason get shortchanged, so does America's future. What we are seeing in the current presidential race is not so much a clash between religion and science as a fundamental disregard for rational and scientific thinking. All but two of the Republican front runners won't even consider that man-made global warming might be causing climate change, despite a great deal of evidence that it is. We know CO_2 warms the planet through the greenhouse effect, and we know humans have created a huge increase in CO_2 in the atmosphere by burning coal and oil. ⒶThat man-made climate change is not proved with 100% certainty does not justify its dismissal.

In fact, an important part of science is understanding uncertainty. When scientists say we know something, we mean we have tested our ideas with a degree of accuracy over a range of scales. Scientists also address the limitations of their theories and define and try to extend the range of applicability. When the method is applied properly, Ⓑ_____ over time.

Public policy is more complicated than clean and controlled experiments, but considering the large and serious issues we face — in the economy, in the environment, in our health and well-being — it's our responsibility to push reason as far as we can. Far from being isolating, a rational, scientific way of thinking could be unifying. Evaluating alternative strategies; reading data, when available, either in the U.S. or other countries, about the relative effectiveness of various policies; and understanding uncertainties — all features of the scientific method — can help us find the right way forward.

1 Choose the one closest in meaning to the underlined Ⓐ.

① Because it is not certain whether humans are culprits of climate change, we must reconsider our current climate measures.

② Though it is not completely verified that human activities cause climate change, we must not exclude the possibility that it is true.

③ Because we cannot control climate artificially with all certainty, it is not right to give up adjusting ourselves to climatic conditions.

④ Though there is no obvious evidence to the contrary, it is doubtful that human beings have changed climate throughout history.

2 Choose the one that best fills in the blank Ⓑ.

① the right results emerge   ② the initial goals change

③ we grow more superstitious   ④ it is forgotten gradually

3 What is the main idea of the passage?

① We should not make little of science and reason on the ground that we adhere to religious beliefs.

② Scientists can make more contribution to America's future prosperity than politicians.

③ It is regretable that almost all runners in the presidential race have little knowledge of science.

④ Politicians should make and implement public policies on the basis of science and reason.

4 Which of the following CANNOT be inferred about "today's politicians"?

① They are poor at dealing with scientific facts and statistical numbers.

② They have a tendency to take no account of science and reason.

③ They take up the position that religion will bring success in career.

④ They need a more rational way of thinking to meet the current issues.

Caste is not a word that modernizing India likes to use. It has receded into the background. Newspapers reserve their headlines for the newer metrics of social hierarchy: wealth and politics, and those powerful influencers of popular culture, actors and cricket stars.

There are two stories we tell ourselves in urban India. Ⓐ One is about how education transforms lives. It is the golden key to the future, allowing people to rise above the circumstances of their birth and background. And sometimes, it does. Ⓑ In my own neighborhood, a few sons and daughters of cooks and gardeners are earning their engineering and business degrees, and sweeping their families into the middle class. Not many, certainly. Ⓒ But enough that this is a valid hope, a valid dream. Ⓓ The other story is about how the last two decades of economic growth have fundamentally changed the country, creating jobs and income and nurturing aspiration where earlier there was none. Ⓔ

These are exciting stories, even revolutionary in a country where, for centuries, the social order was considered immutable. Traditionally, Indian society was divided into four main castes. At the top, Brahmins, as priests and teachers; second came the Kshatriyas, the warriors and rulers; third, Vaishyas, who were merchants; last, Shudras, the laborers. And below them all, the Dalits, or untouchables, called Harijans, or "children of God," by Mahatma Gandhi. The castes were ostensibly professional divisions but were locked firmly into place by birth and a rigid structure of social rules that governed interaction between and within them.

That, famously, was then. Discrimination based on caste has been illegal in India for more than six decades. In today's urban India, this land of possibility, separated from rural India by cultural and economic chasms, it seems reactionary even to speak of caste. Certainly it shouldn't — and usually doesn't — come up at work or at play or in the apartment elevator.

1 **What does the passage mainly discuss?**

① The conflict between urban India and rural India

② The dazzling progress of Indian democratization

③ The extinction of caste system in modern India

④ The middle class emerging as an influencer

⑤ The polarization between haves and haves not

2 The following sentence can be added to paragraph 2. Where would it best fit in the paragraph?

New money and an increasingly powerful middle class are supposedly displacing the old social hierarchies.

① A　　　　　　　　　② B
③ C　　　　　　　　　④ D
⑤ E

3 According to the passage, the biggest benefit Indians can have from the abolishment of the caste system is _____.

① upward mobility
② cultural literacy
③ political liberty
④ financial prosperity
⑤ learning opportunity

4 According to the passage, why does speaking of caste seem "reactionary"?

① Because caste has now become obsolete in Indian urban society.
② Because comment on caste incites people to revive the caste system.
③ Because comment on caste is forbidden under the Indian statute.
④ Because caste highlights the importance of urban India.
⑤ Because caste is prevalent in every corner of the country.

07

경제·경영

01

A fundamental misunderstanding of the Robin Hood legend in the current discussion of tax policy undergirds a mistaken idea, too rarely evaluated — that hurting the "rich" helps the "poor." Right now, this is played out in proposals to reduce tax deductions for charitable giving. Government-spending advocates argue that they should be able to seize more funds from the wealthy by limiting deductions for nonprofit giving. The "rich" will hand over their money to the government in higher taxes and continue to give charitably, and the "poor" will receive largesse from both. This strained reading of Robin Hood makes several very flawed assumptions, including the idea that government is an effective source of help for the poor and that wealth builders deserve to be penalized. In fact, the Robin Hood of legend took back from tax collectors the money seized from the poor and returned it — a medieval tax refund. The heroic act was helping people keep their own money, unjustly seized by the ruling class who did not use those resources to help the needy.

1 Why does the author mention the Robin Hood legend?

① To encourage the rich to donate more money to charities and the government
② To explain that government's efforts to cut tax reductions for charitable giving were little understanding of Robin Hood
③ To show how effective implementing a medieval tax refund is for the poor
④ To emulate the generous actions of Robin Hood — robbing from the rich and giving to the poor

2 According to the passage, the author argues that _____.

① the proposed tax policy has a negative effect on acts of good will
② limiting deductions for nonprofit giving will hurt the rich
③ giving the rich the tax break is irrelevant to a personal philanthropy
④ the rich's donation sponsored by the government will help the poor

02

Ⓐ<u>It</u> is also known as "Ricardo's Law" and it explains why it's beneficial for two parties to trade even though one of them may be able to produce every item more cheaply than the other. Ricardo used an example involving England and Portugal. Producing both wine and cloth does not require as much work in Portugal as it does in England. In England, it's not easy to produce cloth and even less so to produce wine. By contrast, Portugal can produce both easily. At first glance, it's difficult to see why Portugal would want to trade with England but look at it this way. If Portugal just concentrates on producing wine and produces enough to be able to export it to England, and if England focuses on making cloth and exchanges that for cheaper Portuguese wine, both countries benefit. Therefore, Portugal doesn't have the cost of making cloth and England benefits from cheaper Portuguese wine.

1 The above passage is _____.

① mythical   ② fictional
③ sarcastic   ④ informative
⑤ alarmed

2 According to the "Ricardo's Law", Portugal can _____.

① reduce exportation costs
② share the results of production
③ produce a higher quality of a product
④ trade products in an unstable economy
⑤ specialize in the production of one good

3 What does the underlined Ⓐ"<u>It</u>" mean?

① comparative advantage
② bartering
③ free trade
④ monetary system
⑤ controlled economy

03

The classical economists, going back to Adam Smith, rightly conceived of economics as a branch of moral and political philosophy. But the version of economics commonly taught today presents itself as an autonomous discipline, one that does not pass judgment on how income should be distributed or how this or that good should be valued. The notion that economics is a value-free science has always been questionable. But the more markets extend their reach into noneconomic aspects of life, the more entangled they become with moral questions.

In pluralist societies, we disagree about how to value goods, and so it is tempting to try to resolve our differences without bringing moral argument into politics. But this impulse is a mistake; it has contributed to the empty, hollow public discourse of our time. We should not ask citizens to leave their moral convictions at the door when they enter the public square. Instead, we should _____ a morally more robust public discourse, one that engages rather than avoids the moral convictions that citizens bring to public life.

1 Which of the following is true of the passage?

① To the classical economists, economy is completely separate from politics.

② These days, nobody doubts the essential principles of the classical economics.

③ Adam Smith surveyed economics from the moral point of view.

④ As a value-free science, economics disregards the possibility of the continuous economic growth.

2 Which of the following best fits into the blank?

① embrace   ② repudiate

③ utilize   ④ abandon

04

Every manager has a few go-to employees who take on any special project thrown at them. But Ⓐif your go-to employees have too much on their plates, they will not be productive. In fact, they won't be able to do their day jobs, let alone the extra work you have them tackle.

ⒷRon Ashkenas, a managing partner of Schaffer Consulting, writes in Harvard Business Review about the problem of overtaxing your reliable lieutenants. "Managers sometimes 'round up ⓐthe usual suspects' because they only trust a small number of people to handle key projects or initiatives. Every organization has its 'glue people,' the ones who don't show up in organization charts but are assigned to every task force or initiative because they are respected and trusted," he writes.

But Ⓒif you draft the more capable, loyal, and trustworthy employees other than the same overworked group every time to handle new business challenges, you won't get any results. "These task force members usually end up with multiple specialty assignments piled on top of their regular duties," Ashkenas writes. "And Ⓓbecause these few go-to people are spread so thin, they ultimately don't accomplish all that much."

1 Which of the following does NOT fit in the context?

① Ⓐ   ② Ⓑ

③ Ⓒ   ④ Ⓓ

2 According to the passage, what is the main idea?

① Managers should newly discover competent employees and develop them into their new glue people.

② Overtaxing your trustworthy employees with too much burden kills their abilities.

③ Managers depending on their go-to employees too much are very susceptible to betrayal.

④ Developing reliable lieutenants will be ultimately indispensible for every manager.

3 According to the passage, what does the underlined ⓐ refer to?

① highly rebellious employees

② highly naive employees

③ highly dubious employees

④ highly faithful employees

05

Some regions of the world have been marginalized by globalization. Economists once thought that, over time, inequalities between both regions and countries would naturally even out. Some believe that the global economy can be imagined to be a self-equilibrating mechanism of the textbook variety. Others believe that it can be recognized as subject to processes of cumulative causation whereby if one or more countries fall behind the pack, there may be dangers of them falling further behind, rather than enjoying an automatic ticket back to the equilibrium solution path. These two alternative, conflicting views of real-world economic processes have very different implications regarding institutional needs and arrangements. The same applies to regions. There is no reason in theory, nor evidence in practice, why they should enjoy virtuous circles of convergence rather than vicious cycles of divergence. Thus, at the time of the Brexit referendum it was said that income per head in Britain was back above pre-financial crisis levels. As Andy Haldane, the chief economist at the Bank of England, pointed out subsequently, this was true in aggregate, but at a disaggregated level it applied to only two of Britain's regions: London and the South-East.

1 According to the passage, which is NOT true?

① All countries do not enjoy equal benefits from globalization.
② Different views of world economy result in different institutions.
③ An economically unequal result can be a cause of greater inequality.
④ Both regions and countries will be equally well off in the future.

2 The author cites the case of Britain to show that _____ is likely to occur.

① a vicious cycle of economic inequality between regions
② a vicious cycle of economic inequality between countries
③ a virtuous circle of economic equality between regions
④ a virtuous circle of economic equality between countries

06

Findings from several studies on corporate mergers and acquisitions during the 1970s and 1980s raise questions about why firms initiate and consummate such transactions. One study showed, for example, that acquiring firms were on average unable to maintain acquired firm's pre-merger levels of profitability. A second study concluded that post-acquisition gains to most acquiring firms were not adequate to cover the premiums paid to obtain acquired firms. A third demonstrated that, following the announcement of a prospective merger, the stock of the prospective acquiring firm tends to increase in value much less than does that of the firm for which it bids. Yet mergers and acquisitions remain common, and bidders continue to assert that their objectives are economic ones. Acquisitions may well have the desirable effect of channeling a nation's resources effectively from less to more efficient sectors of its economy, but the individual acquisitions executives arranging these deals must see them as advancing either their own or their companies' private economic interests. It seems that factors having little to do with corporate economic interests explain acquisitions. These factors may increase the incentive compensation of executives, lack of monitoring by boards of directors, and managerial error in estimating the value of firms targeted for acquisition.

1 Which of the following is true about the corporate mergers and acquisitions during the 1970s and 1980s?

① Most such acquisitions produced only small increases in acquired firms' levels of profitability.

② Most such acquisitions were based on an overestimation of the value of target firms.

③ The gains realized by most acquiring firms did not equal the amounts expended in acquiring.

④ About half of acquisitions led to long-term increases in the value of acquiring firm's stocks.

2 According to the passage, which of the following is true?

① The known benefits of acquisitions to national economies explain their appeal to firms during the 1970s and 1980s.

② Acquisitions will be less prevalent in the future, since their dubious effects will gain wider recognition.

③ Despite their adverse impact, acquisitions are the best way to channel resources from less to more productive sectors.

④ Factors other than economic benefits to the acquiring firm help to explain the frequency with which they occur.

07

We need to reflect on the very concept of growth. "Zero growth" was seen as a possible option from the 1970s, but the idea of reconciling economic development with environmental protection won out. Four decades later, we must admit that this approach failed. Clearly our planet cannot support the same levels of consumption for all its inhabitants — the ultimate goal if we are to have equity. We could perhaps pit frugality against consumption, but that means reaching a degree of equality, now or in the future. It is not possible at the moment. Some Latin American countries use a concept, ancestral for indigenous Andean communities, but new to us — "wellbeing" or "full life", *buen vivir* or *vida plena*. Though drawn from other traditions, it resembles something Father Lebret advocated 60 years ago: putting human beings at the centre of the economy. That concept is written into the constitutions of Ecuador and Bolivia, and challenges "the traditional concept of progress with its productivist excesses". It promotes a sustainable economy through solidarity, abandoning "_____, understood as ever greater material accumulation." Clearly this kind of change is more apparent in speeches than on the ground: we need to carefully examine the relationship between the markets, state and society.

1   The author's main idea is that _____.

① we have to revive the policy of "Zero growth"

② frugality is the only way to curb excessive consumption

③ we can find a permanent truth in our cherished tradition

④ we need to find out concrete ways of realizing a sustainable economy

⑤ we can overcome every challenge we face through economic growth

2   Which of the following would be best for the blank?

① the logic of efficiency

② the logic of equality

③ the logic of liberty

④ the logic of emancipation

⑤ the logic of justice

08

The whole view of industrial organization embodied in managerial ideology has long since been abandoned by most social scientists as incongruent with reality and useless for purposes of analysis. A more convincing approach sees the organization as a plural society containing many related but separate interests and objectives which must be maintained in some kind of equilibrium. These separate interests and objectives, manifested in the numerous and diverse work groups which make up the organization, often make common cause with similar interests in other organizations. Thus we have manual workers, technicians, and clerical workers with their respective trade unions, and perhaps professionals and technologists with their associations and institutes. Through these horizontal links with groups outside, the members of the organization owe loyalty to, and come under the authority of, leaders other than their own management. Industrial government therefore faces one of the most taxing of all tests of government, in that substantial sections of its empire owe only a partial allegiance which they may choose at certain moments to withdraw altogether. It cannot claim the right to full allegiance, for its functions and responsibilities sometimes Ⓐ_____ the interests of organization members as they see them.

1 Choose the one that best fills in the blank Ⓐ.

① oblige it to act against   ② go hand in hand with

③ get restricted or checked by   ④ require it to strive for

2 Which of the following CANNOT be inferred about "today's industrial organization"?

① It is a complex society where the diverse interests and objectives of its members must be in balance.

② It defies the explanation by previous managerial ideologists who saw an organization as a whole.

③ The conflict between management and labor in it is likely to be extended to the nationwide level.

④ It is imperialistic in that it can easily be a conglomerate through the horizontal links with other organizations.

3 What is the purpose of the passage?

① To compare the two approaches to industrial organizations

② To explain the characters of modern industrial organizations

③ To analyze the strong and weak points of a new approach

④ To urge industrial government to protect laborers' interests

09

All leaders do not lead in the same way or focus on the same goals. Some leaders take an instrumental approach, focusing on getting specific jobs done, while others take a(n) Ⓐ_____ approach, concerning themselves with the emotional well-being of the group. Groups actually have a need for both types of approaches. In meetings, for example, groups have to accomplish whatever task is at hand and also negotiate relationships between group members.

Leaders also differ in regard to how they motivate others and what they seek to achieve. Ⓑ_____ leaders are task-oriented and focus on getting group members to achieve goals. These leaders reward accomplishing routine goals but do not especially inspire performance beyond the routine. In other words, their group members accomplish their tasks but generally do not make extra efforts beyond those required. In an accounting department, for example, the billers would get the monthly invoices out as required but not do more. Ⓒ_____ leaders encourage others to go beyond the routine by building a different type of organization that focuses on future possibilities. They use enthusiasm and optimism to inspire others. They encourage innovation and creativity. They exhibit characteristics that others can identify with, trust, and follow. They also focus on mentoring others as leaders. In an accounting department headed by this type of a leader, Ⓓ_____.

1 빈칸 Ⓐ, Ⓑ, Ⓒ에 들어갈 가장 알맞은 것을 고르시오.

① transformational — Expressive — Transactional
② transactional — Expressive — Transformational
③ expressive — Transformational — Transactional
④ expressive — Transactional — Transformational

2 글의 내용상 Ⓓ에 들어갈 가장 알맞은 것을 고르시오.

① the staff might be punished for noncompliance with the leader's orders
② the staff might hold a meeting to determine the priority of routine tasks
③ the staff might be easily influenced to agree with the group perceptions regardless of their individual opinions
④ the staff might devote time to testing new software that would help the department improve its efficiency

10

The fact that superior service can generate a competitive advantage for a company does not mean that every attempt at improving service will create such an advantage. Investments in service, like those in production and distribution, must be balanced against other types of investments on the basis of direct, tangible benefits such as cost reduction and increased revenues. If a company is already effectively on a par with its competitors because it provides service that avoids a damaging reputation and keeps customers from leaving at an unacceptable rate, then investment in higher service levels may be wasted, since service is a deciding factor for customers only in extreme situations.

This truth was not apparent to managers of one regional bank, which failed to improve its competitive position despite its investment in reducing the time a customer had to wait for a teller. The bank managers did not recognize the level of customer inertia in the consumer banking industry that arises from the inconvenience of switching banks. Nor did they analyze their service improvement to determine whether it would attract new customers by producing a new standard of service that would excite customers or by proving it difficult for competitors to copy. The only merit of the improvement was that it could easily be described to customers.

1 The primary purpose of the passage is to _____.
   ① contrast possible outcomes of a type of business investment
   ② suggest more careful evaluation of a type of business investment
   ③ illustrate various ways in which a type of business investment could fail to enhance revenues
   ④ criticize the way in which managers tend to analyze the costs and benefits of business investments

2 The passage suggests that bank managers failed to consider whether or not the service improvement _____.
   ① was too complicated to be easily described to prospective customers.
   ② could be sustained if the number of customers increased significantly
   ③ was an innovation that competing banks could have imitated
   ④ was adequate to bring the bank's general level of service to a level that was comparable with that of its competitors

11

The centuries-old debate over the profitability of slavery has flared again. It's a debate that has been discussed in academic circles for more than 150 years, with one of the most notable evaluations done by economist Thomas Gowan in 1942. Gowan concluded that plantation slavery was indeed most often profitable to the larger class of slave owners, despite his efforts to prove it was not, and many economists have supported Gowan's theory over the years, with little evidence to suggest otherwise forthcoming. Robert Fogel and Stanley Engerman wrote in their 1974 book, "Time on the Cross: The Economics of American Negro Slavery," that slavery was perhaps more profitable than other investment opportunities in similar industries, such as farming. Slavery was "generally a highly profitable investment that yielded rates of return that compared favorably with the most outstanding investment opportunities in manufacturing," they wrote. Instinctively it would make sense that free labor would bring more profits than paid labor, but many authors on the subject suggest that slavery was not as lucrative as has been thought. Irishman John Elliott Cairnes, often referred to as the last great classical economist, believed that Ⓐ_____ on the economy of the South in 19th century America. His basic argument was that reluctant workers had no interest in learning new farming techniques and therefore weakened soils much quicker because they didn't have the basic requisites for farming. This meant that the South was less competitive than the North, where free slaves were being paid to learn and maintain farms to a better standard, thus growing more and better crops.

1 위 글의 내용과 일치하지 <u>않는</u> 것을 고르시오.

① Thomas Gowan tried to discredit his own hypothesis that slavery makes economic sense.

② Some suggested that slavery in the South was a lucrative enterprise for planation owners.

③ John Elliott Cairnes reckoned that slavery stifled economic growth in the South.

④ The slaves were eventually replaced with paid laborers for enriching soils.

2 문맥상 빈칸 Ⓐ에 들어갈 가장 알맞은 것을 고르시오.

① the movement against slavery was a drag

② slavery had an overall negative impact

③ the emancipation of slaves was a break

④ slave trade was an inevitable consequence

12

Until well into the seventeenth century, surgery was performed not by doctors but by barbers who, untaught and unlettered, applied whatever tortures they had picked up during their apprenticeship. Doctors, observing a literal interpretation of their oath Ⓐ_____, were too 'ethical' to cut and were not even supposed to watch. But the operation, if performed according to the rules, was presided over by a learned doctor who sat on a dais well above the struggle and read what the barber was supposed to be doing aloud from a Latin classic (which the barber, of course, did not understand). Needless to say, it was always the barber's fault if the patient died, and always the doctor's achievement if he survived. And the doctor got the bigger fee in either event.

There is some resemblance between the state of surgery of four centuries ago and the state of organization theory of now. There is no dearth of books in the field; indeed, organization theory is the main subject taught under the heading of 'management' in many of our business schools. There is a great deal of importance and value in these books — just as there was a great deal of genuine value in the classical texts on surgery. But the practising manager only too often feels the way the barber must have felt. It is not that he, as a 'practical man,' resists theory. Most managers, especially in the larger companies, have learned that performance depends greatly upon proper organization theory. But the practising manager does not as a rule understand the organization theorist, and vice versa.

1 Choose the one that best fills in the blank Ⓐ.

① to try their best to save life
② not to neglect any disease
③ to co-work with their fellows
④ not to inflict bodily harm

2 What does the passage mainly discuss?

① the doctor's advantages over the barber in the past
② the state of surgery of four hundred years ago
③ the state of organization theory of now
④ the practising manager's dilemmas in modern times

3 Which of the following CANNOT be inferred about "the practising manager"?

① It is probable that he is less educated or less learned than the organization theorist.
② He tends to put practice before theory, but does not turn a deaf ear to theory.
③ He knows the importance of organization theory, but rarely wins the organization theorist's understanding.
④ He is blamed for all the managerial failure, but never credited with any success.

13

In business, the rest of the world keeps on knocking. When the kingdom of Saudi Arabia decided to build the world's biggest clock on the world's tallest clock tower, it had every reason to seek out designers close to home: the setting was Mecca, after all, which only Muslims are permitted to visit. But this was a project that required specialists, and so a meeting was arranged at a Geneva hotel between a representative of the Saudi royal family and three men from Calw, a small town 30km west of Stuttgart. The German company, Perrot Turmuhren, opened its doors in 1860, and is today run by a fifth generation of the founding family. A world leader in "tower clocks as well as all other related clock and clockwork technology" it won the Saudi contract.

This is the definition of Mittelstand success: to be a world leader in a niche market, the "go-to" company even if the customers are half-way around the world, a "hidden champion" that benefits from globalization rather than being washed away by it. To be part of the Mittelstand is also to be capable of employing 50 to 500 people in a small town, meaning talented youth needn't head to the big city to find success. It is another way power — this time economic — is Ⓐ_____. The success of the Mittelstand, which generates the bulk of corporate revenues in Germany, is deeply intertwined with the country's support for manufacturing. The federal and state governments help fund research — often through NGOs such as the Fraunhofer Institute, with a research budget of €2 billion — that small and medium-sized businesses can use to maintain and improve the quality of their products.

1 Which of the following best fits into the blank Ⓐ?

① decentralized   ② centralized

③ nullified   ④ neutralized

2 Which of the following is NOT true of the German Mittlestand?

① It refers to small and medium-sized enterprises.

② It accounts for much of total economic output in Germany.

③ It tends to take a long-term approach to business, based on strategies to the region.

④ It creates comparatively low level of youth employment.

3 Which of the following is the passage mainly about?

① Mittelstand's model as the welfare state in globalization

② Germany's Mittelstand as postwar economic miracle

③ Germany's Mittelstand as a model of business success

④ Germany's Mittelstand as a new industry with great prospects

14

One reason capitalism has been able to deliver great success is that it never stays static. It has survived and thrived because it has reformed, again and again, in response to the ills of the moment. The suffering brought on by the Great Depression sparked a movement to make capitalism equitable and stable, which led to greater government protection and regulation — the New Deal and the European welfare state. Then, to overcome the stagflation of the 1970s, capitalism had to be more productive and innovative. Ronald Reagan and Margaret Thatcher ushered in an era of deregulation, free trade and free flows of capital that spawned a global economic boom. Today, amid the protracted downturn, capitalism has reached another inflection point. The world's financial sector remains so unsound, and the pain inflicted on the average family has been so great, that capitalism needs to morph yet again, to become more inclusive and balanced and less prone to recurrent meltdowns. The question is not whether capitalism must be reformed. It is how.

On that, there is no agreement. The answer lies with the never-ending waltz of the state and market that has determined the many historical twists and turns of capitalism. Many today believe that financial crisis was caused, like the Great Depression, by capitalism gone wild, fueled by 30 years of _____. Left to their own devices, this thinking goes, bankers and executives can never be trusted to act responsibly. They'll risk the well-being of the economy to ring up bigger profits or work people to death without paying a decent wage. The solution is a renewed government role to control the worst excesses of capitalism.

1 **What is the main idea of the passage?**

① Capitalism has flourished because it repeatedly revised itself to correct evils in the market.
② Every sector of the world economy is now so stagnant that capitalism has to be changed again.
③ The government should intervene in the market to restore seriously aberrant capitalism.
④ Immoral bankers and executives can not act responsibly but only endanger our economy.

2 **Choose the one that best fills in the blank.**

① restricted competition   ② willy-nilly deregulation
③ unfettered redistribution   ④ helter-skelter nationalization

3 **According to the passage, which aspect of capitalism is associated with its hitherto success?**

① dynamism   ② liberalism
③ equilibrium   ④ stoicism

15

Learning begins with perception. Neither an individual nor a company will even begin to learn without having seen something of interest in the environment. That is why surviving and thriving in a volatile world requires, first of all, management that is sensitive to its company's environment. At least a few of the company's leaders should be attentive and responsive to the world in which they live, even to the extent of playing an active role in that outside world. <u>Navel gazers</u> are necessary in every company, but they see little of the forces that will affect the future of that company. By contrast, an open and extroverted management will perceive whatever is happening outside much earlier. Only after seeing that something is about to change or has already begun to change outside the company will management be ready to deal with the effects of that change. Many of these effects lie in the future and are uncertain. In the desire to know and reduce that uncertainty, most managers spend far too much time on the relatively useless question: What will happen to us? But managers who perceive change early should spend more time on a far more useful question: What will we do if such-and-such happens? Only this latter question can lead managers to make changes inside the company that will allow it to survive and thrive in the new world. Indeed, as experience shows, fundamental and painful change may be necessary, possibly even including the abolition of a company's core business.

1   **Choose the closest in meaning to the underlined "Navel gazers."**

    ① Those who think only about themselves

    ② Those who have a fresh point of view

    ③ Those who consistently stick to tradition

    ④ Those who are content with what they are

2   **Which of the following CANNOT be inferred from the passage?**

    ① A company's environment is one of the major factors determining its success in the business industry.

    ② The changes in a company's environment tend to stabilize its future business activities.

    ③ The personality or attitude of a manager has something to do with his or her managerial success.

    ④ Companies can give up even their most profitable business not to be driven out of the industry.

3 What is the main idea of the passage?

① Nothing can be learned until we find something fascinating and change it for survival.

② Companies should give a top priority to change in order to change their business environment.

③ We need active and broad-minded managers who can make innovations in the business.

④ Managers must be alert and prepared for any possible change in their company's environment.

16

Corporate managers often work in groups because of the complexity of strategic problems. A consensus-seeking group's effectiveness may be impaired, however, if the group values harmony over open evaluation of ideas. Consequently, some theorists advocate building decisional conflict into the group process. Doing so, they argue, should yield better decisions. While conflict potentially offers benefits, a group's effectiveness also depends on members' reactions to group experiences. Ideally, the group process wins commitment of its members. The process, though, may generate so much divisiveness that implementation and future cooperation are undermined. Management groups thus face an apparent dilemma: Decisional conflict may yield better decisions at the risk of weakening managerial Ⓐ_____. Conversely, the harmony that facilitates cooperations and implementation may come at the cost of Ⓑ_____.

Efforts to build conflict into group decision making have focused on two approaches, dialectical inquiry and devil's advocacy. Both work by dividing the group into competing subgroups, relying on formal debate to prevent uncritical acceptance of the seemingly obvious, and continuing until participants agree on a decision. The approaches differ in the roles played by the subgroups. In dialectical inquiry, the subgroups present opposed sets of assumptions and recommendations, and debate until they reach agreement. In devil's advocacy, the second subgroup critiques the assumptions and recommendations of the first, but offers no alternative. The first subgroup revises its ideas and presents them for a second critique. The process continues until the subgroups agree.

1 What is the purpose of the passage?

① to advocate dialectical inquiry of group decision making over devil's advocacy

② to emphasize the benefits of group decision making and reconcile two different approaches

③ to argue that group decision making is superior to any other decision making approach

④ to describe the benefits and risks of decisional conflict and alternative means of its use

2 Advocates of both the dialectical inquiry and devil's advocacy processes are likely to agree that _____.

① superior decisions often reflect compromises made between opposing views

② managers should avoid changing their customary ways of thinking

③ formal debate can lead to a more thorough understanding of a problem

④ good decisions stem from a one-sided criticism by the opposite subgroup

3 Which of the following is the most appropriate for the blanks Ⓐ and Ⓑ?

① divisiveness — superior decisions

② effectiveness — inferior decisions

③ cooperation — effectiveness

④ harmony — conflict

17

From countless films and books we all know that, historically, pirates were criminally insane, traitorous thieves, torturers and terrorists. Anarchy was the rule, and the rule of law was nonexistent.

Not so, Ⓐdissents George Mason University economist Peter T. Leeson in his book, *The Invisible Hook*, which shows how the unseen hand of economic exchange produces social cohesion even among pirates. Piratical mythology can't be true, in fact, because no community of people could possibly be successful at anything for any length of time if their society were utterly anarchistic. There is honor among thieves, as Adam Smith noted in *The Theory of Moral Sentiments*: "Society cannot subsist among those who are at all times ready to hurt and injure one another. If there is any society among robbers and murderers, they must at least Ⓑabstain from robbing and murdering one another."

Pirate societies, in fact, provide evidence for Smith's theory that economies are the result of bottom-up spontaneous self-organized order that naturally arises from social interactions, Ⓒas opposed to top-down bureaucratic design. Just as historians have demonstrated that the "Wild West" of 19th-century America was a relatively ordered society in which farmers and miners concocted their own rules and institutions for conflict resolution way before the federal law reached them.

From where, then, did the myth of piratical lawlessness and anarchy arise? From the pirates themselves, who helped to perpetrate the myth to minimize losses and maximize profits. Consider the Jolly Roger flag that displayed the skull and crossbones. It was a signal to merchant ships that they were about to be boarded by a marauding horde of heartless heathens; the Ⓓviolent surrender of all booty was therefore perceived as preferable to fighting back.

---

1 Which of the following words is NOT suitable for the context?

① Ⓐ   ② Ⓑ

③ Ⓒ   ④ Ⓓ

2 Which of the following is true of pirates according to the passage?

① Pirates receive violent resistance from shipping crews and their owners.

② Pirates try to prevent bloody battle that would needlessly injure or kill others.

③ A pirate king centrally designs and imposes a common code on all sea bandits.

④ Pirates generally engage in violence to loot the citizens of many treasures.

3 What is the attitude of Adam Smith toward the pirate myth?

① neutral   ② agreeable

③ indifferent   ④ disapproving

4 Which of the following can be inferred from the passage?

① Markets operating in a lawless society are actually the same as free markets.

② Pirates probably elected their own captains and made their own rules.

③ Pirates were reluctant to negotiate the transactions quickly and peacefully.

④ Pirate myth reveals how economic forces generate social disorder.

18

There are anchor stores in many shopping centers like Macy's, Nordstrom, Bloomingdale's, Sears, and the Mall of America. Anchor stores are larger department stores that are used to provide a major point of interest for a shopping mall or center. Sometimes referred to as a draw tenant or key tenant, it is usually a well-known chain store that is popular with consumers. The presence of this type of store can entice consumers to visit the shopping center or mall, and possibly continue to shop at the smaller stores in the complex. The expectation is that the smaller stores surrounding it will sell goods and services that are complementary to, but not in competition with, those offered by the bigger store. As a result, consumers could possibly _____.

With the advent of the shopping mall during the 1940s and 1950s, an anchor store's value to a shopping venue was expanded. Instead of including one anchor in the venue, malls began to be constructed with a minimum of two anchor stores. With an anchor tenant at each end of the mall, smaller retailers would occupy storefronts that connected the two together. A shopper may enter the mall at one, then shop at the smaller stores while on the way to the other main store at the opposite end of the mall.

Anchor stores are so important to a mall's success that management regularly give them discounted rental rates to entice them. The departure of key tenants portends the atrophy of a shopping mall. Without the larger stores to help maintain consumer interest, the smaller stores usually begin to seek retail space in other malls or centers as soon as possible. Once the anchors and most of the smaller retail outlets have left the facility, it is usually referred to as a dead mall.

1 **Choose the one that best fills in the blank.**

① be given more care and attention

② use the mall as a point of reference

③ complete their shopping at one place

④ purchase better items at lower prices

2 **Choose the closest in meaning to the underlined "portends the atrophy of a shopping mall."**

① puts a shopping mall into an economic hardship

② is the first sign of the decline of a shopping mall

③ leads a shopping mall to turn over a new leaf

④ proves to be a hurdle to the growth of a shopping mall

3 Which of the following CANNOT be inferred about "anchor stores"?

① They were initiated by the shopping malls in the mid-twentieth century.

② They can contribute to increasing the occupancy rate of the shopping mall.

③ They tend to be given financial advantages by the shopping mall management.

④ They are scientifically positioned to get as much consumer traffic as possible.

4 What is the best title for the passage?

① How Have the Modern Malls Evolved?

② How Does a Mall Manage Its Stores?

③ What Does an Anchor Do for Consumers?

④ What Is an Anchor Store in the Mall?

19

Gold originally came into use as a common unit of currency because of its rarity, toughness, and ease of identification. In the pre-industrial world, gold coins were often used as a way to trade goods such as cows or wheat without having to transport bulky products to the marketplace. Eventually, as modern banking systems began to be established, gold coins themselves were replaced by bank notes that represented a specific amount of gold stored in a vault. As the world economy further evolved, the use of gold as a common currency helped to standardize trade practices between countries. Over time, the international use of gold for commercial purposes became known as the gold standard.

For centuries, the gold standard was of vital economic importance because the extremely limited supply of the precious metal created a nearly constant amount of wealth in the world. Although mining companies occasionally discovered and vigorously exploited new sources of gold, Ⓐthe metal could not be produced at the whim of governments in order to redistribute wealth or try to micro-manage the economy. This, in turn, helped to prevent inflation, which occurs when currency loses its value due to an increase in the amount of currency in circulation. During the early twentieth century, however, most nations abandoned the gold standard in favor of national currencies whose values were based on a complicated formula that measured world trade levels as a whole. This development in the world economy was a result of an international economic collapse in the 1920s.

1 Which of the following statements is most likely true of bank notes?

① Bank notes, like gold coins, were used to make the trade of bulky goods easier.
② The value of bank notes varies depending on consumer prices.
③ Bank notes possess a large amount of value because their materials are so rare.
④ Bank notes became so popular that nations adopted a note standard.

2 The author of the passage implies that the amount of wealth in the world _____.

① rose once the gold standard was adopted by many nations
② increased gaps between rich and poor nations under the gold standard
③ became less constant once the gold standard was abandoned
④ did nosedive dramatically shortly after the economic collapse of the 1920s

3 Which of the following can be inferred about the economic collapse of the 1920s?

① It was caused by nations hoarding too much gold before it occurred.

② It led many nations to abandon the gold standard for one based on trade levels.

③ It was caused by a decrease in the amount of gold available for consumption.

④ It affected wealthy nations much less dramatically than poorer ones.

4 Choose the one closest in meaning to the underlined Ⓐthe metal could not be produced at the whim of governments.

① governments could produce gold with conditions attached

② governments couldn't produce gold without aid of governments

③ governments could produce gold in an arbitrary way

④ governments couldn't produce gold at discretion

20

There are higher-yielding varieties of groundnut than those that farmers in Malawi tend to plant, but getting them to switch is tough. Better seed is pricey, increasing their risk. So researchers from the World Bank ran an experiment. With local NGOs, they offered the farmers loans. Some loans even came with a crop-insurance policy: if the season was dry and the yield a dud, the debt would be forgiven. The farmers' risk was lowered. Of farmers offered conventional loans, 33% signed up. With the added incentive of insurance, 18% did. The researchers were puzzled.

Xavier Giné, a World Bank economist in Malawi, has seen microinsurance Ⓐsputter time and again, even in areas where microloans thrive. Unforeseen economic behavior is driving these opposite outcomes, he says. "When we think about credit, lenders need to trust the borrower. But in insurance, it's the exact opposite. You have to trust that the insurance company will pay the claim." It's hardly a stretch that people new to financial institutions don't. (My crop fails, and you pay me? Ha!) In India, Giné has found, it's actually Ⓑ_____ who are more willing to buy insurance policies: the thing meant to hedge against risk is seen as risky. And perhaps not without reason. Insurers didn't pay off in Bangladesh in the 1990s, one of the earliest attempts at microinsurance.

In *Portfolios of the Poor*, New York University economist Jonathan Morduch and his co-authors toss out other reasons microinsurance may be a hard sell. First, being poor is not without complications, and that's part of what makes a loan attractive. Sure, microcredit is typically meant to help build a business, but cash is fungible — if there's no money for dinner one night, a line of credit, whatever its intent, solves the problem. Not so for insurance, which asks people to decide in advance which of the many risks they face they should hedge. Plus, even without formal insurance, most people already have some version of a safety net: friends, family and — in truly catastrophic situations — government. "The challenge for insurance is to beat those other mechanisms, not to beat nothing," says Morduch.

1 According to the passage, which of the following is the most significant factor of the poor not signing up for the insurance?
   ① Poor management of the insurance
   ② Deficiency of lender's capital
   ③ Distrust for the insurers
   ④ Insufficient coverage of the insurance
   ⑤ A burden of expenses to pay for a possible risk

2 The word Ⓐ"<u>sputter</u>" can be best replaced by _____.

① fail   ② thrive

③ operate efficiently   ④ challenge

⑤ leap

3 Choose the word that can best fill in the blank Ⓑ.

① the far-sighted

② opportunity averters

③ destitute people

④ risk takers

⑤ downbeat pessimists

4 According to the passage, it can be inferred that the poor who take out microcredit loans _____.

① implement their business ideas for self-financing

② plan their future for the possibility of bad things happening

③ are likely to unthread a dept trap

④ take up microinsurance for recovering the loss

⑤ use them for a means of subsistence

5 According to the passage, which of the following is most likely true?

① The poor new to microinsurance suspect that insurers have something to hide.

② The more incentives of insurance are given, the more likely the farmers are to sign up for insurance.

③ Policyholders in Bangladesh in the 1990s didn't pay their premiums.

④ Many think that the microfinance can function as a safety net.

⑤ The poor think of microinsurance as a tool to be compensated in case of a bad harvest.

과학·기술

08 과학·기술

▶▶▶ ANSWERS P.407

01

Science is the popular conception of truth. For most people, truth means a state of being absolutely proven. Of course, as the great philosopher of science Karl Popper pointed out, science never really proves anything. For example, most people understand that water freezes at 32 degrees Fahrenheit at sea level. Every time we have ever put this to the test, we have gotten the same result. Popper, however, argued that we can only say that water freezing under these conditions is the best theory we possess. After all, the water might not freeze the one-millionth time we test it. Popper put it this way: suppose that every swan ever observed was white. Would science then be justified in saying that it has proven that swans are white? No, all science could say is that no black swan has ever appeared. The possibility remains that one will someday. Science can never prove; it can only disprove. And in attempting to disprove, it provides an account for events as they exist now while remaining open to the possibility that new events may demand a modification of our view. In short, science is forever looking for the black swan.

1 Which of the following would be the best title of the passage?

① Realism and the Aim of Science
② The Falsification by Science
③ Validity of Pseudoscience
④ Rational Speculation of Science

2 Which of the following can be inferred about the Karl Popper's viewpoint toward science?

① Science empowers men to pursue the absolute truth.
② Some unchanging principles lie deep in the scientists.
③ The more science develops, the more immutable theories are discovered.
④ Belief in any theory is never absolute; it's always provisional.

02

Pure science does not always stimulate innovation — rather, technological change often springs naturally from human inventiveness. Writer Matt Ridley makes this provocative point in a essay in *The Wall Street Journal* called 'The Myth of Basic Science' that fuelled heated and thoughtful responses on social media about the role and benefits of science and technology. Ridley says that government-funded basic research is not the only path toward innovations that improve society. But others countered that publicly-funded research has many benefits. "The causes of technical and social change are manifold, and scientific research forms just part of the ecosystem, but this doesn't make it inconsequential," wrote Jack Stilgoe, a science-policy expert at University College London, in an article commenting on Ridley's essay for *The Guardian*. Ridley responded to his critics on Twitter, saying that basic research is important but that government is not the only way to fund it. Ridley takes aim at the popular 'linear model' that holds that basic science fuels new technology, which, in turn, benefits society. "When you examine the history of innovation, you find, again and again, that scientific breakthroughs are the _____, not the cause, of technological change," he writes. The steam engine did not come about because of breakthroughs in the science of thermodynamics, he notes, but thermodynamics certainly benefited from its invention.

1 The most appropriate expression for the blank would be _____.

① theory   ② practice

③ effect   ④ intuition

⑤ speculation

2 According to the passage, which of the following is true?

① Ridley supports the linear model.

② Ridley prefers basic science to new technology.

③ Ridley invented the steam engine using thermodynamics.

④ The opinion of Jack Stilgoe is not different from that of Ridley.

⑤ Ridley is more concerned with human inventiveness than pure science.

03

It was in the 1920s that the idea of freezing fresh vegetables into preserved, edible rectangles first caught hold, when inventor Clarence Birdseye developed a high-pressure, flash-freezing technique that operated at especially low temperatures. The key to his innovation was the flash part: comparatively slow freezing at slightly higher temperatures causes large ice crystals to form in food, damaging its fibrous and cellular structure and robbing it of taste and texture. Birdseye's super-cold, super-fast method allowed only small crystals to form and preserved much more of the vitamins and freshness. In the 90 years since, food manufacturers have added a few additional tricks to improve quality. Some fruits and vegetables are peeled or blanched before freezing, _____, which can cause a bit of oxidation — the phenomenon that makes a peeled apple or banana turn brown. But blanching also deactivates enzymes in fruit that would more dramatically degrade color as well as flavor and nutrient content. _____, the blanching process can actually increase the fibrous content of food by concentrating it, which is very good for human digestion.

1 **Choose the set of words that best fill in the blanks.**

① for example — What's more
② on the other hand — In addition
③ in a similar way — On the contrary
④ as a consequence — In contrast

2 **Which is true according to the passage?**

① Freezing is the first method of preserving food that people have developed.
② Birdseye's major contribution to food preservation was his no-ice-crystal skill.
③ Moderate oxidation can help preserve food in a fresh state and for a long time.
④ Blanched foods are more nutritious and digestible than those not so treated.

04

Big tech companies investing billions in AI development need to do a better job of explaining what they're working on, without sugarcoating or soft-pedaling the risks. Right now, many of the biggest AI models are developed behind closed doors, using private data sets and tested only by internal teams. When information about them is made public, it's often either watered down by corporate PR or buried in _____ scientific papers. Playing down AI risks to avoid backlash may be a smart short-term strategy, but tech companies won't survive long term if they're seen as having a hidden AI agenda that's at odds with the public interest. And if these companies won't open up voluntarily, AI engineers should go around their bosses and talk directly to policy-makers and journalists themselves. Similarly, the news media needs to do a better job of explaining AI progress to nonexperts. Too often, journalists rely on outdated sci-fi shorthand to translate what's happening in AI to a general audience.

1 The most appropriate expression for the blank would be _____.

① immiscible
② inscrutable
③ irrefutable
④ imperceptible
⑤ indomitable

2 The main point of the passage would be '_____'.

① AI giants should not monopolize their technologies.
② AI technologies have not only benefits but also risks.
③ We need to talk openly about what is happening in AI.
④ Journalists have to work with insiders to monitor AI firms.
⑤ No one can grasp how fast progress is being made in AI.

05

Mercury is the only metal that keeps its liquid form at normal temperatures. It is possible to pour mercury from one vessel to another in exactly the same way that it is possible to pour water. Because of this, people for a long time were not certain that mercury was a true metal. The silver-white substance was known to the ancient Chinese and Hindus. It has been found in Egyptian tombs dating back to 1500 B.C. One ancient Greek writer described the metal as "liquid silver," and even today it is often called quicksilver.

Mercury is a very Ⓐ_____ metal. It is used widely in the making of many useful drugs and medicines. Large amounts of mercury are also used in mixing paints, in making explosives, and in manufacturing electrical and scientific apparatus. Mercury is perhaps most commonly known for its use in thermometers. It is the substance that expands or contracts according to changes in temperature.

Occasionally, mercury is found in its free state among rocks. Most often, however, it is found mixed with sulfur in a beautiful red ore called cinnabar.

1 위 글에서 수은에 관해 언급되지 <u>않은</u> 것은?

① versatility   ② liquidity

③ antiquity   ④ fragility

2 다음 중 수은에 대한 설명으로 옳은 것은?

① Mercury was known to the ancient Middle East and Asia only.
② We can only find mercury as mixed with other base metals.
③ Mercury and apparatuses made from it are edible.
④ All metals except mercury are solid at room temperature.

3 문맥상 빈칸 Ⓐ에 들어갈 단어로 가장 적당한 것은?

① curious   ② valuable

③ scientific   ④ fluid

06

From the beginning of human history innovators have experimented with all kinds of elements, from the ordinary to the invisible, to try to come up with new, improved materials. The invention of plastic in 1907 inaugurated the era of synthetic materials that are stirred up in laboratories, greatly expanding the possibilities for creating an endless variety of useful products.

Researchers at the Wyss Institute at Harvard invented a miraculous new substance called "Shrilk" by combining shrimp shell and silk proteins. Shrilk is inexpensive to manufacture but has invaluable virtues: It's tough, flexible, and biodegradable. In the future it may be used to make everything from wound dressings to trash bags to disposable diapers. And it might make many landfill-choking plastics obsolete. However, scientists sometimes concoct materials that have no clear use at first. That's the case with the complex, record-holding kinds of carbon highlighted at night. Other new materials may seem trivial in our high-tech world but will undoubtedly bring joy to convenience-seeking consumers. For example, a team from MIT has come up with a patent-protected, food-based formula called LiquiGlide, a slippery coating for the inside of containers that will make thick liquids like ketchup and mayonnaise glide right out.

1 Choose the one closest in meaning to the underlined "bring joy to convenience-seeking consumers."

① be available for entertainment and function

② make consumer goods more attractive

③ be employed to produce easy-to-use goods

④ make consumers prefer convenience stores

2 Which of the following is NOT among the qualities of "Shrilk"?

① versatility　　　　　　　　② eco-friendliness

③ viscosity　　　　　　　　④ plasticity

3 According to the passage, what is true about "new materials"?

① Plastic is the first new material to be utilized in human history.

② The complex carbon was intended to be highlighted at night from the start.

③ The more cutting-edge the materials are, the more appealing they are.

④ LiquiGlide can be used to line the inside of the condiment bottles.

The family AV(autonomous vehicle) will ferry children to school; adults to work, malls, movies, bars and restaurants; the elderly to the doctor's office and back. For some, car ownership will be a thing of the past, as the cost of ride-hailing services like Uber and Lyft tumbles once human drivers are no longer needed. Ⓐ Going driverless could cut hailing costs by as much as 80%, say optimists. Welcome to the brave new world of mobility-on-demand. Ⓑ All these things may come to pass one day. But they are unlikely to do so anytime soon, despite the enthusiasm of people like Elon Musk. Within two years, says the Tesla boss, people will be napping as driverless vehicles pilot them to their destinations. Mr Musk has defied conventional wisdom before, and proved critics and naysayers wrong. Ⓒ In this case, however, too many obstacles lie ahead that are not amenable to brute-force engineering. It could take a decade or two before AVs can transport people anywhere, at any time, in any condition — and do so more reliably and safely than human drivers. Ⓓ Consider how long it has taken something as simple as battery-powered vehicles to carve a niche for themselves. After a couple of decades, hybrid and electric vehicles still account for no more than 2% of new-car sales in most countries. Ⓔ Battery prices and storage capacities are finally approaching a point where sales could feasibly take off. Ⓕ But even under the most optimistic of assumptions (say, electrics accounting for half of all new-car sales), it would be 2035 at the earliest before they represented half the vehicles on American roads. Expect fully autonomous vehicles to face an equally long and winding road.

1 When the above passage can be divided into three paragraphs, which would be the best boundary?

① Ⓐ and Ⓒ   ② Ⓐ and Ⓓ
③ Ⓑ and Ⓓ   ④ Ⓑ and Ⓔ
⑤ Ⓒ and Ⓕ

2 According to the passage, the writer _____.

① is positive about Elon Musk's ambitious plan that fully autonomous vehicles will be mainstream within two years
② has high expectations that fully autonomous vehicles will soon become more common, just as battery-powered cars have
③ argues that companies like Uber will not survive as the number of autonomous vehicles increases
④ is skeptical about some views that fully autonomous vehicles will be commercialized in two years or so
⑤ expects autonomous vehicles to take up half of the U.S. roads within a decade

The laser light is different from ordinary light. Ordinary light is composed of waves which are called incoherent light. This means that the waves have different frequencies; they are all mixed together and the waves of light run off in every direction. Ⓐ_____, the light waves produced by the laser are coherent. This means that the waves are parallel and of the same size and frequency, each wave of light fitting closely with the one next to it. Because the waves travel long distances without dispersing, the laser has many uses in long distance communication.

While radio waves are measured in meters, and television waves are measured in inches, the laser waves are measured in ten-millionths of an inch. As the shorter the wavelengths are, the greater the amount of information that can be carried, lasers can be used to transmit great volumes of messages.

The laser has many uses Ⓑ_____ transmitting information, and recently scientists are discovering even more. One of its most remarkable uses is in doing bloodless surgery. Its beam is so strong that it can painlessly burn away warts and wrinkles, and seal blood vessels with its great heat. Oculists use it to weld detached retinas into place and to remove cataracts. Dentists can use lasers to drill teeth painlessly.

1 빈칸 Ⓐ와 Ⓑ에 들어갈 가장 알맞은 것은?

① In the same vein — in addition to
② Besides — In the same breadth
③ On the other hand — besides
④ In contrast — regarding
⑤ Besides — besides

2 다음 글의 내용과 일치하지 <u>않는</u> 것은?

① The radio light has longer wavelengths, compared to laser light.
② The light waves of general light scatter in all directions.
③ The laser will probably be found to have more diverse uses.
④ The only drawback the laser has is that it costs too much.
⑤ The light waves produced by a laser are all the same frequency.

09

Work based skills are changing as more and more jobs are displaced by digital technologies. Software, apps and online technology such as Uber, Airbnb, Legal Zoom and TurboTax to name a few, have already had an impact on many professions. Online shopping has eliminated tens of thousands of retail store positions. Ⓐ And with self-driving vehicles on the way, how many taxi, trucking, express delivery — and even aviation jobs — will <u>go the way of</u> the telephone switchboard operator? Ⓑ If history is a reliable guide, the technologies that are eliminating one set of jobs will create others: jobs that require twenty-first century — mainly digital — skills. The explosion in industrial robotics, for example, is eliminating thousands of assembly line jobs but it is creating a demand for people who can design, manufacture, program and maintain those machines. Ⓒ The questions are — what will the net impact on jobs be and how well are our schools preparing young people for those new, higher skilled jobs as we head toward <u>the fourth industrial revolution</u>? Ⓓ Any assessment is disheartening. Most schools lack the resources to keep up with the technological curve. They don't have robotic labs, 3D printers, code writing courses, and so forth. America is not the only nation facing this problem. Ⓔ U.K. schools are no better positioned to educate young people for the digital age even though, according to the Bank of England, up to 15 million jobs are at risk of being automated out of existence. Ⓕ According to one leading U.K. institution, the Edge Foundation "The U.K.'s future workforce will need technical expertise in areas such as design and computing, plus skills which robots cannot replace — flexibility, empathy, creativity and enterprise."

1 The underlined "<u>go the way of</u>" means _____.

① get lost in a maze   ② break new ground

③ hinder growth   ④ get their own way

⑤ tread in another's step

2 Which of the following is NOT the characteristic of the underlined "<u>the fourth industrial revolution</u>"?

① internal combustion engine   ② 3D printing

③ robotology   ④ autonomous vehicles

⑤ digitization

3 If the above passage is divided into three paragraphs, the best boundary would be _____.

① Ⓐ — Ⓒ   ② Ⓐ — Ⓓ

③ Ⓑ — Ⓓ   ④ Ⓑ — Ⓕ

⑤ Ⓒ — Ⓓ

10

A scientific theory summarizes a hypothesis or group of hypotheses that have been supported with repeated testing. If enough evidence accumulates to support a hypothesis, it moves to the next step — known as a theory — in the scientific method and becomes accepted as a valid explanation of a phenomenon. When used in non-scientific context, the word "theory" implies that something is unproven or speculative. As used in science, however, a theory is an explanation or model based on observation, experimentation, and reasoning, especially one that has been tested and confirmed as a general principle helping to explain and predict natural phenomena.

Any scientific theory must be based on a careful and rational examination of the facts. In the scientific method, there is a clear distinction between facts, which can be observed and/or measured, and theories, which are scientists' explanations and interpretations of the facts. Scientists can have various interpretations of the outcomes of experiments and observations, but the facts, which are the cornerstone of the scientific method, do not change.

A scientific theory must include statements that have observational consequences. A good theory, like Newton's theory of gravity, has unity, which means it consists of a limited number of problem-solving strategies that can be applied to a wide range of scientific circumstances. Another feature of a good theory is that it formed from a number of hypotheses that can be tested independently.

A scientific theory is not the end result of the scientific method; theories can be proven or rejected, just like hypotheses. Theories can be improved or modified as more information is gathered so that the accuracy of the prediction becomes greater over time. Theories are also foundations for furthering scientific knowledge and for putting the information gathered to practical use. Scientists use theories to Ⓐ_____.

1 **According to the passage, what is the best title?**

① Deductive Reasoning of the Scientific Method

② The Good Grasp of a Scientific Theory

③ Debunking a Myth on Nature with a Theory

④ How to Tell a General Theory from a Scientific One

2 **Choose the one that best fills in the blank Ⓐ.**

① phase out all the established scientific order

② harbor doubts about the foundations of a theory

③ expunge evidences unfavorable to theories

④ bring out inventions or find a cure for a disease

11

Say "pseudoscience," and immediately a bunch of doctrines leap to mind: astrology, phrenology, eugenics, ufology, and so on. Do they have anything in common? Some are advocated by outsiders to the scientific community, while others have been backed by the elite. And the status of each can fluctuate over time. Astrology, for example, was considered an exemplary field of natural knowledge from antiquity through the Renaissance. For millennia, philosophers have attempted to erect a boundary between those domains of knowledge that are legitimate and those that are not. The renowned philosopher Karl Popper coined the term "demarcation problem" to describe the quest to distinguish science from pseudoscience. As Popper argued in a 1953 lecture, "The criterion of the scientific status of a theory is its falsifiability." In other words, if a theory articulates which empirical conditions would invalidate it, then the theory is scientific; if it doesn't, it's pseudoscience. That seems clear enough. Unfortunately, it doesn't work. How would you know when a theory has been falsified? Suppose you are testing a particular claim using a mass spectrometer, and you get a disagreeing result. The theory might be falsified, or your mass spectrometer could be on the fritz. Scientists do not actually troll the literature with a falsifiability detector, knocking out erroneous claims right and left. Ⓐ_____, they consider their instruments, other possible explanations, alternative data sets, and so on. Rendering a theory false is a lot more complicated than Popper imagined — and thus determining what is, in principle, falsifiable is fairly muddled.

1 The best title of the passage would be _____.

① Why People Believe Pseudoscience

② Prevalence of Pseudoscience within Science

③ Flaws in Experiments Leading to Pseudoscience

④ Uncertainty in Separating Pseudoscience from Science

⑤ Tracing the History of Pseudoscience

2 Which of the following is most appropriate for the blank Ⓐ?

① Rather

② Luckily

③ In addition

④ Nevertheless

⑤ Consequently

3 According to the passage, which of the following is true?

① It is not until recently that astrology was accepted as valid scientific knowledge.

② The scientific status of a theory is not subject to change once it is deemed legitimate.

③ Karl Popper was the first person to recognize the existence of pseudoscience.

④ Philosophers contributed to facilitating accurate scientific analysis.

⑤ Scientists do not take black-and-white approaches in proving the validity of a theory.

12

Tom is late for his train and doesn't know the way to the station. Racing around a corner, he runs into a plaza full of tourists snapping and uploading photos to Instagram and Facebook. Which way should he go? He tells his Internet-connected contact lenses to load a map, meanwhile tapping at his smartwatch to pull up his ticket and platform information. An alarm flashes in his peripheral vision, only 15 minutes until the train departs, but the map is not loading. He looks around in dismay, frantically yelling "refresh" to his lenses against the clamour of the street.

Welcome to the chaotic future of wearable electronics: devices that promise to connect real to digital lives seamlessly. These gadgets are rapidly multiplying, and within five years there could be half a billion devices strapped onto, or even embedded in, human bodies. Today, the most familiar gadgets are fitness trackers and smart watches, which monitor health and provide ready access to online services. But there are already devices that claim to do more than monitor, such as headbands that alert wearers when they become distracted or wristbands that administer electric shocks to smokers who want help quitting. Electronics companies promise to transform medicine with wearables that can treat symptoms or manage care. Devices are emerging that alert people with epilepsy to incipient seizures, help prevent anxiety attacks, and enable blind people to navigate. But the potential of wearables crucially depends on the large amounts of data they access and generate. And that leads to two problems that researchers and technology developers are struggling to solve: finding improved ways to transmit data to and from wearables, and keeping all that information safe.

1 **What is the passage mainly about?**

① We need some knowledge and a little preparation to use wearable electronics with effect.

② As wearable electronics become more and more common, major electronics companies rake in money.

③ Though having a lot of application fields, wearable electronics have some problems to be solved.

④ Because of the apprehension concerning internet security, the future of wearable electronics is very gloomy.

2 **Choose the closet in meaning to the underlined "refresh" in the context.**

① to make lens or glasses clean

② to fill up a drink again

③ to renew someone's memory by stimulation

④ to update the information displayed on a screen

3   Which of the following can be inferred from the passage?

① Because of the decrease in the number of users, global mobile-data traffic is going to become smaller in the future.

② It is unlikely that wearable electronics are leading to new security concerns.

③ A key hurdle for the wearable revolution arises from the attitude of people viewing wearables as just toys.

④ Wearable electronics are going to be used widely in the field of medicine.

13

Could any comic book superheroes exist in real life? Ⓐ According to a physics professor who studies the way science concepts are applied in comics, Superman is a surprising nominee as one who might actually have a chance. Ⓑ Not the flying, heat-vision-using version we know today, says Dr. James Kakalios of the University of Minnesota, but rather the Superman who first appeared in 1938. Ⓒ Jerry Siegel and Joe Shuster imagined a rocket-borne infant refugee whose alien physiology gave him bullet-resistant skin, the strength of 15 strong men, and the ability to leap (not fly) "tall buildings in a single bound." Ⓓ Whereas today's Superman gets his strength from our "yellow sun," the original Superman's power derived from his planet of origin. Ⓔ According to Kakalios, a compact planet with extreme gravity could produce a being who, as a result of adaptation to environmental factors, would have superhuman strength in Earth's lesser gravity. But that planet's ability to bring forth such a being would ultimately result in the planet's own destruction. Its gravitational collapse would be very similar to the planetary death that resulted, fictionally of course, in Superman being sent to our world in the first place.

1 **Which of the following is true according to the passage?**

① The author believes that a superhuman being might really exist somewhere on Earth.

② The character of Superman is more likely to exist in reality than the character of Batman.

③ Superman as he is portrayed today is more powerful than the Superman of 1938.

④ Dr. James Kakalios has a large comic book collection.

⑤ Looking for a planet with beings of superhuman strength is pointless because any such planets would have been destroyed.

2 **According to Dr. Kakalios, which of the following abilities would be possible in a superhuman being?**

ⓐ The ability to travel unaided through outer space

ⓑ The ability to bench-press many times more weight than a normal man

ⓒ The ability to jump over a house

① ⓐ   ② ⓐ, ⓑ

③ ⓑ   ④ ⓑ, ⓒ

⑤ ⓒ

3 Select the sentence in the passage that identifies the scientific rationale for the possibility of a superhuman being.

① Ⓐ   ② Ⓑ

③ Ⓒ   ④ Ⓓ

⑤ Ⓔ

14

There are three chief ways in which science is presented to the public. The first way is simple popularization, mostly concerned with the content of science — discoveries and their applications. This suffers from journalistic desire for sensation which tends to cheapen science in the minds of thinking laymen, while it gives rise to unreasoning dogmatism in the uncritical.

The second method is indirect and consists of references to scientific theories in works of a non-scientific character, particularly in modern philosophic, religious and psychological literature. The writers of these books are not scientists: they obtain their information on science in general from popular works, and if the science they contain is inaccurate or tendentiously twisted, the fault lies with the scientists who have failed either to provide them with accurate information or to correct them in their mistakes by a vigorous polemic.

The third, and the most important, class of popularizers are those eminent scientists who from time to time write about their own science in relation to wider problems, philosophical, political, or religious, etc., of the time. They are important because they are taken, rightly or wrongly, to be speaking for science, which for greater proportion of people must be taken on authority — and they are the holders of that authority. It is by considering their writings that we can see how the state of harmony between science and other methods of thought has arisen.

1 Which of the following is true about "the first way of popularizing science"?

① It is chiefly associated with how science should be studied and criticized.
② It is most frequently used by scientists to get across to the public.
③ It can imbue the public with wrong ideas of and attitudes toward science.
④ It can help scientists to be immersed in their work beyond yellow journalism.

2 Which of the following CANNOT be inferred about "the second way of popularizing science"?

① Experts in other fields than science often write their books by referring to scientific theories.
② If non-scientific writers address scientific theories or findings wrongly in their books, it's entirely their fault.
③ Books on philosophy, religion, or psychology also can indirectly contribute to popularizing science.
④ Scientists are expected to rectify non-scientific experts' mistakes, if any, through a lively discussion.

3 Which of the following can be inferred about "the third way of popularizing science"?

① Even the eminent scientists need to be concerned about what is going on outside their own field of science.

② The more books a scientist writes about other disciplines than his own, the less authoritative he is taken to be.

③ Scientists have the responsibility of propagate the superiority of their own science whenever they can.

④ Scientists who write about their own science for those outside the campus walls are important because they are authoritarians.

15

A This abundance of data changes the nature of competition. Technology giants have always benefited from network effects: the more users Facebook signs up, the more attractive signing up becomes for others. With data there are extra network effects. By collecting more data, a firm has more scope to improve its products, which attracts more users, generating even more data, and so on. The more data Tesla gathers from its self-driving cars, the better it can make them at driving themselves — part of the reason the firm, which sold only 25,000 cars in the first quarter, is now worth more than GM, which sold 2.3m. Ⓐ_____.

B Access to data also protects companies from rivals in another way. The case for being sanguine about competition in the tech industry rests on the potential for incumbents to be blindsided by a startup in a garage or an unexpected technological shift. But both are less likely in the data age. The giants' surveillance systems span the entire economy: Google can see what people search for, Facebook what they share, Amazon what they buy. They own app stores and operating systems, and rent out computing power to startups. They have a "God's eye view" of activities in their own markets and beyond. They can see when a new product or service gains traction, allowing them to copy it or simply buy the upstart before it becomes too great a threat. Many think Facebook's $22bn purchase in 2014 of WhatsApp, a messaging app with fewer than 60 employees, falls into this category of "shoot-out acquisitions" that eliminate potential rivals. By providing barriers to entry and early-warning systems, Ⓑ_____.

1 What would be the most appropriate content for the paragraph preceding this passage?

① Bricks and mortar industry and its market shares

② High-tech firms and their increasing volume of data

③ Limitations of the traditional antitrust law

④ Market exclusivity of technology giants

⑤ Difficulty in information processing and protection

2 What does the above passage mainly discuss?

① New markets in the Big Data era

② Growth and limitations of data economy

③ Data quantity that has a competitive value all its own

④ The adverse effects of antitrust laws on the data economy

⑤ Strengthening competitiveness of existing large corporations

3 Which of the following is NOT true about the above passage?

① Technology giants see growth of startups as a threat and try to get rid of them.

② Tesla's corporate value is higher than that of GM.

③ As more and more people join Facebook, more people are attracted to Facebook.

④ In the data age, technological innovation has made it easier to beat existing conglomerates.

⑤ When startups can survive in existing businesses, it can be said that a healthy competitive environment has been created.

4 Which of the following can best fill in the blank Ⓐ in paragraph A?

① Old ways of thinking about competition, devised in the era of oil, look outdated in what has come to be called the "data economy".

② Vast pools of data can thus act as protective moats.

③ Google and Facebook accounted for almost all the revenue growth in digital advertising in America last year.

④ The emergence of upstarts like Snapchat suggests that new entrants can still make waves.

⑤ Smartphones and the internet have made data abundant, ubiquitous and far more valuable.

5 Which of the following can best fill in the blank Ⓑ in paragraph B?

① data can stifle competition

② startups have the privilege of preemptive attack

③ startups have unique competitiveness

④ Facebook acts as a protector of the social media industry

⑤ Big Data is a key concept in the future industrial revolution

우주·지구

09

우주·지구

▶ ▶ ▶ ANSWERS P.417

01

The Big Bang theory, an explanation of the origins of our universe, is one of the greatest intellectual achievements of the twentieth century. According to this theory, about ten to twenty billion years ago, the matter of which the universe is made was infinitely tightly compressed. Something — called the Big Bang — turned this matter into a gigantic fireball. As the matter was set into motion and flew away from its compressed state, bits of it became glued together to create galaxies and later, stars and planets. The motion of the matter that flew out of the fireball continues today, and the universe appears to be expanding. The theory grew out of observations of the Doppler effect. It explains that the frequency of radiation given off by a moving body decreases as the source recedes from the observer. In 1965, scientists discovered that the radiation bathing the earth is at the precise microwave frequency that would be expected if the universe began with a big bang. Some scientists think the expansion of the universe will continue to infinity, while others theorize that gravity will, at some point in the far distant future, collapse back onto itself in a "big crunch," returning it to a state of Ⓐ_____ matter.

1 Which best fits Ⓐ?

① neutral   ② augmented

③ positive   ④ condensed

⑤ negative

2 Choose a statement that is NOT related to the content of the passage above.

① The Doppler effect explains that as the source gets further from the observer, the frequency of radiation emitted by the source lessens.

② Scientists do not unanimously agree about the fate of the universe in the future.

③ The Big Bang theory explains that the matter of which the universe is made was originally tightly packed.

④ Scientists believe that the Doppler effect originally created the universe in which we live.

⑤ The author thinks the Big Bang theory is a very important contribution to knowledge.

02

Point Nemo is officially known as "the oceanic pole of inaccessibility," or, more simply put, the point in the ocean that is farthest away from land. Located at 48°52.6′S 123°23.6′W, the spot is quite literally the middle of nowhere, surrounded by more than 1,000 miles of ocean in every direction. The closest landmasses to the pole are one of the Pitcairn islands to the north, one of the Easter Islands to the northeast, and one island off of the coast of Antarctica to the south.

Clearly, there are no human inhabitants anywhere near Point Nemo (the name "Nemo" itself is both Latin for "no one," as well as a reference to Jules Verne's submarine captain from *20,000 Leagues Under The Sea*). In fact, the location is so isolated that the closest people to Nemo are actually not even on Earth. Since the inhabited area closest to Point Nemo is more than 1,000 miles away, the humans in space are far closer to the pole of inaccessibility than those on land.

As for non-human inhabitants, there aren't very many of those around Point Nemo either. The coordinates are actually located within the South Pacific Gyre: an enormous rotating current that actually prevents nutrient-rich water from flowing into the area. Without any food sources, it is impossible to sustain any life in this part of the ocean (other than the bacteria and small crabs that live near the volcanic vents on the seafloor).

1 Which of the following is <u>not</u> true about Point Nemo?

① Once you're there, you've got just as far to go to get back to land.
② Its moniker is a fitting name for a spot so lonely.
③ With no-one around, it is home to many other endangered marine animals.
④ It's an invisible spot in the Southern Pacific Ocean furthest from land.

2 According to the passage, the closest humans to Point Nemo at any given time are likely to be _____.

① astronauts   ② oceanographers
③ submariners   ④ aborigines

03

According to Viking mythology, eclipses occur when two wolves, Skoll and Hati, catch the sun or moon. At the onset of an eclipse people would make lots of noise, hoping to scare the wolves away. After some time, people must have noticed that the eclipses ended regardless of whether they ran around Ⓐ<u>banging on</u> pots.

Ignorance of nature's ways led people in ancient times to postulate many myths in an effort to make sense of their world. But eventually, people turned to philosophy, Ⓑ<u>that is</u>, to the use of reason — with a good dose of intuition — to decipher their universe. Today we use reason, mathematics and experimental test — in other words, modern science.

Albert Einstein said, Ⓒ<u>"The most incomprehensible thing about the universe is that it is comprehensible."</u> He meant that, unlike our homes on a bad day, the universe is not just a conglomeration of objects Ⓓ<u>each going</u> its own way. Everything in the universe follows laws, without exception. Newton believed that our strangely habitable solar system did not "Ⓔ<u>arise</u> chaos by the mere laws of nature." Instead, he maintained that the order in the universe was "created by God at first and conserved by him to this Day in the same state and condition."

1 According to the passage, which of the following is NOT true?

① Irrespective of the noise people made, eclipses faded away.
② Ancient people used to depend on the rationality to understand the universe.
③ Einstein believed the universe was not a mere collection of independent objects.
④ Newton and Einstein did not share the perspective about the universe.

2 What does the underlined Ⓒ mean?

① The fact that we cannot understand the universe is the only thing understandable.
② The seemingly mysterious universe is made out of the rules we can understand.
③ Like ordinary homes, the universe has a universal rule without exception.
④ What is understandable is the universe is created by God, not by laws of nature.

3 Which of the following is NOT grammatically correct?

① Ⓐ   ② Ⓑ
③ Ⓓ   ④ Ⓔ

04

The Polynesians did not need a compass because the stars told them with unerring accuracy the direction in which they were traveling at night. These sailors knew the positions of 150 rising and setting stars. To reach his destination the navigator would steer towards the star on the horizon that rose over the island to which he wished to go. ⒶJust as the stars were the compass of the Polynesian, the patterns formed by the ocean waves were his navigational charts. The navigator knew that the ocean waves traveled in predictable ways. Their size, frequency, and direction all provided valuable information. ⒷThese patterns were like an open map to the Polynesian sailors. Even on dark, cloudy nights, the navigator could tell from the angle at which the waves hit his canoe the direction in which he was traveling. ⒸThe day sky, filled with birds and clouds, also gave unmistakable signs to the Polynesians. Some seabirds were known to leave their island nests during the day to hunt for fish in the open sea and then to return at night. The sailors who encountered these birds in the evening could follow them home, or, finding them in the mornings, know how to travel in an opposite direction. ⒹBecause land was warmer than the ocean, the clouds that formed over islands were different from those over the open sea. Those over land tended to be large and stationary, while those over the ocean were usually smaller and moved with the wind. The sight of a large, stationary cloud, therefore, was another sure signpost for the navigator. Also, a cloud that was light green on the bottom indicated to the Polynesians that it was located over shallow water.

1 Which is the best place in the passage for the following sentence?

For example, the waves running towards an island bounced back, creating swell patterns different from waves in the open ocean.

① Ⓐ　　　　　　　　　　　　　② Ⓑ
③ Ⓒ　　　　　　　　　　　　　④ Ⓓ

2 Choose the one that the passage does NOT mention.

① Polynesians' navigational references in nature
② Polynesians' navigation during a violent storm at sea
③ The differences among the waves patterns
④ The size, movement, and color of the clouds

05

A spiral galaxy is shaped like a disk with a bulge of old stars in the center known as the nucleus. The nucleus contains very hot gases such as hydrogen, ionized oxygen, nitrogen, neon, sulfur, iron, and argon. The entire galaxy resembles a pinwheel, with arms that curve outward. Spiral galaxies usually have just one arm, although some have two or three arms. The Milky Way galaxy has four arms. The arms of spiral galaxies are either normal or barred. Normal arms emerge right out of the nucleus, while barred spirals have a thick band of bright stars that cuts through the middle of the galaxy. An arm emerges from each tip of the band, creating semi-circles around the galaxy.

How spiral galaxies evolved to develop arms and why these arms continue to exist is puzzling to scientists. The way the galaxy rotates should affect the appearance of the arms. The nucleus of a galaxy rotates somewhat like a wheel, while the arms follow more slowly. Because of this, after a few rotations, the arms should begin to break up, producing a fairly continuous mass of stars. One theory asserts that the arms do not break up because there are differences in gravitational force in the galaxy. These differences in force result in dust and gas being pushed and pulled. The movements produce compression waves. Because the galaxy is rotating, Ⓐ<u>they</u> seem to be moving in a spiral path, making the dust and gas appear like spiral arms. The dust and the gas in these spiral arms are the matter from which the stars form.

1   It can be inferred from paragraph 1 that stars in the arms of spiral galaxies _____.

① converge on one part of the galaxy

② are brighter than those in the nucleus

③ have extremely high temperatures

④ are younger than stars in the nucleus

2   Which of the following can be inferred about the rotation of spiral galaxies in paragraph?

① The rotational speed of a spiral galaxy is capable of destroying its arms.

② It is not clear how spiral galaxies retain their arms despite rotation.

③ The rotation of a spiral galaxy is largely an illusion.

④ A spiral galaxy's rotation is likely caused by strong gravitational forces.

3   According to the passage, what does the underlined Ⓐ refer to?

① dust and gas   ② movements

③ compression waves   ④ differences

06

As the biologist Jacques Monod once put it, life evolves not only through necessity — the universal workings of natural law — but also through chance, the unpredictable intervention of countless accidents. Chance Ⓐhas reared its head many times in our planet's history, dramatically so in the many mass extinctions that wiped out millions of species and, in doing so, created room for new life-forms to evolve. Some of these baleful accidents appear to have been caused by comets or asteroids colliding with Earth — most recently the impact, 65 million years ago, that killed off the dinosaurs and opened up opportunities for the distant ancestors of human beings. Therefore scientists look not just for exoplanets, or planets orbiting stars other than the sun, identical to the modern Earth, but for planets resembling the Earth as it used to be or might have been. "The modern Earth may be the worst template we could use in searching for life elsewhere," notes Caleb Scharf, head of Columbia University's Astrobiology Center.

1   Which of the following best represents the main idea of the passage?

① Life evolves through unexpected occurrences of numerous accidents.

② Mass extinctions of some species allowed new forms of life to evolve.

③ The comet collision is most likely to have enabled life to appear on Earth.

④ Planets resembling the ancient Earth may help to find life in the outer space.

2   Choose the one closest in meaning to the underlined Ⓐ.

① has vanished   ② has worked

③ has changed   ④ has overdone

3   Which of the following can be inferred from the passage?

① According to Jacques Monod, life chiefly evolves through absolute necessity.

② New forms of life evolved from the few survivors of an annihilated species.

③ Exoplanets may not be similar to the modern Earth.

④ Human beings appeared on Earth shortly after dinosaurs had become extinct.

07

The rocky object that wiped out the dinosaurs 65 million years ago may have been a comet, rather than an asteroid, scientists say.

Ⓐ The 112-mile Chicxulub crater in Mexico was made by the impact that caused the extinction of dinosaurs and about 70 percent of all species on Earth, many scientists believe. A new study suggests the crater was probably blasted out by a faster, smaller object than previously thought, according to research presented at the 44th Lunar and Planetary Science Conference in The Woodlands, Texas.

Ⓑ Evidence of the space rock's impact comes from a worldwide layer of sediments containing high levels of the element iridium, which could not have occurred on Earth naturally.

Ⓒ The new research suggests the often-cited iridium values are incorrect, however. The scientists compared these values with levels of osmium, another element delivered by the impact.

Ⓓ In order for the smaller rock to have created the giant Chicxulub crater, it had to have been going exceedingly fast, the researchers Ⓐ_____ the conclusion.

"How do we get something that has enough energy to generate that size of crater, but has much less rocky material? That brings us to comets," study author Jason Moore, a(n) Ⓑ_____ at Dartmouth College in New Hampshire, told BBC News.

---

1 What does the following sentence best fit in the passage?

Their calculations suggested the space rock generated less debris than previously thought, implying the space rock was a smaller object.

① Ⓐ   ② Ⓑ
③ Ⓒ   ④ Ⓓ

2 What is the main theme of the above passage?

① The new study proves how the Chixulub crater occurred.
② Iridium is a smoking gun in solving the extinction mystery.
③ What made dinosaurs evaporate still eludes scientists.
④ Comet, not asteroid, may have cost dinosaurs their life.

3   **Which of the following best fits in the blanks Ⓐ and Ⓑ?**

    ① repudiated — archaeologist

    ② derived — paleoecologist

    ③ adjourned — materialist

    ④ drew — anthropologist

4   **Which of the following can be inferred from the passage?**

    ① Iridium and Osmium are the only space rocks found in the Earth.

    ② The new research showed the possibility that a comet is the main culprit behind the extinction of dinosaurs.

    ③ The Chicxulub crater itself triggered the extermination of all the species including dinosaurs.

    ④ Incorrect iridium values demonstrate that the rocky object that made dinosaurs extinct is an asteroid.

08

As far back as the 1600s, people studying maps have noticed that the coastlines of the continents had some interesting similarities. In studying them, particularly the coastline of South America and Africa, it looked like the two continents could fit together, implying that they were joined at one time in the distant past. This was Ⓐan orthodoxy because the accepted theory of the continents was that they were stationary and constant. There was no evidence other than the similarities of the coastlines to support such Ⓑa radical theory.

In 1911, a German meteorologist named Alfred Wegener began looking for additional evidence to support the idea that the continents might actually move around on the earth's surface. He discovered many scientific papers that described puzzling data that did not seem to fit Ⓒthe received opinion of inert continents.

One observation was that geologists noticed that rocks of similar type and formation existed in Canada and in Scandinavia as well as other locations. Other geologists found fossils, or evidence and remains of once-living organisms, of the same plants and animals on widely separated continents, sometimes in locations where they never could have existed, such as tropical plant fossils in Antarctica.

Still other scientists noted that similar deposits left behind by glaciers also appeared on different continents like Africa and South America. In Ⓓthe conventional wisdom of static earth surface, this data did not make much sense because there was no theory that adequately explained how continents separated by great distances and vast oceans could produce these similarities. So, in 1915, Wegener published a new book called *The Origin of Continents and Oceans*, where he proposed a new theory — that the continents were connected at one time in Earth's history and have drifted to their present location.

1   Which is <u>not</u> appropriate in the context?

① Ⓐ   ② Ⓑ
③ Ⓒ   ④ Ⓓ

2   According to the passage, which of the following is <u>not</u> mentioned?

① the parallelism between continental coastlines
② the reason why Alfred Wegener brought out a book
③ the identical anthropological evidence in different regions
④ the challenge against the established theory about continents

3 Which of the following is most likely to be mentioned right after the passage?

① the gradual evolution of cartography

② the controversy about Wegener's continental drift theory

③ the pacific rim susceptible to earthquake

④ the meteor impact with the Earth's atmosphere

09

Astronomers have identified areas in space which they call black holes. They believe these black holes are super-dense stars from which nothing, not even light, can escape. Astronomers think black holes form when a very large star dies and begins to collapse inward upon itself. A star dies when it uses up its nuclear fuel and thus loses heat. As it cools, it begins to shrink. The collapsing star becomes more and more dense, and the pull of gravity becomes stronger. At the point when its density becomes a million billion times greater than that of water, the gravity becomes so strong that everything near the black hole, including light, planets or even other stars, is dragged into it. For our Sun, an ordinary-size star, to become a black hole, it would have to collapse to a point where its radius was a mere three kilometers. Surrounding any black hole is a spherical "horizon," a boundary through which light can enter but not escape. Because no light can leave the star, it appears to be totally black. Black stars can be detected only because, just before material enters the hole, it becomes hot and gives off X-rays, which can be detected from Earth. The only other way to detect these "invisible" black holes is by their influences on other stars. Black holes may be small, but they exert the same gravitation attraction as an ordinary, uncollapsed star of the size would, and so large black holes can be powerful enough that they can pull visible stars into orbit around them, and the movements of this second, visible star can be observed. Astronomers are now suggesting that all large galaxies may have gigantic black holes in their center.

1   According to astronomers, black holes are _____.

① stars which are far darker than ordinary stars

② stars of a very large size

③ areas in space which are as black as night

④ super-dense stars from which nothing can escape

2   The basic reason why a star begins to collapse and shrink is that _____.

① light can enter but can not escape

② a star runs out of fuel

③ the pull of gravity becomes stronger than that of water

④ the weight is added by planets and nearby stars

3 According to the passage, why can't light escape from a black hole?

① The pull of gravity is so strong.

② The sun has little nuclear fuel.

③ It is obstructed by the falling planets and stars.

④ Material blocks the hole.

4 Which of the following is NOT an accurate statement about the detection of black holes?

① Black holes can only be observed directly with great difficulty.

② Black holes can be detected by the X-rays given off by materials which are entering.

③ Black holes can not be observed because they omit no light.

④ Black holes can be detected by their effects on other stars.

10

What sets white dwarfs aside from the rest of the stellar universe? It seems they are a form of degenerate stars, an instance of stars that are dying out. How do we know that? First, they are so much dimmer than more mature bright stars. Second, they are also much tinier in cosmic terms. Some are even smaller than planets. Like Sirius B, for instance, it's barely as large as our planet Earth.

What makes these white dwarfs different is their mass. Sirius B, for example, packs half the density of the Sun into its little frame. That makes white dwarfs the heaviest forms of matter in the universe apart from black holes and neutron stars.

So what does that mean for this celestial body? How was it possible it acquired so much mass in spite of its reduced volume? White dwarfs are the last phase in the existence of a star. When a star has spent all of its hydrogen to fuse into helium, it goes through a red giant phase. That means it gets to shed its outer layer to create a planetary nebula. This spelling of its surface takes up lots of energy. The star has no more hydrogen left to sustain nuclear fusion. Since it's no longer emitting energy, it shows up like a _____ on the night sky — and that's our white dwarf.

Now, what happens to white dwarfs is that they start to cool down — seeing as there's no energy to sustain them. This gradual shift in temperature causes the core mass to shrink within itself — so that's why white dwarfs have such abnormally high densities. What usually happens is that density pressure causes gravitational collapse — or, in other words — a giant explosion of the supernova type. But most white dwarfs don't meet such violent ends. Actually, most of them gradually fade and burn off until they disappear completely. In this last stage, they are actually called black dwarfs because they emit so little radiation that they can't even be detected by current astronomic devices.

1 Which of the following is NOT characteristics of white dwarfs?

① Their mysterious radiation from space
② Their lack of interior energy
③ Their high densities in their little frames
④ Their dissipation of the outer layer

2 Why does the author mention Sirius B in the passage?

① To introduce the topic of the passage on white dwarfs
② To give a visual example of what the author is explaining
③ To explain the relation between stars and their companions
④ To compare and contrast two stages in the formation of stars

3　According to the author, what is one important result of the red giant phase?

① the creation of a new planet

② the onset of a supernova explosion

③ the cessation of dwarf stars

④ the beginning of star degeneration

4　Which of the following best fits in the blank?

① gale　　　　　　　　② glint

③ blur　　　　　　　　④ beacon

10

환경·기상

10 환경·기상

01

Many stratigraphers have come to believe that human beings have so altered the planet in just the past century or two that we've ushered in a new epoch: the Anthropocene. If we have indeed entered a new epoch, then when exactly did it begin? When did human impacts rise to the level of geologic significance?

William Ruddiman, a paleoclimatologist at the University of Virginia, has proposed that the invention of agriculture some 8,000 years ago, and the deforestation that resulted, led to an increase in atmospheric CO_2 just large enough to Ⓐ_____ what otherwise would have been the start of a new ice age; in his view, humans have been the dominant force on the planet practically since the start of the Holocene. Some scientists have suggested that the Anthropocene began in the late 18th century, when, ice cores show, carbon dioxide levels began what has since proved to be an uninterrupted rise. Others put the beginning of the new epoch in the middle of the 20th century, when the rates of both population growth and consumption accelerated rapidly. Still others argue that we've not yet reached the start of the Anthropocene — not because we haven't had a dramatic impact on the planet, but because the next several decades are likely to prove even more stratigraphically significant than the past few centuries.

1 **Choose the one that best fills in the blank Ⓐ.**

① trigger off   ② stave off

③ wrap up   ④ heave up

2 **Which of the following CANNOT be inferred about "the Anthropocene"?**

① It is a new name for a new geologic epoch: age of man.

② It is an epoch defined by our own massive impact on the planet.

③ It started after the Holocene ended and continues to this day.

④ It is related with human activities raising carbon dioxide levels.

3 **According to the passage, where would future geologists look for the evidence of the Anthropocene?**

① the historical landmarks   ② the rain forests

③ the lower atmosphere   ④ the earth's layers

234 김영편입 영어 독해 워크북 2단계

02

The animal habitats where gorilla doctors work are surrounded by some of the highest rural human-population densities on the planet. And people, as it turns out, make terrible neighbors. Mountain gorillas have always faced habitat destruction and poaching at the hands of the humans in their midst. They die because of civil unrest and military conflict; they get caught in snares hunters set for antelope; and they risk catching human respiratory diseases. As a result of all that, the mountain-gorilla population has languished between 300 and 400 for most of the last 30 years.

When a species is so critically endangered, the survival of every individual matters. Such a serious situation calls for 'extreme conservation'. Conventional wildlife conservation efforts try to limit the negative human effects on an individual species or specific ecosystem — by protecting wildlife habitat against industrial pollution, say, or by enforcing rules against hunting. The extreme version takes Ⓐ_____ by increasing our positive influence. For gorilla doctors, that means protecting the species by saving them one at a time. Forty-two groups of habituated gorillas — those families that have grown accustomed to humans — are continually monitored during daylight hours by trackers who follow them through the forest. They also receive monthly health checks by local field veterinarians who examine stool samples and watch for visible signs of injury or disease, such as weight loss, weakness, laboured breathing or a discolored coat. When a gorilla shows any of these symptoms, the team discusses whether or not to step in.

1 **Which expression best fits Ⓐ?**

① account of environment

② a laissez-faire attitude

③ after a first-aid treatment

④ some precautionary steps

⑤ a more hands-on approach

2 **What is the most appropriate title of the passage above?**

① The Great Apes on the Brink of Extinction

② Conservation Efforts for Endangered Species

③ Vets Saving Mountain Gorillas from Extinction

④ Rapport Between Humans and Wildlife Groups

⑤ Research by Doctors on Habituated Gorillas

03

Carbon dioxide emissions are colorless, odorless, and in an immediate sense, harmless. But their warming effects could easily push global temperatures to levels that have not been seen for millions of years. Some plants and animals are already shifting their ranges toward the Poles, and those shifts will leave traces in the fossil record. Some species will not survive the warming at all. Meanwhile rising temperatures could eventually raise sea levels 20 feet or more.

Long after our cars, cities, and factories have turned to dust, the consequences of burning billions of tons' worth of coal and oil are likely to be clearly discernible. As carbon dioxide warms the planet, it also seeps into the oceans and acidifies them. Sometime this century they may become acidified to the point that corals can no longer construct reefs, which would register in the geologic record as a "reef gap." Reef gaps have marked each of the past five major mass extinctions. The most recent one, which is believed to have been caused by the impact of an asteroid, took place 65 million years ago, at the end of the Cretaceous period; it eliminated not just the dinosaurs, but also the plesiosaurs, pterosaurs, and ammonites. The scale of what's happening now to the oceans is, by many accounts, unmatched since then. To future geologists, our impact may look as _____ as that of an asteroid.

1 **Choose the one that best fills in the blank.**

① widespread and shallow

② gradual and recoverable

③ sudden and profound

④ transient and superficial

2 **Which of the following CANNOT be inferred about "carbon dioxide"?**

① It is extremely difficult to perceive with our senses.

② It warms the earth, which can reduce biodiversity.

③ It chemically reacts with sea water, making it more acid.

④ It obstructs the formation of coral reefs by scattering corals.

3 **Which of the following is true about "reef gaps"?**

① They caused, and were caused by, the acidification of ocean water.

② They coincided with when ocean carbon dioxide concentrations dropped.

③ There have been five reef gaps so far and another is expected to be added.

④ They refer to the sudden deaths of coral reefs causing mass extinctions.

04

Disturbingly, scientists have observed something similar happening in the ocean. Much of the carbon dioxide humans release into the atmosphere is eventually absorbed by the sea, gradually making the water more and more acidic. This process of ocean acidification can wreak havoc on marine invertebrates, dissolving their shells and then their fragile bodies. But just like in the tropical forest, "there are always the winners as well as the losers of climate change," says Ivan Nagelkerken, a marine ecologist at the University of Adelaide in Australia. To get an idea of which species might thrive under ocean acidification, he headed to two places where underwater vents already spew carbon dioxide into the sea: Vulcano Island in Italy and White Island in New Zealand. "These CO_2 vents are natural laboratories where you can get a peek into the future," Nagelkerken explains. As in Winter's experiment, that future was far from lifeless. But the kind of life it supports has Nagelkerken worried. Carbon dioxide vents can occur in any marine ecosystem, from coral reefs to kelp forests to seagrass plains. But no matter where you are, life in the most acidic pockets looks strikingly similar. Immediately around a vent, all ecosystems "transform into systems that are dominated by turf algae — very short, fleshy algae with very little structural complexity," Naglekerken explains. What's more, "we did not observe a single predator on those vents."

As a result, the food web is dramatically simplified, the number of fish species drops, and the ecosystem becomes "much less valuable and productive." Small grazing fish that love turf algae will probably excel in the acidic oceans of the future. But as they take over, "everywhere will start to look like everywhere else," Nagelkerken says. The new, homogenous ocean won't be good for humans. The fish that are likely to thrive in the oceans of the future — small, adaptable species such as gobies and blennies — are, simply, not fish people like to eat. And even if human tastes evolved, those fish wouldn't fill us up; most gobies clock in at fewer than 4 inches long. Humans like to eat big predators, like tuna and marlin — exactly the kind of species that had disappeared from the CO_2 vents Nagelkerken studied. As ocean acidification _____ marine ecosystems, the first to go will be the fish that people rely on for money and food.

1 위 글에서 빈칸에 들어가기에 가장 적합한 것을 고르시오.

① enriches ② restructures

③ diversifies ④ fosters

2 위 글의 내용과 일치하지 않는 것을 고르시오.

① The emission of carbon dioxide is related with ocean acidification.

② Ocean acidification does not mean the complete extinction of sea creatures.

③ Ocean acidification will have an adverse effect on the diversity of marine ecosystems.

④ Humans will adapt to homogenous ocean caused by ocean acidification with ease.

05

Wildfires aren't the only extreme weather-related events seen in recent weeks. Heavy rains have Ⓐ_____ parts of the U.S. East Coast, and heat waves around the world have set multiple temperature records. A group of leading climate scientists warned that the Earth is at risk of being driven into "hothouse" state from which it cannot recover. "Our study suggests that human-induced global warming of 2°C may trigger other Earth system processes, often called 'feedbacks', that can drive further warming — even if we stop emitting greenhouse gases," Will Steffen said in a news release. Once that Ⓑ_____ is crossed, the "Hothouse Earth" would reach temperatures never seen in human history.

The impact on human societies "would likely be massive, sometimes abrupt, and undoubtedly disruptive," the author writes. Mann, the Penn State climate scientist, said "we're walking out onto a minefield." "As we continue to move forward onto that minefield, as we continue to burn fossil fuels, we're likely to encounter more and more extreme and damaging and irreversible impacts on our climate," he said. Ⓒ_____. "The only sensible thing to do is to stop walking forward on to that minefield," he said. "And we can do it. We can move away from the burning of fossil fuels. The Paris agreement has set a course for us that, if we follow, and if we improve on that agreement in the years ahead, we can prevent the worst impacts of climate change from occurring."

1 **Which pair best fits Ⓐ and Ⓑ?**

① sustained — line

② supplanted — border

③ trespassed — section

④ drizzled — path

⑤ inundated — threshold

2 **Which expression best fits in the blank Ⓒ?**

① But he said it's not too late for changes to be made

② Climate change is affecting conditions in both our summers and winters in ways that contribute to wildfires

③ If we put carbon pollution into the atmosphere, we are going to continue to warm the surface of the Earth

④ It's actually worse than that

⑤ We're going to get worse and worse droughts and heat waves and superstorms and floods and wildfires

3 Which of the following CANNOT be inferred?

① If we move away from the burning of fossil fuels, we can prevent climatic changes from continuing to worsen.

② It's up to us whether to do something about climate change.

③ Climate change is kind of turning up the dial on everything.

④ Devastating wildfires are regarded as results of climate change.

⑤ We have reached a period of "new normal" and a state of little fluctuation.

The Galapagos are a stretch of 13 major islands that live as much in myth as on the map — a finch-crowded Brigadoon where Darwin arrived in 1835 and began to make observations that eventually would show him, and us, how life on Earth evolves. His *On the Origin of Species* would inform "almost every component in modern man's belief system," wrote evolutionary biologist Ernst Mayr.

As isolated as they may seem, the Galapagos aren't immune to the impacts of modern life: Climate change is coming to the cradle of evolutionary theory. Iconic species such as tortoises, finches, boobies, and marine iguanas could suffer. The famed ecosystems that taught the world about natural selection may teach us a lesson yet again, offering us insights into what's in store elsewhere. The Galapagos are a fabulous laboratory for studying species' responses to climate change.

Before they were the Galapagos, they were Las Encantadas — "the enchanted ones" — warty islands laced with foam, flowing lava, and odd animals. "Man and wolf alike disown them," wrote Herman Melville. "The chief sound of life here is a hiss."

Whalers tossed those hissing tortoises into their ships' holds for food, filled water casks, and sailed on. Ⓐ<u>They were right about the strangeness</u>: Cut off from mainland South America by about 600 miles of water, nature here ran wild. Among the animals that made the voyage to the islands from the mainland, few survived. Those that did evolved into different forms by adapting to the conditions on each island. Those that could not adapt vanished into extinction.

But there are other changes happening here now — not just the evolutionary kind. Few places on Earth give scientists front-row seats to watch ecosystems shocked so drastically, sometimes repeatedly, in such a short time.

1 **Which of the following is the best topic for the passage?**

① The Galapagos as the cradle of Darwin's *On the Origin of Species*

② The Galapagos as a lab for studying climate change's effects on ecosystems

③ The Galapagos as home to globally rare and endangered species of animals

④ The Galapagos as a Brigadoon inaccessible and treacherous to outlanders

2 **Which of the following best explains Ⓐ?**

① Whalers were wise enough not to land on the Galapagos, feeling strange.

② It was nothing other than hissing tortoises that made the Galapagos strange.

③ The Galapagos were so strange that they immediately aroused whalers' curiosity.

④ It was strange that whalers should have caught tortoises before sailing on.

3 Which of the following is NOT mentioned about the Galapagos?

① froth, streaming magma, and odd creatures
② being where Darwin started his study of evolution
③ the possibility of being damaged by climate change
④ pristine landscapes and seascapes long kept intact

07

A change in our essential character is not possible without a realistic hope that we can make change happen. But hope itself is threatened by the realization that we are now capable of destroying ourselves and the earth's environment. _____, the stress of coping with the complicated artificial patterns of our lives and the flood of manufactured information creates a pervasive feeling of exhaustion just when we have an urgent need for creativity. Our economy is described as post-industrial; our architecture is called post-modern; our geopolitics are labeled post-Cold War. We know what we are not, but we don't seem to know what we are. The forces that shape and reshape our lives seem to have an immutable logic of their own; they seem so powerful that any effort to define ourselves creatively will probably be wasted, its results quickly erased by successive tidal waves of change. Inevitably, we resign ourselves to whatever fate these powerful forces are propelling us toward, a fate we have little role in choosing.

Perhaps because it is unprecedented, the environmental crisis seems completely beyond our understanding and outside of what we call common sense. We consign it to some seldom visited attic in our minds where we place ideas that we vaguely understand but rarely explore. We tag it with the same mental labels we might use for Antarctica: remote, alien, hopelessly distorted by the maps of the world we inhabit, too hard to get to and too unforgiving to stay very long. When we do visit this attic, when we learn about how intricately the causes of the crisis are woven into the fabric of industrial civilization, our hope of solving it seems chimerical. It seems so forbidding that we resist taking even the first steps toward positive change.

1 **Choose the one that best fills in the blank.**

① Moreover ② Therefore

③ However ④ For instance

2 **Choose the closest in meaning to the underlined "tag it with the same mental labels we might use for Antarctica."**

① take the environmental crisis as seriously as the exploration of Antarctica

② classify Antarctica as where we feel the environmental crisis most prominently

③ regard the environmental crisis as not real or urgent, and even insurmountable

④ fight against our mental negligence when focusing on the environmental crisis

3 Which of the following CANNOT be inferred from the passage?

① Our modern life style and conditions undermine the creativity needed for meeting the environmental crisis.

② Our essential character of the moment is far from desirable for enhancing the earth's environmental status.

③ We have not been and will not be a creative master of the stream of change in the history of civilization.

④ The environmental crisis is the first mentally challenging issue that human beings have ever experienced.

4 What is the tone of the passage?

① indifferent   ② pessimistic

③ inspirational   ④ argumentative

The Montreal Protocol on Substances that Deplete the Ozone Layer, also known simply as the Montreal Protocol, is an international treaty designed to protect the ozone layer by Ⓐphasing out the production of numerous substances that are responsible for ozone depletion. Open for signature on 16 September 1987, it was made pursuant to the 1985 Vienna Convention for the Protection of the Ozone Layer, which established the framework for international cooperation in addressing ozone depletion. The Montreal Protocol entered into force on 1 January 1989, and has since undergone nine revisions.

As a result of the international agreement, the ozone hole in Antarctica is slowly recovering. Climate projections indicate that the ozone layer will return to 1980 levels between 2050 and 2070. The Montreal Protocol's success is Ⓑattributed to its effective burden sharing and solution proposals, which helped Ⓒmitigate regional conflicts of interest, compared to the shortcomings of the global regulatory approach of the Kyoto Protocol. However, global regulation was already being installed before a scientific consensus was established, and overall public opinion was convinced of possible imminent risks with the ozone layer.

The Vienna Convention and the Montreal Protocol have each been ratified by 196 nations and the European Union, making them the first universally ratified treaties in United Nations history. Due to its widespread adoption and implementation, the Montreal Protocol has been Ⓓupbraided as an example of exceptional international cooperation, with the UN Secretary-General describing it as "perhaps the single most successful international agreement to date".

1 Which of the following is not appropriate in the flow of the passage?

① Ⓐ
② Ⓑ
③ Ⓒ
④ Ⓓ

2 According to the passage, which of the following is not true?

① Based on the Vienna Convention, the Montreal Protocol is unanimously approved in the UN history.
② When the Montreal Protocol was made, it didn't come into effect immediately among UN member countries.
③ According to the Montreal Protocol, the production of substances that deplete the ozone layer should be stopped by stages.
④ When the Montreal Protocol was approved, previous international agreements on greenhouse gases were nullified.

3 According to the passage, which of the following can be inferred?

① Public opinion was polarized around the world on signing the Montreal Protocol, with backlash springing up everywhere.

② The Kyoto Protocol, designed to protect the ozone layer, was conducive to the ratification of the Montreal Protocol.

③ Thanks to the Montreal Protocol, we can expect a tangible result about the ozone hole.

④ Once the international protocol or convention becomes valid, it can neither be amended nor complemented.

09

As global temperatures increase, the warming is not uniform throughout the earth. Different parts absorb more or less heat from the sun depending on the angle at which the rays of the sun strike the surface. But another important factor also determines the amount of heat absorbed by different parts of the earth: the extent to which the surface reflects the sun's rays back into space. Ice and snow glare back at the sun almost like mirrors, reflecting more than 95 percent of the heat and light that strike them. By contrast, the partly transparent blue-green water of the ocean absorbs more than 85 percent of the heat and light it receives from the sun.

This critical difference between reflective and absorptive surfaces has the most impact on the climate at the two poles. The freezing point is a threshold of change marking the boundary between two different states of equilibrium for H2O: water above and ice below. At the edge of the polar region, at the boundary of the ice-covered surface, there is another threshold of change. Wherever the temperature pushes above the freezing point and the edge of the ice begins to melt, that tiny change transforms the relationship between that part of the earth's surface and sunlight, which the earth now absorbs instead of reflects back into space. As it absorbs more heat, the retreating edge of the ice is pressed by the accumulating warmth to melt at a faster rate. Though clouds _____, the process tends to feed upon itself, leading to a faster increase in temperatures at the poles than at the equator, where the sunlight-absorbing quality of the surface is mostly unaffected by increasing temperatures.

1 **Choose the one that best fills in the blank.**

① may be rare in the sky

② give way to sunshine

③ can mitigate the effect

④ trap the radiated heat

2 **According to the passage, which of the following does NOT affect the temperature in a given region?**

① how glancingly the sun's rays strike the surface

② how much heat the surface absorbs from the sunlight

③ how much of the sunlight received the surface reflects

④ how vulnerable the surface is to the sun's rays

3 Which of the following CANNOT be inferred from the passage?

① It is colder at the poles than at the tropics because the sun's rays spread more thinly over a larger area.

② The region near the lake is hotter than elsewhere because water absorbs more sunlight than it reflects.

③ It is after the freezing point has been reached that the melting of the ice begins to be accelerated at the poles.

④ The amount of heat transferred from the equator to the poles decreases as global warming proceeds.

4 What is the best title for the passage?

① Global Warming More Pronounced at the Poles

② Light Absorption and Reflection for the Melting of Ice

③ Two Thresholds of Change from Global Warming

④ The Slowly Retreating Edge of the Ice at the Poles

10

A Last September, Jeanne Haegele, a 28-year-old Chicago resident resolved to cut plastics out of her life. She was concerned about what the chemicals leaching out of some common types of plastic might be doing to her body. She was also worried about the damage all the plastic refuse was doing to the environment. So she hopped on her bike and rode to the nearest grocery store to see what she could find that didn't include plastic. "I went in and barely bought anything," Haegele says. She did purchase some canned food and a carton of milk — only to discover later that both containers were lined with plastic resin. "Plastic," she says, "just seemed like it was in everything."

B She's right. The U.S. produced 28 million tons of plastic waste in 2005 — 27 million tons of which ended up in landfills. Our food and water come wrapped in plastic. It's used in our phones and our computers, the cars we drive and the planes we ride in. But the infinitely adaptable substance has its <u>dark side</u>. Environmentalists fret about the petroleum needed to make it. Parents worry about the possibility of toxic chemicals making their way from household plastic into children's bloodstreams. Which means Haegele isn't the only person trying to cut plastic out of her life — she isn't even the only one blogging about this kind of endeavor. But those who've tried know it's far from easy to go plastic-free. "These things are so _____ that it is practically impossible to avoid coming into contact with them," says Frederick vom Saal, a biologist at the University of Missouri.

C We think of plastic as essentially inert; after all, it takes hundreds of years for a plastic bottle to degrade in a landfill. But as plastic ages or is exposed to heat or stress, it can release trace amounts of some of its ingredients. Of particular concern these days are bisphenol-A (BPA), used to strengthen some plastics, and phthalates, used to soften others. Each ingredient is a part of hundreds of household items; BPA is in everything from baby bottles to can linings to protect against E. coli and botulism, while phthalates are found in children's toys as well as vinyl shower curtains. And those chemicals can get inside us through the food, water and bits of dust we consume or even by being absorbed through our skin. Indeed, the Centers for Disease Control and Prevention reported that 92% of Americans age 6 or older test positive for BPA — a sign of just how common the chemical is in our plastic universe.

1 According to paragraph Ⓑ, which of the following best summarizes the underlined dark side of plastic?

① Our dependence on plastics is unlikely to be easily solved, although the environment is polluted when producing plastics and human health can deteriorate when plastics are consumed.

② A huge amount of plastic waste cannot be recycled and is just being landfilled.

③ Plastics are all around our lives, but alternative materials have not yet been developed to replace them.

④ Despite the usefulness of packaging our food and drinking water in plastic, plastics generate excessive waste.

⑤ The harmful chemicals of plastics are absorbed into the bodies of children, harming the health of children.

2 Which word best fits the blank in paragraph Ⓑ?

① plastic   ② ubiquitous

③ flexible   ④ futile

⑤ adaptable

3 According to paragraph Ⓒ, BPA and phthalates are mentioned because _____.

① they are the most representative constituents of plastic

② they are the main constituents of plastics, the safety and plasticity of which has increased

③ the writer wants to remind the readers how many plastic products are used in our lives

④ they are all around our lives and their ingredients can easily be absorbed into our bodies and can cause health problems

⑤ the writer wants to tell the readers that plastics are inherently inert but some are easily leached

4 According to the above passage, which of the following is true?

① Canned food and a carton of milk do not contain plastic.

② Most of the plastic waste made in the United States in 2005 was landfilled.

③ Phthalates are used to strengthen plastics, and BPA is used to soften some plastics.

④ When the plastic is old, or exposed to heat or pressure, a large amount of its component is released.

⑤ Ninety-two percent of Americans aged 6 or older have a positive attitude toward plastic products.

22만 6천 편입합격생의 선택

**김영편입 영어
독해**

워크북 **2**단계

11

의학·건강

11

의학·건강

01

At the age of 7, Peter experienced his first auditory hallucination: a comforting voice that told him everything would be all right. By the time he was 10, he recalls, it had turned into 20 demonic voices; they compelled him to steal, convinced him he was Jesus, and persuaded him to attempt suicide. Years of psychiatric treatment offered no relief, so he joined the Hearing Voice Network(HVN), a support group for people similarly afflicted. This group brings voice hearers together to exchange personal stories and coping strategies. Drawing on research indicating that up to one in 25 people hears voices, it seeks to recast the phenomenon as a Ⓐ_____ experience, encouraging members to maintain a dialogue with their voices so they can live peacefully with and even appreciate their presence. This HVN prescription flies in the face of traditional psychiatry, which prefers that patients take antipsychotic medication and ignore their voices, and warns that acknowledging them intensifies hallucinations. But HVN argues that accepting voices is the one precondition to start the process of recovery, and that the mind uses this internal chatter to alert people to unresolved traumas, causes of hallucinations, including the death of a loved one or outright abuse.

1 Choose the one that best fills in the blank Ⓐ.

① psychotic ② normal
③ mystic ④ special

2 Which of the following can be inferred about "auditory hallucination" according to the passage?

① Auditory hallucination can disappear over time without any particular treatment.
② Vulnerable to shock, the elderly are apt to suffer from auditory hallucination.
③ HVN recommends its members to use the ignoring strategy for treating auditory hallucination.
④ Psychiatrists generally accept auditory hallucination as a symptom of a mental disease.

02

To make progress, we need to be able to imagine alternative realities — better ones — and we need to believe that we can achieve them. Such faith helps motivate us to pursue our goals. Optimists in general work longer hours and tend to earn more. Economists at Duke University found that optimists even save more. And although they are not less likely to divorce, they are more likely to remarry — an act that is, as Samuel Johnson wrote, the triumph of Ⓐ_____.

Even if that better future is often an illusion, optimism has clear benefits in the present. Hope keeps our minds at ease, lowers stress and improves physical health. Researchers studying heart disease patients found that optimists were more likely than nonoptimistic patients to take vitamins, eat low-fat diets and exercise, thereby reducing their overall coronary risk. A study of cancer patients revealed that pessimistic patients under the age of 60 were more likely to die within eight months than nonpessimistic patients of the same initial health, status and age.

1 **Choose the one that best fills in the blank Ⓐ.**

① hope over experience

② wisdom over knowledge

③ pride over prejudice

④ pathos over ethos

2 **According to the passage, which aspect is associated with "optimists"?**

① workaholic   ② daydreaming

③ relaxed   ④ pro-life

3 **Which of the following CANNOT be inferred about "optimism"?**

① It can be conducive to the progress of human history.

② It makes people less prepared for their future financial needs.

③ It is a common feature of successful and healthy businessmen.

④ It can be a means of enhancing the survival rates of cancer patients.

03

Thumb-sucking and nail-biting can cause health problems for kids and potential financial problems for parents paying for Ⓐ_____. Thumb-sucking can interfere with the alignment of children's teeth and nail-biting can increase the risk of spreading harmful germs from their fingers to their mouths.

Those two childhood habits, however, come with a surprising Ⓑ<u>upside</u>, according to a study published in the journal Pediatrics. Children who suck their thumbs or bite their nails may have a lower risk of developing allergies, said Bob Hancox, a co-author of the study and an associate professor at the University of Otago's Dunedin School of Medicine in New Zealand.

"The study was done to test the hygiene hypothesis: the idea that Ⓒ_____ exposure to microbial organisms, in other words increased hygiene, is responsible for the rise in allergic diseases seen over recent decades," Hancox said. The hypothesis also has been described as including the use of antibiotics. "We didn't know what to expect," he said. "We had hypothesized that we would find a reduced risk of allergies in children with these habits, but really had no idea whether this would turn out to be true."

1 According to the passage, which of the following is most appropriate for the blank Ⓐ and Ⓒ?

① dentures — augmented

② crutches — bolstered

③ braces — diminished

④ compresses — prolonged

2 According to the passage, what is the topic?

① Thumb-sucking and nail-biting are encouraged.

② Why does the hygiene hypothesis matter now?

③ Bad habits formed in the childhood die hard.

④ Can thumb-sucking and nail-biting do good?

3 According to the passage, what does the underlined Ⓑ refer to?

① Parents whose children suck their thumbs may be burdened by the medical care costs.

② Children who suck thumbs or bite nails are less likely to be subject to allergic diseases.

③ The study to test the hygiene hypothesis has found a loophole in an unexpected part.

④ It turns out that increased hygiene conditions account for the rise in allergic diseases.

04

As a general anesthetic, propofol acts on the brain's GABA receptors, which cause inhibitory neurons — those that quiet other circuits — to fire; that's how it induces unconsciousness. Propofol also increases levels of the feel-good neurotransmitter dopamine, triggering a sense of reward not unlike sex or cocaine. Some patients experience euphoria, sexual disinhibition, and even hallucinations, followed by a feeling of calm. Since propofol is so widely used — it revolutionized ambulatory anesthesia, allowing a physician to knock someone out in seconds to perform, say, a colonoscopy, and have them up and about after only 10 minutes — scientists have had no shortage of subjects able to describe the experience. About one third don't remember a thing, and another third say they dreamed, but don't recall specifics. The rest experience vivid, strange dreams, sometimes of a sexual nature.

Soon after the drug was introduced in 1989, reports of abuse surfaced — all among medical professionals. Since propofol is not a controlled substance like morphine, hospitals tend not to keep it locked up, making it fairly easy for someone to swipe. Last year, alarmed by the growing abuse, the American Society of Anesthesiologists formally endorsed a proposal by the Drug Enforcement Administration to classify it as a controlled substance. No action has been taken.

1 According to the passage, which of the following is NOT one of the side effects of propofol?

① upbeat mood ② high libido
③ restorative sleep ④ feeling of oblivion

2 Which of the following CANNOT be inferred from the passage?

① Propofol has a significant potential for abuse.
② Anesthesiologists recognize profopol as the safest opiate drug.
③ Hospitals can't possibly avoid being criticized for neglecting management of propofol.
④ The Drug Enforcement Administration recognizes propofol as a controlled substance.

3 According to the passage, why is propofol widely used?

① It has a rapid onset and termination of action.
② It can be commonly prescribed at a local clinic.
③ It is delivered by injection without surgical instruments.
④ It is less effective in the relief of severe pain.

05

The idea that dietary fat causes heart disease is deeply, deeply ingrained. We all know the Atkins diet kills people — that's what we've been told, anyway. But over the past decade, dozens of studies have finally looked at the Atkins diet, and they show that heart disease risk factors improve more on this kind of low-carbohydrate diet than on the low-fat, low calorie diet that doctors and the American Heart Association want you to eat. Your HDL(good cholesterol) goes up, which is the most meaningful number in terms of heart health. Small, dense LDL(bad cholesterol) — which is particularly dangerous — becomes large, fluffy LDL. And not only does your cholesterol profile get better, your insulin goes down, and your insulin resistance goes away, and your blood pressure goes down. The low-fat diet that people have been eating in hopes of protecting their heart is actually bad for their heart, because it's high in carbohydrates. The public health effort to get everyone to eat that way is one of the fundamental reasons that we now have obesity and diabetes epidemics.

1 According to the passage, which of the following is NOT true about the Atkins diet?

① It goes against a conventional wisdom about diet and heart health.

② It is a diet containing a high level of fat and a low level of carbohydrate.

③ It improves cholesterol profile and lowers insulin and blood pressure.

④ It is recommended by public health workers to ward off obesity and diabetes.

2 What is the purpose of the passage?

① To give information of a myth-breaking diet good for heart health

② To call attention to the long forgotten effects of a traditional diet

③ To publicize the American Heart Association and its medical activities

④ To urge those who suffer from obesity and diabetes to go on a diet

3 What is the best title for the passage?

① Your Heart Needs More Vegetable

② High Fat Is Better for Your Heart

③ Unhealthy Heart Brings Diseases

④ Dietary Fat Causes Heart Disease

06

Inflammation occurs when you're injured or exposed to disease-causing germs. In response, your body's immune system releases proteins called cytokines to fight off harmful microbes and repair damage. But now some experts believe that chronic exposure to cytokines — from inflammation caused by stress, diet and environmental toxins — may lower the feel-good hormone serotonin and contribute to depression.

Scientists first made the connection in the 1980s when they injected animals with bacteria to trigger inflammation. The animals exhibited symptoms of depression: lethargy, loss of appetite and avoiding social contact. Subsequent studies have found that depressed people have higher levels of inflammatory chemicals such as C-reactive protein in their blood. Intrigued, a team of researchers gave infliximab — an anti-inflammatory drug that treats auto-immune diseases — to people with major depression and found that subjects with high levels of C-reactive protein reported _____ than those without inflammation.

While inflammation isn't likely the primary cause of depression, experts increasingly agree that it can prolong or worsen it. Treating depression in patients who have high levels of inflammation with anti-inflammatory drugs may have a big impact on their mood.

1 **Choose the one that best fills in the blank.**

① greater improvement in depression symptoms

② smaller improvement in depression symptoms

③ greater improvement in inflammatory symptoms

④ smaller improvement in inflammatory symptoms

2 **Which of the following is true about "inflammation"?**

① It impedes the release of cytokines and facilitates that of serotonin.

② Its relation to bacteria was first shown by animal experiments in the 1980s.

③ Its level is in direct proportion to that of C-reactive protein in the blood.

④ It is a process in which germs attack impaired body parts and cause disease.

3 **What is the main idea of the passage?**

① Depression is caused by low levels of the feel-good hormone serotonin.

② Inflammation resulting from the ways of modern life may trigger depression.

③ A scientific team has developed a cure for depression called infliximab.

④ Treating depression with anti-inflammatory drugs may be just a makeshift.

07

Can a cup of coffee motivate you to relish your trips to the gym this winter? That question is at the heart of a notable study of caffeine and exercise, one of several new experiments suggesting that, whatever your sport, caffeine may allow you to perform better and enjoy yourself more.

Scientists and many athletes have known for years, of course, that a cup of coffee before a workout jolts athletic performance, especially in endurance sports like distance running and cycling. Caffeine has been proven to increase the number of fatty acids circulating in the bloodstream, which enables people to run or pedal longer (since their muscles can absorb and burn that fat for fuel and save the body's limited stores of carbohydrates until later in the workout). As a result, caffeine, which is legal under International Olympic Committee (IOC) rules, is the most popular drug in sports. More than two-thirds of about 20,680 Olympic athletes studied for a recent report had caffeine in their urine, with use highest among triathletes, cyclists and rowers. But whether and how caffeine affects other, less-aerobic activities, like weight training or playing a stop-and-go team sport like soccer or basketball, has been less clear.

1 **What is the main topic of the passage?**

① Can the IOC rules about coffee be amended?

② Should athletes drink coffee before workout?

③ Is drinking coffee controversial for athletes?

④ Can coffee contribute to athletic performance?

2 **Which of the following can be inferred according to the passage?**

① Fatty acid has nothing to do with athlete's physical performance.

② Caffeine is performance-enhancing drug for athletes, which is recommended by the IOC.

③ Many players may have resorted to coffee to perform better in the marathon.

④ Caffeine, considered legitimate by the IOC, is only contained in coffee.

3 **According to the passage, how do people create energy?**

① by taking regular exercise

② by burning off fat

③ by burning caffeine

④ by taking a trip

08

Since 1997, when the U.S. Food and Drug Administration first allowed big pharmaceutical firms to advertise prescription drugs on television, viewers have been bombarded by commercials touting everything from anti-inflammatories and cholesterol-lowering drugs to anti-histamines. Most hurriedly list side effects and urge viewers to ask their physicians for further information. Permitting such advertising no doubt encouraged the creation of the twenty-four-hour cable-TV Discovery Health Channel. This _____ of health-related information, misinformation and knowledge hurled at the individual varies in objectivity and credibility. But it directs more and more public attention to health issues — and changes the traditional relationship between doctors and patients, encouraging a more take-charge attitude on the part of the latter.

Ironically, while patients have more access to health information of uneven quality, their doctors, driven by pressures to speed up, have less and less time to peruse the latest medical journals, whether online or off, and to communicate adequately with relevant specialists — and with patients. Patients come with printouts of Internet material, photocopies of pages from the Physicians' Desk Reference or clips from medical journals and health magazines. They ask questions and no longer <u>tug their forelocks in awe of the doctor's white lab coat</u>.

1 **Choose the one that best fills in the blank.**
① fallout
② avalanche
③ dearth
④ aggregate

2 **Choose the one closest in meaning to the underlined "<u>tug their forelocks in awe of the doctor's white lab coat</u>."**
① respect the doctor's high level of education
② are satisfied with what the doctor explains
③ pay attention to what clothes the doctor wears
④ are overwhelmed by the doctor's authority

3 **Which of the following can be inferred about today's patients?**
① They are harmed by the abundance of advertising for prescription drugs.
② Most of them have trust in the effects of the drugs advertised on TV.
③ They are very attentive to, and willing to take care of, their own health.
④ Some of them have more health information and knowledge than doctors.

09

If you pay careful attention to the way Ikarians have lived their lives, it appears that a dozen subtly powerful, mutually enhancing and pervasive factors are at work. The big "aha!" for me is how these factors that encourage longevity reinforce one another over the long term. For people to adopt a healthful lifestyle, I have become convinced, they need to live in an ecosystem, so to speak, that makes it possible. It's easy to get enough rest if no one else wakes up early and the village goes dead during afternoon nap time. It helps that the cheapest, most accessible foods are also the most healthful — and that your ancestors have spent centuries developing ways to make them taste good. It's hard to get through the day in Ikaria without walking up 20 hills. You're not likely to ever feel the existential pain of not belonging or even the simple stress of arriving late. At day's end, you'll share a cup of the seasonal herbal tea with your neighbor. And thus even if you're antisocial, you'll never be entirely alone. Every one of these factors can be tied to longevity. There's no silver bullet to keep death and the diseases of old age at bay. Ⓐ<u>If there's anything close to a secret, it's silver buckshot.</u>

1   Which of the following best rephrases Ⓐ?

① You had better take a multi-pronged approach to longevity.

② You had better have a transcendental viewpoint of death.

③ You had better concentrate on one magic tool for longevity.

④ You had better use up your wealth before you get ill and die.

2   Which of the following is NOT mentioned as a longevity factor?

① enough repose

② routine exercise

③ seasonal herbal tea

④ interpersonal relationship

3   Which of the following does the above article most likely to appear in?

① textbook   ② magazine

③ diary   ④ encyclopedia

10

Are you socially jet-lagged? ⒶA The term, coined by Till Roenneberg, a chronobiologist at Ludwig-Maximilians University in Munich, refers to what happens when your internal body clock wants you to stay asleep but your external social clock wants you to wake up. ⒷB By getting up with our alarms all week and sleeping late on the weekends, Ⓐit's like sending our body clock to the West Coast and dragging it back East Monday morning. ⒸC The result, says Roenneberg, is that "there are people who, caught in a cycle of sleep loss and oversleeping, hardly ever get a normal night's sleep at all." ⒹD

The problem is that this increasingly describes most of us. If majoritarian rules applied to society, and we weren't chasing the global economy, most people would happily nod off between 12 a.m. and 1 a.m. and wake between 8 a.m. and 9 a.m. Instead, "85 percent of us need an alarm clock to wake up," says Roenneberg, with the result that "two thirds of normal people suffer from one hour or more of social jet-lag, 16 percent two hours, and shift workers considerably more."

Shift work is particularly vicious. Orfeo Buxton, a sleep researcher at Harvard University Medical School, recently led the first study in humans where sleep was disrupted for several weeks to simulate the effects of shift work. The result was metabolic chaos: glucose spiked to levels that could, over time, trigger diabetes, while energy expenditure slumped to the point where subjects would have gained up to 13 pounds in a year.

1 Which of the following is NOT stated or implied in the passage?

① Workers who maintain a rotating night-shift schedule are likely to be overweight.

② Disrupted sleep wreaks havoc on the body's metabolic processes.

③ Getting more sleep on weekends in order to fill a need may help you keep slim.

④ Many people are woken by the alarm clock in the middle of their biological night.

2 Which is the best place in the passage for the following sentence?

If you need an alarm clock to wake up, then you probably are.

① Ⓐ   ② Ⓑ

③ Ⓒ   ④ Ⓓ

3 The underlined Ⓐ implies that our internal body clock _____.

① wants us to stay asleep

② resets itself to Eastern Time

③ adjusts to gradual changes between time zones

④ lets us know it's time to wake up

11

Some jobs are so bad that they are actually worse for employees' psychological well-being than not having a job at all, according to a new study in the journal *Occupational and Environmental Medicine*. Researchers analyzed annual data over several years from 7,155 adults, evaluating links between the nature of their jobs and their mental health. They found the mental health of those who were unemployed was Ⓐ_____ those in jobs of the poorest quality.

Poor-quality jobs were defined as those with high demands, low pay and a lack of autonomy and security. Participants were asked, for example, whether a job was "more stressful than I ever imagined," whether it was "complex and difficult," or whether it caused them to "worry about the future." The worse the job, the poorer the worker's mental health.

To make sure the pattern wasn't caused by a Ⓑselection effect, the researchers studied what happened when the unemployed subjects finally landed work. They found those who moved into high-quality jobs showed significant improvements in mental health. But those who took poor-quality jobs showed clinically significant declines in mental well-being, compared to their own previous mind-states and to their jobless counterparts.

1   Which of the following best fits the blank Ⓐ?

① equivalent or inferior to

② in proportion to

③ more or less different from

④ comparable or superior to

2   What does the underlined Ⓑ mean?

① intentional falsification of research data

② distortion of a statistical analysis due to sampling error

③ giving preference to a specific group of individuals

④ a scientific method especially designed for anthropology

3   What is the author's main purpose?

① To warn us not to quit bad jobs if there's no other job offer in hand

② To inform the negative impacts of poor quality jobs on the mind

③ To urge job seekers to take into account the work characteristics

④ To stress the benefit of having jobs with high psychosocial quality

12

Faced with the prospect of chemotherapy, many patients wonder if there is a more "Ⓐ_____" option. The hope is that cannabis, homeopathy or a herbal supplement will eradicate cancer whilst sparing the patient the potentially unpleasant treatment effects of chemo and radiotherapy. There's also always the prospect that something "Ⓐ_____" might be more efficient than something manufactured by a drug company.

Cannabis and derivatives such as cannabis oil are pretty much top of the list when it comes to non-chemotherapy "treatment". This is not surprising as cannabis has been used recreationally and medicinally for centuries. THC in cannabis has known anti-emetic properties, and for decades agents derived from it have been used in the clinical management of pain and nausea.

Beyond this, however, claims that cannabis has any efficacy as a cancer treatment are unsupported by evidence, as a wide-ranging US study recently concluded. Cannabis may not have an impact on cancer, but at least THC has some helpful effects. Homeopathy, however, is a different story. In multiple studies, homeopathy has been shown to have no effect beyond placebo. In fact, its central tenets are completely at odds with known physics and are demonstrably wrong. Yet homeopathy remains popular. While the preparations might be in themselves biologically inert, there is a serious danger that patients will cling to the false hope offered by them and reject medical intervention that could be beneficial, which can have fatal consequences.

1   Which of the following best fits in Ⓐ?

① natural   ② exclusive

③ practical   ④ synthetic

2   What is the best title of the passage?

① Efficacy of Homeopathy in Cancer Treatment

② Guidelines for Prescribing Medical Cannabis

③ Pernicious Myths Surrounding Cancer Treatment

④ How Alternative Medicines Became Popular

3   According to the passage, which of the following is true?

① Cannabis that suppresses the nausea may be helpful in cancers but cause serious side effects.

② Cancer patients are vulnerable to dodgy information that homeopathy can treat cancer.

③ Homeopathy is effective at combating the nausea caused by cancer treatments such as chemo.

④ Homeopathic medicines when taken with chemo and radiotherapy can aggravate illness.

13

At some point in your life you've probably been tickled — repeatedly touched in a way that induced smiling, laughter, and involuntary movements. Ticklishness can occur in many places on the body, but the most common are the ribcage, the armpit, and the sole of the foot. ⒶTickling usually occurs in the context of intimate relationships. Parents tickle their babies and small children; siblings, romantic partners, and close friends sometimes tickle each other. Some people seem to be more ticklish than others. One of the strangest things about tickling is that it's pretty much impossible for a person to tickle himself or herself. ⒷIf someone else can make you laugh and twitch by poking you in the ribcage, shouldn't you be able to do the same thing to yourself?

The reason you can't tickle yourself is that when you move a part of your own body, a part of your brain monitors the movement and anticipates the sensations that it will cause. ⒸThat's why, for example, you don't really notice if your arm rubs against your side when you walk, but you would be startled if somebody else touched you in a similar way. If our brains didn't have the ability to keep track of our own body movements and the sensations they cause, we would constantly feel as though we were being brushed, poked, and prodded, and it would be hard to devote our attention to anything else. Self-tickling is an extreme example of ⓐthis phenomenon. Your brain knows that the fingers poking you in the ribcage are your own fingers, so it dials down the sensory response. ⒹScientists also found that the somatosensory cortex is thicker in migraine sufferers, though it is not known if this is the result of migraine attacks.

1 According to the passage, which of the following is <u>not</u> appropriate in the context?

① Ⓐ   ② Ⓑ

③ Ⓒ   ④ Ⓓ

2 According to the passage, what does the underlined ⓐ refer to?

① In the context of intimate relationships such as parenthood and brotherhood, tickling mainly occurs.

② The somatosensory cortex is likely to be developed among migraine sufferers.

③ In case of the touch of somebody, you notice it, but in case of your own motion, you don't.

④ We have difficulty devoting our attention to anything else.

3 According to the passage, which of the following is true of ticklishness?

① It happens only on certain parts of our human body.

② When it comes to its degree, each person may feel differently.

③ It never occurs among acquaintances in our society.

④ We feel it most on the ribcage, the armpit, and the sole.

14

Sugar is especially challenging, because children respond to it in ways that aren't obviously related to taste, and almost all of them consume too much of it, at least in developed countries. Sweet Ⓐ_____ expressions of pain during childhood. It will reduce crying in a baby, and it's used as an analgesic during circumcisions and heel-stick blood draws. (The effective agent is sweet taste rather than sugar, because aspartame works too.) A child's response to sweetness can be so gratifying to parents that they end up reinforcing it: How many other mood-altering tricks work so quickly and so well?

But there are public health implications, and they go beyond increases in childhood obesity and type 2 diabetes. There is much worry in particular about "baby-bottle caries" — tooth decay caused by sugar-containing beverages, including fruit juice — especially in children who are put to bed with bottles. Some children's permanent teeth come in already decayed. It's a major preventable disease of childhood, and it's reaching epidemic proportions.

Increasing the concentration of sweetness-enhancing volatiles in certain foods may make it possible to reduce their sugar content without making them taste less sweet. But Ⓑthere can be unintended consequences. As soon as we can produce a sweet experience that has no calories, isn't toxic, and has no nasty characteristics, what will that mean for the brain? We know that sweetness uses neural pathways that look very much like the ones used by drugs of addiction, which are believed to hijack circuitry that evolved for food and particularly for sweet. Getting something for nothing looks good, but Mother Nature has a nasty side.

1 Which of the following best fits in Ⓐ?

① sharpens   ② blunts

③ diversifies   ④ measures

2 Which of the following is most relevant to Ⓑ?

① Clouds always follow the sunshine.

② Every cloud has a silver lining.

③ Don't bite off more than you can chew.

④ Never judge a book by its cover.

3 Which of the following is true?

① It is recommendable that parents soothe a crying child by giving sweets.

② Like childhood obesity and type 2 diabetes, baby-bottle caries are hereditary.

③ Too much sugar consumption can cause obesity, diabetes and baby-bottle caries.

④ Natural sweeteners have a bad side, but artificial sweeteners have a good side.

15

Antipsychotic drugs are widely used to blunt aggressive behaviour in people with intellectual disabilities who have no history of mental illness, a UK survey of medical records finds, even though the medicines may not have a calming effect. The finding is worrisome because antipsychotic drugs can cause severe side effects such as obesity or diabetes. Psychiatry researcher Rory Sheehan and colleagues at University College London studied data from 33,016 people with intellectual disabilities from general-care practices in the United Kingdom over a period of up to 15 years. The researchers found that 71% of 9,135 people who were treated with antipsychotics had never been diagnosed with a severe mental illness, and that the drugs were more likely to be prescribed to those who displayed problematic behaviours. "We should be worried because the rates are high," says James Harris, a psychiatrist at Johns Hopkins University in Baltimore, Maryland. But he adds that it is hard to determine whether treatment with antipsychotics is appropriate without knowing what other forms of treatment were available to people in the study.

It is possible that medication was the only option available or that it was used to dampen a person's behaviour enough that they could participate in therapy or other types of treatment. But evidence suggests that the drugs are not effective at treating aggressive and disruptive behaviour, says psychiatrist Peter Tyrer of Imperial College London. In 2014, he and several colleagues gave a placebo to people who had intellectual disabilities but no mental illness, and exhibited aggressive behaviour. Because the placebo reduced aggressive behaviour by 79%, Tyrer notes, it may be that antipsychotics are so prevalent simply because they seem to have an effect and can be administered by untrained caregivers in an emergency. "It's impossible to do a psychological intervention at two in the morning," Tyrer says.

1   위 글을 통해 추론할 수 <u>없는</u> 것으로 가장 적합한 것을 고르시오.

① Some of the intellectually challenged sometimes reveal aggressive tendencies.

② Antipsychotic drugs have some by-effects which are inimical to people's health.

③ The intellectually challenged with no disease of the mind did not respond to the placebo.

④ The impracticability of psychological intervention led to the use of antipsychotic drugs.

2   위 글의 제목으로 가장 적합한 것을 고르시오.

① The Effect of Antipsychotic Drugs

② The Side Effect of Antipsychotic Drugs

③ The Abuse of Antipsychotic Drugs

④ The Danger of Antipsychotic Drugs

16

Hepatitis B is a virus mainly transmitted through blood to blood contact. It can also, in some cases, be transmitted through unprotected penetrative sex. The virus can also be found in vaginal fluids and saliva, although it is not known whether it is present in large enough quantities to transmit. Hepatitis B is a strain of the Hepatitis family, which means it is a virus that affects the liver. It affects people differently, however. Some people may only have the virus and feel ill for a few weeks, and then make a full recovery. For others, the virus may stay with them for life and cause fatal liver damage. Some people may carry the virus but never experience any symptoms or disease. It is more infectious than HIV or even Hepatitis C. This means that a tiny amount of body fluid infected with the virus may be enough to infect someone else. It is also a very Ⓐ_____ virus, which means it can survive outside of the body for long periods of time. It takes about 6 months for Hepatitis B to show up in a blood test, from the moment of exposure to the virus. This is known as Ⓑ_____, and during this time, some people may experience symptoms such as abdominal pain, jaundice, flu-like illness and joint aches and pains. Other people may not experience any symptoms at all. Often it is not necessary to start treatment if you have Hepatitis B. This is because many people get over the illness within six months. Treatment such as Interferon may, however, benefit those who have had the virus longer than six months. A vaccine does exist to protect against Hepatitis B. Three doses of the vaccine are needed for full protection. A blood test to check for Ⓒ_____ to the virus may be advisable a few months after the course of injections is finished, to check immunization is complete. There are some people who may require a repeat course of injections after not responding fully to the first course. The vaccine may be advisable for anyone perceived to be "at risk". This includes healthcare workers, sex workers, injecting drug users and gay men.

1 빈칸 Ⓐ, Ⓑ, Ⓒ에 들어가기에 가장 적합한 것을 고르시오.

① contagious — the grace period — antioxidant

② resilient — the incubation period — antibodies

③ polymerized — the natural duration of life — antigen

④ anti-plague — probationary period — antibiotics

2 위 글의 내용과 일치하지 <u>않은</u> 것을 고르시오.

① Some people are not immunized after a full course of injections.

② Some people who carry the virus don't show any symptoms.

③ Many people get over the illness during the latent period.

④ You'd better check whether you are immunized right after you get the injections.

17

If everybody over 40 had their blood pressure checked once a year, that would really save lives. There's nothing Ⓐ_____ about it. People with unhealthily high blood pressure may have no symptoms at all however. They can appear very fit, and feel very well, and still be a ticking time bomb. The trouble is that you can't see the damage being done. I don't want Ⓑ<u>to pussyfoot around this</u>: someone with high blood pressure can often feel fine right up until the day they have a stroke.

Some pharmacists have a blood pressure machine in their shop. A few very with-it general practitioners keep one for everyone to use in the waiting room. All that happens is that you sit down, roll your sleeve up and they'll wrap the band around your upper arm, pump it up, and then take the reading. Something like 120 over 70 would be nice. It's your relaxed pressure, the lower number, that is most relevant. It tends to rise as you age, but you really don't want to see a lower figure getting close to 100.

This is not about being Ⓒ<u>neurotic</u>; keeping an eye on your body is just in everybody's interest. And if you do have high blood pressure, there is still a good chance of lowering it successfully. For some people, a change of lifestyle will be enough; others may need medication as well.

1 **Choose the one that best fills in the blank Ⓐ.**

① racial or ethnic

② hereditary or acquired

③ moral or ethical

④ magical or mysterious

2 **Choose the one closest in meaning to the underlined Ⓑ.**

① to make a fuss over such a trifle

② to beat around the bush

③ to sound pretentious or self-righteous

④ to give misleading information

3 According to the passage, which of the following is NOT true?

① It is important for your health to maintain blood pressure as low as possible without getting it too low.

② High blood pressure is a silent killer as it exhibits no obvious symptoms but is the major cause of heart disease.

③ There are different ways to control high blood pressure but adopting healthy lifestyle habits will be an effective first step.

④ Middle-aged adults must have their blood pressure checked biannually to keep a normal blood pressure.

4 Choose the one closest in meaning to the underlined ©"**neurotic**".

① acceptable   ② sensible

③ obsessive   ④ generous

18

We've known for some time that garlic is a nutritional powerhouse. It's been shown to boost immunity; relax blood vessels to open up blood flow and reduce blood pressure; ⓐ_____ inflammation, a known trigger of premature aging and disease; protect blood vessels from damage, thus lowering the risk of heart disease; and even protect against osteoarthritis.

Now, a new study shows Ⓐthis may hold some promise for weight control as well. Researchers fed mice a fattening diet for eight weeks to plump them up, then served them the same diet supplemented with garlic for another seven weeks. The addition of garlic reduced the mice's body weights and fat stores, and lessened the effects of the unhealthy diet on the animals' blood and liver. And there is another reason to ⓑ_____ the "stinking rose," as it's affectionately called by those who love it.

To get the most bang for your bulb, crush fresh garlic, then let Ⓑit sit at room temperature for a full 10 minutes before cooking. Several studies have shown that Ⓒthis helps retain about 70 percent of Ⓓits beneficial natural compounds compared to cooking it immediately after crushing. That's because crushing the garlic releases an enzyme that's been trapped in the cells of the plant. The enzyme boosts levels of health promoting compounds, which peak 10 minutes after crushing. If the garlic is cooked before this, the enzymes are destroyed.

1 Which of the following best fits in the blanks ⓐ and ⓑ?

① quell — savor
② foment — relish
③ quench — dodge
④ commove — satiate

2 According to the passage, which of the following is NOT true of "stinking rose"?

① It impedes degenerative joint disease.
② It may serve to regulate the weight.
③ It expedites premature aging and disease.
④ It is beneficial to health 10 minutes after crushing.

3 Choose the one that best replaces the underlined part.

① To last the fragrance of the beautiful rose
② To attain the maximum potency from the garlic
③ To make the most of the renown of the garlic
④ To gain the stamina from the extract of the garlic

4 Which of the following refers to something different?

① Ⓐ <u>this</u>　　　　　　　② Ⓑ <u>it</u>

③ Ⓒ <u>this</u>　　　　　　　④ Ⓓ <u>its</u>

19

Traumatic events have an element of randomness, making them almost impossible to prepare for or protect against. In real life, a wound like this reveals a person's inner core of strength or weakness, and while we all hope to respond well in these situations, we often don't. The shock of the experience can leave raw emotional gouges that are slow to heal.

A wound that is sudden and shocking often deprives a person of closure, leaving him with only questions: *Why did this happen? Why me? How can the world be so cruel?* Not only will a person be shaken by the experience, he may also question his own reactions and assign himself blame for not ensuring a better outcome. This self-blame is usually irrational, damages self-worth, and creates guilt (including survivor's guilt, in some cases). A traumatic event leaves a person especially changed and perhaps jaded. His fear of something similar happening again can lead to extreme shifts in personality and behavior, especially when it comes to safety and security. It is also the category most likely to lead to a character suffering from post-traumatic stress disorder (PTSD).

PTSD is a recognized disorder affecting some people who have experienced a significantly frightening or dangerous event. Someone suffering from PTSD may relive what happened via dissociative episodes that can last for moments, hours, or days. The person might also be triggered by reminders of the event, avoid emotions or thoughts associated with the trauma, have nightmares and difficulty sleeping, and be tense and on edge due to a chronic state of hypervigilance. Emotional volatility (including self-blame and guilt) is common, along with negative self-thoughts and depression-like symptoms such as isolation and losing interest in passions or hobbies.

1 According to the passage, which of the following is NOT true?

① Traumatic events will not let go of us however hard we try.

② Self-blame is a natural result of the majority of wounding events, even if the we were in no way at fault.

③ Not all personality changes resulting from a wound will be negative.

④ Those suffering from PTSD may have symptoms that are severe enough to impact their daily lives.

2 Which of the following statements can be inferred from the passage?

① It's normal for victims to experience a range of PTSD responses following a trauma.

② Of all the wounds, childhood-specific ones can do the most damage.

③ A large part of resiliency has to do with the amount and kind of support that's available for a person when tragedy strikes.

④ While the wound itself is life changing, it can be worsened when the victim also has to deal with hardships that follow.

3   Which of the following best describes the author's view in paragraph 3?

① How PTSD will manifest is highly individual, depending on who we are.

② People who experience traumatic events directly are likely to be more affected than those who are farther removed from them.

③ When the same traumatic occurrence happens repeatedly, those wounds dig deep.

④ The person's emotional closeness to the assailant can affect how intimate the victimization is.

20

Led by Suzanne Craft, a psychiatrist at the University of Washington in Seattle, researchers conducted a small pilot study involving 104 men and women with mild cognitive impairment — a common precursor to more advanced dementia — as well as the early stages of Alzheimer's itself. The researchers gave each participant two daily doses of a nasal spray, randomly containing either insulin or placebo. Over four months, the researchers found that those who took insulin improved or at least maintained their scores on tests of memory and general cognitive abilities; people who got a placebo did worse over time. The participants who received insulin actually got one of two doses: a lower dose of 20 international units (I.U.) or a higher dose of 40 I.U. At the end of four months, nearly 80% of those in the low-dose group showed improvements in a memory test. The placebo group showed worse performance on the task. People getting the higher dose of insulin also did not show enhancement in memory, but they did improve in overall cognitive functions. In addition to the memory tests, scientists also compared patients' levels of proteins and other substances in the body, which are known to be markers of Alzheimer's. Participants who showed improvements in memory also showed slight declines in levels of disease-related plaques and tangles in the brain. Brain scans further showed that people in the insulin-treated group were able to preserve their ability to process glucose properly in the brain. Glucose helps brain cells work normally and perform functions related to memory and other cognitive abilities. Alzheimer's brains show less metabolism of glucose, and in the study's placebo group, scans showed gradual declines in the brain's ability to break it down. "It's well known that insulin plays an important role in blood-sugar regulation in the body, but work from our lab and others suggests that it has a number of different and important roles in the brain as well. Those include mediating glucose or energy metabolism in the parts of the brain important for memory and other cognitive functions. When there is a problem with insulin's ability to carry out these functions, we believe that the stage is set for development of age-related conditions such as Alzheimer's disease." says Craft. But it is a small study and very preliminary — only the first of many steps toward figuring out whether insulin could become a weapon against dementia. It's still unclear, for example, why the lower dose of insulin appeared to improve people's memory, while the higher dose did not; and yet the higher dose enhanced other cognitive functions. The finding suggests _____. "We can't know for sure what mechanism is underlying this pattern, but, potentially, the dose that is optimal for memory may be different from the dose that is optimal for other types of cognitive abilities. Too little is bad, and too much is bad." says Craft.

1 빈칸에 들어가기에 가장 적합한 것을 고르시오.

① it is impossible to cure the disease completely with contemporary medicine

② there's a fine line between too little insulin and too much

③ the interaction between amount of insulin and glucose metabolism is mysterious

④ with the development of these findings, a road to complete recovery has been opened

2 위 글을 통해 추론할 수 있는 것으로 가장 적합한 것을 고르시오.

① The participants took insulin orally.

② The researchers selected patients who were supposed to take insulin.

③ The placebo group showed the lower levels of glucose in their brains.

④ It's not clear what is the mechanism between quantity of insulin and improvement in the Alzheimer's.

생물학·생명과학

12 생물학·생명과학

01

The term hormone was first used with reference to secretin. Starling derived the term from the Greek word hormon, meaning to excite or set in motion. The term endocrine was introduced shortly thereafter. Endocrine is used to refer to glands that secrete products directly into the bloodstream such as the pancreas, thyroids, and pituitary glands. Because the lack of any one of them may cause serious disorders, many hormones are now produced synthetically and used in treatment where a deficiency exists. Insects also have a unique hormone, ecdysone. Much like steroids stimulate muscle formation in humans, ecdysone strengthens the exoskeleton of insects while they metamorphose into the adult stage. Plants rely on a variety of hormones such as auxin and cytokinin that assist in flower, tuber, bulb, and bud formation. Ethylene, a synthetic hormone used by horticulturists, is believed to accelerate the ripening of fruit.

1 According to the passage, which of the following is affected by the hormone ethylene?

① Correcting digestive disorders

② Ripening fruits

③ Bud and flower formation

④ Insect metamorphosis

2 According to the passage, ecdysone is a hormone that _____.

① debases reproductive power

② inhibits the immune system

③ helps insects harden their outer shells

④ camouflages certain insects from predators

278 김영편입 영어 독해 워크북 2단계

02

Basic biology tells us that bravery emerges from a primal struggle between the brain's decision-making hub, the prefrontal cortex, and the focal point of fear, the amygdala. When we find ourselves in an unexpected and dangerous situation, the amygdala sends a signal to the prefrontal cortex that interferes with our ability to reason clearly. In extreme cases, that can be paralyzing. But the brave don't succumb to fear. In some cases, they're strengthened by the muscle memory that comes from intense training.

The ability to carry out duties in the face of imminent danger lies in the area of the brain known as the basal ganglia. When you practice an act again and again, the responsibility for performing the action switches from the brain's outer cortex, where it is experienced consciously, to the basal ganglia, which executes the action automatically and isn't affected by fear. Armies have understood this principle for thousands of years. Boot camps the world over deeply embed the fundamentals of combat into a recruit's brain through _____. That way, when intense fear shuts down a soldier's rational brain, he or she will still be able to function on autopilot.

1 Which of the following is true about "the brave"?

① They are not made but born, for they are endowed with strong prefrontal cortex and weak amygdala.

② When they are safe, the amygdala sends a signal facilitating decision-making to the prefrontal cortex.

③ They can behave courageously when a warning signal is sent from the brain's outer cortex to the basal ganglia.

④ When their prefrontal cortex is paralyzed by strong fear, they can do their duties by the muscle memory.

2 Choose the one that best fills in the blank.

① spiritual discipline   ② relentless repetition

③ subconscious learning   ④ cutthroat competition

3 What is the tone of the passage?

① inspiring   ② argumentative

③ admiring   ④ informative

03

It may _____ be said that natural selection is daily and hourly scrutinizing, throughout the world, the slightest variations; rejecting those that are bad, preserving and adding up all that are good; silently and insensibly working, whenever and wherever opportunity offers, at the improvement of each organic being in relation to its organic and inorganic conditions of life. We see nothing of these slow changes in progress, until the hand of time has marked the lapse of ages, and then so imperfect is our view into long past geological ages that we see only that the forms of life are now different from what they formerly were.

In order that any great amount of modification should be effected in a species, a variety, once formed, must again, perhaps after a long interval of time, vary or present individual differences of the same favorable nature as before; and these must be again preserved, and so onward, step by step. Seeing that individual differences of the same kind perpetually recur, this can hardly be considered as an unwarrantable assumption. But whether it is true, we can judge only by seeing how far the hypothesis accords with and explains the general phenomena of nature. On the other hand, the ordinary belief that the amount of possible variation is a strictly limited quantity is likewise a simple assumption.

1   Which of the following is most appropriate in the blank?

① metaphorically   ② ironically

③ paradoxically   ④ scientifically

⑤ philosophically

2   Which of the following can be inferred from the passage?

① Only after some decades pass, we can see the effects of slow changes in a species.

② If we had a clear view into long past geological ages, we could know how a species changes slowly in evolution.

③ For a species to advance in a large amount, it requires a large population.

④ It is unjustifiably assumed that for great progress a variety must again vary or present individual differences of the same favorable nature as before.

⑤ It turns out that the amount of possible variation is a strictly limited quantity.

04

The truth is that the question of life's origins is about as vexing a problem as science has ever faced. Ask a hundred random scientists to tell you how they think life originated and you will probably get a hundred slightly different answers. To compound matters, technology keeps opening new doors out of which new questions spill. Still, the past half-century has seen a bewildering array of findings that speak to life's origins not as something weird, but as something just about unavoidable. The discovery of hydrothermal systems spewing chemical feedstock in the depth of the oceans is a great example. Revolutions in genomics and proteomics have revealed a whole new map of life, illuminating core pieces of life's function and evolution during the past 4 billion years. And across fields as diverse as physics and economics we've seen the emergence of a spontaneous generation of order, or process, or behavior, that can occur from the interaction of many simpler players, be they molecules or birds in a flock. Therein lies one of the most frustrating aspects of the study of the origins of life; juicy pieces of the puzzle appear all around us, but we still can't fit them together successfully. Even defining what life really is represents a challenge. Without a good quantitative measure of "aliveness," it's actually difficult to talk about origins. That puts us in danger of falling into the ancient Greek philosophical mosh pit, debating whether or not a flame is alive.

1 What is the meaning of the underlined expression in the context?

① The ancient Greek philosophers discovered a lot of scientific truths.
② The ancient Greek philosophers knew the nature of a flame.
③ The question of life's origins can be an empty argument.
④ The question of life's origins must be studied by scientists earnestly.
⑤ The question of life's origins was already solved by the ancient Greek philosophers.

2 According to the passage, what is the most difficult problem of the study of the origins of life?

① Founding new scientific theories
② Integrating scientific discoveries systematically
③ Putting scientific theories into practice
④ Inventing new scientific technologies
⑤ Producing bioethics experts and scientists

05

Allelopathy, from the Greek words *allelo* (one another or mutual) and *pathy* (suffering), refers to the release of chemicals by one plant that have some type of effect on another plant. These chemicals can be given off by different parts of the plant or can be released through natural decomposition. Allelopathy is a survival mechanism that allows certain plants to compete with and often destroy nearby plants by inhibiting seed sprouting, root development or nutrient uptake. Other organisms, such as bacteria, viruses and fungi, can also be allelopathic. The term allelopathy is usually used when the effect is harmful, but it can apply to beneficial effects too. And even when the effect is harmful to plants, it can be a benefit otherwise. Think of how corn gluten meal is used as _____. Many turf grasses and cover crops have allelopathic properties that improve their weed suppression. Or how about the way the fungus penicillin can kill bacteria. You've probably heard of the problems experienced by plants growing near black walnut trees. All parts of the trees produce hydrojuglone, which is converted to an allelotoxin when it is exposed to oxygen. Roots, decomposing leaves and twigs all release juglone into the surrounding soil, which inhibits the growth of many other plants, especially those in the Solanaceae family, like tomatoes, peppers, potatoes and eggplants. Even trees and shrubs, like azaleas, pine and apple trees, are susceptible to juglone. On the other hand, many plants are tolerant of juglone and show no ill effects at all.

1 Choose the one that best fills in the blank.

① a growth promotor

② an organic food

③ a natural herbicide

④ an artificial biofuel

2 Which of the following is NOT true about "allelopathy"?

① It occurs not only while allelopathic plants are alive but also after they die.

② It has helped some organisms survive the struggle for existence in the wild.

③ It is a process by which a plant can either inhibit or benefit other plants.

④ It contradicts the way the first discovered antibiotic kills pathogenic microbes.

3 Which of the following CANNOT be well cultivated near black walnut trees?

① melons   ② peppers

③ carrots   ④ beans

06

Nearly twenty years ago, biochemists found that a separable constituent of deoxyribonucleic acid (or DNA) appeared to guide the cell's protein-synthesizing machinery. The internal structure of DNA seemed to represent a set of coded instructions which dictated the pattern of protein-synthesis. Experiments indicated that in the presence of appropriate enzymes each DNA molecule could form a replica, a new DNA molecule, containing the specific guiding message present in the original. This idea, when added to what was already known about the cellular mechanisms of heredity (especially the knowledge that DNA is localized in chromosomes), appeared to establish a molecular basis for inheritance.

Proponents of the theory that DNA was a "self-duplicating" molecule, containing a code that by itself determined biological inheritance, introduced the term "central dogma" into scientific literature. They did so in order to describe the principles that could explain DNA's governing role. The dogma originally involved an admittedly unproven assumption that, whereas nucleic acids can guide the synthesis of other nucleic acids and of proteins, the reverse effect is impossible; that is, proteins cannot guide the synthesis of nucleic acids. But actual experimental observations deny the second and crucial part of this assumption. Other test-tube experiments show that agents besides DNA have a guiding influence. The kind of protein that is made may depend on the specific organism from which the necessary enzyme is obtained. It also depends on the test tube's temperature, the degree of acidity, and the amount of metallic salts present.

1   What is the author's purpose in the passage?

① to describe the various processes that take place in a living cell

② to compare an old theory about cells with a new theory as an alternative

③ to reveal a discrepancy between a scientific theory and some experimental results

④ to change the way of separating DNA from a cell with the help of a new technology

2   The author presents his argument primarily by _____.

① contrasting two fields of science

② incorporating the former theory into a new one

③ providing experimental evidence against a point of view

④ starting new theories of the structure

07

Scientists and researchers rely on mice and rats for several reasons. One is convenience: rodents are small, easily housed and maintained, and adapt well to new surroundings. They also reproduce quickly and have a short lifespan of two to three years, so several generations of mice can be observed in a relatively short period of time. Most of the mice and rats used in medical trials are inbred so that, other than sex differences, they are almost identical genetically. This helps make the results of medical trials more uniform.

Another reason rodents are used as models in medical testing is that their genetic, biological and behavior characteristics closely resemble those of humans, and many symptoms of human conditions can be replicated in mice and rats. Over the last two decades, those similarities have become even stronger. Scientists can now breed genetically-altered mice — called "transgenic mice" — that carry genes that are similar to those that cause human diseases. Likewise, select genes can be turned off or made inactive, creating "knockout mice," which can be used to evaluate the effects of cancer-causing chemicals (carcinogens) and assess drug safety.

Mice are also used in behavioral, sensory, aging, nutrition and genetic studies, as well as testing anti-craving medication that could potentially end drug addiction.

1 **Choose the one that is NOT mentioned as features of laboratory rats.**

① the same genetic traits among generations

② resemblances to human inheritance

③ potential genetic variability

④ high reproduction rate

2 **Which of the following might be the best title of the passage?**

① Why Do Medical Researchers Use Mice?

② Good News for Alcoholics and Drug Addicts

③ A Medical Breakthrough in Cancer Treatment

④ Mice: The Ease of Genetic Modification

3 **Which of the following is true according to the passage?**

① Studying transgenic mice makes it possible to obtain cure-all.

② Knockout mice are the ones in which some specific gene under study is disabled.

③ The organ from transgenic mice can be transplanted into humans.

④ Doubts have never been raised concerning the reliability of testing rodents.

08

Once polymers were formed, the next step in creating life on Earth would have been the formation of molecular aggregates and primitive "cells." The term "cells" is used very loosely here. When polypeptides or polynucleotides are combined in solution, they form one of two types of complex units: one that Oparin called coacervate droplets and the other that Stanley Fox called proteinoid microspheres. Coacervate droplets are macromolecules that are surrounded by a shell of water molecules which are rigidly oriented relative to the macromolecule forming a "membrane." The coacervate droplets will absorb each other and absorb chemicals from the surrounding. The coacervate droplets can become complex and show internal structures which become more and more pronounced as more materials pass the membrane and are incorporated into the droplet.

Proteinoid microspheres are formed when hot aqueous solutions of polypeptides are cooled. Proteinoid microspheres are much more stable than coacervate droplets and Ⓐ_____: swell in a high salt solution, shrink in a low salt solution, have a double-layered outer boundary which is very similar to a cell membrane, show internal movement similar to cytoplasmic streaming, grow in size and complexity, bud in a manner superficially similar to yeast cell reproduction, have electrical potential differences across the outer boundary which is necessary for cell membranes to generate ATP, and aggregate into clusters. In either case (coacervate droplets or proteinoid microspheres) these "prebionts" are structurally complex and sharply separated from their environment, creating a situation in which chemical reactions can take place inside the prebionts that would not happen in the surrounding medium.

1 Which of the following is most appropriate for the blank Ⓐ?

① can use ATP to make polypeptides and nucleic acids

② have the following characteristics for primitive reproduction

③ aggregate spontaneously to form small round bodies

④ can be reviewed from a theological point of view

2 Which of the following can be inferred from the passage?

① Coacervates are droplets formed in an anaerobic solution.

② The synthesis of proteinoid microspheres refutes the theory that proteinoids were a precursor to the first living cells.

③ Unlike proteinoid microspheres, coacervates can't be regarded as prebionts.

④ Proteinoid microsphere forms when solutions of certain polymers are cooled.

09

You may have heard people describe themselves as strictly "right-brained" or "left-brained," with the left-brainers bragging about their math skills and the right-brainers touting their creativity. That's because the brain is divided into two hemispheres, with each half performing a fairly distinct set of operations. According to Roger Sperry, the human brain's hemispheres operate both independently and in concert with each other. The two hemispheres communicate information, such as sensory observations, to each other through the thick corpus callosum that connects them. The brain's right hemisphere controls the muscles on the left side of the body, while the left hemisphere controls the muscles on the right side of the human body.

In general, the left hemisphere is dominant in language: processing what you hear and handling most of the duties of speaking. It's also in charge of carrying out logic and exact mathematical computations. When you need to retrieve a fact, your left brain pulls it from your memory. The right hemisphere is mainly in charge of spatial abilities, face recognition and processing music. It performs some math, but only rough estimations and comparisons. The brain's right side also helps us to comprehend visual imagery and make sense of what we see. It plays a role in language, particularly in interpreting context and a person's tone.

As for whether a person is right-brained or left-brained or even right-handed or left-handed the uses and preferences of the brain's two sections are far more Ⓐ_____ than just a simple left vs. right equation. For example, some people throw a ball with their right hand but write with their left. "Brain Ⓑ_____ is essential for proper brain function," professor Stephen Wilson of University College London told Live Science. "It allows the two sides of the brain to become specialized, increasing its processing capacity and avoiding situations of conflict where both sides of the brain try to take charge."

1 빈칸 Ⓐ와 Ⓑ에 들어갈 가장 알맞은 것은?

① simple — symmetry
② complex — asymmetry
③ intriguing — structure
④ original — appearance

2 윗글의 목적으로 가장 알맞은 것은?

① to emphasize the importance of the left-brain as a source of the command of a language
② to ague that the left-brain would not function properly without the cooperation of the right-brain
③ to discuss the structure of the brain through the differing functions of the left and right sides of the brain
④ to criticize the notion that Brain asymmetry allows us to process many things at once

10

Ecologists have been debating the origin of the high degree of rain forest biodiversity for a long time, and so far have not come up with a satisfying explanation. Ⓐ What causes this great amount of diversity is a Ⓐ_____ and still enigmatic question. Initially it seemed that the high productivity afforded by large quantities of rainfall and hot temperatures would promote much diversity. However, when ecologists examined this idea closely it did not prove to be true. Ⓑ Indeed there are convincing arguments that greater productivity could actually result in much Ⓑ_____ diversity. From the point of view of how much material is actually produced per unit time, the most productive ecosystem in the world is a modern cornfield. Ⓒ But here too there are opposing arguments, and this "time hypothesis" remains at best controversial. We could go on with a variety of other explanations, but the story is the same for each one of them. Ⓓ While Newton was able to explain the laws of gravity, and Darwin explained how biological organisms evolved, no comparable explanation yet exists for why some places (like the tropics) have so many species, while other places (like the arctic) have so few.

1 Choose the words that fit best for blanks Ⓐ and Ⓑ.

① clairvoyant — higher

② persistent — lower

③ long-lasting — higher

④ glaring — lower

2 Which of the following cannot be inferred from the passage?

① Cornfields show that farmers are pursuing the productivity of their crops at the expense of biodiversity.

② Much precipitation and scorching heat in tropics do not contribute to the high degree of biodiversity there.

③ Many hypothetical explanations about rain forest biodiversity are being set forth, but remain controversial.

④ We will be able to explain tropical biodiversity by comparing it with gravity and evolution, but not yet.

3 Which would be the best place for the following sentence?

Other ecologists have suggested that the longer duration the tropics have been free of the ice sheets that covered much of the temperate zone during the great ice ages has allowed for the evolution of the more different kinds of organisms.

① Ⓐ

② Ⓑ

③ Ⓒ

④ Ⓓ

11

The human appendix, also known as the vermiform appendix, is an organ located near the transition between the large and small intestines. Normally, it is situated on the right-hand side of the body, below the stomach and above the legs. Only about one to two inches long, the appendix is approximately the size of a finger. Many other mammals besides humans have appendixes. Despite this fact, scientists still disagree over the precise function of the appendix. Some biologists have argued that the organ is a part of the human immune system, helping the body to fight diseases. This theory, however, has several flaws.

The hypothesis that the human appendix helps keep the body healthy is based on research of rabbit appendixes. In rabbits, the organ is home to certain important tissues involved in the immune response, and rabbits without appendixes often have health problems. However, it is not clear that rabbit appendixes can tell us anything about how human appendixes function. Comparisions between the two are problematic because rabbit appendixes are shaped differently from those of humans and are relatively larger. Additionally, many biologists believe that two organs resulted from convergent evolution. Convergent evolution occurs when organisms independently develop similar attributes. For example, although ducks and bees both have wings, they evolved separately, and did not inherit their wings from a common ancestor. This is important, because while organs acquired through convergent evolution are alike, they do not always have the same purpose or function.

1 **Which of the following is NOT true of the human appendix?**

① It is situated between the stomach and intestines.

② Some scientists believe it plays a role in human health.

③ A number of different animals have similar organs.

④ Biologists are still unsure of its exact function and purpose.

2 **Comparisons between human and rabbit appendixes are problematic EXCEPT _____.**

① because rabbit appendixes and human appendixes may have evolved separately

② because rabbit appendixes may not perform the same function as human appendixes

③ because human appendixes have unique tissues that are part of the immune system

④ because rabbit and human appendixes are not shaped the same way

3 The author's description of convergent evolution mentions all of the following EXCEPT
_____.

① it is exemplified by a comparison between the wings of bees and the wings of ducks

② it indicates that similar organs in different species might not be used for the same purpose

③ it occurs when two species that have evolved independently develop similar traits

④ it proves that two animals with similar organs likely shared a common ancestor

12

Proteins, in short, are complex entities. Hemoglobin is only 146 amino acids long, a runt by protein standards, yet even it offers 10190 possible amino acid combinations, which is why it took the Cambridge University chemist Max Perutz twenty-three years — a career, more or less — to unravel it. For random events to produce even a single protein would seem a stunning improbability — like a whirlwind spinning through a junkyard and leaving behind a fully assembled jumbo jet, in the colorful simile of the astronomer Fred Hoyle.

Yet we are talking about several hundred thousand types of protein, perhaps a million, each unique and each, as far as we know, vital to the maintenance of a sound and happy you. And it goes on from there. A protein to be of use must not only assemble amino acids in the right sequence, but then must engage in a kind of chemical origami and fold itself into a very specific shape. Even having achieved this structural complexity, a protein is no good to you if it can't reproduce itself, and proteins can't. For this you need DNA. DNA is a whiz at replicating — it can make a copy of itself in seconds — but can do virtually nothing else. So we have a paradoxical situation. Proteins can't exist without DNA, and DNA has no purpose without proteins. Are we to assume then that they arose simultaneously with the purpose of supporting each other? If so: wow.

And there is more still. DNA, proteins, and the other components of life couldn't prosper without some sort of membrane to contain them. No atom or molecule has ever achieved life independently. Pluck any atom from your body, and it is no more alive than is a grain of sand. It is only when they come together within the nurturing refuge of a cell that these diverse materials can take part in the amazing dance that we call life. Without the cell, they are nothing more than interesting chemicals. But without the chemicals, the cell has no purpose. As the physicist Paul Davies puts it, "If everything needs everything else, how did the community of molecules ever arise in the first place?"

It is rather as if all the ingredients in your kitchen somehow got together and baked themselves into a cake — but a cake that could moreover divide when necessary to produce more cakes. It is little wonder that we call it the miracle of life. It is also little wonder that we have barely begun to understand it.

1 위 글의 제목으로 가장 적합한 것을 고르시오.

① DNA: The Whiz of Replication

② The Complexity of Proteins

③ The Purpose of DNA

④ Life Comes from Life

2 위 글의 내용과 일치하지 <u>않는</u> 것을 고르시오.

① DNA is good at replicating but it can do virtually nothing else.

② It would seem almost improbable that a single protein could be produced through random events.

③ Even if any atom is separated from your body, it could be alive when it includes DNA.

④ It can be said that DNA and proteins arose coincidentally with the purpose of supporting each other.

13

Human breast milk contains lactose, a sugar. What we know about babies is that they're born preferring sweet. It's only been a couple of centuries since the time when, if you didn't breast-feed from your mother or a wet nurse, your chance of survival was close to zero. The aversion to bitter foods is inborn too and it also has survival value: It helps us avoid ingesting toxins that plants evolved to keep from being eaten — including by us. Ⓐ

Food or poison? Vertebrates arose more than 500 million years ago in the ocean, and taste evolved mainly as a way of Ⓐsettling that issue. All vertebrates have taste receptors similar to ours, though not necessarily in the same places. There are more taste receptors on the whiskers of a large catfish than there are on the tongues of dozens of people. Ⓑ

Anencephalic infants, who are born with virtually no brain beyond the brain stem — the most primitive, ancient part — react to sweetness with the joyful-seeming facial expressions. The broccoli grimace is also primitive. In fact, although our tongues have just one or two types of receptor for sweet, they have at least two dozen different ones for bitter — a sign of how important avoiding poison was to our ancestors. The challenge many of us face these days is different: It's the pleasure we get from food that gets us into trouble. Ⓒ

Our preoccupation with food has led to a boom in research on taste. It has turned out to be a very complicated sense — more complicated than vision. Scientists have made great progress in recent years in identifying taste receptors and the genes that code for them, but they are far from fully understanding the sensory machinery that produces our experience of food. Ⓓ

1 Which of the following is NOT true?

① Evolutionarily speaking, no wonder babies dislike vegetables with bitter tastes.
② Being able to avoid bitter plant toxins gave our ancestors an evolutionary advantage.
③ Food manufacturers keep developing flavors which reflect consumers' preference.
④ Babies born with only a partial brain cannot taste other kinds of flavors than bitterness.

2 The following is removed from the passage. In which of the Ⓐ to Ⓓ may it be inserted to support the author's argument?

The modern food environment is a tremendous source of pleasure, far richer than the one our ancestors evolved in, and the preferences we inherited from them — along with a food industry that's increasingly adept at selling us what we like — often lead us to adopt unhealthy habits.

① Ⓐ   ② Ⓑ
③ Ⓒ   ④ Ⓓ

3 Choose the one that is closest in meaning to the underlined part Ⓐsettling that issue.

① distinguishing toxins from foods

② indulging appetite for sweets

③ corresponding taste receptors on the tongue

④ solving a food shortage

Using recovered DNA to "genetically resurrect" an extinct species — the central idea behind the *Jurassic Park* films — may be moving closer to reality with the creation of a new company that aims to bring back woolly mammoths thousands of years after the last of the giants disappeared from the Arctic tundra.

Flush with a $15 million infusion of funding, Harvard University genetics professor George Church, known for his pioneering work in genome sequencing and gene splicing, hopes the company, in the bold words of its news release, can usher in an era when mammoths "walk the Arctic tundra again." To be sure, what Church's company, Colossal, is proposing would actually be a Ⓐ_____ created using a gene-editing tool known as CRISPR-Cas9 to splice bits of DNA recovered from frozen mammoth specimens into that of an Asian elephant, the mammoth's closest living relative. The resulting animal — known as a "mammophant" — would look, and presumably behave, much like a woolly mammoth.

But even if the researchers at Colossal can bring back mammoths — and that is not certain — the obvious question is, should they? Joseph Frederickson, a vertebrate paleontologist and director of the Weis Earth Science Museum in Menasha, Wis., was inspired as a child by the original Jurassic Park movie. But even he thinks that the more important goal should be preventing extinction rather than reversing it. If you can create a mammoth or at least an elephant that looks like a good copy of a mammoth that could survive in Siberia, you could do quite a bit for the white rhino or the giant panda. Especially for animals that have "dwindling genetic diversity," Frederickson says, adding older genes from the fossil record or entirely new genes could increase the health of those populations. Speaking with NPR in 2015, Beth Shapiro, a paleogeneticist at the University of California, Santa Cruz and author of *How to Clone a Mammoth: The Science of De-Extinction*, said emphatically, "I don't want to see mammoths come back." "It's never going to be possible to create a species that is 100% identical," she said. "But what if we could use this technology not to bring back mammoths but to save elephants?"

1   **Which of the following best fits into Ⓐ?**

① hybrid   ② fetus

③ embryo   ④ purebred

2 Which of the following can be inferred from the passage?

① Creating mammophant in the lab is the most effective way to restore the tundra.

② The mammophant would be more like an woolly mammoth with a number of elephant traits as well.

③ Some animals will be removed from the endangered species list thanks to the fossil record.

④ Genetically engineered mammoths don't need to adjust to the Arctic tundra.

3 Which of the following is the main idea of the third paragraph?

① Reintroduced mammoths in the Arctic tundra could help reverse climate change.

② The process of returning an extinct species is slow and cumbersome.

③ The techniques to resurrect mammoths might be better used to help endangered species.

④ The proposed 'de-extinction' of mammoths will be achieved in the near future.

15

A The immune system is a complex structure, built over a person's life in response to environmental conditions. Antibodies, proteins that tag and attack viruses and bacteria, "remember" past invaders, allowing white blood cells to quickly respond during subsequent infections. Because different groups of people encounter different diseases — the European settlers had high exposure to smallpox, measles, and influenza thanks to close contact with livestock — they develop different antibodies. But what about the genes behind the immune system? Could those also change vulnerability to certain diseases?

B To find out, a team led by Ripan Malhi, an anthropologist at the University of Illinois in Urbana, sought permission from the Tsimshian, a First Nations community in the Prince Rupert Harbor region of British Columbia in Canada, to examine DNA from the skeletal remains of 25 individuals who lived in the region between 500 and 6000 years ago. These ancient indigenous inhabitants, many of them ancestors to the modern Tsimshian, were a seafaring people who first encountered Europeans in the early 1700s.

C Using a technique known as whole exome sequencing, researchers sifted through the DNA for genes related to immune response. They then sequenced DNA samples from 25 Tsimshian living near Prince Rupert today. Comparing the two sets of genes, the team discovered several immune-related gene variants that were rare among the living. For example, a variant of a gene known as a *HLA-DQA1*, which codes for proteins that sort healthy cells from invading viruses and bacteria, was found in nearly 100% of ancient individuals, but in only 36% of modern ones.

D That finding suggests that the immune-related genes of the ancient Tsimshian were well-adapted to local diseases but not to novel infections like smallpox and measles, the team reports today in *Nature Communications*. Because European-borne epidemics altered the disease landscape, survivors were less likely to carry variants like *HLA-DQA1*, which were less able to cope with the new diseases. "Ⓐ_____," Malhi says.

E Measuring differences between the ancient and modern DNA, Malhi and colleagues calculated a rough date for the genetic shift, about 175 years ago. At that time, smallpox epidemics raged throughout the Americas, including in Prince Rupert Harbor. Those with the most susceptible immune system genes were killed. Based on the new findings and historical accounts, the team says that close to 80% of the community died in the decades following initial European contact.

1 **What is the best title for the above passage?**

   ① Genetic Differences between Westerners and Native Americans
   ② Genetic Causes of Indigenous Population Decline
   ③ Past Diseases' Mark On Modern-day Indigenous Population
   ④ Massacre of Indigenous People
   ⑤ Pathological Causes of Indigenous Population Decline

2 According to the paragraph Ⓐ, which of the following is NOT true?

① Human immune system is the result of the body reacting to stimuli in the environment.

② Antibodies are a kind of protein that remembers previous attacks by pathogens.

③ People who have lived in different environments have different immune systems.

④ Without information about the disease provided by the antibodies, white blood cells alone cannot perform their immune function.

⑤ Although the antibodies in the body are different for each person, the genes encoded for antibody formation are essentially the same.

3 Which of the following is TRUE about the above passage?

① Even though they are exposed to different diseases, people have the same antibodies.

② A variant of a gene known as a *HLA-DQA1* picks up healthy cells that are not infected.

③ The genes of the ancient Tsimshian were well adapted to local diseases such as smallpox.

④ European-borne epidemics completely destroyed the immune system of the indigenous people.

⑤ The Tsimshian descendants have an improved immune system compared to their ancestors.

4 In paragraph Ⓓ, which of the following would best fit in the blank Ⓐ?

① Those ancient genetic variants that were once adaptive were no longer adaptive after European contact

② The genetic variants of Europeans were unable to adapt to the diseases of indigenous peoples

③ *HLA-DQA1* didn't have the information to generate proteins that separate healthy cells from infecting viruses and bacteria

④ The contact between Europeans and indigenous people was genetically mutually beneficial

⑤ This example demonstrates the maladaptation of the body against foreign diseases

5 Which of the following CANNOT be inferred from the passage?

① Demographic data from past Prince Rupert Harbor seem to remain today.

② European settlers had developed the antibody for smallpox before they came to the Americas.

③ When the environment changes, the genes that were useful can disappear.

④ The immune systems of ancient natives were more complex than those of Europeans.

⑤ European-borne epidemics were spread rapidly among natives.

13

동물·식물

13 동물·식물

01

The unusually long, oval egg of the Indonesian maleo may look a lot like a potato, but this bird is no slouch. When the chicks of these anvil-headed animals hatch, they're almost immediately able to fly. For years, scientists have wondered why bird species have different egg shapes. Some theorized shapes may protect eggs from shattering or allow them to fit snugly in the nest. Aristotle had even (wrongly) asserted that long, pointy eggs were female while rounder eggs were male. But no comprehensive studies had ever been conducted to test these ideas, which left Mary Stoddard and colleagues skeptical. "It has not gone unnoticed that birds have evolved to shapes that are quite diverse in form — everything from a spherical owl egg to a pointy sandpiper egg," said Stoddard, an ecologist at Princeton University. In a new study, the team revealed a surprise: _____.

. The results showed that birds with the higher hand-wing index — the most efficient and thus best fliers — were the ones with the most asymmetric or elliptical eggs. "We were shocked to see that one of the best explanations for egg shape variation was flight ability," says Stoddard. "This is something that has not gotten a lot of airtime in the hypotheses that are out there for egg shape variation."

1 According to the passage, which of the following is true?

① Egg shape will help protect the eggs from breaking while being incubated.
② Flight ability may have been critical drivers of egg shape variation in birds.
③ Elliptical shape helps birds camouflage their eggs in open nest dug into the ground.
④ There are no birds born with the ability to fly because flying takes some practice.

2 Which of the following best fits in the blank?

① Birds lay eggs in a wide range of shapes and colors
② Birds adapted for flight may have generally smaller bodies
③ All flightless birds would have perfectly spherical and pointy eggs
④ Egg shapes evolved as birds themselves evolved for better flight

02

An estimated 25,000 species of orchids, over the past 80 million years or so, have managed to colonize six continents and virtually every conceivable terrestrial habitat, from the deserts of western Australia to the cloud forests of Central America, from the forest canopy to the underground, from remote Mediterranean mountaintops to living rooms, offices, and restaurants the world over.

The secret of their success? In a word, dupery. Though some orchids do offer conventional food rewards to the insects and birds that carry their pollen from plant to plant, roughly a third of orchid species long ago figured out, unconsciously of course, that they can save on the expense of nectar and increase the odds of reproducing by _____, whether that ruse be visual, aromatic, tactile, or all three at once. Some orchids lure bees with the promise of food by mimicking the appearance of nectar-producing flowers, while others, as in the case of a Dracula orchid, attract gnats by producing an array of nasty scents, from fungus and rotten meat to cat urine and baby diaper. Some orchids promise shelter, deploying floral forms that mimic insect burrows or brood rooms. Others mimic male bees in flight, hoping to incite territorial combat that results in pollination.

1   Choose the one that best fills in the blank.

    ① drawing on natural enemies

    ② hiding in their surroundings

    ③ evolving a clever deceit

    ④ sharpening their sensibility

2   Which of the following can be inferred about "orchids"?

    ① They primarily use fragrant smell to decoy flying bees and bugs.

    ② They are of ancient origin and are nearly ubiquitous on the earth.

    ③ They are vulnerable to extreme weather, as their appearance implies.

    ④ They cannot but provide their pollinators with reciprocal rewards.

3   What is the purpose of the passage?

    ① to describe the ecological features of various orchids

    ② to compare the ways orchids camouflage themselves

    ③ to give various information on how to identify orchids

    ④ to explain a reproductive strategy of orchids in detail

03

Plant pores, called stomata, are essential for life. When they evolved about 400 million years ago, they helped plants conquer the land. Plants absorb carbon dioxide through stomata and release oxygen and water vapour as part of the Earth's carbon and water cycles. Stomata need to be evenly spaced to maximise breathing capacity. But how they establish an even spatial pattern during plant growth has been a mystery.

In a paper to be published in *Science*, the JIC scientists show that the ability of cells to divide and form stomata is retained in only one of the two daughter cells generated by each division. This pattern, known as stem cell behaviour, is also found in certain animal cells, like those that form skin or bone. In the case of stomata, the stem cell property depends on a protein called SPEECHLESS (SPCH) being kept active in a single daughter cell. The daughter cell is kept at the centre of her cellular relatives through a sort of molecular dance through which the polarity of cells switches at each division. The daughter eventually forms a stoma, surrounded by non-stomatal relatives, ensuring that the stomatal pores are spaced out.

"Unravelling this mechanism was only possible because of advances in live imaging and computational modelling," said Professor Enrico Coen from JIC. The computer modelling predicted rules that the scientists were able to validate experimentally in the plant Arabidopsis. They tracked various markers such as a fluorescent protein to see the patterns that formed in growing leaves. The research could help scientists to tailor the number and arrangement of stomata to different environments. This could regulate Ⓐ_____.

1 빈칸 Ⓐ에 들어갈 가장 적합한 표현을 고르시오.

① the number of daughter cells that are made during cell division

② growth rate of plants growing in a specific environment

③ the rate at which plants photosynthesize using carbon dioxide and water

④ the efficiency at which plants absorb carbon dioxide or diffuse water vapour

2 위 글의 내용과 가장 일치하는 것을 고르시오.

① Plants account for the largest portion of the Earth's carbon and water cycle.

② Plants' spatial arrangement patterns of pores change irregularly during the growing season.

③ The experimental results by the scientists were consistent with the predictions of the computer modeling.

④ All of the cells after division contain a protein called SPCH.

04

One of the standard ways of testing for animal intelligence involves examining their reaction to their own reflection in a mirror. In fact, only very few species, including chimpanzees and dolphins, seem to recognize the image for what it is. In various experiments with captive elephants, scientists have noted behavior that indicates that elephants also realize that their reflection is a self-image. The most telling clue is that no elephant has ever been known to engage its reflection in the sort of social greeting behavior that normally occurs when two elephants meet. In addition, elephants looking into mirrors act in much the same way humans do. If they are dirty, they will attempt to clean themselves, using their reflection as a guide. That elephants can recognize their reflection for what it is impresses scientists because it means that elephants apparently have a sense of self lacking in many other animals. This sense of self is considered one of the fundamental characteristics of a truly sentient intelligence.

Another striking aspect of elephant behavior that indicates they possess a high level of intelligence is their seeming awareness of death. Elephants react to death in many of the same ways that humans do. When a member of the herd perishes, the rest of the herd members gather around the corpse, stroking and touching it with their trunks. This behavior indicate that elephants are capable of grasping death as an intellectual concept.

1 What can be inferred from the passage about the testing for animal intelligence?

① Elephants should not be put in front of mirrors.

② Dolphins may also possess a high level of intelligence.

③ Elephants are very anti-social animals.

④ Chimpanzees are more intelligent than elephants.

2 Which of the following is NOT mentioned as evidence that elephants can recognize their own reflection?

① They do not try to engage their reflection in social behavior.

② They use their reflection to help them clean themselves.

③ They attempt to rub their trunks against their reflection in greeting.

④ They explore their reflection to see what they look like.

3 What is one indicator that elephants possess a concept of death?

① They will gather around a fresh elephant corpse.

② They have been known to bury the dead.

③ They sometimes seek revenge on those who kill elephants.

④ They will avoid areas where an elephant has died.

05

The great white shark Carcharodon carcharias is easily one of the most recognizable species of shark — and yet knowledge of them is incredibly _____. This is truly remarkable, considering these creatures can be more than 6m long and weigh over 2,000kg. However, they're incredibly adept at hiding themselves, mainly due to their colouration, which makes them difficult to make out from above and below — and they're also known to retreat to very deep water, where they're almost impossible to track.

Their behaviour is hard to predict, too, as they adopt seemingly random pathways across the oceans. These differ between males, females, and juveniles: some will hug the coastline, some choose to stay in the wider ocean, with no consistency. As a result, scientists aren't even sure how many white sharks exist, but it's agreed they're a vulnerable species with their numbers decreasing.

Remarkably, they've never been documented mating or giving birth, however it's thought they go to deep waters in the Pacific Ocean to mate. Their gestation period is estimated to be around 12 months, but very little is known about where the females deliver the pups. This giant of the deep guards its secrets well!

1 What is the best title of the passage?

① Enigma of the Great White Shark
② Conservation Efforts for the Great White Shark
③ The Habitat of the Great White Shark
④ The Great White Shark in Danger

2 Which is the most appropriate for the blank?

① robust   ② scant
③ fascinating   ④ detailed

3 According to the passage, which of the following is <u>not</u> true of great white sharks?

① Because of their color, it is hard to spot them in the ocean.
② They spend most of their time in shallow and near-shore waters.
③ Not much is known about the mating habits of them.
④ Accurate global population numbers of them are unavailable.

06

Oriental Sacred Lotus seeds collected from the sediment of a dry lake bottom near a small village in northeastern China have germinated after being dormant for over 1,200 years. They are presumed to be the oldest living seeds ever found.

These Sacred Lotus seeds have managed to Ⓐ_____. Existing in an impenetrable seed coat and mired in an oxygen deficient mud, the seeds have intact genetic and enzymatic systems that reactivated when they were split open and soaked in water. (Enzymes are proteins that speed up chemical reactions in the cell.) A key enzyme that repairs proteins was present during germination; this enzyme has been found in similar quantities in modern day Sacred Lotus seeds. The repair enzyme functions in converting damaged amino acids back to their naturally occurring functional form. This is especially important in "repairing" the proteins of the cell membrane. Without intact membranes, cells are not able to function and such damage will lead to the death of the cell and eventually of the organism.

The architecture of the fruit no doubt plays a key role in the longevity of these seeds. The fruits of the Sacred Lotus are round to oblong, 10-13 cm long, 8-10 cm in diameter, and each contains a single seed. The fruit wall or pericarp, which is impervious to water and is also airtight, is initially green and then turns purplish brown as it becomes dry and notably hard. The hard, airtight fruit walls are the most significant of the structural features that contribute to the exceptional longevity of the seeds.

1 Choose the one that best fills in the blank Ⓐ.

① ward off the ravages of time ② figure out the change of weather

③ show up in the nick of time ④ take fortune at the tide

2 What is the best title for the passage?

① The Repair Enzyme: A Miracle Material

② The Origins of Oriental Sacred Lotus

③ The Seeds That Have Slept for 1,200 Years

④ The Contributors to the Longevity of Plants

3 Which of the following is NOT favorable to the longevity of the Sacred Lotus seeds?

① the oxygen-deficiency of the mud

② the intactness of enzyme systems

③ the structure of the fruit

④ the size and shape of the fruit

07

There is a limit to how small an animal's body can be. Many of the constraints derive from the fact that for any given shape, the ratio of surface area to volume increases with decreasing size. This is a major issue for warm-blooded birds and mammals; the smaller they get, the faster they lose heat, so they have to generate heat faster to compensate. Minute birds and mammals push their metabolism to the absolute limits. The classic evidence of this size limitation is in the smallest shrews, where they are constantly eating to renew the energy that is being rapidly lost through their skin. This is why the smallest recorded bird, the 30mm-long bee hummingbird of Cuba and the smallest known mammal, the 40mm Etruscan pygmy shrew found across Europe, north Africa and Southeast Asia are much larger than the smallest known reptile, a dwarf gecko from the Caribbean that measures just 14mm from snout to anus. But while heat loss isn't an issue for cold-blooded creatures, water loss is. This is a special problem for amphibians. If a tiny frog gets out into dry air it could dry out in a matter of minutes. Fish would appear to have things easier. Being cold-blooded and aquatic, heat loss and desiccation are not a problem. There are other constraints that kick in at such sizes, though. Losing a few bones here or there might not make much difference to a very small animal, but all its parts still have to work. And there are fundamental limits on how far organs can be scaled down. One is that organs are made of cells, a certain number of which are needed to make complex organs like brains and eyes. The upshot is that an organ in a small animal is usually _____ its size than in a big animal.

1 Choose the one that best fills in the blank.

① smaller relative to

② larger relative to

③ smaller regardless of

④ larger regardless of

2 According to the passage, what does NOT influence an animal's body size?

① the time of the day the animal is active

② the ability to regulate body temperature

③ the class which the animal belongs to

④ the number of cells needed for organs

3 Which of the following can be inferred from the passage?

① Their volume being equal, a short animal loses heat faster than a long one.

② The smaller an animal's size is, the slower metabolism it should have.

③ The frog is a cold-blooded animal which belongs to the amphibian class.

④ The brains and the eyes of animals are made of the same number of cells.

4 What is the tone of the passage?

① admonitory   ② introspective

③ exclamatory   ④ descriptive

08

There are around 800 species of urchins in the world. They're found in almost every major marine habitat from the poles to the Equator, and from shallow inlets to depths of more than 5000m. All have roe that's edible, though not necessarily palatable. Urchins have hundreds of adhesive tube feet and move over the seafloor at a leisurely pace. The test — its spiny outer shell — protects what is basically an eating and breeding machine. Ⓐ The skeleton is divided into sections running from top to bottom, like the segments of an orange. Ⓑ Inside the body are five corals of roe, sometimes called tongues. Ⓒ This chewing apparatus is known as Aristotle's lantern, from a description in the Greek philosopher and naturalist's *Historia Animalium*. (Scholars recently proposed that he was actually referring to the test, which resembles the bronze lamps of ancient Greece.) Ⓓ

Both fragile and destructive, the urchin is a tempest in an environmental seapot. In every corner of the planet, there seem to be either too few or too many. The French and Irish exhausted their resident stocks years ago. In Maine, Nova Scotia and Japan, urchin populations have been drastically reduced by overfishing and disease. Ⓐ_____, off the coasts of California and Tasmania, overfishing the animal's natural predators and large-scale change in ocean circulation — believed to be an effect of climate change — have turned vast stretches of seafloor into "urchin barrens" that remind you of moonscapes. The urchins multiply, chew down the kelp and devastate marine ecosystems.

1 **Which is the most appropriate place for the sentence below?**

On the underside of the test are a muscular system and five self-honing calcium carbonate teeth that allow the urchin to chomp through stone.

① Ⓐ   ② Ⓑ

③ Ⓒ   ④ Ⓓ

2 **Which of the following is most suitable for the blank Ⓐ?**

① Meanwhile   ② Similarly

③ Otherwise   ④ Nonetheless

3 According to the passage, which of the following is NOT true about urchins?

① They are ubiquitous and unevenly distributed in the oceans of the world.

② The structure of their body resembles that of an orange.

③ They were described as something like a lantern by Aristotle.

④ They are both victims and beneficiaries of human fishing activities.

4 According to the passage, "urchin barrens" in the second paragraph mean the sea floors where _____.

① warm ocean currents meet cold ones, causing the over-multiplication of kelp, an urchin's prey

② urchins have been extinguished by their overpopulated predators and too hot ocean currents

③ urchins are fighting their competitors, kelps, for habitats optimal to them under the sea

④ the urchin population has grown unchecked, causing destructive grazing of kelp beds

09

Honeybees are generalists. According to the International Bee Research Association, a third of our diet comes from flowering crops and honeybees are responsible for pollinating about 80 per cent of them. They are essential in the production of at least 90 commercially grown foods. Bee-pollinated forage and hay crops like alfalfa and clover are also used to feed the animals that supply meat, milk and cheese. It doesn't matter whether you're a vegetarian or a meat-eater. A report by the National Research Council in Washington Ⓐhit the nail on the head: "Pollinator decline is one form of global change that actually does have credible potential to alter the shape of the terrestrial world." Pollinators, especially bees, are a keystone species, at the very centre of the entire food web. Remove the keystone and the whole edifice collapses.

To Ⓑ_____ matters, there is mounting evidence that native bees and other pollinators like moths, butterflies, bats and humming birds are also in steep decline. Disease is the main suspect in the decline of the North American bumblebees. Dr Laurence Packer, a world expert in wild bees at York University in Toronto, believes US greenhouse growers are the most likely culprit. Bumblebees are widely used for 'buzz pollination' of greenhouse crops like tomatoes and peppers. In the 1980s growers sent bees to Europe to perfect breeding techniques. The bees returned infected with nosema ceranae, a single-celled protozoa originally from southeast Asia, which destroys the bees' digestive tract. Before long the disease had spread to wild bumblebees.

The globalization of the bee industry has helped Ⓒ_____ pathogens around the world — mites, bacteria, fungi, parasites and a whole host of deadly viruses. But there is consensus among scientists that habitat loss, the intensification of agriculture and the routine use of agrochemicals are also playing havoc with bee populations and opening the door to disease. Bees need a varied diet to thrive. No single pollen source contains the vitamins, proteins, minerals and fats necessary for good nutrition.

1 **According to the passage, which of the following is true?**

① Pesticides are the main contributing factor in destruction of pollinating insects.

② Most pollinator species rely on steady and various pollen sources.

③ Wild bumblebees have avoided an infection to the disease.

④ Vegetarians are most affected by rapid decline in population of pollinators.

2 **What does Ⓐ"hit the nail on the head" mean?**

① to fall short of one's expectations

② to take credit for other people's work

③ to say something that is exactly right

④ to make a wrong guess and blame the wrong thing

3 Which of the following best describes the author's tone in the passage?

① detached and impartial

② resentful and blunt

③ self-deprecatory

④ anxious and concerned

4 Which of the following would be best for the blanks Ⓑ and Ⓒ?

① simplify — transmit

② complicate — spread

③ illuminate — scatter

④ deteriorate — eradicate

10

Ⓐ For decades, scientists have known that trees communicate with one another through a network of underground fungi, which even allows them to trade nutrients back and forth. This incredible discovery was first made by ecologist Suzanne Simard when she was researching her doctoral thesis over 20 years ago. She discovered that a very complex social relationship exists between various forms of plant life. One incredible example is the "hub tree," or "mother tree," which is the tallest tree in the forest that usually acts as a central hub for the underground network of fungi. Mother trees help the rest of the trees in the forest grow by supplying them with nutrients. In a similar fashion, older trees supply nutrients to younger trees that are just getting started.

Ⓑ In some cases, trees that are sick and unhealthy will receive a boost of nutrients for their neighbors. Conversely, if a tree determines that they are going to die, they will get rid of all of their nutrients and distribute them among its neighbors so they don't go to waste.

Ⓒ These processes make it possible for trees to survive through the harsh conditions that they will inevitably encounter, and allow older trees to nurture their offspring while they are more vulnerable.

Ⓓ On rare occasions, the web of fungi used by trees to communicate can be Ⓐ_____ by more selfish trees who use the network to enrich themselves at the cost of surrounding trees, but this type of activity is limited to a few select plant species. Generally, researchers have found trees to be altruistic and very generous with their nutrients.

Ⓔ This astonishing system explains why plant life has been so resilient through many centuries here on earth. The trees around us are not inanimate fixtures of our environment, but a living breathing ecosystem filled with relationships that are just as complex as, if not more so than, our human relationships.

1 According to paragraph Ⓐ, hub trees are called "mother trees" in that they _____ other trees in the forest.

① dissent

② care for

③ drop by

④ lie under the knife

⑤ teem with

2 According to paragraph ⒞, which of the following best summarizes the underlined These processes?

① underground communication systems that send and receive nutrients

② determinations to cut nutrients and get ready to die

③ willingness to distribute redundant nutrients to neighbouring trees

④ appropriations to make use of nutrients for themselves at the sacrifice of other trees

⑤ collaborations to send a boost of nutrients to the sick neighboring plant

3 Which word best fits the blank Ⓐ in paragraph ⒟?

① supplanted   ② bypassed

③ nurtured   ④ ameliorated

⑤ appropriated

4 According to the above passage, which of the following is true?

① Trees are able to send their nutrients to other trees but can't receive them.

② Trees will suffer retarded growth if they distribute nutrients among their neighbors.

③ Trees must provide underground fungi with nutrition to communicate with other trees.

④ A forest is not just an assembly of trees, but makes a kind of ecosystem where trees care for one another.

⑤ Trees are unwilling to share their nutrients with an ailing tree beside them.

해설편

01

흑사병은 큰 재앙이었다. 역사학자들은 여전히 흑사병이 발병한 시기에 대해 의견이 분분하다. 하지만 1348년과 1351년 사이 그리고 1361년과 1362년 사이에 유럽 대부분의 지역에서 (흑사병은) 절정에 달했다. 유럽 인구의 약 3분의 1이 목숨을 잃었다. 역사학자들은 흑사병의 경제 효과에 대해 의견 충돌했다. 대개 사람들은 흑사병이 발병한 당시와 그 후의 소작농들의 고난에 초점을 맞춘다. (그 시기에) 노동력 공급에 엄청난 감소가 있었다. 그리고 일반 경제이론에 따르면 노동자의 수가 줄어들면 임금 및 근무환경이 향상된다고 한다.

중세 정부들은 흑사병이 처음 발병한 후에 증대하는 노동력에 대해 분명히 우려했다. 영국에서 1348년 흑사병이 발발하고 약 1년 후에 처음 제안된 노동자 법령은 1345년 수준으로 임금을 정했다. 1351년에 통과된 프랑스 법령은 (영국 노동자 법령과) 매우 똑같은 것을 이루려고 했다. 그리고 1381년 노동자들의 반란 후에 영국의 고용주들은 심지어 더 구속적인 법안을 요구했다. 14세기 사회의 상류계층은 살아남은 노동자들이 그들의 특권적인 지위를 이용하는 것에 대해 우려했다.

1 ③   ▶ **내용파악**
노동자수가 줄어들면 임금 및 근무환경이 개선된다는 일반적인 경제이론과 달리 흑사병이 발병했을 때 실제로 노동자 수는 줄어들었지만 중세 정부들은 이를 우려하여 임금을 흑사병 발병이전 수준으로 정했다고 했으므로 이는 일반적인 경제이론이 그 당시의 상황을 설명할 수 없음을 지적하기 위해서이다. 따라서 ③이 정답이다.

2 ②   ▶ **내용일치**
흑사병이 발병한 시기에 대해서 역사학자들의 의견이 다르며, 두 번째 단락에서 영국에서 제안된 노동자 법령에서 노동자의 임금을 1345년 수준으로 정한 것을 봤을 때 1345년은 흑사병이 발병한 시기가 될 수 없다.

perish v. 멸망하다, 사라지다
peasant n. 농부, 소작농
uprising n. 반란, 폭동
clamour v. (큰 소리로) 요구하다
stratum n. (사회) 계층

02

마르쿠스 툴리우스 키케로(Marcus Tullius Cicero)는 공화정 마지막 시기의 로마의 정치가 겸 철학자로, 서구 역사상 가장 위대하고 가장 영향력 있는 연설가로 남아 있다. 그의 많은 유명한 정치적 소책자와 연설 중 가장 주목할 만한 것 가운데 하나는 카탈리나에 대한 첫 번째 연설로, 이것은 공화정을 전복시킬 음모를 꾸민 것에 대해 원로원 의원인 루시우스 세르기우스 카탈리나(Lucius Sergius Catiline)를 비난하는 내용을 담고 있다. 그 전 해의 집정관 선거에서 그의 정적(政敵) 키케로에게 패배한 데 화가 난 카탈리나는 기원전 63년에 있었던 선거에서 승리하고자 키케로와 다른 원로원 의원 몇몇을 암살하려는 음모를 꾸몄다. 그 음모가 발각되어 좌절되었을 때, 선거는 연기되었고, 원로원 회의는 다음날 보다 안전한 장소로 옮겨서 진행되어 그 음모에 대해 서로 이야기했다. 카탈리나는 원로원에 도착하여 모든 의원들을 놀라게 했으나, 키케로는 신속하게 제자리를 잡은 후에 카탈리나에 대한 첫 번째 연설을 했는데, 이것은 능숙한 솜씨를 자랑하는 기념비적인 연설로, 이로 인해 나머지 원로원 의원들은 카탈리나를 반역자로 탄핵하게 되었다. 카탈리나는 모반 음모를 함께 꾸민 이들과 그 도시를 떠났으며, 1년 후에 공화국 군인들과의 전투 중에 사망했다.

1 ④   ▶ **글의 주제**
키케로가 명연설을 통해 카탈리나의 모반 음모를 저지하고 반역자로 탄핵하게 한 이야기가 주를 이루고 있는데, 본문에서는 이 연설을 "the first Catilinarian Oration"으로 나타내고 있으므로, 정답으로는 ④가 적절하다.

influential a. 영향력을 미치는, 유력한
orator n. 연설자, 웅변가
tract n. (특히 종교·정치 관계의) 소책자
condemnation n. 비난; 유죄 판결
conspiracy n. 공모, 음모; 모반
consulship n. 집정관의 지위
weave v. (이야기·음모 등을) 꾸미다
assassinate v. 암살하다
foil v. (계략 따위를) 좌절시키다
prompt v. 자극[격려]하다; 촉구하다
denounce v. 공공연히 비난하다; 탄핵하다
traitor n. 반역자; 배신자
conspirator n. 공모자, 음모자

2 ③ ▶ **내용일치**

"카탈리나에 대한 '첫 번째' 연설"로 표현하고 있는 것은 이러한 주제의 연설이 더 있다는 것을 암시한다. 따라서 ③이 정답이다. ① 키케로의 연설은 카탈리나를 비난하는 내용이었다. ② 모반 음모는 실행에 옮겨지기 전에 발각되었다. ④ 집정관으로 선출된 사람은 키케로였다. ⑤ 탄핵당한 사람은 카탈리나였다.

03

프랜시스 베이컨(Francis Bacon)이 오늘날 중요한 점은 그가 자신의 불행에서 거리를 두고 야망의 문제들을 보편적으로 적절한 정도로 명백하게 분석할 수 있었다는 것이다. 그는 자신이 설교한 미덕과 정직의 원칙들을 그대로 지킬 수 없었다는 것을 부끄러워하지 않고 인정했다. 그의 말에 따르면, 그는 별개의 두 인생을 살았으며 그의 이상은 예견치 못한 유혹으로 좌절되었다. "지금까지 나의 순례(인생) 여정에서 내 영혼은 낯선 사람이었습니다."라고 그는 말했다. 야망의 보상은 그가 기대한 것이 아니었다. 그는 자신이 권력을 추구하고 자유를 잃어버리려는, 즉 다른 사람들에 대한 지배력은 추구하고 자신에 대한 지배력은 잃어버리려는, 낯선 욕망의 함정에 아무 생각 없이 빠져버렸음을 너무나 늦게 깨달았다. 그는 그것을 설명할 수 없었으며, 왜 그렇게 많은 다른 사람들이 그 낯선 욕망의 고통을 겪는지도 설명할 수 없었다. 그로서는 놀랍게도, 고위직은 그를 판에 박힌 행정업무를 맡은 하인의 지위로 격하시켰다. 권력을 성취하는 과정은 때때로 비열했으며, 권력을 유지하는 것은 교활했고, 자신이 더 이상 과거의 자신이 아니라고 느낄 때 인생에 대한 모든 흥미를 잃어버리기 때문에 권력을 잃는 것은 우울한 일이다. 성공은 너무나 비싼 대가를 치르고 얻어진다. 달리 말해, 사람들은 모욕에 의해 고위직에 오른다. 권력에 대한 그의 굶주림은 사실인즉 그를 영향력 있는 사람에게 아첨하고 약속을 하고 한때 친구였으나 더 이상 쓸모가 없는 사람들을 배신하는 그런 기술의 대가로 만들어버렸다. 그는 권력이 그를 다른 사람들로부터 고립시켰다고 결론지었다. 그는 다른 사람들의 잘못은 가장 먼저 책잡으면서도 자신의 잘못은 가장 늦게 인정하는 사람이었다.

1 ④ ▶ **글의 주제**

이 글은 베이컨이 어떤 삶을 살았는지를 주로 다루고 있는데, 가장 두드러진 특징은 '자신이 설교한 미덕과 정직의 원칙들을 그대로 지키지 않았다'고 한 것과 '그는 다른 사람들의 잘못은 가장 먼저 책잡으면서도 자신의 잘못은 가장 늦게 인정하는 사람이었다'고 한 것에서 알 수 있듯이 겉 다르고 속 다른 '위선적인 면'이다. 따라서 ④가 글의 주제로 적절하다. 이런 자신의 삶의 위선적인 면을 베이컨은 솔직히 인정했다는 것이 그의 삶을 오늘날 우리에게도 중요하게 만든다고 저자는 지적한다.

2 ② ▶ **부분이해**

앞 문장에서 '자신이 설교한 미덕과 정직의 원칙들을 그대로 지킬 수 없었다'고 했으므로 베이컨은 미덕과 정직의 원칙들을 설교하는 삶과 이 원칙들에 위배된 실생활의 삶이라는 두 가지 인생을 살았다고 할 수 있다. 미덕과 정직의 원칙들에 위배된 실생활은 곧 자신의 세속적인 야망을 추구하는 삶이므로 ②가 적절하다. 이것은 이상을 꿈꾸는 삶과 이상을 저버리고 현실에 타협한 삶이라고도 할 수 있다.

3 ③ ▶ **부분이해**

lick the boots of는 '~에게 아첨하다'는 뜻이고 the influential(영향력 있는 사람)은 곧 상위자(superordinate)나 직장 상사(boss)를 의미하는데, 이런 사람에게 아첨한다는 것은 이런 사람의 눈에 들려고 하고 환심을 사려는 것이므로 ③의 '직장상사의 환심을 사다'가 ⓑ가 의미하는 것이다.

---

distance oneself from ~로부터 거리를 두다, 초연하게 바라보다

lucidity n. 명백함, 명료함

preach v. 설교하다

pilgrimage n. 순례

unthinkingly ad. 생각 없이, 경솔하게

reduce v. 격하시키다

base a. 비열한

slippery a. 미끄러운, 잡기 힘든, 교활한

melancholy a. 우울한

indignity n. 모욕, 경멸

dignity n. 존엄, 위엄, 품위; 고위

betray v. 배신하다

find fault with ~의 흠을 잡다, 비난하다

04

일시적으로 왕가가 축출되었던 기간이 지나 영국의 왕정이 공식적으로 다시 복고된 것은 1660년 5월 8일 찰스 2세(Charles II)가 왕권을 회복하면서부터였다. 왕위가 비어 있었던 이유는 1640년대 초반의 사건들 때문이었는데, 당시 왕정에 반발하는 내란(청교도 혁명)이 최초로 일어났었다. 이후 1640년대가 끝나기 전에 두 번째 봉기가 일어났고, 봉기가 끝나기 전인 1649년에 찰스 1세(Charles I)에 대한 사형선고가 승인되어 찰스 1세는 퇴위당하고 처형되고 말았다. 청교도군 사령관 올리버 크롬웰(Oliver Cromwell)이 그 빈자리를 메우며 새로운 청교도 코먼웰스의 수장으로 등극했다. 크롬웰의 새로운 국가는 종교적 이상 수호를 추구하고 왕정 억압을 청산했으나 결국 제한적인 성공으로 끝나고 말았다. 그가 죽은 뒤, 아들 리처드 크롬웰(Richard Cromwell)이 그의 자리를 이어받았으나 아버지의 위업을 지속시킬 만큼 강력한 지도자가 아닌 것으로 밝혀지게 되었다. 그는 이내 군 통제권을 상실하고 권좌에서 물러났다.

리처드 크롬웰이 축출된 직후 왕정 체제로 다시 돌아가려는 움직임이 점진적으로 일어났지만, 크롬웰 정부에 남아 있는 총독들 일부의 반발이 〈촉진되었다〉. 영국 의회, 즉 국회는 처음에 부분적으로 군부에 의해 복원되었다. 이는 유명한 '잔여국회'라고 통칭되는데, 그 규모와 무력함 때문이었다. 하지만, 곧바로 국회는 완전히 회복되었으며 1660년 4월 25일 영국 국회는 12년 만에 처음으로 다시 개최될 수 있었다. 5월 8일이 되자, 코먼웰스와 호국경 전 시대에 걸쳐 찰스 1세의 아들 찰스 2세가 사실상 나라의 정당한 통치자라고 발표했다. 망명 중이었던 찰스 2세는 영국 국회의 추대를 승낙하고 귀국하여 1660년 5월 29일 왕위에 복귀하였다.

1 ④　▶ **논지의 흐름상 적절하지 않은 어구 고르기**
왕정체제의 반대편에 서있는 크롬웰의 아들이 축출당한 이후, 왕정 체제로 다시 돌아가려는 움직임이 점진적으로 있었다고 했는데, 이에 대해 크롬웰 정부의 잔여세력의 저항이 있었다고 했으므로 왕정복고에 '방해가 되었을' 것이다. 그런데, ⓓ에서 expedite는 '촉진하다, 신속히 처리하다'는 뜻이므로 글의 흐름상 적절치 않다. 따라서 expedited를 impeded(방해받다)로 고쳐야 한다.

2 ④　▶ **내용일치**
① 찰스 1세는 추방된 후 처형된 것은 아니었다. ② 올리버 크롬웰은 찰스 1세를 처형했을 뿐, 왕족의 씨를 말렸다는 말은 언급되지 않았다. ③ 왕정복고의 움직임은 크롬웰 정부세력의 반발로 방해를 받았다고 했다. ④ blue-blooded는 '왕족 혈통의'라는 뜻으로 처형당한 찰스 1세의 아들 찰스 2세가 크롬웰의 아들인 리차드 이후 왕좌에 올랐으므로 ④가 정답이다.

3 ②　▶ **부분이해**
monarchy는 '군주제'라는 뜻으로 통치권이 군주에게 있는 국가를 의미하므로 ②가 정답이다.

restoration n. 회복; 복구, 부흥
monarchy n. 군주제[정치, 국]
temporary a. 일시적인, 임시의
eliminate v. 없애다, 제거하다
throne n. 왕좌, 왕위, 왕권
civil war 내란, 내전
break out (전쟁 등이) 발발[발생]하다
uprising n. 봉기, 반란, 폭동
death warrant 사형 집행 영장
depose v. 물러나게 하다, 퇴위시키다
behead v. 목을 베다, 참수하다
void n. 빈자리, 공석
do away with 버리다, 처분하다, 폐지하다
repression n. 탄압, 진압, 억압
take over 인계받다
remove v. 쫓아[몰아]내다, 해고하다
expedite v. 촉진시키다; 신속히 처리하다
resistance n. 저항, 반대
Rump Parliament 잔부(殘部) 의회
the Protectorate n. (Cromwell 부자(父子)에 의한) 호민관 정치
rightful a. 합법적인, 적법한, 정당한
exile n. 망명, 추방
invitation n. 초대, 안내; 유인

05

조셉 이그나스 기요틴(Joseph Ignace Guillotin) 박사는 자신의 이름을 딴 처형 기계를 발명하지 않았다. 그러나 사형 선고를 받은 모든 죄수들이 인도주의와 평등에 입각해 참수형에 처해져야 한다고 1789년 10월 10일 (프랑스의) 국민의회에 제안한 사람은 기요틴 박사였다.

Ⓓ 그 당시 참수형은 단언코 가장 인간적인 처형 방식으로 간주되었고 많은 국가에서 귀족들에게만 허락되었다. 평민인 죄수들은 느린 속도로 교수형에 처해지거나 바퀴에서 몸이 부러지거나 (끔찍할 정도로 잔인한 형태의 처형) 화형을 당했다. 획일화된, 속도가 빠르고 인도적인 죽음이라는 발상은 혁명적인 사고와 보다 같은 선상에 있었다.

Ⓒ 국민의회는 1791년 3월 25일 참수형을 유일한 처형 방식으로 인정하는 법령을 정식으로 통과시켰으며, 이는 1792년 3월 25일 법률화되었다. 그러나 사형 선고를 받은 모든 사람들을 칼로 처형하는 것은 실행 불가능하다고 지적한 당시 공식 사형집행인이었던 산손(Sanson)이 가리켰듯이 여기에는 작은 문제점이 있었다.

execution n. 처형
bear v. (칭호 등을) 가지다
propose v. 제안하다
Constituent Assembly (프랑스의) 제헌 국민의회
condemned a. 유죄 선고를 받은, 사형수의
criminal n. 범인, 범죄자
behead v. 목을 베다, 참수형에 처하다
on the grounds of ~때문에
humanity n. 자비, 인도
humane a. 인도적인

Ⓐ 죄수의 머리를 단칼에 베려면 숙련된 사형집행인은 참수를 하기 위해 엄청난 힘, 떨지 않는 손과 좋은 시력을 필요로 한다. 산손은 옳았다. 왜냐하면 공포정치 시대에는 처형률이 몇 명 되지 않는 숙련된 사형집행인들의 수행 능력을 훨씬 넘어서는 압도적인 비율에 도달했기 때문이다.

Ⓑ 모종의 기계가 필요하다는 것이 명백해졌기에 외과학회 회원인 앙뚜안 루이(Antoine Louis) 박사의 자문을 통해 그러한 기계가 고안되었고 만들어졌다.

처음에는 이 기계가 루이종이나 루이제트로 알려졌었지만 이 선한 외과의사에게는 의심할 여지없이 다행스럽게도 제안자의 이름을 따서 기요틴으로 알려지게 되었다.

1 ④ ▶ **단락배열**

제시된 첫 문장에서 기요틴 박사는 "모든 죄수들이 인도주의와 평등에 입각해 참수형에 처해져야 한다"고 제안했다. 따라서 이어지는 단락에서는 왜 참수형이 인도주의 정신과 들어맞는지에 관한 내용이 와야 할 것이다. 따라서 이에 대한 부연설명을 하는 Ⓓ가 제일 처음에 와야 하며, Ⓓ에서 참수형이 그 당시 가장 인간적인 방법으로 여겨졌으며, 귀족에게만 허락되는 비교적 덜 고통스러운 처형 방법이라는 '긍정적인 면'을 언급하고 있다. 따라서 Ⓓ 다음에는 이런 긍정적인 면을 가진 참수형을 기요틴 박사가 제안한 것에 대한 결과인 '참수형의 법제화'를 다룬 Ⓒ가 와야 한다. 그러나 Ⓒ에서 이런 인도주의적인 처형 방법인 참수형에 대한 문제점이 있다는 내용이 나오므로, Ⓒ 다음에는, 참수형에 대한 문제점으로 '죄수의 머리를 단칼에 베기 위해서는 엄청난 힘과 떨리지 않는 손 등이 필요하다', '공포정치 시대에는 처형 비율이 일부 사형집행인의 능력을 넘어섰다'는 내용이 나오는 Ⓐ가 그다음에 와야 하며, Ⓐ에서 인간의 힘으로는 이런 참수형을 감당할 수 없다고 했으므로, 이어지는 내용으로는 참수할 때 사람을 대신하는 '기계'에 대한 내용인 Ⓑ가 맨 마지막에 와야 한다. 또한 Ⓑ에서 언급된 앙뚜안 루이 박사의 이름이 맨 마지막 단락에 이어지므로 ④가 전체 글의 흐름상 자연스럽다.

2 ① ▶ **동의어**

staggering은 '엄청난'이란 뜻으로 쓰였으므로 ①의 enormous가 정답이다. ② 대수롭지 않은, 사소한 ③ 종교(상)의 ④ 흥미 있는, 재미있는

3 ④ ▶ **내용일치**

① 기요틴은 참수형을 집행하기 위해 만들어진 기계이다. ② 기요틴은 참수형을 제안한 기요틴 박사의 이름을 땄을 뿐, 기요틴 박사가 만든 것은 아니었다. ③ 기요틴은 소름끼치는 다른 처형 방법을 대체하는 참수형을 위해 만들어진 기계였다. ④ 기요틴은 귀족과 평민 모두에게 허용되도록 법제화된 참수형을 위한 기계로 평민에게만 기요틴이 이용된다는 것은 사실과 다르므로 ④가 정답이다.

06

미국의 독립선언문은 13개의 미국 식민지로 이루어진 대륙회의가 영국과 분리할 것을 만장일치로 내린 결의를 전 세계에 공표하였다. 그러나 미국 독립선언문의 진정한 혁명적인 의미는 지금과 마찬가지로 그때도 정치적 합법성의 새로운 기초가 국민이 주권을 가진다는 데 있다는 선언이라는 점이다. 미국인들의 궁극적인 호소는 인위적인 법령이나 변하는 시대정신에 대한 호소가 아니라, 모든 인간이 선천적으로 가지고 있는 권리에 대한 호소였다. 이들 권리들은 영구적인 '자연계와 자연신의 법칙'에서 발견된다. 그러한 것으로서 독립선언문의 의미는 시간과 환경이라는 특성을 초월한다.

독립선언문을 작성하는 데 있어 주변 상황들은 독립선언문의 예외주의적인 주장들을 우리가 더욱 정당하게 평가하도록 만든다. 1776년 6월 7일 리처드 헨리 리(Richard Henry Lee)의 결의안 이후 대륙회의가 영국으로부터 식민지들의 독립을 연구할 목적으로 위원회를 지정했을 때는 영국을 상대로 전쟁이 2년 이상 맹렬히 계속되던 중이었다. 존 애덤스(John Adams), 벤저민 프랭클린(Benjamin Franklin), 로저 셔먼(Roger Sherman), 그리고 로버트 리빙스턴(Robert Livingston)은 공식 독립선언문의 초안을 작성하기 위해 그들의 동료인 토머스 제퍼슨(Thomas Jefferson)에 의지했는데, 그들은 이 독립선언문의 초안을 거의 수정하지 않은 채 대륙회의에 제출하였다. 7월 2일 대륙회의는 (미국의) 독립에 찬성하는 투표를 하였으며, 독립선언문의 단어선택을 계속해서 논의했으며(이 논의 속에서 눈에 띄는 점은 토머스 제퍼슨의 격렬한 노예제도를 비난한 대목을 삭제했다는 것이다.) 7월 4일 저녁에 독립선언문이 만장일치로 승인되었다.

---

noble a. 고귀한

horrendously ad. 끔찍하게

be burnt at the stake 화형을 당하다

be in line with ~와 같은 선상에 있다

duly ad. 정당하게

decree n. 법령, 명령

executioner n. 사형집행인

impracticality n. 실행 불가능함

sever v. 절단하다, 자르다, 분리하다

stroke n. (손을) 한 번 놀리기, 일격

the Terror 공포정치

staggering a. 압도적인, 엄청난

headsman n. 목 베는 사람, 사형집행인

initially ad. 처음에는

guillotine n. 기요틴, 단두대

---

declaration n. 선언

independence n. 독립

unanimous a. 만장일치의

colony n. 식민지

legitimacy n. 합법성

sovereignty n. 주권, 통치권

appeal n. 매력, 호소

decree n. 법령, 포고

transcend v. 초월하다

exceptionalist a. 예외주의(자)의

rage v. 맹렬히 계속되다

turn to ~에 의지하다

draft v. 초안을 작성하다

wording n. 표현법, 단어선택

1 ①　▶ **빈칸완성**
'not A but B' 구문이 쓰였다. 따라서 빈칸 Ⓐ에는 man-made(인위적인)와는 반대되는 의미인 inherently(선천적으로), indigenously(타고나서)가 적절하며, 빈칸 Ⓑ 앞에 이런 선천적인 권리는 영구적인 자연법에서 발견된다고 했으며, 빈칸 Ⓑ 다음에 독립선언문의 의미는 시간과 환경이라는 특성을 초월한다고 했으므로, Ⓑ에는 인과적인 뜻인 As such(그러한 것으로서)와 On that account(그래서)가 적절하다. 따라서 두 빈칸 모두에 적절한 ①의 inherently ― As such가 정답이다. ② 인위적으로 ― 후불로 ③ 타고나서 ― 이에 반하여 ④ 세심하게 ― 그래서 ⑤ 교묘하게 ― 귀납적으로

2 ⑤　▶ **빈칸완성**
"미국의 독립선언문은 13개의 미국 식민지로 이루어진 대륙회의가 영국과 분리할 것을 만장일치로 내린 결의(unanimous decision)를 전 세계에 공표하였다."고 했다. 따라서 빈칸 Ⓒ에도 독립선언문을 발표한 주체인 대륙회의가 독립선언문을 '만장일치로' 승인했다는 말이 되어야 하므로 ⑤의 without dissent가 정답이다. ① 태연하게 ② 조건부로 ③ 서론 없이, 단도직입적으로 ④ 원한을 가지고

3 ③　▶ **내용일치**
① 대륙회의는 독립선언문의 단어선택을 계속해서 논의했다고 했으며, 이 논의 속에서 토머스 제퍼슨의 격렬한 노예제도를 비난한 대목을 삭제했다고 했다. ② 13개의 식민지가 영국으로부터 독립을 선언하자마자 독립국가로 인정을 받았는지는 본문의 내용만으로는 알 수 없다. ④ 벤자민 프랭클린과 로버트 리빙스턴은 토머스 제퍼슨이 초안으로 작성한 독립선언문을 거의 수정하지 않은 채 대륙회의에 제출했다고 했으므로 제퍼슨의 초안에 동의했다고 볼 수 있다. ⑤ 독립선언의 의미는 시간과 환경이라는 특성을 초월한다고 했다. ③ "미국 독립선언문의 진정한 혁명적인 의미는 지금과 마찬가지로 그때도 정치적 합법성의 새로운 기초가 국민이 주권을 가진다는 데 있다는 선언이라는 점이다."라고 했으므로, ③이 정답이다.

07

앨버트 아인슈타인(Albert Einstein)은 독일태생의 이론물리학자로, 일반 상대성 이론을 개발했는데, 이 일반 상대성 이론은 양자역학과 함께 현대 물리학의 양대 기둥 중 하나이다. 자신의 질량에너지 등가법칙인 E=mc2('세계에서 가장 유명한 방정식'이라 불려왔다)로 가장 널리 알려져 있지만, 아인슈타인은 '이론물리학에 대한 그의 공로와 특히 광전효과법칙을 발견한 것'으로 1921년에 노벨물리학상을 받았다. 이 광전효과법칙은 양자이론을 세우는 데 아주 중요했다.
그의 활동 초창기 즈음에, 아인슈타인은 고전역학 법칙들과 전자기장 법칙을 조화시키기에는 뉴턴역학이 더 이상 충분하지 않다고 생각했다. 이런 생각이 그의 특수 상대성 이론을 개발하게끔 했다. 그러나 아인슈타인은 이 특수 상대성 이론이 중력장으로도 확대될 수 있다는 것을 알았으며, 1916년 후속이론인 중력이론으로 일반 상대성 이론에 관한 논문을 발표했다. 아인슈타인은 계속해서 통계역학과 양자이론 문제를 다루었는데, 이로 인해 입자이론과 분자의 운동을 설명할 수 있게 되었다. 아인슈타인은 또한 빛의 열 특성을 조사했는데, 이것은 빛에 대한 광자이론의 토대를 마련해주었다. 1917년, 아인슈타인은 일반 상대성 이론을 적용하여 우주의 대규모 구조의 모형을 만들었다.

1 ③　▶ **내용파악**
① 전자기장 법칙, ② 빛의 열 특성, ④ 빛의 광자이론은 모두 아인슈타인이 이론을 만들기 위한 조사대상이거나 이론을 만드는 계기가 되는 것인 반면, ③의 광전효과법칙은 아인슈타인이 직접 발견한 것이므로 ③이 정답이다.

2 ③　▶ **내용파악**
아인슈타인은 기존의 뉴턴역학이 고전역학 법칙들과 전자기장 법칙을 조화시키기에 충분하지 않다고 생각했다고 했으며, 이런 생각으로 특수 상대성 이론이 나오게 되었다고 했다. 또한 아인슈타인은 특수 상대성 이론을 중력에도 적용이 가능하다는 것을 깨닫고 일반 상대성 이론을 발표하게 되었다고 했으며, 이 이론을 통계역학과 양자이론과 빛의 열 특성 그리고 우주이론 등 여러 다른 분야에도 적용했다고 했으므로 ③이 이 글의 내용과 부합된다. ① 아인슈타인이 일반 상대성 이론에 반하는 입자이론과 분자의 운동을 설명한 것은 아니다. ② 아인슈타인이 일반 상대성 이론으로 떼돈을 벌었는지 여부는 본문

theory of relativity 상대성 이론

pillar n. 기둥, 지주

in company with ~와 함께

quantum n. 양자

mechanics n. 역학

equivalence n. 등가, 동치

equation n. 방정식, 등식

photoelectric a. 광전기의

inception n. 처음, 시작

reconcile v. 조화시키다, 조정하다

electromagnetic field 전자기장

gravitational field 중력장

subsequent a. 뒤이어 일어나는, 뒤이은

particle n. 극소량; 입자

molecule n. 분자; 미립자

thermal property 열 특성

photon n. <물리> 광자

에서 알 수 없으며, 특수 상대성 이론의 응용으로 나온 것이 일반 상대성 이론이다. ④ 특수 상대성 이론의 응용으로 나온 것이므로 두 이론은 깊은 관련이 있다고 봐야 할 것이다.

3 ④　　▶ **내용파악**
첫 번째 문단의 마지막 문장에서 후자인 광전효과법칙이 양자이론을 세우는 데 있어 아주 중요했다고 했으므로 ④가 정답이다.

4 ①　　▶ **동의어**
이 글에서 inception은 '시작'이라는 뜻으로 쓰였으므로 ① beginning이 동의어로 적절하다. ② 꼭대기, 정점 ③ 절정, 정점 ④ 밑바닥, 최악의 순간

08

홀로코스트 기간 동안, 때때로 '모슬렘'이라고 불린 '무젤만'은 건강 상태가 매우 좋지 않고 삶에 대한 의지를 포기한 나치의 포로수용소에 있던 포로를 지칭하는 속어였다. 무젤만은 '걸어 다니는 시체' 또는 '산송장'으로 여겨졌는데, 이들에게 세상에 남은 시간은 거의 없었다.
Ⓒ 포로수용소의 포로들이 이런 상황에 빠지는 것은 어려운 일이 아니었다. 아주 고된 강제 노동 수용소에서 마저 배급량이 매우 제한되었으며 옷은 포로들을 악천후에서 적절히 보호하지 못했다.
Ⓐ 오랜 시간의 강제 노동에 더하여 이런 열악한 상황으로 인해 포로들은 체온을 조절하는데 필수적인 칼로리만 소모하게 되었다. 체중 감량이 급속히 일어났으며, 많은 포로들의 신진 대사 시스템은 이런 제한된 칼로리 섭취로 신체를 유지할 만큼 충분히 강하지 않았다.
Ⓑ 게다가 매일 이어지는 굴욕과 고문은 지극히 평범한 일도 어려운 일이 되게 만들었다. 면도는 유리조각으로 해야 했으며, 신발끈이 끊어져도 대체되지 않았다. 화장실용 휴지가 부족했으며, 눈이 오는 겨울철에 입을 옷이 없었고 몸을 씻을 수 있는 물이 없던 것은 포로수용소의 수감자들이 겪었던 일상적인 위생 문제 중 일부에 불과했다.
Ⓓ 이러한 가혹한 상황만큼이나 중요했던 것은 희망이 사라진 것이었다. 포로수용소의 포로들은 얼마나 오랫동안 이 시련을 견뎌야할지 알 수 없었다. 매일이 한주처럼 느껴졌기 때문에, 몇 해는 수십 년처럼 느껴졌다. 많은 사람들에게, 희망이 사라진 것은 그들이 살아갈 의지를 없애버렸다.
포로들이 '무젤만' 상태에 추락하게 되는 것은 이들이 병에 걸려 굶주리고 어떠한 희망도 사라질 때였다. 이 상황은 신체적으로나 심리적으로 무젤만이 살아갈 모든 욕구를 상실하게 만들었다.

1 ③　　▶ **단락배열**
홀로코스트 기간 동안, 건강 상태가 좋지 않고 삶에 대한 의지를 포기한 "무젤만(Muselmann)"에 대해 첫 단락에서 설명한 다음, 앞 문장에서 이들이 처한 상황을 this condition으로 받은 Ⓒ가 와야 한다. 그리고 Ⓒ에서 배급과 악천후에 몸을 보호하지 못하는 옷을 예로 들었는데, 이 상황을 these poor conditions로 받은 Ⓐ가 그 뒤에 와야 한다. 그리고 Ⓑ에서 수용소의 포로들이 겪는 추가적인 어려움을 설명하고, 이로 인해 살아갈 의지를 잃게 되었다고 한 Ⓓ로 글이 이어져야 마지막 단락과 문맥상 어울리게 된다.

2 ①　　▶ **글의 제목**
이 글은 홀로코스트 기간에 포로들이 나치 수용소의 열악한 상황에서 삶에 대한 의지를 잃고 어떻게 무젤만이 되는지를 설명하고 있으므로 ①이 글의 제목으로 적절하다.

3 ②　　▶ **내용일치**
나치 강제 수용소의 열악한 상황으로 인해 포로수용소의 포로들이 시련을 못 견디고, 병에 걸려 굶주리고 살아갈 욕구를 상실하게 됐다고 했으므로 ②가 이 글의 내용과 일치하지 않는다.

Holocaust n. 홀로코스트(1930~40년대 나치에 의한 유대인 대학살)
Muselmann n. 무젤만(수용소에서는 살아 있으나 살아 있다고 말할 수 있는 특성을 갖지 못한 자들을 가리킴)
concentration camp 강제 수용소
metabolic a. 신진 대사의
intake n. 섭취(량)
humiliation n. 굴욕, 굴복
banal a. 지극히 평범한, 따분한, 시시한
inmate n. 입소자, 수감자
slip into (상태에) 빠지다
ration n. (식료품·연료 등의) 일정한 배급량, 할당량
the elements 악천후, 비바람
ordeal n. 호된 시련, 고된 체험

09

로버트 맬서스(Robert Malthus)는 그의 역사적인 저서 『인구론(Essay on the Principle of Population)』에서 인구가 계속 통제되지 않는다면 빈곤과 기근이 전 세계적인 재앙이 되리라는 가설을 세웠다. 맬서스는 식물과 동물이 생존 가능한 개체수보다 항상 더 많은 자손을 생산한다는 개념을 자신의 이론의 근거로 삼았다. 그는 더 나아가 인간들, 즉 하층계급이 그와 다를 바 없으며, 인류의 파멸을 막기 위해 억제 조치가 필요하다고 생각했다. 맬서스에 따르면, 인구가 균형을 이룬 사회에서는 인구 증가가 질병과 같은 '적극적인 억제'와 결혼의 연기와 같은 '예방적인 억제'의 통제를 받는다고 한다.

정치경제학자였던 맬서스는 19세기 영국사회에서 사회가 나아가는 방향에 대해 우려했다. 그에 따르면, 높은 출산율과 자원의 공급 부족, 무책임한 노동 계층에 의해 생활 여건이 계속 악화되고 있었다. 그는 하층민 스스로가 경제적으로 부양할 수 있는 정도의 자녀만을 낳는다면 인구는 통제될 수 있다는 견해를 제시했다. 또한 하층계급이 사치에 맛을 들이면 가정을 이루는 것을 늦추게 되고, 그 결과 자녀도 적게 낳을 것이라고 생각했다. 맬서스는 많은 논란을 불러일으킨 이 논문으로 저명인사가 되었지만, 많은 사람들, 특히 노동 계층은 그의 비관주의를 개탄했으며 심지어는 그를 '파멸의 예언자'라고 부르기도 했다. 찰스 다윈(Charles Darwin)은 맬서스의 에세이를 읽고 자연도태에 관한 이론의 영감을 얻었다. 다윈은 식량이 모자랄 정도로 자손이 많아지면 형제자매 간의 경쟁이 보다 심해진다는 점에서 인구과잉을 필요한 현상으로 보았다. 이런 발상에서 그의 적자생존 이론이 나오게 된 것이다.

1 ③ ▶ **내용파악**
첫 단락의 마지막 문장에서 맬서스는 인구가 균형을 이룬 사회에서는 질병과 같은 '적극적인 억제'와 결혼의 연기와 같은 '예방적인 억제'가 있다고 주장했다.

2 ① ▶ **내용파악**
맬서스는 하층계급 스스로가 경제적으로 부양할 수 있는 정도의 자녀만을 낳는다면 인구가 억제될 수 있다고 했다. 이는 맬서스가 하층계급이 부양 능력 이상으로 아이를 낳는 것을 인구 증가의 주요 원인으로 보고 있었음을 의미한다.

3 ③ ▶ **내용파악**
찰스 다윈은 맬서스의 에세이를 읽고 '자연도태설'에 관한 영감을 얻었고, 적자생존의 이론을 내놓았다. 저자가 다윈을 언급한 것은 맬서스의 이론이 당대에 또 하나의 중요한 이론에 큰 영향을 미쳤다는 것을 설명하기 위해서다. 저자는 두 학자를 비교하거나 차이를 설명하고 있지 않으므로, ①, ②는 정답이 될 수 없으며, 생물학자인 다윈은 맬서스와 동시대 인물이므로 ④ 또한 정답이 될 수 없다.

4 ① ▶ **빈칸완성**
맬서스는 무책임한 노동계층에 의해 생활여건이 안 좋아진다는 생각을 하였으므로 그의 논란은 노동계층 사이에 논란을 불러일으켰을 것이며, 빈칸 뒤에서 노동계층은 맬서스를 '파멸의 예언자'라고 했으므로 그의 이런 비관주의에 대해 노동계층의 사람들은 '개탄했을' 것이다. 따라서 ①이 정답이다. ② 인정하다 ③ 헤아리다 ④ 묵인하다

unregulated a. 규제되지 않은
offspring n. 자손, 자식
postponement n. 연기
steadily ad. 지속적으로
take it upon oneself to ~의 책임을 떠맡다
go as far as to ~정도까지 하다
doom n. 파멸
natural selection 자연 선택[도태]

10

제2차 세계대전 후인 전후시대는 미국 각지에 있는 아프리카계 미국인에게 부여된 2류 시민권에 반대하는 전례 없는 에너지가 폭발한 시기로 특징지어졌다. 시민 불복종, 비폭력 저항, 행진, 항의, 보이콧, 그리고 집회 같은 전략을 동원해서 인종 분리와 인종 차별에 맞선 저항은 신문과 라디오와 TV 기자들과 카메라맨들이 인종 불평등을 끝내고자 하는 투쟁을 상세히 기록해서 널리 알림에 따라 전국적인 관심을 받게 되었다. 1955년 12월 앨라배마(Alabama) 주 몽고메리(Montgomery)에서 로사 파크스(Rosa Parks)가 한 백인 남성에게 자리를 양보하는 것을 거절하고 체포되었을 때 그녀는 미국의 흑인 민권 운동이 일찍이 경험한 적이 없었던 결정적인 모멘텀을 만들어내는 일련의 사건들을 촉발시켰다. 버스를 보이콧하는 운동을 벌이기로 결정하고 나서 아프리카계 미국인 공동체는 곧 보이콧 운동을 지휘할 새로운 조직을 만들었다. 그 어떤 누가 희망했던 것보다 성공적이었던 보이콧 운동은 흑인과 백인을 분리하는 버스를 금지하는 1956년의 대법원 판결을 이끌어 냈다. 1960년 그린즈버러(Greensboro)에 위치한 노스캐롤라이나 농업 기술 대학에 적을 두고 있는 4명의 흑인 신입생이 울워스(F. W. Woolworth) 식당에 걸어 들어가 조용히 간이식당 식탁에 앉았다. 그들은 음식을 서빙 받지 못했다. 그러나 그들은 간이식당이 문을 닫을 때까지 식탁에 앉아있었다. 다음 날 아침 그들은 스물다섯 명의 다른 학생들을 더 데리고 그 간이식당에 갔다. 2주 후에 유사한 시위들이 몇몇 도시들로 퍼져 나갔고 1년이 채 지나지 않아 남부와 북부에 있는 100여개 이상의 도시들에서 유사한 평화적 시위가 벌어졌다. 1963년 8월 28일 행해진 워싱턴의 위대한 행진은 전 미국인들의 관심을 사로잡았다. 이 행진에는 애초에 예상했던 10만 명을 훌쩍 뛰어넘어 20만을 헤아리는 인파가 모여들어 행진을 조직한 사람들조차 깜짝 놀라게 만들었다. 흑인들과 백인들은 나란히 케네디 대통령과 국회를 향해 아프리카계 미국인들에게도 공공시설물, 양질의 교육, 충분한 고용, 그리고 정갈한 주택 등의 혜택을 누릴 수 있는 동등한 권리를 달라고 요구했다. 링컨 기념관 앞에서 열린 대중 집회가 진행되는 동안 앨라배마 주 몽고메리에서 성공적인 버스 보이콧 운동을 이끌었던 젊은 목사 마틴 루터 킹(Martin Luther King, Jr.)은 "나는 꿈이 있습니다."라는 후렴구가 들어가는 감동적인 연설을 했다.

1 ④   ▶ **글의 제목**

이 글은 제2차 세계대전 이후 전개된 미국 흑인민권운동의 역사를 기술하고 있다.

2 ⑤   ▶ **내용추론**

마틴 루터 킹은 인종 차별에 맞서 집회를 이끌었다고 했으므로 정부의 요구를 따랐다고 볼 수 없으며, 또한 이것이 이유가 되어 워싱턴의 위대한 행진을 비폭력적으로 이끈 것이 아니므로 ⑤가 정답이다.

3 ③   ▶ **빈칸완성**

빈칸 앞의 형용사가 similar이므로 앞에 나온 그냥 식당 안에 앉아 있기만 하는 비폭력적인 방법과 같이 ③ peaceful(평화적인)이 와야 한다. ① 폭력적인 ② 활기 없는 ④ 경솔한 ⑤ 선정적인

era n. 연대, 기원, 시대

unprecedented a. 전례가 없는, 새로운

accord v. 부여하다

segregation n. 분리, 인종차별

disobedience n. 불순종

document v. 상세히 기록하다

momentum n. 운동량; 타성; 여세, 힘; 추진력

stroll v. 한가롭게 거닐다

lunch counter (미) 간이식당(의 식탁)

rivet v. 고정시키다; 사로잡다

preacher n. 설교자

refrain n. 후렴구

02 심리·교육

01

"헬레나(Helena)가 연봉이 올랐어. (그런데) 나는 하나도 놀랍지 않아. 사장에게 추파를 날리던 걸 보면 뻔하지."라고 자신이 승진하길 원하는 한 동료가 투덜거린다. "아 그 깡마른 애 말이지? 걔 말이야. 신경성 식욕 부진증에 걸린 게 분명해."라고 그녀의 친구가 답한다.

아, 뒷담화가 주는 안락함이란! 은밀하게 주고받는 악의적인 말 몇 마디가 우리에게 활기를 불어넣어 줄 수 있다. 친구들과, 동료들과, 또는 가족들과 다른 사람들에 대해 나쁜 말을 하면 기분이 좋아진다는 것이다.

이론(논리)적으로는 아무리 우리가 뒷담화를 못마땅해 할지라도, 뒷담화는 (우리에게) 매우 흔한 행동이라고 사회심리학자인 로랑 베그(Laurent Bègue)는 주장한다. "어른들 사이에 나누는 대화의 거의 60%가 그 자리에 없는 사람에 관한 대화이며, 이런 뒷담화의 대부분이 (그 자리에 없는 사람에 대해) 비난을 하는 것"이라고 로랑 베그는 말한다.

뒷담화를 하는 것이 나쁜 것이라는 것을 우리 모두는 알고 있으며, 아무도 악의적으로 보이기를 원치 않는다. 그렇다면 왜 우리는 이 떳떳하지 못한 즐거움에 빠지게 되는가? 험담을 주고받는 것이 긍정적인 이야기를 주고받은 것보다 훨씬 더 강력한 유대감을 형성해주기 때문에, 뒷담화는 사회적 유대감을 강화시켜 준다. 서로에 대해 알지 못하는 두 사람이 제3자에 대해 좋은 이야기를 할 경우보다 제3자에 대해 어떤 짓궂은 말들을 주고받을 경우 두 사람이 더 친밀감을 느끼게 될 것이라는 말이다. 그것은 (말하는 사람의) 공유된 가치관과 유머감각을 보여주는 것이다. 그리고 여기에 더해 일탈이 주는 짜릿함도 있다. 왜냐하면 우리는 늘 친절해야 하고 긍정적이어야만 하기 때문이다.

1 ③　　▶ **글의 제목**

이 글은 사회적 유대감 및 친밀감 형성과 가치관의 공유 등 나쁜 것인 줄 알면서도 하게 되는 '뒷담화를 하는 이유'에 대해 설명하고 있으므로, 글의 제목으로 ③의 '우리가 은밀하게 뒷담화에 빠져들게 되는 이유'가 가장 적절하다.

2 ②　　▶ **부분이해**

this guilty pleasure는 본문에서 언급한 '뒷담화'를 가리키는데 ① 근거 없는 소문에 대해 의견 교환하기, ③ 소셜미디어 상에 옛 여자 친구를 몰래 비방하기, ④ 타블로이드 신문에 게재된 유명인들의 사생활에 대해 이야기하기는 모두 뒷담화에 해당하는 반면, ② 아무도 없는 방안에서 자기 만족감을 느끼기 위해 셀카 찍는 행동은 뒷담화와 무관한 것이므로 ②가 정답이다.

---

flirt with ~에 추파를 던지다
grumble v. 투덜거리다
skinny a. 깡마른
anorexic a. 신경성 식욕 부진증에 걸린
gossip n. 험담, 뒷담화
spiteful a. 악의적인
in confidence 은밀하게
give a person a boost 남에게 활력을 불어넣다
disapprove v. 못마땅해 하다
pass v. (공식적으로) 말하다
malicious a. 악의적인
indulge in ~에 빠지다
guilty pleasure 죄의식을 동반한 즐거움, 떳떳하지 못한 즐거움
bond n. 유대감
add to that 이에 더하여
transgression n. 일탈

02

가끔 호저 딜레마라고도 불리는 고슴도치 딜레마는 인간의 친밀함이 낳는 문제에 대한 유추다. 그것은 한 무리의 고슴도치들이 모두 추운 날씨 동안 열기를 나누려고 서로 가까워지고자 하는 상황을 묘사한다. 그러나 그들은 날카로운 가시로 서로 상처를 줄 수밖에 없기 때문에 서로 떨어져 있어야 한다. 그들은 모두 친밀한 상호관계를 유지하고자 하는 의도를 공유하고 있지만, 피할 수 없는 이유로 이런 일은 일어나지 않을 것이다.

아서 쇼펜하우어(Arthur Schopenhauer)와 지그문트 프로이트(Sigmund Freud)는 이 상황을 이용하여 그들이 보기에 사회에서의 타인과 관련한 개인의 상태를 설명했다. 고슴도치 딜레마는 선한 의지에도 불구하고 인간이 친밀해지면 반드시 사실상 서로 해를 입히게 되고 그 결과 행동을 조심하게 되고 관계가 약해진다는 것을 시사한다. 고슴도치 딜레마로 인해, 우리는 타인에 대한 고려에서뿐 아니라 자기 이익 때문에도 타인과의 일에서는 적당히 절제하라는 권유를 받는다. 고슴도치 딜레마는 내향성과 고립주의를 정당화하거나 변명하는 데 이용된다.

---

hedgehog n. 고슴도치, 호저
porcupine n. 호저
analogy n. 유사, 유추
spine n. 가시, 바늘
reciprocal a. 상호적인
substantial a. 실질적인, 사실상의
recommend v. 권고하다, 권유하다
moderation n. 절제, 적당, 중용
introversion n. 내향성
isolationism n. 고립주의

---

1 ① ▶ **내용일치**
고슴도치가 추운 날씨에 보온을 위해 서로 가까워지려고 하는 상황을 가정해본 것일 뿐 고슴도치가 실제로 무리를 지어 사는지는 알 수 없으며 가시에 독이 있다고는 할 수 없으므로 ①이 사실이 아닌 진술이다. ③ 쇼펜하우어는 철학자이고 프로이트는 심리학자이다. 따라서 이 딜레마가 철학과 심리학의 연구 주제가 될 수 있음을 알 수 있다. ④ despite good will이라고 했다. ⑤ use moderation in affairs with others라고 했다.

2 ⑤ ▶ **부분이해**
ⓐ는 '인간끼리 서로 친밀해지는 것이 갖고 있는 문제'라는 뜻인데 너무 친밀해지다보면 상대방에 대해 멸시하는 태도를 보일 수 있으므로 ⑤ "친밀함이 멸시를 낳는다."가 ⓐ를 가장 잘 반영하고 있다. ① 수에 안전이 있다.(주위에 여러 사람이 있을 때 안전하다.) ② 표범은 자기 점을 못 바꾼다.(천성은 못 바꾼다.) ③ 음식 주는 손을 깨물지 마라.(은혜를 원수로 갚지 마라.) ④ 모든 구름 뒤에 밝은 면이 있다.(부정적인 일에도 희망적인 면이 있다.)

3 ② ▶ **빈칸완성**
고슴도치 딜레마가 '가까워지면 서로에게 해가 되어 거리를 둘 수밖에 없다'는 것이므로 이것은 다른 사람과 가까워지기를 싫어하는 사람이 자신의 비사교적인 행동을 정당화(합리화)하거나 변명하는 데 이용될 수 있다. 따라서 ⓑ에는 ② '내향성과 고립주의'가 적절하다. ① 협력과 집단주의 ③ 단결과 박애 ④ 이기심과 개입 ⑤ 외향성과 소외

03

아이들의 흥미와 능력이 사회가 기대하는 것과 다를 때 그들은 종종 차별과 집단 괴롭힘을 당하게 된다. 부모들이 그들의 자녀가 사회적으로 용납되기를 바라는 것은 당연하다. 그러나 자녀의 강점이 항상 사회나 부모의 기대와 일치하는 것이 아니라면, 그들을 강제적으로 현재나 전통적인 (남녀)성별 행동의 틀에 맞추는 것이 아니라 그들이 자신의 고유한 잠재력을 성취하도록 도와주는 것이 중요하다. <일부 어린아이들의 경우에는 자신을 다른 성으로 인식하는 것이 일시적일지 모르지만 또 다른 아이들의 경우에는 그렇지 않다.> 즉, 초기 아동기에 남녀성별 면에서 비순응적인 일부 아이들은 자라서 (자신의 성을 출생 시에 부여받은 성과 다른 성으로 지속적으로 인식하는) 트랜스젠더 성인이 되고, 또 다른 아이들은 그렇지 않다. 이렇게 되는 원인은 생물학적 원인일 수도 있고 사회적 원인일 수도 있다. 그러나 부모의 가정교육이나 어려서 정신적 외상을 입는 것과 연관 있다는 증거는 없다. 아이들이 살아가면서 나중에 자신을 어떻게 인식할지를 예측할 방법은 없다. 이 불확실성이 부모로서 성별-비순응적인 아이를 교육하는 데 있어 가장 어려운 점들 중 하나다. 부모들이 자신의 집을 자녀가 안전하고, 무조건적으로 사랑받고, 있는 그대로의 모습으로 부모에게 받아들여진다고 느끼는 곳으로 만들어주는 것이 중요하다. 연구는 성별은 우리가 가지고 태어나는 것이며 그 어떤 개입에 의해서도 변화될 수 없다는 것을 암시한다.

subject v. 당하게 하다
discrimination n. 차별
bully v. (약한 자를) 괴롭히다
conform to 일치하다, 순응하다
potential n. 잠재력
mold n. 주형, 틀
identify v. 확인하다, 인지하다, 식별하다
nonconforming a. 비순응적인
trauma n. 정신적 외상, 쇼크

1 ③ ▶ **빈칸완성**
앞 문장에서 '아이들이 살아가면서 나중에 자신을 어떻게 인식할지를 예측할 방법은 없다'고 했는데 예측할 수 없다는 것은 확실히 알 수 없다는 뜻이므로 빈칸 ⓐ에는 uncertainty(불확실성)가 적절하고, 앞에서 '아무 조건 없이 사랑 받는다'고 한 것과 같은 취지로 빈칸 ⓑ에는 '있는 그대로의 자신(모습)'의 뜻인 who they are가 적절하다.

2 ② ▶ **문장삽입**
제시문의 의미를 'That is(즉)'로 시작되는 Ⓑ 다음 문장에서 설명하므로 제시문은 Ⓑ에 들어가는 것이 적절하다.

04

일반적으로 말해, 내성적인 사람은 대인관계에 의해서 신체적으로 그리고/혹은 정신적으로 지치게 될 수 있는 사람이다. 그래서 그들은 '재충전'을 위해 어느 정도의 고독을 추구한다. 반면 외향적인 사람은 다른 사람들에 둘러싸여 있는 상황에서 힘을 얻고 평상시 사회적 관계의 형태를 추구한다. 그러나 내향성과 외향성을 이분법적인 것이 아니라 하나의 척도, 즉 연속체의 양 끝으로 생각하는 것이 도움이 된다. 완전 내성적이거나 혹은 완전 외향적인 사람은 거의 없다. 이와 같이 대부분의 사람들은 '양향 성격자' 혹은 내성적인 특징과 외향적인 특징이 혼합된 성향을 가졌다고 여겨진다. 그러므로 당신은 '내성적인 외향적인 사람'이거나 '외향적인 내성적인 사람'이다. 그래서 당신은 '내성적인 외향적인 사람'이 다른 사람들에 둘러싸여 있고 사교적 이벤트에 가는 것을 즐긴다는 사실, 달리 말해 다른 사람들과 관계 맺는 일에 대해 편안함을 느낀다는 사실을 발견하게 된다. 그러나 내성적인 외향적인 사람은 또한 때때로 혼자 있는 시간을 즐기기 위해 노력한다. '외향적인 내성적인 사람'의 경우, 당신은 그 사람이 비록 말이 많은 타입이 아니라고 할지라도 그룹 속에서의 교류에 가치를 부여하고 사교적인 환경 속에 있고자 하는 의지를 보여 준다는 사실을 발견하게 된다. 그러나 만일 선택할 수 있는 기회가 주어진다면 외향적인 내성적인 사람은 하룻밤을 친구들과 어울려 외출을 하기보다는 집에서 보낼 것이다.

1 ② ▶ **빈칸완성**
내성적인 사람과 외향적인 사람만이 존재하지 않는다는 것이 빈칸 다음에 이어지는 문장의 핵심적인 내용이므로 빈칸 Ⓐ에는 역접의 연결사인 ②의 But이 와야 한다. ① 그래서 ③ 사실 ④ ~에 반하여

2 ② ▶ **동의어**
Ⓑ dichotomy는 '분기', '갈라섬', '나누어짐'의 의미를 가지고 있으므로 ②의 split이 정답이다. ① 유사성 ③ 한 점으로 집합함, 집중성 ④ 발산, 보급

3 ① ▶ **부분이해**
ⓒ have a night in than go out on the town이라는 문장의 의미는 사람들과 어울려 시내에 나가 밤을 보내기보다 홀로 집에서 고독한 시간을 갖는다는 것이다.

4 ③ ▶ **내용일치**
"그러나 내성적인 외향적인 사람은 또한 때때로 혼자 있는 시간을 즐기기 위해 노력한다."라는 진술로부터 정답을 추론할 수 있다.

introvert n. 내향적인 사람
extrovert n. 외향적인 사람
interaction n. 상호 작용, 상호의 영향
recharge v. 재충전하다
continuum n. 연속체, 연속물
ambivert n. 양향성격자

05

창의적인 사람들에 대한 연구를 통해 창의성은 새로운 생각에 대한 개방성, 모험심, 그리고 내부지향성과 관계가 있다고 계속해서 입증되고 있다. 그러나 창의적인 많은 학생들이 교육제도는 물론 그들 주변의 다른 사람들과 마찰을 빚는 것을 알고 있다. 창의적인 학생들은 주로 우뇌로 생각하는 학생들이지만, 많은 공립학교의 환경은 이런 학생들이 잠재적인 창의력을 발휘하는 데에 도움을 주거나 격려하지 않는다.

공립 교육하에서 대체적으로 좌뇌적인 전략이 몇 세대 전과 마찬가지로 여전히 지배적이다. 학교가 설립된 이래로 학교에서는 다양한 지식을 암기하는 것은 잘하지만, 문제 해결 능력이 없는 학생들을 배출해왔다. 학생들은 권위에 도전하기보다는 순종하도록 교육받았고, 그 때문에 새롭거나 창의적인 방식으로 생각하지 못했다. 지금까지 지속되고 있는 이런 형태의 교육은 보다 분석적이지만 창의적이지 못한 학생들에게 최대의 이득을 준다. 그러나 이런 과도하게 조직된 학교 환경은 강력한 창의력을 가진 학생들에게는 도전 의식을 북돋지 못한다. 그들은 객관식 시험에서 저조한 점수를 받기 때문에, 종종 평균 이하로 분류되었고, 이것은 그들에게 좌절감과 자존심에 상처를 준다. 이는 왜 창의적인 아이들이 학교에서 어려움을 느끼는가에 대해 어느 정도 깨닫게 해준다. 교사가 그들에게 정보를 외우라고 할 때, 그들의 우뇌적 생각은 그것에 집중하지 못한다. 이런 전통적 교육방식은 학생들이 자극에 그다지 노출되지 않은 대부분이던 시절엔 어떤 문제도 없었지만, 요즘 창의적인 아이들은 본능적으로 이런 암기식 학습을 인생의 '대국적인 측면'을 이해하는 것과

consistently ad. 일관되게
be at odds with 다투다, 갈등하다
setting n. 환경
latent a. 잠재적인
tactics n. 전술, 전략
churn out 대량으로 생산하다, 배출하다
persist v. 집요하게[끈질기게] 계속하다; 지속하다
objective a. 객관적인
memorize v. 암기하다
overstimulate v. 지나치게 자극하다
irrelevant a. 무관한, 상관없는

비교할 때 무의미하거나 중요하지 않다고 생각한다. 문제는 현재 학생들이 과거의 학생들과는 근본적으로 다르다는 것이다.

1 ③ ▶ **내용파악**
과거에서부터 현재까지 공립학교 교육의 목표가 지식전달과 주입식 교육이기 때문에 창의적인 교육을 실행할 수 없었다. 따라서 ③이 정답이다.

2 ③ ▶ **빈칸완성**
공교육의 목표가 '좌뇌적' 전략에 의거해서 지식을 분석하고 저장한다는 내용을 통해 ⓐ에 창의적인 학생은 '우뇌적' 사고를 가지고 있다는 것을, 또한 전통적인 교육이 주입식 교육을 지향한다면 그런 시스템하에서 '우뇌적' 사고 성향의 창의적 학생들이 학습에 집중할 수 없는 것을 알 수 있다.

06

확증 편향은 사람들이 정보를 수집하는 방식에 영향을 미치지만, 사람들이 정보를 해석하고 기억해내는 방식에도 영향을 미친다. 총기 규제에 관한 토론을 생각해보라. 샐리(Sally)는 총기 규제를 지지한다. 그녀는 총기 소유를 제한해야 할 필요성을 거듭 긍정하는 뉴스 기사와 오피니언(의견) 글을 찾아낸다. 언론매체에 나오는 총기사고 관련 기사를 들으면, 그녀는 그 기사를 자신의 기존 신념을 지지하는 식으로 해석한다. 반면에, 헨리(Henry)는 총기 규제에 완강하게 반대한다. 그는 자신의 입장을 펀드는 뉴스 취재(공급)원을 찾아내고 총기사고에 대한 뉴스 기사를 우연히 발견하면, 그는 그 기사를 자신의 현재 관점을 지지하는 식으로 해석한다. 많은 실험이 사람들은 자신의 기존 신념을 확증하는 정보를 찾는 경향이 있다는 것을 보여준다. 불행하게도, 이런 유형의 편향은 상황을 객관적으로 보지 못하게 할 수 있으며, 우리가 내리는 결정에 영향을 미칠 수 있고, 서툴거나 잘못된 선택을 초래할 수 있다. 예를 들어, 선거철에 사람들은 그들이 지지하는 후보자를 좋게 그려 보이는 긍정적인 정보를 찾기 쉬운 반면에 반대 후보자를 부정적으로 보이게 하는 정보를 찾는다. 객관적인 사실을 찾지 않고 정보를 자신의 기존 신념을 지지하는 식으로만 해석하고 이런 신념을 지지하는 세부사항들만을 기억함으로써 사람들은 종종 중요한 정보를 놓쳐버리는데, 만일 놓치지 않았으면 어느 후보자를 지지할 것인가에 대한 결정에 영향을 미쳤을지도 모를 정보이다.

1 ③ ▶ **빈칸완성**
객관적인 사실을 찾지 않고 기존의 자기 신념에 맞게만 해석하고 기억하면 중요한 정보를 얻지 못하고 놓칠 것이므로 ③이 적절하다. ④ 새로운 아이디어를 외부에 의뢰하지 않았으면 그 새로운 아이디어가 결정에 영향을 미쳤을지 모른다는 말은 어색하다.

2 ① ▶ **내용추론**
① 샐리가 총기 규제를 지지하는 사람이므로 that절의 내용은 맞으나 찬성론을 반대론과 비교하여 고찰한다는 것은 편향적이지 않고 공정한 태도이므로 추론할 수 없는 것이다. ② that절의 내용이 각자 자신의 안전을 위해 총기를 가질 수 있다는 논리이므로 국가에 의한 규제를 반대하는 헨리의 생각과 일치한다. ③ 총기사고의 피해자는 총기 때문에 피해를 입었으므로 총기 규제를 지지하는 생각일 것이고 가해자는 비록 사고는 냈지만 이런 저런 이유로 총기를 사용할 수밖에 없었다고 변명할 것이므로 총기 규제를 반대하는 편일 것이다. ④ 총기사고의 발생은 주로 총기 규제의 필요성을 부각시킬 것이므로 총기 규제를 반대하는 헨리는 총기사고 보도 기사를 처음부터 묵살해버릴지도 모른다.

3 ④ ▶ **글의 목적**
이 글은 확증 편향이라는 특정한 심리적 성향을 예를 들어 명료하게 설명한 글이므로 ④가 글의 목적으로 적절하다.

confirmation n. 확인, 확증
bias n. 편견, 편향
in support of ~를 옹호[지지]하여
gun control 총기 규제
seek out 찾아내다
reaffirm v. 다시 긍정하다
adamantly ad. 완강하게
be aligned with ~와 제휴하다, 일치되다, 편들다
come across 뜻밖에 만나다, 우연히 발견하다
confirm v. 확실히 하다, 확증하다
in a good light 잘 보이는 곳에, 좋은 면을 강조하여
uphold v. 지지하다

07

공격성의 본질과 이유에 대한 서로 다른 두 가지 이론이 있다. 본능과 사회학습 이론이다. 많은 이론에 따르면, 공격성은 원초적이고 자연스러운 인간의 본능이라 한다. 공격 본능 이론에 따르면, 공격성이란 생물학적인 현상이다. 지그문트 프로이트(Sigmund Freud)에 의하면, 공격성은 자기 파괴적인 선천적인 충동이며, 프로이트가 타나토스(죽음의 본능)라고 지칭했던 인간의 가장 기본적인 본능의 결과이다. 만약 프로이트의 말이 옳다면 왜 모든 인간들이 자살을 하지 않는 것일까? 그런 이유 가운데 하나는 다행이도 타나토스와 에로스(삶을 추구하는 본능)간의 갈등에서 에로스가 대부분 승리하기 때문이다. 그러나 이것은 또한 외적 전이(displacement)가 자기 파괴적인 에너지를 다른 곳으로 방향을 돌리기 때문이기도 하다. 우리 자신을 공격하는 것이 아니라, 다른 사람을 공격하게 되는데, 바로 이런 과정을 전이라고 한다. 그렇다면 사람들은 과연 어떻게 서로에 대한 극단적인 폭력충동을 억제할 수 있는 것일까? 프로이트는 그 해답은 카타르시스(감정의 정화)라고 한다. 폭력적인 장면을 보거나 또는 분노를 소소하게 표출하는 행위를 하게 되면서 공격적 충동이 줄어들고 우리의 감정이 정화되고 진정된다는 것이다. 이런 본능 이론이 주장하는 것처럼 공격성이 외부 도발과 무관하게 커져서 마침내 외부 도발이 거의 혹은 전혀 없어도 공격적 행동이 발생하는 것이다. 이 이론을 지지하는 사람들은 야생 서식지에 사는 동물들의 행태에 대한 연구를 근거로 한다. 공격성을 본능으로 보는 이론에 따르면, 이런 본능은 인간과 동물 모두가 공유한다고 한다.

1 ①　　▶ 뒷내용 추론
글 첫머리에서 공격성의 본질과 이유에 대한 두 가지 이론으로 본능 이론과 사회학습 이론이 있다고 한 다음 본능 이론에서의 공격성에 대해 설명했으므로, 이 글 다음에는 두 번째 이론인 사회학습 이론에서의 공격성에 대한 내용이 이어질 것이다.

2 ③　　▶ 내용파악
전이는 본능적인 자기방어기제인데 셋째 문장에서 본능 이론은 공격성이 생물학적인 것이라고 주장한다고 했으므로 "전이는 공격성이 생물학(본능)적 현상이라는 생각에 근거한다."는 ③이 정답이다.

aggression n. 공격성
instinct n. 본능
consequence n. 결과
biological a. 생물학적인
primary a. 주요한, 최초의
innate drive 선천적인 충동
disintegration n. 분해, 분열, 파멸
commit suicide 자살하다
instinctive force 본능
displacement n. 전이(轉移)
divert v. 방향을 전환하다, 딴 데로 돌리다
catharsis n. 감정의 정화
dwindle v. 줄어들다, 쇠퇴하다
regardless of ~와는 상관없이
provocation n. 도발, 자극

08

다음번에 당신의 어린 아들이 난폭하게 굴면, 꾸짖기보다는 오히려 북돋우어주고 싶어 할지도 모른다. 라이브사이언스(LiveScience)에 의하면, 몇몇 교육 전문가들과 연구원들은 교실에서 난폭한 장난을 금지하는 것은 남자아이들에게 해로울 수 있다고 주장하고 있다. 또한 '영웅'놀이나 경찰관과 도둑놀이를 하는 것을 막으려는 엄마들과 교사들은 잘못 인식하고 있는 것이라고 전문가들은 말하고 있다. "그들은 남자아이들이 이런 식으로 놀면 그로 인해 폭력에 둔감해지고 자라서는 더욱 폭력적이게 될 것이라는 ─ 그것을 도시 괴담이라고 부르자 ─ 믿음을 갖고 있다. 그러나 그것은 무엇이 성인을 난폭하게 만드는지를 잘못 알고 있는 것이다."라고 『Raising Cain: Protecting the Emotional Life of Boys』의 공동 저자인 심리학자 마이클 톰슨(Michael Thompson)이 말했다.
B "남자아이들은 선천적으로 지배욕구와 밀접한 관련이 있고, 그것은 그들이 좋아하는 이야기의 종류와 그들이 노는 게임의 종류에 영향을 미친다."라고 그는 덧붙였다. 사실, '악동'들과 같이 노는 것은 남자아이들이 성장하도록 도와준다고 4세의 남자아이들을 가르치는 98명의 여자 선생님들을 대상으로 조사한 메인(Maine) 대학의 메리 엘린 로그(Mary Ellin Logue)가 말했다.
C "그들은 또한 충동을 억제하려고 노력하는데, 얌전하게 굴기 위해 무척 애를 쓰지만 그러기는 정말 어렵다. 이러한 악동들은 자신들이 정복하려 노력하는 것들의 일부를 밖으로 드러나게 하는 방법을 스스로에게 제공해준다."라고 그녀는 말했다.
A 사실, 거칠게 놀고자 하는 남자아이들의 자연스러운 본능을 억압하는 것은 그들을 더욱 폭력적으로 만드는 결과를 가져올 수도 있다. "그것을 억누르려 할 때, 그것은 교묘한 방식으로 표출된다."라고 『Under Deadman's Skin: Discovering the Meaning of Children's Violent Play』의 저자인 제인 캐치(Jane Katch)가 말했다.

roughhouse v. 크게 떠들다, 난폭하게 굴다
scold v. 잔소리하다, 꾸짖다
misguide v. 그릇되게 지도하다; 잘못 인식시키다
desensitize to ~에 대해 둔감하게 하다
conduct a survey 조사하다; 측량하다
suppress v. 억압하다, 진압하다; 억누르다
innately ad. 선천적으로, 본질적으로
dominance n. 우세, 우월; 지배
externalize v. 외면화하다, 구체화하다

1 ①   ▶ **지시대상**

B, C, D는 모두 남자아이들을 지칭하지만 A의 They는 the moms and teachers를 가리킨다.

2 ③   ▶ **단락배열**

주어진 문단 내용은 남자아이들이 폭력적 놀이를 하는 것에 대한 오해이므로, 이를 풀기 위해 폭력적 놀이를 하는 배경과 긍정적인 면에 대한 설명인 B가 바로 이어질 수 있다. 부연 설명으로 이런 놀이의 역할에 관한 C가 이어지고 A에서 이런 놀이를 제지할 때의 부작용에 대한 경고로 글을 마무리하는 것이 자연스럽다.

3 ④   ▶ **내용추론**

일방적으로 폭력성의 표출을 차단하면 역효과가 있다고 했으므로 ④는 옳지 않다. 남자아이들이 폭력적인 놀이를 하는 데에는 본능적인 정서적 배경이 있다고 했으므로 ①과 ③처럼 남자아이들의 감정을 이해해주는 것이 중요하다.

09

가구에서 동물들과 개념들에 이르기까지 모든 것을 뇌 안의 서로 다른 여러 폴더에 분류해 넣는 것은 자동적으로 일어나는 일이며 우리가 제 기능을 다하도록 도움을 준다. 사실, 범주화는 진화론적 목적을 갖고 있다. 모든 버섯은 독이 있다고 생각하고 모든 사자는 당신을 잡아먹기를 원한다고 생각해버리는 것이 주변 환경에 대처하는 아주 효과적인 방법인 것이다. 독이 없는 버섯이나 때로는 배고프지 않은 사자들과 관련한 미묘한 차이를 무시해버리면 확실성이 사람을 안전하게 해준다. 그러나 어떤 특정한 범주화 방식이 부정확할 수 있으며 그 잘못된 범주들이 편견과 고정관념을 초래할 수 있다. 편견에 대한 많은 심리학 연구는 사람들이 어떻게 특정한 범주들을 본질적인 것으로 여기는가에 초점을 맞추었는데, 이것은 이 범주들이 여러 본유적이고 불변적인 특성들과 연계된 하나의 근본적인 본성을 갖고 있다고 가정하는 것으로 요약된다.

성(性), 연령, 성적 지향과 같은 인간의 다른 속성들과 마찬가지로 인종도 강력하게, 그리고 부정확하게, 본질적인 것으로 여겨지는 경향이 있다. 이것은 사람들을 그 범주(인종)에서 생각할 때는 재빨리 심지어 자동적으로 그들의 특성들에 대한 가정들을 생각해내게 된다는 것을 의미한다. 예를 들어, '미국 흑인'이라는 범주와 관련된 일반적인 고정관념에는 '시끄럽다'와 '춤을 잘 춘다'와 '스포츠에 능하다'가 포함된다. 그 어떤 인간 집단에 대한 본질주의도 의심스러운 것이어서 노인들이 본래부터 마음이 약한 것은 아니고 여자들이 선천적으로 온순한 것은 아니다. 그리고 인종에 관해 말하자면, 거기에 뿌리 깊고 근본적인 차이들이 있다는 생각은 잘못임이 과학자들에 의해 철저하게 밝혀져 왔다.

1 ③   ▶ **글의 요지**

두 번째 단락에 나타나 있는 이 글의 요지는 (범주화가 긍정적인 결과를 낳기도 하지만) 잘못된 범주화는 고정관념을 초래하고 고정관념의 작용으로 인해 특정 범주들을 본유적이고 불변적인 특성을 갖는 본질적인 것으로 여기는 본질주의를 낳는다는 것인데, 마지막 문장에서 이런 본질주의가 잘못임이 과학자들에 의해 밝혀졌다고 했으므로 빈칸에는 ③의 '잘못임이 과학적으로 증명된 본질주의'가 적절하다. ① 신속하고 자동적인 범주화 ② 본유적이고 불변적인 특성들 ④ 충분히 정당화된 인종 차별

2 ④   ▶ **내용일치**

노인들은 본질적으로 마음이 약하다거나 여성은 본질적으로 온순하다고 여기는 본질주의의 시각에서 보면 의지가 강한 노인이나 난폭한 여성은 설명할 수 없는 것이므로 ④가 글의 내용과 일치하지 않는 것이다. ① 첫 단락은 긍정적인 효과를, 그 이하는 부정적인 효과를 설명하고 있다. ② 지나친 일반화(overgeneralization)는 첫 단락 마지막 문장의 독이 없는 버섯이나 배고프지 않은 사자들과 관련한 미묘한 차이를 무시해버리는 것에 해당한다. ③ 범주의 특성들을 본유적이고 불변적이라고 생각하는 본질주의가 잘못이므로 그것들은 후천적이고 가변적인 것일 수 있다.

categorization n. 범주화

be nuanced 미묘한 차이를 지니다

certitude n. 확신, 확실성

essentialize v. ~의 본질을 나타내다[말하다], ~를 본질적인 것으로 여기다

boil down to ~로 요약되다

inherent a. 본래 갖고 있는, 타고난

immutable a. 불변의

attribute n. 속성

roundly ad. 단호히, 완전히

debunk v. 정체를 폭로하다, 가면을 벗기다

10

불안을 낳는 그런 세상은 실제로는 비교적 안전한 세상이며, 그 누구도 자신이 갑작스런 죽음을 맞이하게 될 거라고는 생각지 않는 세상이다. 갑작스런 죽음은 아마도 일정 수의 신원미상의 다른 사람들에게는 닥쳐올지 모르지만 자신에게는 오지 않는 것이다. 불안은 불편한 마음상태로서 존재하는데, 이런 마음상태에서 사람은 불특정하고 확정지을 수 없는 어떤 일이 잘못되어 가고 있을지 모른다고 느낀다. 세상이 잘 돌아가고 있다고 여겨질지라도 좋은 시절이 끝날지도 모르니까 이것이 불안을 낳는다. 세상이 잘못 돌아가고 있으면, 더 나빠질지도 모른다.(그래서 또 불안을 낳는다.) 불안은 초점이 없기가 쉽다. 불안한 사람은 자신을 탓해야 할지 남을 탓해야 할지 모른다. 그는 이런 막연한 불안감이 금년 탓인지, 행정부 탓인지, 기후변화 탓인지, 원자폭탄 탓인지 모른다.

적정량의 불안이 있어야 사회가 잘 돌아가게 되는 그런 사회를 우리가 발달시켜온 것은 분명하다. 정신과의사들이 "그는 회복되기에는 불안이 충분치 않았어요."라고 말하는 것을 듣게 되는데, 이 말은 우리가 너무 많은 불안은 정신 건강에 해롭다는 것에 동의하지만 다른 한편으로는 불안에 힘입어 암 증세일지도 모를 증세에 대해 알아보려 병원을 찾기도 하고, 그 안에 연한이 지난 낡은 조항이 있을지도 모르는 오래된 생명보험증서를 뒤져 확인도 하고, 빌리(Billy)의 성적표가 괜찮아 보여도 그의 선생님과 면담을 갖기도 하게 되었다는 것을 보여준다. 결국, 우리의 불안 시대는 미개한 농경문화에 비해 크게 발전한 모습을 보여준다.

1 ④   ▶ **빈칸완성**
빈칸 다음 문장에서 의사가 "그는 회복되기에는 불안이 충분치 않았어요."라고 말하므로 빈칸에는 ④가 적절하다. ① 불안이 다른 감정을 압도하는 것 ② 유머로 불안을 쫓아버리는 것 ③ 적절한 방법으로 불안을 극복하는 것

2 ②   ▶ **글의 제목**
이 글은 첫 문장에서도 알 수 있듯이, 불안이 이 세상에서 행하는 긍정적인 역할을 서술하며 불안을 역설적으로 예찬한 글이다. 따라서 ②의 '이 불안의 시대에 한 표(찬성표)를'이 가장 적절한 제목이다.

3 ③   ▶ **내용추론**
①은 첫 문장에서, ②는 첫 단락 마지막 두 문장에서, 각각 추론의 단서를 찾을 수 있다. 셋째 문장에서 '불안은 불편한 마음상태로서 존재하는데'라고 했으므로 불안은 우리가 싫어하는 것이지만, 둘째 단락 첫 문장에서 언급했듯이 적절한 양의 불안이 있어야 사회가 잘 돌아가므로 불안은 우리가 필요로 하는 것이라 할 수 있으므로 ④도 추론할 수 있다. 그러나 ③ 원시사회에서 문명사회로 변천하면서 불안이 줄어들었다고 추론할 수는 없다.

unidentified a. 정체불명의, 신원 미상의
unspecified a. 특정하지 않은
undeterminable a. 결정[확정]지을 수 없는
psychiatrist n. 정신과의사
inimical a. 적의가 있는, 유해한
prod v. 자극하다, 촉구하다
life-insurance policy 생명보험증서
have a conference with ~와 협의하다
on balance 모든 것을 고려해 보면, 결국은
savage a. 미개한
peasant a. 소작농[농민]의, 시골뜨기의

11

과학 지식은 인간화되고 잘 가르쳐지면 우리 삶에 영속적인 균형을 이룰 수 있는 관건이 된다. 생물학자가 완전히 풍성한 생물계에 대해 더 많이 알게 될수록 알아낸 생물계의 모습은 그만큼 더 이득이 된다. 마찬가지로, 심리학자가 인간 정신의 발달에 대해 더 많이 알게 될수록 자연계가 우리의 영혼과 정신을 끌어당기는 중력에 대해 더 많이 이해하게 된다.

우리가 이 지구와 화해하고 우리들 서로서로와 화해하려면 아직 멀었다. 우리는 신석기 혁명을 시작하면서 잘못된 전환을 했다. 그 후 줄곧 우리는 자연에 이르는 쪽으로 발전하려는 것이 아니라 자연에서 멀어지는 쪽으로 발전하려 하고 있다. 우리가 인류의 자연 유산이 주는 대단히 만족스런 혜택을 받기 위해 이미 얻은 삶의 질을 잃지 않고 방향을 돌려 돌아가기에 시간이 너무 늦은 것은 아니다.

딜레마의 일부는 전 세계 대부분의 사람들이 자연환경에 대해 걱정하지만 왜 걱정하는지, 왜 자연환경에 대해 책임을 느껴야 하는지 모른다는 것이다. 대체로 그들은 자연이 인간을 위해 행하는 청지기의 일이 그들 개개인에게 무엇을 의미하는지 분명히 말할 수 없었다. 이러한 혼동은 미래 세대뿐 아니라 현대 사회에도 큰 문제가 된다. 그것은 세계 어디에나 있는 과학교육의 부적합성이라는 또 하나의 큰 문제와 연관되어 있다. 두 문제 모두 부분적으로는 현대 생물학의 폭발적인 발전과 복잡성에서 비롯된다. 가장 뛰어난 과학자들조차도 21세기의 가장 중요한 과학으로 등장한 것(생물학)의 작은 일부만을 뒤떨어지지 않고 따라갈 수 있을 뿐이다.

biosphere n. 생물계
rewarding a. 이득이 되는, 보람 있는
gravitational a. 중력의
pull n. 끌어당김
have a long way to go 갈 길이 멀다, 전도요원하다
make peace with 화해하다
launch v. 착수하다, 개시하다
come around 방향을 바꾸다
fulfilling a. 충족시키는
heritage n. 유산
articulate v. 분명히 말하다
stewardship n. 청지기의 직책[일]
keep up with 뒤떨어지지 않다

1 ④   ▶ **내용추론**

이 글의 저자는 인간과 자연이 일체로서 서로 조화를 이루어야 하는 것으로 보고 있으므로 ④가 추론할 수 없는 것이다. ① '교육받은 사람은 과학 지식을 제대로 가진 사람'을 말하므로 첫 단락의 생물계와 자연계라는 '자연'과 인간의 정신 발달이라는 '인간'에 대해 모두 알고 있어야 하는 것이다. ② 셋째 단락에서 자연이 인간을 위해 청지기의 일을 한다고 했다. ③ 자연이 살아야 인간도 산다는 말이다.

2 ①   ▶ **빈칸완성**

생물학자가 아는 것과 심리학자가 아는 것이 마찬가지의 결과를 낳게 되므로 ⓐ에는 ① Similarly(마찬가지로)가 적절하다. ② 반대로 ③ 놀랍게도 ④ 결과적으로

3 ③   ▶ **지시대상**

Both가 가리키는 것은 앞 두 문장의 This confusion과 the inadequacy of science education인데, This confusion은 그 앞 문장에서 설명된 대부분의 사람들이 자연(자연환경)에 대해 모르는 것을 말하므로 Both가 가리키는 것으로 ③이 적절하다.

4 ②   ▶ **내용일치**

둘째 단락에서 신석기 혁명을 시작하고 나서 인간이 점점 더 자연과 멀어지고 자연과 불화를 빚게 되었다고 했으므로 신석기 혁명 이전에는 자연과 더 조화를 이루었을 것이다. 따라서 ②가 사실인 진술이다.

12

소크라테스식 주장은 비민주적이지 않다. 사회적으로 소외된 자들의 정당한 주장을 파괴하는 것도 아니다. 사실, 소크라테스가 간파하였듯이, 소크라테스식 주장은 강력한 민주주의와 정의를 지속적으로 추구하는 데 있어서 필수적이다. 단지 경쟁하는 이익단체들의 시장이 아닌, 성찰적이고 신중한 민주주의, 공익을 진정으로 고려하는 민주주의를 육성하기 위해, 우리는 자신의 신념에 관해 판단을 내릴 줄 아는 소크라테스적 능력을 갖춘 시민들을 양성해야 한다. 사람들이 라디오 토론프로그램을 듣고 그것에 대해 이의를 제기해 본 적도 없는 심리상태로 투표하는 것은 민주주의에 이롭지 않다. 비판적으로 사고하는 능력이 결여된 곳에서 만들어지는 민주주의는 사람들이 서로 이야기는 주고받지만 참된 대화는 하지 못하는 그런 민주주의다. 그런 분위기에서는 나쁜 주장이 좋은 주장으로 통하고, 편견이 사리에 맞는 것으로 매우 쉽게 가장될 수 있다. 편견을 폭로하고 정의를 보장하기 위해 우리는 논쟁이 필요한데, 그것은 시민적 자유의 필수적인 도구다. 우리 대학의 일반 교양교육은 소크라테스적인 것이고, 또 그렇게 되어야 한다. 다시 말해 각 학생들의 독립심을 활성화하고, 어떤 문제에 대해 단지 주장과 반대주장을 교환하는 정도가 아니라, 문제에 대해 함께 합리적으로 추론할 수 있는 공동체를 만들어내는 데 헌신하여야 한다. 가족과 전통에 대해 우리가 충성하고, 우리나라 안의 여러 집단들에 대한 불의를 시정하는 데 우리가 다양한 관심사들을 갖고 있긴 하지만, 우리는 소크라테스적인 방식으로 함께 추론할 수 있고 또 해야 하며, 대학은 우리가 그렇게 할 수 있도록 우리를 준비시켜줘야 한다. 소크라테스 및 그리스 스토아학파의 사고 속에서 등장하는 이성적 공동체를 우리의 목표로 이해함으로써, 우리는 민주적인 자치를 위해 이성이 가지는 존엄성과 중요성을 입증할 수 있다. 이러한 생각을 오늘날 다양한 종류의 학부 과정에 있는 철학교육에 적용해보면, 우리 사회의 건전성에 치명적인 것은 소크라테스적 교육이 아니라, 오히려 그것의 부재라는 사실을 알 수 있다.

1 ①   ▶ **글의 제목**

오늘날 대학 교양교육이 소크라테스적인 방식으로 이루어져야 할 필요성이 있다는 것이 이 글의 주제다.

2 ④   ▶ **내용일치**

논쟁은 시민 자유의 필수적인 도구라고 했으며 대학의 교양교육이 소크라테스적인 것이 되어야 한다고 했다. 따라서 소크라테스적인 교육은 비판적인 사고와 참된 대화를 하는 데 도움이 될 것이므로 ④가 정답이다.

---

subversive a. 체제전복적인, 파괴적인

exclude v. 제외하다, 배제하다

reflective a. 숙고하는; 반성적인, 사려 깊은

deliberative a. 신중한; 심의의

common good 공익

critically ad. 비판적으로; 위급하게

prejudice n. 편견, 선입관

unmask v. 정체를 나타내다, 폭로하다

committed a. (주의·주장에) 전념하는, 헌신적인

counterclaim n. 반대주장, 맞고소

allegiance n. 충성, 충절; 충실

emerge v. 나오다, 나타나다

dignity n. 존엄, 위엄, 품위

3 ① ▶ 빈칸완성

빈칸 Ⓐ 앞의 In such an atmosphere는 참된 대화가 이뤄지지 못하는 민주주의 사회의 분위기이며, 나쁜 주장이 좋은 주장으로 통한다고 했으므로, 편견 또한 사리에 맞는 것이 된다는 의미가 되어야 한다. 따라서 빈칸 Ⓐ에는 '가장하다'라는 뜻의 masquerade가 적절하다. 그리고 소크라테스적인 교육 방식의 중요성에 대해서 언급하고 있고 대학에서는 학생들이 소크라테스적인 방식으로 추론할 수 있도록 준비시켜줘야 한다고 했으므로 현재 대학에서는 이런 소크라테스적인 교육이 잘 이루어지지 않고 있음을 알 수 있다. 따라서 우리 사회의 건전성에 위험이 되는 것은 소크라테스적인 교육의 부재이므로, 빈칸 Ⓑ에는 absence가 적절하다. ② 생략하다 — 풍부 ③ 가치를 떨어뜨리다 — 실행; 연습 ④ 조화시키다 — 존재론

13

스톡데일 패러독스(희망의 역설)는 미군 장교로 베트남 전쟁 당시 8년 동안 포로로 잡혀있던 해군 대장 제임스 스톡데일(James Stockdale)의 이름을 따라 붙여졌다. 스톡데일은 그를 억류한 사람들에 의해 스무 번이 넘는 고문을 당했으며, 포로수용소에서 살아남아 언젠가 자신의 부인을 다시 만나게 될 것이라고 생각할 이유가 많지 않았다. 그러나 그는 시련을 당하는 동안 신념을 잃지 않았다. "저는 제가 (수용소에서) 나갈 수 있을 뿐만 아니라 결국 이겨낼 것이고 그 경험이 저의 삶의 결정적 순간이 될 것이며, 이것은 돌이켜 생각해보면 바꿀 수 없는 것이라는 것을 전혀 의심치 않았습니다."

그로 인해 역설이 생겼는데 스톡데일은 알 수 없는 (미래의) 일에 대한 확고한 신념이 있었지만, 그는 항상 수용소에서 살아 나가지 못했던 사람은 그의 수용소 동료들 중에 가장 낙관적인 동료들이었다는 점에 주목했다. "그들은 '크리스마스쯤에는 나갈 수 있을 거야.'라고 말했고, 크리스마스가 찾아오고 크리스마스가 지나가면 다시 '부활절쯤에는 나갈 수 있을 거야.'라고 말했다. 그리고 부활절이 찾아오고 부활절이 지나면 추수감사절쯤에는 나가게 될 것이라고 믿지만 다시 크리스마스가 찾아오고 결국 비탄에 빠져 죽게 되었다."

낙관주의자들이 하지 못했던 일은 자신들의 상황의 현실에 맞서는 것이었다. 그들은 타조 접근법(현실도피책)을 택했다. 자기 망상은 그들로 하여금 단기적으로 상황을 쉽게 받아들이게 했지만, 그들이 결국 현실에 맞서야 했을 때 그 상황은 너무 과한 것이 되었으며 그것을 감당할 수 없었다. 스톡데일은 매우 다른 사고방식으로 역경에 맞섰다. 그는 그가 처한 상황의 현실을 받아들였다. 그는 그가 지옥에 있다는 것을 알고 있었지만, 현실을 외면하기보다 앞으로 나아가 자신과 함께 수감된 동료들의 사기를 높이고 삶을 연장하기 위한 모든 것을 했다.

1 ③ ▶ 내용파악

제임스 스톡데일은 베트남 전쟁 당시 포로로 잡혀서 풀려날 수 있다는 신념을 잃지 않았지만, 그에게 처해진 가혹한 현실도 받아들였다고 했다. 반면 그의 수용소 동료들 중 낙관주의자들은 조만간 일이 잘 풀릴 것이라고 낙관하여 무너졌다고 했으므로 이 둘의 차이를 설명한 것으로 옳은 것은 ③이다.

2 ④ ▶ 내용파악

스톡데일 패러독스는 "역경에 처하게 됐을 때 그 현실을 외면하지 않고 정면 대응하면 살아남을 수 있는 반면, 조만간 일이 잘 풀릴 거라고 낙관하면 무너지고 만다."는 '희망의 역설'을 뜻하므로 희망이 모든 상황에서 근본적인 해결책이 아니라는 것을 밝히고 있다. 따라서 ④가 적절하다.

3 ① ▶ 부분이해

수용소에서 낙관주의자들은 현실을 외면하고 어려움이 사라지길 희망했으므로 이들이 택한 '타조 접근법'을 가장 잘 설명한 것은 ①이다.

name v. ~에[이라고] 이름을 붙이다, 명명하다

admiral n. 해군 대장

captive n. 포로

torture v. 고문하다; 괴롭히다

captor n. 잡는 사람, 체포자

prison camp 포로수용소

ordeal n. 호된 시련, 고난

prevail v. 우세하다, 이기다

in retrospect 돌이켜보면

paradox n. 역설

optimistic a. 낙관적인, 낙천적인

Easter n. 부활절

optimist n. 낙천주의자, 낙관론자

confront v. 직면하다; 대항하다, ~와 맞서다

self-delusion n. 자기기만

adversity n. 역경

bury one's head in the sand 현실을 외면하다

lift v. 향상시키다; 높이다

morale n. 사기

prolong v. 늘이다, 연장하다

14

도덕성은 이해하기 힘든 개념일지 모르지만 우리는 도덕성을 빠르게 습득한다. 하버드 대학의 심리학 교수인 마크 하우서(Marc Hauser)는 대부분의 언어학자들이 믿는 우리가 태어날 때부터 갖춘 기본적인 언어 습득에 상당하는 것, 소위 도덕 문법 감각을 우리 모두가 가지고 있다고 믿는다. 그러나 우리가 태어날 때부터 도덕 프로그램을 단지 갖고 있다고 해서 도덕적 행동을 실행에 옮기는 것은 아니다. 무언가가 그 소프트웨어를 작동시키고 적절하게 배열해야 한다. 단어들이 모여 문장을 이루기 전까지 문장론이 아무것도 아니듯, 옳고 그름 또한 누군가가 어떻게 그것을 적용하는지 가르쳐 주기 전까지 소용이 없다. 그러한 가르침을 주는 사람은 우리 주변에 있다. 인간은 누군가는 도와야 하고 누군가는 도우지 말아야 할 상황에서 아주 갈등을 느끼게 되는데, 이에 대한 일반적인 규칙은 "집에서 가까운 사람은 도우며 멀리 사는 사람은 내버려 두라."는 것이다. 그것은 부분적으로 어떤 이의 고통을 당신이 직접 볼 수 있을 때가 단지 누군가의 고통이 설명으로 전해질 때 보다 더 현실로 와 닿기 때문이다. 하지만 부분적으로는 당신이 속한 지역의 번영이 당신의 생존에 필수적이고 상대 지역의 번창은 당신과 무관했을 때도 그러하다. 집단의 도덕을 강제하는 가장 강력한 도구들 중의 하나는 배척을 하는 것이다. 한 집단의 구성원이 되는 것이 자신의 식량 및 가족 그리고 약탈자로부터의 보호를 보장하는 길이라면, 배척을 당하는 것은 끔찍한 일이 될 수 있다. 클럽, 사회단체 그리고 우애단체에서는 바람직하지 않은 구성원들을 탈퇴시키고, 미 군부는 징계도구로써 강제 전역시키겠다는 위협을 가하다가 심지어 '불명예'라는 처분을 내려 전직군인에게 평생 따라다닐 기록을 더럽히기도 한다. 인간은 약하고 무방비상태에 있으며 약탈자에게 공격받기 쉽다. 추방당하지 않는 것은 우리에게 중요하다.

1 ② ▶ 빈칸완성
우리는 도덕성을 빨리 습득하며, 하우서는 이를 도덕 문법이라고 칭하며 우리에게 주어져 있는 것이라고 주장한다. 이에 대한 부연 설명으로, 태어날 때부터 주어져 있는 기본적인 언어습득에 상당하는 것이므로 Ⓐ에는 'equivalent(동등한 것, 상당하는 것)'가 들어간다. 또한 도덕 프로그램이 주어져 있어도 누군가 어떻게 적용할 것인지 가르쳐주기 전까지는 아무 소용이 없는 것이라고 하였다. 따라서 이러한 도덕 프로그램이 있다고 해서 도덕적 행동을 실행에 옮기는 것이 아니므로 Ⓑ에는 'practice(실행하다, 실천하다)'가 들어가야 한다. ① 일관성 ― 운동[연습]시키다; 행사하다 ③ 선례 ― 보유[유지]하다 ④ 성질 ― 바꾸다

2 ① ▶ 부분이해
문장 Ⓒ는 하나하나도 중요하지만 완성과 실행의 중요성을 강조하는 말이다. 따라서 ① "구슬이 서 말이라도 꿰어야 보배다."가 정답이다. ② 티끌 모아 태산 ③ 호미로 막을 것을 가래로 막는다 ④ 행동과 말은 맞아야 한다

3 ② ▶ 동의어
blackball은 '배척하다'는 뜻으로 ② exclude(배척하다, 제외하다)가 정답이다. ① 괴롭히다 ③ 협박[위협]하다 ④ 의심하다

4 ③ ▶ 내용파악
도덕성을 자신의 안전을 보장하기 위한 수단의 측면에서 설명하고 있으므로 ③이 정답이다.

---

grasp v. 붙잡다; 이해하다
acquire v. 손에 넣다; 획득하다; 취득하다
ethical a. 도덕상의; 윤리적인
linguist n. 언어학자
syntax n. 통어법; 구문론
plight n. 곤경; 어려운 입장
shun v. 피하다; 비키다
blackball v. 반대 투표하다; 배척하다
fraternity n. 동포애; 우애 단체
disciplinary a. 훈련상의; 규율의
defenseless a. 무방비의; 방어할 수 없는
predator n. 약탈자; 육식동물
banishment n. 추방; 유형, 유배

15

교육 과정은 유치원 이전부터 시작하여 완벽한 대학교에 입학해서야 끝나는 하나의 경주처럼 더욱 더 느껴지고 있다. 자녀들이 성공하는 데 도움을 줄 수 있는 최선의 방법에 대한 수많은 충고들이 있지만, 우리가 충분히 생각하지 않은 점은 자녀들이 덕성을 기르는 데 도와주는 방법이다. 뉴욕주립대(State University of New York) 버팔로 캠퍼스의 마크 시리(Mark Seery)가 이끈 심리학자들로 구성된 연구팀에 의한 최근 연구는 자라면서 역경을 거의 경험하지 않은 성인들은 어린 시절에 몇 가지 상당한 좌절을 겪은 이들보다 사실상 덜 행복하고 자신감이 없다는 것을 밝혔다. 연구원들은 장애를 극복하는 것이 "효과적인 대처 능력을 가르치고, 사회지원망을 이용하도록 도와주고, 과거 역경을 자기 것으로 만들고, 미래에 성공적으로 대처할 수 있는 능력을 가지고 있다는 믿음을 갖게

---

thrive v. 번창하다, 잘 자라다
adversity n. 역경, 곤궁
setback n. 차질, 좌절
overcome v. 극복하다, 이기다
obstacle n. 장애, 장애물
hypothesize v. 가설을 세우다, 가정하다
cope v. 잘 대처하다, 잘 처리하다

해줄 수 있다."라고 가정하였다.

우리가 선생님들에게 전화를 하여 숙제를 연장하고 모두가 장난감을 나누어 놀도록 모래 놀이통에 간섭하고 자녀들이 잘하는 과목만 선택하도록 종용할 때와 같이 우리 아이들을 가능한 모든 역경으로부터 보호할 때, 우리는 아이들이 이와 같은 덕성함양 경험을 쌓지 못하도록 하는 것이다. 심리학자인 마델린 레빈(Madeline Levine)과 댄 킨들런(Dan Kindlon)이 기술하였듯이 이는 청소년기와 성인기 내 어려움을 초래할 수 있는데, 이때 과잉보호를 받은 청년들은 결국 진짜 문제들을 홀로 부딪치면 어떻게 극복해야 할지를 모른다.

학교 안팎에서 부모들은 어린이들이 모험하고 스스로 도전하도록 독려해야 한다. 역설적이게도 어린이들에게 실패를 할 여지를 제공하는 것이 성공을 하도록 도와주는 가장 좋은 방법일 수 있다.

1 ⑤ ▶ **단락 나누기**

Ⓒ 이전에는 어린이들의 역경 경험에 대한 긍정적인 효과를 소개하고 Ⓒ부터 Ⓔ까지 부모의 과잉보호가 낳을 수 있는 우려를 설명한다. Ⓔ부터는 작가의 주장이 시작된다.

2 ③ ▶ **빈칸완성**

역경과 좌절을 겪은 어린이들이 성장했을 때 보다 사회 및 정서적으로 성숙하게 된다고 설명하였으므로 ③의 '자녀들에게 실패를 할 여지를 제공하는 것'은 해로운 일이 아니라 오히려 성공에 도움이 될 수 있을 것이다.

3 ② ▶ **내용일치**

세 번째 문장을 통해 ②의 "자녀를 과잉보호하는 부모들은 자녀가 자신감을 기르는 것을 방해하는 것일 수 있다."를 알 수 있다.

mastery	n. 지배, 숙달, 정통
adolescence	n. 청년기, 사춘기
overprotect	v. 과보호하다
confront	v. 직면하다, 마주보다
paradoxically	ad. 역설적으로, 역설적이지만

16

게임이론의 기본 가정은 모든 의사결정자가 자신의 이익에 의거해서 행동한다는 것이다. 사람들은 자신의 이익을 극대화하고자 하며 다른 사람의 이익은 부수적인 것으로 생각한다. 이런 상황에서 개인의 이익은 종종 집단 전체의 이익과 상충된다. 이것은 죄수의 딜레마로 알려진 유명한 가상 상황에 잘 나타나 있다.

죄수의 딜레마에서 두 죄수 A와 B는 서로 다른 방에서 경찰에게 심문을 받고 있다. 각 죄수는 두 가지 선택이 있는데 침묵을 지키든지 아니면 경찰에게 말해서 다른 죄수를 배신하는 것이다. 세 가지 가능한 결과가 있다. 먼저 둘 다 침묵을 지키면 그들은 6개월간 복역하게 된다. 만약 죄수 A가 침묵을 하고 다른 죄수 B가 A를 배신하면, 죄수 A는 10년을 복역해야 하지만 죄수 B는 석방된다. 만약 죄수 B가 침묵을 지키고 죄수 A가 B를 배신하면 그 반대가 된다. 두 명의 죄수가 서로 배신하게 되면 그들은 2년간 복역하게 된다. 이런 상황에서 최선의 선택은 죄수 두 명이 침묵을 지키는 것이다. 그러나 이것은 서로간의 큰 신뢰를 필요로 한다. 만약 한 죄수가 침묵을 지키고 다른 죄수가 그를 배신하게 되면 그는 최악의 결과에 처하게 된다. 그러나 두 명의 죄수는 서로를 100% 신뢰하지 못하기 때문에 가장 논리적인 선택은 서로를 배신하는 것이다.

이것은 언뜻 보기에 비논리적인 많은 의사결정에 작용하고 있는 기본 원칙이다. 예를 들어, 어떤 나라가 공해 문제를 완전히 없애거나 대폭 줄이는 것은 가능하지만 공해를 감소시키기 위해서는 에너지를 적게 생산하고 더 비싼 기술을 사용해야 하기에 그 나라의 경제는 손해를 보게 된다. 이런 경우 다시 한 번 지구 전체를 위한 최선의 선택은 모든 나라가 이런 결정(오염시키는 것을 멈추기)을 하는 것이다. 그러나 한 나라가 오염시키는 것을 멈춘다 해도, 다른 나라들이 그렇게 하지 않는다면 그 나라는 공해의 피해를 겪게 되는 것이다. 왜냐하면 공해는 지구 전체에 영향을 미치는 것이지, 공해를 발생하는 나라들에만 영향을 주는 것이 아니기 때문이다. 따라서 나라마다 가장 논리적인 결정은, 비록 공해 때문에 지구 전체에 더 부정적인 결과를 가져오더라도, 계속해서 지구를 오염시키는 것이다.

1 ① ▶ **글의 제목**

협력할 경우 서로에게 가장 이익이 되는 상황일 때조차도 개인의 이익과 상호불신 때문에 비논리적인 결정을 하는 게임이론에 대해서 설명하고 그 예를 들고 있으므로 이 글의 제목으로 ①이 적절하다.

assumption	n. 가정, 이론
self-interest	n. 이기심, 자기 이익
welfare	n. 복지, 행복
hypothetical	a. 가설의, 가정의
betray	v. 배반하다, 폭로하다
suffer	v. 형을 살다
at work	일하고 있는, 영향력을 미치는
eliminate	v. 제거하다
avert	v. 피하다
negative	a. 부정적인

2 ④ ▶ **내용일치**

④ 죄수들이 서로를 배신하는 것은 개인적인 욕심이나 이익 때문이지 게임이론 때문에 서로에게 이득이 되는 결정을 내리지 못하는 것은 아니다.

3 ③ ▶ **지시대상**

밑줄 친 ⓐ가 들어있는 문장은 앞 단락의 죄수의 딜레마에서 최선의 선택과 대구를 이루고 있으며, 죄수의 딜레마에서 최선의 선택은 두 죄수가 '서로 침묵을 지키는 것'이다. 따라서 죄수의 딜레마를 환경과 관련하여 각 나라의 상황에 적용시키면 경제적인 손실이 있을 수 있겠지만, 모든 나라가 환경오염을 멈추는 것이다. 따라서 ③이 정답이다.

4 ② ▶ **빈칸완성**

빈칸 ⓑ가 들어있는 문장은 앞 단락의 죄수의 딜레마에서 가장 논리적인 선택과 대구를 이루고 있다. 따라서 죄수의 딜레마에서 가장 논리적인 선택으로 '상대방을 배신하는 것'이라고 했으므로 빈칸 ⓑ에도 가장 논리적인 선택으로 '부정적인' 내용이 들어가야 할 것이다. 따라서 '계속해서 지구를 오염시키다'는 ②가 정답이다.

17

편승효과는 행동과학에서 잘 입증된 집단 사고의 한 형태이며 적용되는 곳이 많다. 이 효과의 일반적 규정은 행동이나 신념은 그 어떤 개인이 그것을 채택할 확률이 이미 그렇게 한 사람들에 비례해서 증가하는 가운데 사람들 사이에 퍼져나간다는 것이다. 더 많은 사람들이 어떤 것을 믿게 됨에 따라 다른 사람들도 그 근원적인 증거는 상관하지 않고 시류에 편승하는 것이다. 다른 사람들의 행동이나 신념을 따라가는 경향이 발생할 수 있는 이유는 사람들이 곧바로 순응하기를 더 좋아하기 때문이거나 다른 사람들에게서 정보를 얻어내기 때문이다.

편승효과는 투표에서 일어난다. 일부 사람들은 결국 승자의 편에 서기를 바라면서, 선거에서 이길 것 같거나 이길 것 같다고 언론매체에 의해 공언되고 있는 후보자나 정당에 표를 던진다. 그리고 그것은 사람들이 자신의 의견을 다수의 견해로 바꾸는 다수 의견과 관련한 상황에 적용되어왔다. 그런 의견 전환은 사람들이 다른 사람들의 결정에서 추론을 끌어내기 때문에 일어날 수 있다.

미국에서는 여러 다른 시간대들 때문에, 서부에서는 투표가 아직 진행 중인데도 동부에서는 선거결과가 방송되는 일이 있다. 이런 차이로 인해 미국 서부 유권자들의 행동이 다른 시간대의 유권자들의 결정에 대한 소식에 어떻게 영향을 받는지 연구하게 되었다. 1980년에 NBC 뉴스는 출구조사를 근거로 하여 로널드 레이건(Ronald Reagan)이 대통령 선거에서 당선되었다고 선언했는데, 이것은 서부의 투표소들이 문을 닫기 몇 시간 전의 일이었다.

그것은 또한 미국 대통령 예비선거에서도 중요하다고 한다. 미국의 주들은 어느 날 하루에 모두 투표하는 것이 아니라 몇 달에 걸쳐 모두 서로 다른 시간에 투표한다. 다른 주들은 어떤 특정한 날까지 기다려야 하는 반면에 일부 주들(아이오와 주, 뉴햄프셔 주)은 특별히 앞서 일찍이 투표를 진행한다. 이것은 종종 이 주들에게 부당한 영향력을 부여한다고 하며, 투표를 일찍 진행하는 이 주들에서 이기는 것이 후보자에게 큰 힘을 주어 그가 여세를 몰아 대통령 후보지명전에서 이기도록 해준다고 한다.

1 ① ▶ **부분이해**

대부분의 사람들이 하는 행동이나 생각을 따라 하는 것을 의미하므로 ①이 가장 가깝다. ② 사회 주류층의 일원이 되다 ③ 다른 사람의 성취에 의지하다 ④ 출세의 사다리를 타고 올라가다

2 ③ ▶ **내용추론**

편승효과는 시류나 대세에 따라가는 것이므로 "세상을 바꾸는 데 창의적인 소수가 평범한 다수보다 더 많은 역할을 한다는 것을 편승효과는 보여준다."고 한 ③이 추론할 수 없는 진술이다.

3 ④ ▶ **내용파악**

④처럼 어떤 사람이 바느질 솜씨와 수명과 옷감 때문에 디자이너 의상을 사겠다고 하는 것은 다른 사람들의 생각이 아니라 한 개인의 주관적인 판단에 따른 것이므로 편승효과의 예가 아니다.

bandwagon n. (서커스행렬 선두의) 악대차; 우세한 세력; 유행, 시류

bandwagon effect 편승효과

group-think n. 집단 사고, 집단 순응적 사고

hop on the bandwagon 시류에 편승하다, 영합하다

exit poll 출구조사

voting booth 투표소

momentum n. 여세, 힘, 추진력

propel v. 추진하다, 몰아대다

nomination n. 후보지명

4 ②   ▶ **태도**

이 글의 필자는 편승효과에 대해 자신의 의견을 말하지 않고, 있는 그대로 객관적으로 설명하고 있다. 마지막 단락이 편승효과의 불공정성이 문제될 수도 있는 내용이지만 'is said to V(~하다고 한다)'로 표현하여 객관적 진술태도를 유지한다. 따라서 ②의 '중립적인(neutral)' 태도가 적절하다. ① 긍정적인 ③ 일관성 없는 ④ 비판적인

18

DVD와 TV에서 하는 교육용 프로그램은 어린이들이 학습하는 데 있어 점점 더 커진 위상을 차지하고 있다. 그러나 이 DVD와 TV에서 하는 교육용 프로그램이 옛날 방식인 대화만큼 효과적이지는 않을지도 모른다는 새로운 증거가 있다.

심지어 태어나기도 전에, 어린이들은 소리와 단어들을 들으며 결국 언어가 될 다양한 소리를 옹알이 할 수 있다. "생후 9개월 전에, 아기는 수백 개의 언어에 들어있는 수백 개의 음소로 만들어진 옹알이를 합니다."라고 Ecole Internationale de New York의 언어치료사인 엘리자베스 크로스(Elisabeth Cros)가 4월 『타임(TIME)』과의 인터뷰에서 말했다. "부모는 그들의 모국어에서 그들이 인식하는 음소에 대해 반응을 할 것이며, 이것은 아기의 선택된 음소 사용을 강화시켜 줍니다."

효율적인 언어 학습에 있어 중요한 것은 유아와 유아를 돌보는 사람간의 바로 역동적인 상호작용으로 이것은 고정된 비디오나 TV 프로그램이 제공할 수 없는 말 주고받기이다. 그리고 워싱턴 대학교, 템플 대학교, 델라웨어 대학교 출신의 일단의 연구원들은 이에 대한 이유를 설명한다.

그 과학자들은 세 가지 다른 방식으로 동사를 학습하라고 임의로 배정된 두 살짜리 아기 36명을 연구했다. 이들 중 1/3은 실제 사람과 훈련했고, 또 다른 1/3은 스카이프와 같은 화상채팅기술을 통해 학습했으며, 마지막 1/3은 똑같은 사람이 가르치는 미리 녹화된 언어수업 동영상을 보면서 학습했다. 『아동발달(Child Development)』이라는 저널에 발표된 이 결과는 사람과 직접 대하고 실시간 화상채팅으로 했을 때 아이들이 학습을 잘했다는 것을 보여주었는데, 이는 아마도 두 가지 시나리오(사람과 직접 대하는 것과 실시간 화상채팅)가 아이와 교사의 상호작용을 가능하게 해서 어린이들이 더 반응을 잘하고 따라서 그들의 학습경험으로부터 더욱 더 많은 것을 간직하도록 해주기 때문인 것으로 보인다. 이와는 대조적으로 미리 녹음된 동영상을 이용해 학습한 아이들은 10분 학습이 끝난 후 시험 치는 방식으로는 새로운 어휘를 학습하지 못했다.

1 ④   ▶ **글의 제목**

이 글은 우리가 알던 DVD와 TV에서 하는 교육용 프로그램이 생각만큼 효과적이지 않으며, 그보다 쌍방향 의사소통이 가능한 방법들이 아이들의 언어학습에 유익하다는 글이다. 따라서 ④의 '동영상이 아이들의 학습에 있어 최고의 방법이 아닌 이유'가 글의 제목으로 적절하다.

2 ①   ▶ **부분이해**

옛날 방식인 대화는 DVD와 TV에서 하는 교육용 프로그램을 사용하지 않고 아이들과 직접 나누는 대화이므로 ①이 정답이다.

3 ①   ▶ **빈칸완성**

첫 번째 문장 다음에서 "생후 9개월 된 아기가 수백 개의 음소로 만들어진 옹알이(말을 트는 과정에서 아직 말을 못하는 어린아이가 혼자 입속말처럼 자꾸 소리를 내는 짓)를 한다."고 했으므로, 다양한 소리가 결국 말로 '합쳐질(coalesce)' 것이다. 그리고 두 번째 빈칸에서 '역동적인' 상호작용과 비디오는 서로 대조되는 말이 되므로, 비디오를 꾸며주는 말은 '역동적인'과 반대되는 '정적인(static)'이 적절하다. 따라서 이 두 빈칸에 적절한 ①이 정답이다. ② 묵인하다 ― 미적인 ③ 건강을 회복하다 ― 운동의 ④ 청년[사춘]기에 이르다 ― 마취의

4 ④   ▶ **내용일치**

세 가지 다른 방식으로 동사를 학습시킨 연구에서처럼, 언어를 배우는 아이에게 있어 학습방법은 단일하지 않고 다양하므로 ④가 정답이다.

---

effective a. 효과적인
old-fashioned a. 옛날식의, 구식의, 전통적인
conversation n. 대화, 회화
babble v. 종알종알 지껄이다 n. 중얼거림
phoneme n. 음소
native tongue 모국어
reinforce v. 보강하다; 강화하다, 증강하다
randomly ad. 무작위로, 생각나는 대로, 임의로
assign v. 할당하다, 배정하다

19

우리나라 국민에게는 어떤 병폐라고 진단이 내려지는 것이 하나 있는데, 그것은 곧 "양쪽 모두 일리가 있다"라는 식의 사고방식이다. 그것은 공정을 기하고 싶은 욕구에서 비롯되며, 실제 문제는 양쪽 각각의 지지자들이 종종 생각하는 것 이상으로 더 복잡하다는 인식에서 비롯된다. 그러나 그것은 건강한 사고 작용을 병적으로 회피하는 결과를 낳는다. 그것은 또한 때때로 "진리는 양쪽 사이 어디쯤에 있다"라는 식의 사고방식이나 "봤지? 난 균형 잡힌 사람이야"라는 식의 사고방식으로 나타나기도 한다.

습관적으로 "양쪽 모두 일리가 있다"라고 생각하는 것은 종종 사람들로 하여금 자신은 한 가지 주제에 대해 한 가지 의견을 갖는 따위는 하지 않는 사람이라는 착각에 빠지게 한다. (어느 한쪽이 옳다고 명확한 의견을 가진 사람은, "양쪽 모두 일리가 있다"라는 식의 논리대로라면, 자신이 반대하는 의견에 담겨 있는 진리는 알아차리지 못하는 셈이니까.) 이것은 논쟁 중인 문제의 알맹이를 회피하게 만든다. 이런 병폐를 가진 사람들은 종종 사실적이고 철학적인 문제에 있어서 개별적인 의견 차이점들을 발견하지 못하게 된다. 이는 그들이 자신들이 직접 논쟁을 탐구해봐야 소용없다고 생각하고 다른 사람들에 의존하여 명확한 의견을 형성하기 때문인데, 그들에게 명확한 의견이란 단지 다른 사람들의 의견을 인상적으로 배열해놓은 것을 의미할 뿐이다. 그들은 자신들의 생각도 중요하다는 것을 잊고, 그들의 역할은 '사람들로 하여금 각자의 생각을 정하게 하는 것'이라고 생각한다.

때로는 논쟁의 양쪽이 모두 강력한 근거를 실제로 갖고 있는 것이 사실이기도 하다. 어쩌면 심지어 대개의 경우 그게 사실일지 모른다. 쟁점의 복잡성을 인식하면, 그 결과 여러 가지를 다 생각하고 났을 때 여러 복잡한 의견들이 나오게 된다. 그러나 "진리는 양쪽 사이 어디쯤에 있다"라는 것이 선험적으로 사실인 것은 결코 아니다. 즉, 양쪽 모두 일리가 있다는 것이 사실일 때도, 그것은 양쪽이 하는 말에 세심한 주의를 기울이며 생각해보고서야 비로소 알 수 있는 것이다. "양쪽의 말을 경청해보자"라는 것은 건전한 생각이다. 그러나 양쪽이 똑같이 옳다고 미리 가정해버리는 것은 나태한 생각일 뿐인데, 불행하게도 흔히들 그렇게 생각한다.

이런 종류의 생각이 생겨난 원인의 일부는, 자신들의 생각과 다른 분석이나 자신들로서는 감추고 싶은 사실을 신문이 게재할 때 광고주들에게 편지를 써 보내는 호전적인 우익 인사들의 비판을 피하는 방법으로 기자들이 이런 종류의 생각에 의지해왔다는 데 있다. 오늘날 기자들은 대개 열띤 논제에 대한 기사에서 그냥 진실을 말하는 대신, 어느 한쪽의 말이 실제로 얼마나 허위인가와는 상관없이 '양쪽 모두'에게 의견 개진의 장을 마련해준다. 많은 일반인들도 이런 종류의 '균형'이 객관성과 같은 것이라 생각하고 기자들처럼 해버린다. 그러나 그것은 객관성과 같지 않다. 그것은 이런 사고 습관이 갖고 있는 너무나 해로운 점이다. 객관성은 결론을 도출할 수 있지만 선험적 '균형'은 그렇게 할 수 없다. 결론을 도출할 만큼 객관적인 논쟁에 참여하는 대중이 없다면, 누가 그런 논쟁을 이끌어 가는가?

1 ② ▶ 부분이해
'건강한 뇌 기능'이란 '활발한 사고 작용'을 의미하므로 이것을 회피한다는 것은 활발하게, 철저하게 생각하지 않으려 한다는 말이 된다. 이 글에서 논의되는 사고방식을 필자는 malady라고 진단 내리므로 bypass에 pathological이라는 수식어를 붙인 것이다.

2 ① ▶ 내용파악
세 번째 단락의 마지막 문장에서 "양쪽 모두 일리가 있다"라는 사고방식은 나태한 생각이라고 했으므로, ①의 생각 부족에 대한 변명으로 이용될 수 있다. ②의 양쪽 모두를 인정하는 것은 진리의 상대성을 의미하며, ③의 흑백논리나 ④의 종교적 근본주의와 반대되는 것이다.

3 ③ ▶ 내용추론
글의 마지막 문장에서 "who leads?"라고 한 것은 곧 journalists lead의 의미다. 마지막 단락의 요지도 진리를 말하고 객관성에 기초해 결론을 내리는 일을 기자들이 먼저 솔선해서 해야 한다는 것이다. 따라서 ③이 정답이다. ① "양쪽 모두 일리가 있다"라고 하는 양시론자(兩是論者)들은 공정을 기하고 싶은 욕구를 갖고 있고 자신은 균형 잡힌 사람이라고 말은 하겠지만 실제로 그들이 공정하고 균형 잡힌 생각을 가진 것은 아니다. ② 진리는 양측의 명확한 의견을 단지 모아서 얻어지는 것이 아니라 객관적으로 탐구하고 평가한 결과로 얻어지는 것이다. ④ 세 번째 단락에서 복잡한 문제에 대해 생각을 다하고 나면 복잡한 의견들이 나오게 되는 것은 사실이라고 인정했지만, 그것이 결론을 도출하는 데 방해가 된다고 말한 것은 아니다.

---

body politic 정치통일체, 국가; 국민

reflex n. 반사, 반영; (습관적인) 사고방식

allow v. 허용하다, 인정하다; 생각하다

pathological a. 병적인

bypass n. 우회로, 회피

meat n. 고기; 내용, 알맹이

at issue 논쟁 중인, 의견이 엇갈리는

there is no point in ~ing ~해도 소용이 없다

add up to 총계가 ~이 되다, 결국 ~이 되다

tableau n. 그림; 인상적인 배열

a priori 선험적으로

salutary a. 건전한, 유익한

presumption n. 추정, 가정

bellicose a. 호전적인

suppress v. 억압하다, 감추다

platform n. 연단; 근거; 토론회장

bogus a. 가짜의, 허위의

follow suit 선례를 따르다

cancerous a. 암(癌)의

4 ④ ▶ 내용파악

필자는 양시론을 반대하는 입장인데, ④의 how절 내용이 부르카를 반대하는 것과 여성의 부르카 착용 권리를 옹호하는 것을 모두 인정하는 양시론적 시각이고 그 앞에 I can't understand라고 했으므로 ④가 필자가 동의하는 내용의 진술이다.

5 ① ▶ 글의 요지

이 글은 우리 사회에 존재하는 양시론이라는 병폐를 지적하고 이를 시정해야 한다는 내용을 특히 두 번째, 세 번째, 네 번째 단락의 끝 문장에서 암시하고 있다. 따라서 ① "우리는 양쪽 모두를 탐구하여 양쪽 중 어느 하나로 결정하려고 애써야 한다."가 이 글의 요지다.

20

동물로서의 인간은 본성의 근본적인 변화를 통해 본능적 목표들뿐 아니라 본능적 가치들, 즉 본능적 목표들의 성취를 지배하는 원칙들도 변화시킴으로써만이 문명인이 된다.

프로이드(Freud)는 이 변화를 쾌락원칙이 현실원칙으로 바뀌는 것이라고 설명했다. 인간의 정신구조를 이 두 가지 원칙으로 해석하는 것은 프로이드 이론의 기본을 이루는 것으로, 무의식 과정과 의식 과정의 구별과 (전적으로는 아니지만) 대체로 일치한다. 쾌락원칙에 지배되는 무의식은 보다 더 오래된 근원적 과정들로 구성되어 있다. 이것들이 단지 쾌락만을 추구하다보니, 인간의 정신활동은 불쾌(고통)를 유발할 수 있는 모든 작용을 기피한다.

그러나 무제한의 쾌락원칙은 자연 및 인간 환경과 충돌을 일으킨다. 개인은 자신의 욕구를 완전히, 고통 없이 충족시킬 수는 없다는 것을 충격 속에 깨닫는다. 그리고 이렇게 실망을 경험한 후, 정신적 기능의 새로운 원칙이 지배하게 된다. 현실원칙이 쾌락원칙의 자리를 대신하여, 인간은 지연되고 제한되지만 확실히 보장된 쾌락을 위해 일시적이고 불확실하고 파괴적인 쾌락을 포기할 줄 알게 되는 것이다.

현실원칙의 확립으로 인해, 지금까지 쾌락원칙의 지배 하에서 거의 동물적 충동 덩어리에 불과했던 인간은 이제 하나의 조직된 자아가 되었다. 조직된 자아로서의 인간은 유용한 것을 추구하고 자신과 자신의 중요한 환경에 피해를 주지 않고 획득할 수 있는 것을 추구한다. 현실원칙 하에서 인간은 이성의 기능을 발달시킨다. 즉, 현실을 시험하고 선과 악, 진리와 허위, 유용한 것과 해로운 것 등을 구별하는 법을 배우는 것이다. 인간은 주의력과 기억력과 판단력을 갖게 된다. 그는 의식적이고 사고하는 주체가 되어 외부로부터 자신에게 부과되는 합리성에 부응해간다.

쾌락원칙의 지배 하에서 정신구조에 들러붙는 자극을 덜어주는 역할을 했던 운동에너지 방출 기능이 이제는 적절한 현실 개조에 이용된다.

이리하여 인간의 욕망 범위와 욕망충족 수단은 엄청나게 증가하고, 현실을 유용한 것에 일치되게 의식적으로 개조할 수 있는 인간의 능력은 욕망충족에 대한 외부 장애들을 점차적으로 제거할 것 같아 보인다. 그러나 인간의 욕망들도 인간의 현실개조도 이제부터는 인간의 것이 아니다. 그것들은 이제 인간의 사회에 의해 조직된다. 그리고 이런 조직이 인간이 원래 가졌던 본능적 욕구들을 억압하고 변질시킨다.

1 ③ ▶ 글의 요지

이 글의 중심사상은 첫 번째 단락에 나와 있으므로 ③이 가장 적절하다. 이 글은 단순히 프로이드의 이론을 소개한 글이기보다 프로이드의 이론을 빌어 인간의 문명화를 인간의 욕구충족 면에서 이해하고 설명한 글이므로 ④는 적절하지 않다.

2 ④ ▶ 내용파악

무의식 작용 과정은 쾌락원칙에 지배되므로 ① 무한한 욕구충족을 추구하고, ② 환경과의 충돌로 환경에 피해를 입히고, ③ 선악은 생각지 않지만, ④는 현실원칙에 따른 의식 과정과 연관된 것이다.

3 ② ▶ 내용추론

마지막 단락에서 문명인의 욕구충족도 사회적 제약에 봉착함을 알 수 있으므로 ②가 정답이다. ① 두 번째 단락에서 무의식을 이루는 원초적 과정들이 쾌락만을 추구한다고 한 것은 추구의 방향성을 말한 것이지 추구 과정에서 의식적 노력을 할 필요가 없다는 말은 아니다. ④ 적절한 현실개조로 인간의 욕구와 그 충족 능력은 늘어난다는 것을 마지막 단락에서 말하고 있다.

apparatus n. 장치, 기계, 기구; 구조
primary a. 제1의; 원시적인, 근원적인
draw back 물러서다, 손을 떼다
traumatic a. 외상성의; 충격적인
ascendency n. 우월, 우세, 지배
supersede v. 대신하다, 자리를 빼앗다
assured a. 보증된; 확실한
bundle n. 묶음, 다발
drive n. 충동, 욕구
gear v. (계획·요구에) 맞게 하다, 조정하다
motor discharge 운동에너지 방출
supremacy n. 최고, 우월
unburden v. 덜어주다, 내보내다
accretion n. 부착, 증가
instrumentality n. 수단
extraneous a. 외부의
transmute v. 변형시키다, 변질시키다

4 ③　▶ **내용파악**

네 번째 단락의 설명에 의하면 ③이 사실인 진술이다. ① 현실원칙에 지배된다. ② 자신의 피해도 없이 얻을 수 있는 것을 추구한다. ④ 환경에 피해를 주지 않으려 하고 외부에서 부과되는 합리성에 부응하려 한다.

5 ①　▶ **내용파악**

외부에서 자극이 들어오면 신경중추의 지시에 따라 운동기관이 행하는 반응을 motor discharge라 하는데, 이것이 현실원칙 하에서는 현실을 개조하므로 쾌락원칙 하에서보다도 더 생산적인 기능을 하는 셈이다. 갈증을 해소하기 위해 경쟁자를 완력으로 물리치고 하나뿐인 샘을 독차지하기보다 샘을 하나 더 파는 것이 더 생산적이라 할 수 있는 것이다. ② 원시의, 초기의 ③ 수동적인, 소극적인 ④ 금지의; (값이) 터무니없는

6 ②　▶ **내용파악**

인간의 가치체계는 쾌락원칙에서 현실원칙으로 바뀌는데, 억압의 부재는 곧 쾌락원칙에 해당하므로 빈칸에는 현실원칙에 해당하는 것이 들어가야 한다. 세 번째 단락 마지막 문장에서 현실원칙 하의 쾌락은 일시적이고 불확실하고 파괴적인 것이 아니라 지연되고 제한되지만 확실히 보장된 것이라 했으므로 ②의 '안전'이 적절하다. ① 방종 ③ 해방 ④ 환상

01

1970년에 출판되어 많은 논란을 빚은, 이상향적인 새 시대의 시작에 대한 예찬서『미국의 의식혁명(The Greening of America)』에서, 찰스 A. 라이히(Charles A. Reich)는 청바지를 반(反)물질주의적이고 공동체의식이 강하고 자유를 사모하는 사랑과 평화와 희망의 시대로 미국을 이끌어갈 새로운 제3의식 세대가 가진 해방 정신의 상징으로 찬양했다. 그는 제3의식 세대의 공인된 구성원들이 입는 옷은 기본적으로 기계로 만든 옷이며, 그 사실을 숨기려고도 하지 않고, 대량생산 상품을 부끄럽게 여기지 않으며, 미국 전역에서 4달러 99센트에 팔리며 모두가 읽을 수 있게 옷 바깥에 치수들이 인쇄되어 있는 그런 옷을 입어도 사교상의 점수를 전혀 잃지 않는다고 썼다.

말할 필요도 없이, 청바지와 그 외 다른 모든 것에 대한 라이히 씨의 예측은 지금까지 실현되지 못했다. 제임스 설리반(James Sullivan)이 자신의 산문적인 신문화 역사서에서 지적하고 있듯이, 청바지는 바니스(Barneys)와 프레드 시걸(Fred Segal) 같은 곳에서 일상적으로 100달러 내지 200달러에 팔리는 명품이 되었고 희귀한 빈티지 청바지는 값이 수만 달러에 이를 수도 있다. 청바지는 끊임없이 새롭게 만들어지고, 다시 디자인되고, 아름답게 꾸며지고, 더욱 공격적인 마케팅이 행해지면서, 이제는 평등주의와 보통사람을 의미하는 실용적인 옷이 아니라 신분의 상징이 되었다.

1 ① ▶ **동의어**
paean은 '기쁨의 노래, 찬가'의 뜻이므로, '찬사'라는 뜻의 ①이 가장 가깝다. 주절의 동사 hailed가 단서가 된다. ② 역설 ③ 비탄; 애가 ④ 묘책, 묘약

2 ④ ▶ **내용일치**
두 번째 단락에서 "청바지는 바니스와 프레드 시걸 같은 곳에서 비싸게 팔리는 명품이 되었다."고 했을 뿐, 바니스와 프레드 시걸이 고품질 청바지 애호가들만을 위한 전문점이라는 말은 아니므로 ④가 사실이 아니다.

3 ② ▶ **글의 목적**
이 글은 제3의식이 아니라 청바지에 대한 글이며, 청바지가 라이히의 예측과는 달리 고가의 명품이 되었다는 주장을 하기 위한 글이다. 따라서 ②가 글의 목적으로 적절하다.

paean n. 기쁨의 노래, 찬가
dawning n. 새벽녘; 시작
hail v. 환영하다, 찬양하다
Consciousness III 제3의식(자유, 해방에 기초하여 풍요로운 사회를 떠나 보다 자연적인 생활양식을 추구한 1960-1970년대 미국 젊은이 세대의 반문화적 의식)
certified a. 공인된, 보증된
just about everything 모조리, 몽땅 다
pedestrian a. 보행자의; 평범한; 산문적인
staple n. 주요상품; 주요소
a designer staple 명품
fetch v. (상품이 얼마에) 팔리다
vintage a. 오래되고 가치 있는, 유서 있는
utilitarian a. 공리적인, 실용적인
garment n. 옷, 의상
egalitarianism n. 인류평등주의
relentlessly ad. 가차 없이; 끊임없이
embellish v. 아름답게 꾸미다, 미화하다

02

1915년 무렵까지는, 영화는 길이가 짧았고 프로그램은 여러 작품으로 이루어져 있었다. 그런 후에, 그리피스(D. W. Griffith)와 그 밖의 사람들이 완전한 길이의 영화를 만들기 시작했는데, 그것은 멜로드라마가 주었던 것과 똑같은 강렬한 감정적 호소력을 제공했으며, 연극이 줄 수 있었던 것을 훨씬 넘어서는 구경거리를 보여주었다. 따라서, 제1차 세계대전 후에는 점점 더 많은 관객들이 영화를 보기 위해 연극을 저버리게 되었다. 이러한 추세는 1920년대 후반에 두 가지 새로운 요인 때문에 가속되었는데, 1927년에는 이전의 무성영화에 소리가 첨가되었고, 그리하여 연극이 우월하다고 주장할 수 있는 주된 근거 중의 하나가 사라지게 되었다. 1929년에는 심각한 경기 침체가 시작되었다. 특히 불황이 깊어짐에 따라, 관객들은 연극을 보는데 드는 비용의 몇 분의 1만 있으면 영화를 보러갈 수 있었기 때문에 연극을 보러 가는 것은 일부 소수의 사람들만이 할 수 있는 사치가 되었다. 제2차 세계대전이 끝날 무렵, 미국의 극장은 뉴욕 시에 있는 약 30개의 극장과 그곳에서 생긴 소수의 순회공연회사 만이 남게 되었다.

1 ① ▶ **내용파악**
1920년대까지의 '영화의 결함'에 대해 묻고 있다. '1927년이 되어서야 영화에 소리가 첨가되었다'고 했다. 따라서 ①이 정답으로 적절하다.

appeal n. 호소; 간청, 애원; 매력
spectacle n. 광경; (호화로운) 구경거리, 쇼
spectator n. 구경꾼, 관객
desert v. 버리다
accelerate v. 가속하다; 진척[촉진]시키다
principal a. 주요한; 제1의; 중요한
superiority n. 우월
vanish v. 사라지다
economic depression 경기 불황, 불경기
luxury n. 사치

2 ② ▶ 내용파악

사람들이 연극보다 영화를 택하게 된 이유로 본문에서 언급하고 있는 것 중의 하나는 '경기 불황(a depression)'이다.

3 ④ ▶ 내용파악

"제2차 세계대전이 끝날 무렵, 미국의 극장은 뉴욕에 있는 약 30개의 극장과 그곳에서 생긴 소수의 순회공연회사 만이 남게 되었다."고 했다. 따라서 "전문적인 연극 공연은 주로 뉴욕에서만 국한되어 행해졌다."고 볼 수 있다.

03

신고전주의는 회화와 또 다른 시각예술들에 널리 확산된 영향력 있는 운동이었는데, 1760년대에 시작하여 1780년대, 1790년대에 절정에 이른 후 1840년대, 1850년대까지 계속되었다. 회화에서 신고전주의는 고고학적으로 정확한 배경과 의상을 사용하여 고전적인 주제와 제재(題材)를 묘사하는 데 있어 간소한 선형적 디자인(구성)을 강조하는 형태를 일반적으로 띠었다. 부분적으로, 신고전주의는 1720년대부터 유럽 예술을 지배해온 감각적이고 경박하게 장식적인 로코코 양식에 대한 반동으로 일어났다. 신고전주의는 고대 그리스 로마 예술의 이상을 되살리고자 했다. 신고전주의 예술가들은 고전적인 형태들을 사용하여 용기, 희생, 조국애에 대한 그들의 사상을 표현했다. <로코코는 때때로 바로크 시대의 마지막 국면이라고 여겨진다.>

비록 이 운동이 서유럽 전역으로 확산되었지만 프랑스와 영국이 그들의 예술과 건축에 이 양식을 가장 빈번하게 사용한 나라들이었다. 이 운동은 허큘라니엄과 폼페이의 폐허에서 고대 이탈리아 유물들이 발견된 것에 의해 촉발되었다. 신고전주의는 합리성과 전통의 부활을 강조했다. 신고전주의 예술가들은 기둥, 박공벽, 소벽, 또 다른 장식 설계를 포함한 고전적인 양식과 제재를 그들의 작품에 통합시켰다.

1 ③ ▶ 문맥상 적절하지 않은 문장 고르기

첫 단락 끝에서 네 번째 문장에서 신고전주의가 로코코 양식에 대한 반동으로 일어났다고 하고, 이어서 두 문장에 걸쳐 신고전주의에 대해 기술했으므로, 그다음 또 다시 로코코의 시기에 대해 언급한 ⓒ가 문맥상 부적절한 진술이다.

2 ② ▶ 내용파악

첫 단락 마지막 부분에서 신고전주의 예술가들은 고전적인 형태들을 사용하여 용기, 희생, 조국애에 대한 그들의 사상을 표현했다고 했으므로 ②가 옳은 진술이다. ① 간소한 선형적 디자인을 강조했다. ③ 고고학적으로 정확하게 그 시대의 배경과 의상을 사용했다. ④ 화려한 장식이 아니라 간소한 선형적, 고전적 양식이다. ⑤ 현실을 초월한 종교적 신앙에 대한 언급은 없다.

visual art 시각예술
reach one's height 절정에 이르다
austere a. 꾸미지 않은, 간소한
theme n. 주제
subject matter 제재(題材)
archaeologically ad. 고고학적으로
setting n. 배경
costume n. 의상, 의복
sensuous a. 감각적인, 심미적인
frivolously ad. 경박하게
decorative a. 장식적인
revive v. 소생시키다, 되살리다, 부흥시키다
artifact n. 인공물, 문화유물
ruins n. 폐허
resurgence n. 재기, 부활
incorporate v. 통합하다
pediment n. 박공벽
frieze n. 소벽(小壁)
scheme n. 계획, 설계

04

제1차 세계대전의 공포가 엄청난 환멸을 가져다주었다. 이 환멸의 표현 가운데 하나가 곧 '다다이즘'이라 불리는 운동의 탄생이었다. ('다다'라는 단어 — '목마'에 해당하는 프랑스어 — 가 언제 어떻게 선택되게 되었는지에 대해서는 상당한 논쟁이 있다. 다다이스트 자신들은 이 단어를 아기가 처음 말하는 단어들 가운데 하나처럼 무의미한 두 음절로 받아들였다.) 1915년에서 1916년 사이에 많은 예술가들이 서구 세계가 나아가고 있는 방향에 대한 그들의 혐오감을 표현하기 위해 전쟁에 중립적인 유럽 국가들의 수도에 모여들었다. 다다이즘은 그래서 정치적인 시위였고 많은 곳에서 다다이스트들은 예술보다 좌익 선전물을 더 생산해냈다.

1916년에는 이미 소수의 예술작품들이 나타나기 시작했는데, 그 작품들 중에는 발견된 물건과 실험이 많았으며 여기에는 우연이라는 것이 중요한 역할을 했다. 예를 들어, 진 아르프(Jean Arp)는 아무렇게나 자른 종이조각들을 물체의 표면 위에 떨어뜨리고 떨어지는 대로 풀로 붙여서 콜라주 작품들을 만들었다. 막스 에른스트(Max Ernst)는 이상하고 아무 관계없는 물건들을 나란히 놓아

tremendous a. 무서운, 굉장한; 엄청난
disillusionment n. 환멸
dada n. 다다이즘(= dadaism: 전통적인 도덕적, 미적 가치를 부인하는 허무주의적 예술 운동)
hobby-horse n. (회전목마의) 목마
syllable n. 음절
neutral a. 중립의; 불편부당의, 공평한
propaganda n. 선전, 선전활동
collage n. 콜라주(관계없는 것을 짜 맞추어 예술화하는 화법의 일종)

설명할 수 없는 현상을 창출했다. 이렇게 보통의 물건을 이용해 그 전통적인 의미를 변화시키는 환경에 놓아두는 것이 다다이즘 예술의 특징이다. 『여자, 노인, 그리고 꽃(Woman, Old Man, and Flower)』에서 보이듯이 불합리성, 무의미성, 거칠고 기계적인 이미지 등이 전형적인 효과다. 이것은 기이한 특징과 비율을 가진 가짜 인간형태가 악의적인 비현실을 암시하는 무의미한 세계다.

1 ① ▶ **빈칸완성**
빈칸 다음 문장의 haphazardly가 단서가 되므로, 빈칸에는 ①의 '우연'이 적절하다. ② 계획 ③ 동기 ④ 결과

2 ④ ▶ **내용파악**
첫 번째 단락의 괄호 안에서 '다다'라는 단어가 언제 어떻게 선택되게 되었는지에 대해서는 상당한 논쟁이 있다고 했으므로 ④ '논란의 여지가 있는'이 정답이다. ① 이중적인 ② 신화적인 ③ 명확한

3 ④ ▶ **내용파악**
두 번째 단락의 네 번째 문장에서 '보통의 물건을 그 전통적인 의미를 변화시키는 환경에 놓아두는 것이 다다이즘 예술의 특징'이라고 한 것은 전통적 미학을 무시했다는 말이고, 그다음 문장에서 불합리성, 무의미성 등을 특징적 효과로 들고 있으므로 ④가 사실이다. ① 제1차 세계대전 중에 시작되었고, 환멸을 '벗어난' 것이 아니라 '표현한' 것이다. ② 예술을 위한 예술을 옹호하는 예술지상주의의 예가 아니라, 첫 번째 단락 마지막 문장에서 알 수 있듯이 오히려 정치적 성향의 예술 운동이다. ③ 새로운 기계와 무관하고, 두 번째 단락의 첫 번째 문장의 실험은 과학 실험이 아니라 예술 창작에서의 실험적 시도를 의미한다.

---

haphazardly ad. 우연히, 아무렇게나
juxtapose v. 나란히 놓다, 병렬하다
phenomenon n. 현상, 사건
conventional a. 전통적인, 인습적인
characteristic n. 특질, 특색, 특징
irrationality n. 불합리, 부조리
nonsensical a. 무의미한, 부조리한
bizarre a. 기괴한, 별난
proportion n. 비율; 조화, 균형
malevolent a. 악의 있는

05

많은 20세기 작곡가들은 지난 150년 동안 음악에서 사용되어왔던 화성법으로부터 등을 돌렸다. 프랑스 출신인 클로드 드뷔시(Claude Debussy)(1862-1918)는 파리의 음악학교에서 가르쳐진 19세기 화성법들을 거부했다. 그 대신 그는 그의 작곡 방식에 동아시아와 러시아의 화성 기법을 불어넣었다. 드뷔시와 함께, 우리는 오늘날까지 이어진다고 가정되는 시대인 서구 음악 예술의 '현대시대'로 들어선다. 드뷔시에게 음악은 리듬, 화성, 질감, 색깔 등의 많은 다양성으로부터 유기적으로 발전했다. 그는 스트라빈스키(Stravinsky)나 쇤베르크(Schoenberg) 같은 유형의 교훈적인 혁명가는 아니었다. 비록 그가 출판을 위해 보낸 많은 곡들은 그 곡들을 완성하는데 몇 달이 걸리거나 심지어는 몇 년이 걸리기도 했지만, 그의 곡들은 한 순간의 번득이는 영감에 의해서 착상되었다는 인상을 만들어 낸다. 드뷔시의 후기 음악은 인상파 화가들, 특히 모네(Monet)와 어떤 특징들을 공유하고 있다고 여겨졌다. 드뷔시는 그러한 비교에 동의하지 않았지만, 대상의 구조적인 윤곽선을 부드럽게 하는 것을 향한 인상주의 화가들의 경향성 및 빛과 색깔에 대한 그들의 열광과 드뷔시의 피아노곡인 『Préludes』 및 관현악곡인 『Images』와 『La mer』 사이에 존재하는 두드러진 연관성에 주목하는 것을 피하기는 어렵다.

1 ⑤ ▶ **내용파악**
후기 드뷔시 작품은 인상주의 화풍의 특징을 공유하고 있다.

2 ② ▶ **빈칸완성**
빈칸 앞과 뒤에 있는 문장은 역접관계에 있다. 따라서 ②의 yet이 적절하다. ① 따라서 ③ 마침내 ④ 그러므로 ⑤ 한편

---

harmony n. 화성법; 조화
Conservatoire n. 음악 학교, 미술 학교, 예술 학교
presumably ad. 생각건대, 추측하건대
didactic a. 교훈적인
mould n. (사람·사물의) 타입[유형]; 거푸집, 주형
correspondence n. 일치, 조화; 상응, 대응

06

한 방 가득 저명한 남자들이 예복에 넥타이를 한 채 품격 있는 저녁식사에 앉아 있는데, 그들 각자는 교양과 사회적 계급이라는 측면에서 다른 사람보다 더 뛰어나 보이려는 데 열중해 있는 듯 보인다. (이때) 어떤 남자가 버터가 담긴 접시를 가져오기 위해 식탁 너머로 팔을 내밀었는데, 그의 팔이 소금통에 부딪혔고, 그 소금통은 한두 번 흔들거리다가 넘어지고 만다. 소금 알갱이들이 비단 식탁보 쪽으로 쏟아지자마자 곧바로 그 신사는 앞으로 손을 내밀어 한 번 집을 정도로 몇 알갱이를 집은 다음 그의 왼쪽 어깨위로 던진다. 소금을 엎지른 것에 대해 그 신사가 보여준 이 미신행위는 아무 지적하는 말없이 행해지며, 저녁식사는 계속 진행된다.

소금을 엎지르는 것은 액운으로 여겨진다. 그러나 소금을 엎지르는 행동과 가장 연관된 미신은 소금을 엎지른 행동이 아니라, 소금을 엎지른 다음 하는 행동이다. 소금을 엎지른 사람에게 액운이 미치는 것을 막기 위해, 소금을 엎지른 사람은 엎질러진 그 소금을 자신의 왼쪽 어깨 위로 던져야 한다. 이런 매우 독특한 행동은 방패막이(액막이) 역할을 하는 것으로 추정된다. 그러나 이 방패막이가 효력이 있으려면 즉시 행해져야 한다.(소금을 엎지른 즉시 왼쪽 어깨 위로 소금을 던져야 한다.) 이런 매우 흥미로운 미신행위는 (역사적으로) 매우 오랫동안 계속되어 왔다. 비록 이 미신의 정확한 기원이 역사적으로는 불분명하지만 말이다.

소금을 엎지르는 것이 액운으로 여겨지기 오래전에 소금을 엎지르는 것이 결례로 여겨졌다는 사실에서 소금을 엎지르는 것과 관련한 미신의 기원이 있을지도 모른다. 먼 옛날 소금은 값비싼 필수품이었으며, 많은 유용한 용도로 쓰이는 필수품이었다. 따라서 소금을 낭비하는 것은 눈살이 찌푸려지는 것이어서, 소금을 쏟는 것이 '액운'이라는 경고가 조심성 없는 사람들에게 귀중한 양념을 낭비하지 못하도록 하기 위한 한 가지 방책으로 생겨난 것이라고, 일부는 주장하고 있다.

1 ② ▶ **글의 제목**
이 글은 소금을 쏟았을 때 미신행위를 하는 이유와 이 미신행위의 유래를 다루고 있으므로, 글의 제목으로 ②의 '어떤 미신행위와 이 미신행위의 유래'가 적절하다.

2 ④ ▶ **부분이해**
밑줄 친 ⒜는 '신사가 앞으로 손을 내밀어 한 번 집을 정도로 몇 알갱이를 집은 다음 그의 왼쪽 어깨 위로 던지는 행동'을 가리키는 것으로, 이러한 행동을 한 목적은 ⒝ 이후에서 언급한 'to prevent the bad luck from settling on the salt spiller(소금을 엎지른 사람에게 액운이 미치는 것을 막기 위해)'에 해당하므로, 같은 맥락의 ④ '액운을 미연에 방지하기 위한 방패막이를 제공하기 위해'가 정답이다.

3 ② ▶ **단락 나누기**
이 글은 식사 도중 소금통을 쏟은 사람이 하는 미신행위에 관한 이야기, ⒝ 그 미신행위를 하는 이유와 미신행위의 구체적인 방법, 그리고 ⒞ 이런 미신행위가 생겨난 유래에 대한 추측이라는 세 가지 이야기를 담고 있으므로, 세 단락으로 나누기 위해 적절한 구분으로 ②가 정답이다.

tails n. 연미복	
distinguished a. 저명한; 기품 있는	
bent on 열중하고 있는	
out-shine v. ~보다 뛰어나다	
breeding n. 번식	
retrieve v. 가져오다, 집다	
salt cellar 소금통	
wobble v. 비틀거리다	
grain n. 알갱이	
superstition n. 미신	
take hold 효력이 있다	
be around 계속되다	
bad form 무례, 결례	
commodity n. 필수품	
frown upon ~에 대해 눈살을 찌푸리다	
admonition n. 충고, 경고	
come about 생기다, 나타나다	

07

세잔느(Cezanne)는 한 편지에서 "화가에게 빛은 존재하지 않는다."라고 썼다. 이 역설적인 말로 그는 빛이 사물의 실제 형태를 왜곡할 수 있고 또 대개 왜곡한다는 점을 암시하고자 했다. 빛의 일반적인 효과는 빛이 접촉하여 반사되는 그 두드러진 점들에 말살시키는 힘을 가진 채 내려앉아 빛이 직접 닿는 부분 밖의 모든 부분들을 중요하지 않은 그늘 속으로 던져버리는 것이다. 물론 그 결과 얻어지는 명암비가 그 자체로 하나의 목적으로 이용될 수 있으며, 그것은 17세기와 18세기 매너리즘 화가들의 주된 즐거움이었다. 세잔느는 그가 그리는 물체의 입체적 부피와 촉각적 표면들을 실감나게 하려고 애쓰다가 그런 과장된 장치에 적절하게도 반감을 느끼게 되었다. 그는 색깔들을 순수한 상태로, 즉 고르게 분포된 빛 속에서 색깔들이 가진 정확한 색조 값으로 표현하려고 최선을 다했으며, 물체의 진정한 형태는 그때 생겨난다고 믿었다. "색깔이 풍부해졌을 때 형태도 풍부해졌다. 자의적인 빛의 효과를 이렇게 피하는 것이 3차원 형태를 2차원의 캔버스 표면에 나타내는 화가에게 중요하다면, 그것은 감각에 직접 호소하는 3차원 형태를 만들려고 노력하는 조각가에게는 분명 훨씬

paradoxical a. 역설적인, 모순된	
distort v. 왜곡하다, 일그러뜨리다	
obliterating a. 말살하는, 삭제하는	
prominent a. 두드러진, 돌출한	
realize v. ~에 현실감을 주다	
chiaroscuro n. 명암의 배합, 명암법	
exploit v. 개발하다; 이용하다; 착취하다	
tactile a. 촉각의; 입체감의	
rhetorical a. 수사적인, 화려한, 과장된	
render v. ~로 만들다; 주다; 묘사하다	

더 중요하다."라고 그는 말했다.

1 ①　　▶ **빈칸완성**
빈칸 다음에서 빛이 직접 닿는 부분 밖의 모든 부분들을 중요치 않은 그늘 속으로 던져버린다고 한 것은 그런 부분들을 죽이는 것이므로 빈칸에는 ① '말살하는 힘을 갖고서'가 적절하다. ② 깜박거리며 ③ 소생력을 가지고 ④ 초자연적인 방법으로

2 ④　　▶ **내용파악**
마지막 문장으로 미루어 ④에서 painting과 sculpture를 서로 맞바꾸어 놓아야 사실인 진술이 된다. 따라서 ④가 정답이다. 다섯 번째 문장의 'such rhetorical devices'는 chiaroscuro, 즉 빛과 그늘의 강한 대조를 가리키므로 ①과 ②는 사실이며, 여섯 번째 문장의 '순수한 상태의 색깔' 즉 '고르게 분포된 빛에서 정확한 색조 값을 가진 색깔'이란 빛에 의해 왜곡되지 않은 색깔을 의미하므로 ③도 사실이다.

3 ②　　▶ **글의 제목**
이 글은 세잔느가 그림에 미치는 빛의 효과에 대해 어떻게 생각했나를 설명한 글이므로 ②가 제목으로 가장 적절하다. 세잔느가 빛을 부정적으로 보고 피했으므로 Light가 들어간 ④는 제목으로 부적절하다.

purity n. 청정, 순수
plenitude n. 풍부; 충실
evasion n. 회피, 기피
arbitrary a. 자의적인; 전횡적인, 멋대로의
appeal n. 호소; 매력, 사람을 이끄는 힘

08

20세기로의 전환기는 유럽과 미국에서 생활이 몇 가지 극적인 변화를 겪음에 따라 일반적으로 인습 타파의 시대였다. 산업주의가 대두하고 있었고, 많은 나라가 제1차 세계대전에 참전했고, 사회는 급속히 변하고 있었다. 생활의 법칙들이 변함에 따라 일부 무용가들은 고전 발레의 형식적 규칙들이 너무 제약적이라고 느끼기 시작했으며, 그들 나름의 자유로운 흐름의 무용양식을 개발하기 시작했는데, 고전 발레와 차별화하여 '현대' 무용으로 알려지게 되었다.
현대 무용은 이제는 재즈무용, 발레, 탭댄스 같은 다른 분야와 더욱 밀접하게 혼합되어 있으며 일부 무용가들은 현대무용 양식과 고전무용 양식 모두에서 활약하며 두 양식에서 기술들을 이끌어낸다. 현대 무용 공연에서 무용가는 종종 맨발이거나 부드러운 신발을 신고 있다. 무용가는 자유롭고 거의 즉흥적인 방식으로 몸을 움직이며, 통제된 낙하와 또 다른 흥미로운 체중과 중력의 상호작용을 보는 것은 흔한 일이다. 도약과 하이 킥 동작으로 주인공들을 향해 몸을 뻗는 발레와 달리, 현대 무용은 종종 무대 바닥면 가까이서 머무는데, 심리와 강한 감정상태의 영향을 많이 받은 작품에서 특히 그러하다.

1 ④　　▶ **빈칸완성**
빈칸 이하에서 변화(산업혁명)와 파괴(제1차 세계대전)에 대한 언급이 있으므로 빈칸에는 ④ 'iconoclastic(인습 타파의)'이 적절하다. ① 경박한 ② 쾌락주의의 ③ 배반하는

2 ②　　▶ **내용파악**
현대 무용은 고전 발레의 형식적 규칙들이 너무 제약이라고 느끼고 자유로운 흐름의 무용양식을 개발하기 시작한 것이므로 ②가 현대 무용의 특징이 아니다. ① 즉흥적으로 연기하기 ③ 다양한 요소를 결합하기 ④ 몸을 마룻바닥에 가깝게 낮게 유지하기

3 ④　　▶ **내용추론**
현대 무용이 20세기 사회적 병폐의 해결책으로 각광받던 것은 아니므로 ④가 추론할 수 없는 것이다. ①은 둘째 단락 첫 문장이, ②는 둘째 단락 셋째 문장이, ③은 둘째 단락 마지막 문장이 각각 단서다.

underfoot ad. 발밑에서
restrict v. 제한하다, 한정하다
differentiate v. 구별하다, 차별하다
mingle v. 섞다, 혼합하다
discipline n. 학과, 교과, (학문의) 분야
barefoot a. ad. 맨발의[로]
improvisational a. 즉흥의
linger v. 오래 머무르다

09

그 어떤 조각칼 제조공도 고용주에게 "당신은 내가 예리한 조각칼을 만들기를 바라지만 나는 반대로 무딘 조각칼을 만들어야만 나 자신을 마음껏 표현할 수 있습니다."라고 말하지 않을 것이다. 예술가도 조각칼 제조공과 마찬가지로 주인을 위해 일하지만, 그렇게 하면서 그는 주인에게 주인이 결코 기대하지 않은 어떤 것을 준다. 렘브란트(Rembrandt)는 『야경(The Night Watch)』이라는 그림을 그렸을 때, 겉으로는 배닝 코크(Banning Cocq)라는 어떤 단장과 그의 사냥 단체 단원들의 초상화를 그리고 있었다. 아마도 학교 하키 팀의 단체 사진 같은 그림이면 단원들 모두를 만족시켰을 테지만, 렘브란트는 단장과 그의 친구들의 초상과는 무관한 어떤 할 말, 즉 빛이 어떻게 어두운 곳에 떨어지고, 어떻게 여기는 세게 부딪히고, 저기는 부드럽게 쓰다듬는가에 대해 해야 할 말들을 갖고 있었다. 그리고 그는 그 말들을 꼭 하기를 고집했다. 그렇게 하면서 그는 그가 그리는 그림의 원래 목적을 잊기 시작했다. 배닝 코크와 그의 친구들은 그가 하고자 하는 말을 명암을 배합하는 실험을 하기 위한 구실에 지나지 않게 되었다. 단원들은 화가 났다. 어떤 단원들은 자기 얼굴이 어둠속에 잠겨버렸다고 불평했다. 그들은 명암 배합보다 자신의 모습에 더 관심이 있었던 것이다. 이와 달리 우리는 즐겁다. 우리는 17세기 사냥 클럽에 대해서는 흥미를 잃어버렸지만, 렘브란트가 빛이 살에 어른거리는 것에 대해 말하고자 했던 것은 오늘날에도 1642년 때만큼이나 흥미롭다.

1 ③ ▶ **부분이해**
'주인이 기대하지 않은 어떤 것'은 그다음 다음 문장의 두 개의 대시 사이의 내용을 가리키는데 그것은 곧 ③의 '빛의 어른거림에 대한 것들'이다. 이것에 대해 말한다는 것은 이것을 그림으로 그려 보인다는 뜻이다. ①과 ④는 같은 것으로, 초상화를 그리는 겉으로 드러난 행위를 가리킨다.

2 ① ▶ **내용파악**
글의 첫 부분에서 조각칼 제조공이 한 말은 '장인이 하는 일은 주인이 바라는 물건을 바라는 대로 만들어주는 것이 전부'라는 의미다. 그다음 문장은 '예술가가 하는 일은 주인이 바라는 바를 충족시키는 것에 그치지 않고 더 나아가 주인이 기대하지 않은 어떤 것을 주는 것'이라는 의미다. 이렇게 주인이 바라는 바를 충족시키는 것 이상의 일을 하는 것이 장인과 다른 점이다. 따라서 ①이 정답이다.

3 ② ▶ **빈칸완성**
빈칸이 속한 문장의 but 앞에서 have lost interest, 즉 '흥미를 잃어버렸다'라고 했으므로, 빈칸에는 interest와 관계있는 ② fascinating이 적절하다. ① 혼란시키는 ③ 자극하는 ④ 힘을 북돋아 주는

chisel n. 끌, 정, 조각칼	
to the full 마음껏, 철저히	
blunt a. 무딘; 둔감한	
bargain for 기대하다	
ostensibly ad. 표면적으로는, 겉으로는	
presumably ad. 추측상; 아마도	
correspond v. 상당하다; 부합[일치]하다	
likeness n. 유사함; 초상	
caress v. 애무하다, 쓰다듬다	
lose sight of (시야에서) 놓치다, 잊다	
chiaroscuro n. 명암법, 명암의 배합	
semidarkness n. 어둑어둑함	
play n. (빛의) 어른거림	

10

입체파는 파블로 피카소(Pablo Picasso)와 조르주 브라크(Georges Braque)에 의해서 창안된 진정으로 혁명적인 현대 미술의 한 양식이었다. 입체파는 전례 없는 속도로 변화하는 세계에 반응해서 20세기 초에 진화한 추상미술의 초기 양식이었다. 입체파는 (젊은) 예술가들에 의해서 시도되었는데, 그들은 (입체파 운동을 통해서) 이미 과거의 것이 되어버린 서구미술의 진부한 전통에 새로운 활력을 주고자 했다. 입체파 화가들은 르네상스 시대 이후 미술의 규범이 돼버린 원근법과 같은 전통적인 재현형식에 도전했다. 그들의 목적은 현대를 반영하는 새롭게 보는 방법을 개발하는 것이었다. 1870-1910년에 이르는 40년 동안, 서구사회는 이전 4백 년 동안 이루어진 것보다 더 많은 기술적 진보를 목격했다. 이 기간에 사진, 영화, 축음기, 전화, 자동차 그리고 비행기 등의 발명은 새로운 시대의 도래를 알렸다.

그 시대 예술가들의 문제의식은 어떻게 지난 4세기 동안 미술에 기여해 온 진부하고 신뢰받고 있는 전통을 사용해 당대의 현대성을 반영할 수 있는지였다. 사진은 시대를 자세히 기록하는 도구로서 그림을 대체하기 시작했다. 이러한 상황에서 화가들이 앉아서 자동차들, 비행기들 그리고 새로운 기술의 이미지들을 그린다는 것은 도전에 정확하게 부응하는 것이 아니었다. 화가들에게는 더 <보수적인 접근방식>이 필요했는데, 그 접근방식이란 기술이 소통과 여행의 경계를 넓힌 것과 똑같은 방식으로 예술의 가능성을 넓히는 '새롭게 세계를 보는 방식'이었다. 이 새롭게 세계를 보는 방식은 입체파라고 불렸는데, 입체파는 현대미술에 등장한 최초의 추상적인 양식이었다. 피카소와

Cubism n. 입체파	
revolutionary a. 혁명적인, 개혁적인	
abstract art 추상미술	
unprecedented a. 전례가 없는, 공전의	
revitalize v. 새로운 활력을 주다	
representation n. 재현	
perspective n. 원근법	
dawn n. 새벽녘, 여명; 시작	
common interest 공통된 관심	

브라크는 입체파에 대한 그들의 생각을 1907년 파리에서 발전시켰다. 그들의 출발점은 폴 세잔 (Paul Cézanne)의 후기 그림에 대한 공통된 관심이었다.

1 ④ ▶ **글의 제목**
이 글은 입체파가 탄생하게 된 배경과 역사에 대해서 기술하고 있다.

2 ④ ▶ **논지의 흐름상 적절하지 않은 어구 고르기**
ⓓ 다음에 온 'a new way of seeing(새롭게 세계를 보는 방식)'에 맞게 conservative approach를 radical approach로 고쳐야 한다.

11

마르셀 뒤샹(Marcel Duchamp)의 1912년 작 『계단을 내려오는 나부 No.2(Nude Descending a Staircase, No. 2)』가 처음 선보였을 때, 예술계에서는 지금까지 알려진 가장 엄청난 논란을 유발했다. 그러나 수많은 거절, 냉소, 심지어 대통령의 비방에 직면하고 난 후, 이런 논란을 일으킨 그림은 걸작의 대열에 올라섰다. 『계단을 내려오는 나부 No. 2』는 인간의 형상을 입체파의 형식에 따라 기계화된 단색의 렌즈를 통해 재구성한다. 그리고 작품이 완성된 이후로 20세기 내내 계속해서 입체파 예술 전시회에서 전시되고 있다. 그러나 뒤샹은 이십 개의 서로 다른 정적인 자세를 사용해서 운동감과 시각적인 격렬함을 만들어 냈는데 이것으로 인해 입체파 화가들은 그의 그림이 그들의 아방가르드 미술 운동의 전형적인 예라기보다 미래파 그림에 가깝다고 주장했다.

그 프랑스 예술가(뒤샹)는 입체파의 작품이 전시되는 앙데팡당전(Salon des Indépendants) 봄 전시회에서 그 그림을 출품하기를 희망했다. 그러나 알듯 말듯 감질나게 만드는 제목인 『계단을 내려오는 나부 No.2』는 뒤샹의 형제인 자크 비용(Jacques Villon)과 레이몽 뒤샹 비용(Raymond Duchamp-Villon)이 포함된 심사위원회에 의해 단호하게 거부되었다. 그 형제는 뒤샹의 뇌이쉬르센 스튜디오로 뒤샹을 찾아갔고 그곳에서 그들은 뒤샹이 그 그림을 회수하거나 그 제목을 바꾸거나 덧칠을 하라고 부탁했다. 그 살롱 위원회는 뒤샹 형제들의 의견에 동의하며 "나부는 계단을 내려오는 것이 아니라 몸을 기대어 눕힌다."라고 주장했다.

그의 형제들의 만류에도 불구하고 마르셀 뒤샹은 작품에 변화를 가하기를 완강히 거부했다. 그는 후에 "저는 저의 형제들에게 아무 말도 하지 않았어요. 저는 바로 그 전시장으로 가서 저의 그림을 택시에 싣고 집으로 가져왔어요. 이것이 정말 제 인생의 전환점이 되었다는 것을 나는 당신에게 확실히 말할 수 있어요. 저는 그 이후에 그 단체에 대해 그다지 관심이 가지 않을 것이라는 것을 알았다."라고 말했다. 그럼에도 불구하고 뒤샹의 형제들이 포함된 입체파 화가 단체인 살롱도르(Salon d'Or)는 가을 전시회에서 고치지 않은 본래의 『계단을 내려오는 나부 No.2』를 수락했지만, 뒤샹 형제들 간의 유대관계는 영원히 금이 가게 되었다.

1 ① ▶ **내용파악**
뒤샹의 작품이 선보였을 때 많은 논란을 불러일으켰으며, 입체파 화가들과 살롱의 심사위원회마저 그의 그림을 이해하지 못했다고 했으므로 ①이 글의 내용과 다르다.

2 ③ ▶ **빈칸완성**
빈칸 앞에서 뒤샹이 자신의 그림을 전시장에서 집으로 가져왔다고 했으며 그 이후 자신의 형제가 소속된 단체에 대해 흥미를 잃었다고 한 다음, 그런데도 결국은 살롱도르의 가을 전시회에서 『계단을 내려오는 나부 No.2』가 걸렸다고 했으므로 빈칸에는 역접의 접속부사 ③ Nonetheless가 적절하다. ① 결과적으로 ② 더욱이, 게다가 ④ 마찬가지로

debut v. 데뷔하다, 첫 무대에 서다
uproar n. 소란, 소동; 엄청난 논란
scad n. 많음, 다수
put-down n. 헐뜯기, 비방
mechanized a. 기계화된
monochromatic a. 단색의
in keeping with ~와 일치[조화]하여
static a. 정적인, 고정된, 움직임이 없는
Futurist n. 미래파(현대 기계에 대한 자신감 표출이 특징)
tantalizing a. 애타게 하는, 감질나게 하는
hanging committee (미술 전람회 등의) (입선) 심사위원회
entreat v. 원하다, 간청[부탁]하다
reservation n. 보류, 조건; 의구심, 거리낌
flat out ad. 똑바로; 전혀, 완전히
turning point 전환점, 전기
fracture v. 분열되다[시키다]

12

마그리트(Magritte)에게 있어서의 초현실주의 운동의 중요성은 강조되어야 한다. 벨기에 예술을 완전히 매료시킨 세기말의 상징주의가 그에게 영향을 주긴 했지만, 당시의 그 어떤 다른 주의도 분명 그에게 어울리지 않았다. 초현실주의가 제공해준 기초의 도움으로 그는 비이성적이고 설명할 수 없는 세계로 나아갔다. 그럼에도 불구하고, 마그리트는 초현실주의자들의 주된 관심사를 항상 공유한 것은 아니었다. 특히, 무의식은 그들(초현실주의자들)에게 있어 핵심 개념이었다. 꿈에서의 무의식적 욕망의 표현에 대한 프로이드(Freud)의 사상 없이는 달리(Dali)의 1920년대 후반과 1930년대 작품을 상상할 수 없다. 앙드레 브레튼(Andre Breton)과 시인 폴 엘루아드(Paul Eluard)를 포함한 초현실주의 창시자들은 이성적 사고를 무시하고 무의식으로부터 직접 작품의 제재(題材)를 얻어내려는 자동(무의식) 글쓰기 및 그리기 같은 자유연상 기법에 몰두해 있었다. 그러나 마그리트는 그의 그림들을 꼼꼼하게 구상했고 그 어떤 자동적인 것(기법)에도 관심이 없었다. 마그리트가 초현실주의자들과 공유한 것은 혁명적 임무에 대한 의식이었는데, 그것은 예술은 사람들을 자유롭게 할 수 있다는 사상이었다. 그는 한때 자신의 그림을 "생각의 자유를 상징하는 물질적 증거"라 불렀다. 그의 1937년 작『자유의 문턱에서(On the Threshold of Liberty)』에는 마그리트의 작품에 기인하면서도 자주 등장하는 몇 가지 모티프, 즉 말방울과 도일리(꽃병 밑에 까는 자수 천) 형태의 벽지 무늬 같은 것들 뿐 아니라 섹스, 하늘, 자연 등, 매일 우리를 현혹하는 관습적 기호체계를 나타내는 이미지들을 대포 하나가 겨냥하고 있다. 대포가 발사하면 무슨 일이 일어날까? 또 한편, 대포가 발사하지 않으면 무슨 일이 일어날까?

1 ②　　▶ 빈칸완성
빈칸 앞에서 마그리트가 초현실주의의 영향을 결정적으로 받았음을 언급한 후 빈칸 다음에서 "마그리트는 초현실주의자들의 주된 관심사를 항상 공유한 것은 아니었다."고 했으므로 ②의 '그럼에도 불구하고(All the same)'가 적절하다. ① 결과적으로 ③ 게다가 ④ 예를 들어

2 ④　　▶ 부분이해
끝에서 네 번째 문장에서 '그는 한때 자신의 그림을 "생각의 자유를 상징하는 물질적 증거"라 불렀다'고 했는데, 그림에서 여러 이미지들을 겨냥하고 있는 대포는 그것이 발사되면 혹은 발사되지 않으면 어떻게 될까 하는 의문을 불러일으켜 관람자들의 자유로운 생각을 유발하는 것이다. 따라서 ④가 연관된 것이다. ① 무의식적 욕망 ② 자유연상 ③ 자동 그리기

3 ①　　▶ 내용추론
둘째 문장에서 '당시의 그 어떤 다른 주의도 분명 그에게 어울리지 않았다'고 한 것에서 초현실주의자임을, 그다음 though절에서 벨기에 화가임을, 빈칸 다음에서 다른 초현실주의자들과 다름을 추론할 수 있다. 따라서 ①이 정답이다. ② 달리와 더 많은 공통점이 있었는지는 알 수 없고, 빈칸 앞 문장에서 '비이성적이고 설명할 수 없는 세계로 나아갔다'고 했으므로 ③도 추론할 수 없고, ④ 초현실주의 창시자들이 이성적 사고를 무시하고 무의식으로부터 직접 제재를 얻어내는 자동(무의식) 그리기에 몰두한 것과 달리 마그리트는 이런 것에 관심이 없었다고 했으나 그렇다고 자신의 의식적이고 이성적인 세계에 갇혀있었던 것은 아니다.

---

ism n. 주의, 학설
suit v. 어울리다, 적합하다
fin de siecle a. (19)세기말의, 퇴폐파의, 현대적인
cast a[one's] spell over ~에 마법을 걸다, 완전히 ~의 사랑을 획득하다
leave one's mark 영향을 주다
foray n. 침략; (다른 분야로의) 진출
irrational a. 비이성적인
insoluble a. 용해하지 않는; 설명할 수 없는
founding father 창시자
free association 자유연상
bypass v. 우회하다, 회피하다, 무시하다
dredge up 캐내다, 들추어내다
material n. 제재(題材), 소재
plot out (이야기를) 구상하다
meticulously ad. 꼼꼼하게
token n. 증거, 표시
threshold n. 문턱, 문지방
beguile v. 속이다, 현혹시키다
doily n. 도일리(탁상용 작은 그릇을 받치는 레이스로 된 깔개)
cut n. 형, 모양
odd a. 이상한, 기묘한
recurrent a. 재발하는, 재현하는

13

19세기 초 런던에서 가장 유명하고 영향력 있는 남자로 묘사되는 조지 브라이언 '보' 브러멜(George Bryan "Beau" Brummell)은 혁명의 중심에 있었다. 그는 웅변술 혹은 무력으로 변화를 일으킨 것이 아니라 남성 의복 스타일과 양식에 대한 혁명으로 변화를 일으켰다. 남성들은 그가 입었던 옷, 버릇 그리고 심지어 그의 일상적인 차림새를 모방했다.
오늘날 그는 세계 최초의 멋쟁이 남자로 기억되는데, 그의 이름이 댄디라는 꼬리표와 같은 것을 의미했지만, 그는 그것을 만드는 데 영감을 주지 않았다. 『옥스퍼드 영어 사전(Oxford English Dictionary)』에서는 그 용어(댄디)를 "그 무엇보다 우아하고 세련되게 옷을 입기 위해 연구하는 사람"으로 정의하고 있으며, 이 용어는 브러멜이 태어난 지 불과 2년 후인 1780년에 기원을 찾을 수

rhetoric n. 수사법, 화려한 문체
military might 무력
masculine a. 사내다운; 남자[남성]의
sartorial a. (특히 남성용) 의류의, 재봉의
grooming n. 차림새, 몸단장
dandy n. 멋쟁이 (남자)
synonymous a. 동의어의, 같은 뜻의

있다. 그럼에도 불구하고, 브러멜은 오늘날 사람들이 옷을 입는 방식에 여전히 영향을 끼치는 새로운 남성 스타일의 상징이 되었다.

브러멜의 패션 모토는 '최소한의 장식으로 화려함을 극대화'하는 것이었다. 즉 오늘날 사람들이 '간결한 것이 더 아름답다(멋지다)'고 말하는 것처럼 말이다. 우아함이란 색과 장식이라기보다는 (옷의) 마름질과 품질과 관련한 것이었다. 그는 "사람들이 길거리에 있는 당신을 돌아서 쳐다본다면, 당신은 옷을 잘 입은 것이 아닙니다. 너무 경직되어 보이거나, 옷이 너무 몸에 꽉 조이거나, 너무 유행을 따르기 때문입니다."라고 경고했다.

브러멜은 또한 개인위생의 혁신을 주장했다. 옷이 세련되고 단정하게 보여야하는 것처럼, 사람도 그래야 한다. 그는 향수나 헤어 파우더에 대한 의존을 매일 목욕하는 것으로 대체했다. 그와 같은 시대를 살던 사람들에게 목욕은 종종 찬물로 얼굴, 손, 팔만 씻는 것을 의미했고, 땀을 흘리는 것은 몸의 독소를 제거하는 것으로 여겨졌다. 매일 따뜻한 물로 목욕을 하자는 브러멜의 제안은 혁명적인 것이나 다름없는 것이었다.

1 ① ▶ 내용파악
19세기 초에 오늘날 사람들이 옷을 입는 방식에 영향을 끼치게 만든 브러멜이 그 당시 유행한 옷을 살 수 있는 여유가 있었음에도 자신만의 스타일을 만들게 되었는지는 이 글을 통해 알 수 없으므로 ①이 정답이다.

2 ② ▶ 부분이해
브러멜은 '최소한의 장식으로 화려함을 극대화'하는 것을 권했는데, "less is more"는 "더 간결하게 함으로써 더 아름답다"는 뜻이므로 군더더기 없는 디자인 혹은 옳은 방식으로 조화된 단순한 옷은 우아하고 세련되게 보일 것이다. 따라서 ②가 정답이다.

3 ③ ▶ 빈칸완성
그 당시 사람들은 위생 관리를 제대로 하지 않았고, 땀을 흘리는 것을 독소 제거로 여겼다고 했다. 따뜻한 물로 목욕을 하자는 브러멜의 제안은 혁명적인 것이나 다름없는 것이라고 했으므로 마지막 단락에서 브러멜이 주장한 것은 '개인위생'과 관련된 것이라고 볼 수 있다. ① 패션 디자인 ② 합성 세제 ④ 향료

dictate v. 명령하다; ~에 영향을 끼치다
mantra n. 만트라, 진언(眞言); 슬로건, 모토
ostentation n. 겉치레, 허식, 과시
stiff a. 딱딱한, 뻣뻣한, 경직된
hygiene n. 위생
polished a. 윤[광]이 나는, 세련된
clean-cut a. 말쑥한, 맵시 있는; 단정한
contemporary n. 같은 시대의 사람; 현대인
nothing short of 거의 ~이나 마찬가지인, ~이나 다름없는

14

아방가르드란 개념은 주로 주류 문화적 가치에 반대하고 뚜렷한 사회적·정치적 날카로움을 가진 작품을 창작하는 예술가들, 작가들, 작곡가들 그리고 사상가들을 가리킨다. 많은 작가들, 비평가들 그리고 이론가들은 모더니즘의 형성 시기 동안 일어난 전위문화에 주목했다. 전위문화는 역사적으로 "고급" 문화 혹은 "주류" 문화에 반대해왔다. 그리고 전위문화는 산업화에 의해서 만들어진 인공적으로 종합된 대중문화도 거부해왔다. 이들 미디어(대중문화를 만들어내는) 각각은 자본주의의 직접적인 산물로서 이제 모두 중요한 산업이 되었다. 그리고 그러한 산업으로서 이들 미디어들은 진정한 예술의 이상이 아니라 다른 제조업의 분야들처럼 이익만을 추구하는 동기들에 의해서 추동되고 있다. 아방가르드 예술가들에게 있어서, 이런 형태의 예술(대중예술)은 그러므로 '키치(kitsch)'에 지나지 않는데, 키치란 전위문화로부터 훔친 형식적인 장치들을 사용해서 본래의 장치들보다 더 그럴듯해 보이게 만든 가짜이고 위조된 기계적인 문화이다. 예를 들어, 1930년대 광고 산업은 초현실주의로부터 시각적 매너리즘을 재빨리 취했다. 그러나 그렇다고 해서 1930년대의 광고 사진들이 진실로 초현실적이라는 것을 의미하지는 않는다. 정반대로 그 사진들은 중요한 실체가 없는 스타일만을 표현하고 있다. 이런 의미에서 아방가르드 예술가들은 진정한 아방가르드의 창조성을 때때로 새로운 소비자 문화의 이러한 제조된 형태에 대해 특권적 지위를 주장하곤 하는 시장 주도적인 패션과 표피적인 스타일의 혁신으로부터 신중하게 구별했다.

1 ③ ▶ 빈칸완성
전위예술이 주류 문화에 반대한다는 것이 이 글의 주제다. 따라서 빈칸 Ⓐ에는 ③이 들어가야 적절하다.

2 ① ▶ 빈칸완성
이런 예술이 자본주의 산물이라는 진술로부터 Ⓑ에 들어갈 표현을 추론할 수 있고, but

primarily ad. 주로; 첫째로; 본래, 원래
trenchant a. 날카로운, 통렬한, 뚜렷한
edge n. 날카로움, 격렬함
assertion n. 단언, 주장
vanguard n. 전위, 선봉
formative a. 모양을[형태를] 이루는, 형성하는
synthesized a. 합성의
industrialization n. 산업화, 공업화
substantial a. 상당한; 본질적인, 중요한
phony a. 가짜의
pretend v. ~인 체하다, 가장하다
superficial a. 피상적인, 표면적인

이라는 역접이 접속사로부터 ⓒ에 들어갈 표현을 유추할 수 있다.

3 ②   ▶ **빈칸완성**
창조성과 표피성에 대한 대조로부터 정답을 추론할 수 있다. ① 거부하다 ③ 확인하다
④ 받아들이다

4 ③   ▶ **내용추론**
전위 예술가들이 저항 정신을 포기했다는 진술은 본문 어디에도 없다. 따라서 ③이 정답
이다.

15

몇몇 사람들은 음악을 언어에 비유해 왔는데, 언어를 통해서는 음악과는 다른 기호와 의미가 청중
에게 전달된다. 이 이론에 따르면, 작곡가들은 자신의 다양한 경험에 대해 '비언어적 이야기'를 만
들어내고 이를 음악 작품을 통해 표현한다. 음악은 커뮤니케이션이다. 그것은 신성한 문서에 비유
되어 왔는데, 무언의 이야기, 조용한 속삭임을 담고 있고, 곡을 창작하는 동안의 정신적 과정과 연
결되는 심상, 기억, 의미, 사물들에 대해 큰 소리로 외쳐준다. 이러한 표현들은 작곡자의 매우 주관
적인 내부의 정신세계와 그 현실에 깊숙이 묶여 있다.
그러한 현실을 이해하기 위해서는, 음악작품을 통해 제시된 동일한 구조들(심상, 기억, 감정 등)을
자신의 주관적 정신세계를 통해 포착함으로써 음악을 이해하려는 단호한 청취자가 되어야 한다.
음악을 창조하거나, 연주하거나, 듣는 주체는 그래서 스스로의 세계를 쌓아 의미 있고 조화로운 전
체로 나가기 위해 의미 있는 음악적 구조들을 사용할 수 있다. 음악을 창조하거나 밑그림을 그리는
과정에서, 작곡가나 연주가의 외적 공연은 자신의 내적 세계를 형성하는 내적 작업 과정과 일치하
게 되고, 이로 인해 소리라는 외적 산물은 비로소 그것의 최종적인 형식을 얻게 된다.

1 ②   ▶ **글의 요지**
이 글은 음악이 작곡가의 주관적 경험이 음악적 기호를 통해 청자에게 전달되고, 청자의
주관적 세계를 통해 받아들여지는 소통(communication)의 과정임을 상세히 설명하고
있다.

2 ④   ▶ **내용파악**
음악이 언어에 비유된다는 내용의 바로 다음에, "이 이론에 따르면, 작곡가들은 자신의
다양한 경험에 대해 비언어적 이야기를 만들어내고 이를 음악 작품을 통해 표현한다."라
는 부분에서 우리는 음악이 비록 전달 수단은 다르지만 이야기를 만들어 표현된다는 점
에서 언어와 유사함을 알 수 있다.

3 ①   ▶ **빈칸완성**
빈칸 바로 앞에 "음악은 곡을 창작하는 동안의 정신적 과정과 연결되는 심상, 기억, 의
미, 사물들에 대해 큰 소리로 외쳐준다."라는 말을 통해, '음악적 표현들은 작곡자의 매
우 주관적인 내부의 정신세계와 그 현실에 깊숙이 묶여 있음'을 알 수 있다. ② 완전히
떨어져 있다 ③ 일으키다 ④ 효율적으로 활용하다 ⑤ 치열하게 경쟁하다

formulate v. 공식화하다; 명확하게 말하다
composition n. 구성: 작곡; 작품
sacred a. 신성한, 성스러운
whisper n. 속삭임, 귓엣말
psychic a. 마음의, 심적인
anchor v. 고정시키다; 단단히 묶어 두다
emphatic a. 어조가 강한; 강조한
constantly ad. 변함없이, 항상
entirety n. 완전, 모두 그대로임, 전체
coincide v. 동시에 일어나다, 일치하다
configuration n. 형태, 외형

16

아마도 1990년대의 힙합과 보다 현대적인 트랙(힙합 트랙) 사이에 존재하는 가장 두드러진 차이점은 가사에 있다. 일반적으로 지난 10년 동안의 힙합은 상대적으로 한정적인 영역에만 초점을 맞췄다. 힙합노래들은 아티스트의 성공 그 자체에 대해서 노래하기 보다는 아티스트가 성공에 이르게 된 과정에 대해서 노래하는 경우가 더 많았다. 심지어 가장 상업적으로 성공한 래퍼조차도 폭력, 범죄, 그리고 가난에 시달린 인생에 대한 가사를 쓰는 경우가 많았다. Billboard's Hip-Hop chart의 매니저인 Rauly Ramirez에 따르면, 90년대의 래퍼들은 그들 자신들을 폭력배나 갱스터로 묘사하는 것을 통해서 '자신의 페르소나(예술가로서의 가면, 혹은 이미지)를 만들어 내곤했는데,' 그 이유는 그러한 페르소나가 '그들을 성공으로 이끌어준 캐릭터'이기 때문이었다. 이런 캐릭터를 창조하고 유지하는 것에 대한 아티스트의 필요성은 90년대 랩 노래들의 공통적인 주제를 이끌어 냈다. 랩은 빈민가의 삶에 대한 이야기였고 갱스터들의 노래였는데, 90년대 랩의 이러한 측면은 랩이 주류 음악인 팝과 록에 합류하는 것을 가로막았다.

반면 10년이 지난 뒤, 랩의 가사들은 여전히 아티스트의 이야기를 노래하지만, 각각의 래퍼는 서로 다른 이야기를 한다. 아티스트들은 이제 더 이상 대형 음반사와 계약을 하기 위해서 '빈민가에서의 삶'에 대한 가사를 쓸 필요가 없다. 래퍼가 누구일 수 있는가와, 힙합이 무엇을 말할 수 있는가에 대한 정의는 2000년대 중반 이후 거의 무한정 확장되었다. Ramirez는 이런 전환의 기원이 2004년에 발표된 Kanye West의 데뷔 앨범 "The College Dropout"부터라고 꼭 집어서 지적한다. 이 앨범은 마약 밀매 혹은 폭력 혹은 거리에서의 삶에 초점을 맞추기보다는 종교, 음악에 대한 웨스트의 추구, 그리고 그가 "Breathe In Breathe Out"이라는 트랙에서 말했듯이 '무엇인가 중요한 것을 말하고자 하는' 그의 욕망 등에 초점을 맞추고 있다. Kanye의 첫 번째 앨범이 발표되고 난후, 이어지는 세월 속에서 더욱더 많은 래퍼들이 '갱스터 랩'에서 벗어나서 예술가로서 그들의 개성을 발전시키는 쪽을 향해 나갔다. 오늘날 가장 성공한 힙합 아티스트들은 중고품 가게에서의 쇼핑에서부터 지나칠 정도로 풍요로운 삶의 방식에 이르는 모든 것에 대해서 랩을 통해 노래한다.

1 ⑤   ▶ 글의 제목
이 글은 1990년대 힙합과 2000년대 힙합의 차이점을 가사의 관점에서 서술하고 있다. 따라서 ⑤가 이 글의 제목으로 적절하다.

2 ④   ▶ 내용파악
④는 본문에 언급되지 않은 내용이다. 그리고 ②는 '~ more about his or her rise to it'라는 단서로부터 정답이 되지 않음을 추론할 수 있다.

3 ①   ▶ 빈칸완성
Kanye West's 2004 debut album부터 가사의 내용이 바뀌었다는 사실로부터 정답을 유추할 수 있다. 따라서 '변화, 전환'을 의미하는 ① transition이 빈칸에 적절하다. ② 침체 ③ 퇴화 ④ 인식, 인지 ⑤ 편견, 선입관

striking a. 이목[주의]을 끄는, 인상적인; 현저한

poverty n. 가난, 빈곤

thug n. 폭력배

ghetto n. 슬럼가, 빈민가

anthem n. (국가·단체 등에 중요한 의미가 있는) 노래; 성가, 찬송가

pinpoint v. 정확하게 지적하다

individuality n. 개성, 개인성

17

프랑스 인상주의의 발전은 예술사상 가장 중요한 분수령 중 하나였다. 인상주의파 화가들은 새로운 화법을 개척하여 예술을 개혁하였으며, 그런 과정에서 수없이 많은 예술 영역의 발전에 영향을 미치는 한편, 전통과 사실주의를 강조하던 이전 화법을 탈피하는 배경을 수립하였다. 클로드 모네(Claude Monet)가 1872년의 한 전시회에서 『인상: 일출(Impression: Sunrise)』이라는 제목의 작품을 공개했을 때, 한 프랑스 예술비평가는 그의 작품을 비롯한 몇몇 화가들의 작품들은 한 장면의 느낌을 스케치한 것일 뿐 완성된 예술작품이 아니라고 퇴짜를 놓았다. 이리하여, 이 전시회에 출품했던 그 화가들 무리가 인상주의파라고 알려지게 되었다.

인상주의파의 주제와 화법은 독특했다. 이 화가들은 하녀들이나 농부, 세탁부의 일상 모습 등 순수예술에 적합하지 않다고 여겨졌던 많은 주제들을 화폭에 담았다. 그렇게 함으로써, 화가들이 보다 많은 관람객들의 취향에 맞추어 초점을 바꾸어 작품들을 '민주화' 시키기 시작했다고 할 수도 있다. 몇몇 비평가들은 인상주의파 화가들을 비웃었고 이들 인상주의파 화가들의 인기를 불쾌하게 생각했다. 대다수의 경우, 인상주의파들은 화단의 주류로 대접받지 못했거나 또는 '살롱'이라 불렸던 프랑스 국립예술전시회에 작품을 전시할만한 역량을 갖추었다는 인정도 받지 못했지만, 살롱에서 성공을 거둔 인상주의파 화가들도 몇 명 있었다. 하지만, 전반적으로 전통적인 예술계는 이들을 반항자들로 치부했다. 혹평에도 굴하지 않고, 이들은 자체적인 전시회를 개최했고 살롱과의 관계를 제한시켰다.

그 이름이 시사하는 것처럼 인상주의파 화가들은 명확한 묘사보다는 이미지의 느낌만으로 표현하고자 했다. 이들은 빠짐없이 고르게 물감을 칠하는 대신, 붓으로 캔버스를 두드리듯 짧게 붓터치를 하는 방식을 선호했다. 인상주의파의 화법은 부드럽고, 흐릿하며, 거의 몽환적인 느낌을 창출했다.

1 ③　　▶ **내용추론**

인상주의파 화가인 클로드 모네가 한 전시회에서 작품을 처음 공개했을 때, 한 비평가로부터 퇴짜를 맞았다고 했으나, 이후 새로운 화법을 개척해서 많은 예술 영역의 발전에 영향을 주었다고 했으므로 ③이 정답이다. ① 인상주의파 화가들은 수없이 많은 예술 영역의 발전에 영향을 주었다고 했다. ② 인상주의에서 자연적인 형태가 기하학적인 모양으로 표현된다는 말은 없다. ④ 인상주의는 (자연의) 장면들을 명확히 묘사하기 보다는 이미지의 느낌만을 표현하고자 했다.

2 ④　　▶ **내용파악**

화단의 주류로 인정받지 못했고, 살롱에 전시할만한 역량을 갖추었다고 인정받지 못했던 인상주의파의 화법은 거의 몽환적인 느낌을 창출했다고 했으며, 명확한 묘사대신 이미지의 느낌을 표현하려고 했다고 했으므로 이와 대조되는 대다수의 작품들은 인상주의 화가와 비교했을 때 ① 더 사실적이었을 것이다. 또한 ② 더 많은 명확한 묘사를 했을 것이며, ③ 인상주의 작품들은 순수예술에 적합하지 않다고 여겨졌던 하층민의 일상모습을 화폭에 담았다고 했으므로 이와 비교되는 대다수의 작품들은 하층민의 일상모습에는 관심이 없었을 것임을 알 수 있다. 하지만 ④ 대다수의 작품들이 인상주의 그림보다 오늘날 더 평가를 받는다는 내용은 본문에서 알 수 없다.

3 ④　　▶ **내용추론**

처음에 인상주의파의 작품이 공개되었을 때, 한 비평가가 한 장면의 느낌을 스케치한 것일 뿐 완성된 작품이 아니라고 퇴짜를 놓으면서, 이들 화가들이 '인상주의파'라고 알려지게 되었다고 했으므로 처음에는 인상주의파라는 용어가 안 좋은 이미지임을 알 수 있으나, 인상주의 화가들이 예술을 개혁하고 예술발전에 영향을 미쳤다고 했으므로 나중에는 결국 좋은 이미지로 바뀌었음을 알 수 있으므로 ④가 정답이다.

4 ①　　▶ **동의어**

watershed는 '분수령, 중대한 분기점'을 나타내므로 '중대한 시점, 중대한 국면'을 나타내는 ①의 junctures가 가장 의미상 유사하다. ② 끌어내기, 꾀어내기 ③ 예비 교섭; 제안 ④ 취미, 여가 활동

---

impressionism n. 인상주의, 인상파

watershed n. 분수령, 중대한 분기점

revolutionize v. 혁명[대변혁]을 일으키다

pioneer v. 개척하다

set the stage for ~을 준비하다, ~의 자리를 마련해주다

rejection n. 거절, 각하, 부인

emphasize v. 강조하다

dismiss v. 묵살[일축]하다; 해고하다

unique a. 유일무이한, 독특한

maidservant n. 하녀

peasant n. 농부

washwomen n. 세탁부(= washerwoman)

democratize v. 민주화하다

deride v. 조롱[조소]하다, 비웃다

resent v. 분개하다

popularity n. 인기

rebellious a. 반역하는, 반항적인

undaunted a. 불굴의, 기가 꺾이지 않는

brushstroke n. 솔질, 붓놀림

dab v. 가볍게 두드리다; 살짝 칠하다

blurry a. 흐릿한

18

버배팀(축어적) 연극은 사고나 재난에 연루된 사람들의 말을 통해 실화를 들려준다. 대사는 배우들이 말하지만, 어쩌다가 특별한 상황 속에 있었던 보통 사람들과의 인터뷰 기록에서 직접 뽑아온 것이다. (때때로 조사위원회 같은 출처에서 얻은 공적 증언을 더하기도 한다.) 일반적으로 무대배경은 추상적으로 최소한이며, 설명되고 있는 그 사건들을 그대로 재현할 의도는 없다. 이 연극의 힘은 전적으로 말해지고 있는 말에 있다. 전통적인 연극의 간략하게 절제되고 다듬어진 대화와는 달리, 버배팀 연극에는 실제 말의 특징인 '음~'과 '아~'와 끝맺지 못한 문장들이 들어있다. 효과는 깜짝 놀랄만할 수 있다. 이 연극들을 본 실제 사고 경험자들은 "처음 연극이 시작되자 두 손으로 얼굴을 가렸어요. 그러나 놀라웠어요. 정말 굉장했어요."라고 말한다.

버배팀 연극을 잘 모르는 사람들은 때때로 그것이 누군가의 가슴 아픈 개인적인 이야기를 오락용으로 이용할 것이라고 걱정한다. 그러나 연극은 여러 가지 일이나 사물에 대해 이야기하기 위한 큰 매체이며 어느 정도로는 치유를 위한 매체이다. 우리는 버배팀 연극에 의해 무언가를 정면으로 다룰 수 있고 공동체사회가 그 이야기에 나오는 사람들을 지지하고 포용하고 있다는 느낌을 가질 수 있다. 또 하나의 일반적인 오해는 버배팀 연극의 극본이 오려붙이기 작업에 불과한 것이고 모든 일이 인터뷰 받는 사람들에 의해 행해진다는 것이다. 그 문제라면, 이것을 다큐멘터리 영화 제작 과정과 비교해보는 것이 유용한데, 다큐멘터리 영화에서도 극작가의 역할은 누구를 인터뷰할 것이고 무엇에 대해 물어볼 것인지를 결정한 다음 어느 인터뷰의 어느 부분을 사용할 것인지를 결정하고 그 모든 것을 함께 짜 맞추어 하나의 일관성 있는 이야기를 들려주는 것이다.

1 ② ▶ **빈칸완성**
주절에서 버배팀 연극의 대사를 '음~, 아~'나 불완전한 문장 같은 실제 상황에서 입에서 나오는 그대로의 말이라고 설명하므로 전통적인 연극의 대사로는 실제 그대로가 아닌 ②의 '절제되고 다듬어진'이 적절하다. ① 장황하고 성가신 ③ 꾸밈없고 솔직한 ④ 불안정하고 민감한

2 ① ▶ **부분이해**
여기서 address는 '다루다, 처리하다'는 뜻이고 head-on은 '정면으로, 직접적으로'의 뜻이므로 ①이 가장 가깝다. ② 무언가에 대중들의 주의를 환기시키다 ③ 무언가에 대해 솔직히 말하다 ④ 무언가를 토론의 의제로 삼다

3 ④ ▶ **내용추론**
셋째 문장 대시 다음에서 '그 사건들을 그대로 재현할 의도는 없다'고 한 것과 첫 단락 마지막에 나온 사고 경험자들의 말에서 알 수 있듯이 사고를 재현해서 생존자들을 가슴 아프게 하는 것은 아니므로 ④는 추론할 수 없는 진술이다.

4 ③ ▶ **글의 목적**
이 글은 버배팀 연극이 어떠한 것인가를 설명한 글이므로, 글의 목적으로 ③이 가장 적절하다. 둘째 단락의 버배팀 연극에 대한 두 가지 오해는 버배팀 연극에 대한 설명의 일부이지 그 오해를 풀기 위해 이 글을 쓴 것은 아니다.

---

verbatim a. 축어적인, 말 그대로인
ad. 축어적으로, 말 그대로
transcript n. 베낀 것, 사본, 필기한 기록
abstractly ad. 추상적[관념적, 이론적]으로
clip v. 잘라내다, 오려내다, 단축하다
polish v. 윤을 내다, 다듬다
electrify v. 깜짝 놀라게 하다, 충격을 주다
sensational a. 놀라운, 굉장한, 선정적인
heartache n. 마음아픔, 비탄
address v. 역점을 두어 다루다
head-on ad. 정면으로
playscript n. 극본
cut-and-paste n. 오려붙이기
weave v. 천을 짜다
cohesive a. 일관성 있는

19

종교와 집단적 삶의 제도적 제약으로부터 예술이 이처럼 "자유"를 얻게 됨으로써, 예술은 훨씬 더 비판적인 사회적 역할을 할 수 있게 되었다. 보통의 관람객들에게 많은 현대 미술은 전혀 "영적"으로 보이지 않을 수도 있고, 오히려 현대 사회와 인간의 상태에 대해 자기 분석적이고 매우 비판적으로 보일 수 있다. 비록 현대 미술이 영적으로 보이지 않을 수도 있지만, 이 비판적 기능은 종교의 전통적인 역할을 예술이 장악하게 된 것의 연장선에 있다. 예술은 도덕의 새로운 심판자가 되었는데, 이것은 종종 관습적인 도덕률을 지지하기보다는 전도시키는 것과 관련되어 있다. 바르쥔(Barzun)이 주장했듯이, 20세기 초에 상징주의자들 및 여타 초기 모더니스트들의 전략은 예술을 현실의 정수로 대변하고, 그렇게 함으로써 다른 모든 것들은 거짓이고 인위적인 것들로서, 결국 의심의 대상이 되도록 하는 것이었다. 예술이 진정한 생명력의 척도가 되었다. 다른 모든 가치들은 니체(Nietzsche)가 저항이라고 부르는 것 안에서 뒤집히거나 의심받았다.

이러한 영적, 물질적 저항은 영향력 있는 20세기 후반과 21세기 예술가들에게 계속해서 동기를 부여하고 있다. 유명한 공연 미술작품 『Coyote: I Like America and America Likes Me』(Rene Block Gallery, 1974년 뉴욕)에서, 미술가 요셉 보이스(Joseph Beuys)는 펠트 담요로 몸을 감싸고 1주일 동안 코요테가 있는 방에서 지냈다. 방안의 몇 안 되는 소품 중 하나가 『월스트리트 저널(Wall Street Journal)』이었다. 코요테가 그토록 집요하게 오줌을 싸는 『월스트리트 저널』은 보이스에게 현대의 삶에 대한 생각을 고통스럽게 하는, "최후의 사후 경직"을 전형적으로 표현한 것이었다. 경제적 자본의 이름으로 다른 모든 것을 희생할 태세가 된 문화가 숭상하는 유일한 "실체"가 바로 경제적 자본이다. 보이스가 말하는 "실체"(또는 자본)의 의미는 완전히 다른 것으로서, 창조적이고 정령 신앙적인 에너지와 상상력으로서의 예술(자본)에 대한 샤머니즘적 인식에서 자라난, 사회적, 우주적 총체성을 반영하는 비전체주의적 세계를 향한 모든 성장 가능성의 궁극적 뿌리였다. 보이스의 정치 예술은 20세기 후반의 "영적" 예술이 현대 문화에서 비판적 역할을 하여, 100여 년 전 아방가르드의 탄생과 함께 시작되었던 한 경향성을 확장시킨 방식을 예시하고 있다.

1 ②   ▶ **글의 제목**
이 글은 '종교의 전통적인 역할인 비판적 기능을 예술이 장악하게 되었다', '예술은 도덕의 새로운 심판자가 되었다'는 요지를 전달하고 있다.

2 ③   ▶ **빈칸완성**
'다른 모든 것들은 거짓이고 인위적인 것들로서, 결국 의심의 대상이 되도록 하는 것', '다른 모든 가치들은 뒤집히거나 의심받는 것', '예술만이 진정한 생명력의 척도가 되도록 하는 것' 등의 진술에서 예술을 통해 사회의 전반적 가치에 대한 총체적 '저항'을 말하고 있음을 추론할 수 있다. ① 화해 ② 불멸 ④ 초월 ⑤ 미학

3 ④   ▶ **부분이해**
문맥상 보이스에게 있어 '경제적 자본만을 유일한 실체'로 숭상하는 이 사회는 '전체주의적 사회'나 다름없을 것이다. 보이스는 자신의 작품에서 그러한 사회를 비판하면서 '창조적이고 정령 신앙적인 에너지와 상상력을 바탕으로 모든 가능성'을 꿈꾸었다.

4 ⑤   ▶ **내용일치**
앞부분에서 '보통의 관람객들에게 현대 미술은 전혀 "영적"으로 보이지 않을 수 있다'고 하였지만, 필자는 '보이스의 정치 예술은 20세기 후반의 "영적" 예술이 현대 문화에서 비판적 역할을 했던 방식을 예시하고 있다'고 하였다.

constraint n. 제약

contemporary a. 현대의

assumption n. 장악, 인수

arbiter n. 결정권자

inversion n. 전도

affirmation n. 확언, 지지

vitality n. 활력

overturn v. 뒤집히다

motivate v. 동기를 부여하다

prop n. 소품

persistently ad. 집요하게

urinate v. 오줌을 누다

epitomize v. 전형적으로 보여주다

rigor mortis 사후 경직

afflicting a. 비참한, 고통스러운

animistic a. 물활론(우주 만물에 영혼이 있다는 믿음)의, 정령 신앙의

totality n. 총체성

non-totalitarian a. 전체주의가 아닌

exemplify v. 전형적인 예가 되다

20

사람들이 맨 처음 옷을 입게 된 이유를 설명하기 위해 정숙성 이론은 우리의 원시 조상들이 특정 신체 부위의 노출로 인한 죄책감과 수치심을 피하기 위해 옷을 입었다고 주장한다. 몸에 옷을 입게 만드는 모든 원초적 동기들의 기저에 정숙 의식이 깔려있다고 사람들이 흔히 생각하고 있는지 모르지만, 이 분야 학자들이 일반적으로 받아들이는 것도 아니고 관찰 가능한 사실들이 뒷받침해주고 있는 것도 아니다.

의복 착용에 대한 한 가지 주요한 설명으로서의 정숙성 이론을 버려야 하는 첫 번째 이유는 정숙과 벌거벗음을 구성하는 요소에 대해 사람들이 갖고 있는 생각이 너무나 다양하다는 점이다. 세계의 대부분의 사람들이 신체 부위를 가리기 위해 옷을 사용하지만 옷이 가리는 부위는 문화마다 다르다. 아마존 정글의 수야(Suya) 족(族) 여성들은 원통 모양의 큰 나무 마개를 귓불에 착용하고 원판을 아랫입술에 착용한다. 그들은 벌거벗은 몸에 대해서는 부끄러워하지 않지만, 만일 제자리에 있어야 할 원판이 없는 모습을 외부인이 보면 그들은 굉장히 당황스러워한다. 남태평양 야프(Yap) 섬의 여성들은 대단히 엄격한 정숙의 전통을 고수하지만 노출시켜서는 안 되는 것은 젖가슴이 아니라 허벅지다.

정숙성 이론을 버려야 하는 또 하나의 이유는 정숙은 본능이 아니라 시간과 장소에 따라 다른 문화적으로 생겨나는 습관이라는 것을 보여주는 증거가 이제 있기 때문이다. 우리 사회의 어린아이들에게는 정숙 의식이 전혀 없는데, 이들은 세 살 나이에 당연하게도 집 앞 잔디밭에서 옷을 벗고 있고 이웃집에 갈 때도 옷을 입지 않고 간다.

그 밖에도, 정숙이라는 개념은 나이에 따라 변한다. 벌거벗은 아기의 사진은 잡지나 가족사진첩에 실린다. 벌거벗은 아기의 사진을 찍는 것은, 여러 해가 지난 후 아기 때의 자기 사진을 보는 아이들로서는 당황스러운 일이지만, 사람들이 널리 인정할 뿐 아니라 종종 부추겨지기도 한다. 아기나 어린 아이는 사람들이 있는 곳, 예를 들어 해변에서 옷을 벗고 있어도 되고 거기서 아기 기저귀를 갈아도 된다. 그러나 나이가 좀 더 들면 이런 일은 꼴사나운 노출이 되고 대부분의 나라에서 엄격한 법의 처벌을 받을 수 있다.

결론적으로 말해, 오늘날 사회의 많은 사람들이 정숙이라는 이유로 옷을 입지만 그것이 아마도 가장 중요한 이유는 아닐 것이며 따라서 그것은 옷의 기원을 설명해줄 수 없다.

1 ③ ▶ 글의 제목
이 글은 사람들이 맨 처음 옷을 입게 된 이유를 설명하는 이론 중 하나인 정숙성 이론을 설명하고, 그 이론의 부적절함을 지적하고 있다. 따라서 ③이 제목으로 가장 적절하다.

2 ③ ▶ 내용파악
①는 두 번째 단락에, ②는 세 번째 단락에, ④는 네 번째 단락에 각각 설명되어 있다.

3 ② ▶ 내용파악
첫 번째 단락의 "사람들은 맨 처음 옷을 입게 된 동기의 기저에 정숙 의식이 깔려 있다고 생각한다."라고 한 것은, 정숙성 이론이 보통 사람들의 상식에는 부합될지도 모른다는 말이다. 따라서 ②가 정답이다. ① 세 번째 단락에 언급된 '증거'는 정숙성 이론의 부적절성에 대한 증거다. ③과 ④에 관한 언급은 없다.

4 ① ▶ 내용파악
정숙성 이론은 인류가 맨 처음 신체 노출에 따른 부끄러움을 피하기 위해 옷을 입었다는 주장이므로, ①이 사실이라면 이 이론을 지지해준다. ② 부끄러워해야 할 신체 부위를 오히려 옷을 통해 부각시키는 것이다. ③ 신체 보호를 위해 옷을 입게 되었다는 주장이다. ④ 아름답게 보이기 위해 옷을 입게 되었다는 주장이다.

5 ④ ▶ 내용추론
정숙성 이론은 '정숙 때문에 옷을 입게 되었다'라는 이론이므로, cause가 아니라 result라 해야 한다. 따라서 ④가 정답이다.

6 ③ ▶ 뒷내용 추론
이 글은 정숙성 이론을 버려야 하는 이유를 세 가지로 들고 마지막 단락 끝에 it cannot account for the origin of clothes라고 결론을 내리므로, 이 글 다음에는 정숙성 이론 이외의 다른 이론에 대한 설명이 이어질 것이다.

---

modesty n. 수줍음, 정숙

modesty theory 정숙성 이론(신체 노출에 대한 수치심에서 의복을 착용하게 되었다는 이론)

bear out 지지하다; 입증하다

reject v. 퇴짜 놓다, 버리다

cylindrical a. 원통 모양의

plug n. 마개

earlobe n. 귓불

disk n. 원판

hold to 고수하다

thigh n. 허벅지

induce v. 야기하다, 유발하다

diaper n. 기저귀

indecent a. 꼴사나운, 상스러운

04 언어·문학

01

소쉬르(Saussure)의 두 가지 핵심 개념은 '언어학 연구의 대상은 무엇인가?'와 '단어와 사물의 관계는 어떤 것인가?'라는 질문에 대한 새로운 답을 제시한다. 그는 랑그와 파롤 사이를, 즉 언어의 실제 예보다 앞서 존재하는 언어 '체계'와 개별적인 '발화' 사이를, 근본적으로 구별한다. 랑그는 언어의 사회적 측면으로, 우리가 화자로서 (무의식적으로) 이용하는 공유된 체계이다. 파롤은 이 체계를 언어의 실제 예에서 개별적으로 실현하는 것이다. 이러한 구별은 이후의 모든 구조주의 이론에 필수적이다. 언어학 연구의 적절한 대상은 개별적인 발화가 아니라 인간의 모든 특정한 의미화 실행의 기저를 이루고 있는 체계이다. 이것은 만일 우리가 특정한 시나 신화나 경제관행을 조사한다면, 우리는 어떤 규칙체계가, 즉 어떤 문법이, 사용되고 있는지 발견하기 위해 그렇게 한다는 것을 의미한다. 결국, 인간은 앵무새와 아주 다르게 말을 한다. 즉, 전자(인간)는 무수히 많은 문법에 맞는 문장을 만들 수 있게 해주는 규칙체계를 이해하고 있는 것이 분명한 반면, 앵무새는 그렇지 못하다.

1 ② ▶ **빈칸완성**
콜론(:) 다음에서 '공유된 체계'라 한 것은 사회 구성원들이 모두 함께 갖고 있는 체계라는 의미이므로 빈칸에는 '사회적인'이라는 의미의 ② social이 적절하다. ① 인식의 ③ 청각의 ④ 역사의

2 ③ ▶ **내용파악**
① 랑그와 파롤은 기원과 파생의 관계가 아니라 추상적 체계와 구체적 발화의 관계이다. ② 언어학의 연구 대상은 랑그이다. ④ 랑그에 대한 진술이다. 끝에서 셋째와 둘째 문장에서 ③이 사실임을 알 수 있다.

langue	n. 랑그(체계로서의 언어)
parole	n. 파롤(구체적 언어행위, 발화)
pre-exist	v. ~보다 전에 존재하다
utterance	n. 발화
draw upon	의존하다, 이용하다
underlie	v. 기저를 이루다
signify	v. 의미하다
have a grasp of	~를 이해하다
well-formed	a. 적격의

02

"부조리극(Theater of the Absurd)"은 1940년대 중반에서 1950년대까지 주로 프랑스에서 쓰여진 일군의 드라마 작품들을 가리키기 위해 사용된 용어이다. 이들은 인간 실존의 명백한 부조리함을 표현하기 위해 보통 비논리적인 상황, 비인습적인 대화, 최소의 플롯을 사용한다. 알베르 카뮈(Albert Camus)나 장 폴 사르트르(Jean-Paul Sartre) 같은 프랑스 사상가들은 인간 삶에 대한 어떤 합리적인 설명도 찾을 수 없는 무기력함을 인정하여 1940년대에 '부조리'라는 용어를 사용했다. 이 용어는 혼잡스럽고, 적대적이며, 냉담한 세계에서 근본적으로 의미 없는 인간의 상황을 이해한 것을 묘사했다.
사무엘 베케트(Samuel Beckett)와 외젠 이오네스코(Eugene Ionesco)는 논리, 등장인물, 언어, 플롯에 관한 가정을 거부하면서 전통적인 서양연극의 인습에 반발하였다. 예를 들어 베케트의 『고도를 기다리며(Waiting for Godot)』(1954)는 고도(Godot)라는 인물을 기다리고 있는 두 명의 떠돌이를 그리고 있다. 고도가 누구인지, 그가 그들을 만나기 위해 나타날 것인지, 실제로 존재하는지 알지 못하지만 그들은 그를 기다리며 매일 시간을 보내며 자신이 살고 있는 세계를 이해하려고 한다. 베케트는 등장인물, 플롯, 대화를 최소화해서 인간 실존에 관한 근본적인 질문에 초점을 맞춘다.

1 ③ ▶ **내용파악**
부조리극이란 '파격적인 극의 형식'과 더불어 '의미 없는 인간 상황'을 묘사하고 있는 것이 특징이다. 『고도를 기다리며』에서 두 명의 부랑아가 존재유무조차 알 수 없는 '고도'라는 인물을 마냥 기다리고 있는 무의미한 상황을 제시하고 있다는 점에서 전형적인 부조리극의 특징을 보여주고 있다.

identify	v. 확인하다
employ	v. 사용하다
illogical	a. 비논리적인
unconventional	a. 비인습적인
plot	n. 구성
apparent	a. 명백한
absurdity	n. 부조리
rational	a. 합리적인
tramp	n. 부랑자, 떠돌이
highlight	v. 강조하다

2 ②   ▶ 내용파악
'부조리'라는 낱말은 1940년대 프랑스 실존주의 사상가들이 사용한 용어다.

03

사피어-워프 가설은 언어와 사고 간의 관련성을 탐구한다. 사피어와 워프의 가설에 따르면, 말의 다른 형태를 요구하는 언어들은 그 언어들을 사용하는 사람들로 하여금 그러한 언어의 형태를 본떠 생각하게 만들고, 결국 다른 언어를 쓰는 사람들과 다른 행동 방식을 취하게 만든다고 한다. 그러므로 만약 이 가설이 타당하다면, 한 가지 언어를 쓰면서 성장한 사람은 다른 언어를 쓰면서 성장한 사람과는 생각하는 방식과 행동이 다를 것으로 예측할 수 있다.

분명히 매우 관심을 끄는 가설이긴 하지만, 사실상 사피어-워프 가설에는 어느 정도 과장된 측면이 있다. 사람들이 날마다 접하는 자극이 엄청나게 다양하다는 것을 고려하면, 언어가 생각을 결정하는 유일한 요인이라고 할 수 없다. 하지만 언어가 어떤 식으로든 간에 정신 작용에 영향을 전혀 미치지 않는다고 하기도 어렵다. 그보다는, 언어가 실제로 사고와 행동에 영향을 미치긴 하지만, 제한적이고 포괄적이지 않은 범위로 국한된다는 데 현대 학자들 대다수가 동의하고 있다. 최근 연구들은 이처럼 언어가 미치는 영향의 정확한 수준을 파악하는 데 전념하고 있다. 사피어-워프 가설이 대부분의 현대 학자들의 견해에 따라 수정될 필요는 있지만, 인간의 사고가 말과 언어에 의해 영향을 받는다는 근본적인 개념은 여전히 언어학자들에게 중요한 개념으로 남아있다.

1 ①   ▶ 내용파악
사피어-워프 가설은 한 개인이 말하는 언어에 의해 사고와 행동이 결정된다는 것이므로 ①이 정답이다.

2 ②   ▶ 내용파악
두 번째 단락에서 현대 학자들은 언어가 사고와 행동에 영향을 미치는 데는 동의하지만 사람들이 접하는 자극이 엄청나게 다양하다는 것을 고려하면 사피어-워프 가설은 수정될 필요가 있다고 보고 있다. 따라서 ②가 정답이다.

hypothesis n. 가설; 추측, 가정
explore v. 탐험[답사]하다; 탐구하다, 조사하다
teaching n. (주로 pl.) 가르침, 사상, 교리
employ v. 고용하다; 쓰다, 이용하다
emulate v. 모방하다
adopt v. 취하다; 채용[채택]하다
valid a. 유효한, 정당한; 타당한
undoubtedly ad. 의심할 여지없이; 명백히
provocative a. 도발적인, 자극적인
overstate v. 과장하여 말하다
encounter v. (우연히) ~과 만나다, 마주치다
occupy v. (공간·시간 등을) 차지하다; ~에 바쁘다
modify v. 수정하다, 변경하다
underlying a. 기초를 이루는, 기본적인

04

J. D. 샐린저(J. D. Salinger)의 『호밀밭의 파수꾼(The Catcher in the Rye)』은 출간된 이래 지속적으로 읽히는 미국문학의 고전이 되었다. 이 소설은 소설속의 유머, 미국 중산층 사회와 가치관에 대한 빈정대는 비판, 그리고 구어적인 말과 어휘들을 구사하는 샐린저의 작가적 역량 때문에 사랑을 받아왔다. 충분히 역설적이게도 『호밀밭의 파수꾼』은 홀든 콜필드(Holden Caulfield)가 비난하기 위해서 인용한 거친 언어들 때문에 오랜 세월동안 일부 비판을 받아왔다. 소설의 이야기는 캘리포니아에 있는 정신병원에 머무르고 있는 것이 분명해 보이는 주인공 홀든의 회상을 통해 전개된다. 홀든이 말하고 있는 것은 그의 삶의 미몽에서 깨어난 이야기와 그 미몽으로부터 깨어남이 그를 인도해준 방향이다. 소설을 통해 홀든은 그의 외로움과 절망에 대해서 말한다. (소설 속에서 다루어지고 있는) 그의 삶에서의 며칠간의 이야기는 도덕적 가치를 심하게 결여하고 있는 사회 속에서 도덕적 가치를 추구하고자 하는 그의 여정이 얼마나 슬프고 외로운 것인지를 나타내 보여주고 있다. 홀든은 펜실베이니아에 위치한 배타적인 명문 사립 고등학교에서 크리스마스 전날 퇴학을 당하는 것으로 이야기는 시작된다. 그는 그의 부모들이 화를 낼 것임을 잘 알고 있다. 그래서 그는 집으로 돌아가기 전에 며칠 동안을 뉴욕에서 보내기로 결심한다. 뉴욕에서 홀든은 몇 가지 모험을 겪고 나서 집으로 돌아간 후, 그의 유일한 진정한 친구인 그의 여동생 피비(Phoebe)에게 그가 믿고 있는 것에 대해 설명한다. 그러나 어떤 도덕적 정체성의 발견은 홀든을 정신병원으로부터 구해내지 못한다.

1 ⑤   ▶ 내용파악
본문에 따르면 『호밀밭의 파수꾼』은 주인공이 사용하는 거친 언어 때문에 비판받아 왔다.

enduring a. 지속하는, 영속적인
mordant a. 빈정대는
colloquial a. 구어의
denounce v. (공공연히) 비난하다
disenchantment n. 미몽에서 깨어남
sorely ad. 심하게; 아주 많이
expel v. 쫓아내다; 추방하다, 면직시키다
exclusive a. 배타적인
preparatory school 사립 고등학교
hospitalization n. 입원

2 ①　▶ 내용파악
　　　　　퇴학을 당한 학생이 모범생이라고 볼 수 없다.

05

언어를 습득하는 것과 배우는 것의 차이는 무엇인가? 우선, 언어를 배우는 것은 지속적인 사회적 상호 작용을 요구한다. 그리고 이 가설은 '언어습득지원체계', 혹은 요약해서 LASS라는 브루너(Bruner) 이론의 기반을 이루고 있다. 브루너에 따르면, 어떤 형식의 LAD(언어습득장치)가 존재할 수도 있지만, 아이의 언어 발달에 있어서 부모나 형제자매도 중요한 역할을 한다고 한다. "안녕"이나 "잘 가"와 같은 말을 건네는 일상행동이나, 식사나 목욕과 같은 일상생활에 아이들을 참여시키는 방식으로 말이다. 따라서 '모국어'라는 표현이 나오게 된 것도 놀라운 일은 아니다. 어쨌든 우리 모두가 어릴 때 엄마가 사용하던 익숙한 소리나 반복적인 어구를 들었던 것을 기억한다. 사실, 모어크(Moerk)라는 이름의 학자는 이런 식의 언어 모형을 가리켜 '모성어'라고 칭했다. 브루너 이론의 두 번째 가설은 언어 학습에 발달성이 있다는 점이다. 다시 말해, 아이가 언어 능력을 쌓아가면서 부모와 형제자매들은 아이를 위한 학습 환경을 조장한다. 처음에는 부모와 형제자매들의 목소리가 크고 아이는 다소 수동적이다. 하지만 아이의 언어 능력이 발달하면서 아이는 더욱 능동적으로 변한다. 이런 관점에서, 언어 학습은 발견의 과정이라는 측면이 두드러진다. 아이들은 이전에 쌓은 지식과 경험과 결부시켜 새로운 개념들을 정립하는 법을 배운다. 따라서 브루너의 이론은 언어 발달에 있어서 양육이 본성만큼 필수적이라는 개념을 강력히 지지하고 있음이 분명하다.

1 ②　▶ 내용파악
　　　　　브루너의 언어습득지원체계에서는 부모와 가족이 아이의 언어 발달에 중요한 역할을 한다고 했다. 이에 mother tongue과 motherese를 언급하였으므로 ②가 정답이다.

2 ③　▶ 내용추론
　　　　　브루너의 이론은 아이가 언어를 습득하는 데 있어 부모를 비롯한 주변 사람들의 관계와 사회적 상호 작용을 중시한다. 이 내용에 가장 부합하는 ③이 정답이다.

---

acquire v. 취득[획득]하다; 습득하다
ongoing a. 계속하고 있는, 진행 중인
interaction n. 상호 작용
assumption n. 가정, 추정, 가설
acquisition n. 취득, 획득; 습득
for short 생략하여, 요약해서
sibling n. 형제자매
involve v. 관련[연루]시키다; 참여하다
routine a. 정해 놓은, 판에 박힌, 일상적인
ritual n. 의식 절차; 습관적 행위
evolve v. 발전[진화]하다
familiar a. 익숙한, 친숙한
repetitive a. 되풀이되는, 반복적인
nickname v. 별명을 붙이다
passive a. 수동적인, 소극적인
perspective n. 관점, 시각
evident a. 분명한, 명백한
nurture n. 양육, 양성, 육성
essential a. 불가결한, 절대 필요한, 필수의

06

애드거 앨런 포우(Edgar Allan Poe)는 섬뜩하거나 공상적인 내용의 단편소설과 시를 통해 많은 현대 독자에게 잘 알려져 있지만, 그의 문학에 대한 공헌은 추리소설과 공상과학소설뿐만 아니라 비평에까지 미치고 있다. 사실, 광범위한 장르와 다양한 작가들이 직접적으로나 간접적으로 포우의 작품에 영향을 받았다.

흥미로운 점은, 그의 많은 소설들이 오늘날의 독자들에게는 공포소설로 읽히고 있지만 그의 초기 독자들에게는 공상과학소설로 읽혔다는 사실이다. 공상과학소설의 핵심은 새로운 기술이 사회에 어떤 영향을 미칠 것인가를 탐구하려는 시도가 근간을 이룬다. 그러므로 포우가 『아서 고든 핌 이야기(The Narrative of Arthur Gordon Pym)』에서 소재로 삼았던 남극이나 최면술에 대해 이야기할 때, 그는 당시의 대중에게는 생소한 개념들을 다루고 있었던 것이다. 예를 들어, 한 소설에서 어떤 남자가 죽기 직전에 최면 상태에 빠진다. 그리고 소설의 결말에 가서 남자는 최면에서 깨어나고 비로소 죽는다. <포우 시대의 독자들은 이런 이야기를 새로운 과학의 놀라운 응용으로 이해했을 것이다.> 오늘날에 이런 것은 유령 이야기처럼 읽힌다. 『프랑켄슈타인(Frankenstein)』의 작가 메리 셸리(Mary Shelley)처럼 포우도 인간의 발견이 충격적인 결과를 초래한다는 이야기를 대중에게 널리 확산시켰다. 이러한 이야기 양식은 후대의 지적 산물들에서도 찾아볼 수 있는데, 방사선을 쬐어 거대해진 개미가 등장하는 영화에서부터 지구를 공격하는 난폭한 외계인이 등장하는 것에 이르기까지 다양하다. 공상과학소설의 고전으로 여겨지는 작품들의 작가인 H.G. 웰스(H.G. Wells)는 포우가 이 장르의 작가가 무엇을 해야 하는가를 보여준 인물이라고 썼다. 즉, 작가는 지성인이 상상할 수 있는 것을 보여주어야 하는 것이다.

---

macabre a. 섬뜩한, 기분 나쁜
extend v. (영향을) 미치다
owe v. ~의 덕이다, ~의 신세를 지다
interestingly ad. 흥미롭게도
hypnosis n. 최면술
trance n. 최면상태
popularize v. 대중[통속]화하다
descendent n. 자손, 후예
radiation n. 방사선

1 ① ▶ 내용추론

두 번째 단락에서 포우의 독자들이 시대에 따라 그의 작품을 다르게 보고 있다고 소개하고 있다. 오늘날의 독자는 그의 소설을 공포소설이라고 생각하지만, 포우가 살았던 시대의 사람들은 공상과학소설로 받아들였다고 했으므로 독자들은 그의 작품에 대해 시대마다 다른 해석을 할 수 있다고 유추할 수 있다.

2 ③ ▶ 문장삽입

제시문에서 "그 당시 독자들이 그것을 과학의 놀라운 응용으로 이해했다."고 했으므로 포우 소설에 나온 생소한 개념에 대한 이야기가 제시문 앞에 와야 하며, 이와는 달리 오늘날의 독자들이 그 내용에 대해 어떻게 생각하고 있는지에 대한 설명이 제시문 뒤에 와야 한다. 따라서 제시문은 ⓒ에 삽입이 되어야 한다.

3 ① ▶ 태도

H.G. 웰스는 포우가 공상과학소설의 작가가 무엇을 해야 하는가를 보여준 인물이라고 썼다고 했으므로 H.G. 웰스는 포우에 대해 '존경하는(admiring)' 태도를 가졌다고 볼 수 있다. ② 강박 관념의 ③ 조롱하는 ④ 중립적인

07

『1984(Nineteen-Eighty-Four)』는 1949년에 조지 오웰(George Orwell)에 의해 출간된 소설이다. 그 소설은 1950년 결핵성 출혈로 사망하기 직전에 그가 쓴 마지막 작품이었다. 그 소설은 전체주의에 의해 장악된 세계에 대한 반(反)이상향적 세계관을 보여준다. 이 소설의 주인공인 윈스턴 스미스(Winston Smith)는 명목상의 최고위자인 빅브라더가 통치하는 당에 대한 소규모의 저항을 잠시 시도한다.

실제로 소설의 엄청난 인기 때문에 버나드 크릭(Bernard Crick)과 같은 오웰을 연구하는 학자들은 소설의 널리 퍼진 잘못된 해석에 대해 불평해왔다. 크릭은 『1984』가 조나단 스위프트(Jonathan Swift)의 경우와 유사하게 풍자로 읽혀야 한다고 주장했다. 그러한 해석은 유머의 순간과 끊임없는 암울한 어조가 공존하는 것을 설명한다. 우리는 '구둣발이 인간의 얼굴을 영원히 짓밟는' 그런 모습의 미래관을 갖게 된다. 그러나 이것은 예언이라기보다 경고를 위한 것이다.

소설의 많은 표현과 많은 생각들은 일반적으로 널리 쓰이게 되었다. 이 표현들에는 특정한 유형의 사상을 강요하는 언어의 형태인 'Newspeak(모호하고 기만적인 표현, 신언어)'와 'War is Peace(전쟁은 평화이다), Freedom is Slavery(자유는 예속이다), Ignorance is Strength(무지가 힘이다), Hate is Love(미움이 사랑이다), 2+2=5'와 같은 표현을 만들어 낼 수 있는 '이중사고(모순되는 두 가지 생각을 동시에 갖는 것)'가 포함된다. 이와 반대로 독립적인 사고는 '반사회적인[범죄적인] 생각'으로 특징지어지며, 사상경찰(사람들의 사상을 통제하는 경찰)에 의해 잔인하게 처벌된다. 많이 남용되고 있는 'Orwellian(전체주의적인)'이라는 형용사는 선전을 보여주고 당국이 카메라를 통해 추종자들을 감시할 수 있게 해주는 '텔리스크린'을 통해 당에 의해 확립된 철저한 감시에서 기인한다. 이것은 '빅브라더가 당신을 감시하고 있다'는 현재 어디서나 볼 수 있는 문구를 만들어냈다.

1 ② ▶ 빈칸완성

크릭은 『1984』가 풍자로 읽혀야 한다고 했으므로, Such an interpretation은 풍자임을 알 수 있다. 풍자는 문학 작품에서 '현실의 부정적 현상이나 모순 따위를 빗대어 비웃는' 것이다. 따라서 이러한 해석은 유머(웃음)와 반대되는 현실의 부정적인 어조가 함께 쓰여야 할 것이므로 빈칸 Ⓐ에는 ② bleakness가 적절하다. ① 선견지명 ③ 소문 ④ 딴데로 돌림, 전환

2 ④ ▶ 빈칸완성

『1984』에서 쓰인 표현 중 이중사고는 War is Peace와 같이 두 개의 상반되는 내용을 가진 표현법이다. 따라서 ① 자유와 예속, ② 무지와 힘, ③ 미움과 사랑은 전쟁과 평화와 같이 상반된 내용을 가지지만 ④ 감시는 제한하는 것이므로 이중사고의 표현법으로 적절하지 않다.

tubercular a. 결핵(성)의

haemorrhage n. (인체 내부의) 출혈

dystopian a. 반(反)이상향의

totalitarianism n. 전체주의

protagonist n. 주인공

figurehead n. 명목상의 최고위자

misinterpretation n. 오해, 오역

satire n. 풍자

vein n. 기질, 성질; (특징적인) 표현 양식

unremitting a. 끊임없는

stamp on ~을 짓밟다

phraseology n. 표현; 어구

telescreen n. 대형 TV 화면

ubiquitous a. 어디에나 있는, 아주 흔한

3 ②   ▶ 내용추론
    Newspeak와 Doublethink와 달리 Independent thinking은 반사회적인[범죄적인] 생
    각으로 특징지어지며 처벌된다고 했으므로, 사상경찰에 의해 허용되는 Newspeak와
    Doublethink는 사상을 통제하기 위한 수단이었다고 추론할 수 있으므로 ②는 expand
    가 아니라 narrow가 되어야 한다.

08

오늘날 많은 사람들은 역사적으로 대부분의 문화에서 여성은 남성만큼 대우받지 못해왔다고 느낀
다. 서구세계에서는 백 년 전까지만 해도 여성은 선거에 참여할 수 없었고 대부분의 직업에서 제외
되었었다. 하나의 성을 다른 성보다 선호하는 태도 (이 경우, 남성을 선호)는 성차별주의라고 불리
며, 많은 사람들은 우리가 사용하는 바로 그 언어에 존재한다고 생각한다. 예를 들어, 지문의 뒷부
분에 사용되는, 동사 to mother는 대개 '돌보다, 보호하다' (예를 들어, "저 선생님은 그녀의 모든
학생들을 돌본다.")를 의미한다; 반면 동사 to father는 주로 간단히 '불러일으키다 아니면 유래하
다' (예를 들어, "그는 아들 세 명을 낳았다.")는 의미로 쓰인다. 여기서 남성이 아닌 여성이 아이들
을 돌봐야한다는 생각이 우리가 일상 언어에 갇혀있는 것이다.
페미니스트들은 영어의 단어 그리고 심지어 문법 안에도 성차별주의의 예시가 담겨있다고 주장한
다. 흔한 예로 단어 man 혹은 mankind가 전체 인류를 가리키는 용법이다: "인간은 도구를 사용하
는 유일한 동물이다.... 농경시대가 시작된 이후 인류의 업적은 시작되었다..." 일부 페미니스트를
비난하는 사람들은 모두가 단어 man과 mankind가 여성도 포함한다는 것을 알기 때문에 이 용법
은 사실 문제가 되지 않는다고 주장했다. 그러나 페미니스트들은 일반적으로 이런 방식의 말하기
는 여성이 조용히 옆에 앉아서 남성들을 도와주는 동안, 남성들이 역사에서 적극적인 참가자들 —
일하고, 건설하고, 탐험하고, 발명하고 — 이었다는 인상을 심어준다고 믿는다.
일부 사람들은 언어 개혁을 찬성하고, 단어 people 혹은 humanity가 이런 맥락에서 사용되어야
한다고 생각한다. 다른 사람들은, "뭐, 솔직히 말해봅시다! 남성이 역사가 흐르는 내내 적극적인 참
가자였잖아요."라고 말한다.

1 ①   ▶ 빈칸완성
    본문 전반에 걸쳐 우리가 평소에 쉽게 사용하는 단어들에 담겨있는 성차별에 대해 설명
    하고 있으므로 ① '우리가 사용하는 바로 그 언어'가 적절하다. ② 우리가 살고 있는 문화
    ③ 교육 제도 ④ 몇몇 특정 사회

2 ④   ▶ 빈칸완성
    여성이 부수적인 역할을 할 때 남성이 일하고, 건설하고, 탐험하고, 발명하는 역할을 했
    다면 남성은 ④ '적극적인 참가자'로 표현되어야 적절하다. ① 거만한 참가자 ② 억눌린
    참가자 ③ 겁을 내는 참가자

3 ②   ▶ 어법상 적절하지 않은 표현 고르기
    ② 우리가 사용하는 언어에 성차별이 담겨있다는 내용을 담은 문장이다. 그러므로 여기
    서 present는 '있는, 존재하는'의 의미로 사용되어야 할 것이다. present가 동사나 명사
    가 아닌 형용사로 사용되려면 문법적으로 by many to be present가 되도록 present
    앞에 be가 와야 옳다.

treat v. 다루다, 대우하다
exclude v. 제외하다, 배제하다
profession n. 직업, 직종
sexism n. 성차별, 성차별주의
latter a. 후자의, 마지막의
engender v. 낳다, 불러일으키다, 생기다
originate v. 비롯되다, 유래하다; 발명[고안]하다
lock v. 잠그다; 고정되다; 걸러들다
species n. 종
agricultural a. 농업의, 농사의
sideline n. 부업

09

언어학은 언어에 대한 과학적 연구다. 그것은 "언어란 무엇인가, 그리고 언어는 생각 속에서 어떻게
표현되는가?"라는 질문에 답변하려고 노력한다. 언어학자는 언어를 기술하고 설명하는데 집중하며
언어를 규정하는 규칙, 즉 예를 들어 "부정사는 분리하지 않는다"는 것과 같은 규칙에는 관심이 없
다. 언어학자들은 많은 언어들을 반드시 알아야 하는 것은 아니며 언어학자들은 통역가가 아니다.

endeavor v. 노력하다, 애쓰다
be concerned with ~와 관련되어 있다
prescriptive a. 규정하는

언어학자의 근본적 목표는 언어에 관련된 일반개념을 발견하려고 애쓰는 것이다. 즉, "모든 언어에 공통적인 요소는 무엇인가"하는 것이다. 언어학자는 그런 다음 이러한 요소들을 정리하여 모든 언어들을 기술할 수 있는 이론적 구조를 정립하고, 또한 특정 언어에서 발생할 수 없는 것을 예측하려고 애쓴다. 언어학은 심리학, 인류학, 사회학 그리고 고고학 같은 다른 사회과학들과 공통적 기반을 갖고 있는 사회과학이다. 언어학은 커뮤니케이션 연구와 컴퓨터 과학 같은 다른 학문분야에 영향을 줄 수도 있다. 그러나 언어학은 일반적으로 인지과학으로 간주될 수 있다. 심리학, 철학 그리고 컴퓨터 과학과 함께, 언어학은 궁극적으로는 인간의 두뇌가 어떻게 기능하는지에 관심이 있다.
이 학문은 몇 가지 서로 다른 분야를 포함하고 있다. 음성학, 음운론, 형태론, 통사론, 의미론 그리고 언어습득이론 같은 분야들이 언어학의 핵심 분야이며, 더욱 수준 높은 주제들을 해결하기 위해서는 이 분야들에 대한 확고한 지식이 필요하다.

1 ④　▶ **글의 주제**
　　이 글은 전체적으로 언어학에 대한 개론적 입문이다.

2 ①　▶ **빈칸완성**
　　빈칸 다음 문장의 the common elements of all languages가 곧 '언어에 관한 일반개념들'을 말한다.

3 ⑤　▶ **내용일치**
　　마지막 문장에서 언어학의 상위 주제를 다루기 위해서는 하위 분야에 대한 확고한 지식이 필요하다고 말하고 있다.

split v. 쪼개다, 분리하다
infinitive n. 부정사
interpreter n. 통역, 번역가
underlying a. 밑에 있는, 근원적인
place A in B A를 B의 형태로 정립하다
theoretical framework 이론적 틀
common ground 공통의 근거
anthropology n. 인류학
archaeology n. 고고학
discipline n. 학문분야
for the most part 대개, 대부분의
ultimately ad. 궁극적으로
function v. 기능하다
comprise v. 포함하다, ~로 구성되어 있다
phonetics n. 음성학
phonology n. 음운론
morphology n. 형태론
syntax n. 통사론
semantics n. 의미론
aquisition n. 습득
tackle v. 달려들다, 맞붙다
advanced a. 진보된, 고급의

10

새로운 사상은 종종 속물적이고 반(反) 지성적인 반응을 불러일으키는데, 구조주의 범주에 들어가는 이론들이 받은 반응의 경우가 특히 그러했다. 문학에 대한 구조주의적 접근은 일반 독자가 갖고 있는 가장 소중한 신념들 중 일부에 이의를 제기한다. 문학작품은 작가의 창의적 생활의 산물이며 작가의 본질적인 자아를 표현하는 것이라고 우리는 오랫동안 생각해왔다. 문학작품은 우리가 정신적으로나 인간적으로 작가와 생각과 감정을 함께하기 시작하는 곳이다. 독자들이 종종 내세우는 또 하나의 기본적인 가정은 좋은 책은 인간의 삶에 대해 진실을 말한다는 것, 즉 소설과 희곡은 실상이 어떠하냐를 우리에게 말해준다는 것이다. 그러나 구조주의자들은 작가는 '죽은' 것이고 문학적 이야기는 진실을 말하는 기능을 전혀 하지 않는다는 것을 우리에게 설득시키려 애써왔다. 조나단 쿨러(Jonathan Culler)가 쓴 책에 대한 서평에서 존 베일리(John Bayley)는 반(反) 구조주의자들을 옹호하며, "그러나 기호학의 죄악은 픽션 안의 진실에 대한 우리의 의식을 파괴하려 하는 것이다. … 좋은 이야기에서 진실은 픽션보다 앞서며 여전히 픽션에서 떼어낼 수 있는 것이다."라고 선언했다. 1968년에 쓴 글에서 롤랑 바르트(Roland Barthes)는 구조주의적인 견해를 매우 강력하게 표현하여 다음과 같이 주장했다. 작가는 단지 이미 존재하는 글들을 혼합하고 재조립하거나 재배치할 수 있는 능력만을 갖고 있다. 작가는 글을 이용하여 자신을 표현할 수는 없고 글을 이용하여 단지 (바르트가 좋아한 표현을 사용하자면) '항상 이미 써진' 방대한 언어와 문화의 사전에 있는 것을 끌어낼 수 있을 뿐이다. 구조주의의 정신을 기술하기 위해 '반(反) 인간주의적'이라는 용어를 사용해도 오해를 낳지는 않을 것이다. 사실 이 단어는 인간을 문학적 의미의 원천이자 기원으로 삼는 모든 형태의 문학비평에 반대한다는 것을 강조하기 위해 구조주의자들 자신이 사용해 온 단어이다.

1 ③　▶ **동의어**
　　philistine은 '교양 없는, 속물적인'이라는 뜻이므로 ③의 uncultured와 그 의미가 가장 가깝다. ① 무제한의 ② 공격적인 ④ 무자비한

provoke v. (감정 따위를) 일으키다
philistine a. 속물적인, 교양 없는
accord v. 주다, 수여하다; 일치시키다
structuralism n. 구조주의
cherish v. 소중히 하다; (소원 등을) 품다
communion n. 함께함, 친교
fundamental a. 기초의, 기본의, 근원적인
assumption n. 가정, 억측, 가설
discourse n. 강연, 설교; 이야기, 담화
semiotics n. 기호학
precede v. ~에 선행하다
emphasize v. 강조하다; 역설하다

2 ② ▶ **내용추론**

구조주의가 "일반 독자가 갖고 있는 가장 소중한 신념들 중 일부에 이의를 제기한다."라고는 했지만 이것이 문학작품은 난해해야 한다고 주장하는 것은 아니므로 ②가 정답이다. ①는 첫 번째 문장에서, ③은 "문학적 담화(이야기)는 진실을 말하는 기능을 전혀 하지 않는다."라고 한 것에서, ④는 끝에서 세 번째 문장에서 각각 추론할 수 있다.

3 ① ▶ **내용파악**

"작가는 '죽은' 것이고"라고 했으므로 ①의 '작가 예찬'은 구조주의와 무관한 것이다. ② 인간주의의 배격 ③ 기호학적 분석 ④ 롤랑 바르트의 글

4 ④ ▶ **글의 요지**

이 글은 일반 독자들의 문학관과 상충되는 구조주의의 문학적 주장을 설명한 글이므로 ④가 글의 요지로 적절하다. ③은 구조주의의 한 가지 특징에 불과하다.

11

단어는 게임의 맥락에서만 의미를 가진다. 축구 경기를 보는 동안, 이 철학적인 생각이 비트겐슈타인(Wittgenstein)에게 떠올랐다. 축구 경기에 대한 어떠한 사전 지식도 없는 사람이 경기를 보고 있다면, 그에게 있어 그것은 아주 임의적이고 의미가 없는 것처럼 보일 것이다. 그것이 의미를 가지기 위해서, 그는 우선 게임의 규칙을 이해해야 한다. 축구 경기에는 양 팀이 있고, 각 팀은 11명의 선수로 구성되어 있으며, 각 팀은 상대편 네트에 공을 넣음으로써 상대와 겨루어 득점을 하려고 한다. 일단 그가 이 게임의 전반적인 상황을 이해할 수 있다면 공을 쫓아 이리저리 뛰어다니는 선수들은 더 이상 미친 것처럼 보이지 않고 게임 속에서 의미를 가지게 된다.

<그것은 언어의 경우에서도 마찬가지라고 비트겐슈타인은 결론을 내렸다.> 한 사람이 언어의 맥락과 특정한 담화에 적용된 규칙을 이해하지 못한다면, 본질적으로 그 사람은 가장 진정한 형태의 말(글)을 이해할 수 없다. 그는 한 게임(예를 들면, 미식축구)의 규칙을 이해하는 사람들은 다른 게임(예를 들면, 럭비)에서 유사점을 발견할 수 있지만, 이 두 게임은 본질적으로 다르며 이에 따라 완벽하게 이해하기 위해서, 그 사람은 해당 게임의 특정한 규칙과 다른 게임과의 차이점을 이해해야 한다는 것을 인정했다.

비트겐슈타인이 말했던 것은 언어는 특정한 맥락에서만 의미를 가진다는 것이었다. 그 맥락에서 벗어나 다른 문맥에 넣어지면 같은 것을 의미하지 않을지도 모른다. 비트겐슈타인은 규범주의와 한 가지 생각 방식에 너무 갇혀 있는 것에 대해 우리에게 경고를 했다. 비트겐슈타인은 누구도 어떤 게임 밖에 서 있으면서 그것에 대해 규정하거나 다른 게임의 규칙을 강요해서는 안 된다고 생각했다. 즉, 당신은 미식축구 경기처럼 농구를 할 수 없다는 것이다! 마찬가지로 그는 한 게임의 선수는 우선 다른 게임의 규칙을 배우고 게임에 참여하지 않으면 다른 게임의 선수를 비판할 수 없다고 말했다.

context n. 맥락; (어떤 일의) 정황, 배경

random a. 임의의, 멋대로의

chase v. 뒤쫓다, 쫓아다니다

impose v. 지우다, 과(課)하다

discourse n. 담론, 이야기

essentially ad. 본질적으로

inherently ad. 생득적으로; 본질적으로

prescriptivism n. 규범주의

legislate v. 제정하다

1 ① ▶ **내용추론**

비트겐슈타인은 언어의 활동을 게임에 비유해서 설명했는데, 예를 들어, 축구 경기에 대해 제대로 알지 못하면 축구 경기를 보는 것이 아무런 의미가 없다고 생각했다. 언어에서도 이와 같이 특정 언어를 제대로 이해하지 못한다면 대화를 제대로 이해하지 못할 것이므로 상대방에 관한 판단이나 비판 등을 할 수 없을 것이다. 따라서 ①이 정답이다.

2 ③ ▶ **빈칸완성**

빈칸 Ⓐ는 앞 문장을 부연 설명할 수 있는 예가 들어가야 하는데 "비트겐슈타인은 누구도 어떤 게임 밖에 서 있으면서 그것에 대해 규정하거나 다른 게임의 규칙을 강요해서는 안 된다고 생각했다."라고 했으므로 본질적으로 다른 어떤 게임들에 대해서는 같은 규칙을 사용하여 게임을 할 수 없다는 의미가 되는 ③이 빈칸에 적절하다.

3 ② ▶ **문장삽입**

제시문에서 "그것은 언어의 경우에서도 마찬가지라고 비트겐슈타인은 결론을 내렸다."라고 했으므로 제시문 다음에는 언어와 관련된 사항이 와야 한다. 첫 단락에서 언어의 경우를 설명하기 위해 축구 경기의 예를 들은 다음, 이와 같은 예가 적용되는 언어의 경우가 두 번째 단락에 제시되고 있으므로 제시문은 Ⓑ에 들어가야 한다.

12

『월든(Walden)』은 대부분의 사람들의 운명인 '절망적인' 존재를 초월함에 있어서 고독, 명상, 그리고 자연과의 친화 등의 중요성을 강조한다. 이 책은 전통적인 의미의 자서전이 아니라, 자서전과 당대 서구문화에 만연해 있던 소비주의적이고 물질주의적인 태도, 서구문화의 자연과의 거리와 자연의 파괴 등에 대한 사회 비평을 결합시킨다. 이 책이 단순히 사회를 비판하는 것뿐만 아니라 당대 문화의 바람직한 경향들에 창조적으로 참여하고자 시도하고 있다는 사실은 소로(Thoreau)가 (당대 저명한 미국의 지식인들이 모여 있었던) 콩코드(Concord) 지역의 사회와 가까웠다는 점과 소로가 고전문학을 흠모했다는 점을 통해서 드러난다. 『월든』은 세 가지 이유 때문에 읽기 어려운 책이다. 첫 번째로, 이 책은 외과적으로 정확한 언어, 확장된 비유적인 은유, 길고 복잡한 단락과 문장, 그리고 생생하고 세세하고 통찰력이 넘치는 묘사 등을 사용한 오래된 스타일의 산문체로 쓰여졌다. 소로는 은유, 암시, 삼가는 표현, 과장, 의인법, 아이러니, 풍자, 환유, 제유, 그리고 모순어법 등을 사용하는 데 주저함이 없다. 그리고 그는 문장 중간에 과학적 관점에서 초월론적 관점으로 이동하기도 한다. 두 번째로 이 책에서 전개되고 있는 논리는 대부분의 사람들이 상식이라고 부르는 것과 정반대되는 삶에 대한 다른 이해에 기초하고 있다. 아이러니하게도, 이 논리는 대부분의 사람들이 믿고 있다고 말하는 것에 기초하고 있다. 이것을 인식하고 있던 소로는 빈정거리는 표현, 역설, 이중 의미 등을 사용해서 『월든』을 채운다. 그는 그의 독자들을 괴롭히고 도전하고 심지어 속이는 것을 좋아한다. 그리고 세 번째로 매우 자주 어떤 단어들도 진실에 대한 소로의 많은 비언어적인 통찰을 표현하는 데 있어서 충분하지 않다는 것이다. 소로는 이들 개념을 표현하기 위해 비문자적인 언어를 사용해야 했고 그 덕에 독자들은 그 의미를 이해하기 위해서 많은 애를 써야 했다.

1 ②   ▶ 빈칸완성
       『월든』이 다양한 비유와 길고 난해한 문장을 빈번하게 사용하고 있다는 진술로부터 정답을 추론할 수 있다.

2 ③   ▶ 빈칸완성
       『월든』이 읽기 힘든 이유들 가운데 하나는 한 문장 안에서 과학적인 관점으로부터 초월론적인 관점으로 이동하는 것 같은 빈번한 관점의 이동 때문이다. 따라서 ③이 정답이다. ① ~을 고수하다 — ~때문에 ② ~을 방해하다 — ~에 의하면 ④ 결과적으로 ~이 되다 — ~에도 불구하고

3 ①   ▶ 빈칸완성
       '비언어적인'과 '진리에 대한'이라는 단서로부터 통찰력을 유추할 수 있다. ② 환각; 오해 ③ 주관성 ④ 정체, 신원

4 ④   ▶ 내용추론
       ④의 "미국의 모든 중요한 가치를 전복시키려는 의도를 가지고 있었다."는 것은 본문에 진술되지 않은 내용이다.

---

contemplation n. 숙고, 명상

proximity n. 근접, 근사치

allusion n. 인유, 암시

understatement n. 삼가는 표현

metonymy n. 환유

synecdoche n. 제유

oxymoron n. 모순어법

sarcasm n. 풍자, 빈정거림

paradox n. 역설

double entendre 이중의미

tease v. 괴롭히다

non-literal a. 비문자적인

rhetorical figure 수사법

13

고대영어(1150년경 이전의 영어)에서, you는 원래 주격 대명사도 아니었다. you는 2인칭 복수 대명사인 ye의 목적어 형태였다. 다시 말해서, you는 직접 목적어, 간접 목적어, 전치사의 목적어는 될 수 있었지만, 주어는 될 수 없었다. 옥스퍼드 영어사전(OED)에서 15세기의 한 인용문에는 you가 다음과 같이 나온다. "너희들 속에 내가 (있고), 내 속에 너희들이 (있다.)" you는 "너희들 자신을 집에 데려다 주다(즉, 귀가하다)"에서처럼, 재귀적 용법으로도 또한 사용되었다.

you는 그 이후 조금씩 주어 자리로 이동했다. 옥스퍼드 영어사전에서 you의 첫 번째 인용문은 14세기에 나왔는데, 복사상의 오류일 가능성이 있다는 특별한 표시가 있다. 15세기 무렵에는, 이 you의 어법은 다음과 같이 분명해졌다. 즉, you는 ye와 함께 사용되고 있었다는 것이다. you와 ye 모두 다음과 같이 1611년 흠정역 성서에 등장한다. 너희(ye)는 결코 죽지 아니 하리라. (창세기 3장 4절) 너희(you)가 어찌 나와 함께 가려느냐? (룻기 1장 11절)

원래 복수였던 ye는 프랑스어 vous의 영향을 받아 한 사람을 지칭하는 공식적인 방식으로도 또한 사용되기 시작했다. you가 ye의 영역을 침범할 때, 양쪽 모두로 침범하여, you는 복수와 공식적인 단수로 쓰였다.

(you의) 비공식적인 단수는 여전히 thou였는데, 그 당시 영어는 tu-vous, du-Sie, tú-usted 등과 같이 많은 현대 유럽언어들의 구분처럼 비공식 대명사와 공식 대명사간의 구분을 유지했다. 그러나 사회적 변화로 인해 you의 승리가 점차 확정되었다.

한 사람을 지칭하기 위해 복수를 사용하는 것은 한때 최상류층들만 그렇게 했지만, 하류층으로까지 내려가서 마침내 사회적 상위권자이면 누구든지 간에 you로 지칭될 수 있었다. 하지만 vous와 Sie가 그랬던 것처럼 you는 거기서 멈추지 않았다. 대신 한때 ye를 밀어내었던 you는 이제 근현대 시기에 thou를 서서히 몰아냈다.

요약하면 다음과 같다: you는 목적어로 시작해서, 주어의 위치에서도 사용이 가능해졌다. 그러다가 you는 복수로 사용하다가 결국 단수로도 사용이 가능해졌다. 그 후 you는 공식적인 사용에서 비공식적인 사용까지 반경을 넓혔다. ye, thou, thee(thou의 목적어 형태)는 모두 역사책 속으로 잊혀졌다. 대명사 you는 대단한 정복자였던 것이다. 대명사인 you여, 훌륭하도다!

1 ② ▶ 빈칸완성

빈칸 ④는 대명사인 you가 어떻게 쓰일 수 있느냐에 관한 것인데, 빈칸 다음에 나오는 get you home에서의 you는 yourselves의 의미로 쓰인 것이라고 했다. 즉 '재귀적 용법'을 의미하는 것이므로 빈칸 ④에는 '재귀적으로'라는 뜻의 reflexively가 적절하며, 마지막 단락은 본문 전체 내용을 요약 정리한 글이므로 빈칸 ⓒ에는 '요약하다'는 뜻의 abridge나 recap이 적절하다. 따라서 두 빈칸 모두에 적절한 ②의 reflexively — recap이 정답이다. ① 비현실적으로 — 요약하다 ③ 되풀이해서 — 철회하다 ④ 이분법적으로 — 찰과상을 입히다

2 ④ ▶ 글의 제목

이 글은 2인칭 복수대명사인 ye의 목적어 형태에 불과했던 you가 2인칭 대명사인 ye, thou, thee의 역할까지 다 하게 되는 대세로 급부상했던 반면, 나머지 2인칭 대명사들은 쇠락의 길을 걷게 되었다는 내용이므로, ④의 '2인칭 대명사들의 흥망성쇠'가 제목으로 적절하다.

3 ④ ▶ 부분이해

밑줄 친 ⑧는 "사회적 변화로 인해 you의 승리가 점차 확정되었다"는 뜻으로 you의 비공식적인 단수인 thou가 있음에도 you가 승리를 거두었다는 것은 '사회적 변화로 인해 you가 thou 대신 비공식적인 단수로도 차츰 쓰였다'는 말이 된다. 따라서 "사회가 비공식적인 단수로도 thou보다 you를 역시 선호함에 따라 thou가 차츰 뒷전으로 밀려났다"는 ④가 정답이다.

4 ① ▶ 글의 어조

이 글은 목적어에 불과했던 복수대명사인 you가 주어도 되고 단수로도 쓰이고 비공식적으로도 사용되는 등 2인칭 대명사로서 천하통일을 이룬 것에 대한 you의 업적을 기리는 찬가이다. 따라서 이 글의 어조로 ①의 panegyrical(칭찬의)이 적절하다. ② 불명예스러운 ③ 감각을 마비시키는 ④ 신랄한

---

originally ad. 원래

creep v. 살금살금 걷다; 천천히 나아가다

citation n. 인용문

flag v. (중요한 정보 옆에) 표시를 하다

potential a. 잠재적인, 가능성 있는

usage n. (언어의) 관용법, 어법

clear a. 분명한, 명백한, 명확한

encroach v. 침범하다, 침해하다

distinction n. 구별, 차별

seal v. 결정하다, 확정하다

triumph n. 승리

by piecemeal 조금씩, 점차로

reserve v. 떼어두다; (권리·이익을) 유보[보류]하다

highborn a. 명문 출신의, 집안이 좋은

crowd out 밀쳐내다, 밀어 젖히다

edge out 서서히 몰아내다

14

역사학자들이 그 사실을 아무리 개탄할지라도 그들은 과거에 대한 독점권이 없으며 대중들에게 특권을 가진 해설가로서의 독점 사용권이 없다. 한때는 달랐을지 모르지만, 역사학자가 눈에 띄지 않는 지위로 좌천된 것에 대해 더 이상 의심의 여지가 없다. 대중들의 규모와 그것들이 미치는 영향력으로 평가해 볼 때 역사서를 뛰어 넘는 것은 소설이며 연극, 영화, 텔레비전에 사용된다. 주로 이러한 자료들로부터 역사책을 한 번도 읽어보지 않은 수백만 명의 사람들은 그들이 과거에 대해 알고 있는 개념, 해석, 신념 혹은 환상들을 얻는다. 과거에 대한 지배적인 생각을 구체화하는 것은 무엇이든 역사가에게 중요하며 이것에 소설이 의심할 여지없이 포함된다.
대체로 두 가지 형식의 소설(역사소설과 허구적인 역사)은 과거를 다룬다. 두 가지 형식 중 더 일반적인 것은 역사소설로 거의 확실한 역사적 배경 안에서 등장인물과 사건들을 배치한다. 이런 예는 『전쟁과 평화(War and Peace)』에서 『바람과 함께 사라지다(Gone With the Wind)』에까지 이른다. 소수를 제외한 거의 모든 소설가들은 어떤 시대에 등장인물을 배치해야 하기 때문에 거의 모든 소설은 어느 정도 역사적인 것으로 생각될 수 있다. <그러나 이 용어(역사소설)는 역사적인 사건들이 주요한 부분이 되는 소설에서만 주로 적용된다.> 한편 허구적인 역사는 실제 역사적인 인물과 사건을 묘사하고 주목하지만, 소설가는 자유롭게 상상하고 글을 쓴다. 톨스토이(Tolstoy)의 대작에 버금가는 작품이 아직 나오지 못했다. 몇몇 허구적인 역사는 허구의 등장인물과 사건을 이용하고, 역사소설은 때때로 허구와 실제 인물을 섞는다. 그 결과 두 장르는 때때로 겹치지만, 겹치는 일이 그다지 빈번하지 않아 (이 둘을) 구별하는 것은 여전히 중요하다.
둘 중에서 역사에 장난을 치는 것은 허구적인 역사인데 지어낸 이야기와 사실, 허구와 실화가 섞이고 혼돈될 가능성이 높기 때문이다. 물론 역사가들 스스로가 때때로 사실과 허구를 섞지만 의식적으로 또는 고의적으로 그것을 하는 역사가는 드물고 그것이 밝혀지면 그의(역사가의) 소명을 저버린 것으로 낙인이 찍힌다는 것을 잘 알고 있다. 한편 허구적인 역사소설의 작가는 이것을 하는 것을 당연지사로 생각하고 아무 거리낌 없이 어떤 것이든 한다.

deplore v. 한탄[개탄]하다
franchise n. 특권; 지배권
relegation n. 좌천, 격하, 귀속
back seat 눈에 띄지 않는[부차적인] 위치
exert v. (영향력 등을) 발휘하다, 쓰다
give shape to (생각·계획 등을) 구체화하다, 구체적으로 설명하다
of concern to ~에 중요한
broadly speaking 대충 말하면, 대체로
more or less 거의, 대략
authentic a. 믿을 만한, 확실한
all but 거의, ~외에는 모두
focus attention on ~에 주의를 집중시키다, ~에 주목하다
fabrication n. 위조물; 허구, 지어낸 이야기
stand convicted of ~의 죄를 선고받다
as a matter of course 당연지사
compunction n. 양심의 가책, 후회, 회한

1 ④ ▶ **내용추론**
① 역사소설과 허구적인 역사 모두 역사적인 사건에 바탕을 두고 있다. ② 역사소설의 작가는 확실한 역사적 배경에서 등장인물과 사건을 배치한다고 했으므로 그가 쓰려고 하는 시기에 대한 확실한 이해가 필요하다고 볼 수 있다. ③ 역사소설이 연극, 영화, 텔레비전에 사용된다고 하였으며 이것을 본 사람들은 TV에서 나오는 역사적인 사건을 사실로 받아들일 가능성이 높다. ⑤ 이 글의 마지막 문장에서 역사가들이 사실과 허구를 고의적으로 섞어버리면 역사가의 소명을 저버린 것으로 낙인이 찍힌다는 것을 알고 있다고 하였다. 하지만 ④ 허구적인 역사가 성공을 한 이유와 관련하여 독자들이 역사적인 배경에 관심이 높기 때문이라는 내용은 이 글을 통해 유추할 수 없다.

2 ② ▶ **내용파악**
역사소설의 특징은 확실한 역사적인 배경에 허구의 등장인물을 배치하는 것이라고 하였으므로 ②가 정답이다.

3 ② ▶ **문장삽입**
제시문의 the term은 '역사소설'을 가리키므로 앞 문장에는 역사소설과 관련한 내용이 나와야 한다. 따라서 Ⓑ에 제시문이 들어가야 한다.

4 ⑤ ▶ **빈칸완성**
빈칸의 앞 문장에서 역사가들이 사실과 허구를 섞는 경우가 있지만 이것이 밝혀지면 역사가의 소명을 저버린 것으로 낙인찍힌다고 한 다음 허구적인 역사소설의 작가는 사실과 허구를 섞는 것을 당연시 한다고 했으므로 아무 거리낌 없이 사실과 허구를 섞는다는 말이 되도록 ⑤ compunction이 적절하다. ① 탐욕 ② 친밀, 친교 ③ 존경, 경의 ④ 조합, 혼성

15

39세의 맨해튼 헤지펀드 매니저인 앤서니 셰이슨(Anthony Chiasson)은 내부자 거래와 관계된 범죄로 6년 6개월의 징역형과 5백만 달러의 벌금을 부과 받았다. 피고는 기술주 관련정보를 이용해 자신의 헤지펀드 회사인 레벨 글로벌(Level Global)에 6,800만 달러의 수익을 올렸을 때, 이미 1년에 1,000만 달러에서 2,300만 달러를 버는 '굉장한 부자'였다.

하지만 셰이슨의 행동이 그토록 이해하기 어려운 것인가? 부자가 더 부자가 되길 원한다거나 한 사람이 자신의 운을 과신하려고 하는 것이 그렇게 이해하기 어려운 것인가? 그 주제는 세계적인 대작가들의 상상과 부합한다.

돈에 대해 잘못된 태도를 가진 남자와 여자를 주제로 한 책과 이야기들로 전체 도서관을 가득 채울 수 있다. 1906년에 레오 톨스토이(Leo Tolstoy)는 셰이슨과 매우 비슷한 파홈(Pahom)에 대한 교훈적인 이야기를 썼다. 파홈은 많은 것을 가지고 있었지만 더 많은 것을 원했고 자신의 탐욕과 지략에 배신당했다.

파홈이나 셰이슨과 같이 운이 좋은 사람이 더 많은 것을 바라고 무모한 위험을 추구하게 하는 것이 무엇인가? D. H. 로렌스(D. H. Lawrence)는 암울한 이야기인 『목마와 소년(The Rocking-Horse Winner)』에서 부유한 사람들의 불만과 씨름했다. 대공황 3년 전인 1926년에 출판된 그 이야기는, 안락한 환경에도 불구하고 엄마의 돈에 대한 열망에 의해 시달려 고통을 받으며 자라는 한 소년의 이야기를 다룬다. 엄마는 아들에게 행운은 '네가 돈을 벌수 있게 하는 것'이라고 말한다. 그리고 자신의 남편은 어떤 운도 없다고 한다. 아들은 어떻게 해서든 운이 좋은 사람이 되기로 결심한다. 그는 놀이방에서 흔들 목마를 미친 듯이 타면 경주에서 경마의 우승마의 이름을 맞추는 능력을 갖게 되는 것을 알게 된다. 그 결과는 돈을 버는 것이지만, 그 결말은 비극적이다.

흔들 목마 우승자의 예상은 초자연적인 것이었지만, 셰이슨의 정보는 불법이었다. 하지만 두 투기꾼 모두 운에 너무 많은 것을 의지했다. 셰이슨에게 판결을 내린 판사는 "돈과 관련한 이런 종류의 행동에 관여하는 사람들은 잡히면 어떻게 될지 알 필요가 있다."라며 그를 비난했다.

레벨 글로벌의 셰이슨의 비윤리적인 행동은 변명의 여지가 없다. 그러나 밝혀진 바로는 그가 왜 그런 행동을 했고 왜 그가 그러고도 무사히 지나갈 수 있으리라 생각했는지를 상상하긴 어렵지 않다. 그에 대한 설명은 작가들에 의해 예시되고 미리 설명되어 이미 문학에 존재한다. 작가의 평생의 걸작은 정의를 행하지는 못하지만 인간 본성의 모순을 보여준다. 우리가 현재 사는 방식이 잘못됐든 옳은 것이든 간에 우리가 오래 전에 살았던 방식으로 되풀이된다. 과거의 문학에 모든 것이 기록되어 있다. 오늘날의 주요 뉴스들이 과거의 소설에 있다.

---

1 ① ▶ **동의어**
dispense justice는 '법을 시행하다, 정의를 행하다'라는 뜻이므로 ① apply가 정답이다.
② 견디다 ③ 칭찬하다 ④ 고민하다 ⑤ 결백을 입증하다

2 ③ ▶ **글의 요지**
이 글은 내부자 거래로 형을 받게 된 셰이슨의 사례를 소개한 다음 탐욕으로 파멸하는 주인공을 주제로 한 세계적인 작가의 글을 소개하고 있다. 따라서 ③이 정답이다.

3 ④ ▶ **내용파악**
『목마와 소년』은 대공황 3년 전인 1926에 출판되었다고 했을 뿐 작가가 실제로 대공황의 여파를 예상한 것은 아니므로 ④가 정답이다.

4 ④ ▶ **내용파악**
네 번째 단락에서 "셰이슨에게 판결을 내린 판사는 돈과 관련한 이런 류의 행동에 관여하는 사람들은 잡히면 어떻게 될지 알 필요가 있다며 그를 비난했다."라고 하였으므로 그 판사가 의도한 것은 다른 사람들이 이런 행동을 하지 않는 것이다.

---

slap v. (세금·벌금 따위를) 부과하다, 매기다

defendant n. 피고

incomprehensible a. 이해할 수 없는

defy v. 문제 삼지 않다; ~을 허용하지 않다

cautionary tale 교훈적인 이야기

covetousness n. 탐욕스러움

cleverness n. 영리함, 빈틈없음

wrestle with ~을 해결하려고 애쓰다

discontent n. 불만, 불평

well-off a. 복을 받은, 부유한

torment n. 고통, 고뇌

resolve v. 결의하다, 결정하다; 분해하다

maniacally ad. 광적으로, 열광적으로

rocking horse 흔들 목마

nursery n. 아기방, 놀이방

epiphany n. 에피파니(계시나 통찰의 순간을 상징적으로 묘사하는 수법이나 작품)

chide v. 꾸짖다, 비난하다

unethical a. 비윤리적인, 파렴치한

prefigure v. 예시(豫示)하다, 예상하다

dispense v. 분배하다; 실시[시행]하다

contradiction n. 부인, 부정; 반박, 모순

echo v. 되풀이되어 나타나다

05 철학·종교

01

휴머니즘은 진보의 이념을 품고 있었고 이번에는 또한 진보의 이념이 휴머니즘을 지탱해 왔다. 콘도르세(Condorcet)가 살았던 시대 이래, 진보는 인간의 역사가 반드시 복종해야만 하는 법칙으로 다루어져 왔다. 그리고 도덕적 진보란 마치, 불가피하게 이성, 민주주의, 그리고 과학, 기술 그리고 경제의 진보와 더불어 가는 것처럼 보였다. 이런 믿음은 서구에서 기원했다. 그리고 20세기 전체주의와 세계대전들이 가져다준 진보와는 정반대되는 끔찍한 증거에도 불구하고 서구는 이 믿음을 유지했고 이 믿음을 전 세계로 퍼져나가게 했다. 1960년대, 서구자유진영은 조화로운 미래를 약속했고 동구공산진영은 빛나는 미래를 약속했다. 이들 두 미래는 20세기가 끝나기 전에 무너져 내렸고 불확실성과 불안에 의해서 대체되었다. 이제 진보에 대한 믿음은 약속이라기보다는 가능성의 문제가 돼버렸다. 이제 우리는 새롭게 재창조된 휴머니즘이 필요하다. 이전 형태의 휴머니즘은 세계화에 의해서 창조되어지고 지속적으로 확장되어 온 단일한(인류라는) 운명 공동체 안에서 모든 인간들 간의 구체적인 상호의존성을 품고 있지 못했다.

1 ④ ▶ **내용일치**
진보의 이념이 가능성으로 남아 있다는 것은 진보의 이념이 여전히 사라지지 않았음을 의미한다.

2 ④ ▶ **내용파악**
① Condorcet가 살았던 시대에 시작된 것이지, Condorcet에 의해서 시작된 것은 아니다. ② 진보의 이념과 기술 및 과학의 발전은 그 궤를 같이 했다. ③ 새로운 휴머니즘이 진보의 이념을 대체하리라는 보장은 없다.

radiant a. 빛나는, 눈부신
collapse v. 붕괴되다
regenerated a. 개선된, 갱생된, 새로워진
interdependence n. 상호의존
categorical imperative 지상명령(근본적 도덕으로서의 양심의 명령)
take place of ~을 대신하다

02

유물론적 견해가 어떻게 그리 우세했던 것일까? 유물론을 단순히 부정하는 정도를 넘어서 있는 이원론자의 견해가 더 나은 형태라는 것이 명료하지 않다는 점이 그 원인 가운데 하나다. 하지만 이원론의 부족함이 그 자체로 유물론의 강력한 근거가 되지는 못한다. 철학에서는 소거에 의한 주장은 언제나 의심스러운 것인데, 지금 여기서, 우리가 논의하고 있는 그 중심적 현상 — 다시 말해 의식 — 에 대해 우리는 설사 이해할 수 있다 하더라도 사실상 거의 이해하지 못하고 있기 때문에 더더욱 그러하다. 오히려, 유물론은 철학이나 여타 다른 학문들이 취약한 면을 보이는 여러 불행한 지적 시류들 중의 하나인 듯 보인다. 그런 면에서 유물론은 논리행동주의, 현상학, 모든 철학적 논점들은 언어와 관련을 갖는다는 주장 등, 한때 유행했지만 지금은 단지 어리석은 얘기처럼 보이는 그런 견해들과 비슷하다. 그러나 이런 식으로 비교하는 데에는 한 가지 중요한 측면에서 볼 때 오해의 소지가 있다. 그렇게 본다면 그것은 유물론적 견해들이 펼쳐지는 그 열성을 축소해서 말하는 셈이 된다. 이런 관점에서 볼 때, 유물론은 종종 종교적 확신과 많이 닮았다. 그래서 나는 다음에 나올 내용에서 유물론에 대한 옹호 및 유물론에 반대하는 주장에 대한 그들의 응답이 종종 특징적으로 스콜라 철학적이거나 신학적인 특색을 지닌다는 점을 아래에서 지적할 것이다.

1 ③ ▶ **빈칸완성**
오늘날 유물론이 세력을 떨치는 원인을 설명하는 글이다. 유물론의 반대편에 서 있는 이원론적인 설명이 부족하기 때문에 유물론이 근거를 갖게 된다는 주장은 소거에 의한 주장은 의심스럽다는 철학적 원칙 때문에 받아들이기 힘들다. 그 대신(Instead) 유물론은 인기는 끌지만 결국 잘못된 것으로 판명될 여러 불행한 시대적 조류들 중의 하나라고 보아야 한다는 것이다. 하지만(However), 단지 그런 식으로만 보기에는 유물론의 인기를 오해할 수 있는 여지가 있다. 유물론의 인기에는 종교적, 신학적 특징이 가미되어 있기 때문이다. 따라서, '그 대신 — 하지만'의 짝으로 이루어진 ③이 정답이다. ① 그러므로

materialist n. 물질주의자, 유물론자
dualist n. 이원론자
inadequacy n. 부적절함, 불충분함
bandwagon n. (많은 사람들이 함께 하는) 행사, 시류(時流)를 탄 움직임
on a par with ~와 동등한, ~와 같은
pertain to ~와 관련되다
misleading a. 오해의 소지가 있는
understate v. (실제보다) 축소해서 말하다
fervency n. 열렬, 열성, 열정

— 게다가 ② 그러므로, 이와 같이 — 참으로, 실로 ④ 그럼에도 불구하고 — 오히려, 차
라리

2 ④　　▶ **내용추론**
글의 중간 부분에서 논의의 대상이 되고 있는 것이 의식이라고 한 것으로 보아 ④는 타
당하다고 볼 수 있는 진술이므로 정답이다. ① 유물론에 종교적, 신학적 열정이 느껴진
다는 진술이 곧 유물론이 종교, 신학에서 유래했다는 진술과 같은 것은 아니다. ② 필자
는 모든 철학적 논점들이 언어와 관련이 있다는 주장이 지금은 어리석은 것으로 여겨지
고 있다고 본다. ③ 철학에서 소거에 의한 주장은 의심스럽게 여겨진다고 하였다.

03

현대 회의론은 고대 세계 지성인들의 회의론과는 전혀 다른 종류의 것이다. 그것은 종교 정신의 외
면적 형식들, 즉 종교 정신의 특수화된 교리들 뿐 아니라 종교 정신의 본질 그 자체, 즉 의미 있고
목적 있는 세계에 대한 믿음도 공격하여 파괴시켰다. 새로운 종교의 창설을 위해서라면 새로운 예
수 그리스도나 부처가 나타나야 할 것이지만 이것은 본질적으로 매우 있을 법하지 않은 사건이며
어떤 경우든 우리가 가만히 앉아서 기다릴 수 없는 사건이다. 그러나 새로운 예언자나 새로운 종교
가 나타난다 하더라도 그 예언자와 종교는 현대 세계에서 실패할 것이라고 우리는 예측할 수 있다.
오랫동안 아무도 그들을 믿지 않을 것인데, 이는 현대인은, 모든 종교에 기본적인, 세계의 질서정
연한 계획과 목적을 볼 수 있는 눈을 잃어버렸기 때문이다. 그들의 정신적 시야에는 목적 없는 세
계의 모습이 펼쳐져 있으며, 그런 세계의 모습은 기독교만이 아니라 모든 종교에 치명적임에 틀림
없다.
우리는 종교 정신의 부흥이 이따금씩 나타나는 것에 현혹되어서는 안 된다. 사람들이 삶의 공허함
에 혐오와 환멸을 느끼고 다시 한 번 종교에 의지하고 있거나 새로운 메시지를 찾고 있다는 말을
우리는 듣는다. 그럴지도 모른다. 우리는 필경 정신의 그런 생각 깊은 열망을 기대할 것이며 우리
는 필경 사람들이 꺼져버린 빛이 다시 되살아나기를 바라고 또 되살리려 노력하기를 기대할 것이
다. 그러나 사람들이 아무리 바라고 노력해도 빛은 적어도 우리가 속한 문명에서는 다시 비치지 않
을 것이다.

1 ③　　▶ **내용파악**
첫 두 문장에서 현대 회의론은 과거와 달리 종교 정신의 본질 자체도 공격하여 파괴시켰
다고 했으므로 ③ '공격의 표적'이 다른 점이다. ① 그 무의미한 목적 ② 지지자들의 계층
④ 과학적 논증

2 ④　　▶ **내용추론**
둘째 단락에서 ④를 추론할 수 있다. seek in vain after ~는 '~를 찾으나 헛수고로 끝난
다'는 뜻이다.

3 ②　　▶ **글의 어조**
첫 단락에서 "실패할 것이라고 우리는 예측할 수 있다"라고 한 것이나 둘째 단락 끝에서
"아무리 바라고 노력해도 빛은 적어도 우리가 속한 문명에서는 다시 비치지 않을 것이
다"라고 한 것에서 이 글의 논조로 ② '비관적인(pessimistic)'이 적절함을 알 수 있다.
① 희망에 찬 ③ 초연한 ④ 관망하는, 방관적인

skepticism n. 회의론, 무신론
order n. 질서; 상태; 종류
particularize v. 특수화하다
dogma n. 교리, 교조
purposeful a. 목적이 있는
prophet n. 예언자
ordered a. 질서정연한
fatal a. 치명적인
wistful a. 그리워하는, 동경하는 듯한, 생각에 잠긴

04

"신은 죽었다"라는 유명한 선언은 니체(Nietzsche)의 작품들 여러 곳에서 등장한다. (주목할 만한 것은 1882년에 발표된 『즐거운 과학(The Gay Science)』이다) 그리고 이 선언 때문에 대부분의 해설자들은 니체를 무신론자로 여긴다. 그는 현대 과학과 유럽사회의 증가된 세속화가 천년 이상의 기간 동안 서구사회에서 의미와 가치의 기초로서 역할을 수행해온 기독교적인 신을 실질적으로 '죽였다'고 주장했다. 그는 신의 죽음이 결국 사물에 대한 모든 보편적 관점의 상실과 객관적인 진리의 모든 논리 정합적인 의미의 상실을 이끌어 내면서, 우리에게 일종의 인식론적인 상대주의인, 관점주의라고 알려진 견해인, 우리 자신의 다양하고 많은 유동적인 관점들을 남겨주었다고 주장했다. (상대주의의 본질을 잘 드러내 보여주는 또 다른 인용구(니체의 말)는 "사실들은 없다. 단지 해석들이 있을 뿐이다"이다) 니체의 많은 사유들의 핵심에는 그것이 경치를 보기 위해 산에 오르는 것이든 아니면 좋은 삶을 사는 것이든, 어떤 가치 있는 것을 성취하기 위해서는 고난과 노력이 필요하다는 것이다. 그는 심지어 모든 사람들이 삶의 고통, 질병, 삶의 반전까지 모두 사랑하고, 그 사랑을 통해서 그 혹은 그녀가 그와 같은 좌절들을 극복하는 이점을 경험했으면 한다고 말하기까지 한다. 그의 사상은 전형적인 "고통 없이는 얻는 것이 없다"는 철학이다. 그리고 그는 삶에서 커다란 행복을 얻기 위해서는 도전으로 가득 찬 위험천만한 삶을 살아가고 위험을 감수해야 한다고 믿었다. 그러므로 니체에게 슬픔과 고난은 부정당하거나 회피되어져야 하는 것이 아니라(그는 특히 술과 종교로 관심을 돌리는 사람들을 경멸했다) 환영받고 잘 이용되어져서 자신에게 유리하게 전환되어야 하는 것이었다.

1 ② ▶ 글의 제목
  이 글은 니체의 핵심적인 사상들 가운데 몇 가지를 설명하고 있다.

2 ⑤ ▶ 내용파악
  "신은 죽었다"는 진술 때문에 니체는 무신론자로 여겨진다는 단서로부터 니체의 이론이 유신론이라는 보기는 부적절하다.

3 ② ▶ 태도
  슬픔과 고난을 긍정했다는 사실로부터 정답을 추론할 수 있다. ① 비관적인 ③ 암담한 ④ 순진한 ⑤ 일관성 없는

05

자유에 대한 핵심 주장들 중 하나는 19세기 철학자 밀(J.S. Mill)이 자신의 저서 『자유론(On Liberty)』에서 제시했다. 그는 모든 '이기적인' 행동(달리 말해, 자신과만 관계된 모든 것)에는 절대적인 자유가 있어야 한다고 주장했다. 자유에 대한 유일한 제한은 그의 용어를 빌리자면 '유해' 원칙이었다. 즉, 다른 사람에게 해를 입히는 행동은 아무것도 하지 말아야 한다는 것이었다. 그리고 물론, 그것은 자신을 위해 추구하는 것과 같은 정도의 자유를 다른 사람에게도 허용해야 한다는 말이 된다.
이 말에 함축된 의미는 만일 당신이 하는 모든 일이 당신 자신(혹은 동의하는 다른 성인)과만 관계된 것이면 그 과정에서 당신이 자신에게 해를 입힌다 하더라도 그 일을 자유롭게 할 수 있어야 한다는 것이다. 법이 개입해야 하는, 혹은 당신이 도덕적으로 비난받아야 하는 유일한 시점은 당신의 행동 — 혹은 말이나 생각 — 이 다른 사람에게 해를 입히는 경우이다.
밀이 이런 주장을 내놓은 배경(맥락)은 그가 모든 사람이 다른 사람들의 규범에 순응해야 할 필요 없이 자기 능력껏 최대한 자기 개발을 할 수 있기를 원했다는 것이다. 그는 자유를 그렇게 하기 위한 필수적인 요건으로 보았다.

1 ① ▶ 빈칸완성
  even if이므로 앞뒤가 서로 상반되어야 하는데, 앞에서 you should be free to do it이라고 긍정적으로 기술했으므로 빈칸의 동사는 benefit가 아니라 부정적인 harm이어야 하고 harm others는 유해 원칙에 위배되므로 harm yourself가 적절하다.

2 ②　▶ **부분이해**

본문에서 for that의 that이 develop themselves to their maximum potential을 가리키므로 ②의 '최대한의 자기 개발을 위한 선결요건'에 가장 가깝다. ① 자신의 철학이론의 핵심 ③ 많은 자기희생을 요구하는 장애요소 ④ 사회규범에 순응하기 위한 도구

3 ③　▶ **내용파악**

③은 'you should do nothing that causes harm to another person'라는 유해 원칙에 위배되므로 밀이 지지하지 않을 것이다.

06

그리스와 로마 사회는 개인을 공동체에, 시민을 국가에 종속시킨다는 개념 위에 세워졌다. 그 사회는 현세이건, 내세이건, 개인의 안정보다는 국가의 안정을 가장 중요한 행위의 목표로 삼았다. 어렸을 때부터 이런 비이기적인 이상 속에서 훈련된 시민들은 공무에 자신의 삶을 헌신했으며, 공동선을 위해 스스로의 목숨을 기꺼이 내놓을 수 있었다. 궁극적인 희생을 못하고 몸을 사릴 경우, 자신이 국가의 이익보다 개인의 존재를 앞세우는 비열한 행동을 하고 있다는 생각만 들었다. 신(神)과의 교감과 영원한 구원만을 유일한 삶의 목표로 삼는, 그런 목표에 비하면 국가의 번영과 생존 따위는 무의미할 뿐이라는 생각을 심어주는 동양의 종교들이 확산됨으로써 이 모든 것은 변하였다. 이런 이기적이고 부도덕한 교리의 필연적인 결과, 그 신봉자는 점점 더 자신의 생각을 자신만의 영적 감정에만 집중하게 되고, 현세의 삶을 경멸하게 되었으며, 그에게 현세란 단지 더 나은 영원한 내세를 맞이하기 위한 수습기간에 불과하게 되었다. 현세를 경멸하고 천상의 황홀한 무아지경에만 몰두하는 성인과 은둔자가 인류의 최고 이상이라는 생각이 퍼져나갔고, 자신을 잊고 국가의 선익을 위해 죽을 준비가 되어 있는 애국자와 영웅에 관한 낡은 이상들은 밀려나 버렸다. 구름을 뚫고 다가오는 천상의 도성을 주시하는 이의 눈에 지상의 도성은 형편없고 경멸스러운 것이었다. 따라서 무게중심은, 이를테면 현세에서 내세로 옮겨간 것이며, 다른 세상이 아무리 많은 것을 얻었을지 몰라도 이 세상이 변화에 의해 잃은 것이 많았다는 데에는 의심의 여지가 없다. 국가는 전반적으로 해체되어갔다. 국가와 가족의 유대관계는 느슨해졌다. 사회의 구조는 개인적 요소들로 해체되어 갔고, 야만주의의 병은 다시 도졌다. 문명이란 시민들의 적극적인 협력과 자신들의 사적인 이해관계를 공동선에 종속시키려는 의지를 통해서만 가능하기 때문이다.

1 ②　▶ **빈칸완성**

이 글의 요지는 동양에서 기원한 내세지향적 교리가 들어오면서, 그리스-로마 사회의 근간이 되었던 '공동선을 지향하고 개인보다 국가의 선익을 앞세우는 공동체 정신'이 붕괴되었다는 것이다. 빈칸 앞의 objects in comparison with which에서 which의 선행사는 objects이다. 이것을 해석해보면 '신과의 교감과 영원한 구원이라는 목표에 비하면'이라는 의미가 된다. 글 전체의 주제를 고려하면 '국가의 존재나 번영은 중요하지 않다'라는 말이 빈칸에 와야 적절하다.

2 ④　▶ **내용일치**

"종교와 국가의 연합이 전례 없던 규모로 강화되었다."라는 진술은 글 전체의 내용과 무관하므로 ④가 정답이다.

---

subordination n. 예속시킴; 하위; 종속

commonwealth n. 국가, 국민; 공화국; 연방

unselfish a. 이기적이지 않은

basely ad. 천하게, 비열하게

shrink from ~을 꺼리다, 피하다

inculcate v. (사상·지식 따위를) 가르치다, 되풀이하여 가르치다

communion n. 교감, 친교; 종교단체

salvation n. 구조, 구제; 구조수단

inevitable a. 피할 수 없는, 부득이한

devotee n. 열성적인 애호가; 광신자

probation n. (직장에서의) 수습; 수습기간

recluse n. 은둔자, 세상을 버린 사람

rapt a. 완전히 몰입한, 열중한

ecstatic a. 무아지경의

contemplation n. 숙고, 명상; 기대

contemptible a. 경멸할 만한, 비열한

disintegration n. 분해; 분열

behold v. 보다, 주시하다

body politic 정치적 통일체, 국가; 국민

relapse v. (병이) 재발하다, 도지다

07

고대 그리스인들은 미신이나 종교에 의지하지 않고 논리적인 생각만으로 자연을 이해할 수 있다고 생각한 역사상 최초의 사회 중 하나의 구성원들이었다. 기원전 6세기 이전에 그리스 사상가들은 종종 세상을 이해하기 위해 신화 쪽으로 눈을 돌렸다. 예를 들어, 불이 어떻게 생겨나는가를 설명하기 위해 제우스(Zeus)신에게 반항하여 신들의 고향인 올림포스 산에서 불을 훔쳐 나온 프로메테우스(Prometheus)의 신화를 이야기했다. 하지만 (고대) 철학자 밀레투스의 탈레스(Thales)로부터 시작하여 그리스인들은 실제적 세계의 본질에 대해 탐구하기 시작했으며, 논리적인 사고만을 토대로 하여 현상의 본질에 관한 가설을 세웠다. 비록 이들의 과학적 지식은 한정적이었는데, 이는 자신들의 생각을 검증할 수 있는 실험을 수행하지 못했던 탓이 컸다. 그럼에도 불구하고 고대 그리스 철학자들은 오늘날까지 높이 존중되고 있는 현상의 체계적이고 과학적인 현실관의 기초를 닦았다. 탈레스 이전의 사상가들과 이후의 사상가들 간의 핵심적인 차이점 하나는 이들이 현상의 특질에 대해 내렸던 근본적인 가설에서 찾아볼 수 있다. 탈레스 이전의 많은 저술가들은 자연이 예측할 수 없으며, 신의 변덕에 따라 좌우된다고 믿었다. 탈레스는 이러한 전통을 깨고 혼란스러워 보이는 자연 현상 속에는 신중한 사색을 통해 발견할 수 있는 근본적인 질서가 존재한다고 주장했다. 아마도 생명에 대한 중요성과 기체 상태에서 액체 및 고체 상태로 변화될 수 있는 능력, 그리고 다양한 물질 내의 그 존재성 때문이었겠지만, 탈레스는 '물'이야말로 모든 물질의 기본적 요소라고 생각했다. 과학적 견지에서 본다면 탈레스의 업적은 구체적인 가설, 즉 어떤 주어진 현상에 대해 타당하고 체계적인 설명을 제공하는 방법을 발전시킨 것이었다.

1 ②   ▶ **내용일치**

밀레투스의 탈레스는 논리적인 생각으로 자연을 이해할 수 있다고 생각했으며 실제적 세계의 본질에 대해 탐구하려고 했다. 하지만 과학적인 지식이 한정되어 있어 자신들의 생각을 검증할 수 있는 실험을 수행하지 못했다고 했다. 따라서 ②가 이 글의 내용과 일치한다.

2 ④   ▶ **빈칸완성**

빈칸 앞에 탈레스 이전의 많은 저술가들은 자연이 예측할 수 없다고 했으므로 빈칸에는 자연 예측이 불가능했던 것과 관련된 사항이 와야 하는데, 첫 단락에서 그리스 사상가들은 종종 세상을 이해하기 위해 신화 쪽으로 눈을 돌렸고 이와 관련하여 신들의 고향인 올림포스 산에서 불을 훔쳐 나온 프로메테우스의 신화에 대한 예를 들었다. 따라서 빈칸에는 ④가 오는 것이 적절하다.

without recourse to ~에 의지하지 않고	
originate v. 일어나다, 생기다	
in defiance of ~를 무시하여, 무릅쓰고	
speculate v. 숙고하다, 사색하다	
carry out ~을 수행[이행]하다	
set the stage for ~을 준비하다, ~의 기초를 닦다	
unpredictable a. 예언[예측]할 수 없는	
whim n. 일시적인 생각, 변덕	
chaos n. 무질서, 대혼란	
transform v. 변형시키다	
gaseous a. 기체의, 가스의	
solid a. 고체의, 고형의	
substance n. 물질, 물체	
hypothesis n. 가설, 가정	

08

시뮬라크르는 오랫동안 철학자들의 관심사였다. 그의 저서 『소피스트(Sophist)』에서, 플라톤은 두 종류의 이미지 만들기에 대해서 말한다. 첫 번째 이미지 만들기는 원본을 정확하게 복제하고자 시도하는 (원본에) 충실한 재현이다. 두 번째 이미지 만들기는 복제된 것이 관람자들에게 올바른 것이라고 보이도록 하기 위해서 의도적으로 왜곡하는 것이다. 그는 아랫부분 보다 윗부분을 더 크게 조각해서 땅에서 조각을 보는 관람자들로 하여금 조각이 올바른 것처럼(올바르게 실물을 재현한 것처럼) 보이게 하는 그리스 조각의 예를 든다. 만일 관람자들이 일정한 비율로 조각상을 본다면 그들은 조각상이 기형적이라는 것을 깨닫게 될 것이다. 시각 예술로부터 유래한 이 예(시뮬라크르)는 진실을 왜곡하고 그 왜곡된 진실이 적절한 각도에서 보여지지 않는 한, 정확한 것처럼 보이게 하고자 하는 철학적 예술들과 일부 철학자들의 경향을 위한 은유로서 역할을 수행한다. 니체는 (시뮬라크르라는 용어를 사용하지는 않았지만) 그의 저서 『우상의 황혼(Twilight of the Idols)』에서 시뮬라크르의 개념을 다루었다. 니체에 따르면 대부분의 철학자들은 그들의 감각에 들어오는 신뢰할만한 입력들(감각적 정보들)을 무시하고 언어와 이성에 의해 만들어진 구성물에 의존하는 것을 통해서 (실체가 아니라) 실체의 왜곡된 복제에 도달한다고 한다. 포스트모더니스트로서 프랑스의 사회이론가인 장 보드리야르(Jean Baudrillard)는 시뮬라크르가 실재의 복제가 아니라 그 자체로 진리가 됐다고 수상한다. (그에게 시뮬라크르는 이제 실재의 복제가 아니라 실재보다 더 실재다운) 하이퍼리얼이다. 플라톤이 충실한 재현과 의도적으로 왜곡된 재현(시뮬라크르)이라는 두 가지 종류의 재현을 보았다면, 보드리야르가 보는 것은 네 가지 재현이다: 기초적인 현실의 반영; 현실의

simulacrum n. 모방의 모방; 그림자, 환영	
statuary n. 조상, 조각상	
in scale 일정한 비율로, 균형을 이루어	
malformed a. 기형인, 흉하게 일그러진	
perversion n. 곡해, 왜곡	
pretence n. 위장, 겉치레; 주장	
avenue n. 대로; 길, 수단, 방법	

왜곡; (모델을 갖지 않는) 현실에 대한 위장; 그리고 '어떤 종류의 현실과도 관련을 맺고 있지 않은' 시뮬라크르. 니체처럼, 보드리야르의 개념 속에서 시뮬라크르는 부정적으로 인식된다. 그러나 이 토픽을 다룬 또 다른 현대 철학자인 질 들뢰즈(Gilles Deleuze)는 다른 견해를 가지고 있다. 질 들뢰즈는 시뮬라크르를 받아들여진 이상이나 특권적인 위치(한 마디로 기존의 체제)에 도전하고 (기존의 체제를) 전복시킬 수 있는 수단으로 여긴다. 들뢰즈는 시뮬라크르를 차이가 차이 그 자체에 의해서 차이와 관계를 맺는 그러한 체계로서 정의 내린다. 여기서 중요한 것은 이 체계 속에서(순수한 차이로 이루어진 시뮬라크르라는 체계 속에서) 우리가 그 어떤 이전부터 있어 온 정체성도, 그 어떤 내적 유사성도 발견할 수 없다는 것이다.

1 ② ▶ **글의 제목**
이 글은 철학사에서 다양한 의미로 사용되고 있는 시뮬라크르라는 개념을 다루고 있다.

2 ③ ▶ **내용일치**
Jean Baudrillard에게 시뮬라크르는 현실의 재현이 아니라 그 자체로 존재하며 현실보다 더 현실 같은 하이퍼리얼이다.(가령 현재 세계 경제를 지배하고 있는 수많은 금융상품을 생각해보라. 그들이 바로 원본이 없는 시뮬라크르들이다.)

09

아나키즘은 강압적인 정부 혹은 강압적인 통치를 거부하고 그것들의 제거를 옹호하는 정치철학으로서 사회는 강압적인 국가 없이 조직될 수 있다는 (되어야만 한다는) 견해를 가지고 있다. 이러한 태도는 어떤 종류의 권위도 모두 거부하는 것을 포함할 수도 있고, 포함하지 않을 수도 있다. 아나키스트들은 정부가 해롭고 불필요하다고 믿는다. 철학적인 아나키즘은 국가가 도덕적 정당성을 결여하고 있고, 국가에 복종해야 하는 개인적인 의무도 없고, 역으로 국가가 개인들에게 명령할 권리를 가지고 있지 않다고 주장한다. 그러나 아나키즘은 국가를 제거하기 위한 혁명을 적극적으로 옹호하지 않고, 현대 국가의 억압적인 법과 사회적 구속으로부터 개인을 자유롭게 해줄 점진적인 변화를 요구한다. "아니키(anarchy)"라는 용어는 '통치자 없는'이라는 의미를 가지고 있는 그리스어 "anarchos"로부터 유래했다. 19세기가 될 때까지 아나키즘이란 용어는 대개 논리정합적인 정치적 믿음을 설명하는 긍정적인 방식으로 사용되었다. 아나키즘이라는 용어가 혼란과 유사한 어떤 것을 의미하는 비난 투로 사용된 것은 후대의 일이다.
아나키즘은 개인의 권리와 자유의지를 최대치로 하고 국가의 역할을 최소화하는 것을 옹호하는 자유의지주의와 연관이 있다. 그리고 특히 개인의 자유를 최대치까지 끌어올리고 권력 혹은 권위의 집중을 최소화하고자 시도하는 노동자 지향적인 체제를 옹호하는 자유의지주의 사회주의와 연관이 있는데, 아나키즘과 자유의지주의 사회주의는 거의 동의어다. <무정부주의자와 마르크스주의 간의 갈등은 이론, 전략, 실행, 그리고 즉각적인 정치적 목적이라는 관점에서 등장했다.> 강압적인 정부와 '국가'를 반대하는 것을 넘어서, 모든 아나키스트들의 주장들을 담아낼 수 있는 단일하게 정의된 입장은 없다. 아나키즘의 옹호자들은 극단적인 개인주의(인간의 독립을 강조하고 개인의 자립과 자유의 중요성을 강조하는 정치적 전망)에서부터 완벽한 집단주의(인간의 상호의존성과 집단의 중요성을 강조하는 정치적 전망)에 이르는 그 어떤 것이나 아마도 지지할 것이다.

1 ④ ▶ **문맥상 적절하지 않은 문장 고르기**
이 글은 아나키즘과 마르크스주의를 비교하고 있지 않다.

2 ③ ▶ **글의 제목**
이 글은 아나키즘의 특징을 서술하고 있다.

3 ② ▶ **내용추론**
아나키스트들은 혁명을 선호하지 않는다.

compulsory a. 강제적인, 필수적인, 의무적인
coercive a. 강제적인, 강요하는
constraint n. 강제, 압박, 속박
pejorative a. 경멸적인, 비난 투의
Libertarianism n. 자유의지주의
worker-oriented a. 노동자 지향적인
interdependence n. 상호의존

10

교황은 로마의 주교이자 전 세계 가톨릭교회의 지도자다. 로마 주교의 중요성은 대체적으로 성 베드로(Saint Peter)의 전통적인 계승자로서의 역할에서 비롯되는데, 예수 그리스도는 성 베드로에게 천국의 열쇠와 '(무엇이든) 매고 푸는' 권능을 주었으며, 성 베드로를 교회가 세워지는 '반석'이라고 불렀다. 현재의 교황은 프란치스코(Francis)로 2013년 3월 13일 선출되었으며, 교황 베네딕토 16세(Benedict XVI)를 계승했다.

교황권은 papacy(교황 제도)라고 불린다. 교황의 교회 관할구역은 사도 성 베드로와 사도 성 바울(Saint Paul)이 로마에서 순교했던 교회의 전통에 바탕을 둔 '교황청' 또는 '로마 교황좌'라고 종종 불린다. 교황은 또한 이탈리아의 수도인 로마에 둘러싸여 고립되어 있는 독립된 도시국가 바티칸(Vatican) 시국의 국가원수다.

<교황 제도는 세계에서 가장 오래 지속되는 제도 중 하나이며, 세계사에서 주목할 정도의 역할을 해왔다.> 고대의 교황들은 기독교의 포교를 도왔으며, 다양한 교리상의 분쟁을 해결하는 데 도움을 주었다. 중세시대에는 교황들이 서유럽에서 세속적으로 중요한 역할을 맡았으며, 종종 기독교 군주들 사이의 조정자 역할을 하였다. 현재는, 기독교 신앙과 교리의 확산뿐 아니라, 교황들은 세계교회주의, 종교간 대화, 자선사업, 그리고 인권 옹호에 관여하고 있다.

처음에는 세속적인 권력이 없었던 교황은 역사의 어느 시기에, 세속적인 통치자의 광범위한 권력과 유사한 광범위한 권력을 축적했다. 최근 몇 세기 동안, 교황은 점차 세속적인 권력을 포기해야만 했고, 현재 교황의 권력은 또다시 거의 전적으로 종교 문제에만 국한되어 있다.

1 ③ ▶ 문장삽입
제시문은 "교황 제도는 세계에서 가장 오래 지속되는 제도 중 하나이며, 세계사에서 주목할 정도의 역할을 해왔다."라는 내용이다. 따라서 제시문 앞에는 교황 제도에 대한 언급이, 제시문 뒤에는 교황 제도가 세계사에서 행한 역할의 내용이 나와야 하므로 ⓒ가 정답이다.

2 ① ▶ 빈칸완성
세 번째 단락의 내용은 역대 교황이 관여해 온 활동들을 언급하고 있다. 따라서 같은 맥락으로 첫 번째 빈칸에는 교황들이 세계교회주의, 종교간 대화, 자선사업, 그리고 인권 옹호에 '관여하고 있다'는 말이 들어가야 적절하다. 따라서 첫 번째 빈칸에는 engage, participate가 적절하며, 두 번째 빈칸 앞에는 "교황이 처음에는 세속적인 권력이 없었다"고 했던 반면, 빈칸의 다음 문장에서는 "교황이 점차 세속적인 권력을 포기해야만 했다"는 내용이 나온다. 따라서 두 번째 빈칸에는 역사의 어느 시기에, 세속적인 통치자의 광범위한 권력과 유사한 광범위한 권력을 '축적했다'는 말이 들어가야 문맥상 적절하다. 따라서 두 번째 빈칸에는 accrued, amassed가 적절하다. 따라서 ①이 정답이다. ② 청산하다 ― 포기하다 ③ 해산시키다 ― 축적하다 ④ 참가하다, 관여하다 ― 상실하다

3 ④ ▶ 내용일치
① 사도 성 베드로와 사도 성 바울이 로마에서 순교했다고 했다. ② 교황은 성 베드로의 전통적인 계승자라고 했으며, 예수 그리스도가 성 베드로에게 천국의 열쇠와 무엇이든 매고 푸는 권능을 주며, 성 베드로를 교회가 세워지는 반석이라고 불렀다고 했으므로, 1대 교황이 성 베드로임을 알 수 있다. ③ 교황은 이탈리아의 수도인 로마에 둘러싸여 고립되어 있는 독립된 도시국가인 바티칸 시국의 국가원수라고 했다. ④ 교황의 세속적인 권력은 최근 몇 세기 동안 점차 포기되어야만 했고, 지금은 교황의 권력이 종교 문제에만 국한되어 있다고 했으므로 ④가 정답이다.

4 ③ ▶ 내용파악
① 교황청의 위치, ② 기독교 전파, ④ 예수 그리스도의 제자들은 본문에 모두 언급된 반면, ③ '교황청의 계급제도'는 본문에 언급되지 않았으므로 ③이 정답이다.

---

pope n. 교황
bishop n. 주교
be derived from ~에서 유래하다, 비롯되다
rock n. 반석
papacy n. 교황의 지위[통치권, 임기], 교황 제도
ecclesiastical a. 교회의, 성직자의
jurisdiction n. 권한, 지배권; 재판권; 사법권이 미치는 지역, 관할구역
Holy See 교황청
Apostolic a. 사도의; 로마 교황의
Apostolic See 로마 가톨릭 교회; 교황좌
Apostle n. 사도: 그리스도의 12제자
martyr v. 순교자로 만들다, 순교자로 죽이다
head of state 국가원수
sovereign a. (국가가) 자주적인, 독립적인
enclaved a. 외국 영토 안에 고립된
have a part in ~에 관여하다
doctrinal a. 교리상의
arbitrator n. 중재인, 조정자
monarch n. 군주
ecumenism n. (기독교의) 세계교회주의
interfaith a. 다른 종교 간의
charitable work 자선사업
temporal a. 세속의
accrue v. 획득하다, 축적하다
papal a. 로마교황의, 로마 가톨릭교회의

11

알튀세르(Althusser)의 주장에서 가장 핵심적인 사항은 '이데올로기'의 구조와 기능에 관한 것이다. 알튀세르는 두 가지 명제를 제시하는 것을 통해서 이데올로기의 구조와 기능을 설명한다. 첫 번째로, 그는 이데올로기가 그들의 실제 존재 조건에 대해서 개인들이 맺고 있는 상상적인 관계를 나타내 보여주는 것이라고 상정한다. 이러한 현실에 대한 왜곡은 물질적 소외와 이 세계에 대한 거짓된 표상을 통해 억압받는 사람들의 상대적으로 수동적인 마음을 노예화하고 이를 기반으로 해서 그들에 대한 지배와 착취를 일삼는 억압하는 자들의 적극적인 상상에 의해서 이루어진다. 두 번째로, 그는 이데올로기가 구체적 실체나 장치(이데올로기적 국가 장치) 등과 같은 형태를 갖춘 물질적인 존재라고 상정한다. 이처럼 다양한 이데올로기(상상된 현실)에 대한 개인의 믿음은 이데올로기적 국가 장치에 의해서 정의(조작)된 의식을 부여받은 주체인 개인의 생각으로부터 비롯된다. 이러한 (거짓) 의식은 주체로 하여금 특정한 방식으로 행동하고 특정한 태도를 수용하고 더 나아가 자기 자신을 주체라고 인식하는 이데올로기에 순응하는 특정한 규칙적인 관행에 참여하도록 고무하고 선동한다.

알튀세르의 핵심적인 명제는 이데올로기가 호명이라는 과정을 통해서 개인을 주체로 변형시킨다는 것이다. 가족이라는 이데올로기적 국가 장치는 심지어 한 아이가 태어나기 전에도 작동하는데 그 이유는 가족이라는 이데올로기적 국가 장치가 그 아이의 정체성을 그 아이가 태어나기도 전에 앞서 결정하기 때문이다. 이처럼 개인은 이미 항상 (이데올로기에 의해 호명당한) 주체로서 존재한다. 한 개인은 다양한 차원에서 이데올로기에 대한 복종을 강요받는다. 그리고 각각의 차원의 복종 혹은 개인을 복종시키는 이데올로기적 국가 장치는 개인의 일상적인 활동에 영향을 미치고 이를 통해서 그 개인의 실질적인 존재 조건을 결정한다. 더 나아가 알튀세르는 이데올로기 안에서 '자유로운' 주체로서 자기 자신을 인식한다는 것이 단지 오인에 지나지 않는다는 사실을 보여주는데, 그 이유는 이데올로기에 포획된 상태에서 '자유로운' 주체라는 개념이 환상에 지나지 않기 때문이다. 사실상 주체는 항상 이데올로기에 의해 예속되고, 한계 지워지고, 제한되고, 통제될 수밖에 없다. 이와 같은 오인 때문에 주체는 궁극적으로 자신의 이익에 해가 되는, 지배 이데올로기 속에 깊이 침윤된 의례적인 일들을 행하게 되는 것이다.

crux n. 가장 중요한[곤란한] 부분

posit v. 상정하다, 단정하다, 생각하다

exploitation n. 착취; 이용; 개발

domination n. 지배

the oppressed 억압받는 사람들

entity n. 실체; 실재물; 본질, 실질

instigate v. 부추기다, 선동하다

subject n. 주체

interpellation n. (의회에서 장관에 대한) 질문, 설명 요구; 호명

hailing n. 호명

predetermine v. 미리 예정되다; 미리 운명 지어지다; 미리 결정되다

subjection n. 정복; 복종, 종속; 의존

subjugate v. 정복하다, 예속시키다

1 ②   ▶ **글의 제목**
이 글은 이데올로기적 국가장치 개념을 핵심으로 하는 프랑스의 철학자 알튀세르의 이데올로기론이 어떠한 것인지를 설명하고 있는 글이다.

2 ②   ▶ **빈칸완성**
빈칸 Ⓐ는 이데올로기가 일종의 상상 혹은 환상이라는 단서로부터 추론할 수 있다. 이데올로기에 침윤된 우리의 현실에 대한 인식은 불가피하게 왜곡을 수반할 수밖에 없다. 빈칸 Ⓑ는 이데올로기가 형태를 갖춘 물질적인 실체로서 존재한다는 단서로부터 추론할 수 있다. 이데올로기는 단순한 관념이 아니라 구체적 형태를 갖고 존재하는 물질적 실체다.
① 완전, 완벽 ― 추상적인 ③ 묘사 ― 선험적인 ④ 단언, 확언 ― 세속적인

3 ②   ▶ **부분이해**
밑줄 친 문장은 우리가 존재하는 한 어떤 경우에도 이데올로기를 벗어날 수 없다는 정도의 의미를 가지고 있다.

12

처음 명성을 얻고 나서 2천 년도 더 지난 지금 스토아 철학은 중요한 계기를 맞이하고 있다. 물론 스토아 철학과 관련된 내용은 인터넷에 있는데, 온라인에서 스토아 철학과 관련된 가장 큰 토론장인 스토아 철학 관련 서브레딧(subreddit)에는 28,000명이 넘는 구독자가 있으며, 지금까지 라이벌인 에피쿠로스주의(쾌락주의)의 구독자 수인 약 4,000명에 비해 몇 배가 많은 것이다. 하지만 스토아 철학은 또한 그 가장 지독한 형태로나마 실제 삶에 스며들고 있다. 미 해군 특수부대는 신병에게 스토아 철학의 통찰력을 가르치며, 미국 프로 미식축구 연맹(NFL) 전반에 걸쳐 선수들과 감독들은 스토아 철학에 이르는 지침서인 라이언 홀리데이(Ryan Holiday)의 『돌파력(The Obstacle Is the Way)』를 탐독하고 있다.

심지어 고대 시대에도 스토아 철학은 실현 가능성으로 유명했다. 고대 그리스와 로마의 스토아 철학자들은 신학, 논리학, 형이상학과 관련한 글을 썼지만 그들의 초점은 '현시점'이었다. "스토아 철학은 당신에게 삶에서 소유할 가치가 있는 것을 알려주고 그것에 이르는 방법을 제시해줍니다."라고 『올바른 생활에 이르는 지침서(A Guide to the Good Life)』라는 스토아 철학을 담은 핸드북을 쓴 저자인 윌리엄 어빈(William Irvine)은 말한다. 그 핸드북의 핵심은 당신이 가진 것에 만족하는 것을 배우는 것이다. "어떤 일은 우리에게 달려있고 다른 일은 그렇지 않다. 의견, 충동, 욕망 등은 우리에게 달려있지만 신체, 재산, 명성, 지위, 한마디로 말해서 우리 자신의 행동이 아닌 것은 무엇이든 간에 우리에게 달린 것이 아니다."라고 에픽테토스(Epictetus)는 가르쳤다. 일상생활의 안락함에 대한 무관심은 스토아 철학이 냉정하다는 명성을 남겼다. 실제로 스토아 철학을 옹호하는 사람들은 그것을 단순히 기대치 관리에 대한 합리적인 접근이라고 주장한다. 스토아 철학의 중심 통찰력은 삶은 어렵고 변덕스럽기 때문에 어려움에 대비해야 한다는 것이다.

많은 현대의 스토아 학자들은 이 교리가 이미 부분적으로 인지행동치료법(CBT)의 형태로 되살아났다고 주장한다. 인지행동치료법은 '문제 중심의' 치료법으로 현재 우울증, 불안, 모든 종류의 도움이 안 되는 사고에 대한 심리학의 최고 무기로 널리 알려져 있다. 스토아 철학과 같이 CBT는 환자를 치료하는 사람들에게 사건과 인식 사이의 차이를 구별하도록 장려하고 있으며, 거의 모든 CBT 교과서는 에픽테토스의 격언의 일부 견해를 포함하고 있다. "인간은 사물에 의해서가 아니라 그것을 보는 관점에 의해 동요된다." 그러나 CBT의 창시자들은 스토아 철학의 영향을 공개적으로 인정했지만, 그들은 더 넓은 도덕 체계와는 관계없는 기법을 채택하는 경향이 있었다. "스토아 철학은 우리의 정서적 고통의 상당 부분이 자기중심주의나 물질주의 또는 쾌락주의와 같은 잘못된 가치관에 의해 발생한다는 견해를 제시함으로써 대부분의 현대적 자기 수양과 치료법을 능가합니다."라고 스토아 철학 주간을 주최하는 사람 중 한 명인 인지행동 심리치료사인 도널드 로버트슨(Donald Robertson)은 말한다.

1 ① ▶ 내용파악

두 번째 단락에서 스토아 철학의 중심 사상에 대해 자세히 설명하고 있는데, 스토아 철학은 현시점에서 삶에서 소유할 가치가 있는 것을 알려주고 그것에 이르는 방법을 제시해준다고 했다. 또한 스토아 철학의 중심 통찰력은 "삶은 어렵고 변덕스럽기 때문에 어려움에 대비해야 한다는 것이다."라고 했으므로 ①이 정답이다. ③ 거대한 야망으로 계획을 세우는 것은 미래 중심의 비현실성이다. ④ 심리치료법이다.

2 ③ ▶ 빈칸완성

빈칸 다음 문장에서 "고대 그리스와 로마의 스토아 철학자들은 신학, 논리학, 형이상학과 관련한 글을 썼지만 그들의 초점은 '현시점'이었다."라고 했다. 그리고 스토아 철학은 우리가 기대할 수 있는 부분과 그렇지 못한 부분을 나누어서 어려움에 대비할 수 있도록 해준다고 했으므로 '실질적인' 측면이 있는 철학이라고 볼 수 있다. 따라서 빈칸 Ⓐ에는 ③ practicality가 정답이다. ① 방종 ② 구원 ④ 중용

3 ④ ▶ 부분이해

밑줄 친 부분 Ⓑ에서 "인간은 사물에 의해서가 아니라 그것을 보는 관점에 의해 동요된다."고 했는데, 사물은 사건(events)을 가리키는 것이고, 그것을 보는 관점은 지각(perception)을 의미하므로, Ⓑ가 의미하는 것은 "사람들은 사건이 아니라, 그 사건들을 대하는 태도에 의해 영향을 받는다."는 것이므로 ④가 정답이다.

13

종교는 신념체계이며 따라서 사실 일종의 이념이다. 그러나 종교는 그 기원을 신(神)의 영감에 두고 있는 것으로, 다른 이념과는 구별된다. 이로 인해 종교는 다른 이념과 너무나 다른 것이 돼 버려서 우리가 종교를 '이념'이라 부르는 것은 단지 하나의 기술적인 의미에서일 뿐이다. 종교의 핵심이 신적인 것이다 보니 종교에 대해 논쟁하기가 더 어려워지는데, 종교에 대해서는 그 종교의 신적인 기초를 사람들이 믿거나 믿지 않거나 하기 때문이다. 믿음을 공유하는 두 사람은 그 종교 안에서 중요한 해석의 차이에 대해서 논쟁할지도 모르지만, 믿는 사람과 믿지 않는 사람은 단지 서로 의견이 다르다는 것에 동의해야만 한다. 이것은 우리가 대개 이념적 논쟁이라고 생각하는 것과는 아주 다른 담화다.

종교적 담화가 다른 이념적 담화와 얼마나 다른가 하는 것은 부분적으로는 신앙인이 얼마나 근본주의적인가에 따라 달라진다. 근본주의 신앙인은 성경이든 코란이든, 신이 주신 경전의 모든 단어가 신으로부터 온 것이기 때문에 사실이라고 생각한다. 근본주의적 성향이 덜한 신앙인은, 모든 종교적인 책에는 불가피하게 모순된 점들과 모호한 점들이 있다는 것을 알고서, 신앙의 문서가 신앙원리의 중심된 진수를 갖고 있긴 하지만 정확한 규정에 대해서는 이렇게 저렇게 해석할 수 있는 것으로 간주한다. 이런 보다 더 해석적인 신앙인은 예를 들어 황금률에 대해서는 타협하지 않을지 모르지만, 동성애에 대한 신의 말씀은 보다 더 자유롭게 논의할 수 있는 것으로 생각한다. 해석적인 신앙은 종종 진보주의나 사회주의나 보수주의 같은 다른 이념의 요소들과 혼합될 여지를 많이 남겨둔다. 그래서 근본주의 신앙에 기초한 논의보다 그런 (근본주의가 아닌) 믿음에 대한 담화가 결국 다른 이념적 논의와 조금 더 유사한 것이다. 그러나 신의 진리에 대한 이해가 논의의 일부인 만큼, 그 어떤 종교적 담화도 항상 특별한 성격을 띤다.

1 ④ ▶ 부분이해

"믿는 사람과 믿지 않는 사람은 단지 서로 의견이 다르다는 것에 동의해야만 한다."라는 말은 거기서 더 나아가 상대방의 신앙 혹은 불신앙을 자신의 신앙 혹은 불신앙에 기초해 공격하고 비판할 수는 없다는 말이므로 "종교적 신조는 논쟁할 수 없는 것이다."라는 ④가 가장 가까운 의미다.

2 ① ▶ 빈칸완성

but 앞에서 황금률에 대해서는 타협하지 않을지 모른다고 했으므로 빈칸에는 '타협이 가능하고 이렇게 저렇게 해석될 수 있는'에 가까운 ①의 '보다 더 자유롭게 논의할 수 있는'이 적절하다. ② 매우 적절한 ③ 문제가 되지 않는 ④ 더욱 논박할 수 없는

3 ③ ▶ 내용추론

해석적인 신앙은 해석의 자유로움을 허용하지만 신의 진리와 관계된 종교적 특성을 갖고 있다는 점에서는 근본주의 신앙과 같으므로 ③을 추론할 수는 없다. ① 종교는 신념체계이며 신의 영감에 기원을 두고 있다. ② 종교는 신념체계이며 그래서 사실 일종의 이념이라고 했으므로 다른 이념들도 모종의 신념체계라 할 수 있다. ④ 빈칸이 있는 문장에서 예로 나온 황금률은 앞 문장에 나온 신앙원리의 중심된 진수에 해당한다.

4 ② ▶ 글의 제목

특히 첫 번째 단락의 마지막 부분과 두 번째 단락의 첫 부분을 보면, 이 글이 종교적 논쟁이나 담화가 어떻게 해서 일반적인 이념적 논쟁이나 담화와 다른가를 설명한 글이라는 것을 알 수 있다. 따라서 ②의 '종교적 담화의 본질'이 글의 제목으로 가장 적절하다.

ideology n. (사회·정치상의) 이데올로기
origin n. 기원, 발단; 유래
divine a. 신적인, 신성한
inspiration n. 영감, 인스피레이션
technical a. 기술의; 전문의, 특수한
interpretation n. 해석, 설명; 판단
fundamentalist a. 근본주의적인
take it that ~이라고 생각[가정]하다
scripture n. 성서, 경전
inevitable a. 불가피한, 부득이한
contradiction n. 부인, 부정; 모순
ambiguity n. 애매모호함, 불명료함
prescription n. 규범, 규정
interpretive a. 해석의, 해석적인
liberalism n. 자유주의, 진보주의
to the extent that ~인 정도까지, ~이라는 점에서; ~인 한[바]에는

14

포스트모더니즘을 정의내리기가 쉽지 않다는 것은 이제는 진부한 얘기처럼 들린다. 그러나 포스트모더니즘은 현존, 동일성, 역사적 진보, 지식의 자명성, 의미의 일의성 같은 개념들을 해체하기 위해 차이, 반복, 흔적, 시뮬라크르, 하이퍼리얼리티 등의 개념을 사용하는 비판적, 전략적, 수사학적인 실천이다. '포스트모더니즘'이라는 용어는 장 프랑수아 리오타르(Jean-François Lyotard)가 쓴 『포스트모던의 조건(The Postmodern Condition)』의 발간과 함께 1979년 처음으로 철학적 용어 속으로 들어왔다. 나는 선택의 효율성을 고려해서 이 범주에 드는 다른 인물들을 선택했다. 비록 개인적으로 이들 철학자들이 공통의 범주에 함께 묶이는 것에 대해 저항할 것이 분명하지만, 그럼에도 불구하고 나는 철학적 포스트모더니즘의 토론에서 가장 많이 인용되는 철학자들을 선택했는데, 그들은 다섯 명의 프랑스 철학자들과 두 명의 이탈리아 철학자들이다. 국적에 따라 그들을 줄 세우는 것은 그들이 문제시하는 모더니스트적인 기획을 모방하는 것인지도 모른다. 그러나 그들 사이에는 강한 차이가 존재하며, 이러한 차이는 언어학적 경계선과 문화적 경계선을 따라 나누어진다.

예를 들어, 프랑스 철학자들은 마르크스(Marx)와 프로이트(Freud)에 대한 구조주의자들의 독서를 포함하는, 1950년대와 1960년대의 파리에서 일어난 구조주의 혁명기간 동안 발전한 개념을 가지고 연구한다. 이러한 이유 때문에, 그들은 종종 '후기구조주의자들'이라고 불린다. 그들은 또한 1968년 5월에 일어난 사건들을, 특히 대학의 경우에, 모던한 사유 및 제도와 갈라서는 분수령의 순간으로 인용한다.

이와는 대조적으로, 이탈리아의 철학자들은 잠바티스타 비코(Giambattista Vico)와 베네데토 크로체(Benedetto Croce)와 같은 인물들을 포괄하는 미학적이고 수사학적인 전통에 의지한다. 그들이 강조하는 바는 매우 역사적이다. 그리고 그들은 (68혁명 같은) 혁명적 순간에 대한 매혹을 보여주지 않는다. 대신에 그들은 (프랑스 철학자들이 구사하는) 대응전략이나 담론적 차이보다는 지속성, 이야기, 지속성 안에 존재하는 차이를 강조한다. 그러나 양쪽 모두 포스트모더니즘이 모더니티에 대한 공격이라거나 모더니티로부터의 완전한 벗어남은 제안하지 않는다. 차라리, 모더니즘과 포스트모더니즘 사이에 존재하는 차이란 모더니티 그 자체 내부에 존재하는 것이고 포스트모더니즘은 다른 방식으로 모던적 사유를 지속시킨 것이다.

1 ③ ▶ **글의 목적**
이 글은 포스트모더니즘의 탄생 배경과 주된 특징들을 서술하고 있다.

2 ② ▶ **빈칸완성**
Rather, its differences lie within modernity itself라는 진술로부터 모더니즘과 포스모더니즘이 연결되어 있음을 추론할 수 있다. ① 절단 ③ 배신 ④ 복종, 종속

3 ① ▶ **동의어**
이 글에서 destabilize는 '해체하다'의 의미로 볼 수 있다. 포스트모더니즘의 가장 두드러진 특징 가운데 하나는 기존의 것들을 창조적으로 해체하는 것이다. ② 승인하다 ③ 전진하다; 진보하다 ④ 약속하다

4 ② ▶ **내용추론**
① 포스트 모더니스트들은 역사의 진보 같은 거대 담론을 불신한다. ③ 68혁명을 높이 평가하면서 구조주의적 혁명 동안에 발전한 개념을 이용하였다는 진술로부터 잘못된 보기임을 추론할 수 있다. ④ 모더니즘과 포스트모더니즘은 적대 관계가 아니라 영향을 주고받는 관계다.

indefinable a. 정의내릴 수 없는

truism n. 자명한 이치; 뻔한 소리

epistemic a. 지식의

univocity n. 일의성

economy n. 효율성

affiliation n. 결연, 제휴, 연결

draw upon 이용하다, 의지하다

counterstrategy n. 대응전략

discursive a. 산만한, 담론의

deconstruct v. 해체하다

15

비어 있음은 하나의 도전적인 개념이다. 그 정의는 파악하기 힘들고 의미는 탄력적이다. 그것은 지도상에서 사람, 건물, 물체 또는 표시와 같은 내용이 전혀 없음을 의미한다. 추상적으로, 비어 있음은 무(無), 완전한 공동(空洞)과 같다. 그러나 고비 사막이나 사하라 사막, 태평양의 심연 등 비어 있다고 생각될 만한 지구상의 장소들을 생각해보면, 진짜 아무것도 없이 비어 있는 곳은 없다는 점이 금세 명백해진다. 이들 두 지역을 대충 조사만 하더라도, 광물 매장, 복잡한 생태계, 일시적인 형태의 생명체들, 이주하는 동물들 및 순환과 이동의 장기적 패턴과 같은 일련의 내용물들이 드러날 것이다. 심지어 저 궁극의 진공인 우주에도 행성, 항성, 소행성, 파편 및 우주 쓰레기들이 가득 차 있다. 그러나 이러한 내용물들이 비어 있음이라는 명백한 인식과 반드시 모순되는 것은 아니다. 이런 의미에서 비어 있음은 본질적으로 관계적이며, 실제로 존재하는 것만큼이나, 공간을 채우고 있지 않은 것, 혹은 공간을 채울 것으로 예상되는 것들로서 정의될 수 있다.

따라서 비어 있음은 특정 위치에 대한 정량적 평가의 결과라기보다 다른 장소들과의 비교를 통해 인식되는 어떤 것이다. 비어 있는 장소란, 더 적은 사람, 더 적은 생명의 흔적, 더 적은 인간 활동의 흔적을 포함함으로써 다른 곳에 비해 더 비어 있는 것처럼 비치는 것이다. 하나의 상태로서, 비어 있음은 필연적으로 현재 있지 않은 것을 연상시킨다. 그것은 어떤 면에서 부재의 상태다. 따라서 비어 있음은 지각의 문제이므로, 누가 관찰하고 있는지, 그리고 그 주체가 찾고자 하는 것이 무엇인지에 크게 좌우되는 매우 주관적인 현상이다. 한 사람 또는 집단에게 대상이나 의미가 없는 것이 다른 사람이나 집단에게는 '가득 찬' 것이 될 수 있다. <한 걸음 더 나아가, 비어 있음은 장소가 상상되는 방식에 깊이 뿌리를 두고 있으며, 개인과 집단들 간의 힘을 표현하는 강력한 도구다.> 이러한 사실을 염두에 둔다면, 비어 있음을 액면 그대로 받아들일 수는 없다. 그것은 결코 객관적인 상태가 아니다. 근대 초 유럽의 지도들 상에 표현된 글자 그대로 공백으로서의 부재는 역사적 조사와 비판적 분석의 대상이 되어야 한다.

비어 있음에 대한 이러한 검토는 공간사 연구를 향한 오랜 추세 속에서 행해질 수 있다. 역사적으로, 21세기 들어 '공간적 전환'을 이야기하는 경향이 있지만, 공간사는 훨씬 더 깊은 과거에 뿌리를 두고 있다. 그 노력은 계속 쌓이면서, 장소와 풍경의 안정성과 영원성에 중점을 둔 더 오래된 데카르트적 공간 개념을 근본적으로 바꾸었고, 19세기에는 현대적 사고를 통해 공간을 시간에 종속시켰다. 우리 주변 세계를 이해하는 데 있어 중요한 개념으로서 공간에 대한 점진적인 재평가는 19세기 후반과 20세기 초반에 시작되었다. 그 당시 전 세계 학자들은 성장하는 인문지리 분야에 기여하면서 지리와 환경이 문화에 미치는 영향을 연구했다. 그들은 생물군계와 생태계와 같은 자연 과학의 개념을 문화 현상과 연결시켰지만 여전히 공간을 경계가 있고 안정적인 것으로 생각했다. 1970년대 후반과 1980년대 이후에야 담론 분석과 포스트모더니즘 연구의 영향을 받은 역사가들과 지리학자들은 끊임없이 변화하는 사회적 구성물로 공간을 생각하기 시작했다.

1 ② ▶ 문장삽입

제시문은 "비어 있음은 어떻게 인식하느냐에 따라, 그리고 개인과 집단들이 어떻게 관계 맺느냐에 달려 있다."는 내용이므로 앞에는 '비어 있음은 주관적 현상'임을 언급하고 있고, 뒤에는 '객관적인 상태가 아니다'라고 말하는 Ｂ에 들어가는 것이 가장 적절하다.

2 ③ ▶ 내용추론

"19세기에는 현대적 사고를 통해 공간을 시간에 종속시켰다."고 하였으므로 ③은 잘못된 추론이다. 한편, 데카르트는 영원성 즉, timelessness를 강조하는 공간 개념을 상정하였는데 그것은 '시간의 경계를 초월한 공간'이라고 볼 수 있으므로 ②는 타당한 추론이다.

---

slippery a. 미끄러운; 파악하기 힘든

elastic a. 탄력적인

void n. 진공, 공동(空洞)

cursory a. 대충하는, 피상적인

deposit n. 매장물

transitory a. 일시적인

vacuum n. 진공

asteroid n. 소행성

palpable a. 명백한, 감지할 수 있는

quantitative a. 정량적인

invoke v. 불러내다, 연상시키다

articulation n. 표현

timelessness n. 영원함

biome n. (숲·사막 같은 특정 환경 내의) 생물군계

hard science 자연 과학

discourse n. 담론

06 사회·정치

01

미국계 인디언과 미국 원주민이란 용어는, 흑인과 아프리카계 미국인이라는 용어가 종종 서로 호환되어 사용되는 것과 같은 방식으로 사용될 수 있는 본질적인 의미에서 동의어인 것인가? 아니면, 미국 원주민이라는 용어 대신 미국계 인디언이란 용어를 사용하는 것이, 흑인 대신 검둥이라는 용어를 사용할 때와 동등하게 모욕적이고 시대착오적인 것인가? (그리고) 다른 모든 용어들을 배제한 채 미국 원주민이란 용어만을 고집하는 것은 탁상공론적이라는 징후인가? 이와 같은 문제는 문화전쟁이 진행되던 시절에는 매우 민감한 것들이었지만, 다행히도 이들 문제들은 지금은 진정되고 있다. 지난 수년 동안 이들 용어들이 나타냈던 사람들이 그들의 선호를 명확히 했기 때문이다. 대다수의 미국계 인디언들/미국 원주민들은 두 용어 중 하나를 사용하거나 두 용어를 모두 사용하는 것을 받아들이고 있다. (그러나) 많은 인디언들은 또한 그와 같은 일반적인 용어를 사용하는 것보다 구체적인 부족명칭을 사용하는 것을 더 선호한다. 『The Navajo Times』의 편집장은 "나는 미국 원주민 혹은 미국계 인디언 대신에 나바호 부족의 구성원으로 알려지고 싶습니다. 나는 나 자신을 (인디언) 민족 전체와 묶는 것보다 하나의 구체적인 부족의 이름으로 불리게 하는 것을 통해 내가 물려받은 유산에 대한 보다 진정한 설명을 얻을 수 있습니다."라고 말한다.

1 ③ ▶ **빈칸완성**
많은 미국의 인디언들은 자신들이 하나의 민족이라는 개념으로의 인디언에 속하기보다는 개별 부족의 정체성을 지니고 싶어 한다는 단서로부터 정답을 추론할 수 있다. ① 절단하다 ② 왜곡하다 ④ 정정하다

2 ① ▶ **내용일치**
『The Navajo Times』의 편집장의 진술을 통해서 미국의 많은 인디언들이 부족의 정체성을 더 중시하고 있다는 사실을 알 수 있다.

equivalent a. 동등한; 상당하는, 대응하는
offensive a. 싫은, 불쾌한; 모욕적인
anachronistic a. 시대착오의, 시대에 뒤진
doctrinaire a. 순이론적인; 공론의
sort oneself out 진정되다
authentic a. 믿을 만한; 진정한, 진짜의
lump v. 한 덩어리로 하다, 하나로 묶다

02

한편으로, 전쟁이 진보, 외교, 세계화, 그리고 경제 및 과학적 발전에 의해서 사실상 끝이 났다고 생각하는 많은 사상들이 존재했다. <정신이 온전한 사람이라면 전쟁의 위험을 감수하고 세계화된 세계의 경제적 상호의존성을 파괴하려고 하지 않을 것이다.> 그와 동시에 각 나라의 문화는 군비경쟁, 호전적인 경쟁관계, 그리고 자원을 확보하기 위한 투쟁 등, 전쟁을 향해 가는 강력한 흐름으로 가득 차 있었다. 수백만에 달하는 남자들이 징집을 통해 군대를 경험했는데, 이는 군대의 교화를 받은 경험이 있는 사람들이 인구의 상당 부분을 차지하게 만들었다. 이전보다 교육에 더 많이 접근할 수 있었지만, 그 교육이 심한 편견으로 가득 차 있어서 민족주의, 엘리트주의, 인종주의, 그리고 그 외의 호전적인 사상들이 널리 퍼졌다. 정치적 목적을 위한 폭력은 만연했고 러시아의 사회주의자들에서부터 영국의 여성참정권주의자들에 이르기까지 폭넓게 퍼져 있었다. 조국을 위한 폭력은 점차 정당화되었고, 예술가들은 반항하면서 새로운 표현 방식을 찾았고, 새로운 도시문화는 기존의 사회질서에 도전했다. 본질적으로 1914년을 살았던 유럽인들은 파괴를 통해 세계를 재창조할 수 있는 하나의 방법으로서의 전쟁을 받아들일 준비가 되어 있었던 것이다.

1 ② ▶ **동의어**
shot through는 '가득 차 있다'는 의미. 문장 뒤쪽의 "군비경쟁, 호전적인 경쟁관계, 그리고 자원을 확보하기 위한 투쟁"의 내용으로 전쟁을 향한 흐름이 강함을 추론할 수 있다. ① 정체된; 불경기의 ③ 휘발성의; 변덕스러운 ④ 불충분한

armament n. 무기; 군사력
belligerent a. 호전적인, 공격적인
conscription n. 징병 제도, 징병
indoctrination n. 주입, 가르침; 교화
rebel v. 반란을 일으키다, 권력에 반대하다
prime v. 준비시키다, 대비시키다
sane a. 제정신의; 신중한
interdependence n. 상호 의존

2 ①　　▶ **동의어**
　　이 문장에서의 order의 의미는 사회 '질서'의 의미로 사용되고 있다. 질서에 가장 의미적
　　으로 비슷한 보기를 고르면 정답을 추론할 수 있다. ② 종류; 등급 ③ 명령 ④ 요구

3 ①　　▶ **문장삽입**
　　제시문의 앞부분에 전쟁이 실질적으로 일어나지 않을 것이고 세계화된 세계의 상호의
　　존성이 파괴되지 않을 것이라는 낙관적 전망을 가지는 생각을 진술하는 내용이 와야 한
　　다. 따라서 Ⓐ에 제시문이 들어가야 한다.

03

지구상에는 끔찍한 상황에서 살고 있는 많은 사람들이 있다. 국가 간의 전쟁, 내전, 기아, 질병, 인종청소, 문맹, 그리고 가난의 틈에서 지구상의 많은 사람들이 여러 가지 고난에 직면해 있다. 비록 제3세계 사람들이 직면하고 있는 시련이 유감스럽긴 하지만, 미국과 다른 국가들이 그들로부터 그러한 재난을 없애줄 권리는 갖고 있지 않다. 위험을 무릅쓰고 다른 나라의 사건에 개입할 능력이 있는 정치가들은, 어떤 노력을 시작하기 전에 내가 지원하는 행위가 우리나라 국민들의 정당한 이익에 도움이 되는가를 자문해봐야 한다. 많은 경우에 있어, 그러한 행위는 단연코 그렇지 못하다. 왜냐하면 어떤 정치가도 외국인을 자기의 선거구민으로 삼아 대변하지 않기 때문이다. 정치가들은 오직 국가적인 이해관계에만 신경을 써야 한다.
인종 학살은 한 민족이 착수할 수 있는 가장 비열한 잔혹행위 가운데 하나다. 비록 그것이 인류에게는 저주이지만, 미국과 다른 나라들은 그것을 종결시키기 위해 노력해야 할 그 어떤 도덕적 의무도 지지 않는다. 어떤 국가가 문제를 촉발시키지 않았다면, 비록 그럴 능력이 있다 할지라도 그 국가는 그러한 문제를 끝내야 할 도덕적 의무가 없다. 클린턴 행정부에서 국가안보보좌관을 지낸 토니 레이크(Tony Lake)는 "그러한 힘을 갖고 있다고 해서 그것을 사용할 책임을 자동적으로 지게 되는 것은 아니다."라고 말한 바 있다. 미국은 자국의 이익을 증진시키기 위해 무엇을 해야 하는지를 신중하게 판단해야 하며, 다른 모든 주도적인 역할에서 벗어나야 한다.

1 ①　　▶ **내용파악**
　　자국의 이익에 도움이 되지 않는다면, 지구상, 특히 제3세계에서 벌어지는 여러 참상들
　　에 미국을 비롯한 어느 나라도 개입해서는 안 된다는 것이 필자의 일관된 주장이다.

2 ③　　▶ **빈칸완성**
　　빈칸 Ⓐ에는 '인종 학살'을 부연하는 말이 필요하며, 빈칸 Ⓑ를 통해서는 필자가 일관되
　　게 주장하는 주제인 '자국 이익의 도모'의 의미가 완성되어야 한다. 따라서 ③이 정답이
　　다. ① 솜씨 좋음 — 나아가게 하다, 촉진하다 ② 야만, 잔인 — 방해하다 ④ 용기; 용감한
　　행위 — 나아가게 하다, 전진시키다

detestable a. 혐오스러운
starvation n. 기아, 굶주림
ethnic cleansing 인종 청소[말살]
illiteracy n. 문맹
hardship n. 역경, 고난
tribulation n. 고난, 시련
bane n. 독; 재난
undertake v. 떠맡다, 감당하다
endeavor n. 노력, 수고
just a. 정당한, 당연한
constituent n. 선거구민; 구성물
concern oneself with ~에 관심을 가지다
genocide n. 인종 말살
despicable a. 비루한, 비열한, 천한
atrocity n. 포악, 잔학행위
embark upon ~에 착수하다
humanity n. 인류, 인간
further v. 증진하다, 촉진하다
deviate away ~으로부터 벗어나다
initiative n. 선제, 주도, 주도권

04

사회학자 해럴드 가핑클(Harold Garfinkel)이 창시한 민속방법론은 우리가 일상적인 상황을 어떻게 이해하는가를 살펴보는 이론이다. 비록 우리는 하나의 상황을 주변 사람들과 다르게 볼지도 모르지만, 우리의 배경은 일상생활에 대한 몇 가지 기본 가정을 우리에게 제공해준다. 민속방법론은 그 배경적 가정들이 무엇인지, 우리는 어떻게 그런 가정들에 도달하는지, 그리고 그런 가정들이 우리의 현실 인식에 어떤 영향을 주는지를 연구한다. 이런 가정들을 이해하기 위해 민속방법론 학자들은 우리가 일상생활에 대해 갖고 있는 당연시 되는 가정들을 위반하거나 거기에 이의를 제기하라는 가르침을 받는다. 미국에서 한 가지 배경적 가정은 경찰관 같은 응급 구조원들은 근무 중에 식별 가능한 정복을 입는다는 것이다. 사고 현장에서 일상복을 입고 있는 경찰관은 자신이 경찰관이라고 주장하지만 정복을 입지 않은 사람의 말은 군중들이 따르려 하지 않는다는 것을 알게 될 것이다. 그 경찰관은 구경꾼들을 가까이 오지 못하게 하거나 차량들을 사고 현장에서 멀리 돌아가게 하는 데 애를 먹을지도 모른다. 배경적 가정이 충족되지 않으면 그 경찰관이 정복을 입었을 경우만

ethnomethodology n. 민속방법론
emergency personnel 응급 구조원들
identifiable a. 식별 가능한
keep ~ at bay ~를 접근시키지 않다
redirect v. 방향을 바꾸다
respectfully ad. 경의를 표하여, 공손하게
required a. 필수적인

큰 대중들이 공손하게 반응하지 않을 것이며 그 경찰관은 필수적인 직무를 수행하는 데 어려움을 겪을 것이다.

1 ② ▶ **빈칸완성**

or 뒤의 '차량들을 사고 현장에서 멀리 돌아가게 하는 것'과 마찬가지로 군중들의 행동을 통제하는 내용이 빈칸에 적절하므로 ⓐ에는 ②가 적절하다.

2 ① ▶ **내용파악**

첫 문장의 how we make sense of everyday situations에서 일상적인 상황을 이해한다는 것은 주변 세계를 이해한다는 말이므로 ①이 적절하다. ②는 인류학, ③은 사회학, ④는 민속학(folklore)에 대한 정의다.

3 ③ ▶ **내용파악**

배경적 가정은 우리가 당연시하는 것이고 그래서 이것에 부합되게 생각하고 행동할 때 우리의 생활이 안정되는 것이므로 이에 이의를 제기하면 일상생활은 더 나빠질 것이다. 따라서 ③이 사실이 아니다.

05

아메리칸 드림은 항상 세계적인 것이었다. 1931년, 역사학자인 제임스 트러슬로우 애덤스(James Truslow Adams)가 처음으로 이 개념을 소개했을 때, 그는 그 꿈이 "모든 국가들로부터 온 수천만 명의 사람들을 우리의 해안(땅)으로 불러들인" 것이라고 믿었다. 그러나 최근에, 이 애초의 꿈과 세계의 나머지 나라들을 향해 대놓고 말하지 않는 새로운 꿈 사이에 골치 아픈 차이가 생겨났다. 애초의 아메리칸 드림은 세 가지 부분을 가지고 있다. 첫 번째 부분은 번영에 관한 것이다. 그것은 그들의 가족을 중산층에 올려놓기 위해서 열심히 일하는 무일푼인 노력하는 사람의 영웅적인 이야기다. 이 영웅적인 이야기에서 필수불가결한 부분은 세대 간의 연속성 ― 부모의 희생을 통해서 아이들이 성공하고, 성공한 아이들이 '그들이 어디에서 왔는지'를 절대로 잊지 않는 것 ― 이다. 말할 나위 없이, 성실한 노동과 세대 간의 유동성(소통)이라는 이야기를 담고 있는 이 꿈은 미국인이 아닌 사람들의 95%에 의해서 공유되고 있다. 그럼에도 이 꿈은 아메리칸 드림이라고 불리는데, 그 이유는 미국이 그 꿈이 많은 사람들에게 실제로 실현된 역사상 최초의 국가이기 때문이다.

미국은 또한 어떤 개인이나 집단을 아메리칸 드림으로부터 의도적으로 배제하는 것을 비난하는 국가였다. 이것은 아메리칸 드림의 두 번째 부분과 세 번째 부분이 무엇인지를 지적해준다. 그것은 바로 민주주의와 자유다. 아메리칸 드림이 제대로 작동하기 위해서는 개인들의 기본적인 권리가 존중되어져만 한다. 애덤스는 바로 이 점을 명백히 한다. "아메리칸 드림은 단지 자동차를 소유하고 높은 임금을 받는 꿈만이 아닙니다. 아메리칸 드림은 모두가 저마다 타고난 능력에 걸맞은 사회적 지위를 획득할 수 있는 사회적 질서에 대한 꿈이기도 합니다."

1 ③ ▶ **글의 목적**

이 글은 아메리칸 드림의 진정한 의미를 곱씹어 보는 내용이다.

2 ④ ▶ **빈칸완성**

빈칸 ⓐ는 "lured tens of millions of all nations to our shores."라는 단서로부터 정답을 추론할 수 있다. 빈칸 ⓑ는 콜론(:) 이하에서 이어지는 내용의 성격을 통해 정답을 추론할 수 있다. ① 시의, 자치 도시의 ― 자유 ② 국가의 ― 평등 ③ 지방의, 지역의 ― 박애, 자선

credit A with B A를 B의 공로자[행위자]라고 믿다
lure v. 유혹하다, 불러들이다
strand n. (실·전선·머리카락 등의) 가닥[줄]; (생각·계획·이야기 등의) 가닥[부분]
saga n. 전설, 무용담
striver n. 노력하는 사람; 싸우는 사람
philanthropy n. 박애주의

06

우리는 정치권력이 없는 사회, 즉 경찰, 군대, 법체계, 공무원조직, 기타 국가 구성 기관들이 모두 제거된 사회에서의 생활을 상상해보라고 독자에게 요구함으로써 정치권력을 옹호할 수 있다. 그러면 어떻게 될까? 이와 같은 가장 유명한 사고실험은 1651년에 발간된 토마스 홉스(Thomas Hobbes)의 『리바이어던(Leviathan)』에서 찾아볼 수 있을 것이다. 홉스는 잉글랜드 내전으로 인해 정치권력이 부분적으로 붕괴되는 것을 경험했었고 그래서 그가 그려 보인 정치권력이 없는 상태에서의 삶의 모습은 끊임없이 황폐한 모습이었다. 그는 정치적 통치가 없는 '인간의 자연 상태'를 생필품에 대한 경쟁이 치열한 상태로 기술했는데, 그런 치열한 경쟁으로 인해 인간은 남에게 빼앗기거나 얻어맞을까 항상 두려워하게 되고 그래서 남을 먼저 공격하고 싶은 마음이 항상 생기게 된다고 했다. 홉스는 사람은 본래 이기적이거나 욕심이 많고 그래서 정치권력에 의해 제한되지 않으면 가능한 한 많은 것을 자신을 위해 움켜쥐려 한다고 믿기 때문에 이런 비관적인 결론에 이르게 된다고 때때로 말해진다. 그러나 이것은 홉스가 말하려는 진짜 요점을 놓치고 있는데, 그의 요점은 신뢰가 없으면 사람들 사이의 협력은 불가능하다는 것과 법을 집행할 상위 권력이 없으면 신뢰는 없을 것이라는 것이다. 홉스가 '자연 상태'에서는 없는 것으로 설명하는 것들은 그 무엇보다 많은 사람들로 하여금 남들도 자기 역할을 다 할 것이라는 기대 속에 서로 협력하도록 요구하는 것들이며 정치권력이 없으면 그런 기대를 조금도 안심하고 가질 수 없게 된다.

1 ④   ▶ 내용일치
홉스의 요점이 '신뢰가 없으면 사람들 사이의 협력은 불가능하고 법을 집행할 상위 권력이 없으면 신뢰는 없을 것'이라는 것이므로 ④가 글의 내용과 가장 가깝다. ① 이상주의나 관념론에 대한 언급은 없다. ② 이기적 욕심을 억제하는 것이 아니라 신뢰를 구축하여 사회 협력을 가능하게 하는 것이다. ③ compromising(타협)이 아니다. ⑤ 폭력적 정치권력으로 인해 전쟁이 일어나는 것을 보여주는 것이 아니라 정치권력이 없는 상태로 인해 삶이 황폐해지는 것을 보여준다.

2 ①   ▶ 빈칸완성
'describe+목적어+as+보어'이므로 빈칸에는 as가 먼저 오고 one은 '하나'라는 뜻이 아니라(상태≠경쟁) condition을 대신한 대명사이므로 of 다음에 추상명사로 단수형의 competition이 와야 한다. 따라서 ①이 적절하다.

authority n. 권위, 권력, 권한
thought-experiment n. 사고실험(사물의 실체나 개념을 이해하기 위해 가상의 시나리오를 이용하는 것)
along these lines 이런 방침의, 이와 같은
unremittingly ad. 끊임없이
bleak a. 황폐한, 냉혹한
rule n. 통치
necessities of life 생필품
pessimistic a. 비관적인
grab v. 움켜쥐다
restrain v. 제지하다, 제한하다
enforce v. 실행하다, 집행하다

07

라스베가스(Las Vegas)에서 벌어진 끔찍한 총격사건 이후, 정치인들이 본능적으로 하는 일은 조기를 달고, 묵념을 하며, 죽은 이에게 슬픈 헌사를 바치는 것이다. 그러나 우리가 가장 필요로 한 것은 애도가 아니라, 미국에서 총기사고로 인한 사망자 수를 낮추는 것이다. 우리는 이러한 잔인한 살인을 그저 묵인해서는 안 된다. 호주가 1996년 총기난사사건을 겪었을 때, 호주는 총기에 대한 보다 강경한 법을 만드는 데 힘을 합쳤다. 그 결과 총기로 인한 살인사건은 거의 절반으로 줄었으며, 총기로 인한 자살 또한 절반이나 줄었다고 『보건정책저널(The Journal of Public Health Policy)』이 밝혔다. 미국의 총기 살인율은 현재 호주의 거의 20배에 달한다.

회의론자들은 (이런 총기사고에 대해) 마법의 지팡이처럼 즉각적인 해결책은 존재하지 않는다고 말할 것이며, (즉각적인 해결책이 없다는) 그들의 말이 맞다. 그러나 (그렇다고 해서) 정치인들이 이런 비율로 살인자들의 힘을 계속해서 키워주는 것은 불합리하다. 미국독립전쟁까지 거슬러 올라가는 미국 역사상 모든 전쟁에서 죽은 미국인들을 모두 합친 것보다 더 많은 미국인들이 1970년 이후 총기로 인해 죽었다.(이는 자살, 살인, 사고를 포함한다.) 하버드 대학교의 데이빗 헤멘웨이(David Hemenway)에 따르면, 매일 약 92명의 미국인들이 총기로 인해 목숨을 잃으며, 미국의 아이들이 다른 선진국의 아이들보다 총기로 인해 사망할 확률은 14배나 더 높다고 한다. 그러나 우리는 속수무책인 것은 아니며, 변화를 이끌어 내기 위해 적절한 수단을 찾아야 한다.

offer moments of silence 묵념하다
somber a. 슬픈 듯한
tribute n. (특히 죽은 사람에게 바치는) 헌사[찬사]
acquiesce v. 묵인하다, 굴복하다
slaughter n. 잔인한 살인, 대학살
mass shooting 총기난사사건
fire arm (라이플·권총 등의) 소형화기(火器)
homicide n. 살인
halve v. 반으로 줄이다, 이등분하다
suicide n. 자살
magic wand 마술 지팡이; 즉각적인 해결법
helpless a. 무력한; 속수무책인
take order to V ~하도록 적절한 수단을 취하다
make a difference 변화를 가져오다

1 ① ▶ **빈칸완성**
라스베가스의 끔찍한 총격사건 이후, 정치인들이 본능적으로 하는 일은 조기를 달고, 묵념을 하며, 죽은 이에게 슬픈 헌사를 바치는 것이라고 했는데, 그다음에 But이 나왔으므로, 우리가 가장 필요로 하는 것은 But 앞에 언급한 것이 아니라는 말이 되어야 하므로, 첫 문장을 한 단어로 표현한 mourning이나 lamentation이 빈칸 ④에 적절하다. 그리고 이 글은 단순히 총격사건의 애도를 표하기 위한 글이 아니라 앞으로는 이런 '사상자'가 발생하지 않도록 실질적인 대책을 강구하라는 목적의 글이므로, 빈칸 ⑧에는 toll이나 casualties가 적절하다. 따라서 ① '애도 — 사망자 수'가 정답이다. ② 배은망덕 — 승차요금 ③ 관대함 — 사상자 수 ④ 슬퍼함 — 규제

2 ③ ▶ **내용추론**
① 저자는 총기사고에 대해 즉각적인 해결책이 존재하지 않는다는 회의론자들의 말에 '동의한다'고 했다. ② 우리가 '가장' 필요로 하는 것이 애도가 아니라고 했지, 우리가 유족들에게 애도를 표할 필요가 없다는 말은 아니다. ④ 우리가 이런 총기사건에 대해 묵인해서는 안 된다고 했으며, 총기사건에 대한 즉각적인 해결책이 없다고 해서 정치인들이 '이런 비율로' 살인자의 힘을 계속해서 키워주는 것은 불합리하다고 했을 뿐, 정치인들이 끔찍한 총격사건을 너그러이 봐줬던 것은 아니다. ③ 우리가 가장 필요로 하는 것은 총기로 인한 사망자 수를 줄이는 것이라고 했으며, 마지막 문장에서 속수무책인 것은 아니며, 변화를 이끌어내기 위해 적절한 수단을 찾아야 한다고 했으므로 ③이 정답이다.

3 ④ ▶ **뒷내용 추론**
끔찍한 총격사건 이후 가장 필요로 하는 것은 미국의 총기로 인한 사망자 수를 낮추는 것이라고 했으며, 마지막 문장에서도 속수무책인 것은 아니며, 변화를 이끌어 내기 위해 적절한 수단을 찾아야 한다는 내용으로 글이 끝났으므로, 이어지는 내용으로는 ④의 '총기사건을 미연에 방지하기 위한 적극적인 대책 취하기'가 문맥상 가장 적절하다.

08

유한(有閑)계층은 고도로 조직화된 모든 현대 산업사회에 팽배해있는 절박한 경제적 어려움을 그다지 겪지 않는다. 생활 수단을 놓고 벌이는 경쟁의 긴박함은 다른 어떤 계층에서보다 이 계층에서는 덜 가혹하다. 그리고 이런 특권적 지위의 결과로, 우리는 이 계층이 모든 계층 중에서 사회제도를 더욱 발전시키고 변화된 산업 여건에 맞게 재조정해야 하는 상황적 요구에 가장 미약한 반응을 보일 것으로 예상할 것이다. 사회의 일반적인 급박한 경제 상황이 이 계층의 사람들에게는 거리낌 없이 직접적으로 영향을 주지 않는다. 지키지 않는 경우 재산을 몰수한다는 조건을 달고서, 변화된 산업 기술의 요구에 맞도록 생활 습관을 바꾸고 외부세계에 대한 이론적 생각을 바꾸라고 그들에게 요구하지 못한다. 이는 그들이 완전한 의미에서 산업사회의 유기적 일부가 아니기 때문이다. 따라서 이런 급박한 상황이 다른 계층 사람들에게는 그것만으로도 습관화된 견해와 생활방식을 포기하게 할 수 있을 정도의 기존 질서에 대한 불편함을, 이 계층 사람들에게는 쉽게 불러일으키지 못한다. 사회 발전에 있어 유한계층이 하는 역할은 발전을 지체시키고 케케묵은 것을 지키는 것이다. 이런 주장은 결코 새로운 것이 아니며, 오래전부터 사람들이 일반적으로 해온 흔한 말이다.

1 ③ ▶ **태도**
필자가 유한계층에 대해 '비판적인(critical)' 태도를 취하고 있음을 특히 마지막 두 문장에서 알 수 있다. ① 무관심한 ② 지지하는 ④ 반대 감정이 병존하는

2 ① ▶ **내용추론**
변화에 맞게 재조정해야 하는 상황적 요구에 가장 미약한 반응을 보인다는 것과 케케묵은 것을 지킨다는 것은 '보수적'이라는 뜻이다.

3 ④ ▶ **빈칸완성**
첫 번째 문장에서 경제적 어려움을 겪지 않는다고 했으므로 ④에는 less가 적절하고, 경제적 어려움이 없다보니 변화된 상황에 맞는 재조정 요구에도 무반응일 것이므로 ⑧에는 least가 적절하다.

leisure class 유한(有閑)계층(생산적 노동에 적극적인 의욕을 가지지 않고 비생산적 소비생활을 하는 귀족·자본가·이자생활자 등의 계층)
stress n. 압박, 긴장, 시련, 곤경
exigency n. 긴급성, 절박한 사정
exacting a. 엄한, 가혹한
institution n. 제도; 관례, 관습, 법령
readjustment n. 재조정
impinge v. 침범하다; 영향을 주다
forfeiture n. 몰수(물)
uneasiness n. 불안, 걱정
office n. 임무, 직책
retard v. 지체시키다, 늦어지게 하다
conserve v. 보존하다, 유지하다
obsolescent a. 쇠퇴한, 노후한, 진부한
proposition n. 명제, 진술, 주장
novel a. 새로운, 참신한
commonplace n. 평범한 것, 진부한 것

4 ② ▶ **내용파악**
유한계층은 변화에 저항하는(change-resistant) 태도를 보인다. ① 사회적으로 깨어있는 ③ 매우 가난한 ④ 자급자족의

09

전쟁에서 한 집단이 다른 집단에게 하려고 하는 것은 살인에서 개개인들에게 일어나는 일과 같다. 전쟁에 가담한 군인들은 "적군"에 대한 폭력 행위에 대해, 그 군인들이 행동하기를 거부했더라면 그 폭력이 일어나지 않았을 것이라는 의미에서, 책임이 있다. 제2차 세계대전 후의 뉘른베르크 재판은 군인들 개개인도 또한 도덕적으로나 법적으로 책임이 있다는 것을 확립하려 시도했지만, 이 시도는 폭력의 제도화가 폭력의 도덕적 차원을 어느 정도로 바꾸어놓는지를 간과하고 있었다. 한편으로, 군인 개개인은 자발적으로 그리고 자기 책임으로 행동하고 있지 않으며, 믿을만한 정보를 얻고 정부 주장에 시의 적절하게 대처하기가 엄청나게 어렵다보니 군인들과 민간인들은 말할 것도 없고 미국 상원의원들조차도 군사적 행동의 정당성에 대한 필요한 판단을 내리기에 적절한 위치에 있지 않다. 다른 한편으로, 집단은 영혼이 없으며 개개인들의 행위를 통해서만 행동할 수 있다. 그래서 그런 제도적 폭력에 대해 책임을 부여하기가 정말로 어렵다. 폭력의 다른 쪽인 폭력의 대상도 똑같이 모호한데, 이는 "적군"은 개개인으로서가 아니라 조직화된 정치세력으로서 공격을 받고 있지만 집단은 영혼이 없듯이 육체도 없어서 "적군"은 개별 사병들의 육체에 대한 공격에 의해서 공격을 받기 때문이다.

1 ① ▶ **부분이해**
첫 문장은 집단 사이의 전쟁은 폭력 행위라는 점에서 개인 사이의 살인과 같다는 뜻이다. 따라서 ①이 가장 가깝다. ② 개인의 살인이 집단 사이의 전쟁의 원인이 된다. ③ 전쟁도 살인도 모두 인간이 하는 행동이다. ④ 살인은 개인이 저지르고 전쟁은 집단이 저지른다.

2 ④ ▶ **내용추론**
① 군인도 평화 시에 사람을 죽이는 것은 살인이다. ② who didn't refuse여야 한다. ③ 국가에도 군인 개개인에게도 전쟁 책임을 묻기는 어렵다고 했다. ④ 뉘른베르크 재판은 군인들 개개인도 도덕적으로나 법적으로 책임이 있다는 것을 확립하려 시도했지만, 이 시도는 폭력이 제도화되면 폭력의 도덕적 차원이 달라짐을 간과한 것이라고 했으므로 이런 경우 전범들을 처벌하는 것은 문제의 소지가 있게 될 것이다.

3 ③ ▶ **글의 목적**
이 글은 서두에서 전쟁과 살인이 폭력 행위라는 면에서 같다고 한 다음, 셋째 문장 but 이하부터 전쟁이 살인과 달리 그 책임을 묻기가 어렵다는 점을 설명한 글이므로 ③이 글의 목적으로 적절하다.

trial n. 재판
on one's own initiative 자발적으로
on one's own responsibility 자기 책임으로
military engagement 군사적 참여, 군사행동
agency n. 기능, 작용; 행위; 대리 행위
ambiguous a. 모호한

10

미국의 사회학은 일반적으로 마르크스 사회학과 정확하게 정반대의 특징들을 보여준다. 나의 경험상, 미국의 사회학자들은 절대로 역사의 법칙에 관해 말하지 않는데, 우선 첫째로 그들이 그 법칙들을 잘 모르기 때문이고, 다음으로는 그들이 그 법칙들의 존재를 믿지 않기 때문이다. 그들은 지적인 사람들이기 때문에, 이러한 법칙들은 어떤 확실성을 가지고도 확립된 적이 없었다고 말하기를 선호할 것이다; 그러나 그들이 자신들의 진정한 생각을 표현한다면, 그들은 아마 소비에트가 역사의 법칙이라고 간주하는 것이 전혀 과학적 타당성이 없으며 오랜 세월에 걸쳐 반복되는 패턴으로부터 혹은 현재로부터 미래에 대한 정확한 예측을 가능케 할 정도로 충분히 명백한 발전의 경향으로부터 그러한 법칙을 유도하는 것에는 전혀 정당성이 없다고 말할 것이다.
미국의 사회학은 근본적으로 분석적이고 경험적이다; 그것은 우리가 익숙한 사회의 개인의 삶의 방식을 탐구할 것을 제안한다. 그것의 활기찬 연구는 교실의 학생들, 대학 내외의 교수들, 공장의

opposite a. 정반대의
characteristic n. 특징, 특질
be acquainted with ~을 알고 있다[알게 되다]
validity n. 정당성, 타당성
justification n. 정당성
derive v. 이끌어내다, 유도하다
recurrent a. 반복되는
familiar a. 익숙한, 친숙한

노동자들, 선거일의 유권자들 등의 생각과 반응들을 확정하는 데 목표를 둔다. 미국 사회학은 개인의 행동의 관점에서 그리고 다양한 사회 집단의 구성원들의 행동을 결정하는 목표, 정신 상태, 동기들의 관점에서 사회 기관과 구조들을 설명하기를 선호한다.

1 ②   ▶ 내용추론
첫 문장에서 미국의 사회학은 마르크스 사회학과 정확하게 정반대의 특징을 보여준다고 했으므로 미국의 사회학이 반대하는 것이 마르크스 사회학이 하는 것이다. 따라서 첫 단락의 마지막에 나오는 ②의 '오랫동안 반복되는 패턴으로부터 도출된 역사의 법칙을 제시하려고 하는 것'이 미국 사회학이 반대하는 것이며 정확하게 마르크스 사회학이 하는 행위라고 추론할 수 있다.

2 ④   ▶ 빈칸완성
빈칸 뒤에 이어지는 내용에서 미국 사회학은 뭔가를 직접적으로 자세히 관찰하고(examine) 설명하는(explain) 것을 목표한다는 말에서, 그것의 학문적 방법론이 '분석적이고 경험적임'을 알 수 있다. ① 종합적이고 역사적인 ② 결정론적일 뿐만 아니라 진보적인 ③ 종합적이고 세심한 ⑤ 개인적이고 논리적인

3 ④   ▶ 글의 서술방식
두 번째 단락의 서술방식은 미국 사회학의 방법론적 특징을 먼저 간결하게 진술하고, 그 이후에 그렇게 말할 수 있는 구체적 근거(이유)들을 전개해 간다.

11

아타튀르크주의(Atatürkism) 혹은 여섯 개의 화살로 알려진 케말주의(Kemalism)는 터키공화국의 건국이념이다. 무스타파 케말 아타튀르크(Mustafa Kemal Atatürk)에 의해 시행된 케말주의는 새로운 터키 국가를 그 전의 오토만 제국으로부터 분리시키고 민주주의 확립, 세속주의, 과학과 무상교육에 대한 국가 지원 등을 포함하여 서구적인 생활 방식을 받아들이도록 계획된 전면적인 정치, 사회, 문화 그리고 종교 개혁으로 정의된다. 그리고 이것들의 대부분은 아타튀르크 대통령이 재임하는 동안 터키에서 처음으로 도입되었다.
케말주의는 터키를 너무 빨리 세속적으로 너무 변모시키다 보니 몇 세대 지속되지 못했다. 이에 따라, 정치적인 이슬람주의의 부활은 터키가 케말주의로부터의 이탈을 자체적으로 준비하고 있다는 것을 보여주고 있다. 어느 누구도 이런 변동이 장래에 터키 사회와 정치에 영향을 어떻게 줄 것인지에 대해 확신하지 못한다. 내가 생각하기에 다음은 터키가 피해갈 수 없는 상황인데, 케말주의, 쿠르드 문제, 터키의 이웃 나라, 터키와 미국의 관계 등과 같이 현재 이 나라에서 일어날지도 모르는 것에 관해 우리가 이해할 필요가 있는 것들이다.
터키는 유럽과 이웃 이슬람 국가들과 달리 매우 독특하다. 아주 엄밀한 의미에서 보면 두 대륙에 걸쳐있으며 무슬림이 대다수를 차지하고 있는 이 나라는 공식적으로 세속적인 국가다. 터키는 무슬림 세계에서 식민지에서 독립한 또 하나의 국가가 아니라, 오히려 동부 유럽, 서아시아, 북아프리카의 지역들을 제1차 세계대전이 끝날 무렵까지 몇 세기 동안 지배해 왔던 강력한 오토만 제국의 중심지인 전(前) 식민 강국이다. 기독교인들에서 무슬림으로의 강제적인 개종과 악명 높은 아르메니아인들에 대한 대량 살상을 포함하여 유럽 국가들에 대한 터키 오토만 제국의 무자비한 정복이라는 유산은 지금도 여전히 유럽 국가들이 터키를 유럽연합에서 제외하는 이면의 요인이다.

1 ①   ▶ 내용파악
케말주의는 과거 오토만 제국의 이슬람 전통에서 탈피해 민주주의, 세속주의 등을 받아들인 서구적인 정치, 사회, 문화, 종교 개혁이라고 했으므로 케말주의의 주요 사상을 가장 잘 설명한 것은 ①이다.

2 ②   ▶ 내용일치
유럽 국가들이 터키가 유럽연합에 들어오는 것을 반대하는 이유가 마지막 문장에 설명되어 있지만, 유럽연합이 터키가 이슬람교를 유지하는 것에 대해서 눈감아주고 있다는 설명은 없으므로 ②는 이 글의 내용과 일치하지 않는다.

implement v. 이행하다, 수행하다
sweeping a. 전면적인, 광범위한
predecessor n. 전임자; 선조
embrace v. 맞이하다, 환영하다; 채택하다
secularism n. 세속주의
resurgence n. (활동의) 재기[부활]
nemesis n. 필연적인 결과, 응보
straddle v. ~에 걸터앉다
postcolonial a. 식민지 독립 후의
ruthless a. 무정한, 무자비한
subjugation n. 정복, 예속
conversion n. 개종; 전향
genocide n. (인종·국민 등의 계획적인) 대량 학살
exclusion n. 제외, 배제

12

전쟁 혹은 내분과 관련된 여러 상황에서 사람들은 예상되거나 현실화된 폭력을 피해서, 종종 자신들의 모든 재산을 버리고 자신들의 고향을 떠날 수밖에 없다. 이런 집단들은 강요된 이주자들이라고 불린다. 이들 이주자들이 결국 어디에 머무느냐에 따라 추가적인 분류가 가능한데, 이는 국제단체가 그들을 지원할 수 있는 방식에 상당히 영향을 미친다.

만약 강요된 이주자들이 자신들의 조국을 떠나 해외에서 피난처를 찾게 되면 그들은 난민이 된다. 이런 일이 벌어지면, 그들을 받아들인 나라가 그들 집단 전체에게 기본적인 생활필수품들을 제공하게 된다. 그보다 더 중요한 것은 국제대응기구들이 그들과 접촉하는 것을 승낙 받아 난민들에게 식량과 거처, 의료지원을 제공할 수 있게 된다는 것이다. 난민들은 또한 그들에게 상당한 정도의 보호를 제공하는 보편적인 법률의 적용을 받고 있다. 결국 그들로 하여금 조국을 떠나게 했던 그 분쟁이 종식되면, 그들이 예전의 삶으로 돌아갈 수 있도록 최선의 지원이 주어진다. 유엔 난민 고등 판무관 사무소(UNHCR)에서는 전 세계적으로 지금 1천만 명 이상의 난민들이 있는 것으로 추정하고 있다. 강요된 이주자들이 그들 나라의 국경을 넘지 못하거나 넘을 의사가 없다면, 그들은 내국유민(IDPs)이 된다. 내국유민들이 그들의 나라를 떠나지 못하는 데에는 인근 국가들이 전쟁 중에 있거나, 장거리를 이동할 능력이 없거나, 국경지역이 폐쇄되는 등 여러 가지 이유가 있다. 내국유민들은 신체적 보호가 매우 취약하여 종종 심각한 식량부족, 물 부족 및 여타 생필품 부족에 시달린다. 그들에게는 국제법에 의한 보호도 거의 주어지지 않고 있으며 제네바협약과 같은 널리 알려진 협약들도 종종 적용하기 어렵다. 내국유민 위기는 확인하는 것조차 어려운 일이며, 일단 확인되었다 하더라도 국제대응기구와 국제구호기구들이 접근하는 것 자체가 어려운데다 위험하기까지 하다. 이처럼 몰려난 국민들을 "국가의 적"으로 바라보는 자국정부가 그들의 운명에 대한 전적인 권한을 갖고 있다. 유엔 난민 고등 판무관 사무소는 지금 현재 전 세계적으로 적어도 50개국에서 2천5백만 명 이상의 내국유민들이 있다고 추정한다.

1 ③ ▶ 빈칸완성

내국유민들이 겪는 상황과 난민들의 상황을 비교하는 글이다. 해당 국가와 국제기구들의 보호 하에 있는 난민들에 비해, 내국유민들은 기본적인 보호를 거의 받지 못한다는 내용이다. 더구나, 내국유민들이 머무르고 있는 자신의 국가의 정부가 그들을 "국가의 적"으로 본다면, 그들의 운명은 그 정부에 의해 좌우될 것이라고 볼 수 있다.

2 ② ▶ 내용일치

난민들의 경우 그들을 떠나게 했던 분쟁이 종식되면 예전의 삶으로 돌아갈 수 있도록 최선의 지원이 주어진다고 하였으므로 ②가 본문의 내용과 일치하지 않는다.

---

internal strife 내분, 국내 분쟁
categorization n. 범주화, 분류
asylum n. 망명; 피난처
refugee n. 난민, 망명자
displaced a. 추방된, 유민의
impassable a. 통행할 수 없는, 폐쇄된
uprooted a. 뿌리 뽑힌, 쫓겨난

13

보수주의는 19세기와 20세기 초에 유럽 전역에서 강력한 세력이었다. 제2차 세계대전과 그 여파로 대대적인 변화가 일어나는 가운데 유럽의 보수주의도 변했다. 귀족계급은 일반적으로 파괴되거나 불신 당했고, 교회는 동요했으며, 대부분의 국가는 국민을 보다 더 평등하게 하기 위해 과세와 사회 서비스를 전면적으로 확장하는 "복지국가"를 도입했다. 전쟁으로 크게 파괴된 후, 보수주의가 지켜야 할 사회 질서(체제)가 있다는 것이 항상 분명하지는 않았다. <그러나 보수주의는 이러한 변화된 환경에 상당히 신속히 적응했다.> 보수주의자들이 (진보주의자들의 입장과 대조적으로) 권력이 집중되는 것을 기꺼이 보고자 하는 것과 아울러 힘 있는 자들이 가난하고 약한 자들을 도와야 하는 책임을 전통적으로 강조해온 것으로 인해 보수주의자들은 복지국가를 상당히 쉽게 받아들이게 되었다. 또한, 보수주의는 국가가 종교를 적극적으로 장려하는 것을 환영하는 반면, 진보주의는 그것을 수상쩍게 여긴다. 비록 최근의 세대들 사이에 종교적 관행이 이제는 급격히 줄어들었지만, 전후의 많은 유럽인들은 종교가 제공하는 가치관의 안정이 매우 필요하다고 느꼈다. 진보주의는 20세기 전체에 걸쳐 유럽에서 쇠퇴했지만, 보수주의는 계속 건강하게 생존해왔다. 보수주의의 지지자들은 복지국가를 인정했지만 복지국가가 전통적인 도덕적 가치와 일치되는 방식으로 세워져야 하며 복지국가가 사회의 평준화를 가져와서는 안 된다고 주장했다. 달리 말해, 보수주의자들은 사회의 일부가 다른 나머지를 이끌 수 있는 어떤 구조가 남아있어야 한다고 생각했다.

---

conservatism n. 보수주의
aftermath n. 여파
nobility n. 귀족계급
discredit v. 불신하다
ferment n. 소란, 동요
sweeping a. 광범위한, 전면적인
conservative n. 보수주의자
liberal n. 진보주의자
liberalism n. 진보주의
drop off 떨어지다, 사라지다, 줄어들다
consistent a. 일치하는
levelling n. 평준화

1 ② ▶ 빈칸완성

바로 앞 문장에서 "보수주의의 지지자들은 복지국가가 전통적인 도덕적 가치와 일치되는 방식으로 세워져야 하며 복지국가가 사회의 평준화를 가져와서는 안 된다고 주장했다."고 했는데, 이는 사회구조적으로, 전통적 가치를 지키려는 (보수주의적인) 지도층이 나머지 일반대중을 이끌어야 하고 그 지도층에게 어느 정도의 특권적 이익을 허용하여 평준화를 막을 수 있어야 한다는 의미다. 따라서 빈칸에는 ②(사회의 일부가 다른 나머지를 이끌 수 있는 어떤 구조가 남아있어야 한다)가 적절하다. ③ 철저한 능력주의 사회를 추구하지 않아도 괜찮다는 식의 생각은 평준화를 지지하는 생각이므로 부적절하다.

2 ③ ▶ 문장삽입

제시문은 "그러나 보수주의는 이러한 변화된 환경에 상당히 신속히 적응했다."이므로 앞에는 '이러한 변화'에 해당하는 설명이 있어야 하고 뒤에는 변화에 '적응하는 과정'의 내용이 있어야 한다. ⒞ 앞에서 제2차 세계대전 후 귀족계급의 몰락, 교회의 동요, 보수적 질서에 대한 회의 등이 변화의 내용으로 언급되었고 ⒞ 이하에서 보수주의가 변화에 신속히 적응하여 계속 번성할 수 있었다고 설명하므로 제시문은 ⒞에 들어가는 것이 적절하다.

3 ⑤ ▶ 글의 요지

이 글은 보수주의와 진보주의의 대립이나 유사점, 상이점을 비교한 글이 아니라 보수주의는 제2차 세계대전 후의 격변에도 불구하고 신속히 적응하여 계속 번성해왔음을 설명한 글이므로 ⑤가 글의 요지로 적절하다.

14

경제학자들은 미국 주(州)별로 230만 명의 미국인들이 제공한 생활만족 점수를 조사하고 이러한 생활만족도와 자살률을 비교했다. 예를 들어, 유타 주는 생활만족도에서 1위를 차지하지만 또한 미국에서 아홉 번째로 높은 자살률을 보이고 있다. 이와 대조적으로, 뉴욕은 생활만족도에서 45위를 차지하지만 미국에서 가장 낮은 자살률을 보이고 있다.

행복과 범죄율은 국가에서뿐만 아니라 주에서의 경제적 불평등의 순위와 관련 있는 경향이 있다. 빈부격차가 커질수록 행복은 줄어들고 범죄는 많아진다. 전반적인 기대수명 또한 불평등에 따라 달라지는데, 임금격차가 더 커지면 비록 가난한 사람들이 훨씬 피해가 심하지만 부자와 가난한 사람 모두 수명은 짧아지고 건강은 악화된다.

연구원들은 이러한 증감률이 사회적 계급제도에서 우리의 위치에 의해 야기되는 스트레스와 관련되어 있다고 생각한다. 예를 들어, 스탠퍼드 대학의 로버트 사폴스키(Robert Sapolsky)는 개코원숭이의 경우에도 낮은 계층의 동물들이 스트레스 호르몬의 수치가 높고 건강이 더 나쁘다는 사실을 발견했다. 그러나 지위에 대한 투쟁이 감소하여 보다 평등한 상황이 되었을 때에는 이러한 차이 또한 줄어든다. 영국 공무원들에 대한 연구 결과 심장병, 비만, 뇌졸중과 같이 스트레스와 연관돼 있는 건강상의 문제는 계급제도와 직접적으로 관련이 있는 것으로 또한 나타났는데, 사람이 계급제도의 가장 말단으로 떨어질 때 이러한 건강상의 문제는 증가했다.

그러면 왜 자살은 이와 같은 증감률을 따르지 않는 것일까? 현재의 연구는 완전한 해답을 주지 않지만 작가 스티븐 우(Stephen Wu)는 다른 사람들과의 비교, 즉 지위보다는 오히려 이 경우에는 상대적 행복의 비교가 중요한 역할을 할지도 모른다고 말했다. "(계급제도의) 바닥에 있는 사람들은 주변의 가까운 사람들이나 이웃과 비교했을 때 어떤 면에서는 상대적으로 그들의 상황이 더 나쁘게 여겨질 수도 있다. 아주 불행한 사람에게 상대적 비교는 불행과 우울증을 더 악화시킬 수도 있다." 유감스럽게도, 이것은 경제적 불평등을 줄임으로써 행복을 증가시키는 것은 역설적으로 '부작용'으로서 더 많은 자살을 초래할 수도 있다는 것을 의미할지도 모른다. 그러나 미국에서 경제적 불평등은 심하고 또한 더 심해지고 있기 때문에 이러한 문제는 우리에게 일어날 것 같지 않다.

1 ③ ▶ 글의 제목

불평등을 줄임으로써 행복은 증가하지만 역설적으로 이러한 행복의 증진이 더 많은 자살을 초래할 수 있음에 대해 이야기하고 있으므로, 글의 제목으로 ③이 적절하다.

gradient n. 기울기; 변화도, 증감률
hierarchy n. 계층제, 계급제도
baboon n. 비비, 개코원숭이
egalitarian a. 평등주의의
obesity n. 비만, 비대
totem pole 계층 조직[제도]
comparison n. 비교; 대조
relative a. 비교상의, 상대적인
depression n. 우울증; 불경기, 불황
paradoxically ad. 역설적으로
side effect 부작용

2 ④　　▶ **내용추론**

사람들의 생활만족도가 높게 나타나는 주(州)가 역설적으로 높은 자살률을 보인다는 언급이 있지만, 선진국이 개발도상국보다 높은 자살률을 보이는지는 이 글에서 추론할 수 없다.

3 ①　　▶ **빈칸완성**

앞에서 개코원숭이의 예를 들면서 낮은 계층의 동물들이 스트레스를 많이 받고 건강이 나쁘다고 했으므로, 계층 간의 차이가 없어지면, 즉 모든 계층이 평등하게 되면 이러한 스트레스나 건강 악화의 정도 차이는 줄어들 것이다. 따라서 '평등주의의'라는 의미의 egalitarian이 들어 있는 ①이 정답이다. ② 인종차별 ③ 전술싸움 ④ 지배계급

15

정치에서 공손함은 도대체 어떻게 된 것인가? 현재 이러한 애통함이 점점 커지고 있다. 끔찍하고 잔인하며 짧막한 홉스주의적인 캠페인 광고가 방송을 오염시키고 있다. 전문적인 논객들은 터무니없는 주장과 비방으로 우리 문화를 오염시키고 있다. 이러한 모든 것에도 불구하고 보다 공손한 정치를 필요로 한다는 개념은 절반만이 맞는 말이고 나머지 잘못된 절반은 위험스러울 정도로 잘못된 말이다. 공손함은 현재 뜨거운 이슈다. 보다 공손한 담론을 촉진하기 위해 미국 전역에서 단체들이 생겨나고 있다. 틀림없이, 공손함과 예의바름은 난폭함과 비난이 가득한 것들보다 바람직하며, 목소리를 높이는 경기보다 대화가 더 좋다. 격렬한 반대를 공손한 어조로 하는 것은 분명히 가능하다. 이것이 우리가 어린이들에게 가르치는 것이며 정치 지도자들은 적어도 이러한 기준에 부합되어야 하는 것처럼 보인다. 문제는 공손함에 집중하는 것은 아주 사소한 이성적인 정치의 한 부분에 불균형적인 집중을 하도록 만든다는 점이다. 민주주의는 대화와 침착함에 대한 것일 뿐 아니라 사실상 그 무엇보다 모진 고통과 쓰라림에 관한 것이기도 하다. 보스턴 차(茶) 사건(Tea Party) 당시의 풀뿌리 민주주의자들과 단명하고 말았던 월스트리트 점령 운동(Occupy movement)의 경우가 바로 그러하였다. 프러시아의 군사이론가 카를 폰 클라우제비츠(Carl von Clausewitz)가 유명하게 표현한 것처럼 만약 전쟁이 '다른 수단에 의한 정치'라면, 대중적인 분노를 담은 절반만 명확한 이러한 두 가지 표현들은 정치는 다른 수단에 의한 전쟁이라는 점을 우리에게 상기시킨다. 인간은 천성적으로 특권, 지위, 권력을 두고 투쟁한다. 우리는 정체성에 도전하고 이익을 위협하여 열정을 자극하는 그런 전투에 가담한다. 이러한 전투적인 본능을 입법 조치라는 비폭력적인 표현으로 개조하길 원하는 것은 정당하다. 하지만 이러한 본능 자체를 법으로 제정하여 소멸시킬 수 있다고 생각하는 것은 잘못된 것이다. 헌법 입안자들이 우리에게 제공한 헌법은 우리가 온순하고 온건하라고 요구한 것이 아니라 우리의 극단적인 본능을 예상하여 발현될 길을 열어놓았다.

1 ①　　▶ **글의 제목**

정치에 있어서 공손함의 제한적인 역할을 설명하면서 정치는 전투적인 성향을 띨 수밖에 없다고 설명하고 있으므로, 이 글의 제목으로는 ① '강력한 특징으로서의 전투적인 정치'가 적절하다.

2 ③　　▶ **내용파악**

공손하게 반론을 제기하는 것은 선호되고 가능하지만 불균형적인 강조라고 피력하고 있으므로, 글쓴이는 정치에 있어 공손함을 '과대평가된 미덕'으로 여기고 있음을 알 수 있다.

3 ④　　▶ **내용파악**

마지막 부분에서 알 수 있듯이 정치에 있어서 우리의 전투적인 본능이 소멸될 수는 없으며 헌법 입안자들 또한 이러한 점을 기대하여 촉진하도록 하였다고 설명하고 있다. 따라서 글쓴이는 "적대적인 태도는 정치에 참여하는 인간에게 자리 잡고 있다."라고 주장함을 알 수 있다.

civility n. 정중함, 공손함

lament n. 애통, 한탄

nasty a. 끔찍한, 형편없는

brutish a. 잔인한, 흉포한

toxic a. 유독한, 독성이 있는

polemicist n. 논쟁자, 논객

infect v. 감염시키다; 영향을 미치다

outrageous a. 너무나 충격적인, 터무니없는

slander n. 모략, 중상, 비방

spring up 휙 나타나다, 갑자기 생겨나다

discourse n. 담론, 담화

preferable a. 더 좋은, 선호되는

coarseness n. 조악함, 거침

snarky a. 무뚝뚝한, 퉁명스러운; 변덕스러운

disproportionate a. 불균형의

rational a. 합리적인, 이성적인

deliberation n. 숙고, 신중함

blood and guts 지독한 적개심

populist n. 대중주의자

convert v. 전환시키다, 개조하다

combative a. 전투적인

instinct n. 본능, 타고난 소질

moderate a. 중도의, 온건한, 적당한

immoderation n. 무절제, 과도, 극단

16

테러리즘은 정당한가? 찬성하는 편에서는 최소한 일부의 경우, 민간인을 향한 폭력 행위를 옹호할 수 있을 것으로 기대한다. 그러나 반대하는 편에서는 유치원을 폭파하는 것이 옹호될 것이라고 확실히 기대할 수 없다.

찬성측은 때때로 억압적인 정권 아래의 소수집단에게는 다른 표현 수단이 없다고 믿는다. 남아프리카 공화국의 ANC가 아파르트헤이트 아래서 그러했듯이 소수집단이 미디어, 정치 체계 혹은 외부세계로 접근할 수 없기 때문이다. 최후의 수단으로, 폭력에 의지하는 것을 옹호할 수도 있을 것이다.

또한, 결과가 수단을 정당화한다(결과가 좋으면 다 좋다); 테러리스트 활동의 최종적인 결과가 이로운 것이고 그 결과가 과정에서 일어난 피해보다 더 클 수 있다. 동파키스탄의 테러리즘이 방글라데시의 건국을 도왔을 때, 혹은 유대인들이 팔레스타인에서 영국인을 몰아내고 이스라엘의 건국을 이끌었던 것처럼, 역사가 심판이 될 것이다.

그러나 반대측은 다른 표현의 수단이 없다는 것이 무고한 시민에게 해를 가하는 것에 대한 명분이 될 수 없다고 말한다. 간디(Gandhi)나 다른 사람들은 평화적 시위가 성공할 가능성이 있음을 보여주었다. 고결한 이유도 폭력을 통해 싸워나간다면 그 가치가 떨어진다.

이들은 또한 테러리즘이 사실상 효과를 내는 경우는 매우 드물다고 주장한다. 일부 경우에 만족스러운 결과는 테러리스트들이 폭력을 버릴 때만 얻어지기도 한다. 그러나 대부분의 경우 분쟁은 지속되고 이루어질건 아무것도 없다. IRA는 폭력적인 활동을 70년 동안 벌이면서 영국 정부로부터 아무런 양보도 얻어내지 못했고, PLO는 협상이 시작되기 전에 테러리즘을 포기하기를 강요받았다.

1 ④　　▶ **부분이해**

a last resort는 '최후의 수단'을 의미한다. 따라서 ④의 '어려움을 해결하기 위해 마지막 방법을 취하기 위해'가 적절하다.

2 ②　　▶ **빈칸완성**

문맥상 과정에 문제가 있더라도 결과가 좋으면 이해받을 수 있다는 내용이 빈칸에 들어와야 할 것이다. ②에서 end는 결과를 means는 수단을 의미한다. 즉 결과가 수단을 정당화한다는 의미로, 결과가 중요하다는 내용이 빈칸에 가장 적절하다. ① 의지가 힘이다 ③ 시대가 다르면 예절도 다르다 ④ 불난 집에 부채질하다

3 ③　　▶ **내용일치**

마지막 단락에서는 테러리즘이 효과를 내지 못한 예를 언급하고 있다. IRA는 폭력적인 활동을 벌이면서 영국 정부로부터 아무런 양보도 얻어내지 못했다고 했을 뿐 IRA가 무장 투쟁을 끝내기로 결정했는지도 알 수 없고, 이에 대한 아일랜드 사람들의 반응도 알 수 없다. 따라서 ③이 정답이다. ① 폭력에 호소하는 것은 동파키스탄이 방글라데시를 건국하는 데 아마 도움이 됐을 것이다. ② 영국은 팔레스타인에 대한 위임 통치를 끝냈고 유대인들은 이스라엘을 건국했다. ③ 공식적으로 무장 투쟁을 끝내기로 한 IRA의 결정을 아일랜드 사람들이 반겼다. ④ 남아프리카의 인종차별 정권은 ANC의 구성원을 반체제인사로 간주했음이 틀림없다.

4 ①　　▶ **빈칸완성**

앞에서 폭력을 멈출 때 무엇인가를 얻게 된다고 하였으므로, 반대로 분쟁이 지속되면 "이루어질건 아무것도 없다"가 뒤에 오는 것이 문맥상 적절하다. ② 국제적 압력이 쌓인다 ③ 휴전회담이 빠르게 진행된다 ④ 그들은 협상에서 더 많은 힘을 얻는다.

---

justifiable a. 정당한, 타당한

proposition n. 제의; 문제, 과제; 찬성(하는 집단)

blow up ~을 폭파하다, 날려 버리다

defend v. 방어하다, 수비하다; 옹호하다, 변호하다

minority n. 소수, 소수집단

oppressive a. 억압하는, 억압적인

regime n. 정권; 제도, 체제

ANC 아프리카 민족회의(= African National Congress)

apartheid n. 아파르트헤이트(예전 남아프리카 공화국의 인종 차별정책)

defensible a. 옹호할 수 있는; 방어가 가능한

justification n. 타당한 이유, 정당한 이유; 해명

protest n. 항의; 시위

noble a. 고결한, 고귀한; 웅장한

devalue v. 평가 절하하다; 가치를 낮춰보다

renounce v. 포기하다; 버리다, 그만두다

concession n. 양보, 양해; 인정

negotiation n. 협상

17

현대사에서 이 원칙에 큰 예외가 하나 있는데, 그것은 미국이다. 미국은 세계적인 강국으로 성장했지만 많은 사람들이 예측했을 그런 반대는 유발하지 않았다. 사실, 오늘날 미국은 세계를 지배하는 강국이면서도 영국, 프랑스, 독일, 일본 등 미국 다음으로 가장 강력한 국가들이 모두 미국과 연합하고 있는 그런 놀라운 위치에 있다. 이것은 설명이 필요한 예외이다.

이유는 분명 미국 패권의 본질과 관계있다. 미국은 식민지나 정복을 추구하지 않는다. 제2차 세계대전 후, 미국은 적국의 부흥과 재건에 도움을 주어 그들을 동맹국으로 만들었다. 비판의 소리에도 불구하고 전 세계의 사람들은 미국을 더 오래된 다른 제국들과 다르다고 생각한다.

그러나 그것은 미국이 힘을 행사해온 방식과도 관계가 있다. 마지못해 하는 방식이다. 역사적으로, 미국은 세계무대에 뛰어들려는 열의가 없었다. 미국은 제1차 세계대전 말기에 참전했는데 늦게 참전하다보니 최악의 유혈은 피하면서도 전세를 영국과 프랑스에 유리하게 바꿀 수 있었다. 미국은 제2차 세계대전도 일본이 진주만을 공격한 후에야 참전했다. 미국은 유럽에서의 소련의 공격을 저지했지만 다른 여러 곳에서는 너무 지나치지 않도록 신중을 기했다. 그리고 미국이 베트남에서처럼 너무 지나쳤을 때는 희생을 치렀다.

미국에는 오래되고 저명한 정치학파가 하나 있는데, 드와이트 아이젠하워(Dwight Eisenhower)에서 헨리 키신저(Henry Kissinger)와 로버트 게이츠(Robert Gates)에 이르는 정치가들로, 이들은 미국은 강한 국력을 유지하고 힘을 아껴 쓰고 안정되고 자유로운 질서를 창조하고 경제적·정치적 개혁을 장려함으로써 자유의 범위를 전 세계에 확대시키는 데 도움을 주고 있다고 믿는다. 미국은 자신의 군사 개입에 대해 규율이 잡혀있다는 것이 이 임무에 핵심적인 것이다.

1 ③ ▶ **부분이해**

미국이 예외라고 한 다음 미국은 세계적인 강국으로 성장했지만 반대는 유발하지 않았고 다른 강력한 국가들이 모두 미국과 연합하고 있다고 했으므로 그 반대인 ③의 "한 국가가 강력해져 자기주장을 하면 다른 국가들이 그 국가를 타도하려고 집단행동을 벌인다."가 이 원칙에 해당한다.

2 ② ▶ **빈칸완성**

빈칸에는 힘을 행사해온 방식에 해당하는 부사가 들어가는데, 그다음 문장에서 역사적으로, 미국은 세계무대에 뛰어들려는 열의가 없었다고 했으므로 ②의 '마지못해'가 적절하다. ① 몰래 ③ 선제적으로 ④ 자랑하듯이

3 ① ▶ **내용추론**

특히 셋째 단락에서 역사적으로 미국이 대외 문제에 개입해왔음을 진술하므로 ①은 추론할 수 없다. ② 마지막 단락의 정치가들이 미국의 대외 (개입) 정책이 다른 나라의 정책에 비해 도덕적으로 우위에 있다고 믿는 사람들이다. ③ 셋째 단락 마지막 문장에 언급되어 있다. ④ 마지막 단락에서 일부 정치가들은 미국이 세계문제에 개입하여 자유로운 질서를 창조하고 자유의 범위를 전 세계에 확대시키는 데 도움을 주고 있다고 믿는다고 했다.

4 ④ ▶ **글의 요지**

둘째, 셋째 단락에서 언급했듯이 ④의 "미국은 현명한 개입을 통해 다른 제국들과는 다른 종류의 세계강국이 되었다."는 것이 이 글의 요지다.

might n. 힘, 세력

hegemony n. 패권, 주도권, 지배권

revive v. 부흥시키다

ally n. 동맹국, 협력자

carping n. 흠잡음

tail end 최종단계, 말기

bloodshed n. 유혈, 학살

tip the balance 사태를[국면을] 바꾸다, 결과에 결정적인 영향을 주다

contain v. 견제하다, 저지하다

push too far 너무 지나치다

husband v. 아껴 쓰다

18

아이러니하게도, 이민자들의 나라인 미국에서 편견과 차별은 계속해서 심각한 문제가 되고 있다. 이미 정착한 이민자 집단과 그 뒤를 이은 이민자 집단 사이에는 종종 긴장감이 감돌았다. 각 집단이 좀 더 금전적으로 성공하고 영향력을 갖게 됨에 따라, 그들은 새로운 이민자들을 사회에 참여하지 못하게 했다. 편견과 차별 대우는 우리 역사의 일부다. 하지만 다른 집단에 대한 이런 차별 대우는 흑인들에게 있어 가장 부당하다.

흑인들은 뚜렷한 불이익을 받았다. 대부분의 경우에 있어, 그들은 노예의 신분으로 '기회의 땅'에 왔으며, 그들의 유산과 문화적 전통을 지키는 데 자유롭지 못했다. 그들은 또한 피부색 때문에 정착된 사회에 쉽게 섞일 수가 없었다. 흑인이 미국 문화에 적응해가는 것은 어려운 일이었다. 심지어 자유민이 된 이후에도, 그들은 여전히 고용, 주거, 교육, 그리고 화장실과 같은 공공시설에서조차 차별을 경험해야만 했다.

20세기까지 대다수의 흑인 인구는 미국의 남부에서 살았다. 그 후 북부 대도시로의 인구 이동이 있었다. 흑인에 대한 편견은 종종 남부와 관련된다. 노예 제도는 그곳에서 대개 더 흔했으며, 차별 대우는 노골적이었다. 식수대, 화장실, 그리고 식당 등에는 종종 '백인 전용'이라고 표시되어 있었다. 1950년대와 1960년대에 흑인들은 공평한 대우를 얻기 위해 투쟁했으며, 이제는 주거, 교육, 고용에서 법의 보호를 받고 있다. 그들이 사는 지역이 격리되어 있기 때문에, 많은 흑인들은 교육의 기회가 자신들의 아이들에게 충분하지 않다고 느끼고 있다.

흑인과 다른 소수 민족을 위해 고용과 교육의 기회를 평등하게 하기 위한 한 가지 시도가 '차별 철폐 조치'다. 차별 철폐 조치는 회사, 조직, 단체의 책임을 맡고 있는 사람들이 차별 철폐 조치를 수용해 소수 민족들을 채용해야 하는 것을 의미한다. 많은 백인들은 이 규정에 대해 화를 낸다. 왜냐하면 소수 민족에 의해 일자리를 채우고 나면, 때때로 매우 능력 있는 백인이 직업을 얻을 수 없기 때문이다. 사람들은 이런 상황을 '역차별'이라고 부른다.

오늘날 흑인들의 상황은 1950년대보다 훨씬 나아졌다. 그러나 인종 간의 긴장은 계속되고 있다. 시간이야말로 인종 문제의 실질적인 해결책이 될 것이다.

1 ②　　▶ 내용파악
마지막 문단에서 인종 차별의 문제는 예전보다 개선됐지만 갈등은 계속되고 있으며, 이것은 '시간이 지나면 실질적으로 해결될 것'이라고 언급하고 있다.

2 ③　　▶ 내용파악
첫 번째 문단에서 미국의 역사는 편견과 차별로 점철되어왔다고 언급하고 있다.

3 ③　　▶ 내용파악
미국은 새로운 기회를 찾아서 왔던 이민자들로 구성된 나라인데, 이민자들끼리 서로 편견과 차별이 존재하는 게 아이러니하다고 할 수 있다.

immigrant n. 이민자
prejudice n. 편견, 선입관
discrimination n. 차별; 차별 대우
tension n. 긴장
succeeding a. 계속되는, 다음의
exclude v. 제외하다, 배제하다
blatant a. 노골적인, 뻔한
segregate v. 분리하다, 격리하다
affirmative a. 긍정적인, 적극적인
in charge of ~을 책임지고 있는
reverse discrimination 역차별
persist v. 지속하다

19

오늘날의 정치가들은 사실이나 숫자를 제시하기보다 신(神)과 종교에 호소하는 것을 더 편하게 생각하는 것 같다. 물론 누구나 종교적 신념을 가질 자격은 있다. 그러나 과학과 이성이 무시당할 때 미국의 미래도 무시당한다. 우리가 현재의 대선 경쟁에서 목격하고 있는 것은 종교와 과학의 충돌이 아니라 합리적이고 과학적인 사고에 대한 근본적인 무시다. 공화당의 선두 주자들 중 두 명을 제외한 모두는 인간의 소행으로 인한 지구온난화가 기후변화의 원인일지도 모른다는 것을, 그렇다는 증거가 많음에도 불구하고 생각조차 하지 않으려 한다. 우리는 이산화탄소가 온실효과를 통해 지구를 따뜻하게 한다는 것을 알고 있고, 인간이 석탄과 석유를 태움으로써 대기 속의 이산화탄소를 크게 증가시켰다는 것도 알고 있다. 인간의 소행으로 인한 기후변화가 100퍼센트 확실하게 입증되지는 않았다는 사실이 그것을 일축하는 것을 정당화하지는 않는다.

사실, 과학의 중요한 부분은 불확실성을 이해하는 것이다. 과학자들이 우리가 무언가를 안다고 말할 때 그것은 우리의 생각을 다양한 척도로 어느 정도 정확하게 검증해보았다는 말이다. 과학자들은 또한 자신의 이론의 한계를 중요하게 다루어 적용 가능한 범위를 규정하고 그 범위를 확장하려고 노력한다. 그 방법이 적절하게 적용될 때, 시간이 지나면 옳은 결과가 나타난다.

공공정책은 순수하고 통제된 실험보다 더 복잡하지만, 경제, 환경, 건강, 복지 면에서 우리가 직면하고 있는 크고 중대한 문제들을 고려해보면, 이성을 최대한 밀고나가는 것이 우리의 책임이다. 합리적이고 과학적인 사고방식은 분리시키는 것이 아니라 통합시키는 것일 것이다. 대안적인 전략들을 평가하는 것, 다양한 정책들의 상대적 효율성에 대한 미국 내외에서 입수 가능한 자료들을 해독하는 것, 그리고 불확실한 점들을 이해하는 것이 — 모두가 과학적 방법의 특징들인데 — 우리가 앞으로 올바른 길을 찾는 데 도움이 될 수 있다.

1 ② ▶ **부분이해**
밑줄 친 문장에서, man-made는 '인공적인(artificial)'의 의미가 아니라 '인간의 소행(human activities)으로 인한'의 뜻이며, its는 man-made climate change를 가리키고, its dismissal은 '기후변화가 인간의 소행으로 인한 것이라는 점을 부인하는 것'을 말한다. 따라서 ②의 "인간의 소행이 기후변화를 일으킨다는 것이 완전히 입증되지는 않았지만 그것이 사실일 가능성을 배제해서는 안 된다."가 가장 가까운 의미의 문장이다.

2 ① ▶ **빈칸완성**
필자는 과학과 이성에 의지하는 것이 옳다고 생각하므로 과학의 방법이 제대로 적용되면 '옳은 결과가 나타날 것'이다. ② 초기 목표는 변한다 ③ 우리는 점점 더 미신을 믿는다 ④ 그것은 점차 잊혀진다

3 ④ ▶ **글의 요지**
이 글의 요지는 마지막 단락의 첫 번째 문장에 나타나 있다. 첫 번째 단락의 facts or numbers도 공공정책과 관련한 과학적 사실이나 통계 수치를 의미하며, 지구온난화 문제를 언급한 것도 공공정책을 수립하고 시행하는 주체인 정치가들의 과학에 대한 무지를 지적하기 위함이다. 따라서 ①, ③이 아니라 ④가 이 글의 요지로 적절하다.

4 ③ ▶ **내용추론**
오늘날의 정치가들이 종교에 호소하기를 좋아하는 것은 사실이지만 종교가 직업적 성공을 가져다줄 것이라는 입장을 취한다고 보기는 어려우므로 ③이 정답이다. ①는 첫 번째 문장에서, ②는 네 번째 문장에서, ④는 마지막 단락의 첫 번째 문장에서 각각 추론할 수 있다.

---

invoke v. 기원하다, 빌다, 호소하다

entitle v. 권리[자격]를 주다

get shortchanged 무시당하다

presidential race 대통령 선거전, 대선 경쟁

justify v. 정당화하다

dismissal n. 해고, 추방, 기각

scale n. 척도; 규모

address v. 역점을 두어 다루다

applicability n. 적용 가능성

isolate v. 고립시키다, 분리하다, 격리하다

alternative a. 양자택일의; 대신의

20

카스트는 현대화되고 있는 인도가 사용하고 싶어 하는 단어가 아니다. 카스트는 (더 이상) 중요하지 않게 되었다. 신문들은 부와 정치, 그리고 강력한 영향력을 행사하는 것(대중문화, 배우들, 그리고 크리켓 인기선수들)이라는 사회적 계급을 나누는 보다 새로운 측정기준들에 관한 기사를 쓰기 위해 그들의 헤드라인을 따로 남겨두고 있다.

도시화된 인도에서 우리 자신에게 들려줄 두 가지 이야기가 있다. 첫 번째 이야기는 교육이 어떻게 인생을 바꾸는지에 관한 것이다. 교육은 미래를 열어주는 황금열쇠여서 사람들이 태생과 배경이라는 환경을 극복하도록 해준다. 그리고 가끔은 교육이 태생과 배경을 (실제로) 극복하게 해준다. 내 이웃들 중에는 부모가 요리사와 정원사인 아들과 딸이 여럿 있는데, 공학 및 경영학 학위를 취득하고 있으며, 그들의 집안 모든 식구들을 중산층으로 탈바꿈시키고 있다. 이런 사례가 분명 많지는 않다. 그러나 이것이 확실한 희망이자 꿈이 되기에는 충분하다. 두 번째 이야기는 지난 20년간의 경제성장이 인도를 어떻게 근본적으로 변화시켜왔으며, 일자리 및 수입을 창출해왔고, 이전에는 없었던 포부를 키우도록 해왔는지에 관한 것이다. <새로 생긴 돈과 점점 강력해지는 중산층은 아마도 오래된 사회적 계급들을 대체할지도 모른다.>

이 두 가지 이야기는 마음을 설레게 하는 이야기이며, 수세기 동안 사회적 질서가 불변이었던 나라에서 심지어 혁명적이기까지 하다. 전통적으로, 인도사회는 네 가지 주요 계급들로 분류되었다. 최상위 계급에는, 승려와 교사와 같은 브라만(Brahmins), 두 번째 계급에는 무사와 지배층인 크샤트리아(Kshatriya), 세 번째는 상인 계급이었던 바이샤(Vaishya), 마지막으로 노동자 계급인 수드라(Shudra)가 있었다. 그리고 이 모든 네 가지 주요 계급들 밑에는 하리잔(Harijan) 또는 '신의 아이들'(마하트마 간디(Mahatma Gandhi)는 이렇게 불렀다)이라고 불리는 불가촉 천민인 달리트(Dalit)가 있었다. 이 계급들은 표면상 직업에 따른 구분이었지만, 혈통과 계급 간 및 계급 내 상호작용을 결정하는 사회규칙이라는 경직된 구조에 의해 확고하게 고착화되었다.

확연하게도 이 계급제도는 이제 다 지나간 일이다. 인도에서 계급에 바탕을 둔 차별대우는 60년 이상 법으로 금지되어 왔다. 오늘날 기회의 땅이자 문화적·경제적 간극에 의해 인도의 농촌과는 구분되는 인도의 도시에서는, 계급을 이야기하는 것조차 (시대에) 역행하는 것처럼 보인다. 분명히 계급을 언급하는 것은 직장에서나 놀이 중에나 아파트 엘리베이터에서 일어나서도 안 되며 일반적으로 일어나지 않는다.

1 ③ ▶ 글의 주제
불과 60년 전만 해도 인도에 존재했던 카스트 제도가 이제는 법으로 금지되어 사라지고 없다는 내용을 다루고 있으므로 ③이 글의 주제로 적절하다.

2 ⑤ ▶ 문장삽입
제시문은 "새로 생긴 돈과 점점 강력해지는 중산층은 아마도 오래된 사회적 계급들을 대체할지도 모른다."는 뜻이므로, 제시문 앞에는 새로 생긴 돈과 중산층과 관련된 이야기가 나와야 할 것이다. 따라서 지난 20년간의 경제성장이 인도를 어떻게 바꾸었는지, 특히 일자리 창출과 수입을 창출하고 이로 인해 생긴 여유로 (중산층으로서) 전에 없던 포부를 가질 수 있게 되었는지에 관한 내용이 Ｅ 앞에 나오므로 ⑤가 정답이다.

3 ① ▶ 내용파악
카스트 제도는 계급에 의해 구분되고 운명이 정해지는 사회제도를 의미한다. 따라서 카스트 제도 폐지로 인도인들이 얻을 수 있는 가장 큰 혜택은 누구나 자신의 능력에 따라 경제적으로, 사회적으로 신분 상승이 가능하다는 것이다. 따라서 ①의 upward mobility가 정답이다.

4 ① ▶ 내용파악
reactionary는 '(시대에) 역행하는'이라는 뜻으로 네 번째 단락 첫 문장에서 인도의 계급제도는 '이제 다 지나간 일'이라고 했으며, 마지막 문장에서도 "카스트 제도를 언급해서도 안 되며, 보통 언급하는 일이 일어나지 않는다."고 했으므로 ①이 정답이다.

caste n. 카스트; 계층, 계급
recede into the background 눈에 띄지 않다, 중요하지 않게 되다
reserve v. 따로 남겨두다
metric n. 측정기준
hierarchy n. 사회적 계급
transform v. 변화시키다
rise above 극복하다
degree n. 학위
nurture v. 조성하다
aspiration n. 열망, 포부
supposedly ad. 추정상, 아마
displace v. 대신하다
untouchable n. 불가촉 천민
ostensibly ad. 표면상
chasm n. 깊이 갈라진 틈, 간격; 차이

07 경제·경영

01

요즘의 세금정책의 논의에서 로빈 후드(Robin Hood)의 전설에 대한 근본적인 오해는 '부자들'의 돈을 더 많이 거둬들여 '가난한 사람들'을 돕는다는 좀처럼 평가되지 않은 잘못된 생각을 뒷받침하고 있다. 현재, 자선 기부에 대한 세금 공제를 축소하자는 제안이 나오고 있다. 정부 지출 지지자들은 비영리 기부에 대해 세금 감면을 제한함으로써 부자들로부터 더 많은 돈을 거둬들여야 한다고 주장한다. '부자들'은 높은 세금으로 정부에게 그들의 돈을 넘길 것이고, 계속해서 그들의 돈을 너그럽게 기부할 것이며, '가난한 사람들'은 정부와 부자 양측으로부터 후한 도움을 받을 것이다. 이렇게 로빈 후드를 억지로 이해하는 것은 정부가 가난한 사람들을 돕는 실질적인 주체이며 부자들은 벌을 받아 마땅하다는 생각을 포함한 몇 가지 매우 잘못된 가정에 있다. 실제로 전설속의 로빈 후드는 (관리들이) 가난한 사람들로부터 빼앗은 세금을 관리들로부터 약탈하여 가난한 사람들에게 되돌려 준 것이며, 이는 중세식의 세금환급이라 할 수 있다. 그 영웅적인 행동은 자신들의 재원을 빈민들을 돕는 데 사용하지 않은 지배계급에 의해 부당하게 몰수된 돈을 지킬 수 있도록 도와주었다.

1 ②　▶ **내용파악**
첫 번째 문장에 로빈 후드에 대한 근본적인 오해가 자선 기부에 대한 세금 공제를 줄이자는 의견이 나오게 했다는 언급이 있고, 마지막 두 문장을 살펴보면 로빈 후드는 자신이 부자들이 가난한 사람들에게 빼앗은 돈을 다시 가난한 사람들에게 돌려준 것이었다고 했으므로, '정부가 기부금에 대한 세금 공제를 줄이자고 제안한 것은 로빈 후드의 전설을 잘못 이해한 것'이라는 점을 설명하기 위해 로빈 후드의 전설을 언급한 것임을 알 수 있다.

2 ①　▶ **내용파악**
이 글의 글쓴이는 기부금에 대한 세금 감면을 줄이면 실제로 가난한 사람들을 돕지 못하고 부자들이 기부를 줄여 실제로는 가난한 사람들에게 악영향을 줄 것이라는 주장을 펼치고 있으므로 ①이 정답이다.

fundamental a. 기초의, 기본의, 근본적인
undergird v. 뒷받침하다, 떠받치다
evaluate v. 평가하다, 가치를 검토하다
play out ~을 유발하다, 발생시키다
deduction n. 공제; 공제액; 추론
charitable a. 자비로운; 자선의
advocate n. 옹호자; 주창자
hand over 넘겨주다, 이양하다
largesse n. 부조; (아낌없이 주어진) 선물
strained a. 부자연스러운, 억지의
flawed a. 결함 있는, 하자 있는
assumption n. 인수, 수락; 가정, 억측
penalize v. 벌하다; 형을 과하다
medieval a. 중세의, 중세풍의
refund n. 반환, 환불

02

그것은 '리카르도의 법칙(Ricardo's Law)'으로도 알려져 있으며, 두 나라 중 한 나라가 모든 상품을 다른 나라보다 더 싸게 생산할 수 있다 해도, 왜 무역이 쌍방에게 이익이 되는지를 설명한다. 리카르도(Ricardo)는 영국과 포르투갈이 관련된 예를 사용했다. 포르투갈에서는 와인과 의류를 생산하는 데 있어 영국만큼의 노동을 필요로 하지 않는다. 영국에서는 의류 생산이 쉽지 않으며, 와인 생산은 더더욱 쉽지 않다. 이와 대조적으로 포르투갈에서는 둘 다 생산하기 쉽다. 얼핏 보기에, 포르투갈이 영국과 왜 무역을 하려고 하는지 이해하기 힘들겠지만 이렇게 생각해보자. 포르투갈이 오직 와인 생산에만 집중하여 영국에 수출할 만큼 충분히 생산하고, 영국은 옷을 만드는 일에 집중하여 그것을 포르투갈의 저렴한 와인과 교환한다면, 두 나라 모두 이익을 얻게 된다. 그러므로 포르투갈은 옷을 만드는 비용이 들지 않고 영국은 더 저렴한 포르투갈 와인으로 이익을 얻는다.

1 ④　▶ **글의 어조**
리카르도의 법칙으로 알려져 있는 비교우위 이론에 대해 예를 들어서 설명하고 있는 글이므로 ④의 'informative(정보를 제공하는)'가 정답이다. ① 신화상의, 가공의 ② 허구적인; 소설의 ③ 빈정대는, 비꼬는 ⑤ 두려워하는

beneficial a. 유익한, 이로운
at first glance 얼핏 보면, 겉으로 보기에
concentrate v. 집중하다, 한 점에 모으다
export v. 수출하다
benefit v. (~에서) 득을 보다
bartering n. 물물 교환

2 ⑤ ▶ **내용파악**

리카르도의 법칙에 따르면 포르투갈이 와인과 의류를 생산하는 데 영국에서 만큼의 노동을 필요로 하지 않지만, 오직 와인 생산에만 집중하여 그 와인을 영국에 수출해 영국에서 생산된 옷과 교환한다면, 포르투갈에게 옷을 만드는 비용은 전혀 들지 않게 된다. 이를 통해 '한 가지 상품을 특화'할 수 있는 것이다.

3 ① ▶ **지시대상**

리카르도의 법칙이란 "국제 무역에서 한 나라의 어떤 재화가 비록 상대국의 것에 비해 절대 우위에서 뒤처지더라도 생산의 기회비용을 고려했을 때 상대적인 우위를 지닐 수 있다."라는 개념이다. 따라서 영국은 포르투갈에 비해서 와인과 옷 생산에서 절대적인 우위에 뒤처지지만 상대적으로 옷 생산에서 우위를 지닐 수 있으므로 이 문장에서 "It"은 '비교우위'를 의미한다고 볼 수 있다.

03

아담 스미스(Adam Smith)까지 거슬러 올라가는 고전주의 경제학자들은 경제학이 도덕과 정치철학의 한 분과라고 올바르게 생각했다. 그러나 오늘날 일반적으로 교수되는 경제학은 스스로를, 어떻게 소득이 분배되어야 하는지 혹은 이런 효용이나 저런 효용이 어떻게 가치평가를 받아야 하는 것인지에 대해 판단을 내리지 않는 자율적인 학문으로 제시된다. 경제학이 가치판단을 하지 않는 과학이라는 개념은 항상 의문시되어 왔다. 그러나 시장들이 더 확장돼서 삶의 비경제학적인 분야들까지 그 손을 더 뻗쳐오면 올수록, 시장들은 도덕적인 문제들과 더 뒤섞이게 된다.

다원적인 사회에서, 어떻게 상품의 가치를 평가해야 하는지에 대해 우리는 저마다 다른 생각을 가지고 있다. 그래서 우리는 도덕적 논쟁을 정치문제에 끌어들이지 않고 우리의 차이를 해결하고자 노력해보고 싶은 유혹을 느낀다. 그러나 이런 충동은 오류이다. 이러한 충동은 텅 비고 공허한 우리시대의 공적인 담론에나 기여할 뿐이다. 우리는 시민들이 공공 광장으로 들어서려고 할 때 시민들에게 도덕적 확신을 문 앞에 두고 갈 것을 요구해서는 안 된다. 그 대신 우리는 도덕적으로 훨씬 더 강력한 공적 담론을 수용해야 하는데, 그 공적 담론은 시민들이 공적인 삶의 영역으로 갖고 들어가는 도덕적 확신을 피하는 대신 관여시키는 담론이다.

1 ③ ▶ **내용일치**

① 아담 스미스 같은 초기 고전 경제학자들은 경제학을 도덕적이고 정치적인 관점에서 바라보았다. ② 가치 판단을 중시하는 고전 경제학의 입장은 의문시(questionable)되고 있다. ④ 본문에 언급되지 않은 내용이다.

2 ① ▶ **빈칸완성**

저자의 입장은 정치적이고 도덕적인 문제를 포괄하는 공적 담론을 활성화시켜야 한다는 것이다. ② 거부하다, 부인하다 ③ 활용하다 ④ 버리다; 단념하다

classical a. 고전주의의, 고전적인
go back to ~로 거슬러 올라가다
conceive v. 상상하다, 마음에 그리다; 생각하다
autonomous a. 자율적인, 자주적인
discipline n. 훈련, 단련; 규율; 학과, 학문(분야)
questionable a. 의심스러운, 의문의 여지가 있는
entangle v. 얽히게 하다; 말려들게 하다
pluralist a. 다원적인
impulse n. 충동, 충격; 자극
hollow a. 속이 빈, 공허한, 무의미한
discourse n. 담화, 담론
conviction n. 확신, 신념
robust a. 강건한, 튼튼한, 강력한

04

모든 경영자들은 그들에게 던져진 어떤 특별한 프로젝트라도 책임을 지는 대단히 믿음직한 직원들이 있다. 그러나 만일 당신이 믿음직하다고 여기는 직원들에게 처리해야 할 일이 너무 많이 있다면 그들은 생산적이지 않을 것이다. 사실 그들은 당신이 맡긴 추가적인 일은 말할 것도 없고, 그들의 본업도 충실히 할 수 없을 것이다.

셰퍼 컨설팅의 매니징 파트너인 론 애시케너스(Ron Ashkenas)는 당신의 믿음직한 부하직원들을 혹사시키는 문제에 관해 하버드 비즈니스 리뷰에 다음과 같이 기고했다. "경영자들은 때때로 '유력한 용의자들을 체포하는데'(아주 믿음직한 직원들에게 일을 맡기는데) 왜냐하면 그들은 오직 소수의 사람들에게만 핵심 프로젝트나 새로운 계획들을 처리하는 것을 맡기기 때문입니다. 모든 조직들에는 'glue people(심복(心腹))'이 존재하는데, 이들은 조직도에는 나오지 않지만, 능력이 높이

go-to a. (사람이) 대단히 믿음직한, 기댈 수 있는
take on (일 등을) 떠맡다, 책임지다
have too much on your plate 일이 산재해 있다, 처리해야 할 일이 너무 많다
let alone ~은 말할 것도 없고, ~은 커녕
tackle v. 달라붙다, 착수하다
overtax v. 지나치게 부담을 지우다, ~을 혹사시키다
lieutenant n. 서장 보좌, 부 서장, 부관; (직위) 부-

평가되고 신뢰를 받기 때문에 모든 프로젝트 팀이나 특별기획에 참여하는 사람들입니다."라고 론 애시케너스는 주장한다.

그러나 <만일 사업상 새로운 도전과제를 처리하기 위해 매번 똑같이 혹사당하는 집단 이외에 더 유능하고, 충실하며, 믿을 수 있는 직원들을 선발한다면, 당신은 (그들로부터) 어떠한 결과도 얻지 못할 것이다.> "이들 프로젝트 팀원들은 보통 그들의 정규업무 이외에도 다양한 특별임무를 맡게 됩니다. 그래서 대단히 믿음직한 소수의 몇몇 사람들은 동시에 너무 많은 일을 맡게 되어서 어떤 것도 제대로 해내지 못하기 때문에, 결국 이들은 그렇게 많은 임무를 달성하지 못하게 됩니다."라고 론 애시케너스는 주장한다.

1 ③ ▶ **문맥상 적절하지 않은 문장 고르기**
이 글은 경영자들이 믿음직한 직원들만 매번 똑같이 의지하면, 원하는 결과를 얻지 못한다는 내용의 글인데 반해, ⓒ에서는 매번 믿음직한 직원들을 의지하는 것이 아니라, 기존에 믿음직한 직원들보다 유능하고 충실하며 믿을 수 있는 직원들을 선발할 경우 어떠한 결과도 얻지 못할 것이라는 내용이 돼서 전체적인 글의 흐름과 어울리지 않는다. 따라서 ⓒ를 if you draft the same overworked group으로 고치는 것이 글의 흐름상 바람직하다.

2 ② ▶ **글의 요지**
이 글은 아무리 유능하고 믿음이 가는 직원이라도 무리하게 일을 시키면 원하는 결과를 얻을 수 없다는 내용의 글이므로, "신뢰하는 직원을 과도하게 혹사시키는 것은 그들의 능력을 죽인다."는 ②가 글의 요지로 적절하다.

3 ④ ▶ **지시대상**
ⓐ the usual suspect는 원래 '유력한 용의자'란 뜻이지만, 여기서는 문맥상 핵심 프로젝트를 맡길 '아주 믿음이 가는 직원'을 의미하므로 ④가 정답이다. ① 아주 반항적인 직원 ② 아주 잘 속는 직원 ③ 아주 수상쩍은 직원

round up the usual suspect 유력한 용의자[혐의자]들을 체포하다
trust v. 위탁하다, 맡기다
initiative n. (특정한 문제 해결·목적 달성을 위한 새로운) 계획
assign v. 할당하다
task force 대책본부; 프로젝트 팀; 기동부대
draft v. 선발하다
end up with 결국 ~하게 되다
specialty n. 전문, 전공; 특수성, 특별문제
pile v. 쌓다, 축적하다
spread oneself too thin 동시에 너무 많은 일을 벌려 놔서 어떤 것도 제대로 해내지 못하다

05

세계 일부 지역들은 세계화로 인해 뒤처지게 되었다. 경제학자들은 한때 지역과 지역 사이의 그리고 나라와 나라 사이의 불평등은 시간이 지나면 자연히 평등해질 것으로 생각했다. 일부 사람들은 세계 경제가 교과서적인 자율균형 메커니즘인 것으로 생각할 수 있다고 믿는다. 그리고 또 다른 사람들은 세계 경제가 누적적인 인과관계의 과정을 따르는 것으로 볼 수 있어서 만일 한두 나라가 다른 나라들보다 뒤처지면 균형을 찾는 해결의 길로 자동적으로 돌아가기보다 이 인과의 과정으로 인해 더욱더 뒤처지게 될 위험이 있을지 모른다고 믿는다. 실제 세계 경제 과정에 대한 이 두 가지 서로 대체적이고 상충하는 견해는 제도적 필요와 제도적 정비와 관련하여 매우 서로 다른 결과를 낳는다. 동일한 것이 지역에도 적용된다. 지역 간 격차가 벌어지는 악순환이 아니라 지역 간 격차가 좁혀지는 선순환이 있어야 할 이론상의 이유는 없으며 실제로 그렇다는 증거도 없다. 그래서 브렉시트 국민투표가 행해졌을 때 영국의 일인당 국민 소득이 금융위기 이전 수준으로 돌아갔다는 말이 있었다. 영국 은행 수석 경제 분석가 앤디 할데인(Andy Haldane)이 뒤이어 지적했듯이, 이것은 전체 총계로서 맞는 말이었지만 지역별로 나누어 보면 영국의 두 지역, 즉 런던과 동남부 지역에만 맞는 말이었다.

1 ④ ▶ **내용일치**
지역 간과 나라 간의 경제 불평등이 시간이 지나면 자연히 사라질 것이라는 것은 일부 사람들의 믿음일 뿐 저자의 생각은 아니므로 ④가 글의 내용과 일치하지 않는다.

2 ① ▶ **내용파악**
글의 마지막 부분에서 영국의 국민소득이 금융위기 이전 수준으로 낮아졌다고 해도 영국의 모든 지역이 똑같이 그렇게 된 것이 아니고 런던과 동남부 지역만 그렇게 되었다고 했으므로, 저자가 영국을 예로 든 것은 한 나라 안에서도 특정 지역이 다른 지역에 비해 점점 더 뒤처지는 경제적 불평등의 악순환이 일어날 가능성이 있음을 보여주기 위한 것이다.

marginalize v. 사회 진보에서 처지게 하다
even out 평평하게 고르다, 평등하게 하다
self-equilibrating a. 자율균형의
cumulative a. 점증적인, 누적적인
causation n. 원인, 인과관계
pack n. 한 무리, 일당
implication n. 영향, 결과; 함축
arrangement n. 배열; 정돈, 정리; 조정
virtuous circle 선순환
vicious cycle 악순환
convergence n. (한 점으로의) 수렴, 집중
divergence n. 발산, 분기; 상이
Brexit n. 브렉시트(영국의 EU 탈퇴)
referendum n. 국민투표
aggregate n. 총계
disaggregated a. 구성요소로 나누어진

06

1970년대와 1980년대 동안의 기업 인수합병에 관한 여러 연구 결과는 회사들이 이와 같은 거래를 시작하고 완성하는 이유에 대하여 의문을 제기한다. 예를 들어, 한 연구 결과, 인수하는 회사는 일반적으로 인수된 회사의 합병 전 수익 수준을 유지할 수 없었다. 다른 어떤 연구에서는 대부분의 경우, 인수한 회사가 얻는 인수 후 이득은 인수된 회사를 얻기 위해 지불된 금액을 보상하기에는 충분하지 않았다고 결론을 내렸다. 또 다른 연구는 합병을 할 것이라고 발표한 후에, 인수하려는 회사의 주식이 인수될 회사의 주식보다 가치가 훨씬 덜 상승하는 경향이 있음을 보여주었다. 그럼에도 불구하고, 인수합병은 흔히 일어나고 있으며 입찰자들은 그들의 목적이 경제적인 것임을 계속해서 주장하고 있다. 인수는 국가의 자원을 국가 경제의 효율성이 낮은 분야에서 높은 분야로 보내는 바람직한 효과가 있겠지만, 이러한 거래를 조정하는 인수 담당 임원은 인수를 그들 자신이나 자신이 속한 회사의 사적인 경제적 이득을 올려주는 것으로 보는 것이 틀림없다. 기업의 경제적 이득과 관련이 없는 요인이 인수를 설명해줄 것으로 보인다. 이러한 요인들은 임원들의 성과급 보상, 이사회의 감독 부족, 인수될 회사의 가치를 평가하는 데 있어 경영자의 착오를 증가시킬 것이다.

1 ③ ▶ **내용파악**
세 번째 문장에서, "인수를 통해 얻는 이득이 인수를 위해 지불한 금액을 보상하기에 충분하지 않다."라고 했으므로 ③이 정답이다.

2 ④ ▶ **내용일치**
'인수합병을 통해 경제적 이득을 얻기 어려움에도 불구하고 기업이 이를 추진하는 것은 경제적 이득과 관련이 없는 요인이 있기 때문'이라고 했으므로 ④가 정답이다.

merger n. 합병	
acquisition n. 인수, 획득	
initiate v. 시작하다, 일으키다	
consummate v. 완성[완료]하다	
transaction n. 업무, 거래; 처리	
profitability n. 수익성, 이윤율	
adequate a. 충분한, 알맞은	
prospective a. 장래의, 예상된	
derive from ~에서 비롯되다, 유래하다	
channel v. 일정 방향으로 돌리다; 보내다	
have little to do with ~와 관계가 거의 없다	
factor n. 요인, 인자, 요소	
compensation n. 배상; 벌충; 보상	
managerial a. 경영의; 관리의	

07

우리는 성장이라는 바로 그 개념에 대해서 사유할 필요가 있다. 1970년대부터 '제로 성장(개발 억제 정책)'은 가능한 선택 사항으로 여겨졌지만, 경제 발전을 환경보호와 조화시키려는 생각이 더 우세했다. 40년이 지난 지금, 우리는 이러한 접근법이 실패했다는 것을 인정해야 한다. 분명히 우리 행성은 우리 행성에 거주하는 모든 거주자들을 위한 동일한 수준의 소비를 — 우리가 공평하고자 한다면 궁극적인 목표인 — 유지할 수는 없다. 우리는 아마도 절약을 소비에 대립시킬 수 있을지도 모른다. 그러나 그것이 의미하는 바는 우리가 가까운 미래에 어느 정도의 평등에 도달하는 것이다. 현재 상태에서 그것은 가능한 일이 아니다. 일부 라틴 아메리카 국가들은 안데스 원주민 공동체에서 그 원형을 찾을 수 있는, 우리에게는 새로운 '웰빙' 혹은 '풀 라이프'라는 의미를 가지고 있는 "buen vivir" 또는 "vida plena"라는 개념을 사용한다. 비록 다른 여러 전통에서 이끌어오기는 했지만 이것은 60년 전 레브레(Lebret) 신부가 옹호했던 것과 닮은꼴이다: 레브레 신부의 주장은 인간을 경제의 중심에 놓는 것이었다. '웰빙' 혹은 '풀 라이프'라는 개념은 에콰도르와 볼리비아의 헌법에 쓰여졌고, '생산주의적 과잉을 앞세운 전통적인 진보의 개념'에 도전하고 있다. 이 개념은 '보다 더 많은 물질적 축적으로 이해되는 효율성의 논리'를 포기하고 연대를 통해서 지속가능한 경제를 촉진하고자 한다. 분명 이러한 종류의 변화는 현장에서 일어나지 못하고 말만 앞서기 십상이다. 때문에 우리는 시장과 국가와 사회 사이의 관계를 보다 신중하게 탐구할 필요가 있다.

1 ④ ▶ **글의 요지**
이 글에서 저자는 지속가능한 경제의 가능성을 타진하고 있다.

2 ① ▶ **빈칸완성**
더 많은 물질적 축적을 지향한다는 진술로부터 정답을 유추할 수 있다. ② 평등의 논리 ③ 자유의 논리 ④ 해방의 논리 ⑤ 정의의 논리

reflect v. 심사숙고하다, 곰곰이 생각하다	
reconcile v. 화해시키다; 조화시키다	
inhabitant n. 주민, 거주자	
pit v. 자국을 남기다; 구멍을 파다; 경쟁하게 하다	
frugality n. 절약, 검소	
ancestral a. 조상의; 원형[선구]를 이루는	
indigenous a. 고유의, 원산의, 토착의	
solidarity n. 연대, 결속	
abandon v. 버리다, 포기하다	

08

경영이념에 구현되어 있는 전체적 산업조직관은 현실과 일치하지 않고 분석의 목적에 쓸모없는 것으로 대부분의 사회과학자들이 오래전에 포기해버렸다. 보다 설득력 있는 접근법에서는, 조직을 모종의 균형 상태를 유지해야 하는, 서로 관련되지만 별개인 많은 이익들과 목표들을 갖고 있는 하나의 다원적인 사회로 간주한다. 이 별개의 이익과 목표들은 조직을 구성하고 있는 갖가지 다양한 노동집단에 나타나 있는데, 종종 다른 조직의 유사한 이익과 제휴를 하기도 한다. 그래서 육체노동자들, 기술자들, 사무직 노동자들은 그들 각각의 노조를 갖고 있고, 어쩌면 전문가들과 과학기술자들도 그들의 협회와 연구소를 갖고 있는 것이다. 이런 바깥 집단들과의 수평적 연계로 인해, 조직의 구성원들은 그들 자신의 경영진 이외 다른 지도자들에게 충성을 해야 하고 그들의 권위에 복종해야 한다. 따라서 산업정부는 그 제국의 상당 부분이 어느 순간에 가서는 전적으로 철회해버릴 수도 있는 그런 부분적인 충성만을 제국에 바친다는 점에서 가장 힘겨운 시련 중 하나에 직면해 있다. 산업정부라는 제국이 완전한 충성을 요구할 권리는 주장할 수 없는데, 제국은 그 역할과 책임으로 인해 조직 구성원들 스스로 생각하는 그들의 이익에 위배된 행동을 때때로 할 수밖에 없기 때문이다.

1 ①　　▶ **빈칸완성**
　조직 구성원들에게 완전한 충성을 요구할 권리를 주장할 수 없는 이유는 그 조직의 이익이 되는 행위를 산업정부가 항상 할 수는 없기 때문으로 보아야 한다.

2 ④　　▶ **내용추론**
　이 글에서 말하는 수평적 연계가 인수합병을 통한 거대기업으로의 성장을 말하는 것이 아니므로 ④는 추론할 수 있는 내용이 아니다. ① 두 번째 문장에 현대 산업조직은 다원적 사회라고 설명되어 있다. ② 첫 번째 문장에 나온 산업조직을 하나의 전체로 보는 전체적 산업조직관으로는 설명하기 어렵다. ③ 세 번째, 네 번째, 다섯 번째 문장의 설명처럼 조직 내 하부 집단들이 직능별로 다른 외부조직과 수평적 연계와 제휴를 맺고 있어 한 조직에 노사 분쟁이 일어나면 전국적으로 확대되기 쉽다.

3 ②　　▶ **글의 목적**
　이 글은 현대 산업조직의 특징을 설명하기 위한 글이다.

---

embody v. 구현하다, 구체화하다
managerial a. 경영(자)의; 관리의
incongruent a. 일치하지 않는; 부적당한
convincing a. 설득력 있는
plural a. 복수의, 다원적인
equilibrium n. 평형, 균형
manifest v. 명시하다, 나타내다
make common cause with ~과 제휴하다
manual a. 손으로 하는, 육체를 쓰는
manual worker 육체노동자
clerical a. 사무의, 사무원의
trade union 노동조합
horizontal a. 수평의; 균일한
taxing a. 수고스러운, 부담이 큰
allegiance n. 충성; 헌신
withdraw v. 철회하다, 취소하다

09

모든 리더들은 동일한 방식으로 팀을 이끌거나 동일한 목표에 집중하지 않는다. 어떤 리더들은 다른 리더들이 팀의 감정적 행복에 신경을 쓰며 감정 표현적 접근을 취하는 데 반해 특정 업무를 이루는 데 집중하며 도구적인 접근을 취한다. 팀들은 사실상 이러한 두 가지 접근 모두를 필요로 한다. 예를 들어 회의에서 팀들은 목전에 닥친 어떤 업무든 완수해야만 하며, 또한 팀 구성원들 사이의 관계를 다룬다.
리더들은 또한 구성원들을 동기부여 시키는 방식과 성취하고자 하는 바에 있어서 서로 다르다. 업무적인 리더들은 업무 중심적이며 구성원들로 하여금 목표를 달성하게 하는 데 집중한다. 이러한 리더들은 일상적인 목표의 달성에 대해서는 보상하지만 일상적 업무를 넘어서는 수행을 특별히 격려하지는 않는다. 다시 말해, 그들의 구성원들은 그들의 업무를 성취하지만 대개 요구된 노력을 넘어서는 추가적 노력을 하지 않는다. 예를 들어 회계 부서에서 청구서를 작성하는 사람들은 매월 청구서를 요구된 대로 발송하지만 그 이상의 일은 하지 않는다. 전환적인 리더들은 장래성에 집중하는 새로운 조직을 만들면서 구성원들이 일상 업무를 넘어서도록 독려한다. 이들은 열정과 긍정을 활용하여 구성원들을 고무시킨다. 이들은 혁신과 창조성을 권장한다. 이들은 구성원들이 동질감을 갖고, 신뢰하고, 따르는 특성을 드러낸다. 이들은 또한 구성원들을 리더로써 조언하는 데 집중한다. 이러한 리더가 이끄는 회계 부서에서 직원들은 부서의 효율성을 개선하는 데 도움이 될 새로운 소프트웨어를 시험하는 데 시간을 쏟을지도 모른다.

1 ④　　▶ **빈칸완성**
　Ⓐ 감정을 고려하며 서로의 관계에 대해 이야기하도록 격려하는 리더를 표현하는 어구는 expressive(감정을 표현하는)가 적절하다. Ⓑ 주어진 업무 성취에 집중을 하는 리더

---

instrumental a. 도움이 되는, 유용한
expressive a. 나타내는, 표현하는
at hand 가까이에, 머지않아
differ v. 다르다, 의견이 맞지 않다
in regard to ~에 관해서
transactional a. 업무상의, 업무적인
inspire v. 격려하다, 영감을 주다
reward v. 보상하다, 보답하다
routine n. (판에 박힌) 일상
invoice n. 청구서, 계산서
transformational a. 변형의, 전환적인
exhibit v. 보여주다, 드러내다

는 transactional(업무적인)로 설명할 수 있다. © 주어진 업무 이외에 장래성을 염두에 두어 새로운 조직을 형성한다고 하였으므로 이는 변화를 추구하는 transformational (전환적인) 리더라고 할 수 있다.

2 ④ ▶ **빈칸완성**
부서의 효율성을 높이고자 새로운 프로그램을 개발하고자 노력하는 직원들의 모습은 일상적인 업무를 넘어서 혁신과 창조성을 추구하는 설명과 일맥상통한다.

10

월등한 서비스 제공이 회사에 경쟁력 있는 강점을 낳는다는 사실이 서비스를 개선하려는 모든 노력이 그러한 이점을 만들어 낸다는 것을 의미하지는 않는다. 서비스 분야의 투자는 생산과 유통 분야에서의 투자와 같이, 비용절감과 수익증대와 같이 직접적이고 실체적인 이익을 토대로 하여 다른 방식의 투자와 비교하여 고려되어야 한다. 회사의 명성에 타격을 주지 않으며, 용납 못할 정도의 속도로 고객이 빠져나가지 않게끔 서비스를 제공하여 이미 경쟁사와 사실상 동등한 위치에 있다면, 서비스는 극히 심한 경우가 아니고서야 고객에게 결정적으로 작용하지 않으므로, 더 높은 수준의 서비스를 위한 투자는 헛되이 될지 모른다.
이러한 사실이 한 지역은행의 경영진들에게는 분명치 않았는데, 그 은행은 은행원을 기다리는 고객의 시간을 줄이는 투자에도 불구하고 경쟁적 위치를 개선하는 데 실패했다. 그들은 은행 업계에서 거래 은행을 옮기는 불편함으로 야기되는 고객의 미비한 이동 수준을 인지하지 못했다. 또한 해당 서비스가 새로운 고객을 이끌어 낼 결정하기 위해 고객의 흥미를 자아낼 새로운 기준의 서비스를 만들거나, 경쟁사가 모방하기 어렵다는 것을 입증하는 식으로 서비스 개선을 분석하지도 않았다. 그 서비스 개선의 유일한 가치는 고객에게 개선된 부분이 쉽게 설명될 수 있다는 것이었다.

1 ② ▶ **글의 목적**
도입부에서 우수한 서비스 제공이 회사의 경쟁력을 항상 높이는 것은 아님을 언급하면서 회사의 경쟁력을 높일 수 있는 다른 투자 방식과 비교하여 결정되어야 한다고 했다. 따라서 투자에 대한 좀 더 신중한 평가를 제안하는 것이 이 글의 목적이 된다.

2 ③ ▶ **내용파악**
경쟁적 위치에 서는 데 실패한 은행(the regional bank)은 타사가 그들이 제공하는 서비스를 모방하지 못하도록 서비스 개선을 분석한 것이 아니라고 하였다. 따라서 그 은행 경영진들은 그들이 제공하는 서비스를 경쟁사가 모방할 수 있는지에 대한 여부를 고려하지 않았다는 점을 유추할 수 있다.

superior a. 우수한, 뛰어난
distribution n. 분배; 배포; 유통
tangible a. 만져서 알 수 있는; 실체적인(= concrete)
revenue n. 소득; (pl.) 총수입
be on a par with 동등하다
inertia n. 불활동, 불활발; 관성
inconvenience n. 불편; 불편한 것
switch v. 바꾸다

11

노예제의 수익성에 대한 몇 백 년 된 논쟁이 다시 고조되었다. 그것은 150년이 넘는 기간 동안 학계에서 토론되어온 논쟁인데, 1942년에 경제학자 토마스 거원(Thomas Gowan)의 평가가 가장 주목을 받았다. 거원은 농장의 노예제가 더 큰 규모의 노예주 계급에게 이익을 가져다주지 않음을 입증하려는 노력에도 불구하고, 실제로 (노예제는) 이들에게 흔히 이익을 주었다는 결론을 내렸다. 반대의견을 뒷받침해주는 증거는 거의 나오지 않은 가운데 많은 경제학자들은 오랫동안 거원의 이론을 지지해왔다. 로버트 포겔(Robert Fogel)과 스탠리 엥거먼(Stanley Engerman)은 『십자가 위의 시간: 미국 흑인 노예의 경제학(Time on the Cross: The Economics of American Negro Slavery)』을 1974년 썼는데 그들은 노예제가 농업과 같은 산업에서 얻을 수 있는 다른 투자기회보다 아마도 더 수익성이 높다고 주장했다. 노예제는 "대체적으로 아주 수익성이 높은 투자였는데 제조업의 가장 좋은 투자기회와 비교하여도 손색이 없을 정도로 수익률을 낳았다."라고 그들은 썼다. 직감적으로도 무급 노동이 유급 노동보다 더 많은 이익을 가져다 줄 것이라는 것은 이치에 맞는 사실이다. 하지만 그 주제를 다룬 많은 작가들은 노예제가 생각한 것처럼 많은 수익을 가져다주지 않았다고 생각한다. 종종 마지막으로 위대한 고전파 경제학자로 불리는 아일랜드 출신의 존 엘

profitability n. 이익률, 수익성
flare v. 갑자기 일어나다, (논쟁 등이) 고조되다
academic circle 학계
plantation n. 재배지, 농원
yield v. (이익 따위를) 가져오다, 산출하다
instinctively ad. 본능적으로, 직감적으로
lucrative a. 수지맞는, 돈이 벌리는
reluctant a. 마음 내키지 않는, 꺼리는
requisite n. 필요물, 필수품, 필요조건
competitive a. 경쟁의

리엇 케언스(John Elliott Cairnes)는 노예제가 19세기 미국 남부 경제에 전반적으로 부정적인 영향을 미쳤다고 생각했다. 그의 기본적인 주장은 마지못해 일하는 노동자들은 새로운 영농기술을 배우는 데 관심이 없고, 따라서 농사를 하는 데 기초적인 필수지식이 없었기 때문에 토양을 훨씬 빨리 약화시켰다고 했다. 이는 미국 남부가 북부보다 덜 경쟁력이 있다는 의미였다. 북부에서 해방된 노예들이 논밭 밭에서 영농기술을 배워 더 높은 기준에 맞춰 농장을 관리했다. 따라서 더 좋은 작물을 더 많이 수확했다.

1 ④ ▶ **내용일치**
존 엘리엇 케언스는 노예제가 미국 남부 경제에 부정적인 영향을 미쳤다고 주장하며 노예들이 농사를 하는 데 필수지식이 없어서 토양을 훨씬 빨리 약화시켰다고 했다. 하지만 토양을 비옥하게 하기 위해 노예들이 유급 노동자들로 대체된 것은 아니므로 ④는 이 글의 내용과 일치하지 않는다.

2 ② ▶ **빈칸완성**
노예제의 수익성에 대한 경제학자들의 논쟁을 소개하고 있는 글이다. 토마스 거원, 로버트 포겔, 스탠리 엥거먼은 노예제가 수익을 가져다줬다고 했고, 이에 대해 존 엘리엇 케언스는 반대의견을 펼쳤다. 따라서 빈칸에는 ②가 적절하다.

12

17세기에 들어와서 한참 후까지도 수술은 의사가 아니라 이발사에 의해 행해졌는데, 당시 이발사는 배우지 못하고 글도 모르는 사람들로서, 도제 기간 동안 익힌 모든 고문(수술방법)을 적용했다. 신체적인 해를 가하지 않겠다는 서약을 문자 그대로 해석해 지킨 의사들은 너무나 '윤리적'이어서 칼로 환부를 벨 수 없었고 지켜보는 것조차 생각할 수 없었다. 그러나 규정대로 행해질 경우 수술은 학식 많은 의사가 관장했는데, 의사는 고군분투하는 수술 현장 위의 높은 자리에 앉아 이발사가 해야 할 일을 라틴어 의학서(물론 이발사는 이해하지 못했다)에서 찾아 큰 소리로 읽어주었다. 말할 필요도 없이, 환자가 죽을 경우는 항상 이발사의 과실이었고 환자가 살아날 경우는 항상 의사의 공로였다. 그리고 두 경우 모두 의사가 더 많은 보수를 받았다.
400년 전의 수술 상황과 지금 조직이론이 처한 상황 사이에는 약간의 유사성이 있다. 이 분야의 책은 부족하지 않다. 사실, 조직이론은 많은 경영 대학원에서 '경영'이라는 표제로 가르쳐지는 주요 과목이다. 수술에 대한 고전적 교과서에 진짜 귀중한 것이 많이 있었듯이, 이 조직이론 책들 속에는 중요하고 가치 있는 것이 많이 있다. 그러나 실무경영자는 과거 이발사들이 분명히 느꼈을 감정과 같은 감정을 매우 자주 느낀다. 실무경영자는 '실무자'로서 이론을 무시하지는 않는다. 대부분의 경영자들은, 특히 대기업에서, 업무성취도가 적절한 조직이론에 크게 달려 있다는 것을 알게 되었다. 그러나 실무경영자는 대체로 조직이론가를 이해하지 못하며, 조직이론가도 실무경영자를 이해하지 못한다.

1 ④ ▶ **빈칸완성**
문자 그대로 해석해 지킨 결과가 칼로 환부를 베지 않고 지켜보는 것조차 하지 않은 것이므로, 빈칸에는 ④의 '신체적인 해를 가하지 않겠다는'이 적절하다. ① 생명을 구하기 위해 최선을 다하다 ② 어떤 질병도 소홀히 하지 않는다 ③ 동료들과 함께 일하다

2 ③ ▶ **글의 주제**
첫 번째 단락은 두 번째 단락의 이해를 돕기 위해 필자가 비교 대상으로 소개한 내용이므로 글의 주제에서 제외되고, ③이 주제로 적절하다. ④는 ③에 포함된다.

3 ④ ▶ **내용추론**
오늘날의 the practising manager가 과거의 the barber와 유사하다고 했는데, 첫 번째 단락에서 the barber가 '배우지 못하고 글도 모르는 사람들'이었다고 했으므로 ①은 추론할 수 있고, 두 번째 단락에서 '이론을 무시하지는 않는다'라고 했으므로 ②도 옳은 추론이다. 마지막 두 문장에서 ③도 옳은 추론임을 알 수 있다. 그러나 과거의 이발사는 과실에 대한 책임만 지고 의사는 성공의 공로만 차지했지만, 오늘날의 the practising manager와 the organization theorist도 그렇다고 할 수는 없으므로 ④가 잘못된 추론이다.

13

비즈니스 분야에 있어, 전 세계의 많은 나라들이 계속 문을 두드리고 있다. 사우디아라비아가 세계에서 제일 큰 시계탑에 초대형 시계를 제작하기로 결정했을 때, (이슬람 교도인) 자신들에게 꼭 맞는 설계자를 찾는 것은 당연한 것이다. 시계탑은 메카(Mecca)에 있었고, 메카는 이슬람 신자만이 방문할 수 있는 곳이기 때문이다. 그러나 이번 공사는 전문가가 필요한 일이었다. 그래서 사우디 왕가의 대표자와 독일 슈투트가르트(Stuttgart)의 서쪽에서 30킬로 떨어진 곳에 있는 작은 마을인 칼브(Calw)에 있는 회사의 직원 3명은 제네바의 호텔에서 모임을 가졌다. 이 독일 기업 페르트 투르무렌(Perrot Turmuhren)은 1860년에 사업을 시작했고, 오늘날 창업주의 5대 후손이 회사를 운영하고 있다. "시계 관련 모든 분야와 시계기술은 물론 시계탑 분야"의 선두기업인 페르트 투르무렌이 사우디와 계약을 했다.

이것이 독일의 중소전문기업(Mittelstand)의 성공을 보여주는 이야기다. 틈새시장 분야에서 세계 일류기업, 고객이 지구 반대쪽에 있다 해도 '대단히 믿음직한' 기업, 세계화 속에서 밀려나는 회사가 아니라 거기서 온갖 이득을 보는 '눈에 띄지 않는 승자'(최고기업)이다. 중소전문기업을 이룬다는 것은 또한 작은 마을에서 50명에서 500명을 고용할 수 있다는 것이고 이것은 재능 있는 젊은이들이 출세하기 위해 대도시로 떠날 필요가 없다는 것이다. 이것은 권력이 이번에는 경제적 권력이 분권화된다는 것이다. 독일 기업 수익의 상당한 부분을 가져오는 중소전문기업의 성공은 제조업 분야에 대한 독일 정부의 지원과 긴밀하게 연계되어 있다. 연방정부와 주정부는 자금 지원에 기여하고 있다. 연구 예산이 연간 20억 유로인 프라운호퍼 연구소 같은 비정부기관을 통해서 도와주고 있는데, 이 자금은 중소전문기업들이 제품의 품질을 유지하고 개선하는 데 필요로 하는 자금이다.

1 ①   ▶ **빈칸완성**
독일 전역에 걸쳐 확고한 기반을 이루고 있는 독일 중소전문기업이 독일의 중소도시에 퍼져있다는 점에서 '분권화'의 의미가 가장 적당하다. ② 집중시키다 ③ 무효로 하다 ④ 중립화하다

2 ④   ▶ **내용파악**
독일 중소전문기업의 특징으로는 50명에서 500명에 이르는 고용효과, 독일 기업 수익의 상당 부분의 창출, 전문분야에 있어 장기적인 사업방식, 그리고 균등한 지역 발전 효과를 지적할 수 있다. 따라서 "중소전문기업은 비교적 낮은 수준의 청년고용을 창출한다."는 것은 본문의 내용과 일치하지 않는다.

3 ③   ▶ **글의 주제**
본문에서 세계화 추세 속에서도 지속적 경제 활성화, 정치, 경제의 균형적인 발전을 가져온 독일 중소전문기업의 장점이 설명되고 있다. 따라서 글의 주제는 ③의 '독일의 기업 성공모델로서의 중소전문기업'이 가장 적절하다.

knock v. 두드리다, 치다; 문의하다	
clock tower 시계탑	
close to home 마음에 와 닿는, 정곡을 찌르는	
setting n. 장소, 환경	
specialist n. 전문가	
contract n. 계약	
niche market 특정시장, 틈새시장	
wash away 씻겨 내려가다	
head to 향하다	
revenues n. (정부·기관의) 수입, 세입	
intertwine v. 뒤얽히다, 밀접하게 연결되다	
budget n. 예산, 지출비용	
decentralize v. (중앙 정부의 권력을) 분권화하다	
manufacturing n. 제조업	

14

지금까지 자본주의가 큰 성공을 가져다줄 수 있었던 한 가지 이유는 자본주의가 결코 정적인 상태로 있지 않다는 것이다. 자본주의는 순간순간의 여러 고난에 반응하여 개혁을 거듭했기 때문에 생존하여 번성해왔다. 대공황으로 초래된 고난이 자본주의를 평등하고 안정되게 만들려는 운동을 촉발시켰고, 이것이 정부의 보호와 규제를 증가시켜 뉴딜정책과 유럽 복지국가라는 결과를 낳았다. 그러다가 1970년대 스태그플레이션을 극복하기 위해 자본주의는 더욱 생산적이고 혁신적으로 되어야 했다. 로널드 레이건(Ronald Reagan)과 마가렛 대처(Margaret Thatcher)는 규제철폐와 자유무역과 자유로운 자본흐름의 시대를 열어 전 세계의 급속한 경제 성장을 야기했다. 오늘날 경기침체가 장기화되는 가운데 자본주의는 또 한 번의 변곡점에 이르렀다. 전 세계의 금융 부문이 여전히 너무나 불건전하고 평균적인 가계에 가해지는 고통이 이제 너무나 심해졌다보니 자본주의는 또 한 번 변화하여 보다 포괄적이고 균형 잡히고 경기 급락의 재발을 덜 일으키도록 되어야 할 필요가 있다. 문제는 자본주의가 개혁되어야 하느냐가 아니라 어떻게 개혁되어야 하느냐이다.

그 점에 대해서는 의견이 분분하다. 해결책은 자본주의의 많은 역사적인 우여곡절을 결정지어온 국가와 시장의 끝없는 왈츠(상호작용)에 있다. 오늘날 많은 사람들은 대공황처럼 이번의 금융위기도 빗나간 자본주의에 의해 야기되었고 30년 간 이어진 마구잡이식의 규제철폐에 의해 부추겨졌

static a. 정적인	
ill n. 병, 재난, 고난	
bring on 초래하다	
spark v. 발화시키다, 유발하다	
stagflation n. 스태그플레이션(경기침체하의 인플레이션)	
usher v. 안내하다, 선도하다	
deregulation n. 규제철폐	
spawn v. 낳다, 야기하다	
boom n. 급속한 발전	
protract v. 오래 끌게 하다, 연장하다	
downturn n. 경기침체	

다고 믿는다. 이렇게 생각하는 사람들은 은행(금융)업자들과 기업경영자들은 제멋대로 하게 내버려두면 책임감 있게 행동할 것으로 결코 믿을 수 없는 사람들이라고 생각한다. 그들은 더 큰 수익을 올리기 위해 국가경제의 건강을 위험에 빠뜨리거나 상당한 임금을 지불하지 않고 사람들을 죽도록 혹사시킬 것이다. 해결책은 자본주의가 최악으로 과도해지지 않도록 통제하기 위해 정부가 새로운 역할을 맡는 것이다.

1 ③   ▶ **글의 요지**
이 글의 요지, 즉 필자가 말하고자 하는 바는 둘째 단락에 나와 있듯이 ③의 "정부는 시장에 개입하여 심하게 정도를 벗어난 자본주의를 바로잡아야 한다."는 것이다. ②는 자본주의를 바꾸는(개혁하는) 방법에 대한 언급이 아니라서 부적절하다.

2 ②   ▶ **빈칸완성**
빈칸 앞의 '30년'은 1980년대 대처와 레이건이 규제철폐와 자유무역과 자유로운 자본 흐름의 시대를 연 이후 지금까지를 의미하므로 빈칸에는 ②의 '마구잡이식 규제철폐'가 적절하다. ①의 '제한된 경쟁'이나 ③의 '무한정한 재분배'나 ④의 '무질서한 국유화'는 모두 규제철폐가 아니라 정부의 개입 내지 규제와 관련된 것들이다.

3 ①   ▶ **내용파악**
첫 문장과 둘째 문장에서 정적이지 않다는 것과 고난에 반응하여 개혁을 거듭했다는 것은 자본주의가 역동적임을 말한다. ② 자유[진보]주의 ③ 평형상태 ④ 금욕주의

15

학습은 인지에서 시작된다. 개인도 회사도 주변 환경에서 뭔가 흥미로운 것을 발견하고 나서야 배우기 시작할 것이다. 그렇기 때문에 (회사가) 끊임없이 변하는 세상에서 생존하고 번성하려면 무엇보다도 회사의 환경에 민감한 경영을 해야 한다. 회사의 지도자들 중 최소한 일부는 그들이 사는 세상에 주의를 기울이고 민감한 반응을 해야 하며 심지어는 그 외부 세계에서 적극적인 역할을 할 정도여야 한다. 자신에게만 신경 쓰는 사람들은 모든 회사에 필요하지만 그들은 회사의 미래에 영향을 미칠 요소들을 거의 보지 못한다. 이와 달리, 개방적이고 외향적인 경영진은 회사 밖에서 일어나는 모든 일을 훨씬 더 일찍 인지할 것이다. 회사 밖에서 뭔가 변하려 한다거나 이미 변하기 시작했다는 것을 알고 난 후에야 경영진은 그 변화의 영향을 다룰 준비를 할 것이다. 이런 영향들 중 많은 것은 미래에 있고 불확실하다. 그 불확실성을 알고 줄이기를 바라는 마음에서, 대부분의 경영자들은 '우리에게 무슨 일이 일어날 것인가?'라는 비교적 쓸모없는 질문에 너무 많은 시간을 보낸다. 그러나 변화를 일찍 인지하는 경영자들은 '만약 이러저러한 일이 일어나면 우리는 무엇을 할 것인가?'라는 훨씬 더 유용한 질문에 더 많은 시간을 보내야 한다. 이 후자의 질문만이 경영자들로 하여금 새로운 세계에서 회사가 생존하고 번성하게 해줄 변화를 회사 내부에서 일으키도록 만들 수 있다. 사실, 경험이 보여주듯이, 근본적이고 고통스런 변화가 필요할지 모르며, 이 변화에는 아마도 회사의 핵심 사업의 폐지조차도 포함될 것이다.

1 ①   ▶ **부분이해**
navel gazer(배꼽 응시자)는 '자기 문제에만 관심 있는 내성적인 사람'을 가리키므로 ①이 가장 가깝다.

2 ②   ▶ **내용추론**
①은 셋째 문장에서, ③은 Navel gazers로 시작되는 다섯째 문장과 여섯째 문장에서, ④는 마지막 문장에서 각각 그 단서를 찾을 수 있다. ②는 일곱째, 여덟째 문장에서 기업의 환경 변화는 불확실성의 요소로 사업 활동을 불안정하게 만드는 것임을 알 수 있다.

3 ④   ▶ **글의 요지**
이 글은 급변하는 기업 환경 속에서 경영자들이 어떤 자세로 임해야 할 것인지를 설명한 글로, 앞에서 셋째 문장과 끝에서 셋째 문장에 요지가 들어있다.

16

회사의 경영자들은 전략적인 문제들의 복잡성 때문에 종종 그룹으로 일을 한다. 그러나 그룹이 발상에 대한 열린 평가보다 화합에 가치를 둔다면 합의를 추구하는 그룹의 효율성은 떨어질지 모른다. 결과적으로 일부 이론가들은 의사결정의 갈등을 그룹 과정으로 만드는 것을 선호한다. 그들은 그렇게 함으로써 더 나은 결정을 내릴 수 있다고 이론가들은 주장한다. 갈등이 잠재적으로 혜택을 제공하지만, 그룹의 효율성은 또한 그룹의 경험에 대한 구성원의 반응에 달려 있다. 이상적으로 말하면 그룹의 과정이 구성원의 헌신을 얻어내는 것이다. 그렇지만 그 과정은 너무나 큰 불화를 일으켜서 이행하고 미래에 협동하는 것을 약화시킬 수 있다. 따라서 관리 그룹은 명백한 딜레마에 직면한다. 결정 과정의 갈등이 관리적인 효율성을 약화키는 위험을 감수하면서 더 나은 결정을 낳을 수도 있다. 이와 반대로 협력과 실행을 촉진하는 화합은 질이 떨어지는 결정이라는 대가로 이어질 수도 있다.

갈등을 그룹의 의사결정으로 만들려는 노력들은 두 가지 접근법 즉, 변증법적인 토의와 악마의 주장(반대를 위한 반대)에 중점을 둔다. 두 그룹 모두 그 그룹을 경쟁하는 하위 그룹으로 나누고, 겉으로 보기에 명확해 보이는 것을 무비판적으로 받아들이는 것을 막기 위해 공식적인 토론에 의지하며 참가자들이 한 결정에 대해 동의할 때까지 토론을 계속한다. 이 접근법들은 하위그룹들의 역할에 있어 다르다. 변증법적인 토의에서 하위그룹들은 의견이 다른 일련의 가정과 건의를 제시하며 그들이 합의에 이를 때까지 토론을 한다. 악마의 주장에서는 두 번째 하위그룹이 첫 번째 하위그룹의 가정과 건의를 비판하지만 아무런 대안은 내놓지 않는다. 첫 번째 하위그룹은 그 아이디어를 수정하여 두 번째 비판을 받기 위해 그 아이디어를 제시한다. 그 과정은 하위그룹들이 서로 동의할 때까지 계속된다.

1 ④   ▶ **글의 목적**

첫 번째 단락에서는 의사결정의 갈등이 주는 혜택과 위험성에 대해 언급하고 있으며, 두 번째 단락에서는 의사결정에 있어 갈등에 중점을 두는 두 가지 접근법에 대해 설명하고 있으므로 ④는 이 글의 목적과 부합한다.

2 ③   ▶ **내용파악**

두 번째 문단에서 변증법적인 토의와 악마의 주장 모두 의사결정에 있어 무비판적으로 받아들이는 것을 막기 위해 공식적인 토론에 의지하여 참가자들이 동의할 때까지 토론을 계속한다고 한 다음 그 두 가지 접근법의 차이점에 대해 설명하고 있다. 따라서 이 두 가지 접근법에 찬성하는 사람이라면 두 가지 접근법의 공통점인 ③에 대해 동의할 것이라고 볼 수 있다. 참고로 ④는 악마의 주장의 접근법에만 해당하는 보기이다.

3 ②   ▶ **빈칸완성**

결정과정의 갈등이 열린 평가보다는 화합에 가치를 둔다면 효율성이 떨어진다고 했다. 그래서 일부 이론가들은 의사결정의 갈등이 더 나은 결정을 내릴 수 있게 한다고 주장한다고 했다. 따라서 의사결정에 있어 결정과정의 갈등은 더 좋은 결정은 내릴 수 있지만 효율성(effectiveness)을 떨어뜨릴 수 있으며, 반대로 화합은 결정의 효율성을 떨어뜨리는 것이므로 안 좋은 결정(inferior decisions)이라는 대가로 이어질 수 있다. 따라서 빈칸에는 ②가 적절하다. ① 구분 ― 우수한 결정 ③ 협력 ― 효율성 ④ 조화, 화합 ― 충돌

complexity n. 복잡성

strategic a. 전략(상)의

consensus n. 일치, 조화; 합의

effectiveness n. 유효성, 효율성

impair v. 해치다, 손상하다

advocate v. 옹호[변호]하다; 주장하다

decisional a. 결정의, 판단의

yield v. 생기게 하다, 산출하다

potentially ad. 잠재적으로

commitment n. 헌신; 약속

divisiveness n. 구분; 불화, 알력

undermine v. 몰래 손상시키다, 약화시키다

apparent a. 분명한, 명백한

dilemma n. 진퇴양난, 궁지, 딜레마

facilitate v. 촉진하다, 조장하다

dialectical a. 변증법의[적인]

inquiry n. 문의; 조사; 연구, 탐구

devil n. 악마

advocacy n. 옹호, 지지; 주장

critique v. 비평하다

alternative n. 대안

17

수많은 영화와 책을 통해서 우리 모두는 역사적으로 해적은 범죄를 저지르는 쪽으로 정신이 나가버린, 법을 어기는 반역적인 도둑, 고문자, 테러리스트였다는 것을 알고 있다. 무질서가 통례였고, 법치주의는 존재하지 않았다.

조지 메이슨(George Mason) 대학의 경제학자 피터 T. 리슨(Peter T. Leeson)은 그의 책『보이지 않는 후크(The Invisible Hook)』에서 그렇지 않다면서 다른 의견을 내고 있다.『보이지 않는 후크』는 경제 교환이라는 보이지 않는 손이 심지어 해적들 사이에서도 어떻게 사회 통합을 이끌어내는지를 보여주고 있다. 사실 어떠한 공동 사회도 그 사회가 완전히 무질서하다면 기간이 얼마든 성공한다는 것은 불가능하기 때문에, 해적의 신화는 진실일 수 없다.『도덕심의 이론(The Theory of Moral Sentiments)』에서 아담 스미스(Adam Smith)가 언급한 것처럼, 도둑들 사이에도 신의가 있다. "서로를 항상 다치게 하거나 상처 입히려는 사람들 사이에서는 사회가 존재할 수 없다. 강도와 살인자 사이에 사회가 있다면 그들은 적어도 서로를 약탈하고 죽이는 것을 삼가야 한다."

사실, 해적 사회는 경제가 하향식의 관료주의적 구조와는 반대로 사회적인 상호작용에서 자연적으로 발생된 상향식의 자발적으로 조직된 질서의 결과라는 스미스의 이론에 증거를 제공한다. 역사가들이 19세기 미국의 '개척시대의 서부'는 농부와 광부가 연방법이 그들에게 영향을 미치기 훨씬 전에 갈등 해결을 위한 그들의 규칙과 제도를 만들었던, 상대적으로 질서 있는 사회였다고 설명했었던 것처럼 말이다.

그렇다면 해적의 무법성과 무질서에 관한 신화는 어디에서 비롯된 것일까? 그것은 해적들 자신으로부터 비롯되었으며, 그들은 손실을 최소화하고 이윤을 극대화하기 위하여 신화를 유지시키는 것을 도왔다. 해골과 대퇴골이 그려진 졸리 로저(Jolly Roger) 깃발을 생각해보라. 그것은 약탈을 일삼는 무정한 이방인의 무리들이 배에 올라탈 것이라는 것을 상선들에게 알리는 것이다. 그러므로 모든 전리품을 <폭력적으로> 해적에게 내주는 것이 맞서 싸우는 것보다 나은 것으로 여겨졌다.

1 ④ ▶ **문맥상 적절하지 않은 표현 고르기**
해적은 손실을 최소화하고 이윤을 극대화하길 원하기 때문에 상선들과 싸우지 않고 그들이 순순히 전리품을 내주기를 원했으므로 ⑩에는 nonviolent가 적절하다.

2 ② ▶ **내용파악**
해적은 그들에 대한 신화를 이용해 약탈할 대상이 전리품을 내주게 하는 방법을 쓴다고 했으므로, ②가 옳은 진술이다.

3 ④ ▶ **태도**
아담 스미스는 도둑들 사이에도 신의가 있으며 서로를 항상 다치게 하거나 상처 입히려는 사회는 존재할 수 없다고 했으므로, 해적이 도둑, 고문자, 테러리스트였다는 통념을 '찬성하지 않는(disapproving)' 입장이다. ① 중립적인 ② 선뜻 동의하는 ③ 무관심한

4 ② ▶ **내용추론**
세 번째 단락에서 해적 사회는 상향식의 자발적이고 스스로 조직된 질서를 유지했다는 것을 알 수 있으므로 ②를 유추할 수 있다.

---

insane a. 제정신이 아닌, 미친

traitorous a. 반역의, 배반적인

anarchy n. 무정부 상태, 무질서

dissent v. 의견을 달리하다, 불찬성하다

mythology n. 신화; 신화학

subsist v. 존재하다; 생존하다

concoct v. 만들다, 날조하다

perpetrate v. (과오를) 범하다; 함부로 하다

marauding a. 약탈을 일삼는

horde n. 약탈자의 무리; 유목민

heartless a. 무정한, 냉혹한

heathen n. 이방인; 미개인

booty n. 전리품; 이득

18

메이시스, 노드스트롬, 블루밍데일즈, 시어스 그리고 몰 오브 아메리카 같은 많은 쇼핑센터에는 핵심가게가 있다. 핵심가게는 상가(쇼핑몰이나 쇼핑센터)를 주요한 관심지점으로 만들기 위해 사용되는 대형 백화점이다. 때때로 고객유인 임차가게나 핵심 임차가게라고 불리는 그것은 대개 소비자들 사이에 인기가 많은 유명 체인점이다. 이런 종류의 가게가 있다는 것은 소비자들을 유인하여 상가를 찾게 하거나 어쩌면 상가 안의 작은 가게들에서 쇼핑을 계속하도록 만들 수 있다. 큰 핵심가게 주위의 작은 가게들은 큰 핵심가게의 상품과 서비스와 경쟁적 관계가 아니라 상보적 관계에 있는 상품과 서비스를 팔 것으로 기대된다. 그 결과, 소비자들은 한 곳에서 쇼핑을 다 마칠 수 있을 것이다. 1940년대와 50년대 상가(쇼핑몰)의 출현과 더불어, 쇼핑장소에 대한 핵심가게의 가치는 더 커졌다. 쇼핑장소 안에 하나의 핵심가게를 두는 대신 최소 두 개의 핵심가게를 가진 상가가 지어지기 시작했다. 상가 양쪽 끝에 핵심가게를 하나씩 두고 그 둘을 서로 연결하는 가게 정면 공간에 작은 소매상들이 입점하곤 했다. 쇼핑객은 상가로 들어올 때 한쪽 끝의 핵심가게에 들어와서 반대쪽 끝의 다른 핵심가게로 가는 도중에 작은 가게들에 들러 쇼핑을 하게 된다.

핵심가게는 쇼핑몰의 성공에 너무나 중요해서 쇼핑몰 경영자들은 그들을 유치하기 위해 그들에게 정기적으로 임대료를 할인해준다. 핵심가게가 떠나는 것이 상가(쇼핑몰) 쇠락의 전조가 된다. 소비자의 관심을 유지하는데 도움을 줄 큰 가게가 없으면 작은 가게들은 대개 가능한 한 빨리 다른 상가에서 소매영업 공간을 찾기 시작한다. 핵심가게와 대부분의 작은 소매 매장들이 상가시설을 떠나고 나면, 그 상가시설은 대개 죽은 상가라 일컬어진다.

1 ③　▶ **빈칸완성**
빈칸 앞에서 핵심가게가 있다는 것은 상가 안의 작은 가게들에서 쇼핑을 계속하도록 만들 수 있다고 했고 작은 가게가 핵심가게와 상보적 관계에 있는 상품을 판다는 것은 핵심가게에 없는 것을 판다는 뜻이므로 소비자는 한 곳(상가)에서 쇼핑을 다 할 수 있을 것이다. 따라서 ③이 빈칸에 적절하다.

2 ②　▶ **부분이해**
밑줄 친 부분은 '상가 쇠락의 전조가 된다'는 뜻이므로 ②의 '상가 쇠퇴의 첫 징조이다'가 의미상 가장 가깝다. ① 상가를 경제적 어려움에 빠뜨린다 ③ 상가가 새로운 장을 열게 한다 ④ 상가 성장의 저해 요소인 것으로 드러난다

3 ①　▶ **내용추론**
둘째 단락 첫 문장에서 '1940년대와 50년대 상가(쇼핑몰)의 출현과 더불어, 핵심가게의 가치는 더 커졌다'고 한 것은 20세기 중반 이전에도 핵심가게가 있었음을 의미하므로 '20세기 중반에 시작되었다'고 한 ①이 정답이다. ② occupancy rate는 상가 전체 점포들 중 임대된 점포가 차지하는 비율인 임대율로 공실율(vacancy rate)의 반대이다. ③ 셋째 단락 첫 문장이 단서이다. ④ 핵심가게는 고객들의 동선과 구매심리를 이용하여 위치가 정해지므로 과학적으로 위치가 정해진다고 할 수 있다.

4 ④　▶ **글의 제목**
쇼핑몰에서 핵심가게란 어떤 것인가를 설명한 글이므로 ④가 제목으로 가장 적절하다.

---

anchor store 핵심가게(쇼핑몰로 많은 고객을 유인하는 주요 매점)

point of interest 관심지점(사람들의 관심을 모으는 지점[업소])

draw n. 사람[이목]을 끄는 것, 인기 있는 것

tenant n. 임차인, 점유자, 거주자

entice v. 유혹하다, 꾀다

complex n. (상가나 주택) 단지

expectation n. 예상, 기대

complementary a. 보충하는, 상보적인

advent n. 출현, 도래

venue n. 장소, 현장

shopping venue 쇼핑장소, 쇼핑가

retailer n. 소매상

storefront n. (길거리에 면한) 가게나 빌딩의 정면

departure n. 출발, 떠남

portend v. ~의 전조가 되다

atrophy n. 위축, 쇠퇴

outlet n. 매장

19

금은 원래 그 희소성과 경도, 그리고 식별의 용이성 때문에 보편적인 통화단위로 사용되었다. 산업혁명 이전 시대에는 부피가 큰 물품들을 시장까지 운반해갈 필요 없이, 소나 말과 같은 상품을 거래하기 위한 수단으로 금화가 종종 이용되곤 했다. 결국, 현대의 은행 시스템이 설립되기 시작하면서, 금화는 금고에 보관된 금의 양을 표기한 은행 어음으로 대체되었다. 세계 경제가 더욱 진화하면서, 보편적인 통화수단으로서의 금의 사용은 국가 간의 무역 업무를 표준화하는 데 도움이 되었다. 세월이 흐르면서 국제적인 거래에 상업적인 용도로 금을 사용하는 일은 '금본위제(金本位制)'라고 알려지게 되었다.

수세기 동안 이 귀금속의 공급이 극도로 한정되어 있는 덕분에 세계의 재화량이 거의 고정적인 상태를 유지할 수 있었으므로, 금본위제는 경제적으로 필수적인 위치를 차지하고 있었다. 채굴회사들이 가끔씩 새로운 금광을 찾아 열심히 채굴해냈지만, 부의 재분배나 경제의 세부적인 조율을 위해 각국 정부들은 멋대로 금을 생산해 낼 수는 없었다. 이는 또한, 유통되는 통화량의 증가로 통화 가치가 하락하는 인플레이션 현상을 방지하는 데에도 도움이 되었다. 하지만 20세기 초반에 대부분의 국가들이 세계 무역 수준을 전체적으로 측정하는 복잡한 공식에 근거하여 가치를 평가하는 국내 통화 기준을 선택하면서 금본위제를 탈피하게 되었다. 세계경제의 이러한 발전은 1920년대의 국제 경제 붕괴의 결과였다.

1 ①   ▶ **내용파악**

부피가 큰 물품들을 시장까지 운반해갈 필요 없이, 소나 말과 같은 상품을 거래하기 위한 수단으로 금화가 종종 이용되곤 했다고 했으며, 현대 은행 시스템이 설립되기 시작하면서, 금화는 은행 어음으로 대체되었다고 했다. 따라서 금화보다 더 편리한 은행 어음 역시 부피가 큰 물품을 보다 쉽게 거래할 수 있도록 사용되었을 것이므로 ①이 정답이다.

2 ③   ▶ **내용추론**

①, ② 세계에 산재한 금의 양은 일정하기 때문에, 많은 국가들이 금본위제를 채택한다고 해서 늘어나지도 않으며, 금본위제 하에서 빈부의 격차가 커지는 것도 아니다. ④ 1920년대 국제 경제 붕괴 이후 금본위제를 탈피하게 되었다고 했는데, 금본위제에서 벗어났다는 말은 통화량이 늘어남을 유추할 수 있으므로 국제경기 하락 이후 급격하게 부가 줄어들었다는 말은 추론할 수 없다. ③ 금을 기준으로 한 금본위제에서 탈피하게 되면 그 일정성이 사라짐을 의미하므로 ③이 정답이다.

3 ②   ▶ **내용추론**

① 세계경제가 붕괴하기 전에 각 국가들이 많은 금을 보유하고 있었다는 말은 언급되지 않았다. ③ 금의 양은 일정하다고 했다. ④ 세계경제가 붕괴했을 때 부유한 국가들이 덜 부유한 국가들보다 덜 영향을 받았다는 말 역시 본문에 언급되지 않았다. ② 1920년대 세계경제의 붕괴로 인해 금본위제를 버리고 세계 무역 수준을 측정하는 방식에 근거한 국내 통화 기준을 채택했다고 했으므로 ②가 정답이다.

4 ④   ▶ **부분이해**

at the whim of는 '~의 기분에 따라, 변덕에 따라'라는 뜻으로 밑줄 친 문장은 "각국 정부들은 멋대로 금을 생산해 낼 수는 없었다."는 뜻으로 해석할 수 있으므로 ④가 정답이다.

---

toughness n. 경도

identification n. 식별; 신원의 확인

pre-industrial a. 산업혁명 이전의

transport v. 운반하다

bulky a. 부피가 큰

note n. 어음

represent v. 표기하다

vault n. 금고

gold standard 금본위제(金本位制)

precious metal 귀금속

constant a. 변함없는, 일정한

whim n. 변덕

redistribute v. 재분배하다

micro-manage v. 세부조율하다

circulation n. 유통

formula n. 공식

collapse n. 붕괴

20

말라위(Malawi)의 농부들이 경작하는 땅콩보다 생산성이 더 높은 다양한 땅콩 품종들이 있지만, 그들로 하여금 그런 품종들로 바꾸도록 하는 일은 어렵다. 더 나은 품종의 씨앗들은 값이 비싸서 그들의 위험이 증가하기 때문이다. 그래서 세계은행의 연구진들은 실험을 해보았다. 현지 비정부 기구들과 함께, 그들은 농부들에게 자금을 대출해 주었다. 일부 대출에 대해서는 심지어 작물보험 증서가 따라왔다. 즉, 날씨가 건조해 농사를 그르치면, 대출금을 면제해 주는 것이었다. 농부들의 위험은 낮아졌다. 기존의 대출을 받고 있던 농부들 가운데 33퍼센트가 이 대출을 받기로 계약했다. 추가적인 보험 혜택을 덧붙이자 신청자는 18퍼센트에 불과했다. 연구자들은 당혹스러웠다.

말라위의 세계은행 경제학자인 사비어 진(Xavier Giné)은 소액 융자가 자리 잡은 지역에서조차 빈번히 소액보험만큼은 실패하는 것을 보았다. 그는 예기치 못했던 경제적 행동이 이런 상반된 결과를 발생시키고 있다고 말한다. "우리가 신용대출에 대해 생각할 때, 대출기관들은 대출인들을 신뢰할 필요가 있습니다. 그러나 보험에서는 그 정반대입니다. 당신은 보험회사가 청구금을 지불할 것이라고 신뢰해야만 합니다." 금융기관에 대해 생소한 사람들이 그렇게 보험회사를 신뢰하지 않을 것이라는 점은 과장이 아니다. (내 농사가 망했는데, 네가 내게 돈을 준다고? 흥!) 인도에서, 진은 보험 증권을 구매할 의사가 높은 이들은 실제로 위험을 감수하는 경향이 있는 사람들이라는 것을 확인했다. 그것은 달리 말해 위험에 대비해 보험에 가입하는 것이 위험하게 비친다는 의미이다. 그것도 그럴 만한 것이, 최초로 소액보험이 시도되었던 사례들 중에, 1990년대 방글라데시에서 보험업자들이 보험금을 지불하지 않은 일들이 실제로 있었다.

뉴욕 대학의 경제학자 조나단 모르두흐(Jonathan Morduch)와 다른 공동저자들은 『가난한 사람들의 포트폴리오(Portfolios of the Poor)』에서 소액보험을 판매하기 어려운 점에 대한 다른 이유를 논했다. 첫째, 가난하다고 해서 복잡하고 귀찮은 일들이 없는 것이 아니며, 그 점이 바로 대출을 받게 되는 원인 중의 하나다. 물론, 소액대출은 일반적으로 소자본 창업을 돕기 위한 것이지만, 현금이란 원래 대체성이 있게 마련이다. 만약 당장 오늘 저녁 식사할 돈이 없을 때, 신용계좌만 있다면, 그 의도가 어떤 것이든 간에 저녁 식사 문제를 해결할 수 있다. 보험은 그렇지 않은데, 왜냐하면 보험은 사람들에게 그들이 직면하는 많은 위험들 가운데 어떤 위험에 대해 손실을 방지할 것인지 미리 결정할 것을 요구한다. 더구나, 공식적인 보험이 없더라도, 대부분의 사람들은 이미 어느 정도의 안전망을 갖고 있다. 친구들, 가족들, 그리고 실제 재난적 상황에서라면 정부라는 안전망을 가지고 있는 것이다. "보험의 진짜 도전은 안전망 역할을 하는 다른 메커니즘들보다 나은 것이어야 한다는 점입니다. 경쟁이 없는 것이 아니죠."라고 모르두흐는 말하고 있다.

1 ③　▶ **내용파악**
첫 번째 단락에서 말라위 농부들에게 소액대출을 해주면서 작물보험을 함께 판매하였지만 실제 보험을 신청하는 사람들이 거의 없었다고 언급하며 그 이유에 대해서 소개하고 있다. 방글라데시를 예로 들며 보험업자들이 실제로 보험금을 지급하지 않았다고 하였으며 위험에 대비하는 것, 즉 보험에 가입하는 것 자체가 저소득층들이 느끼기엔 위험하게 비춰진다고 하였으므로 ③이 정답이다.

2 ①　▶ **동의어**
sputter는 '소리 내어 불꽃이 튀거나 방전하는 것'을 뜻하며 이 글에서는 "소액대출은 활성화된 반면 소액보험은 실패한다."라는 의미가 되어야 하므로 부정적인 뜻의 ① fail이 적절하다. ② 번창하다 ③ 효율적으로 작동하다 ④ 도전하다 ⑤ 도약하다

3 ④　▶ **빈칸완성**
빈칸 뒤에 콜론(:)이 와서 빈칸이 포함된 문장을 부연 설명하고 있다. 즉, 보험에 가입하는 것이 위험하게 보인다고 했으므로, 보험에 기꺼이 가입하는 사람들은 '위험을 무릅쓰는 사람'이라고 볼 수 있다. ① 선견지명이 있는 사람들 ② 기회 회피자 ③ 궁핍한 사람들 ⑤ 음울한 비관주의자

4 ⑤　▶ **내용추론**
마지막 단락에서 소액대출은 일반적으로 소자본 창업을 돕기 위한 것이라고 했지만, 현금이란 대체성이 있기 때문에 만약 당장 저녁 식사를 할 돈이 없을 때 저녁 문제를 해결할 수 있다고 하였으므로 가난한 사람들에게 소액대출은 생계를 위한 수단으로 사용할 수 있다고 추론할 수 있다.

5 ①　▶ **내용일치**
소액보험에 생소한 사람들의 경우 농사가 망했는데도 불구하고 피해액을 내주는 보험 제도를 의심한다고 했으므로 ①이 정답이다.

---

variety n. 변화, 다양성; 종류

groundnut n. 땅콩

switch v. 바꾸다, 전환하다

pricey a. 비용이 드는, 비싼

NGO 비정부 기구(= non-governmental organization)

dud n. 완전한 실패, 실패작

lower v. 낮추다, 내리다

conventional a. 전통적인, 인습적인

microloan n. (저개발국 정부의) 소액 융자

sputter v. 바지직거리며 튀다, 탁탁 튀다; 갑자기 격렬한 소리를 내다

unforeseen a. 생각지 않은, 뜻하지 않은

stretch n. 과장, 남용

risk taker 위험을 무릅쓰는 사람, 모험가

hedge against something (특히 금전적 손실에) 대비하다

toss out (문제·논의 등을) 끝까지 논하다

hard sell 적극적인 판매; 어려운 설득

microcredit n. 소액대출(개발도상국에서 창업을 위한 저리의 소액 자금 대출)

fungible a. 대용할 수 있는, 대체 가능한

safety net 안전(대)책; (금융 등의) 안전망

catastrophic a. 파국의, 파멸의

08 과학·기술

01

과학은 진실에 대한 사람들의 생각이다. 대부분의 사람들에게, 진실은 완전히 증명된 상태의 것을 의미한다. 물론 위대한 과학철학자 칼 포퍼(Karl Popper)가 지적했듯이, 과학은 실제로 아무것도 증명하지 못한다. 예를 들면, 대부분의 사람들은 물이 해수면에서 화씨 32도에 언다고 알고 있다. 우리는 매번 이 실험을 할 때마다 같은 결과를 얻어왔다. 하지만 포퍼는 이런 조건에서 물이 어는 것은 우리가 알고 있는 최고의 이론이라고만 말할 수 있다고 주장했다. 결국, 물은 우리가 물이 어는지를 백만 번째로 실험할 때 얼지 않을 수도 있다. 포퍼는 그것을 다음과 같이 설명했다. 지금까지 보아왔던 모든 백조가 하얗다고 가정해보자. 그럼 백조가 하얗다는 것을 과학이 증명했다고 말하는 것이 정당화될 수 있을까? 아니다. 과학이 말할 수 있는 것은 어떤 흑조도 이제껏 나타나지 않았다는 게 전부다. 언젠가 흑조가 나타날 가능성은 남아 있다. 과학은 결코 증명할 수 없고, 반증만할 수 있을 뿐이다. 그리고 반증을 함에 있어, 새로운 사건들이 우리의 견해에 대한 수정을 요구할지 모른다는 가능성의 여지를 남겨두고 현재 존재하는 사건들을 설명한다. 간단히 말해서, 과학은 흑조를 영원히 찾고 있다.

1 ②　▶ 글의 제목
　　　'사람들이 일반적으로 생각하고 있는 것과는 달리, 과학은 결코 아무것도 증명할 수 없고, 반증만 할 수 있을 뿐'이라는 것이 본문의 주된 내용이다. 따라서 제목으로는 ②가 가장 적절하다.

2 ④　▶ 내용추론
　　　칼 포퍼는 과학이 아무것도 증명하지 못한다고 주장하며, 지금 우리가 알고 있는 어떤 이론도 절대적이지 않으며 바뀔 가능성이 있다고 했다. 따라서 과학에 대한 칼 포퍼의 관점으로 추론할 수 있는 것은 ④가 적절하다.

state n. 상태, 형편, 사정
point out ~을 가리키다; 지적하다
put ~ to the test ~을 시험해보다
justify v. 옳다고 하다, 정당화하다
modification n. 수정, 변경
in short 요컨대, 간단히 말해
falsification n. 위조, 변조; 반증
provisional a. 임시의, 일시적인, 잠정적인

02

순수과학이 항상 혁신을 자극하는 것은 아니다. 오히려 기술적인 변화는 종종 인간의 창의성으로부터 자연스럽게 생겨난다. 작가 매트 리들리(Matt Ridley)는 이런 도발적인 주장을 『월스트리트 저널(The Wall Street Journal)』에 기고한 '기초과학의 허위'라는 글을 통해서 제기했다. 그의 주장은 과학과 기술의 역할과 이점에 대한 뜨겁고 사려 깊은 반응을 소셜미디어 상에서 불러일으켰다. 리들리는 정부가 기금을 댄 기초 연구가 사회를 향상시키는 혁신으로 향해가는 유일한 길이 아니라고 말한다. 그러나 다른 사람들은 공적 기금이 투여된 연구가 많은 이점들을 가지고 있다고 반박한다. "기술적 변화와 사회적 변화의 원인은 다양합니다. 그리고 과학적 연구는 이런 생태계의 단지 일부를 구성할 뿐입니다. 그러나 그렇다고 해서 이것이 과학적 연구를 중요하지 않게 만드는 것은 아닙니다."라고 『가디언(The Guardian)』지에 실린 리들리의 에세이에 대한 기사 논평에서 UCL의 사회 정치 전문가로 있는 잭 스틸고(Jack Stilgoe)는 썼다. 리들리는 그를 비판하는 사람들에게, 트위터를 통해 기초연구가 중요하기는 하지만 정부가 주도하는 것이 기초연구에 기금을 대는 유일한 방법은 아니라고 답변했다. 리들리는 기초과학이 새로운 기술을 촉진하고, 이 새로운 기술 또한 사회에 이익을 준다는 인기 있는 '선형 모델'을 비판하는 것을 목표로 하고 있다. "만일 당신이 혁신의 역사를 조사해본다면, 당신은 과학적 발견이 기술적 변화의 결과이지 원인이 아니라는 사실을 몇 번이고 반복해서 발견하게 될 것입니다."라고 그는 쓴다. 증기기관이 열역학 과학의 발견 때문에 발명된 것이 아니라 열역학이 증기기관의 발명으로부터 분명히 이익을 얻었다는 사실에 그는 주목한다.

provocative a. 도발적인
counter v. 논박하다
manifold a. 다양한
inconsequential a. 중요하지 않은
breakthrough n. 돌파구; (과학·기술 등의)
획기적인 약진[진전, 발견]
thermodynamics n. 열역학

1 ③ ▶ **빈칸완성**

증기기관의 발명으로부터 열역학이 이득을 보았다는 진술로부터 정답을 추론할 수 있다. ① 이론 ② 실행 ④ 직관 ⑤ 추측

2 ⑤ ▶ **내용일치**

리들리는 순수과학보다 인간의 창의성을 더 중시한다.

03

신선한 채소를 냉동시켜 먹을 수 있는 직사각형 모양으로 보존한다는 생각이 처음으로 힘을 갖게 된 것은 발명가 클라렌스 버즈아이(Clarence Birdseye)가 특별히 낮은 온도에서 작용하는 고압 급속 냉동 기법을 개발한 1920년대였다. 그의 기술혁신의 핵심은 '급속'이라는 부분이었다. 약간 더 높은 온도에서의 비교적 느린 냉동은 식품에 큰 얼음결정이 형성되게 하여 식품의 섬유 및 세포 구조를 손상시키고 식품의 맛과 질감을 앗아간다. 버즈아이의 초저온 초고속 방식은 단지 작은 결정만 형성되게 하여 각종 비타민과 신선도를 훨씬 더 많이 보존했다. 그 후 90년 동안, 식품제조업체들은 품질 개선을 위한 몇 가지 추가적인 요령을 첨가했다. 예를 들어, 일부 과일과 채소는 먼저 껍질을 벗기고 데친 후에 냉동시키는데, 이것은 껍질이 벗겨진 사과나 바나나를 갈색으로 변하게 만드는 현상인 약간의 산화를 야기할 수 있다. 그러나 데치는 것은 또한 맛과 영양분 함량뿐 아니라 색깔도 보다 더 극적으로 나빠지게 할 과일 안의 효소의 활동력을 잃게 한다. 더욱이, 데치는 과정은 식품을 농축시켜 식품의 섬유질 함량을 실제로 증가시킬 수 있고 이것은 인간의 소화에 매우 좋다.

1 ① ▶ **빈칸완성**

첫 빈칸의 문장에 나온 '껍질을 벗기고 데친 후에 냉동을 하는 방식'은 그 앞 문장에서 언급한 '식품제조업체들이 품질 개선을 위해 추가한 요령'의 예로 든 것이므로 첫 빈칸에는 for example이 적절하고 둘째 빈칸 앞뒤로 데치기의 좋은 점을 이어서 들고 있으므로 둘째 빈칸에는 What's more나 In addition이 적절하다. ② 반면에 — 게다가 ③ 비슷한 방법으로 — 그와는 반대로 ④ ~의 결과로서 — 그에 반해서

2 ④ ▶ **내용일치**

끝에서 두 번째 문장에서 데치는 것은 효소가 활동하지 못하게 하는데 이 효소가 맛, 영양, 색깔을 나빠지게 하는 것이므로 결국 데치는 것은 영양을 더 좋게 한다고 할 수 있고 마지막 문장에서 식품을 소화하기 좋게 만든다는 것을 알 수 있으므로 ④가 사실이다. ① 냉동이 인류 최초의 식품 보관법인 것은 아니다. ② 버즈아이의 공헌은 냉동 속도를 급속하게 했다는 것이다. ③ 본문에서는 산화로 과일이 갈색으로 변한다고 했을 뿐이다.

edible a. 식용의
catch hold 힘[세력, 지배력]을 갖다
flash-freezing n. 급속냉동
fibrous a. 섬유의
peel v. 껍질을 벗기다
blanch v. 표백하다, 데치다
oxidation n. 산화
deactivate v. 불활성화하다, 활동력을 잃게 하다
enzyme n. 효소
degrade v. (지위나 품질을) 저하시키다
nutrient content 영양분 함량
concentrate v. 집중하다, 농축하다

04

인공지능 개발에 수십억 달러를 투자하는 대형 기술회사들은 그들이 하고 있는 사업에 대해 꾸밈없이 위험을 숨기지 말고 더 잘 설명해야 한다. 바로 지금도 많은 가장 큰 인공지능 모형들이 문을 닫아놓고 개인 정보데이터를 이용하여 개발되고 회사 내의 팀들에 의해서만 검증되고 있다. 그 인공지능 모형들에 대한 정보가 공개되면, 그것은 종종 기업 홍보에 의해 희석되거나 알 수 없는 과학 논문 속에 묻혀버린다. 반발을 피하려고 인공지능의 위험을 대수롭지 않게 다루는 것은 단기적으로는 영리한 전략일지 모르지만, 공익에 위배되는 인공지능 개발사업들을 숨긴 채 예정해놓고 있는 것으로 간주되면 기술회사들은 장기적으로 생존하지 못할 것이다. 그리고 만일 이 회사들이 자발적으로 공개하려 하지 않으면, 인공지능 기술자들이 회사 상사들을 우회하여 정책 입안자들과 기자들과 직접 이야기해야 한다. 마찬가지로, 뉴스 미디어들은 인공지능 발전 상황을 비전문가들에게 더 잘 설명해주어야 한다. 너무나 자주, 기자들은 인공지능 분야에서 일어나는 일을 일반 대중에게 구식의 공상과학 소설 쓰듯이 속성으로 전한다.

do a better job of ~를 더 잘하다
sugarcoat v. 겉을 잘 꾸미다, 좋게 말하다
soft-pedal v. 부드럽게 하다, (격한 어조를) 낮추다
water down 물을 타다; 효력을 약화시키다
inscrutable a. 불가사의한, 알 수 없는
play down 가볍게 다루다, 경시하다
backlash n. 반발, 반격
agenda n. 의사일정, 예정표
outdated a. 구식의, 시대에 뒤진
sci-fi n. 공상과학 소설
shorthand n. 속기 a. 속기의

1 ② ▶ **빈칸완성**
or 앞에서 기업 홍보에 의해 희석된다고 부정적으로 언급된 것과 마찬가지로 정보가 알려지지 않게 매장되려면 논문은 '알 수 없는, 불가해한' 내용이어야 하므로 빈칸에는 ② inscrutable이 적절하다. ① 혼합할 수 없는 ③ 논박할 수 없는 ④ 감지할 수 없는 ⑤ 굴하지 않는

2 ③ ▶ **글의 요지**
이 글은 대형 기술 회사들이 인공지능 개발과 관련하여 정보를 공개하지 않고 개발에 대한 검증도 회사 자체적으로 비공개로 함으로써 인공지능의 위험을 키우고 있다고 경고하는 글이므로 ③의 "인공지능에서 일어나고 있는 일에 대해 공개적으로 이야기해야 할 필요가 있다."가 글의 요지로 적절하다. ④ 인공지능 기술자들과 뉴스 미디어에 정보 공개를 위한 노력을 촉구할 뿐, 회사를 감시하라고 촉구하는 것은 아니다.

05

수은은 상온에서 액체 형태를 유지하는 유일한 금속이다. 물을 따를 수 있는 것과 정확하게 똑같은 방식으로 수은을 한 용기에서 다른 용기로 부어 따를 수 있다. 이 특성 때문에, 사람들은 오랫동안 수은이 진정한 금속인 것에 대해 확신하지 못했다. 이 은백색 물질은 고대 중국인들과 힌두인들에게 알려져 있었다. 수은은 기원전 1500년에 만들어진 이집트의 무덤들에서 발견되었다. 한 고대 그리스 작가는 이 금속을 "액체 은"이라고 표현했으며, 심지어 오늘날에도 이 물질은 종종 퀵실버라고 불린다.
수은은 아주 귀중한 금속이다. 수은은 많은 유용한 의약품과 약물을 만드는 데 널리 사용된다. 대량의 수은은 또한 페인트를 섞고, 폭발물을 제조하고 전자기기와 과학 기구를 제조하는 데도 사용된다. 수은은 아마도 온도계에서 사용되는 물질로 가장 잘 알려져 있을 것이다. 수은은 온도의 변화에 따라 팽창하거나 수축하는 물질이다.
때때로 수은은 바위들 사이에서 유리된 상태로 발견된다. 하지만, 대부분은 진사라고 불리는 아름다운 빨강색 광석에 유황과 섞인 상태로 발견된다.

1 ④ ▶ **내용파악**
수은은 상온에서 액체 형태를 유지하며, 고대 중국인들과 힌두인들에게 알려져 있었다고 했고, 다양한 방법으로 이용된다고 했으므로 ① '다용도,' ② '유동성,' ③ '오래됨'은 수은에 대해 언급된 사실이다. 하지만 ④ '부서지기 쉬운 속성'은 본문에 언급되지 않았으므로 ④가 정답이다.

2 ④ ▶ **내용일치**
① 고대 그리스 작가가 수은을 언급했다는 점을 보아, 중동과 아시아 외의 지역에도 수은이 알려져 있었음을 알 수 있다. ② 종종 바위 사이에서 유리된 상태로 발견된다고 하였다. ③ 수은이 의약품 제조에 사용되기는 하지만 다른 기구들은 식용이 아니다. 수은은 상온에서 액체 형태를 유지하는 유일한 금속이라고 했으므로 ④의 "수은을 제외한 모든 금속은 상온에서 고체 상태이다."는 적절하다.

3 ② ▶ **빈칸완성**
수은이 의약품 제조부터 과학 기구 제조, 온도계까지 다양하게 사용되고 있으므로 '가치 있는(valuable)' 금속이라 할 수 있겠다. ① 호기심이 강한; 진기한 ③ 과학적인 ④ 유동체의

mercury n. 수은
pour v. 붓다, 따르다
vessel n. 그릇, 용기
substance n. 물질
quicksilver n. 수은
explosive n. 폭발물, 폭약
apparatus n. 기구, 장치
thermometer n. 온도계; 체온계
contract v. 줄어들다, 수축하다
sulfur n. 황, 유황
ore n. 광석
cinnabar n. 진사

06

인류 역사가 시작된 후 혁신자들은 개량된 신소재를 내놓으려고 평범한 원소에서 눈에 보이지 않는 원소에 이르기까지 모든 종류의 원소를 실험해보았다. 1907년 플라스틱의 발명은 실험실에서 합성소재가 마구 만들어지는 합성소재의 시대를 열어 무한히 다양한 유용한 제품을 만들 수 있는 가능성을 크게 넓혔다.

하버드대학교 위스 연구소의 연구원들은 새우 껍질과 실크 단백질을 결합시켜 "쉬릴크"라 불리는 기적적인 신물질을 발명했다. 쉬릴크는 제조비용은 저렴하지만 귀중한 장점들이 있다. 질기고 유연하고 생물분해성이 있다. 장차 그것은 상처치료용 연고에서 쓰레기봉지와 일회용 기저귀에 이르기까지 모든 것을 만드는 데 사용될지 모른다. 그리고 그것은 쓰레기 매립지를 질식시키는 많은 플라스틱 제품들을 무용지물로 만들지 모른다. 그러나 과학자들은 때때로 처음에는 용도가 분명치 않은 소재를 만들기도 한다. 밤에 눈에 잘 띄는, 복잡하고 기록적인 종류의 탄소의 경우가 그렇다. 또 다른 신소재들은 우리의 첨단기술 세계에서는 사소해 보일지 모르지만 편리함을 추구하는 소비자들에게 분명 즐거움을 가져다줄 것이다. 예를 들어, MIT 연구팀이 특허 보호를 받는, 리퀴글라이드라 불리는 식품 용기 처리법을 고안해냈는데, 이것은 케첩과 마요네즈 같은 걸쭉한 액체를 바로 용기 밖으로 미끄러져 나가게 할 용기 내면의 미끄러운 코팅이다.

1 ③　▶ **부분이해**

편리함을 추구하는 소비자들에게 즐거움을 가져다준다는 것은 이 신소재들을 사용하여 사용하기 쉬운(편리한) 제품을 만든다는 뜻이므로 ③이 가장 가깝다.

2 ③　▶ **내용파악**

① 상처치료용 연고에서 쓰레기봉지와 일회용 기저귀에 이르기까지 모든 것을 만드는 데 사용될 수도 있다는 것은 다용도성을 말한다. ② 생물분해성이 있고 쓰레기 매립지를 질식시키는 많은 플라스틱 제품들을 무용지물로 만들지 모른다고 한 것은 친환경성을 말한다. ④ 유연하다(flexible)고 했다. 그러나 ③의 '끈적끈적한 점성(viscosoty)'은 언급되지 않았다.

3 ④　▶ **내용파악**

① 인류 역사 이후 개량된 신소재를 내놓으려고 실험을 했다고 했으므로 플라스틱 이전에도 신소재가 나와 사용되었을 것이다. ② 처음에는 용도가 분명치 않은 소재를 만들기도 한다고 한 다음에 탄소의 경우가 그렇다고 했으므로 탄소는 처음부터 그런 의도로 만들어진 것은 아닐 것이다. ③ 최첨단 소재일수록 매력적인지는 이 글에서 알 수 없다. ④ "리퀴글라이드는 양념 병의 안쪽 면을 입히는(코팅하는) 데 사용될 수 있다."는 마지막 문장이 단서다.

innovator n. 혁신자

come up with 생각해내다, 제공하다

inaugurate v. 시작하다, (새 시대를) 열다

stir up 일으키다

miraculous a. 기적적인, 놀랄 만한

shrimp n. 새우

silk protein 실크 단백질(실크를 전환시켜 만드는 단백질 물질)

biodegradable a. 생물분해성이 있는(미생물에 의해 무해한 물질로 분해되는)

dressing n. (외과의) 처치용품, 연고

disposable a. 사용 후 버릴 수 있는, 일회용의

diaper n. 기저귀

land-fill n. 쓰레기 매립지

choke v. 질식시키다

obsolete a. 쓸모없게 된, 케케묵은

concoct v. 혼합하여 만들다, 조작하다

record-holding a. 기록적인, 기록을 보유한

highlight v. 강렬한 빛을 비추다, 눈에 띄게 하다

formula n. (일정한) 방식, 처리법

07

가정용 자율주행 차량들(AV)이 아이들을 학교로, 학교에서 집까지, 어른들을 직장, 쇼핑몰, 영화관, 술집, 레스토랑으로, 또 집까지, 노인들을 진료실로, 또 진료실에서 집까지 데려다줄 것이다. 어떤 사람들에게는 차량 소유는 과거의 일이 될 것이다. 우버나 리프트와 같은 승차이용 서비스의 비용은 더 이상 인간 운전자들이 필요하지 않게 되면서 폭락할 것이기 때문이다. 자율주행을 통해 80%의 비용이 절감될 수 있다고 낙관론자들은 말한다. 고객이 언제든지 사용할 수 있는 교통의 신세계에 오신 것을 환영한다.

이 모든 것들이 언젠가는 눈앞에 펼쳐질지 모른다. 그러나 그것들은 일론 머스크(Elon Musk)와 같은 사람들의 열정에도 불구하고 곧 그렇게 될 것 같지는 않다. 이 테슬라의 사장은 자율주행 차량이 목적지까지 데려다줄 때까지 사람들이 차 안에서 낮잠을 자는 것이 2년 안에 가능하다고 말한다. 머스크는 이전의 일반적 통념을 거부하고, 비평가들과 반대자들이 틀렸다는 것을 입증해 보였다. 그러나 이 경우에는, 거친 공학의 힘으로 해결하기에는 힘든 너무 많은 장애물이 앞에 놓여 있다. 자율주행 차량이 언제 어디서나 어떤 조건에서든 사람들을 수송할 수 있고, 인간 운전자보다 더 안정적이고 안전하게 운행할 수 있기까지 10~20년이나 걸릴 수 있다.

배터리 구동 차량처럼 단순한 것도 스스로 틈새시장을 개척하는 데 얼마나 오랜 시간이 걸렸는지 생각해보라. 몇 십 년이 지난 지금도 대부분의 국가에서 하이브리드차와 전기차는 신차 판매의

ferry v. 나르다, 수송하다

ride-hailing n. 승차이용 서비스 호출

tumble v. 가격이 폭락하다

on demand 요구만 있으면 (언제든지)

naysayer n. 반대론자, 비관론자

amenable a. 고분고분한

brute-force a. 주먹구구식의, 억지스러운

carve (out) a niche 분야[틈새시장]를 개척하다

feasibly ad. 실행할 수 있게

2%를 넘지 못하고 있다. 배터리 가격과 저장 용량은 이제야 비로소 판매가 현실 가능한 수준에 도달하고 있다. 그러나 가장 낙관적인 가정 아래에서도(예를 들어, 전기 차량이 전체 신차 판매의 절반을 차지한다는) 미국 도로의 차량 절반을 차지하기까지는 빨라야 2035년이 될 것이다. 완전 자율주행 차량 역시 길고도 굽이진 도로를 마주할 것으로 예상된다.

1 ③ ▶ **단락 나누기**
자율주행 차량에 대한 낙관적 기대가 서술되고 있는 부분이 Ⓑ 앞까지이다. 이후 Ⓓ 앞까지 이에 대해 회의적인, 신중한 혹은 보수적 견해가 소개되고 있으며 Ⓓ 이후에는 그것에 대한 비근한 예로 전기차 상용화가 얼마나 늦어지고 있는지를 예시하고 있다.

2 ④ ▶ **내용파악**
저자는 자율주행 자동차가 곧 상용화될 것으로 낙관하는 일부 견해에 회의적이므로 ④가 정답이다. ③과 관련하여 필자가 말하는 것은 '우버와 같은 승차이용 서비스들을 사용하는 비용이 폭락할 것이다'는 것이지 '우버와 같은 회사들이 파산할 것이다'는 것은 아니다.

08

레이저 광선은 일반적인 광선과는 다르다. 일반적인 광선은 비간섭성 광선이라 불리는 파동으로 이루어져 있다. 이것은 파동들이 각기 다른 주파수를 가지고 있다는 것을 의미한다. 그것들은 모두 혼재되어 있고, 광선의 파동들은 사방팔방 흩어진다. 이와 반대로, 레이저에 의해 만들어지는 광선은 응집된다. 이것은 파동들이 평행하며, 크기와 주파수가 같고, 각각의 광선 파동이 바로 이웃해 있는 것과 밀접해 있다는 것을 의미한다. 파동들이 흩어지지 않고 장거리를 이동하기 때문에, 레이저는 장거리 통신에서 많은 쓰임새가 있다.
라디오파는 미터로, 텔레비전파는 인치로 측정되는 반면, 레이저파는 수십만 분의 일 인치 단위로 측정된다. 파장이 짧으면 짧을수록 전송될 수 있는 정보의 양은 더욱 커지므로 레이저는 많은 양의 메시지를 전송하기 위해 사용될 수 있다.
정보의 전송 이외에도 레이저는 많은 쓰임새가 있으며, 현재 과학자들은 더욱 많은 사용처를 발견하고 있다. 가장 주목할 만한 사용처 중의 하나는 무혈 수술의 시행이다. 레이저 광선은 매우 강력해서 고통 없이 사마귀와 주름들을 태워 버릴 수 있으며, 강력한 열로 혈관을 봉합할 수 있다. 안과의사들은 분리된 망막을 제자리에 용접하고, 백내장을 제거하기 위해 레이저를 사용한다. 치과의사들은 고통 없이 치아에 구멍을 뚫기 위해 레이저를 사용할 수 있다.

1 ③ ▶ **빈칸완성**
레이저 광선은 일반적인 광선과는 다르다고 했으며, 첫 번째 빈칸 앞에 일반적인 광선에 대한 내용이 언급되었으므로, 첫 번째 빈칸에는 일반적인 광선과는 다르다는 내용이 나오도록 '이와 반대로'라는 내용이 와야 할 것이다. 따라서 첫 번째 빈칸에는 On the other hand와 In contrast가 적절하다. 레이저의 정보전송에 관한 용도가 나온 다음, 의학적인 용도가 나오므로 두 번째 빈칸에는 besides(~외에도)가 들어가는 것이 적절하다. 따라서 두 빈칸에 적절한 ③이 정답이다. ① 같은 맥락에서 — ~에 더하여 ② ~외에도 — 같은 수준에서 ④ 그에 반해서 — ~에 관하여 ⑤ ~외에도 — ~외에도

2 ④ ▶ **내용일치**
① 라디오파는 레이저파와 비교했을 때 더 긴 주파수를 가지고 있다. ② 일반적인 빛의 파동들은 사방팔방 흩어진다고 했다. ③ 현재 과학자들이 레이저의 더 많은 사용처를 발견하고 있다고 했다. ⑤ 레이저가 만들어내는 파동은 주파수가 같다고 했다. ④ 레이저의 단점에 대해서는 본문에 언급되지 않았으므로 ④가 정답이다.

---

incoherent a. 흩어져 있는, 응집하지 않은
frequency n. 주파수
run off 떠나다, 도망치다
coherent a. 응집하는, 서로 밀착된; 논리적인
parallel a. 평행의
disperse v. 흩어지다
wavelength n. 주파수, 파동
transmit v. 전송하다
beam n. 광선
wart n. 사마귀
wrinkle n. 주름
seal v. 봉합하다
blood vessel 혈관
oculist n. 안과의사
weld v. 용접하다
detached a. 분리된
retina n. 망막
cataract n. 백내장

09

기술에 기반을 둔 노동은 더 많은 일자리가 디지털 기술에 의해서 대체됨에 따라 변화하고 있다. 두세 가지만 예로 들면 Uber, Airbnb, Legal Zoom 그리고 TurboTax 등과 같은 소프트웨어, 앱 그리고 온라인 기술은 이미 많은 직종들에 충격을 주고 있다. 온라인 쇼핑은 수 만 개에 달하는 소매업 일자리를 없앴다. 그리고 자율주행 차량의 발전이 진전됨에 따라, 얼마나 많은 택시 업종, 트럭 업종, 신속배달 업종 등과 관련된 일자리들이 — 심지어 항공관련 일자리까지 — 전화교환수의 전철을 밟게 될 지에 대해 그 누구도 알 수 없는 상황이다.

만일 역사가 믿을 수 있는 가이드라면, 적지 않은 직종에서 일자리를 없애고 있는 기술들은 다른 일자리를 만들어 낼 것이다: 21세기가 요구하는 일자리는 주로 디지털 기술과 관련된 것들이다. 예를 들어 산업용 로봇의 폭발적 증가는 조립라인에서 일하는 수천 개의 일자리를 사라지게 할 것이다. 그러나 동시에 그와 같은 현상은 이러한 기계들을 설계하고, 제조하고, 프로그램을 짜고 유지할 수 있는 사람들에 대한 수요도 만들어 낼 것이다. 문제는, 이러한 현상이 일자리에 미치는 최종적인 순영향이 무엇이 될 것이냐 하는 것과, 4차 산업혁명을 향해 가고 있는 지금 우리 학교가 이들 새롭고 높은 기술을 요구하는 일자리에 우리 젊은이들이 적응할 수 있도록 하는 교육 프로그램을 얼마나 잘 갖추고 있느냐 하는 것이다.

이에 대한 대부분의 평가는 대단히 실망스러운 것이다. 대부분의 학교들은 기술적 흐름에 보조를 맞출 수 있는 자원들을 결여하고 있다. 학교들은 로봇 실험실, 3D프린터, (소프트웨어) 코드 쓰기 과정 등을 가지고 있지 않다. 미국만이 이러한 문제에 직면한 유일한 나라는 아니다. 영국중앙은행이 자동화 때문에 1천 5백만 개 이상의 일자리가 영국에서 사라질 것이라고 발표했음에도 불구하고 영국의 학교들은 디지털 시대에 대비해 젊은이들을 교육시키는 데 있어서 미국보다 더 나은 위치에 서 있지 않다. the Edge Foundation이라는 한 주도적인 영국의 연구기관에 따르면, "영국의 미래 노동력은 설계와 컴퓨터 사용과 같은 분야에서의 기술적 전문성을 필요로 할 뿐 아니라 그 외에도 유연성, 공감능력, 창의성, 야망 등, 로봇이 대신할 수 없는 기술도 필요로 하게 될 것이다."라고 한다.

1 ⑤ ▶ **동의어**
go the way of는 '~의 전철을 밟다'의 의미를 가지고 있으므로 ⑤가 적절하다. ① 미로에 빠지다 ② 새로운 분야를 개척하다 ③ 성장을 저해하다 ④ 제멋대로 하다

2 ① ▶ **부분이해**
3D프린트, 로봇, 자율주행 차량, 디지털화는 4차 산업혁명의 특징으로 본문에 나와 있다. 하지만 internal combustion engine(내연기관)은 2차 산업혁명의 총아다.

3 ③ ▶ **단락 나누기**
이 글은 기술에 기반을 둔 노동은 많은 일자리를 없애고 있다고 설명한 다음, B 이런 기술들은 다른 일자리를 만들어 낼 것이지만 문제는 학교가 이런 일자리에 적응할 수 있는 교육프로그램을 갖추고 있느냐 하는 것이라 설명하고, D 대부분의 학교들이 이런 기술적 흐름에 보조를 맞출 수 있는 자원을 가지고 있지 않은 것에 관해 설명하고 있다.

displace v. 대신하다, 대체하다
to name a few 두서너 가지 예만 들면
on the way 진행되어; 도중에
aviation n. 비행, 항공; 비행[항공]술
net a. 순이익의, 공제할 것을 공제한 후에
assessment n. 평가, 가치 평가
disheartening a. 낙심시키는 (듯한)
plus prep. ~외에도, ~를 덧붙여

10

과학이론은 반복되는 실험으로 뒷받침된 어떤 가설이나 일련의 가설들을 요약한 것이다. 만일 어떤 가설을 뒷받침하기 위한 충분한 증거가 축적되면, 그 가설은 과학적 연구법에 있어 이론으로 알려진 다음 단계로 넘어가며 어떤 현상의 타당한 설명으로 인정을 받게 된다. 비과학적인 상황에 쓰일 경우, '이론'이라는 단어는 입증되지 않거나 추측에 근거한 어떤 것이라는 것을 암시한다. 그러나 과학에 쓰일 경우, 이론은 특히 자연현상들을 설명하고 예측하는 데 도움을 주는 일반적인 원칙으로 시험해 보고 확인된 관찰, 실험 작업, 그리고 추론에 기초한 어떤 설명이나 모델이다.

어떤 과학이론이든 간에 과학이론은 사실을 꼼꼼하면서도 논리적으로 조사한 것에 기초해야 한다. 과학적 연구법에서, 관찰되고[관찰되거나] 측정될 수 있는 사실들과 그 사실들에 대한 과학자들의 설명과 해석인 이론들 간에는 분명한 차이가 존재한다. 과학자들은 실험과 관찰의 결과에 대해 다양한 해석을 내릴 수 있지만, 과학적 연구법의 주춧돌인 사실들은 변하지 않는다.

summarize v. 요약하다
hypothesis n. 가설, 가정
support v. 지탱하다, 지지하다
repeated a. 되풀이된
accumulate v. 모으다, 축적하다
valid a. 근거가 확실한, 정당한; 타당한
explanation n. 설명, 해설
speculative a. 이론적인; 사색적인
observation n. 관찰, 주목

과학이론은 관찰 결과가 들어 있는 주장들을 포함하고 있어야 한다. 뉴턴의 중력이론과 같이 훌륭한 이론은 통일성이 있는데, 이것은 훌륭한 이론이 광범위한 과학적 상황에 적용될 수 있는 소수의 문제해결 전략들로 구성되어 있음을 의미한다. 훌륭한 이론의 또 다른 특징은 훌륭한 이론이 독립적으로 검사될 수 있는 많은 가설로부터 형성되었다는 것이다.

과학이론은 과학적인 연구법의 최종적인 결과물은 아니다. 이론들은 가설과 마찬가지로 입증되거나 거부될 수 있다. 이론들은 더 많은 정보가 수집됨에 따라 개선되거나 부분 수정될 수 있어서 예측의 정확성은 오랜 시간을 거치면서 더욱 커지게 된다. 이론들은 또한 과학적 지식을 발전시키고 축적된 정보를 실용화시키기 위한 기초이다. 과학자들은 이론들을 이용하여 발명품을 개발하거나 질병의 치료제를 찾는다.

1 ② ▶ 글의 제목
이 글은 과학이론이 무엇인가에 관한 전반적인 설명을 다루고 있으므로 ② '과학이론의 충분한 이해'가 글의 제목으로 적절하다.

2 ④ ▶ 빈칸완성
빈칸이 들어있는 문장은 바로 앞 문장의 예시문장이다. 따라서 빈칸에는 과학적 지식을 발전시키고 축적된 정보를 실용화시키는 것과 관련된 말이 들어가야 하므로 ④가 정답이다.

11

'사이비 과학'을 말하면 점성술학, 골상학, 우생학, UFO학 등 다수의 학설이 금방 떠오를 것이다. 이러한 학설들은 공통점이 있는가? 일부는 과학계에 문외한인 사람들이 옹호하고 있는 반면, 어떤 학설들은 엘리트들에 의해 지지를 받았다. 각 학설의 지위는 시간에 따라 수시로 변할 수 있다. 예를 들어, 점성술학은 고대부터 르네상스까지 자연과학 지식의 본보기 영역으로 간주되었다. 수천 년 동안 철학자들은 합당한 지식의 영역과 그렇지 않은 영역 사이에 경계를 확립하고자 노력하였다. 저명한 철학자 칼 포퍼(Karl Popper)는 과학과 사이비 과학을 구별하는 탐구를 설명하기 위해 '구획의 문제'라는 용어를 만들었다. 1953년의 강의에서 칼 포퍼가 주장했듯이, "어떤 이론의 과학적 지위에 대한 기준은 반증가능성이다." 다른 말로 하자면, 한 이론이 어떤 실증적 조건들이 그 이론을 반증할 것인지를 명확히 나타내고 있다면 그 이론은 과학적이지만, 그렇지 않다면 사이비 과학이다. 이는 충분히 분명해 보인다. 불행하게도, 그것은 효과가 없다. 이론에 대한 반증이 이루어진 때를 어떻게 알 수 있을까? 질량 분석계를 이용하여 어떤 특정한 주장을 실험하고 있고, 일치하지 않은 결과를 얻는다고 가정해 보아라. 그 이론은 반증될 수 있거나 질량 분석계가 고장 난 것일 수도 있다. 과학자들은 사실상 온 천지의 오류가 있는 이론들을 탈락시키면서 반박가능성 탐지기를 가지고 이론을 찾지 않는다. 오히려 과학자들은 그들이 사용한 도구들, 기타 가능성 있는 설명, 대안적인 자료 등을 감안한다. 어떤 이론을 거짓이라고 하는 것은 칼 포퍼가 생각했던 것 보다 훨씬 더 복잡하며, 원론적으로 무엇이 반박가능한가를 정하는 것은 상당히 혼란스럽다.

1 ④ ▶ 글의 제목
과학과 사이비 과학의 구분하는 기준을 소개하고 이에 대한 한계를 설명하고 있으므로 ④ '과학으로부터 사이비 과학을 구별하는 데 있어서의 불확실성'이 적절한 제목이다.

2 ① ▶ 빈칸완성
빈칸 이후 앞서 설명한 기준이 아닌 다른 접근 방식, 즉 단순히 반증가능성 뿐만 아니라 이론을 반증하는 데 사용된 도구의 정확성 및 대안적인 해설을 고려함을 소개하고 있으므로 연결어로서 '도리어' 또는 '그렇기는커녕'이 자연스럽다. ② 운 좋게; 다행이도 ③ 게다가 ④ 그럼에도 불구하고 ⑤ 그 결과로서

3 ⑤ ▶ 내용일치
마지막 부분에서 과학자들은 단순히 반증가능성만으로 과학과 사이비 과학을 구별하지 않고 대안적인 설명을 찾거나 사용된 도구를 검증하는 등 보다 복잡한 도구를 취하므로, ⑤ "과학자들은 이론의 정당성을 검증하는 데 흑백 논리적 접근을 취하지 않는다."라는 것을 알 수 있다.

12

톰(Tom)은 기차 시간에 늦었고 기차역까지 가는 길을 모른다. 모퉁이를 뛰듯이 돌고나서 그는 사진을 찍고 그 사진을 인스타그램이나 페이스북에 올리는 관광객들로 가득한 광장과 마주친다. 그는 어느 길로 가야만 하는 것일까? 그는 인터넷과 연결된 그의 콘택트렌즈에 지도를 올려달라고 명령하면서, 기차 티켓과 역의 플랫폼 정보를 띄우기 위해 그의 스마트 워치를 두드린다. 기차가 출발하기까지 15분밖에 남아 있지 않다는 경고 문구가 (스마트 안경의) 렌즈의 가장자리에 번쩍이며 나타난다. 그러나 (역까지 가는) 지도는 올라오지 않는다. 그는 당황해서 주변을 둘러보며 거리의 웅성거림 속에서 그의 (스마트 안경의) 렌즈를 향해 지도 올리기를 새롭게 업데이트할 것을 몹시 흥분해서 명령한다.

우리 몸에 착용하는 것이 가능한 전자제품들이 일상화된 혼란스러운 미래에 온 것을 환영한다. 이들 전자장비들은 현실에서의 삶과 디지털적인 삶을 매끄럽게 이어준다고 약속한다. 이러한 전자장비들은 현재 빠르게 기하급수적으로 증가하고 있는 중이다. 그리고 5년 안에, 5억 개 이상의 전자장비들이 인간의 몸에 채워지거나 심어지게 될 것이다. 오늘날, 가장 친숙한 전자장비는 피트니스 트래커(몸의 건강상태를 추적하는 장치)와 스마트 워치인데, 이들 전자장비들은 건강을 모니터링하고 온라인 서비스에 빠르게 접근하는 것을 가능하게 해준다. 그러나 이미 모니터링 기능 이상의 것을 하는 전자장비들도 시중에 나와 있다. 그런 장비로는 착용자가 당혹스러운 상태가 되었을 때 경고 신호를 보내주는 헤드 밴드와 금연을 하고자 하는 흡연자에게 전기 충격을 가하는 손목 밴드 등이 있다. 전자회사들은 증상을 치료하거나 건강을 관리할 수 있는 착용 가능한 전자장비들을 이용해서 의학을 변모시키겠다고 약속한다. 간질병 환자의 초기 발작을 경고해주고, 불안발작의 예방을 도와주고, 시각장애인들이 길을 찾을 수 있게 해주는 전자장비들이 등장하고 있다. 그러나 착용 가능한 전자장비들의 잠재성은 상당 부분을 전자장비들이 접근하고 만들어내는 많은 양의 데이터에 의존한다. 그리고 이것은 연구자들과 기술개발자들이 해결하기 위해 애쓰고 있는 두 가지 문제를 야기한다. 그 두 가지 문제란 착용 가능한 전자장비로부터 나오고 들어가는 데이터를 전송하는 향상된 방법을 발견하는 것과 그 모든 정보를 안전하게 보호하는 것이다.

1 ③ ▶ **글의 주제**
이 글은 착용 가능한 스마트 전자장비의 현황과 전망 그리고 문제점 등을 두루 다루고 있다.

2 ④ ▶ **부분이해**
글의 흐름 속에서 refresh는 컴퓨터가 데이터를 업데이트한다는 의미로 사용되고 있다.

3 ④ ▶ **내용추론**
① 착용 가능한 스마트 전자장비의 수요가 계속 늘어날 것으로 전망되기 때문에 global mobile-data traffic의 양은 커질 것이다. ② 보안 문제는 착용 가능한 스마트 전자장비가 직면하고 있는 두 가지의 큰 문제들 가운데 하나다. ③ 본문에서 전혀 언급되고 있지 않다. ④ 간질병 환자의 초기 발작을 경고해주고, 불안발작의 예방을 도와주고, 시각장애인들이 길을 찾을 수 있게 해주는 착용 가능한 전자장비들이 등장하고 있다고 했으므로 적절하다.

---

refresh v. 새롭게 하다, 원기를 회복하다
clamour n. 떠들썩함, 부르짖음
chaotic a. 혼돈된; 무질서한, 혼란한
seamlessly ad. 이음매가 없이, 균일하게
gadget n. 간단한 기계 장치
multiply v. 늘다; 증식하다
epilepsy n. 간질병
incipient a. 초기의
seizure n. 몰수; 장악; 발작
blind a. 눈먼

13

만화책에 나오는 슈퍼 히어로가 현실에 존재할 수 있을까? 과학 개념이 만화에 적용되는 방식을 연구하는 한 물리학 교수에 따르면, 슈퍼맨은 실제로 존재할 가능성이 매우 유력한 편에 속한다. 오늘날 우리가 알고 있는, 하늘을 날고 눈에서 광선이 나오는 슈퍼맨이 아니라, 1938년에 처음 모습을 드러냈을 때의 슈퍼맨이 그러하다고 미네소타 대학의 제임스 카카리오스(James Kakalios) 박사는 말하고 있다. 제리 시겔(Jerry Siegel)과 조 셔스터(Joe Shuster)는 지구인과 다른 생리 기능을 갖고 있어서 총알이 피부를 관통하지 못하고, 15명의 힘을 갖고 있고, '한 번에 고층건물 사이'를 (날아서가 아니라) 뛰어서 넘을 수 있는, 로켓 추진 능력을 가진 외계에서 도망쳐온 아이를 상상했다. 오늘날의 슈퍼맨은 '태양'에서 힘을 얻지만, 원조 슈퍼맨의 힘은 자신이 태어난 행성에서부터 얻은 것이었다. 카카리오스에 따르면, 중력이 엄청나게 센 소형 행성은, 환경적 요인들에 적

---

nominee n. 지명된 사람, 추천된 사람
refugee n. 난민; 도망자, 망명인
alien a. 외국의; 이질적인; 우주의
physiology n. 생리학; 생리 기능
gravity n. 중력, 지구인력
adaptation n. 적응, 적합, 순응
factor n. 요소, 요인
gravitational a. 중력의

응한 결과 지구의 낮은 중력 하에서는 초인적인 힘을 가지는 존재를 만들어낼 수 있다. 하지만 그러한 존재를 생겨나게 하는 그 행성의 능력은 궁극적으로는 그 행성을 파괴되도록 할 것이다. 그 행성의 중력 붕괴는, 물론 허구적인 것이긴 해도, 슈퍼맨이 지구로 오게 한 결과를 가져온 행성의 죽음과 매우 유사할 것이다.

collapse n. 붕괴, 와해
planetary a. 행성의
fictionally ad. 허구로, 소설적으로

1 ③ ▶ 내용일치
오늘날 우리가 알고 있는 슈퍼맨은 하늘을 날고, 눈에서 광선이 나오지만, 1938년에 처음 모습을 드러낸 원조 슈퍼맨은 총알이 피부를 관통하지 못하고, 15명의 힘을 갖고 있고, 한 번에 고층건물 사이를 뛰어서 넘을 수 있는 정도의 능력을 가지고 있었다.

2 ④ ▶ 내용파악
카카리오스 박사는 원조 슈퍼맨의 능력을 가진 사람의 존재 가능성을 높게 보고 있으므로, 세 번째 문장의 내용을 참고하면 ⓐ는 해당되지 않음을 알 수 있다. 15명의 힘을 갖고 있다고 했으므로 ⓑ는 옳은 진술이며, 고층건물 사이를 날아가서가 아니라 뛰어서 넘을 수 있다고 했으므로 ⓒ도 옳은 설명이다. 따라서 정답은 ④가 된다.

3 ⑤ ▶ 내용파악
"중력이 엄청나게 큰 행성은, 환경적 요인들에 적응한 결과 지구의 낮은 중력 하에서는 초인적인 힘을 가지는 존재를 만들어낼 수 있다."라는 부분이 초인적 존재의 가능성을 이론적으로 설명하고 있는 곳에 해당한다.

14

과학이 대중들에게 제시되는 세 가지 주된 방법이 있다. 첫 번째 방법은 단순한 대중화로 대개 과학의 발견들과 그 응용이라는 과학의 내용과 관련된 것이다. 이것은 대중들의 선풍적인 반응을 일으키고 싶어 하는 언론기자들의 욕망에 시달리게 되는데, 이것이 생각하는 문외한들의 머리에는 과학을 경시하는 생각을 심어주고 무비판적인 사람들에게는 터무니없는 독단적 태도를 발생시킨다. 두 번째 방법은 간접적인 것이며 과학자가 아닌 인물의 저술에서, 특히 현대의 철학, 종교, 심리학 문헌에서 과학 이론들을 참조하는 것으로 이루어진다. 이런 책의 저자들은 과학자가 아니어서, 과학에 대한 정보를 일반적으로 대중적인 저술에서 얻는다. 그리고 만일 그들의 책에 들어 있는 과학이 부정확하거나 의도적으로 왜곡되어 있으면, 그 잘못은 그들에게 정확한 정보를 제공하지 못했거나 열띤 논쟁으로 그들의 실수를 바로잡아주지 못한 과학자들에게 있는 것이다.

과학 대중화의 세 번째이자 가장 중요한 부류의 주역은 그 시대의 철학, 정치, 종교 등의 더 넓은 문제들과 관련하여 자신의 과학에 대해 이따금씩 글을 쓰는 저명한 과학자들이다. 그들이 중요한 이유는 그들은 옳든 그르든 과학을 대변하고 있는 것으로 간주되고 그들이 대변하는 과학은 대다수 사람들에게 분명 권위 있는 것으로 여겨지며 그들이 바로 그런 권위의 소유자이기 때문이다. 바로 그들의 저술을 고려해봄으로써 우리는 과학과 다른 사고방식 사이의 조화가 어떻게 해서 생겨났는지를 이해할 수 있는 것이다.

sensation n. 물의, 화제; 선풍적인 인기
cheapen v. 경시하다, 얕보다
layman n. 문외한; 속인, 평신도
unreasoning a. 생각이 없는, 터무니없는
dogmatism n. 독단주의; 독단적인 태도
tendentiously ad. 편향되게; 의도적으로
twist v. 왜곡하다
polemic n. 논쟁
eminent a. 저명한, 유명한
speak for 대변하다

1 ③ ▶ 내용파악
저널리스트들이 선정적인 목적에서 이 방법을 사용하여 문외한에게는 과학이 값싼 것이라는 잘못된 생각을 심어주고 무비판적인 사람들에게는 터무니없는 독단이라는 잘못된 태도를 심어준다. 따라서 ③이 정답이다. ① 과학의 내용과 관련된 것이다. ② 주로 저널리스트들이 사용한다. ④ 이 방법에서 과학자가 연구에 도움을 받는 점은 없다.

2 ② ▶ 내용추론
두 번째 단락 마지막 문장에서 잘못은 과학자에게 있다고 했다고 했으므로 ②는 추론할 수 없는 진술이다. ① 두 번째 단락 첫 번째 문장에 언급되어 있다. ③ 두 번째 단락 첫 번째 문장에 언급되어 있다. ④ 두 번째 단락 마지막 부분에 언급되어 있다.

3 ① ▶ 내용추론
더 넓은 문제와 관련하여 과학에 대한 책을 쓰려면 다른 분야에서 어떤 일이 일어나고 있는지 관심을 가져야 할 것이므로 ①이 추론 가능한 언급이다. ④ 권위 있는 것으로 인식되어서이지 권위주의자여서가 아니다.

15

Ⓐ 이러한 데이터의 풍요는 경쟁의 본질을 변화시키고 있다. 대형 기술업체들은 언제나 네트워크 효과에서 이익을 창출해왔다. 페이스북에 사용자들이 더 많이 가입할수록 다른 사람들도 페이스북 가입에 더 끌리게 된다. 데이터가 있으면 부가적인 네트워크 효과들이 생겨난다. 더 많은 데이터를 수집할수록 그 기업은 자사의 제품을 향상시킬 수 있는 여지가 더 넓어지고, 이는 다시 더 많은 사용자들을 유인하고, 더 많은 데이터를 발생시키는 식이다. 테슬라가 자율주행 차량들로부터 더 많은 데이터를 모을수록, 그 회사는 자율주행 차량들을 더 잘 만들 수 있다. 이것이 1분기 2만5천 대의 차량을 판매했을 뿐인 이 회사의 가치가 230만 대를 판 GM보다 더 높은 이유 중의 하나다. 데이터라는 거대한 저수지가 방어용 해자 역할을 톡톡히 하는 것이다.

Ⓑ 데이터에 대한 접근은 또한 경쟁기업들로부터 기업을 또 다른 방식으로 지켜준다. 기술 산업에서 경쟁에 관해 낙관하는 근거는 차고에서 시작한 신생 기업이나 예상치 못한 기술적 격변으로 인해 기존 기업들이 힘도 못써보고 당할 가능성에 있다. 하지만 데이터 시대에는 이 두 가지 가능성 모두 대단히 낮다. 거대기업들의 감시 시스템은 경제 전역에 걸쳐 있다. 구글은 사람들이 무엇을 검색하는 지를, 페이스북은 사람들이 무엇을 공유하는 지를, 아마존은 사람들이 무엇을 구매하는 지를 보고 있다. 그들은 자체 앱스토어와 운영체제를 가졌으며 신생 기업들에게 연산 능력을 대여해준다. 그들은 자신의 시장은 물론 그 너머에서 벌어지는 일들까지 살펴보는 "신의 눈"을 가졌다. 그들은 신규 제품이나 서비스가 견인력을 갖기 시작할 때를 눈여겨보면서 그것을 모방하거나 그것이 너무 큰 위협이 되기 전에 아예 그 벼락부자 기업을 사버린다. 많은 사람들은 페이스북이 2014년 60명이 채 안 되는 직원의 메시징 앱 기업 WhatsApp을 220억 달러에 매입한 것이 잠재적 라이벌들을 제거해버리는 "표적 제거식 인수합병"에 해당한다고 본다. 진입장벽과 조기경보 체제를 통해, 데이터는 경쟁 자체를 질식시켜버릴 수 있다.

1 ②   ▶ 앞내용 추론
> Ⓐ 단락의 첫 구절 '데이터의 풍요'라는 표현에 착안한다.

2 ③   ▶ 글의 주제
> 본문은 데이터 시대에 데이터의 방대한 양 자체가 그 기업의 경쟁력이 되고 있음을 진술하고 있다. 그러므로 이 글의 주제는 '그 나름의 독특한 경쟁적 가치를 지닌 데이터 양'이 적절하다.

3 ④   ▶ 내용일치
> "기술 산업에서 경쟁에 관해 낙관하는 근거는 차고에서 시작한 신생 기업이나 예상치 못한 기술적 격변으로 인해 기존 기업들이 힘도 못써보고 당할 가능성에 있다. 하지만 데이터 시대에는 이 두 가지 가능성 모두 대단히 낮다."는 본문의 진술을 참조하면 ④는 잘못된 진술이다.

4 ②   ▶ 빈칸완성
> Ⓐ 단락을 요약하거나, 요지를 담는 문장이 빈칸에 들어가기에 적절하다. 대형 기술업체들은 영업을 통해 더 많은 데이터를 확보하고, 그렇게 얻은 데이터들을 통해 경쟁력을 더욱 강화하고 있다는 것이 Ⓐ 단락의 요지다.

5 ①   ▶ 빈칸완성
> Ⓑ 단락을 요약하거나, 글 전체의 요지를 담는 문장이 빈칸에 들어가기에 적절하다. Ⓑ 단락은 데이터 시대에 대형 기술업체들은 감시, 모방, 인수합병 등을 통해 신생 기업들의 시장 진입과 성장 자체를 막아버리고 있다고 말한다.

---

abundance n. 풍요, 풍부
sign up 가입하다, 등록하다
scope n. 범위, 영역; 여지, 기회
moat n. 호, 해자(성 주위에 둘러 판 못)
startup n. 신규 업체, 신생 기업
garage n. 차고, 주차장
surveillance n. 감시
traction n. 끌기, 견인력
upstart n. 건방진 놈; 벼락부자, 졸부
shoot-out n. 총격전
acquisition n. 기업 인수
stifle v. 질식시키다

09 우주·지구

01

우리가 사는 우주의 기원을 설명한 빅뱅이론(우주 대폭발 이론)은 20세기의 가장 위대한 지적 위업들 중 하나이다. 이 빅뱅이론에 따르면, 약 100억~200억 년 전 우주를 만든 물질이 엄청 단단히 압축되었다고 한다. 빅뱅이라 불리는 어떤 것이 이 압축된 물질을 굉장히 큰 불덩어리로 변화시켰다. 그 물질이 압축된 상태로부터 이동해 멀리 날아감에 따라, 그 물질의 파편들이 서로 달라붙어 은하를 만들었고, 나중에는 항성과 행성을 만들었다. 그 불덩어리에서 날아갔던 물질의 움직임은 오늘날에도 계속되고 있으며, 우주는 팽창하고 있는 것으로 보인다. 이 이론은 도플러 효과를 관측한 것을 바탕으로 정립되었다. 도플러 효과는 발원체가 관찰자로부터 멀어짐에 따라 움직이는 물체에 의해 발산된 복사에너지의 진동수가 줄어든다고 설명한다. 1965년, 지구를 덮고 있는 복사에너지가 만일 우주가 빅뱅으로 시작되었을 경우 예상되는 극초단파의 진동수와 한 치도 틀림없다는 것을 과학자들이 발견하였다. 일부 과학자들은 우주의 팽창이 무한대로 계속될 것이라 생각하는 반면, 다른 과학자들은 아주 먼 미래의 어느 시점에 중력이 붕괴되어 다시 '우주 대수축'이 일어나는 상태가 되어, 압축된 물질상태로 되돌아갈 것이라는 이론을 제시한다.

1 ④　▶ **빈칸완성**
big crunch는 '우주 대수축'이라는 뜻이므로, 빈칸에도 big crunch와 같은 맥락이 되어야 한다. big crunch의 의미를 모를 경우에도 while을 전후로 상반되는 이야기가 나와야 하므로 while 앞에서 우주가 무한대로 팽창할 것이라고 했으므로 while 다음에는 우주가 반대로 '압축된(condensed)' 상태로 되돌아간다고 해야 문맥상 적절하다. 따라서 ④가 정답이다. ① 중립의 ② 증가된 ③ 양성의 ⑤ 음성의

2 ④　▶ **내용일치**
① 도플러 효과는 발원체가 관찰자로부터 더 멀어짐에 따라 어떤 움직이는 물체에 의해 발산되는 복사에너지의 진동수가 줄어든다고 설명한다고 했다. ② 우주의 미래에 대해 일부 과학자들은 계속 팽창할 것이라고 하는 반면, 또 다른 일부 과학자들은 중력이 붕괴되어 대수축을 겪을 것이라는 이론을 제시한다고 했다. ③ 빅뱅이론에 따르면, 약 100억~200억 년 전 우주를 만든 물질이 무한대로 압축되었다고 한다. ⑤ 우리가 사는 우주의 기원을 설명한 빅뱅이론은 20세기의 가장 위대한 지적 위업들 중 하나라고 했다. ④ 빅뱅이론이 도플러 효과를 관측한 것을 바탕으로 정립되었다고 했을 뿐, 도플러 효과가 우리가 사는 우주를 처음으로 만들어낸 것은 아니므로 ④가 정답이다.

origin n. 기원, 근원
turn ~ into ~을 …로 변화시키다, 바꾸다
gigantic a. 거대한, 굉장히 큰
fireball n. 불덩이
set ~ in motion ~을 움직이게 하다, 작동시키다
glue v. 붙이다
galaxy n. 은하
grow out of ~에서 생기다
Doppler effect 도플러 효과(소리나 빛이 발원체에서 나와 발원체와 상대적 운동을 하는 관측자에게 도착했을 때 진동수에 차이가 나는 현상)
radiation n. 방사선, 복사에너지
give off 방출하다, 발산하다
moving body 움직이는 물체
source n. 원천, 근원; 발원체
get further 더 멀리 가다[도달하다]
bathe v. (빛 등으로) 둘러싸다, 덮다
microwave a. 마이크로파의, 극초단파의
to infinity 무한히, 무한대로
big crunch 우주 대수축

02

포인트 니모(Point Nemo)는 공식적으로 '해양도달불능점'으로 알려져 있으며, 더 간단히 말하자면, 육지에서 가장 멀리 떨어진 바다의 지점이다. 남위 48도 52.6분, 서경 123도 23.6분(48°52.6′S, 123°23.6′W)에 위치한 이 지점은 사면팔방으로 1,000마일 이상의 바다로 둘러싸인 문자 그대로 외떨어진 곳이다. 이 지점에서 가장 가까운 육지로는 북쪽에는 핏케언 제도, 북동쪽으로는 이스터섬, 남쪽으로는 남극의 해안에서 떨어진 한 섬이 있다.
분명히, 포인트 니모 근처에는 어떠한 사람도 살고 있지 않다. ('니모(Nemo)'라는 이름 자체가 라틴어로 '아무도 없다'는 뜻이며, 쥘 베른(Jule Verne)의 『해저 2만리(20,000 Leagues Under The Sea)』에 등장하는 잠수함 선장을 언급하는 것이기도 하다.) 실제로 그 지역은 너무 고립되어 있어 니모에서 가장 가까운 곳에 사는 사람들은 실제로 지구상에 있지도 않다. 포인트 니모에 가장 가까운 사람이 거주하는 지역은 1,000마일 이상 떨어져 있기 때문에, 우주에 있는 인간이 육지에 있는 인간보다 도달불능점에 훨씬 더 가까이에 있다.
인간이 아닌 서식동물 또한 포인트 니모 주변에 많지 않다. 그 좌표(니모의 위치)는 영양분이 풍부한 물이 실제로 그 지역으로 유입되는 것을 막는 거대한 회전 해류인 남태평양 소용돌이 안에 실제

landmass n. 광대한 토지, 대륙
pole n. 장대, 기둥
coordinate n. 좌표
South Pacific Gyre 남태평양 소용돌이(지구 자전 해류 시스템의 일부이며, 북쪽은 적도, 서쪽은 오스트레일리아, 남쪽은 남극해류, 동쪽은 남미로 둘러싸인 소용돌이)
inhabited a. (사람·동물이) 사는, 거주하는

로 위치해 있다. 어떤 식량원도 없어서 (해저의 화산 분출구 근처에 사는 박테리아와 작은 게들 말
고는) 바다의 이런 곳에서 생명을 유지하는 것이 불가능하다.

1 ③   ▶ **내용파악**
마지막 단락에서 인간이 아닌 서식동물 또한 포인트 니모 주변에는 많지 않다고 했는데,
포인트 니모가 영양이 풍부한 물이 유입되는 것을 막는 해류인 남태평양 소용돌이 안에
위치해 있다고 했으므로 멸종위기의 해양 동물마저 생명을 유지하는 것이 불가능할 것
이므로 ③이 정답이다.

2 ①   ▶ **내용파악**
두 번째 단락 마지막 부분에서 포인트 니모에서 가장 가까운 곳에 사는 사람들은 실제로
지구상에 있지도 않으며, 이곳에서 가장 가까운 사람이 거주하는 지역은 1,000마일 이
상 떨어져 있기 때문에, 우주에 있는 인간이 육지에 있는 사람들보다 도달불능점에 훨씬
더 가까이 있다고 했으므로 ① '우주비행사'가 정답이다. ② 해양학자 ③ 잠수함 승무원
④ 원주민

03

바이킹 신화에 따르면, 스콜(Skoll)과 하티(Hati)라 불리는 늑대 두 마리가 해나 달을 잡고 있을 때
일식이나 월식이 일어난다고 한다. 일식 혹은 월식이 일어나면, 사람들은 늑대가 겁을 먹고 도망가
도록 큰 소리로 떠들어대곤 했다. 일정 시간이 지난 후, 사람들은 자신들이 냄비를 두들기면서 뛰
어 돌아다니는 것과는 상관없이 일식 혹은 월식이 끝났음을 틀림없이 알아차렸을 것이다.
자연의 섭리에 대한 무지로 인해 고대인들은 그들이 사는 세상을 이해하려는 노력의 일환으로 많
은 신화들을 만들어냈다. 그러나 결국, 사람들은 철학, 즉 — 상당한 직관과 함께 — 이성을 사용하
는 것에 의지하여 우주의 신비를 풀려고 했다. 오늘날 우리는 이성, 수학, 실험, 즉 현대 과학을 이
용한다.
앨버트 아인슈타인(Albert Einstein)은 "우주에 관해 가장 이해할 수 없는 점은 우주가 이해할 수
있다는 점이다."라고 말했다. 그의 말은 일진이 나쁜 날의 우리의 집들과는 달리, 우주는 각자 제멋
대로 돌아가는 개별적인 사물들이 단지 모인 것에 불과한 것이 아니고, 우주의 모든 것은 예외 없
이 법칙을 따른다는 의미다. 기묘하게도 우리가 거주할 수 있는 태양계는 '단지 자연의 법칙에 의
해 혼돈에서 생긴 것'이 아니라고 뉴턴(Newton)은 믿었다. 대신, 뉴턴은 우주의 질서는 "처음 조물
주에 의해 창조되었으며, 조물주에 의해 오늘날까지 같은 상태 및 조건으로 보존되었다."라고 주장
했다.

1 ②   ▶ **내용일치**
첫 번째 문단의 내용과 두 번째 문단 첫 번째 문장, 즉 "자연의 섭리에 대한 무지로 인해
고대인들은 그들이 사는 세상을 이해하려는 노력의 일환으로 많은 신화들을 만들어냈
다."라는 내용을 통해, ②가 잘못된 진술임을 알 수 있다.

2 ②   ▶ **부분이해**
밑줄 친 문장 다음에 이어지는 문장에서 그것에 대해 설명하고 있다. "우주의 모든 것은
예외 없이 자연법칙을 따른다."라는 의미라고 했으므로 ②가 정답이다.

3 ④   ▶ **어법상 적절하지 않은 표현 고르기**
ⓒ의 arise는 뒤에 나오는 chaos를 목적어로 받을 수 없는 '자동사'이므로, 이것을 arise
from이나 arise out of로 고쳐야 한다.

mythology n. 신화
eclipse n. 일식, 월식
onset n. 발병; 개시
run around 뛰어 돌아다니다
bang on pots 냄비를 두들기다
ignorance n. 무지, 무식
postulate v. 가정하다, 추정하다
make sense of ~을 이해하다
turn to ~에 의지하다
that is 즉, 좀 더 정확히 말하면
reason n. 이성, 이치
a good dose of 상당량의
intuition n. 직관, 직감
decipher v. (수수께끼 등을) 풀다, 해독하다
incomprehensible a. 이해할 수 없는
conglomeration n. 집합, 모임, 응집
habitable a. 거주할 수 있는
solar system 태양계
arise v. 일어나다, 생기다
maintain v. 주장하다; 지속하다

04

폴리네시아인들은 별이 야간에 항해하고 있는 방향을 정확하게 알려주었기 때문에 나침반이 필요 없었다. 이 뱃사람들은 150개의 별이 뜨고 지는 위치를 알고 있었다. 목적지에 도달하기 위해서 항해자는 그가 가고자 하는 섬 위로 떠오르는 지평선상의 별을 향해서 배를 조종하곤 했다. 별이 폴리네시아인의 나침반이 되는 것처럼, 파도에 의해 형성된 형태는 그가 항해하는 데 있어서 해도 (海圖)가 되었다. 항해자는 파도가 예측 가능한 방식으로 흘러간다는 것을 알았다. 그 규모와 횟수, 방향 모두 귀중한 정보를 주었다. <예를 들어, 섬을 향해 흐르는 물결은 튕겨져 나오면서 대양의 물결과는 구별되는 큰 파도 패턴을 만들게 되었다.> 이러한 형태는 폴리네시아 선원들에게는 하나의 펼쳐진 지도와 같았다. 심지어 어둡고 구름 낀 밤에도, 항해자는 그의 배를 치는 물결의 각도를 보고 그가 항해하고 있는 방향을 알 수 있었다. 새들과 구름이 가득한 대낮의 하늘을 보고도 폴리네시아인들은 확실한 신호를 얻을 수 있었다. 몇몇 바닷새들은 둥지를 튼 섬에서 떠나 낮에는 해양에서 사냥을 하고 밤에는 돌아오는 것으로 알려져 있다. 저녁에 이러한 새들을 본 선원들은 새들을 따라 섬으로 가거나 아침에 보면 이들과 반대 방향으로 항해할 줄 알 수 있었다. 육지는 바다보다 따뜻하기 때문에 섬 위에 형성된 구름은 해양 위에 형성된 구름과는 달랐다. 육지 위에 있는 구름은 크고 정지해 있는 반면, 해양 위에 있는 구름은 보통 더 작고 바람에 의해 움직였다. 그러므로 크고 정지해 있는 구름의 모습은 항해자에게 또 다른 확실한 지표였다. 또한, 바닥이 푸른빛이 도는 구름을 보면 폴리네시아인들은 구름이 얕은 물 위에 있다는 것을 알 수 있었다.

1 ②　▶ **문장삽입**
이 글의 주제는 폴리네시아인들이 항해에 활용하는 여러 가지 자연의 지표들이다. 별, 파도, 바닷새, 구름이 언급되었는데, 제시문은 '파도'와 관련된 내용이므로 ⒝에 들어가는 것이 가장 적절하다.

2 ②　▶ **내용파악**
맑은 밤에는 별을 보고, 어둡고 구름 낀 밤에는 물결을 보고 방향을 안다고 했지만, 폭풍우가 거센 바다에서 방향을 찾는 방법은 언급되지 않았다.

---

unerring a. 잘못이 없는, 틀림없는

destination n. 목적지, 도착지

steer v. 조종하다

navigational chart 항해용 해도

swell n. 팽창; 큰 파도

unmistakable a. 명백한, 틀림없는

stationary a. 정지한, 움직이지 않는

signpost n. 푯말, 이정표; 명확한 길잡이

shallow a. 얕은

05

나선은하는 원반처럼 생겼으며, 핵으로 알려진 중심부에 오래된 항성들이 불룩할 정도로 모여 있다. 핵은 수소, 이온화된 산소, 질소, 네온, 황, 철 그리고 아르곤과 같은 고온 가스를 포함하고 있다. 전체 (나선) 은하는 밖으로 휘어진 팔을 가진 바람개비를 닮아있다. 나선은하는 보통 팔을 한 개 가지고 있지만, 일부 은하는 2~3개의 팔을 가지고 있다. 은하수 은하는 4개의 팔을 가지고 있다. 나선은하의 팔들은 정상이거나 막대모양이다. 정상 (나선) 은하의 팔들은 핵에서 직접 나오는 반면, 막대나선은 은하계의 가운데를 가로지르는 밝은 항성들이 모여 두꺼운 띠를 형성하고 있다. 팔은 띠의 양쪽 끝에서 발생해서, 은하계 주위에 반원을 형성한다.

나선은하가 어떻게 팔을 형성하도록 진화했으며, 왜 이 팔들이 계속해서 존재하는지는 과학자들에게 수수께끼이다. 은하계가 회전하는 방식은 팔의 모습에 영향을 주어야 한다. 은하계의 핵은 약간 바퀴처럼 회전하는 반면, 팔들은 천천히 뒤따른다. 이 때문에, 몇 번 회전한 뒤에, 팔은 부서지기 시작하면서 꽤 연속적인 별 무리를 만들어 내야 한다. 한 이론은 은하계에서 중력의 차이가 존재하기 때문에 팔은 부서지지 않는다고 주장한다. 이러한 중력의 차이는 먼지와 가스가 밀고 당겨지는 현상을 초래한다. 이런 움직임은 압축파동들을 만든다. 은하계가 회전하기 때문에, 압축파동들은 나선형 궤도로 움직이는 것처럼 보여서, 먼지와 가스가 나선형 팔처럼 보이게 만든다. 이러한 나선형 팔 안에 있는 먼지와 가스가 별이 형성되는 물질인 것이다.

1 ④　▶ **내용추론**
나선형 은하의 핵에는 오래된 항성들이 있다고 했으며, 나선은하의 팔들은 핵에서 직접 나온다고 했으므로, 나선형 은하의 핵에 있는 항성들보다 나선형 은하의 팔에 있는 항성들이 훨씬 젊을 것임을 유추할 수 있으므로 ④가 정답이다.

---

spiral a. 나선형의

galaxy n. 은하

disk n. 원반

bulge n. 툭 튀어 나온 것, 불룩한 것

nucleus n. 핵

contain v. ~이 들어있다, 함유되어 있다

hydrogen n. 수소

ionized a. 이온화된

oxygen n. 산소

nitrogen n. 질소

sulfur n. 황

iron n. 철

pinwheel n. 풍차; 바람개비

Milky Way 은하수, 은하계

bar v. 빗장을 지르다, 가로막대로 폐쇄하다

band n. 띠, 끈; 한 무리 떼

cut through ~을 헤치고 나아가다

tip n. 끝

semi-circle n. 반원

2 ② ▶ **내용추론**

둘째 단락의 첫 문장에서 나선은하가 어떻게 팔을 형성하도록 진화했으며, 왜 이 팔들이 계속해서 존재하는지는 과학자들에게 수수께끼라고 했으므로 ②가 정답이다.

3 ③ ▶ **지시대상**

밑줄 친 Ⓐ의 they는 바로 앞 문장의 compression waves(압축파동)를 가리키므로 ③이 정답이다.

evolve v. 진화하다

puzzling a. 당혹스러운, 어리둥절한

rotate v. 회전하다

gravitational force 중력, 인력

compression wave 압축파동

path n. 궤도

dust n. 먼지

06

생물학자 자크 모노(Jacques Monod)가 말했듯이, 생명은 자연법칙의 보편적 작용이라는 필연을 통해서뿐 아니라 수많은 사건들의 예측 불가능한 개입이라는 우연을 통해서도 진화한다. 우연이 작용한 예는 지구 역사상 여러 차례 있었는데, 수많은 종(種)을 멸절시키고 그렇게 해서 새로운 형태의 생명이 진화할 수 있는 기회를 마련해준 여러 차례의 대량 멸종에서 특히 그러했다. 이런 재앙의 사건들 중 일부는 혜성이나 소행성이 지구와 충돌하여 초래된 것 같으며, 가장 최근의 충돌은 6,500만 년 전에 일어난 것으로, 공룡을 전멸시키고 인류의 먼 조상들이 출현할 기회를 열어준 것이었다. 따라서 과학자들은 지금의 지구와 동일한 외계행성, 즉 태양이 아닌 다른 항성 주위의 궤도를 도는 행성뿐 아니라, 과거의 지구와 유사한 행성도 찾고 있다. "지금의 지구는 외계의 생명을 찾는 데 사용할 수 있는 표본으로는 가장 좋지 못한 것일지 모릅니다."라고 콜롬비아(Columbia) 대학의 천문생물학 연구소장인 칼렙 샤프(Caleb Scharf)는 말한다.

1 ④ ▶ **글의 요지**

글쓴이가 말하고자 하는 바는 진화나 멸종이 아니라, "외계 생명을 찾는 학자들이 과거 지구에서 생명이 발생했을 때와 유사한 조건의 행성을 찾고 있다."라는 것이므로 ④가 이 글의 요지에 가장 가깝다.

2 ② ▶ **동의어**

주어진 문장에서 '머리를 쳐들었다'라는 것은 '나서서 작용하고 개입했다'라는 뜻이므로, ②가 가장 가까운 의미다. ① 사라졌다 ③ 변했다 ④ 너무 지나쳤다

3 ③ ▶ **내용추론**

"과학자들은 지금의 지구와 동일한 외계행성, 즉 태양이 아닌 다른 항성 주위의 궤도를 도는 행성뿐 아니라 과거의 지구와 유사한 행성도 찾고 있다."라는 내용을 통해 '만약 외계행성이 실재한다면, 그것의 모습은 현재의 지구와 유사할 수도 있고 그렇지 않을 수도 있음'을 추론할 수 있다.

unpredictable a. 예측할 수 없는

intervention n. 개입, 간섭

rear one's head 고개[머리]를 들다; 고개를 치켜들다, 두각을 나타내다

wipe out 닦아내다, 일소하다

room n. 공간, 여지, 기회

baleful a. 재앙의, 해로운

comet n. 혜성

asteroid n. 소행성

exoplanet n. 외계행성

orbit v. 궤도를 돌다

template n. 형판, 본뜨는 잣대; 표본

07

과학자들은 6500만 년 전에 공룡을 멸종시켰던 암석으로 된 물체는 소행성이 아니라 혜성이었을 지도 모른다고 말한다.

많은 과학자들은 멕시코에 있는 지름 112마일의 칙술룹(Chicxulub) 크레이터가 공룡과 지구 생물의 약 70%를 멸종시킨 충돌에 의해 생긴 것이라고 믿고 있다. 텍사스 주 우드랜즈(Woodlands)에서 열린 제44차 달·행성 과학회의에 제출된 연구에 따르면, 한 새로운 연구에서는 칙술룹 크레이터가 이전에 생각했던 것보다 더 빠르고 더 작은 물체에 의해 폭파되어 생긴 것일지도 모른다는 것을 시사하고 있다.

외계암석의 충돌 증거는 고농도의 이리듐 원소를 포함하고 있는 지구 전역의 퇴적층에서 찾을 수 있는데, 이는 자연적으로는 지구에 있을 수 없는 것들이다.

그러나 이 새로운 연구는 자주 인용되던 이리듐의 수치가 부정확하다는 것을 보여준다. 연구를 이끈 과학자들은 이 이리듐 수치를 충돌에 의해 들어온 또 다른 원소인 오스뮴의 수치와 비교하였다. <과학자들의 계산 결과는 이 외계암석이 이전에 생각했던 것보다 잔해를 적게 만들어냈음을 암시하고 있는데, 이것은 이 외계암석이 훨씬 작은 물체였음을 의미한다.> 더 작은 암석이 거대한 칙술룹 크레이터를 만들기 위해서는 그 암석이 굉장히 빠르게 움직이고 있었어야 했다고 연구진들은 결론을 내렸다.

"크레이터 크기를 만들어낼 정도로 충분한 에너지를 가지고 있으면서도 훨씬 적은 암석물질을 가진 물체는 무엇일까라고 생각했을 때, 혜성을 떠올리게 됩니다."라고 연구저자이자 뉴햄프셔 주 소재 다트머스(Dartmouth) 대학의 고생태학자인 제이슨 무어(Jason Moore)가 BBC 뉴스와의 인터뷰에서 말했다.

1 ④ ▶ 문장삽입

제시문은 "그들의 계산 결과는 이 외계암석이 이전에 생각했던 것보다 잔해를 적게 만들어냈음을 암시하고 있는데, 이것은 이 외계암석이 훨씬 작은 물체였음을 의미한다."라는 의미다. 따라서 제시문 앞에는 이 '그들'에 해당하는 사람들이 계산하는 내용이, 제시문 뒤에는 '외계암석이 더 작은 암석'이라는 내용을 부연 설명해주는 말이 와야 할 것이다. 따라서 ⒟가 제시문이 들어가기에 가장 적절하다.

2 ④ ▶ 글의 주제

이 글은 공룡을 멸종시켰던 것이 소행성이 아니라 혜성일지 모른다는 주장과 이를 뒷받침하는 부연 설명이 이어진다. 따라서 ④가 글의 주제로 적절하다.

3 ② ▶ 빈칸완성

작은 물체가 큰 크레이터를 만들려면 이동속도가 빨라야 한다는 결론을 물리학적으로 확실하게 내리게 되는 것이므로 빈칸 Ⓐ에는 결론을 '얻다'라는 의미가 되는 derived와 drew가 들어갈 수 있으며, 빈칸 Ⓑ에서는 문맥상 고대에 지구에 온 외계물질에 대해 연구하는 사람이 들어가야 하므로, '지층에서 발견된 화석과 화분 등을 바탕으로 고생물과 환경의 관계, 고생물상, 생물군집의 구성과 변천을 연구하는 학자'인 고생태학자가 가장 적절하다. 따라서 이 둘을 만족시키는 ②가 정답이다. ① 거절하다 ― 고고학자 ③ 중단하다 ― 유물론자, 물질주의자 ④ 끌어내다, 얻다 ― 인류학자

4 ② ▶ 내용추론

이 글은 공룡을 멸종시킨 것이 소행성이 아니라 혜성일 가능성에 대해 이야기하고 있는데, 이리듐의 수치로 볼 때 더 작은 물체가 더 빠르게 이동해야 했다고 과학자들이 결론을 내렸다고 했으므로, "혜성이 공룡멸종의 주범이라는 가능성을 그 연구가 보여주었다."라는 의미의 ②가 정답이다. 첫 번째 문장에서도 may have been a comet라 했다. ① 과학자들이 이리듐의 수치를 오스뮴의 수치와 비교했을 뿐, 이리듐과 오스뮴이 지구에서 발견되는 유일한 우주암석인지는 본문에서 알 수 없다. ③ 공룡 전부와 지구생물의 70%를 사라지게 한 충돌에 의해 생긴 것이 크레이터라고 했을 뿐, 칙술룹 크레이터 스스로가 멸종을 야기한 것은 아니다. ④ 과학자들이 실시한 연구에서 그동안 자주 인용되던 이리듐의 수치가 부정확하다는 것은 더 작은 물체가 더 빠르게 이동해야 했다는 것을 보여주었을 뿐이며 공룡을 멸종시킨 것은 소행성이 아니라 혜성일지도 모른다고 하였다.

---

wipe out ~을 완전히 파괴하다; 죽이다

comet n. 혜성

asteroid n. 소행성

extinction n. 사멸, 절멸

crater n. 분화구; (달 표면의) 크레이터

impact n. 충돌; 충격; 영향

extinction n. 멸종, 절멸

blast v. 폭파하다

sediment n. 앙금, 침전물

exceedingly ad. 대단히, 매우, 몹시

conclusion n. 결말; 결론

08

1600년대에, 지도를 공부하던 사람들은 대륙들의 해안선에 몇 가지 흥미로운 유사점들이 있다는 것에 주목했다. 해안선들, 특히 남미대륙과 아프리카 대륙의 해안선을 연구해보니, 두 대륙이 서로 딱 들어맞을 수 있는 것처럼 보여서, 두 대륙이 아득한 과거의 어느 시점에는 연결되었음을 암시해 주었다. 이것은 <정설>이었는데, 왜냐하면 대륙에 관한 그 당시 일반적으로 인정되는 이론은 대륙이 움직이지 않고 변하지 않는다는 것이었기 때문이다. (그러나) 해안의 유사점들을 제외하고는 그런 급진적인 이론을 뒷받침할만한 증거가 전혀 없었다.

1911년, 알프레트 베게너(Alfred Wegener)라는 이름의 한 독일 기상학자는 대륙들이 실제로는 지구의 표면 위로 돌아다닐지도 모른다는 생각을 뒷받침하기 위한 추가적인 증거를 찾기 시작했다. 알프레트 베게너는 움직이지 않는 대륙이라는 일반적인 통념과 들어맞지 않는 것으로 보이는 당혹스러운 데이터를 설명해 놓은 많은 과학 논문들을 발견하였다.

한 관찰기록에 따르면, 지질학자들이 유사한 유형 및 구조로 이루어진 암석들이 캐나다와 스칸디나비아 반도 그리고 다른 지역에 존재한다는 것에 주목했다고 한다. 또 다른 지질학자들은 동일한 동식물의 화석, 즉 과거 생물의 증거이자 잔존물을 서로 멀리 떨어진 대륙에서 발견했으며, 때로는 열대식물 화석을 남극대륙에서 발견하는 등, 결코 존재할 수 없었을 곳에서 발견하기도 했다.

또 다른 과학자들은 빙하가 남긴 비슷한 퇴적물이 아프리카와 남미대륙과 같은 서로 다른 대륙에서도 나온다는 것에 주목하였다. 움직이지 않는 지구 표면이라는 일반적인 통념으로는, 이런 데이터가 적절하지 않았는데, 왜냐하면 먼 거리와 광대한 바다로 나뉘어 있는 대륙이 어떻게 이런 유사점들을 만들어낼 수 있는지를 적절하게 설명할 수 있는 이론이 전혀 없었기 때문이었다. 그래서 1915년, 베게너는 『대륙과 대양의 기원(The Origin of Continents and Oceans)』이라는 새로운 책을 출판했다. 이 책에서 베게너는 대륙들이 지구의 역사에서 어느 시점에 연결되어 있다가 현재의 지역으로 이동하였다는 새로운 이론을 제안하였다.

1 ① ▶ **문맥상 적절하지 않은 표현 고르기**
ⓑ, ⓒ, ⓓ는 모두 문맥에 맞게 연결된 반면, ⓐ 앞의 this는 "두 대륙이 아득한 과거의 어느 시점에 연결되어 있었다."라는 주장으로, 대륙이 움직일 수 없다는 기존의 정설과는 배치된다. 문맥상 ⓐ의 an orthodoxy(정설)는 ⓑ의 a radical theory(급진적인 이론)와 같은 의미로 쓰여야 하므로 ⓐ를 a heterodoxy(이단)라고 고쳐야 적절하다.

2 ③ ▶ **내용파악**
① 대륙의 해안선들 간의 유사성, ② 알프레트 베게너가 책을 출판한 이유, ④ 대륙에 관한 기존학설에 대한 이의제기는 모두 본문에 언급된 반면, ③ 다른 지역에서의 동일한 인류학적 증거는 본문에 언급되지 않았으므로 ③이 정답이다.

3 ② ▶ **뒷내용 추론**
이 글의 마지막 부분에 대륙의 이동에 관한 주장을 담은 책을 알프레트 베게너가 출판했다고 했는데, 이 책에 실은 이론은 대륙이 움직이지 않는다는 기존의 학설과는 상반되므로, 이 책에 언급된 대륙이동설에 관해 학자들 사이에 펼쳐질 논란이 이 글 다음에 와야 문맥상 가장 적절하므로 ②의 '그의 대륙이동설에 관한 논쟁'이 정답이다.

continent n. 대륙
fit together 연결되다, 딱 들어맞다
other than ~을 제외한
radical a. 급진적인
meteorologist n. 기상학자
puzzling a. 당혹스러운
geologist n. 지질학자
fossil n. 화석
deposit n. 퇴적물, 침전물
leave behind 남기다
glacier n. 빙하
make sense 이치에 맞다

09

천문학자들은 자신들이 블랙홀이라고 부르는 지역을 우주공간에서 확인했다. 그들은 이 블랙홀이 안에서부터 그 어떤 것도, 심지어 빛조차도 빠져나올 수 없는 밀도가 큰 별이라고 믿고 있다. 천문학자들은 매우 큰 별이 소멸하고 안으로 수축할 때 블랙홀이 생성된다고 생각하고 있다. 별은 가지고 있는 핵연료를 다 쓰고 그로 인해 열을 잃게 되면 소멸하게 된다. 별은 식으면서 수축을 시작한다. 수축하는 별은 점점 더 밀도가 높아져서, 중력의 당기는 힘이 더 강해진다. 밀도가 물의 1,000조 배에 이르면, 중력이 무척 강해져서 빛, 행성, 심지어 다른 별을 비롯하여, 블랙홀 주위의 모든 것들을 속으로 끌어당기게 된다. 보통 크기의 별인 태양이 블랙홀이 되려면, 반지름이 겨우 3킬로미터가 될 만큼 수축해야 할 것이다. 블랙홀은 모두 공 모양의 "층"이 둘러싸고 있는데, 빛이 이것을 통해 들어올 수는 있어도 빠져나가지는 못하는 경계선이다. 블랙홀로부터는 빛이 전혀 나오지 못하기 때문에, 완전히 검게 보인다. 블랙홀을 발견할 수 있는 것은, 물질이 속으로 빨려들기 직전에 온도가 뜨거워지고 X선을 방출하는데, 그것을 지구에서 탐지할 수 있기 때문이다. 이 "보이지 않는" 블랙홀을 발견하는 유일한 다른 방법은 다른 별들에 미치는 영향을 통한 것뿐이다. 블랙홀은 크기가 작을 수도 있지만, 그렇더라도 중력은 같은 크기의 수축하지 않은 보통 별과 같으며, 그렇기 때문에, 큰 블랙홀은 매우 강력해서 눈에 보이는 별들을 자신 주위의 궤도로 끌어들일 수 있으며, 이러한 눈에 보이는 종속되는 별의 움직임을 관측할 수 있다. 오늘날 천문학자들은 규모가 큰 은하에는 모두 그 중심에 거대한 블랙홀이 있다는 가설을 내놓고 있다.

1 ④ ▶ 내용파악
이 글은 블랙홀이 무엇인지에 대해 설명하고 있다. 두 번째 문장에서 과학자들은 어떠한 것도 빠져나올 수 없는 밀도가 큰 별이라고 했다. 이 글에서 ①에 관한 언급은 없었고, 블랙홀은 크기가 작을 수도 있다고 했다.

2 ② ▶ 내용파악
별은 가지고 있는 핵연료를 다 쓰고 열을 잃게 되면 수축한다고 했다.

3 ① ▶ 내용파악
블랙홀에서 빛이 빠져나올 수 없는 이유는 중력이 너무나도 강하기 때문이다.

4 ① ▶ 내용파악
블랙홀을 관측하는 방법은 모두 간접적인 것들이다.

---

astronomer n. 천문학자

dense a. 밀집한, 조밀한

collapse v. 무너지다; 실패하다

use up 다 써 버리다

gravity n. 진지함; 중력

density n. 밀집상태; 농도

drag v. 끌어당기다

radius n. 반지름; 행동반경; 범위

boundary n. 경계(선)

detect v. 발견하다; 간파하다

invisible a. 눈에 보이지 않는; 확실하지 않은

gravitation n. 인력(작용); 중력

galaxy n. 은하

gigantic a. 거인 같은, 거대한

10

백색 왜성은 우주의 나머지 별들과 무엇이 다른가? 백색 왜성은 죽어가는 별의 한 예인 퇴화된 별(축퇴성)의 형태로 보인다. 우리는 그것을 어떻게 아는가? 첫째로, 백색 왜성은 더 성숙한 밝은 별들보다 훨씬 어둡다. 둘째, 그것들은 또한 우주의 조건에서 보면 무척 작다. 일부 백색 왜성들은 행성들보다 심지어 더 작다. 예를 들면, 시리우스 B는 겨우 우리 행성 지구 정도의 크기다.

이러한 백색 왜성을 구별되게 하는 것은 그들의 질량이다. 예를 들어 시리우스 B는 그 작은 구조 안이 태양 밀도의 절반으로 채워져 있다. 그것이 백색 왜성을 블랙홀과 중성자별을 제외하고 우주에서 가장 무거운 형태의 물질이 되게 하는 원인이다.

그럼 그것은 이 천체에 무엇을 의미하는가? 그것의 크기가 줄어들었음에도 불구하고 그렇게 많은 질량을 갖게 되는 게 어떻게 가능한 것인가? 백색 왜성은 별의 일생에 마지막 단계다. 별이 헬륨으로 융합하기 위해 수소를 모두 소모할 때, 그것은 적색 거성단계를 통과한다. 이것은 그 바깥층을 발산시켜 행성 모양의 성운을 만들게 됨을 의미한다. 표면의 이러한 발산이 많은 에너지를 소모하는 것이다. 그 별은 핵융합을 지속할 수소가 더 이상 남지 않게 된다. 더 이상 에너지를 방출하지 않기 때문에 밤하늘에서 흐릿한 형태처럼 보이며 이것이 우리의 백색 왜성이다.

이제 백색 왜성이 식기 시작하는 현상이 발생하는데 더 이상 그것을 지탱하는 에너지가 없기 때문이다. 이러한 점진적인 온도의 변화는 핵의 질량이 그 안으로 응집되는 원인이 된다. 따라서 그것이 백색 왜성이 그렇게 비정상적으로 높은 밀도를 가지는 이유다. 대개 일어나는 것은 밀도 압력이 중력의 붕괴 즉, 초신성 형태의 거대한 폭발을 유발시키는 일이 일어난다. 하지만 물론 대부분의 백색 왜성은 그렇게 격렬한 최후를 맞이하지 않는다. 실제로, 그들 중 대부분은 완전히 사라질 때까지 점차 희미해지고 사그라진다. 이러한 마지막 단계에서 그들은 실제로 흑색 왜성이라고 불리는데 현대 천문학 장비로도 감지될 수 없을 정도로 복사 에너지를 거의 방출하지 않기 때문이다.

1 ① ▶ **내용파악**
백색 왜성은 항성의 퇴화 단계에 해당한다. 크기가 작고, 질량이 무거운데 바깥 대기층을 발산시키는 과정에서 별이 많은 에너지를 소모하고, 더 이상 방출할 에너지가 없게 되면 온도가 낮아지기 시작한다. 이것이 핵 안으로 질량이 압축되는 결과를 초래하며 이 압력이 거대한 폭발로 이어지는 것이다. 따라서 ② 내부 에너지 힘의 결핍, ③ 작은 구조안의 높은 밀도, ④ 바깥층의 소산은 백색 왜성의 주요 특징이지만 우주에서 나오는 밝혀지지 않은 복사에너지는 특징이 아니므로 ①이 정답이다.

2 ② ▶ **내용파악**
백색 왜성의 크기와 밝기 등 백색 왜성의 일반적인 특징을 설명하기에 앞서 그에 대한 대표적인 예로 시리우스 B를 들고 있다.

3 ④ ▶ **내용파악**
적색 거성 단계에서는 별 바깥층이 발산되며, 이 과정에서 많은 양의 에너지가 소모되고 결국 더 이상 핵융합을 할 수 없게 되어 희미하게 보이는 백색 왜성으로서의 별의 퇴화가 시작된다는 것을 설명하고 있다.

4 ③ ▶ **빈칸완성**
첫 단락에서 백색 왜성은 더 성숙한 밝은 별들보다 훨씬 어둡다고 했으며 빈칸의 앞 문장에서 백색 왜성은 핵융합을 지속할 때 수소가 더 이상 남지 않게 되어 에너지를 방출하지 않는다고 했으므로 밤하늘에서 흐릿한 형태로 보일 것이다. 따라서 ③이 정답이다. ① 강풍 ② 반짝임, 번득임 ④ 횃불

---

white dwarf 백색 왜성

stellar a. 별의; 별 같은[모양의]

degenerate a. 퇴폐한, 타락한, 퇴화한

dim a. (빛이) 어둑한

cosmic a. 우주의

pack v. (짐을) 꾸리다; 꽉 채우다

density n. 밀도

frame n. 뼈대, 구조

apart from ~외에는, ~을 제외하고

neutron star 중성자 별

celestial body 천체

fuse v. 녹이다; 융합하다[시키다]

shed v. (빛·열·소리·향기 등을) 발산하다

planetary a. 행성의

nebula n. 성운

sustain v. 유지하다, 지속하다, 지탱하다

nuclear fusion 핵융합

emit v. 방출하다

gradual a. 점진적인, 단계적인

shrink v. 오그라들다, 줄어들다, 움츠리다

abnormally ad. 비정상적으로

gravitational collapse 중력 붕괴(천체가 중력 작용으로 수축해 가는 현상)

explosion n. 폭발, 파열; 폭파

supernova n. 초신성

radiation n. 방사; 복사 에너지

detect v. 발견하다, 알아내다

10 환경·기상

01

많은 지층학자들은 지난 한두 세기만에 인간이 지구를 너무나 변화시켜서 인류가 이제 새로운 시대를 열었다고 믿게 되었는데, 그것은 인류세(人類世)라는 시대다. 우리가 정말로 새로운 시대로 들어갔다면, 그 시대는 정확하게 언제 시작됐을까? 인간의 영향이 언제 지질학적으로 의미 있는 정도로까지 증가했을까?

버지니아(Virginia) 대학의 고생대기후학자인 윌리엄 루디먼(William Ruddiman)은 약 8,000년 전에 있었던 농업의 발명과 그 결과 일어난 삼림파괴가 대기 중의 이산화탄소를 증가시켜서, 그렇지 않았다면 새로운 빙하시대가 시작되었을 상황을 모면하게 되었다는 의견을 내놓았다. 그의 의견에 따르면, 인류는 충적세가 시작된 이후 지금까지 사실상 지구에서 지배적인 세력이었다고 한다. 일부 과학자들은 극지방의 빙하 코어가 보여주듯이, 이후 중단 없이 지속되어온 것으로 판명된 이산화탄소의 증가가 시작된 때인 18세기 후반에 인류세가 시작되었다고 말했다. 다른 과학자들은 새로운 시대의 시작을 20세기 중반으로 잡고 있는데, 이때는 인구증가와 소비 모두가 급속히 가속화되었던 때이다. 또 다른 학자들은 아직 인류세가 시작되지 않았다고 주장하는데, 그 이유는 우리가 아직 지구에 큰 영향을 미치지 않아서가 아니라 과거 몇 세기보다도 앞으로 수십 년이 지층학적으로 훨씬 더 중요할 것 같기 때문이다.

1 ② ▶ 빈칸완성
빈칸 앞뒤에서 '대기 중의 이산화탄소를 증가시켜서, 다시 말해 지구온난화를 통해, 그렇지 않았으면 새로운 빙하시대가 시작되었을 상황을'이라고 했으므로 빈칸에 적절한 동사는 '피하다, 모면하다(stave off)'라는 뜻의 ②가 적절하다. ① 촉발하다 ③ 감싸다 ④ 끌어올리다

2 ③ ▶ 내용추론
인류세가 아직 시작되지 않았다고 주장하는 사람들도 있으므로 그 시기를 ③처럼 추론할 수는 없다.

3 ④ ▶ 내용파악
미래의 지질학자들이 인류세의 증거를 찾는 것은 오늘날의 지질학자들이 과거 지질시대의 증거를 찾는 것과 마찬가지일 것이다. 그들은 지층 속의 화석을 증거로 삼으므로 '지층'이라는 의미인 ④가 적절하다. ① 역사적인 건조물 ② 열대우림 ③ 하부 대기층

stratigrapher n. 지층학자
alter v. 바꾸다, 변경하다
usher in 예고하다, ~의 도착을 알리다
Anthropocene n. 인류세
paleoclimatologist n. 고생대기후학자
deforestation n. 삼림벌채, 삼림파괴
atmospheric a. 대기 중의, 공기의
Holocene n. 충적세(약 12,000년 전 홍적세가 끝난 때부터 지금까지의 지질시대)
carbon dioxide 이산화탄소
uninterrupted a. 끊임없는, 연속된, 부단한
consumption n. 소비; 소모, 소진
stratigraphically ad. 층위학[지층학]적으로

02

고릴라 의사들이 일하는 동물 서식지들은 지구상에서 인구밀도가 가장 높은 몇몇 시골지역에 둘러싸여 있다. 그리고 알고 보면, 사람들은 끔찍스러운 이웃이 된다. 산악고릴라는 그들 가운데 있는 사람들의 손에 저질러지는 서식지 파괴와 밀렵에 항상 직면해 있었다. 그들은 민중봉기와 군사적 분쟁 때문에 죽으며, 그들은 사냥꾼들이 영양을 잡으려고 쳐놓은 덫에 걸리며, 그들은 인간 호흡기 질환에 걸릴 위험을 무릅쓴다. 그 모든 것의 결과로, 산악고릴라의 개체 수는 지난 30년 중 대부분의 기간 동안 300마리 내지 400마리로 감소했다.

한 종이 너무나 중대한 멸종 위기에 처해 있을 때는 모든 개체의 생존이 중요하다. 그 정도로 심각한 상황은 '극단적인 보호'를 요청한다. 인간이 개별 종이나 특정 생태계에 미치는 부정적인 영향을 줄이기 위한 통상적인 야생생물 보호 노력은 야생생물 서식지를 이를테면 산업공해의 해를 입지 않게 보호하거나 수렵 금지 규정을 시행하는 것이었다. 극단적인 보호는 우리의 긍정적인 영향을 증대시킴으로써 보다 더 간섭적인 접근방식을 취한다. 고릴라 의사들에게, 그것은 한 번에 한 종씩 구함으로써 고릴라 종들을 보호하는 것을 의미한다. 길들여진 42개 고릴라 집단들 — 인간에게 익

habitat n. 서식지
as it turns out 알고 보면
poaching n. 밀렵
civil unrest 민중봉기
snare n. 덫, 올가미
antelope n. 영양
population n. 개체 수
languish v. 쇠약해지다, 시들다, 침체되다
conservation n. 보호, 보존
conventional a. 전통적인, 통상적인
enforce v. 집행하다, 시행하다

숙해진 고릴라 가족들 — 은 숲속으로 그들을 뒤쫓는 추적 장치들에 의해 낮 시간 동안 계속 모니터링(감시)된다. 그들은 또한 현지의 현장 수의사들에 의해 매달 건강검진을 받는데, 수의사들은 대변 샘플을 검사하고 체중감소나 허약증이나 호흡곤란이나 외피변색 같은, 부상이나 질병의 가시적인 증후를 찾으려고 살펴본다. 고릴라가 이런 증세들 중 어떤 것이라도 보일 때는 고릴라 의사팀은 개입할 것인지 말 것인지를 논의한다.

1 ⑤ ▶ 빈칸완성
앞에서 통상적인 보호는 부정적인 영향을 줄이는 것이라고 한 반면에 뒤에서는 긍정적인 영향을 증대시키는 것이라 했으므로 '보다 더 적극적으로 개입[간섭]하는 방식'이라 할 수 있다. 따라서 ⓐ에는 ⑤의 '보다 더 간섭적인 접근방식'이 적절하다. ① 환경에 대한 고려 ② 자유방임적인 태도 ③ 응급치료를 닮은 ④ 몇 가지 예방조치

2 ③ ▶ 글의 제목
이 글은 고릴라 의사들의 멸종위기에 처한 산악고릴라들을 구하려는 극단적인 보호의 노력을 소개한 글이므로 ③의 '산악고릴라를 멸종으로부터 구하고 있는 수의사들'이 제목으로 적절하다.

03

이산화탄소 배출은 색깔이나 냄새가 없고, 당장은 해가 없다. 그러나 그 온난화 효과는 지구의 온도를 지난 수백 만 년 동안 경험하지 못한 수준으로 쉽게 끌어올릴 수 있을 것이다. 일부 동식물들은 이미 그 서식범위를 극지방으로 이동시키고 있고 그런 이동은 화석기록에 흔적을 남길 것이다. 일부 종들은 온난화에 전혀 살아남지 못할 것이다. 한편, 기온 상승으로 인해 결국 바다의 수위가 20피트 이상 올라갈 수 있을 것이다.
수십 억 톤 상당의 석탄과 석유를 태운 결과들은 인류의 자동차와 도시와 공장들이 사라지고 오래지난 후에도 분명히 알아볼 수 있을 것 같다. 이산화탄소는 지구를 따뜻하게 하면서 또한 바다 안으로 침투해 들어가 바다를 산성화시킨다. 금세기 중에 바다는 산호가 산호초를 만들 수 없을 정도로 산성화될지 모르며, 이것은 지질학적 기록에 '산호초 갭'으로 기록될 것이다. 산호초 갭은 지난 다섯 차례의 주요 대량 멸종 각각의 두드러진 특징이었다. 가장 최근의 멸종은 소행성 충돌에 의한 것으로 믿어지는데, 6,500만 년 전 백악기 말에 일어났다. 그것은 공룡뿐 아니라 수장룡과 익룡과 암모나이트도 없어지게 했다. 많은 설명에 따르면, 오늘날 바다에 일어나고 있는 일의 규모가 그때 이후 유례없는 규모라고 한다. 미래의 지질학자들이 보기에는 오늘날 (생태계에 가하는) 우리의 충격이 소행성 충돌만큼이나 갑작스럽고 심대한 것으로 여겨질지도 모른다.

1 ③ ▶ 빈칸완성
마지막 문장은 오늘날 우리가 이산화탄소를 과다 배출하여 산호초의 멸종을 불러오는 것으로 생태계에 가하는 충격을, 미래의 지질학자들은 오늘날 우리가 과거의 소행성 충돌이 공룡의 멸종을 불러온 그 충격을 보는 것과 똑같이 보게 될 것이라는 의미인데, 오늘날 우리는 과거의 소행성 충돌이 공룡의 갑작스럽고 전면적인 멸종을 불러왔다고 보므로 빈칸에는 ③이 적절하다. ① 광범위하고 얕은 ② 점진적이고 회복할 수 있는 ④ 일시적이고 피상적인

2 ④ ▶ 내용추론
①은 첫 문장에서 무색, 무취라 했으므로, ②는 이산화탄소 배출로 인한 지구 온난화와 그로 인해 일부 종들은 전혀 살아남지 못할 것이라 했는데 이것은 생물의 다양성이 줄어듦을 의미하므로, ③은 이산화탄소가 바다 안으로 침투해 들어가 바다를 산성화시킨다고 했으므로, 모두 추론할 수 있다. 이산화탄소가 산호를 흩어지게 해서가 아니라 바다를 산성화시켜 산호초의 생성을 막는 것이므로 ④는 추론할 수 있는 것이 아니다.

3 ③ ▶ 내용파악
①은 were caused by는 맞지만 그 앞의 caused가 사실이 아니고, ②는 바다의 이산화탄소 농도가 증가한 시기일 것이며, ④는 대량 멸종 시기와 일치한다고 했을 뿐 멸종의 원인이 된 것은 아니며 산호초의 갑작스런 사망이 아니라 생기지 않은 것을 가리키므로 사실이 아니다. 둘째 단락 셋째 문장에서 금세기 중에 또 하나의 산호초 갭이 추가될 것으로 예상할 수 있으므로 ③이 사실인 진술이다.

---

hands-on a. 간섭적인, 참견하는
habituate v. 길들이다, 익숙하게 하다
daylight n. 일광, 낮
tracker n. 추적자
stool n. 대변
laboured breathing 노작성 호흡, 호흡곤란
discolored coat 변색된 외피
step in 개입하다, 간섭하다

odorless a. 무취의
range n. (동식물의) 분포지역, 서식범위
turn to dust 먼지가 되다, 사라지다
discernible a. 식별[분간]할 수 있는
seep v. 침투하다
acidify v. 산성화시키다
coral n. 산호
reef n. 암초
coral reef 산호초
extinction n. 멸종
impact n. 충돌, 충격
asteroid n. 소행성
Cretaceous period 백악기
plesiosaur n. 수장룡
pterosaur n. 익룡
account n. 설명, 이야기
unmatched a. 필적할 상대가 없는, 유례없는

04

걱정스럽게도 과학자들은 바다에서도 유사한 어떤 일이 벌어지고 있다는 것을 관찰해 왔다. 인간이 대기 중으로 배출한 이산화탄소 가운데 상당부분은 결국 바다에 의해서 흡수되고 점진적으로 바닷물을 점점 더 산성으로 만든다. 이러한 바다의 산성화 과정은 그들의 껍질에 이어 그들의 연약한 몸을 녹이면서 해양에 살고 있는 무척추 동물들에게 엄청난 재난을 초래할 수 있다. 그러나 열대 우림의 경우와 마찬가지로, "기후 변화에는 항상 승자와 패자가 있기 마련이다."라고 호주의 애들레이드(Adelaide) 대학의 해양 환경학자인 이반 네이겔커켄(Ivan Nagelkerken)이 말한다. 어떤 종(種)의 생물이 해양 산성화라는 조건 아래서 번성하게 될지를 알아보기 위해, 그는 수중 분화구들이 이미 이산화탄소를 바다에 분출해 놓고 있는 두 장소를 향해 갔다. 한 곳은 이탈리아에 있는 불카노섬(Vulcano Island)이고 다른 한 곳은 뉴질랜드에 있는 화이트섬(White Island)이다. "이들 이산화탄소 분출구들은 당신에게 미래를 엿볼 수 있게 해주는 자연의 실험실입니다."라고 네이겔커켄은 설명한다. 윈터(Winter)의 실험에서 보았던 것처럼 그 미래는 생명이 없는 것과는 거리가 멀었다. 그러나 네이겔커켄을 근심스럽게 만든 것은 미래가 지탱해 줄 생명의 종류다. 이산화탄소 분출구들은 산호 숲, 다시마 숲, 해중 식물 평원 등의 해양 생태계 어디에서도 발생할 수 있다. 그러나 당신이 어느 곳에 있다고 할지라도 가장 산성화된 곳에서 생존하는 생명체들은 놀라울 정도로 비슷하다. 분출구 바로 주변에 있는 모든 생태계는 "구조가 복잡하지 않고 매우 짧으며 살이 찐 잔디 조류에 의해 지배당하는 생태계로 변합니다."라고 네이겔커켄은 설명한다. 한 술 더 떠서, "우리는 이 분출구 주변에서 단 하나의 포식자도 관찰하지 못했습니다."

그 결과, 먹이그물은 극적으로 단순해지고, 물고기 종의 수는 급감하고, 생태계는 '그 가치는 물론 생산력도 훨씬 더 떨어지게' 된다. 잔디 조류를 좋아하는 작은 방목 어류가 미래의 산성화된 바다에서 가장 돋보이는 생물이 될 가능성이 매우 높다. 그러나 그들이 바다를 접수하게 됨에 따라, "모든 곳은 다른 모든 곳과 비슷한 곳이 될 것입니다."라고 네이겔커켄은 말한다. 동질성을 가진 새로운 바다는 인간에게 좋지 않을 것이다. 미래의 바다에서 번성하게 될 가능성이 높은, 작고 적응을 잘하는 종인 망둥이나 베도라치 같은 물고기들은 단순하게 말해서 인간들이 먹기 좋아하는 물고기가 아니다. 그리고 심지어 인간의 입맛이 진화한다고 할지라도 그 물고기들은 인간의 수요를 채워줄 수 없을 터인데, 그 이유는 대부분의 망둥이의 길이가 4인치보다 작은 것으로 측정되기 때문이다. 인간들은 참치나 청새치 같은 커다란 포식자 물고기들을 먹고 싶어 한다. 그러나 네이겔커켄이 행한 이산화탄소 분출구에 대한 연구에 따르면, 정확하게 바로 이런 종의 어류들이 사라졌다. 해양 산성화가 바다의 생태계를 재구축함에 따라 가장 먼저 일어날 일은 인간이 돈과 식량을 위해 의존하고 있는 어류가 사라질 것이라는 것이다.

1 ②   ▶ **빈칸완성**
해양 산성화로 인해 해양 생태계가 지금과는 전혀 다른 생태계로 바뀔 것이라는 내용이므로, 빈칸에는 '재구축되다'라는 의미의 표현이 적절하다. ① 부유하게 하다 ③ 다양화하다 ④ 촉진[조장, 육성]하다

2 ④   ▶ **내용일치**
인간이 먹기 좋아하는 어류들이 사라질 것이라는 진술로부터 정답을 유추할 수 있다.

---

disturbingly ad. 걱정스럽게도, 불안하게도

wreak havoc 파괴하다, 재난을 초래하다

underwater vent 수중 분화구

spew v. 토하다, 분출하다

kelp forest 다시마 숲

seagrass plain 해중식물 평야

turf algae 잔디 조류, 떼조류

goby n. 망둥이

blenny n. 베도라치

clock v. 측정하다

marlin n. 청새치

05

산불이 최근 몇 주 동안 볼 수 있었던 기상이변과 관련된 유일한 사건은 아니다. 미국 동부 해안의 몇몇 지역은 폭우로 범람했고, 전 세계적인 이상 고온은 여러 번 최고 기록을 경신했다. 주요 기상학자들로 구성된 한 집단은 지구가 이제 회복 불가능한 '온실' 상태로 진입하는 위험에 처해있다고 경고했다. 윌 스테픈(Will Steffen)은 보도 자료를 통해 "우리 연구에 따르면 인간이 초래한 2도 정도의 지구 온난화는 흔히 '피드백'이라고 불리는 다른 지구 체계의 공정들을 자극했고, 이는 더 많은 온난화를 불러일으킬 것이다. 우리가 지금 온실 가스 배출을 중단한다고 해도 말이다."라고 말했다. 일단 그 임계점을 넘고 나면 '온실 지구'는 인간 역사에서 유례없던 기온에 도달하게 될 수도 있다.

인간 사회에 미치는 영향은 "아마도 엄청날 것이다. 때로는 예기치 않게 찾아오기도 하고, 의심의 여지없이 엄청난 파괴를 불러올 것이다."라고 그는 썼다. 펜실베이니아 주의 기상학자인 만(Mann)은 "우리는 지뢰밭으로 걸어 들어가고 있다."라고 말했다. "우리가 계속 화석연료를 태우는 한 우리는 그 지뢰밭으로 걸어 들어가는 것이고, 좀 더 끔찍하고 파괴적이고 돌이킬 수 없는 영향을 우리의 기후에 미치는 것이다."라고 그는 말했다. 하지만 그는 변화를 이루기에 아직 너무 늦지는 않았다고 말했다. "우리가 해야 할 유일하게 현명한 일은 그 지뢰밭으로 걸어 들어가길 멈추는 것이다."라고 그는 말했다. "그리고 우리는 그것을 할 수 있다. 우리는 화석연료를 태우는 것에서부터 벗어날 수 있다. 파리협약은 우리를 위한 길을 마련해 주었다. 우리가 그 길을 따른다면, 앞으로 몇 년 동안 협약을 지키며 개선해 나간다면, 우리는 최악의 기상변화라는 결과가 일어나는 일을 막을 수도 있을 것이다."

1 ⑤ ▶ **빈칸완성**

첫 번째 빈칸에는 주어가 '폭우'이므로 물이 범람했다는 내용이 가장 잘 어울린다. 두 번째 빈칸은 우리가 지금 노력하지 않으면 너무 늦을 수도 있다는 내용이므로, 일종의 '임계점'에 해당하는 표현의 낱말이 필요하다. 회복 불가능한 온실 상태, 즉 2℃의 지구 온난화가 임계점을 나타낸다. ① 유지하다 — 선 ② 대신하다 — 경계 ③ 침입[침해]하다 — 구역 ④ 이슬비가 내리다 — 경로

2 ① ▶ **빈칸완성**

빈칸 다음의 내용을 보면 기상이변에 대처해서 우리가 할 수 있고, 해야 할 일이 제시되어 있으므로, 아직 늦지만은 않았다는 내용이 필요하다. 둘을 모두 만족시켜 주는 것은 ①이다.

3 ⑤ ▶ **내용추론**

우리는 이미 어떤 돌이킬 수 없는 지점으로 가고 있을 수도 있다는 내용이므로, ⑤처럼 어떤 '새로운 정상' 상태에 도달해서 더 이상 많은 변화가 없는 일종의 안정된 상태에 이르렀다는 내용은 적절하지 않다.

---

wildfire n. 자연발화 되는 산불

extreme weather 기상이변

inundate v. 범람시키다

heat wave 열파, 이상 고온

hothouse n. 온실

trigger v. 자극하다

news release 보도 자료

threshold n. 한계, 경계

disruptive a. 파괴적인

minefield n. 지뢰밭

irreversible a. 돌이킬 수 없는

06

갈라파고스 제도는 13개의 주요 섬들이 펼쳐져 있는 곳으로 지도상에 만큼이나 신화 속에도 살아 있다. 신화 속의 이곳은 되새들로 붐비는 브리가둔(신비한 곳)으로, 1835년에 다윈(Darwin)이 당도하여 결국 그와 우리에게 지구상의 생명이 어떻게 진화하는지를 보여줄 관찰을 시작했던 곳이다. 그의 『종의 기원(On the Origin of Species)』은 "현대인의 믿음체계 안의 거의 모든 구성요소를" 특징짓게 될 것이었다고 진화생물학자 에른스트 마이어(Ernst Mayr)는 썼다.

갈라파고스 제도는 고립되어 보일지 모르지만 현대생활의 영향을 받고 있어서, 진화론의 요람인 이곳에도 기후변화가 찾아오고 있다. 그래서 거북, 되새, 가마우지, 바다 이구아나와 같은 이곳을 상징하는 종들이 피해를 입을 수 있을 것이다. 세상 사람들에게 자연선택에 대해 가르쳐주었던 그 유명한 이곳 생태계가 어쩌면 지금 우리에게 다시 한 번 가르침을 주어, 다른 곳에 저장되어 있는 것(전 세계 생태계)에 대한 통찰력을 제공해줄지도 모른다. 갈라파고스 제도는 기후변화에 대한 종들의 반응을 연구할 아주 멋진 실험실이다.

갈라파고스 제도는 예전에는 라스 엔칸타다스(마법의 섬들)이었는데, 거품과 흐르는 용암과 이상한 동물로 뒤섞인 사마귀투성이 같은(울퉁불퉁한) 섬들이었다. "인간과 늑대 모두 이 섬들을 외면하고, 여기 생명의 주된 소리는 쉿 하는 소리다."라고 허먼 멜빌(Herman Melville)은 썼다.

포경선 선원들은 여기서 쉿 소리를 내는 거북을 식용으로 잡아 올려 선창에 넣고, 물통을 가득 채우고는 계속 항해했다. 이 제도의 이상함에 대한 그들의 판단은 옳았다. 남미 본토에서 약 600마일 떨어져 고립되어 있는 이곳의 자연은 사나웠다. 본토에서 이 제도로 건너온 동물들 중에 살아남은 동물은 거의 없었다. 살아남은 동물들은 각 섬의 여건에 적응함으로써 서로 다른 여러 형태로 진화했다. 적응할 수 없는 동물들은 멸종되어 사라졌다.

그러나 지금 여기서는 또 다른 변화들이 일어나고 있는데 진화적인 변화만이 아니다. 과학자들에게 생태계가 그렇게도 짧은 기간에 그렇게도 철저하게 때로는 되풀이하여 충격을 받는 모습을 (이곳만큼) 가장 잘 관찰하게 해주는 곳은 지구상에 거의 없다.

1 ② ▶ 글의 주제
이 글은 첫 단락에서 갈라파고스 제도를 ①로 소개하면서 시작하지만, 특히 둘째 단락과 마지막 단락을 볼 때 ②가 말하고자 하는 주된 내용이므로 ②가 이 글의 논제(topic)로 적절하다.

2 ① ▶ 부분이해
앞 문장에서 포경선 선원들이 이 제도에 상륙하지 않고 계속 항해했다고 했고 뒤이은 문장에서 '이곳의 자연은 사나웠다'고 했으므로 ①이 Ⓐ의 뜻을 가장 잘 설명한 것이다.

3 ④ ▶ 내용파악
갈라파고스 제도의 자연은 태곳적의 모습이 변함없이 그대로 전해온 것이 아니라 생태계 변화를 단기간에 급격하게 겪은 곳이라고 설명되므로 ④가 언급되지 않았다.

---

finch n. 피리새, 되새

Brigadoon n. 브리가둔(100년에 한 번 나타나는 스코틀랜드의 신비한 마을)

inform v. 특징짓다

component n. 구성 요소[부분]

isolated a. 고립된, 격리된

immune a. 면한, 면제받은

cradle n. 요람

iconic a. 우상의, 인습적인

booby n. 가마우지

fabulous a. 전설적인, 아주 멋진, 굉장한

warty a. 사마귀투성이의

lace v. 섞어 짜다, 장식하다, 가미하다

lava n. 용암

disown v. 제 것[책임]이 아니라고 말하다, 자기와 무관하다고 말하다, 의절하다

hiss n. 쉿 하는 소리

whaler n. 고래잡이 어부

hold n. 선창

cask n. 통(= barrel)

cut off 고립시키다

front-row seat 앞자리(가장 잘 볼 수 있는 자리)

07

우리의 본성이 변하는 것은 우리가 변화를 일어나게 할 수 있다는 현실적인 희망 없이는 불가능하다. 그러나 우리가 지금 우리 자신과 지구의 환경을 파멸시킬 수 있다는 실상을 알게 됨으로써 희망 자체가 위협받는다. 게다가, 우리에게는 지금 창의성이 시급히 필요한데도, 우리의 복잡한 인공적 생활패턴과 가공된 정보의 홍수에 대처하는 데 따른 스트레스가 극도의 피로감을 만연하게 만든다. 우리의 경제는 후기 산업화시대 경제라고 설명되고, 우리의 건축은 포스트모더니즘 건축으로 불리며, 우리의 지정학은 탈냉전의 상황으로 분류된다. 우리는 어떤 존재가 아닌지는 알지만 어떤 존재인지는 모르는 것 같다. 우리의 삶을 형성하고 재형성하는 요소들은 그 나름의 변함없는 논리를 갖고 있는 것 같다. 그것들은 너무나 강력해서 우리 자신을 창의적으로 정의 내리려는 그 어떤 노력도 아마도 낭비가 될 것이고 그 노력의 성과는 연이은 변화의 파도에 재빨리 지워질 것이다. 불가피하게도, 우리는 이 강력한 요소들이 우리를 그 어떤 운명을 향해 몰아간다 해도 그 운명에 몸을 맡기며 그 운명을 선택하는 데 있어 우리의 역할은 거의 없는 것이다.

지금의 환경 위기는 어쩌면 전례 없는 것이기 때문에 우리로서는 전혀 이해할 수 없고 소위 상식의 범위 밖에 있는 것 같다. 우리는 그것을 우리가 모호하게 이해하지만 거의 탐구하지 않는 생각들을 넣어두는 좀처럼 찾아가지 않는 그 어떤 정신의 다락방으로 보내버린다. 우리는 그것(환경 위기)에 멀고 이질적이고 우리가 사는 세상의 지도에 의해 절망적으로 왜곡되어버린, 당도하기 너무 어렵고 오래 머물기에 너무 가혹한 남극대륙에 붙일 것과 같은 정신적 꼬리표를 붙인다. 우리가 이 다락방을 찾아갈 때, 우리가 위기의 원인들이 얼마나 복잡하게 엮어져서 산업문명의 천(체제)을 만들어내는지에 대해 알게 될 때, 우리가 그것을 해결할 가능성은 비현실적으로 보인다. 그것은 너무나 험악하게 여겨져 우리는 긍정적인 변화를 향해 첫발조차 내딛기를 꺼려한다.

1 ①　　▶ 빈칸완성
빈칸 앞뒤가 우리의 본성을 변화시키기 어렵게 만드는 점들을 연이어 나열하므로 ①의 '게다가'가 적절하다. ② 따라서 ③ 그러나 ④ 예를 들어

2 ③　　▶ 부분이해
남극대륙이 멀리 떨어져 있어 현실감 있게 와 닿지 않고 그곳의 문제가 시급한 문제로 인식되지 않고 혹독한 기후여건으로 극복할 수 없는 곳으로 인식되는 곳이므로, "남극대륙에 붙일 것과 같은 정신적 꼬리표를 환경 위기에 붙인다."는 말은 환경 위기 문제를 앞에서 남극대륙에 대해 언급한 이러한 성격의 문제로 여긴다는 뜻이다. 따라서 ③이 가장 가깝다.

3 ④　　▶ 내용추론
둘째 단락 첫째 문장에서 '환경 위기를 전례 없는 것'이라고 한 것은 지금 정도로 심각한 위기를 맞이한 적이 없다는 뜻이지 최초의 힘든 문제라는 뜻은 아니므로 ④가 추론할 수 없는 진술이다. 나머지 보기는 모두 첫 단락에서 단서를 찾을 수 있다.

4 ②　　▶ 글의 어조
이 글은 지금의 환경 위기를 극복하려면 우리의 본성이 친환경적으로 변해야 하는데 그러한 변화를 위한 창의적인 노력과 적극적 자세가 보이지 않음을 비관적으로 기술한 글이다. 따라서 ②가 적절하다. ① 무관심한 ③ 고무적인 ④ 논쟁적인

cope with ~에 대처하다
pervasive a. 만연한
post-industrial a. 후기 산업화의, 탈산업화의
post-modern a. 포스트모더니즘의
geopolitics n. 지정학
post-Cold War a. 탈냉전의
immutable a. 불변의
tidal wave 해일, 대변동
resign oneself to ~에 몸을 맡기다, 체념하다
propel v. 추진하다, 몰아가다
unprecedented a. 전례 없는
common sense 상식
consign v. 회부하다, 맡기다; 발송하다
attic n. 다락방
vaguely ad. 모호하게
tag v. 붙이다
Antarctica n. 남극대륙
unforgiving a. 용서하지 않는
intricately ad. 복잡하게
fabric n. 직물, 천; 구조, 체제
chimerical a. 공상적인, 터무니없는, 비현실적인
forbidding a. 꺼림칙한, 험악한, 무서운

08

오존층 파괴물질에 관한 몬트리올 의정서는, 간단하게 몬트리올 의정서로 또한 알려져 있는데, 오존 파괴의 원인이 되는 수많은 물질들의 생산을 단계적으로 중단시키는 방식으로 오존층을 보호하고자 만든 국제협약이다. 1987년 9월 16일에 조인하도록 공개된 몬트리올 의정서는 오존 파괴를 다루는 데 있어 국제적인 협력의 틀을 마련한 1985년 오존층 보호를 위한 비엔나 협약에 의거하여 만들어졌다. 몬트리올 의정서는 1989년 1월 1일에 발효되었으며, 그 후 9번의 개정을 거쳤다.

이런 국제적인 합의의 결과, 남극의 오존홀은 서서히 회복 중에 있다. 기후 전망은 2050~2070년 사이에 오존층이 1980년 수준으로 되돌아갈 것임을 보여준다. 몬트리올 의정서의 성공은 효과적인 책임 분담과 해결책 덕분인데, 이것은 교토의정서의 세계적 규제 접근방식이 갖는 결점들과 비교했을 때, 역내 이해충돌을 완화시키는 데 도움을 주었다. 그러나 세계적인 규제는 체계적인 합의가 이뤄지기 이전에 이미 자리를 잡아가고 있었으며, 전반적인 여론도 있을지도 모르는 오존층의 임박한 위험을 확신하고 있었다.

비엔나 협약과 몬트리올 의정서는 196개국과 유럽연합(EU)에서 비준을 받아서, 이 협약과 의정서가 유엔 역사상 최초로 만장일치로 비준을 받은 것이 되었다. 몬트리올 의정서의 광범위한 채택과 시행으로, 몬트리올 의정서는 국제 협력의 매우 우수한 사례로 <신랄하게 비난받았으며>, 유엔 사무총장은 몬트리올 의정서를 '현재까지 단 하나의 가장 성공적인 국제합의일 수 있다'고 평가했다.

1 ④   ▶ **문맥상 적절하지 않은 표현 고르기**
이 글의 마지막 단락은 국제적으로 비준된 몬트리올 의정서에 대한 평가를 다루고 있는데, ⑩ 다음에 유엔 사무총장이 "현재까지 단 하나의 가장 성공적인 국제합의일 수 있다"라고 한 내용을 통해, ⑩에는 '긍정적인' 내용이 와야 할 것이다. 따라서 ⑩ 앞에 온 수동태를 감안해 '신랄하게 비난하다'는 뜻인 ⑩의 upbraided를 '열렬히 지지하다'는 뜻인 hailed로 고쳐야 한다.

2 ④   ▶ **내용일치**
몬트리올 의정서가 승인되었을 때, 이전의 온실가스 관련 국제적인 합의들이 무효화되었다는 내용은 본문에 언급되지 않았으므로, ④가 정답이다.

3 ③   ▶ **내용추론**
몬트리올 의정서라는 국제적인 합의의 결과, 남극의 오존홀이 서서히 회복 중에 있으며, 기후전망은 2050~2070년 사이에 오존층이 1980년 수준으로 되돌아갈 것임을 보여준다고 했다. 이는 '가시적인 성과'로 볼 수 있으므로, ③이 정답이다.

---

protocol n. 의정서

deplete v. 고갈시키다

layer n. 층

treaty n. 조약

phase out 단계적으로 중단[폐지]하다

signature n. 서명, 조인

pursuant to ~에 의하여

convention n. 협약, 조약

establish the framework 틀을 구축하다

address v. (어려운 문제 등을) 대처하다

enter into force (법·규칙 등이) 발효되다

Antarctica n. 남극대륙

be attributed to ~에 기인하다

mitigate v. 완화시키다, 경감시키다

shortcoming n. 결점, 단점

regulatory a. 규제하는, 단속하는

install v. (편안하게) 자리를 잡게 하다

consensus n. 의견일치, 합의

overall a. 전반적인

imminent a. 임박한

ratify v. 비준하다

implementation n. 실행

exceptional a. 매우 뛰어난, 우수한

Secretary-General n. 사무총장

to date 현재까지

09

전 세계적으로 기온이 올라가면서 일어나는 온난화는 지구 전역에서 균일하지가 않다. 지역마다 태양으로부터 흡수하는 열이 태양광선이 지구표면에 부딪치는 각도에 따라 더 많기도 하고 더 적기도 하다. 그러나 또 다른 중요한 요인이 또한 지구의 여러 지역이 흡수하는 열의 양을 결정하는데, 그것은 지표면이 태양광선을 반사시켜 우주로 되돌려 보내는 정도다. 얼음과 눈은 그들에게 부딪히는 열과 빛의 95% 이상을 반사시켜, 거의 거울처럼 태양을 향해 도로 빛을 발한다. 이와 대조적으로, 부분적으로 투명한 청록색 바닷물은 태양으로부터 받는 열과 빛의 85% 이상을 흡수한다.

이러한 반사표면과 흡수표면 사이의 중대한 차이는 남극과 북극의 기후에 가장 큰 영향을 미친다. 기온이 어는점 이상이면 물이고 그 이하이면 얼음이어서, 어는점이 물과 얼음이라는 H2O의 서로 다른 두 평형상태 사이의 경계를 나타내는 변화의 출발점이다. 극지방 가장자리 지역에서는 얼음으로 덮인 지표면의 경계에 또 다른 변화의 출발점이 있다. 기온이 어는점 이상으로 올라가 얼음 가장자리가 녹기 시작하는 곳마다, 그 작은 변화가 지구표면의 그 부분과 햇빛 사이의 관계를 변화시켜서 이제는 땅이 햇빛을 우주로 반사시키지 않고 흡수하게 된다. 후퇴하는 얼음 가장자리는 더 많은 열을 흡수함에 따라 쌓이는 온기에 의해 더 빠른 속도로 녹지 않을 수 없게 된다. 구름이 이 (녹는) 효과를 줄여줄 수는 있지만, 그 (녹는) 과정은 자가 증폭하는 경향이 있어서, 지표면의 햇빛 흡수 성질이 기온 상승에 대체로 영향 받지 않는 적도에서보다 극지방에서 기온이 더 빨리 상승하도록 만든다.

1 ③ ▶ **빈칸완성**
빈칸 다음의 the process는 얼음이 녹는 과정을 가리키므로 빈칸에는 ③의 '(녹는) 효과를 줄여줄 수는 있지만'이 적절하다. 다른 보기는 모두 얼음이 녹는 과정을 더욱 촉진하는 결과를 낳는다.

2 ④ ▶ **내용파악**
표면의 태양열 흡수를 결정하여 기온상승에 영향을 미치는 요인으로 태양광선이 표면에 부딪치는 각도, 흡수량, 반사량은 첫 단락에 언급되었으나 ④ '표면이 태양광선에 취약한 정도'는 언급되지 않았다.

3 ② ▶ **내용추론**
얼음과 반대로 물은 열을 흡수한다고 첫 단락 마지막 부분에서 언급되었지만, 이것은 얼음 가장자리의 물이 열을 흡수하여 얼음을 더욱 빨리 녹게 하는 것을 설명할 뿐이고, 호수의 물은 증발할 때 주변 대기의 열을 흡수하므로 실제 호수 근처 지역은 더 시원할 수 있다. 따라서 ②는 추론할 수 없다. ① 위도가 높은 극지방에서는 태양광선이 비스듬하게 비추고 태양광선이 표면에 비스듬하게 부딪칠수록 태양광선은 더 넓은 면적에 더 엷게 퍼져 지표면에 흡수되는 열의 양이 더 적기 때문에 극지방이 더 춥다. ③ 어는점이 얼음이 녹는 변화의 출발점이어서 기온이 어는점에 이른 후에 얼음이 녹는 과정이 가속화되기 시작한다. ④ 온도차가 클수록 두 지역 사이에 이동하는 열의 양이 많은데, 지구온난화가 진행됨에 따라 적도보다 극지방에서 기온이 더 빨리 상승하여 기온차가 줄어들면 적도에서 극지방으로 이동되는 열의 양은 줄어들 것이다.

4 ① ▶ **글의 제목**
이 글은 첫 문장에서 지구온난화는 지구 전역에서 균일하지가 않다고 한 다음, 극지방의 기온이 더 빨리 상승함을 설명하므로 ①의 '극지방에서 더욱 현저한 지구온난화'가 제목으로 적절하다.

uniform a. 획일적인, 균일한

glare v. 눈부시게 빛나다, 노려보다

transparent a. 투명한

threshold n. 문지방, 출발점, 역(閾: 반응이 시작되는 분계점)

retreat v. 후퇴하다

feed on ~를 희생하여 살아가다

feed on oneself 스스로 증폭하다, 자가 증식하다

10

A 지난 9월, 28살의 시카고 주민인 쟌 헤걸(Jeanne Haegele)은 그녀의 생활에서 플라스틱 사용을 배제하기로 결심했다. 그녀는 흔한 종류의 플라스틱에서 침출된 화학물질들이 그녀의 몸에 미칠 영향들을 우려하였다. 그녀는 모든 플라스틱 쓰레기들이 환경에 미칠 피해에 대해서도 걱정하였다. 그래서 그녀는 자전거를 타고 근처 식료품점으로 가서 플라스틱을 포함하고 있지 않은 물건들을 찾을 수 있는지 살펴보았다. "가게로 들어가 보니 살 수 있는 게 거의 없었어요."라고 헤걸은 말한다. 그녀는 통조림 식품 몇 가지와 우유 한 팩을 샀는데, 두 종류의 제품 용기 모두 안쪽이 플라스틱 수지로 처리되었음을 발견하였다. 그녀는 "플라스틱은 사실상 모든 제품에 들어 있는 것 같았습니다."라고 말한다.

B 그녀의 말이 맞다. 미국은 2005년에 2천8백만 톤의 플라스틱 쓰레기를 만들어냈고, 2천7백만 톤의 플라스틱 쓰레기들이 매립되었다. 우리의 식품과 식수는 플라스틱으로 포장되어 있다. 플라스틱은 전화기, 컴퓨터, 우리가 몰고 다니고 타고 다니는 차량과 비행기에도 사용된다. 그러나 이 무한히 적용 가능한 물질에는 어두운 측면이 있다. 환경문제 전문가들은 플라스틱 생산에 필요한 석유에 관해 고민한다. 부모들은 가정에서 사용하는 플라스틱 제품들에 포함된 독성 화학물질들이 자녀들의 혈관 속으로 들어갈 가능성에 대해 우려한다. 이것은 플라스틱을 자신의 삶에서 제거하려는 사람이 헤걸 한 사람만 있는 것은 아니라는 것을 의미한다. 그녀만 유일하게 이런 종류의 노력에 관해 블로그를 운영하고 있는 것은 아니다. 그러나 플라스틱 없는 삶을 살기 위해 노력해 본 사람들은 그것이 결코 쉽지 않다는 것을 잘 안다. 미주리 대학의 생물학자 프레데릭 봄 살(Frederick vom Saal)은 "플라스틱은 도처에 있기 때문에 그것들과 마주치지 않기란 사실상 불가능합니다."라고 말한다.

C 우리는 플라스틱은 본질적으로 불활성이라고 생각한다. 실제로 플라스틱 병 하나가 쓰레기 매립지에서 분해되기까지는 수백 년이 걸린다. 그러나 플라스틱이 오래되거나 열 또는 압력에 노출되면 그 성분 중 극소량이 방출된다. 그중에서도 특히 오늘날 우려되고 있는 것은 일부 플라스틱을 강화하는 데 사용되는 비스페놀 A(BPA)와 여타 플라스틱들을 연화시키는 데 사용되는 프탈레이트다. 이 두 성분은 모두 수백 여 종류의 가정용 플라스틱 제품들에 들어 있다. BPA는 대장균과 보톨리눔 식중독 예방을 위해 유아용 젖병에서부터 통조림식품 내부 도료에 이르기까지 모든 제품들에 들어 있고, 프탈레이트는 비닐 샤워 커튼은 물론 어린이용 장난감에서도 발견된다. 이러한 화학물질들은 우리가 먹는 식품이나 물, 먼지를 통해 우리 몸속으로 들어오기도 하고 심지어 피부를 통해 흡수되기도 한다. 실제로 미국 질병통제예방센터에서는 6세 이상의 미국인들 중 92%가 BPA 양성반응을 보인다고 보고했는데, 이는 우리의 플라스틱 우주에서 이 화학물질이 얼마나 흔한 것인지를 보여주는 하나의 증거다.

1 ①   ▶ 부분이해
B 단락에서 필자가 플라스틱의 '어두운 측면'으로 지적하고 있는 것은 그 표현 다음에 언급되고 있다. 첫째, 석유를 사용해야 플라스틱을 만들 수 있기 때문에 수반되는 환경문제, 둘째, 가정용 플라스틱 제품들을 사용하다가 그 유독 성분이 어린이들의 몸 속으로 흡수될 가능성의 문제, 셋째, 플라스틱이 우리 주변에 편재하고 있다는 사실로 인해 그것들을 한꺼번에 대체하기 쉽지 않다는 문제가 그것이다.

2 ②   ▶ 빈칸완성
A 단락 끝에 있는 "플라스틱은 사실상 모든 제품에 들어 있는 것 같았습니다."는 문장과 B 단락 빈칸 다음에 있는 진술 "그것들과 마주치지 않기란 사실상 불가능합니다."를 고려하면 '어디에나 존재하는', '편재하는', '도처에 있는'이라는 의미의 표현이 들어가는 것이 적절하다. ① 가소성이 뛰어난 ③ 구부리기 쉬운 ④ 쓸데없는 ⑤ 적응성이 뛰어난

3 ④   ▶ 내용파악
C 단락에서 필자는 '그중에서도 특히 오늘날 우려되고 있는 것'이라고 말하면서 BPA와 프탈레이트에 대한 언급을 시작하였다는 점에 주목한다.

4 ②   ▶ 내용일치
B 단락 앞부분에서 "미국은 2005년에 2천8백만 톤의 플라스틱 쓰레기를 만들어냈고, 2천7백만 톤의 플라스틱 쓰레기들이 매립되었다."고 하였으므로 ②의 진술이 본문의 내용과 일치한다.

---

leach v. 침출되다, 걸러지다

refuse n. 쓰레기

resin n. 수지, 송진

landfill n. 쓰레기 매립지

fret v. 조바심치다

ubiquitous a. 도처에 있는, 편재하는

inert a. 불활성의, 움직이지 않는

degrade v. 분해되다

trace n. 극미량, 조금

E. coli n. 대장균

botulism n. 보톨리눔 식중독

can lining 관내면 도료

positive a. 양성의

11 의학·건강

01

일곱 살 때 피터(Peter)는 처음으로 환청을 경험했는데, 편안한 음성이 들려와 그에게 모든 일이 잘 될 거라고 말하는 것이었다. 지금 기억에 그가 열 살이 되었을 때는 이미 그 음성이 20가지 악마의 음성으로 바뀌어 있었다. 물건을 훔치라고 강요했고, 자신이 예수라는 확신을 갖게 했으며, 자살을 시도하도록 설득하기도 했다. 여러 해 동안의 정신과 치료에도 증세가 완화되지 않아 그는 비슷한 증세로 고생하는 사람들을 돕는 단체인 환청네트워크(HVN)에 가입했다. 이 단체는 환청에 시달리는 사람들을 한데 모아 개인적인 경험담과 대처 방안들을 서로 교환하게 한다. 환청을 경험하는 사람이 25명 중 한 명꼴이나 된다는 연구 결과에 의거하여 이 단체는 환청 현상을 하나의 정상적인 경험이라고 재정의하고, 가입자들에게 환청의 음성과 대화를 지속하여 그 음성과 평화롭게 살고, 심지어 그 음성의 존재에 감사할 수 있도록 하라고 격려한다. HVN의 이러한 처방은 전통적인 정신병 치료법에 정면으로 거스르는 것인데, 전통적인 치료법은 환자가 정신병 치료약을 복용하고 환청의 음성을 무시해버리기를 더 선호하는 치료법이며, 환청의 음성을 인정하는 것은 환청을 더욱 강화시켜준다고 경고한다. 그러나 HVN은 환청의 음성을 인정하는 것이 회복 과정을 시작하는 선결조건이며, 사람의 정신이 이 내부의 수다쟁이를 이용하여 사람들로 하여금 환청의 원인인 사랑하는 사람의 죽음이나 노골적인 학대와 같은 아직 해결되지 않은 정신적 외상(外傷)에 주의를 기울이도록 만든다고 주장한다.

1 ② ▶ 빈칸완성
25명 중에 한 명꼴이나 될 정도로 흔하다는 것은 특별히 비정상적이지 않고 누구나 겪을 수 있는 정상적인 경험이라는 뜻이며 그 음성과 대화를 지속한다는 것도 '정상적인' 상태로 인정한다는 것이다. ① 정신병의 ③ 비전의, 비밀의 ④ 특별한, 특수한

2 ④ ▶ 내용추론
정신과 의사들은 환청을 정신병 증세로 인정하기 때문에 환자에게 정신병 치료약을 복용케 하는 것을 선호한다고 했으므로 ④가 정답이다. ① 가만히 두어도 사라진다는 말은 본문에 없다. ② 노인들이 특히 환청에 시달린다는 말은 본문에 없다. ③ 무시하는 전략은 전통적인 치료법에 해당한다.

auditory hallucination 환청
demonic a. 악마의; 악마 같은
psychiatric a. 정신과의
draw on ~에 의존하다, ~을 이용하다
recast v. 재구성하다, 다르게 제시하다
fly in the face of ~에 반항하다, ~에 정면으로 거스르다
psychiatry n. 정신의학, 정신병 치료법
antipsychotic a. 항정신병성의
precondition n. 선결조건
alert v. 경고하다, 주의를 환기시키다
trauma n. 정신적 외상, 마음의 상처, 쇼크

02

진보하기 위해서는 대체 현실, 즉 더 나은 현실을 상상할 수 있어야 하고 그런 현실을 성취할 수 있다고 믿어야 한다. 그러한 믿음이 우리에게 목표를 추구하도록 동기를 부여하는 데 도움을 준다. 낙관주의자들은 대체로 더 오래 일하고 더 많은 돈을 버는 경향이 있다. 듀크(Duke) 대학의 경제학자들은 낙관주의자들이 심지어 저축도 더 많이 한다는 것을 알아냈다. 그리고 그들도 마찬가지로 이혼할 가능성이 있지만 재혼할 가능성은 더 높은데, 재혼이란 사무엘 존슨(Samuel Johnson)의 표현대로 희망이 경험을 이긴 행동이다.
비록 그 더 나은 미래가 환상일 때가 종종 있긴 하지만, 낙관주의는 현재에 명백한 이익을 갖는다. 희망은 우리 마음을 편안하게 해주고, 스트레스를 낮추고, 건강을 향상시킨다. 심장병 환자들을 연구하는 학자들은 낙관적인 환자들이 낙관적이지 않은 환자들보다 비타민을 복용하고, 저지방 식사를 하고, 운동을 해서 전반적인 관상동맥질환의 위험을 감소시킬 가능성이 더 높다는 것을 발견했다. 암 환자들에 대한 연구 결과, 60세 미만의 비관적인 환자들이 동일한 초기 건강 상태와 신분과 연령의 비관적이지 않은 환자들보다 8개월 이내에 사망할 가능성이 더 높은 것으로 나타났다.

alternative reality 대체 현실
optimist n. 낙관주의자
optimism n. 낙관주의
at ease 걱정 없이, 마음이 편안한
coronary a. 관상(동맥)의
pessimistic a. 비관적인

1 ① ▶ 빈칸완성

여기서 an act는 재혼을 가리키는데, 낙관주의적인 행동의 한 예로서 인용된 것이므로, 과거의 부정적인 경험보다 미래에 대한 희망이 더 커서 하는 것으로 보아야 한다. ② 지식을 넘어선 지혜 ③ 선입견을 넘어선 자만심 ④ 정신을 넘어선 비애감

2 ③ ▶ 내용파악

두 번째 단락의 두 번째 문장에서 "희망은 우리 마음을 편안하게 해준다."라고 했으므로, 낙관주의자는 마음이 느긋한(relaxed) 사람일 것이다. 더 오래 일한다고 한 것이 일중독(workaholic)을 의미하지는 않으므로 ①은 적절하지 않으며, ②는 '백일몽의', ④는 '낙태를 반대하는'의 의미다.

3 ② ▶ 내용추론

낙관주의자가 저축도 더 많이 한다고 했으므로, 미래에 대해 낙관한다고 해서 미래의 금전적 필요에 대해 준비를 게을리하는 것은 아니라는 것을 알 수 있다.

03

엄지손가락을 빠는 것과 손톱을 물어뜯는 것은 아이에게 건강상의 문제를 초래할 수 있으며, 치열 교정기를 부담하는 부모에게는 잠재적으로 경제적인 문제를 초래할 수 있다. (왜냐하면) 엄지손가락을 빠는 것은 아이의 치열을 상하게 할 수 있으며, 손톱을 물어뜯는 것은 해로운 세균들이 아이의 손가락에서 아이의 입으로 퍼지는 위험성을 증가시킬 수 있다.

그러나 소아과 저널에 실린 한 연구에 따르면, 이러한 두 가지 유년기의 습관들에는 깜짝 놀랄만한 좋은 면이 있다고 한다. 엄지손가락을 빨거나 손톱을 물어뜯는 아이들은 알레르기를 일으킬 위험성을 낮출 수 있다고 뉴질랜드의 오타고 대학교 더니든 캠퍼스의 의과대학 부교수이자 이 연구의 공동 집필자인 밥 행콕스(Bob Hancox)가 주장했다.

"이번 연구는 미생물(세균)에 대한 노출이 줄어든 것이, 다시 말해, 위생상태가 보다 좋아진 것이 최근 수십 년 동안 증가추세의 알레르기 질환의 발병원인이라는 위생 가설을 시험하기 위해 실시되었습니다."라고 밥 행콕스 교수가 말했다. 이 가설은 또한 항생물질을 사용한 것도 포함한 것으로 기술되어 있다. "우리는 (실험에서) 무엇을 기대해야 할지 알지 못했습니다. 우리는 이러한 습관(엄지손가락을 빨고 손톱을 물어뜯는 습관)을 갖고 있는 아이들한테서 알레르기의 위험성이 줄어들 것이라고 가설을 세웠지만, 이 가설이 사실로 드러날지 여부는 전혀 알지 못했습니다."라고 밥 행콕스 교수는 말했다.

1 ③ ▶ 빈칸완성

빈칸 Ⓐ 다음에서 엄지손가락을 빠는 것은 아이의 치열을 상하게 할 수 있다고 했으므로, 부모가 돈을 부담하게 되는 것에 해당하는 것은 braces(치열 교정기)가 적절하다. 빈칸 Ⓒ 다음에는 in other words(다시 말해)가 왔으므로 빈칸 Ⓒ의 앞과 뒤의 내용이 같음을 알 수 있다. 따라서 위생상태가 좋아진다는 말은 곧 미생물(세균)에 대한 노출이 '줄어든다'는 것을 의미하므로 Ⓒ에는 diminished(줄어든)가 들어가야 적절하다. ① 틀니 — 증가된 ② 목발 — 강화된 ④ 압박붕대 — 장기간의

2 ④ ▶ 글의 주제

일반적으로 지양되는 엄지손가락 빨기와 손톱 깨물기에 좋은 점이 있다고 소개하고 있으며, 그 근거로 위생가설을 들고 있다. 따라서 ④의 '엄지손가락 빨기와 손톱 깨물기가 이로운가?'가 글의 주제로 적절하다.

3 ② ▶ 부분이해

upside(나쁜 상황 속에서 좋은 면)는 엄지손가락을 빨고 손톱을 깨무는 것의 좋은 면을 가리키므로, "엄지손가락을 빨거나 손톱을 물어뜯는 아이들은 알레르기를 일으킬 위험성이 보다 줄어들 수 있다."와 같은 맥락인 ②가 정답이다.

thumb-sucking n. 엄지손가락 빨기

nail-biting n. 손톱 물어뜯기

alignment n. 정렬

germ n. 세균, 병원균

pediatrics n. 소아과, 소아학

associate professor 부교수

hygiene n. 위생

hypothesis n. 가설

microbial a. 미생물의, 세균의

antibiotics n. 항생물질

04

일반 마취제인 프로포폴은 뇌에 있는 감마-아미노부티르산(GABA) 수용체에 작용한다. GABA 수용체는 다른 신경 회로를 가라앉히는 억제성 뉴런을 활성화시킨다. 그런 방식으로 그것이 사람의 의식을 잃게 한다. 프로포폴은 또한 기분을 좋게 해주는 신경 전달 물질인 도파민의 수치를 증가시키고 성관계 혹은 코카인과 다르지 않은 보상을 느끼도록 유발한다. 일부 환자들은 행복감, 성적 (性的) 억제의 해제, 심지어 환각을 경험하며, 뒤이어 평온함을 느낀다. 프로포폴은 매우 널리 사용되고 있어서 — 프로포폴은 외래 마취에 혁명을 불러일으켜서, 내과의사가 가령 결장 내시경 수술을 하기 위해 몇 초 안에 환자의 의식을 잃게 하고 10분 만에 환자의 의식을 회복하게 한다 — 과학자들은 그 경험을 설명할 수 있는 환자들이 부족하지 않다. 약 3분의 1은 아무것도 기억하지 못하고, 다른 3분의 1의 환자는 꿈을 꿨다고 말하지만, 세부적인 것들을 기억하지 못한다. 나머지는 생생하고, 이상한 꿈, 때때로 성적인 꿈을 경험한다.

프로포폴이 1989년에 소개되고 난 직후, 의사들 사이에서 프로포폴이 남용되고 있다는 사실이 세간에 알려졌다. 프로포폴이 모르핀과 같은 규제 약물이 아니어서 병원들은 프로포폴을 안전한 곳에 넣어 보관하지 않았으며, 그로 인해 누군가 프로포폴을 훔치는 것은 쉬운 일이었다. 작년에 남용이 점점 늘어나고 있는 것에 당황한 미국 마취과의사회는 프로포폴을 규제 약물로 분류하라는 마약 단속국의 제안을 공식적으로 승인했다. (하지만) 아직 아무런 조치가 이뤄지지 않고 있다.

1 ③ ▶ 내용파악
첫 번째 단락에서 프로포폴은 들뜬 행복감, 강한 성 욕구, 망각 등을 경험하게 해준다고 언급하고 있지만, 숙면에 이르게 해준다는 내용은 없다.

2 ② ▶ 내용추론
마취과 의사들이 프로포폴을 가장 안전한 마취제로 인식하고 있다는 것은 본문에서 추론할 수 없으므로 ②가 정답이다. ① 아직 규제 약물로 정해지지 않은 상태인 점과 프로포폴을 투여한 환자들의 증상을 고려하면, 남용될 가능성이 크다고 할 수 있다. ③ "프로포폴이 모르핀과 같은 규제약물이 아니어서 병원들은 포로포폴을 안전한 곳에 넣어 보관하지 않았으며, 그로 인해 누군가 프로포폴을 훔치는 것은 쉬운 일이었다."라고 했으므로, 관리를 소홀히 한 점에 대해 병원은 비난을 피하기 어려울 것이다. ④ 마지막 문장에서 마약 단속국은 프로포폴을 규제 약물로 인식하고 있다고 했다.

3 ① ▶ 내용파악
프로포폴이 널리 사용되는 이유에 대해서 첫 번째 단락의 네 번째 문장에서 설명하고 있다. "내과의사가 결장 내시경 수술을 하는 데 있어서 몇 초 안에 환자의 의식을 잃게 하고 10분 만에 환자의 의식을 회복하게 한다."라고 했으므로 ①이 정답이다.

anesthetic n. 마취제

inhibitory a. 금지의; 제지하는, 억제하는

induce v. 야기하다, 일으키다

neurotransmitter n. 신경 전달 물질

euphoria n. 행복감

upbeat a. 낙관적인, 명랑한

ambulatory a. 이동하는; 보행용의

colonoscopy n. 결장 내시경 수술

knock somebody out ~를 곯아떨어지게 하다, 의식을 잃게 만들다

controlled substance 규제 약물, 불법 약물

swipe v. 훔치다

endorse v. 지지하다; 배서하다

classify v. 분류하다, 등급으로 나누다

05

식이지방이 심장병을 유발한다는 생각이 우리의 머릿속 깊이 뿌리박혀 있다. 우리 모두는 앳킨스(Atkins) 다이어트가 사람의 목숨을 앗아간다고 알고 있다. 어쨌든 그렇다고 들은 적이 있다. 그러나 지난 10년 동안 수십 건의 연구를 통해 앳킨스 다이어트를 살펴본 결과, 의사들과 미국심장협회가 바라는 저지방 저칼로리 다이어트보다 이런 종류의 저탄수화물 다이어트를 할 때 심장병 위험 요인들이 더 많이 개선된다는 것이 드러난다. HDL(좋은 콜레스테롤) 수치가 올라가는데, 이것이 심장 건강의 관점에서 가장 의미 있는 수치. 특히 작고 밀도가 큰 위험한 LDL(나쁜 콜레스테롤)은 크고 보풀보풀한 LDL이 된다. 그리고 콜레스테롤 수치가 개선될 뿐 아니라, 인슐린 수치가 내려가고 인슐린 저항성이 없어지며 혈압이 내려간다. 심장을 보호해줄 것으로 기대하며 사람들이 먹고 있는 저지방 다이어트 식사는 탄수화물 함량이 높기 때문에 실제로는 심장에 나쁘다. 모든 사람들로 하여금 그렇게 먹도록 만들려는 공중보건 노력이 우리가 지금 비만과 당뇨병을 유행병 수준으로 많이 갖고 있는 근본적인 이유들 중 하나다.

dietary fat 식이지방, 식사로 섭취하는 지방

ingrained a. 깊이 스며든, 뿌리 깊은

Atkins diet 앳킨스 다이어트(앳킨스가 고안한 고단백질 식품만 먹고 고탄수화물 식품은 피하는 다이어트로 황제 다이어트라고도 함)

factor n. 요소, 요인

carbohydrate n. 탄수화물

dense a. 밀집한; 밀도가 높은

fluffy a. 보풀이 인, 솜털의; 솜털로 뒤덮인

cholesterol profile 콜레스테롤 수치

resistance n. 저항, 반항, 반대

fundamental a. 기본적인, 근본적인, 주요한

obesity n. 비만, 비대

1 ④　▶ **내용파악**

마지막 문장의 that way는 저지방 고탄수화물 다이어트이므로 공중보건 종사자들이 앳킨스 다이어트를 권장한다는 ④는 사실이 아닌 진술이다. ① 여기서 통념은 첫 번째 문장의 '식이지방이 심장병을 유발한다는 생각'을 말하므로 사실인 진술이다. ② 세 번째 문장의 '이런 종류의 저탄수화물 다이어트'가 앳킨스 다이어트이며 첫 번째 문장과 관련하여 이것은 고지방 다이어트임을 알 수 있다. ③ 끝에서 세 번째 문장이 단서다.

2 ①　▶ **글의 목적**

이 글은 식이지방이 심장병을 유발한다는 잘못된 생각을 깨뜨리고, 앳킨스 다이어트라는 이름의 심장 건강에 좋은 다이어트를 알리기 위해 쓴 글이다.

3 ②　▶ **글의 제목**

앳킨스 다이어트가 고지방이므로 ②가 적절한 제목이다. ①는 "심장을 위해 야채를 더 많이 먹어야 한다," ③은 "건강하지 못한 심장이 질병을 초래한다," ④는 "식이지방이 심장병을 유발한다."라는 의미이므로 정답으로 적절하지 않다.

diabetes n. 당뇨병	
epidemic n. 유행병, 전염병	

06

염증은 다치거나 병원균에 노출될 때 발생한다. 부상이나 감염에 대한 반응으로 몸의 면역계는 유해한 세균을 물리치고 손상된 부위를 회복시킬 시토킨이라 불리는 단백질을 방출한다. 그러나 지금 일부 전문가들은 스트레스, 다이어트, 환경독소 등에 의해 야기되는 염증으로 인한 시토킨에의 만성적 노출은 기분을 좋게 하는 호르몬인 세로토닌의 수치를 떨어뜨려 우울증의 원인이 될 수도 있다고 믿는다.

과학자들은 1980년대에 동물에게 박테리아를 주사하여 염증을 일으켜보고 처음으로 염증과 우울증의 관련성을 확인했다. 주사를 맞은 동물들이 무기력, 식욕상실, 동료와의 접촉 회피 등 우울증의 증세를 보였던 것이다. 뒤이은 후속 연구 결과, 우울증이 있는 사람들은 혈액 속에 C-반응성 단백질 같은 염증성 화학물질의 수치가 높은 것으로 밝혀졌다. 흥미를 느낀 한 연구팀은 자가 면역 질환을 치료하는 항염증성 약물인 인플릭시맙을 우울증이 심한 사람들에게 투여하고, C-반응성 단백질 수치가 높은 피실험자들(우울증환자들)이 염증이 없는 피실험자들(우울증환자들)보다 우울증 증세가 더 많이 호전되었다고 말한다는 것을 알게 되었다.

염증이 우울증의 주된 원인일 것 같지는 않지만, 전문가들은 그것이 우울증을 장기화시키거나 악화시킬 수는 있다는 데에 갈수록 의견이 일치하고 있다. 염증 수치가 높은 환자들의 우울증을 항염증성 약물로 치료하는 것은 그들의 기분에 큰 영향을 미칠지도 모른다.

inflammation n. 염증	
germ n. 세균(= microbe)	
immune system 면역계	
fight off 격퇴하다	
environmental toxin 환경독소	
lethargy n. 무기력, 권태; 기면	
subsequent a. 뒤이은	
intrigued a. 흥미를 가진	
auto-immune disease 자가 면역 질환	
mood n. 기분, 감정	

1 ①　▶ **빈칸완성**

빈칸 앞에서 인플릭시맙을 투여 받은 사람은 우울증이 심한 환자들(people with major depression)이므로 호전된 증세는 우울증 증세일 것이고, 인플릭시맙이 염증을 없애는 항염증제이므로 염증 화학물질(C-반응성 단백질) 수치가 높은 환자가 염증이 없는 환자보다 더 큰 호전을(효과를) 보일 것이다. 따라서 ①이 정답이다.

2 ③　▶ **내용파악**

C-반응성 단백질이 염증 화학물질이므로 염증의 정도는 C-반응성 단백질의 수치와 정비례한다고 할 수 있다. 따라서 ③이 사실이다. ① cytokines와 serotonin을 서로 맞바꾸어야 한다. ② bacteria를 depression으로 고쳐야 한다. ④ 염증은 세균의 공격 과정이 아니라 부상이나 세균감염에 대한 면역계의 반응이다.

3 ②　▶ **글의 요지**

첫 단락의 첫 두 문장은 염증에 대한 일반적 이해를 언급한 것이고 그다음 But 이하가 이 글의 주제를 담은 문장이다. 여기서 스트레스, 다이어트, 환경독소는 현대인의 생활방식의 단면들을 말하고 그로 인한 염증이 우울증을 낳을 수 있다는 것이 이 글의 요지다.

07

커피 한 잔을 먹으면 의욕이 생겨서 올겨울에 체육관에 가는 것을 즐기게 할 수 있을까? 이런 질문은 당신이 어떤 운동을 하던 간에, 카페인이 경기력을 보다 향상시켜 주고 더 즐겁게 운동을 할 수 있게 해줄지도 모른다는 것을 암시하는 몇몇 새로운 실험들 중 하나인 카페인과 운동을 다룬 유명한 어떤 연구의 핵심 주제다.

물론 과학자들과 많은 운동선수들은 운동 전에 커피 한 잔이 특히 오래 달리기와 사이클링과 같이 지구력을 요하는 운동에서 경기력을 향상시킨다는 것을 수년 전부터 알고 있었다. 카페인은 혈류에서 순환하는 지방산의 수를 증가시키는 것으로 입증되었는데, 이 혈류에서 순환하는 지방산이 사람들을 더 오래 달리거나 더 오래 사이클 페달을 밟도록 해준다. (왜냐하면 사람의 근육은 에너지를 만들어 내기 위해 지방을 흡수하고 연소시킬 수 있으며, 운동 후반부까지 한정된 탄수화물을 비축할 수 있기 때문이다.) 그 결과 국제올림픽위원회에서 합법적인 카페인은 스포츠에 있어 가장 인기 있는 약물이다. 최근 보고서에서 다뤄진 올림픽 선수 약 2만6천8십 명 중 2/3 이상의 선수들이 소변에서 카페인이 검출되었으며, 철인3종 경기 선수들, 사이클 선수들, 조정 선수들 중에서 카페인 사용이 가장 높았다. 그러나 근력운동과 같은 산소를 덜 이용하는 운동이나 축구, 농구와 같이 자주 멈췄다가 움직이는 단체운동을 하는 것에 카페인이 영향을 주는지 여부와 어떻게 영향을 주는지는 (아직) 분명하지 않다.

1 ④ ▶ **글의 주제**
이 글은 커피를 마시면 운동이나 경기를 하는 데 있어 활기를 불어넣을 수 있는지 여부에 관한 내용을 다루고 있으므로 ④의 "커피가 경기력 향상에 도움이 될 수 있을까?"가 글의 주제로 적절하다.

2 ③ ▶ **내용추론**
① 혈류에서 순환하는 지방산은 사람들을 더 오래 달리거나 더 오래 자전거 타도록 해준다고 했다. ② 카페인은 국제올림픽위원회(IOC)가 합법적으로 인정하는 약물이지만, 국제올림픽위원회가 이 카페인을 권한다는 내용은 본문에 언급되지 않았다. ④ 카페인이 들어있는 음료로 커피가 언급되었을 뿐, 카페인이 커피에만 들어 있는지는 본문에서 알수 없으며, 상식적으로도 녹차 등 다른 음료에도 카페인이 함유되어 있다. ③ 운동선수들은 운동 전에 커피 한 잔이 특히 오래 달리기와 사이클링과 같이 지구력을 요하는 운동에서 경기력을 향상시킨다는 것을 수년 전부터 알고 있었다고 했으므로 장거리 경주의 대표격인 마라톤에서 선수들이 경기력 향상을 위해 커피에 의존해왔을지도 모른다는 것은 충분히 추론 가능하다.

3 ② ▶ **내용파악**
혈류에서 순환하는 지방산은 사람들을 더 오래 달리거나 사이클 페달을 더 오래 밟도록 해주는데, 왜냐하면 사람의 근육이 에너지를 만들어내기 위해 '지방을 연소시키기' 때문이라고 하였으므로 ②가 정답이다.

---

motivate v. 동기를 부여하다
relish v. (어떤 것을 대단히) 즐기다, 좋아하다
jolt v. 충격을 주다, 정신이 번쩍 들게 하다; 갑자기 움직이게 하다
athletic performance 경기력
endurance sport 지구력을 요하는 운동
distance running 오래 달리기
fatty acid 지방산
circulate v. 순환하다
bloodstream n. 혈류, 혈액순환
pedal v. 페달을 밟다; (자전거를) 타고 가다
burn fat 지방을 연소시키다
fuel n. 연료, (에너지원으로서의) 음식물
urine n. 오줌, 소변
triathlete n. 삼종 경기(원영(遠泳)·장거리 자전거 경주·마라톤) 선수
rower n. 노 젓는 사람, 조정선수
weight training 근력운동
stop-and-go a. 자주 멎었다 가는, 가다가 쉬곤 하는, 느릿느릿한

08

미국 식품의약국이 대형 제약회사들의 처방약 TV광고를 처음으로 허용한 1997년 이후 시청자들은 항염증제와 콜레스테롤 저하제에서 항히스타민제까지 무엇이든 선전하는 상업광고의 공세를 받아왔다. 대부분의 광고들은 서둘러 부작용을 열거하며 더 자세히 알고 싶으면 의사에게 문의하라고 시청자들에게 강력히 권한다. 그런 광고를 허용한 것이 분명 24시간 방송되는 케이블 TV 디스커버리 헬스 채널의 탄생을 촉진했다. 이렇게 각 개인에게 마구 던져지는 건강 관련 정보와 오보와 지식의 쇄도는 객관성과 신뢰도 면에서 천차만별이다. 그러나 그로 인해 건강 문제가 점점 더 많은 대중의 관심을 받으며 의사와 환자 사이의 전통적인 관계가 변하여 후자(환자) 편에서 자기 관리적 태도가 더 많이 장려되고 있다.

아이러니하게도, 환자들은 양질과 저질의 건강정보를 더 많이 접하고 있는 반면에 그들의 의사들은 더욱 신속히 진료해야 하는 상황에 몰린 나머지, 온라인으로든 오프라인으로든 최신 의학 저널을 정독하고 관련 전문의들과 그리고 환자들과 충분히 의사 교환할 시간을 점점 더 갖지 못하고 있다. 환자들은 인터넷에서 출력한 인쇄물이나 미국의사약전에서 복사한 여러 장의 자료나 의학 학술지

---

pharmaceutical a. 제약의, 약학의
prescription drug 처방약(의사의 처방전이 필요한 약)
bombard v. 폭격하다, 퍼붓다
commercial n. 상업광고
tout v. 몹시 칭찬하다, 크게 선전하다
anti-inflammatory n. 항염증제, 소염제
list v. 열거하다, 명단에 올리다
avalanche n. (눈)사태; (질문·편지 등의) 쇄도
misinformation n. 잘못된 정보, 오보
hurl v. 세게 던지다, 퍼붓다

와 건강잡지에서 잘라낸 글들을 갖고 의사를 찾아온다. 그들은 질문을 던지고, 더 이상 의사의 흰 가운에 위압당하여 굽실거리지도 않는다.

1 ②　▶ 빈칸완성
첫 단락 첫 문장에서 시청자들이 상업광고의 공세를 받아왔다고 했으므로 빈칸에는 '공세(bombardment)'와 유사한 ② '쇄도'가 적절하다. ① 낙진, 강하 ③ 부족 ④ 집합, 집계

2 ④　▶ 부분이해
'의사의 흰 가운'은 곧 의사의 권위를 상징하며 tug one's forelock(굽실거리다)는 그 권위에 압도당한 행동이므로 ④가 가장 가까운 의미다.

3 ③　▶ 내용추론
첫 단락 마지막 문장에서 '오늘날의 환자들은 자신의 건강에 많은 관심을 쏟고 스스로 건강관리를 하려고 함'을 알 수 있다. 따라서 ③이 정답이다. ① 환자가 광고의 피해를 입고 있다는 언급은 없다. ② 광고 정보의 신뢰도는 천차만별이라 했다. ④ 오늘날 환자들이 아는 정보나 지식이 많아졌음은 사실이나 의사보다 더 많이 안다고는 할 수 없다.

take-charge a. 관리 능력이 있는, 리더십이 있는

uneven a. 고르지 않은

Physicians' Desk Reference 미국 내과의사 약학사전, 미국의사약전

clip n. 잘라낸[오려낸] 글

forelock n. 앞머리

tug one's forelock (필요 이상으로) 굽실거리다

in awe of ~를 두려워하여, ~에 위압당하여

09

이카리아 사람들이 살아온 방식을 주의 깊게 살펴보면 교묘하게 강력하고 서로 향상시켜주며 널리 퍼져있는 10여 개의 요인들이 작용하는 것 같다. 내가 "아하!"하고 크게 깨달은 점은 장수를 촉진하는 이러한 요인들이 어떻게 장기간에 걸쳐 서로를 강화시키는가 하는 것이다. 사람들이 건강한 생활양식을 택하려면, 말하자면, 그것을 가능케 하는 생태계(환경)에서 살아야 할 필요가 있다고 나는 확신하게 되었다. 다른 누구도 일찍 잠을 깨는 일이 없고 오후에 낮잠 시간 동안 마을 전체가 죽은 듯이 고요하면, 충분한 휴식을 취하기가 쉽다. 가장 싸고 가장 얻기 쉬운 음식이 또한 가장 건강한 음식이라는 것과 조상들이 수세기를 보내며 그 음식을 맛있게 만드는 법을 개발했다는 것이 (장수에) 도움이 된다. 이카리아에서 살다보면 하루에 20개의 언덕을 오르게 되는 것은 흔한 일이다. 당신은 소속되지 못함으로 인한 실존적 고통이나 심지어 늦게 당도함으로 인한 경미한 스트레스조차도 느끼지 못할 것이다. 하루의 끝자락에서 당신은 계절에 맞는 허브 차 한 잔을 이웃과 함께 마실 것이다. 그래서 당신이 사람 사귀기를 싫어한다 해도 결코 완전히 혼자 있게 되지는 않을 것이다. 이런 요인들 모두가 장수로 연결될 수 있다. 죽음과 노인성 질환을 막아낼 묘책은 없다. 비결에 가까운 것이 있다면, 그것은 지속적이고 다각적인 방책이다.

1 ①　▶ 부분이해
앞 문장에서 "죽음과 노인성 질환을 막아낼 묘책은 없다."고 했는데 silver bullet는 ③처럼 그것 하나로 모든 것을 해결할 수 있는 묘책인 반면에, silver buckshot은 지속적이고 다각적인(multi-pronged) 해결책을 말하므로 ①이 Ⓐ를 가장 잘 바꾸어 말한 것이다.

2 ③　▶ 내용파악
끝에서 세 번째 문장에서 "이런 요인들 모두가 장수로 연결될 수 있다."고 했고 그 앞에 장수의 요인들이 나열되어 있다. 그 바로 앞에서 "계절에 맞는 허브 차 한 잔을 이웃과 함께 마실 것이다. 그래서 당신이 사람 사귀기를 싫어한다 해도 결코 완전히 혼자 있게 되지는 않을 것이다."라고 한 것은 장수 요인으로 이웃과 사귀는 대인관계를 말한 것이지 계절에 맞는 허브 차를 말한 것이 아니므로 ③이 장수 요인이 아니다. ② 이카리아에서 살다 보면 하루에 20개의 언덕을 오르게 되는 것은 흔한 일이라고 했다.

3 ②　▶ 내용파악
이 글은 일상생활과 관련된 것이므로 대중적인 ② 잡지에 실려 있을 것이다.

subtly ad. 교묘하게

pervasive a. 널리 퍼진

longevity n. 장수(長壽)

reinforce v. 강화하다

dead a. 죽은 듯한

get through the day 하루를 다 보내다

existential a. 실존적인

simple a. 하찮은

herbal a. 초본의, 풀의

antisocial a. 반사회적인; 비사교적인

silver bullet (문제 해결의) 묘책

keep ~ at bay ~를 저지하다, 막아내다

silver buckshot 지속적인 효과를 낼 수 있는 다각적인 방책

10

당신이 사회적 시차증에 걸렸다고 생각하는가? <일어나기 위해 자명종이 필요하다면 당신은 아마도 그럴 것이다(사회적 시차증으로 고생하고 있는지도 모른다).> 뮌헨에 있는 루드비히-막시밀리안(Ludwig-Maximilians) 대학의 시간 생물학자 틸 뢰네버그(Till Roenneberg)가 만든 그 용어는, 체내 생체시계는 수면 상태를 더 유지하길 원하는데도 체외 사회생활 시계가 일어나라고 할 때 나타나는 현상을 가리킨다. 주중 내내 자명종 소리에 일어나고 주말에 늦잠을 자는 것은 우리 생체시계를 미국 서부해안으로 보냈다가 월요일 아침에 다시 동부해안으로 불러오는 것과 같다. 그로 인해 "수면부족과 수면과다의 순환에 빠져 밤에 정상적인 수면을 거의 하지 못하는 사람들이 있다."라고 뢰네버그는 말한다.

문제는 이런 현상이 우리 대부분의 사람들에게 점점 늘어나고 있다는 것이다. 다수결 원칙이 사회에 적용된다면 그리고 세계 경제를 따라가지 않는다면, 대부분의 사람들은 밤 12-1시 사이에 행복하게 잠자리에 들어 아침 8-9시 사이에 일어날 수 있을 것이다. 대신에 "우리 가운데 85퍼센트는 일어나기 위해 자명종이 필요하다."라고 뢰네버그는 말한다. 그에 따라 "보통 사람 가운데 3분의 2가 1시간 이상의 사회적 시차증에 시달린다. 16퍼센트의 사람들은 두 시간, 교대근무자들은 훨씬 더 긴 사회적 시차증에 시달리고 있다."

교대 근무는 특히 나쁘다. 하버드 의과대학의 수면 연구소장인 오르페오 벅스톤(Orfeo Buxton)은 교대 근무의 영향을 실험하기 위해 몇 주 동안 수면을 제대로 취하지 못한 사람들을 대상으로 최근 첫 연구를 시행했다. 그 결과 신진대사에 큰 문제가 생겼는데, 시간이 지남에 따라 포도당은 당뇨병을 유발시킬 수 있는 수치까지 급등했던 반면, 에너지 소모는 피험자들이 1년에 13파운드까지 체중이 증가하는 수치로 떨어졌다.

1 ③ ▶ **내용일치**
사회적 시차증에 시달리는 사람들이 체중이 증가할 수 있다고는 하였지만 주말에 몰아 자는 것이 날씬한 체형을 유지하는 데 도움이 되는 것은 아니므로 ③이 정답이다. ①, ② 마지막 단락에서 교대 근무는 사회적 시차증에 특히 좋지 않은 영향을 미친다고 하였고, 신진대사에 문제가 생긴다고 하였으며, 이로 인한 영향으로 당뇨병이 유발될 수 있고, 체중이 증가할 수 있다고 했으므로 옳은 진술이다. ④ 많은 사람들이 사회적 시차증에 시달리는 이유는 생체시계가 아직 밤중인데 자명종에 의해 일어나기 때문이다.

2 ① ▶ **문장삽입**
제시문의 you probably are는 you probably are socially jet-lagged에서 socially jet-lagged가 생략된 것이며 지문의 첫 번째 문장에 대한 답변으로 적절한 문장이다. 따라서 제시문은 A에 들어가야 한다.

3 ① ▶ **부분이해**
생체시계를 서부해안으로 보냈다가 다시 동부해안으로 불러온다는 것은 생체시계가 서부시간에 맞춰져 있는데 3시간 빠른 동부시간에 맞춰 일어나야 한다는 것을 의미한다. 따라서 생체시계는 우리가 수면상태를 유지하길 원할 것이라고 볼 수 있다.

chronobiologist n. 시간 생물학자
majoritarian a. 다수결의, 다수결에 의한
chase v. 쫓다, 추적하다
nod off 잠들다, 깜빡 졸다
social jet lag 사회적 시차증
shift work 교대 근무
vicious a. 나쁜, 결점 있는, 옳지 않은
disrupt v. 부수다; 분열시키다; 중단시키다
simulate v. 가장하다; 흉내 내다; 모의실험하다
metabolic a. 신진 대사의
chaos n. 혼돈; 대혼란
glucose n. 포도당, 글루코오스
spike v. (가치 등이) 급등하다
trigger v. (일련의 사건·반응 등을) 일으키다
diabetes n. 당뇨병
expenditure n. 지출, 소비; 경비; 소비량
slump v. 급감하다, 급락하다, 폭락하다
subject n. 실험대상자, 피실험자; 환자

11

학술지 『직업과 환경의학(Occupational and Environmental Medicine)』의 새로운 연구 결과에 따르면, 어떤 직업들은 너무나 형편없어서 직업이 없는 것보다 실제로 근로자들의 정신적 행복에 더 나쁘다고 한다. 연구원들은 몇 년간에 걸쳐 7,155명의 성인들로부터 얻은 연간 데이터를 분석했으며, 그들이 가진 직업의 특징과 정신건강 사이의 관련성을 평가했다. 그들은 실직한 사람들의 정신건강이 가장 질이 낮은 직업을 갖고 있는 사람들의 정신건강과 유사하거나 그보다 더 낫다는 사실을 알게 되었다.

질이 낮은 직업들은 요구사항이 많고, 임금은 적고, 자율권과 안전성이 부족한 것들로 정의 내려졌다. 예를 들어, 참가자들은 직업이 '예상했던 것보다 더 스트레스가 많았는지', 일이 '복잡하고 어려웠는지' 또는 그들로 하여금 '미래에 대해 걱정하도록' 만들지 않았는지에 대해 질문을 받았다. 직업이 나쁠수록 근로자의 정신건강은 형편없었다.

그러한 경향이 선택효과에 의해 초래된 것이 아님을 분명히 하기 위해, 연구원들은 실직한 피실험

analyze v. 분석하다; 분해하다
evaluate v. 평가하다, 가치를 검토하다
autonomy n. 자치(권); 자율
land a work 일자리를 얻다
subject n. 환자; 피실험자
move into (보다 좋은 일자리·주거·생활 등으로) 옮겨가다
clinically ad. 임상적으로
counterpart n. 상대물, 상대방

자들이 마침내 직업을 구하게 됐을 때 무슨 일이 일어났는지를 조사했다. 그들은 질 높은 직업에 종사하게 된 사람들의 정신건강이 상당히 개선되었다는 사실을 알게 되었다. 그러나 질이 낮은 직업을 갖게 된 사람들은 그들의 이전 정신건강 상태와 직업이 없는 피실험자들에 비해 임상적으로 정신건강이 상당히 나빠졌다.

1 ④   ▶ **빈칸완성**

첫 번째 문장에서 "너무 형편없는 직업들은 직업이 없는 것보다 근로자의 정신적 행복에 더 나쁘다."라고 했다. 이는 실직한 사람들의 정신건강이 질이 낮은 직업을 갖고 있는 사람들의 정신건강과 비교해서 '(적어도) 유사하거나 그보다 더 낫다'라는 것을 의미한다. 따라서 정답은 ④가 된다. ① ~와 동등하거나 열등한 ② ~에 비례하여 ③ ~와 다소 다른

2 ②   ▶ **부분이해**

실직한 피실험자를 대상으로 이들이 질이 높거나 낮은 직업을 얻게 됐을 때의 정신건강 상의 변화를 추가적으로 조사한 것은, "어떤 피실험자를 선택해서 조사했느냐에 따라 연구 결과가 달라지지 않을까"를 우려했기 때문이다. 따라서 밑줄 친 "selection effect"는 '연구 조사의 피실험자 샘플을 잘못 선택하는 오류로 인한 통계 분석의 왜곡'을 의미하는 것으로 보는 것이 타당하다. 데이터를 의도적으로 조작하는 것과 관련된 내용은 전혀 없으므로 ①은 정답이 될 수 없다.

3 ②   ▶ **글의 목적**

본문에서 '사회 심리적으로 질이 좋은 직업을 갖는 것의 이점'에 대해 중점을 두기보다는 '질이 낮은 직업이 정신건강에 끼치는 부정적 영향'에 대해 초점을 두고 설명하고 있으므로, 글의 목적으로 ④는 부적절하고 ②가 정답이다.

12

화학 요법을 받을 가능성에 직면해 있는 많은 환자들은 더 '자연적인' 치료 방법이 있는지 궁금해 한다. 그 희망은 마리화나, 동종 요법 또는 식물성 영양보충제가 화학 요법과 방사선 치료로 인해 잠재적으로 환자가 겪게 될 불쾌한 치료의 영향을 면하게 해주는 동시에 암을 없애게 해 줄 것이라는 것이다. 또한 '자연적인' 어떤 것이 제약회사에서 제조된 것보다 더 효과적일지도 모른다는 가능성이 항상 있다는 것이다.

비화학 요법의 '치료'와 관련하여 마리화나와 마리화나 오일 같은 파생물질은 치료법의 목록 중 꽤 높은 위치에 있다. 이것은 마리화나가 몇 세기 동안 기분 전환과 의약용으로 사용되었기 때문에 놀라운 일이 아니다. 마리화나에 들어 있는 THC는 구토 방지 작용을 하는 성분이 있는 것으로 알려져 있고, 수십 년 동안 마리화나에서 추출한 약품은 통증과 메스꺼움을 임상적으로 관리하는 데 사용되어 왔다.

그러나 이것 외에 마리화나가 암 치료에 어떠한 효능이 있다는 주장은 증거로 입증되지 않는데, 광범위하게 진행된 미국의 한 연구는 최근 이런 결론을 내렸다. 마리화나가 암에 영향을 줄 수 없을지도 모르지만, 적어도 THC는 일부 유익한 효과가 있다. 그러나 동종 요법의 경우에는 얘기가 다르다. 여러 연구에서, 동종 요법은 위약 효과 이외에는 효과가 없음을 보여주었다. 실제로, 그 치료법의 주요 원리는 알려져 있는 물리학과 완전히 대립되며 명백히 틀린 것이다. 그러나 동종 요법은 여전히 인기가 많다. 그 조제된 약이 생물학적으로 어떠한 작용도 보이지 않는 동안, 환자들은 동종 요법에 의해 헛된 희망에 매달릴 것이고 유익할 수 있는 의학적인 개입을 거부할 심각한 위험이 있는데, 이것이 치명적인 결과를 초래할 수 있다.

1 ①   ▶ **빈칸완성**

chemotherapy는 '암을 치료하는 화학 요법'이고 이에 대한 대안 치료로 마리화나, 동종 요법, 식물성 영양보충제를 들고 있는데, 이는 화학적인 치료법과 반대되는 '자연적인' 것이므로 빈칸 ⓐ에는 natural이 적절하다. ② 배타적인 ③ 현실적인 ④ 합성의

2 ③   ▶ **글의 제목**

암을 치료하는 것과 관련하여 비화학적인 치료법으로 인기가 많은 마리화나나 동종 요법이 실제로 암을 제거하는 아무런 효과가 없음을 밝히고 있으며 이것이 환자에게 치명적

---

chemotherapy n. 화학 요법

cannabis n. 마리화나

homeopathy n. 동종 요법(질병과 비슷한 증상을 일으키는 물질을 극소량 사용하여 병을 치료하는 방법)

supplement n. 보충물; 영양 보조 식품

spare v. (불쾌한 일을) 모면하게 하다

derivative n. 파생물

anti-emetic a. 구토 방지[억제] 작용의

nausea n. 욕지기, 메스꺼움

tenet n. (특히 집단의) 주의(主義)

at odds with ~와 불화하여, ~와 조화하지 못하는

preparation n. (약·화장품 등으로 사용하기 위한) 조제용 물질

inert a. 약리(藥理) 작용을 보이지 않는

intervention n. 개입, 간섭

인 결과를 초래할 수도 있다고 했으므로 이 글의 제목으로 ③ '암 치료와 관련된 유해한 근거 없는 믿음'이 적절하다.

3 ②　▶ **내용일치**

마지막 단락에서 동종 요법이 위약 효과에 지나지 않는다고 했는데도 불구하고, 여전히 인기가 많다고 했으므로 암환자들은 동종 요법이 암을 치료할 수 있다는 잘못된 정보에 취약하다고 볼 수 있다. 따라서 ②가 정답이다.

13

인생의 어느 순간 당신은 아마도 간지럽힘을 당했을 것인데, 간지럽힘은 미소, 웃음, 그리고 자기도 모르게 하는 행동을 유발하는 방식으로 반복적으로 건드려지는 것을 의미한다. 간지러움은 신체의 많은 부위에서 일어날 수 있는데, 가장 흔한 곳은 흉곽, 겨드랑이, 그리고 발바닥이다. 간지럽힘은 보통 친밀한 관계라는 상황 속에서 일어난다. 즉 부모가 자신의 아기와 아이들을 간지럽히고, 형제자매, 연애상대, 그리고 친한 친구들이 가끔 서로를 간지럽힌다. 어떤 사람들은 다른 사람들보다 간지러움을 더 잘 타는 것으로 보인다. 간지럽히는 것에 관해 한 가지 이상한 점은 자신을 스스로 간지럽히는 것이 불가능하다는 점이다. 만일 누군가가 당신의 흉곽을 찔러 당신을 웃게 하고 씰룩거리게 할 수 있다면, 똑같은 일을 당신 스스로에게도 할 수 있어야 되는 거 아닌가?

당신 스스로를 간지럽힐 수 없는 이유는 당신이 신체 일부를 움직일 때, 당신의 뇌의 어느 부위가 당신의 동작을 추적관찰해서, 그 동작이 초래할 감각을 예상하기 때문이다. 바로 이런 이유로, 예를 들어, 걸을 때 당신의 팔이 당신의 옆구리를 스치더라도 당신이 실제로 알아차리지 못하지만, 다른 누군가가 비슷한 방식으로(그 사람의 팔이 당신의 옆구리를 스칠 경우) 당신을 건드릴 경우 당신은 깜짝 놀랄 것이다. 만일 우리의 뇌가 우리의 신체 동작과 신체 동작이 일으키는 감각을 추적할 능력을 갖고 있지 않다면, 우리는 끊임없이 스치고 찌르는 것을 느끼게 되어 그 밖의 다른 어떤 것에 우리의 관심을 쏟는 것이 어렵게 될 것이다. 스스로 간지럽히는 것은 이런 현상의 극단적인 예다. 당신의 뇌는 당신의 흉곽을 찌르는 손가락이 당신 손가락인지 알고 있어서, 당신의 뇌가 감각반응을 완화시키는 것이다. <과학자들은 또한 체감각피질이 편두통 환자의 경우보다 두꺼웠다는 것을 발견했지만, 이 발견이 편두통 발병의 결과인지는 알려져 있지 않다.>

1 ④　▶ **문맥상 적절하지 않은 문장 고르기**

이 글은 신체의 간지러움에 대해 전반적으로 이야기하고 있다. 반면, ⑩는 이 글에서 언급되지 않은 '편두통 환자에게 나타나는 체감각피질'에 관한 내용이므로, 이 글의 흐름상 어색하므로, ④가 정답이다.

2 ③　▶ **지시대상**

밑줄 친 this phenomenon은 앞에서 언급한 "당신의 팔이 당신의 옆구리를 스치더라도 당신이 실제로 알아차리지 못하지만, 다른 누군가가 비슷한 방식으로 당신을 건드릴 경우 당신은 깜짝 놀랄 것이다."를 가리키므로, ③이 정답이다.

3 ②　▶ **내용파악**

사람들 중 일부는 다른 사람들보다 더 간지러움을 잘 타는 것으로 보인다고 했는데, 이 말을 바꿔 말하면 사람들마다 간지러움을 느끼는 정도가 다르다는 말로 해석할 수 있으므로, ②가 정답이다. ①, ④ 흉곽, 겨드랑이, 발바닥은 간지러움을 느끼는 부위의 대표적인 예로 언급되었을 뿐이다.

---

tickle v. 간지럽히다
ribcage n. 흉곽
armpit n. 겨드랑이
sole n. 발바닥
intimate a. 친밀한
twitch v. 씰룩거리다
poke v. (손가락 등으로) 쿡 찌르다
startle v. 깜짝 놀라게 하다
brush v. 지나가면서 가볍게 닿다
prod v. 쑤시다, 찌르다
dial down 완화하다
somatosensory a. 체성(體性)감각의
cortex n. (대뇌) 피질
migraine n. 편두통

14

설탕은 아이들이 분명 맛과 무관한 방식으로 설탕에 반응하고 적어도 선진국에서는 거의 모든 아이들이 설탕을 너무 많이 먹기 때문에 특히 문제가 되는 것이다. 단것은 아동기 동안에 고통의 표현을 무디게 한다(자제시킨다). 그것은 아기의 울음을 줄일 것이고, 포경수술과 발뒤꿈치를 찌르는 채혈 동안 진통제로 이용된다. (합성감미료 아스파탐도 또한 효과가 있기 때문에 효과를 내는 인자는 설탕이 아니라 단맛이다.) 단것에 대한 아이의 반응이 부모에게 너무나 만족스러워서 부모들이 결국 단것을 더 많이 주게 될 수도 있다. 그렇게도 효과가 신속하고 충분한 기분전환 책략이 이것 이외에 몇 개나 있겠는가?

그러나 공중보건상의 영향은 있으며, 그 영향은 아동 비만과 제2형 당뇨병의 증가 이상의 것이다. 특히 우유병을 들고 잠자리에 들게 되는 아이들에게 있어 과일주스를 포함한 당분 함유 음료수를 마셔서 치아가 썩는 "우유병 충치"에 대해 특히 걱정이 많다. 일부 아이들의 경우 영구치가 이미 썩어서 나온다. 그것은 주요한 예방 가능한 소아질환이며 유행병이라고 할 만한 규모에 이르고 있다. 특정 식품에 단맛을 강화시키는 휘발성물질의 농도를 높이는 것이 그 식품의 단맛을 떨어뜨리지 않고 당분 함량을 줄일 수 있게 해줄지도 모른다. 그러나 의도하지 않은(뜻밖의) 결과가 있을 수 있다. 칼로리가 없고 독성이 없고 나쁜 특성이 없는 단맛을 맛보는 경험을 창출할 수 있는 순간 곧바로 그것이 뇌에 대해 갖게 될 의미는 무엇인가? 우리는 단맛이 중독성 약물이 사용하는 경로와 아주 유사해 보이는 신경 경로를 이용한다는 것을 알고 있는데, 중독성 약물은 식품을 위해 특히 단것을 위해 진화된 신경회로를 강점하는 것으로 믿어진다. 무언가를 공짜로 얻는 것은 좋아 보이지만, 대자연은 위험한 면을 갖고 있다.

1 ② ▶ 빈칸완성
그다음 문장에서 단것이 아이들의 고통 표현이나 고통 인지를 감소시킴을 알 수 있으므로 빈칸 Ⓐ에는 '무디게 하다'는 의미의 ②가 적절하다. ① 날카롭게 하다 ③ 다양화하다 ④ 측정하다

2 ① ▶ 부분이해
그다음 문장에서 Ⓑ의 "뜻밖의 결과가 있을 수 있다"의 내용을 설명하는데, 칼로리가 없고 독성이 없고 나쁜 특성이 없는 단맛을 본다는 것은 좋은 점이지만 그 단맛에 대한 경험이 중독성을 갖게 하는 나쁜 점도 있음을 설명하므로 ①의 "좋은 일에는 항상 나쁜 일이 뒤따른다(호사다마)"가 Ⓑ와 가장 관련이 있다. ② 하늘이 무너져도 솟아날 구멍은 있다 ③ 과욕은 금물 ④ 겉만 보고 판단하지 말라

3 ③ ▶ 내용일치
둘째 단락에서 아이에게 단것을 많이 준 결과로 아동 비만과 제2형 당뇨병의 증가와 우유병 충치를 언급하므로 ③이 사실이다. ④ 셋째 단락의 '단맛을 강화시키는 휘발성물질'이 감미료인데 이어서 나쁜 점을 설명하고 있다. 천연과 인공을 구별하지 않는다.

challenging a. 도전적인, 문제가 되는
blunt v. 무디게 하다
analgesic n. 진통제
circumcision n. 포경수술
heel-stick a. 발뒤꿈치를 찌르는
blood draw 채혈
aspartame n. 아스파탐(합성감미료)
reinforce v. 강화하다
implication n. 내포, 함축; 영향, 결과
baby-bottle caries 우유병 충치
tooth decay 충치
come in 생기다
epidemic a. 유행병의
proportion n. 비율, 규모
volatile n. 휘발성물질
content n. 내용; 함유량
nasty a. 불쾌한, 위험한
hijack v. 강탈하다, 납치하다
circuitry n. 회로

15

영국에서 실시한 의료 기록 조사에 따르면, 항정신병 약들이 진정효과를 가지고 있지 않음에도 불구하고, 정신 병력을 가지고 있지 않은 정신지체장애자들의 공격적인 성향을 무디게 하기 위해서 광범위하게 사용되고 있다. 이러한 발견은 심히 우려가 되는데, 그 이유는 항정신병 약들이 비만이나 당뇨병 같은 심각한 부작용을 야기할 수 있기 때문이다. 유니버시티 칼리지 런던(University College London)의 정신의학 연구원인 로리 쉬핸(Rory Sheehan)과 그의 동료들은 15년 이상의 기간 동안 영국의 보호시설에 있는 33,016명의 정신지체장애자들로부터 얻은 자료를 연구했다. 연구자들은 항정신병 약 치료를 받은 9,135명의 정신지체장애자들 가운데 71%가 심각한 정신병 진단을 받지 않았다는 사실과 항정신병 약이 주로 문제적인 행동을 드러낸 정신지체장애자들에게 더 많이 처방되는 경향이 있었다는 사실을 발견했다. 메릴랜드 주 볼티모어에 있는 존스 홉킨스 대학교(Johns Hopkins University)의 정신과 의사인 제임스 해리스(James Harris)는 "(항정신병 약을 처방하는) 비율이 높기 때문에 우리는 걱정을 해야만 합니다."라고 말한다. 그러나 그는 연구 속에 등장하는 정신지체장애자들에게 다른 형태의 치료가 이용 가능했는지를 알기 전까지는 항정신병 약을 사용한 치료가 적절했는지 여부를 결정하기 힘들다고 덧붙여 말하고 있다.

약의 사용이 유일하게 이용 가능한 선택사항일 수도 있었고, 혹은 치료요법이나 다른 종류의 치료에 참여시키기 위해서 정신장애지체자의 행동을 억누르기 위해 약을 사용했을 가능성도 있다. 그러나 임페리얼 칼리지 런던(Imperial College London)의 정신과 의사인 피터 타이러(Peter Tyrer)는 항정신병 약이 공격적이고 파괴적인 행동을 치료하는 데 효과가 없다는 증거를 제시할 수 있다고 말한다. 2014년, 그와 그의 몇몇 동료들은 정신병은 없지만 공격적인 성향을 보이는 정신지체장애자들에게 위약(僞藥)을 주었다. 위약이 공격적인 행동을 79% 정도 감소시켰다. 타이러는 항정신병 약이 그토록 빈번하게 사용된 이유가, 항정신병 약들이 효과가 있는 것처럼 보였기 때문에 응급실에서 근무하는 훈련이 안 된 간병인들에 의해서 환자들에게 복용되었다고 말한다. "새벽 두시에 (공격적인 성향을 보이는 정신지체장애자들을 상대로) 심리학적인 개입을 시도한다(심리치료사나 정신과 의사가 와서 치료한다.)는 것은 불가능한 일입니다."라고 타이러는 말한다.

1 ③ ▶ **내용추론**
정신지체장애자들에게 위약은 공격적인 성향을 무디게 하는 효과가 있었다.

2 ③ ▶ **글의 제목**
이 글은 정신지체장애자들을 대상으로 한 항정신병 약의 남용을 다루고 있다.

antipsychotic drug 항정신병 약
psychiatry n. 정신의학
general-care practice 보호시설
diagnose v. 진단하다
prescribe v. 처방하다
dampen v. 좌절시키다, 기를 꺾다
aggressive a. 공격적인
disruptive a. 혼란시키는; 파괴시키는; 분열시키는
placebo n. 플라시보, 위약
administer v. (약 등을) 복용시키다, 투여하다

16

B형 간염은 주로 혈액 간 접촉을 통해서 전염되는 바이러스다. 그것은 또한 무방비로 성교할 경우에도 감염될 수 있다. 그 바이러스는 질 분비액과 타액에서도 발견되기도 하는데, 전염성이 있을 만큼 다량으로 존재하는 지의 여부는 알려져 있지 않다. B형 간염은 간염군에 속하는 하나의 변종이므로 당연히 간에 영향을 미치는 바이러스다. 그러나 사람들마다 그 영향은 다르다. 어떤 사람들은 바이러스가 들어오면 몇 주간 몸이 아프다가 완전히 회복한다. 다른 이들의 경우, 그 바이러스는 평생 동안 체내에서 머무르면서 치명적인 간 손상을 일으킬 수 있다. 어떤 이들은 바이러스를 지니고 있어도 어떤 증세나 질병을 겪지 않을 수도 있다. B형 간염은 HIV(인체면역결핍바이러스)나 심지어 C형 간염보다 전염성이 높다. 바이러스에 감염된 소량의 체액만으로도 다른 사람을 감염시키기에 충분하다는 의미다. B형 간염은 또한 매우 회복력이 강한 바이러스로서 오랫동안 체외에서 생존할 수 있다. 바이러스에 노출된 시점으로부터 약 6개월이 지난 뒤에 B형 간염은 혈액 검사에서 나타난다. 이 기간을 잠복기라고 하는데, 이 기간 동안 사람에 따라 복통, 황달, 독감 증세와 유사한 증상, 관절의 통증 등이 나타난다. 어떤 이들은 이런 증상을 전혀 겪지 않는다. 종종 B형 간염을 보유하더라도 반드시 치료를 시작해야 하는 것은 아니다. 많은 사람들이 6개월 안에 이 질병을 극복해내기 때문이다. 그러나 인터페론과 같은 치료는 6개월 이상 지속되는 바이러스를 지닌 사람들에게 도움이 된다. B형 간염을 예방하는 백신도 존재한다. 완전한 방지를 위해서는 3차례 백신을 맞을 필요가 있다. 이 바이러스에 대한 항체를 확인하여 면역 여부를 확인하는 혈액검사는 접종이 완료된 지 2~3개월 뒤에 하는 것이 바람직하다. 접종을 다 마치고 나서도 면역이 충분히 형성되지 않는 사람

hepatitis n. 간염
vaginal a. 질의
saliva n. 침, 타액
strain n. 혈통; 변종; 계통
fatal a. 치명적인
infectious a. 전염성의
abdominal a. 복부의
jaundice n. 황달

들이 일부 있는데, 이들은 다시 접종 과정을 반복해야 한다. 이른바 '위험 직종' 종사자들은 누구나 접종을 받는 것이 바람직하다. 여기에는 보건관련 종사자, 섹스산업 종사자, 주사마약 중독자 및 남성동성애자 등이 포함된다.

1 ② ▶ 빈칸완성
Ⓐ B형 감염 바이러스의 특징을 뒤의 관계대명사절에서 설명하고 있다. 오랜 기간 동안 체외에서 생존할 수 있다고 하였으므로 회복력(resilient)이 있다고 볼 수 있다. Ⓑ 빈칸 앞 문장에서 바이러스에 노출된 시점으로부터 6개월이 지난 뒤에 B형 감염이 혈액검사에서 나타난다고 했으므로 그 기간은 '잠복기(the incubation period)'를 의미한다. Ⓒ 예방주사를 맞는다는 것은 항원(antigen)을 생체 내에 투여하여, 생체 내에서 항원과 특이하게 반응하는 항체(antibodies)가 형성되도록 하는 것이다. ① 전염성의 — 유예 기간 — 산화 방지제 ③ 중합된 — 수명 — 항원 ④ 안티프라그 — 수습 기간 — 항생 물질

2 ④ ▶ 내용일치
면역 형성 여부를 확인하는 혈액검사는 최종접종 2~3개월 후에 하는 것이 바람직하다고 했다.

17

40세 이상의 모든 사람이 1년에 한 번 혈압을 검사한다면, 그것만으로도 정말 많은 사람의 목숨을 살릴 수 있다. 혈압을 측정하는 것에 신비하거나 수수께끼 같은 것은 아무것도 없다. 그러나 건강에 해가 될 만큼 혈압이 높은 사람들이 아무런 증상이 없을 수도 있다. 그들은 매우 건강해 보이고 기분이 좋을 수 있으며, 그럼에도 불구하고 똑딱거리는 시한폭탄이 될 수 있다. 문제는 손상이 가해지고 있다는 것을 당신이 알 수 없다는 것이다. 이 점에 있어서 나는 모호한 태도를 취하고 싶지는 않다. 고혈압이 있는 몇몇 사람들은 종종 발작을 보이는 당일까지도 컨디션이 괜찮다고 느낄 수 있다.
몇몇 약사들은 약국에 혈압 측정 기계를 구비하고 있다. 소수지만 최신식의 혈압 측정기를 구비하고 있는 일반의들은 누구나 대기실에서 이용할 수 있도록 기계를 하나 정도 마련해놓고 있다. 당신이 앉아서 소매를 걷어 올리면 그들은 당신의 위쪽 팔에 밴드를 두르고 펌프로 공기를 불어넣은 후 기록을 잴 것이며, 그게 전부다. 대략 70~120의 수치가 이상적이다. (건강 상태를 파악하는 데 있어) 가장 의미 있는 수치는 바로 낮은 숫자인 이완기의 혈압이다. 그것은 나이가 들면서 높아지는 경향이 있으나 이완기 혈압이 100에 가까워지는 것을 결코 보고 싶지 않을 것이다.
이것은 신경이 과민해지는 것과 관련된 게 아니다. 몸에 관심을 갖고 지켜보는 것은 단지 모든 사람들의 관심일 뿐이다. 그리고 만약 당신이 고혈압을 갖고 있다면, 여전히 그것을 성공적으로 낮출 충분한 기회들이 있다. 어떤 사람들의 경우 생활방식의 변화만으로 충분할 것이고, 다른 이들의 경우 약물치료까지 필요할 수도 있다.

1 ④ ▶ 빈칸완성
본문은 시간이나 비용이 거의 들지 않는 '간단한' 혈압 측정을 통해 목숨까지도 살릴 수 있다는 점을 말하고 있다. 따라서 고혈압의 예방을 위한 혈압 측정에 있어 '신비하거나 수수께끼 같은 것'은 아무것도 없다는 표현이 되도록 ④가 빈칸에 적절하다. ① 민족의 또는 인종의 ② 유전적인 또는 후천적인 ③ 도덕적인 또는 윤리적인

2 ② ▶ 부분이해
pussyfoot은 '모호한 태도를 취하다'라는 의미이므로, '(요점을 직접적으로 말하지 않고) 완곡히 말하다'라는 ②와 유사한 의미를 갖는다. ① 사소한 일로 야단법석을 떨다 ③ 가식적이거나 독선적으로 들리다 ④ 허위 정보를 주다

3 ④ ▶ 내용일치
첫 번째 문장에서 40세 이상의 중년들의 경우 '1년에 1회'의 혈압 측정을 권장하고 있으므로 '1년에 2회'를 뜻하는 ④의 biannually는 잘못된 진술이다. ① 혈압을 낮게 유지하는 것이 좋지만 최소 70 이하가 돼서는 안 된다. ② 첫 번째 단락에서 고혈압은 전조 증상이 없을 수도 있기 때문에 이를 시한폭탄에 비유했다. ③ 마지막 단락에서 언급된 건강한 생활습관은 고혈압을 낮추는 가장 기본적이고 효율적인 방법일 것이다.

blood pressure 혈압
fit a. 좋은 건강 상태인, 컨디션이 좋은
time bomb 시한폭탄, (후일의) 위험을 내포한 정세
stroke n. 타격, 일격; (뇌졸중 등의) 발작
general practitioner 일반의
with-it a. 현대식의, 유행의 첨단을 달리는, (사회적·문화적으로) 최신의
reading n. (온도계 등의) 표시 도수, 기록
age v. 나이를 먹다, 늙다; 오래되다
keep an eye on ~을 감시하다, 주목하다
lower v. 낮추다, 내리다

4 ③ ▶ **동의어**

밑줄 친 부분의 다음 문장에서 부가적인 설명을 통해 "몸의 상태에 지속적으로 주목하는 것은 (일부 예민한 사람들에게만 국한된 일이 아니라) 일반적인 사람들의 공통된 관심사다."라고 말하고 있다. 따라서 '신경과민의, 노이로제에 걸린'을 뜻하는 neurotic의 유의어는 '비정상적일 정도로 집착하는'이라는 뜻의 ③ obsessive가 적절하다. ① 받아들일 만한, 허용할 수 있는 ② 분별[양식] 있는 ④ 관대한, 후한

18

얼마 전부터 우리는 마늘이 영양가면에서 최강자임을 알아왔다. 면역력을 증가시켜 주고, 혈관을 이완시켜 혈류량을 늘려주며 혈압을 낮춰주고, 조기노화 및 질병의 원인으로 알려진 염증을 가라앉히는 것으로 알려져 있다. 또한 혈관손상을 막아 심장병 위험을 줄여주며 심지어 골관절염을 방지해주는 것으로 알려져 있다.

이제, 한 새로운 연구에 따르면, 이 마늘이 체중조절도 보장해 줄지도 모른다고 한다. 연구원들은 쥐들을 살찌우기 위해 8주 동안 살이 찌는 음식을 주었으며, 그런 다음 쥐들에게 7주 동안 마늘이 첨가된 똑같은 음식을 주었다. 첨가된 마늘은 쥐의 체중과 저장지방을 줄여주었고 건강에 해로운 음식이 쥐의 피와 간에 미치는 영향을 줄여주었다. 게다가 이 '냄새 나는 장미'(마늘을 좋아하는 사람들은 애정을 가지고 이렇게 부른다.)를 즐겨야 하는 이유가 또 한 가지 있다.

구근식물인 마늘에서 원기를 최대한으로 얻기 위해서는, 신선한 마늘을 으깬 다음 요리하기 전에 10분 꽉 채워 실온으로 보관해야 한다. 몇몇 연구에 따르면 이런 실온보관이 으깬 즉시 마늘을 요리하는 것과 비교할 때 몸에 좋은 천연 화합물의 약 70%를 유지하도록 도와준다고 한다. 왜냐하면 마늘을 으깨면 마늘의 세포에 갇혀 있던 효소가 나오기 때문이다. 이 효소는 활력을 증진시켜 주는 화합물의 수치를 끌어 올리는데, 으깬 지 10분 후에 이 수치는 절정에 이른다. 만약 마늘을 이렇게 하기 전에 요리하면, 효소는 파괴된다.

1 ① ▶ **빈칸완성**

빈칸 ⓐ는 문맥상 마늘의 좋은 점에 대한 내용이 들어가야 할 것이다. 따라서 염증을 '가라앉히다'는 뜻의 quell이나 quench가 어울리며, 빈칸 ⓑ 뒤에 마늘을 stinking rose라 부르는 이유가 애정이 있어서라고 했으므로 빈칸에도 마늘을 '즐긴다'는 말이 어울릴 것이다. 따라서 이 둘을 만족시키는 ①의 quell — savor가 정답이다. ② 조장하다 — 즐기다 ③ 가라앉히다 — 교묘히 피하다 ④ 동요시키다 — 물리게 하다

2 ③ ▶ **내용파악**

stinking rose는 마늘을 지칭한다. ① 마늘은 골관절염을 방지해 주는 것으로 알려져 있다고 했다. ② 마늘은 체중조절도 보장해줄지 모른다고 했다. ④ 마늘을 으깨면 건강을 증진시켜 주는 천연 화합물이 나오는데, 으깬 지 10분 뒤에 절정에 이른다고 했다. ③ 조기노화 및 질병의 원인으로 알려진 염증을 마늘이 가라앉힌다고 했다. 따라서 '촉진시킨다(expedite)'는 ③은 사실과 다르므로 정답이다.

3 ② ▶ **부분이해**

밑줄 친 부분은 '구근식물(마늘)에서 원기를 최대한으로 얻기 위해서'라는 뜻이므로 ②가 정답이다.

4 ③ ▶ **지시대상**

ⓐ, ⓑ, ⓓ는 모두 garlic을 가리키는 반면, ⓒ는 마늘이 아니라 '마늘을 으깬 후 실온 보관하기'를 가리키므로 ③이 정답이다.

nutritional a. 영양의, 영양상의

powerhouse n. 정력가, 강력한 그룹[조직, 나라]

boost v. 증대[증가]시키다

immunity n. 면역(성); 면제

inflammation n. 염증

trigger n. (반응·사건을 유발하는) 자극, 유인

premature a. 조숙한; 너무 이른; 시기상조의

osteoarthritis n. 골관절염

fattening a. 살을 찌게 하는

plump v. 불룩하게 만들다, 살찌게 하다(up)

supplement v. 보충하다; 추가하다

stinking a. 악취를 풍기는

affectionately ad. 애정을 담고, 애정 어리게

bang n. 원기, 기력

bulb n. 구근(球根); 구근 식물

crush v. 눌러서 뭉개다, 짓밟다, 으깨다

retain v. 보류하다, 보유[유지]하다

enzyme n. 효소

19

외상(外傷) 사건은 무작위적으로 일어난다. 따라서 대비하거나 방비하기가 거의 불가능하다. 현실에서 이 같은 상처는 그 상처를 가진 사람이 내적으로 강한 사람인지 약한 사람인지를 그대로 드러내 보여준다. 우리 모두는 이러한 상황에 의연하게 대처할 수 있기를 바라지만, 보통은 그러지 못한다. 이렇게 충격적인 사건 경험은 치유하기 힘든 커다란 감정의 구멍을 남겨 놓는다.

갑작스럽게 충격적으로 만들어진 상처로 인해 흔히 사람들은 생각을 종결시키지 못하고 "이런 일이 왜 일어났을까? 왜 하필 나에게 일어났을까? 세상이 어떻게 나에게 이토록 잔인하게 굴 수 있을까?"와 같은 질문만을 계속 던지게 된다. 개인은 이 사건 경험 때문에 크게 동요하는 데서 그치지 않고, 또한 자신의 대응에 대해서도 만족하지 못하고, 좀 더 나은 결과를 도출할 수 없었던 자신을 책망하게 된다. 이러한 자책은 대체로 비이성적이고, 자존감을 훼손하고, 죄책감만 만들어 낼 따름이다. (경우에 따라서는 생존자의 죄책감이 나타나기도 한다.) 외상 사건은 사람을 바꾸어 놓는다. 특히 냉소적으로 만든다. 비슷한 일이 다시 일어날 수도 있다는 두려움으로 인해 그의 성격과 행동이, 특히 안전과 안정과 관련된 성격과 행동이 극단적으로 바뀔 수 있다. 이 범주는 또한 외상 후 스트레스 장애(PTSD)을 겪을 가능성이 가장 높다.

외상 후 스트레스 장애는 심각하게 두렵거나 위험한 사건을 경험한 사람들에게 나타날 수 있는 장애다. 외상 후 스트레스 장애를 겪고 있는 사람들은 해리성 삽화를 통해 과거에 일어난 일들을 추체험(追體驗, 이전 경험을 다시 체험하는 것) 할 수도 있는데, 이 삽화는 단발성에 그치지 않고, 몇 시간 혹은 며칠을 지속될 수도 있다. 그 사람은 사건을 상기시켜 주는 것들에 자극을 받을 수도 있고, 외상과 관련된 감정이나 생각들을 피할 수도 있고, 악몽을 꾸고 수면장애를 겪으며, 만성적인 과잉각성 상태로 인해 긴장하고 안절부절못하게 될 수 있다. (자책과 죄의식을 포함한) 변덕스러운 감정 변화는 흔하게 나타나며, 부정적인 자기 생각과 예를 들어 고립감이나 열정 또는 취미에 대한 관심을 잃는 등 우울증 비슷한 증상들이 같이 나타날 수 있다.

1 ③   ▶ 내용일치

③ 외상으로 인한 성격 변화가 모두 부정적이지 않다면 긍정적인 성격 변화의 예가 있어야 하는 데 본문에서 그런 내용은 전혀 찾을 수 없다. ① 두 번째 문단에서 끊임없이 괴롭힌다고 하였다. ② 역시 두 번째 문단에서 자책은 일반적인 반응으로 짐작할 수 있다.

2 ①   ▶ 내용추론

마지막 문단 첫 문장에서 PTSD에 대해 외상 사건을 겪은 사람들에게서 나타나는 질환이라고 하였으므로, ① "외상 이후 피해자들이 다양한 PTSD를 겪는 것은 정상이다."는 짐작 가능하다. ② 모든 상처 중에서 어린 시절의 상처가 가장 커다란 피해를 준다. ③ 외상을 극복하는 정도는 비극이 일어났을 때 주변 사람들로부터 어느 정도의 어떤 종류의 도움을 받을 수 있는가와 관련이 있다. ④ 상처 그 자체는 삶을 바꿔 놓기도 하지만, 피해자가 그 이후 더 많은 고통을 이겨내야만 할 때 더 악화될 수 있다는 내용은 찾아볼 수 없다.

3 ①   ▶ 내용파악

마지막 문단의 요지는 사람에 따라 PTSD의 증상도 다양하게 나타난다는 것이다. 가장 비슷한 내용이 ①이다. ② 외상 사건을 직접 겪은 사람이 외상 사건과 크게 동떨어져 있는 사람에 비해 더 많은 영향을 받는다. ③ 똑같은 외상 사건이 반복되어 일어날 때, 그 상처가 더 깊어진다. ④ 공격한 사람과 정서적으로 가까울 때 피해가 더 밀접하게 느껴진다는 내용은 찾아볼 수 없다.

---

gouge n. 구멍

closure n. 종결; 심리적 확실감

self-blame n. 자책

irrational a. 비합리적인

survivor's guilt 생존자의 죄책감(큰 재난에서 자신만 살아남은 사람이 느끼는 죄책감)

jaded a. 염세적인, 냉소적인

relive v. 다시 살다, 추체험하다

via prep. ~을 통해

dissociative a. 해리적인, 분열적인

on edge 초조한

chronic a. 만성적인

hypervigilance n. 과잉각성

volatility n. 변덕

depression n. 우울증

symptom n. 증상

20

시애틀에 소재한 워싱턴대학의 정신의학자 수잔 크래프트(Suzanne Craft)가 주도한 연구진들은 진전된 치매의 공통된 전조이자 초기 알츠하이머 단계의 전조이기도 한 경미한 인지손상을 겪고 있는 남녀 104명을 대상으로 소규모 시범연구를 하였다. 연구진들은 인슐린 혹은 위약이 임의로 담긴 비강 스프레이를 참가자들에게 매일 2차례씩 투여하였다. 4개월에 걸쳐 연구자들은 인슐린이 기억력 검사 점수와 전반적인 인지능력을 향상시키거나 적어도 유지시켰다는 것을 알아내었다. 하지만 위약을 투여한 사람들은 시간이 지남에 따라 악화되었다. 인슐린을 투여 받은 참가자들은 실제로 두 가지 중 하나를 받았는데 국제단위 기준으로 20 IU 혹은 그보다 많은 40 IU였다. 4개월 뒤 20 IU를 투여한 집단은 기억력 검사에서 거의 80%가 개선을 보였다. 위약 그룹은 같은 시험에서 성적이 더 나빠졌다. 인슐린 40 IU를 투여한 사람들도 기억력 향상은 보이지 않았지만 전반적인 인지 기능은 분명히 향상되었다. 기억력 검사 외에도 과학자들은 알츠하이머의 표시물질로 알려진 체내 단백질 및 다른 물질들의 수치를 비교해 보았다. 기억력 향상을 보인 참가자들은 뇌에서 치매와 관련된 플라크와 엉킴의 수치가 약간씩 감소했다. 뇌 주사로 살펴보았을 때 인슐린으로 치료한 집단의 사람들은 뇌 속의 포도당을 제대로 처리하는 능력을 유지하고 있음이 확인되었다. 포도당은 뇌세포가 정상적으로 기능할 수 있도록 돕고 기억 및 여타 인지능력과 관련된 기능을 수행하는 데 도움을 준다. 알츠하이머 환자들의 두뇌는 포도당 신진대사가 떨어지는데, 위약 그룹의 경우 뇌 주사로 보았을 때 두뇌가 포도당을 분해하는 능력이 점진적으로 떨어지고 있었다. "인슐린이 체내의 혈당 조절에 중요한 역할을 한다는 것은 잘 알려진 사실이지만, 우리의 실험실 연구나 여타 연구결과를 보면 인슐린이 두뇌에서도 다양하면서도 중요한 역할을 한다는 것이 나타납니다. 그러한 역할 중에는 기억력과 여타 인지기능에 중요한 두뇌 부위의 포도당 또는 에너지 신진대사에 영향을 미치는 것도 포함됩니다. 인슐린이 이런 기능을 수행하는 데 문제가 생기면 우리는 알츠하이머 질환처럼 노화 수반성 질환이 촉발되는 것으로 보고 있습니다."라고 크래프트는 말한다. 하지만 이번 연구는 아직 소규모이고 매우 예비적이다. 즉 인슐린이 치매에 맞서는 무기가 될 수 있을지를 알아내기 위한 많은 단계의 겨우 첫걸음일 뿐이다. 예를 들어, 왜 인슐린 투여가 적었을 때는 기억력이 향상된 반면 인슐린 투여가 많았을 때는 기억력은 향상되지 않았지만 다른 인지기능들이 향상되었는지, 그 이유가 여전히 분명하지 않다. 이번 연구 결과는 인슐린 양이 많고 적은 것 사이에 아슬아슬한 차이밖에 없다는 것을 시사한다. "우리는 이러한 패턴의 근간에 있는 기제를 확실히 알지 못합니다만, 잠정적으로는 기억력에 최적한 양의 수준과 다른 유형의 인지능력에 최적한 양의 수준이 다른 것이라고 볼 수 있습니다. 너무 적어도 나쁘고, 너무 많아도 나쁜 거죠."라고 크래프트는 말한다.

1 ②   ▶ **빈칸완성**
인슐린의 양이 너무 적어도 좋지 않고, 너무 많아도 좋지 않으니 그 미세한 차이가 크지 않고 아슬아슬하다(a fine line)는 의미의 표현이 적절하다.

2 ④   ▶ **내용추론**
본문에 보면, "인슐린 투여가 적었을 때는 기억력이 향상된 반면 인슐린 투여가 많았을 때는 기억력은 향상되지 않았지만 다른 인지기능들이 향상되었는지, 그 이유가 분명하지 않다."고 하였으므로 ④가 적절하다.

psychiatrist n. 정신의학자

precursor n. 선도자; 전조; 전구물, 전구체

dementia n. 치매

pilot study 선행 연구, 준비 조사

nasal spray 비강 스프레이

placebo n. 위약

cognitive a. 인지의

dose n. 약의 분량

international unit <약학> 국제 단위(국제 규약으로 정한 열·전기 등의 단위; 略 IU)

tangle n. 엉킴

glucose n. 포도당

metabolism n. 신진대사

mediate v. 영향을 주다, 가능하게 하다

12 생물학·생명과학

01

호르몬이란 낱말은 처음에 세크레틴을 의미하는 말로 사용되었다. 스탈링(Starling)은 이 용어를 '흥분시키다' 혹은 '작동하다'라는 의미의 그리스어 'hormon'에서 가져왔다. 내분비선이라는 용어는 그 후 바로 도입되었다. 내분비선은 췌장, 갑상선, 뇌하수체선과 같이 혈류 속으로 물질을 직접 분비하는 선을 가리킨다. 이 선들 중 어느 것 하나라도 부족하면 심각한 질병을 가져오기 때문에 지금은 많은 호르몬을 합성해서 만들어 결핍된 곳을 치료하는 데 사용하고 있다. 곤충들은 또한 독특한 호르몬인 엑디손(ecdysone)을 가지고 있다. 스테로이드가 인간의 근육 형성을 자극하는 것처럼 곤충에게는 엑디손이라는 호르몬이 성충의 단계로 변태하는 과정에 곤충의 겉껍질을 단단하게 하는 역할을 한다. 식물은 꽃, 줄기, 구근, 봉오리의 형성을 돕는 옥신과 시토키닌 등과 같은 다양한 호르몬에 의존한다. 원예가들이 사용하는 합성 호르몬 에틸렌(ethylene)은 열매의 숙성을 촉진한다고 한다.

1 ②　▶ 내용파악
합성 호르몬 에틸렌은 식물이 열매를 숙성하게 하는 데 필요로 하는 호르몬이라고 언급되고 있다.

2 ③　▶ 내용파악
호르몬 엑디손은 곤충들이 성충으로 변태하는 데 필요한 호르몬이고 곤충의 겉껍질을 단단하게 하는 역할을 한다고 언급되어 있다.

---

set in motion 작동하다
endocrine n. 내분비선, 호르몬
gland n. <생리·식물> 선(腺)
pancreas n. 췌장
thyroid n. 갑상선
pituitary gland 뇌하수체선
synthetic a. 합성의; 종합의
deficiency n. 부족
ecdysone n. 엑디손(곤충의 탈피 촉진 호르몬)
exoskeleton n. 겉껍질
metamorphose v. 변태하다
tuber n. 용기, 결절
horticulturist n. 원예학자
ripe v. 숙성하다

02

기초 생물학은 우리에게 용기는 뇌의 의사결정 중추인 전전두엽과 공포의 중심점인 편도선 사이의 원시적 투쟁에서 생겨난다고 말한다. 우리가 예상치 못한 위험한 상황에 처해있을 때 편도선은 명료하게 추론하는 능력을 방해하는 신호를 전전두엽에 보낸다. 극단적인 경우에 그것은 몸을 마비시켜버릴 수 있다. 그러나 용기 있는 자들은 공포에 굴복하지 않는다. 일부 경우, 그들은 강한 훈련에서 생겨나는 근육기억에 의해 더욱 강해진다.

급박한 위험에도 아랑곳하지 않고 책무를 수행할 수 있는 능력은 기저핵으로 알려져 있는 뇌 부위에 있다. 어떤 행동을 거듭 되풀이해서 행할 때 그 행동을 수행하는 책무는 그 행동이 의식적으로 경험되는 뇌의 바깥피질에서 그 행동을 자동적으로 수행하고 공포의 영향을 받지 않는 기저핵으로 옮겨진다. 군대는 이 원리를 수천 년 전부터 이해하고 있었다. 전 세계의 신병훈련소들은 혹독한 반복훈련을 통해 전투 기본수칙들을 신병의 뇌에 깊이 새겨 넣었다. 그런 식으로 해서, 강한 공포가 군인의 이성적인 뇌를 닫아버릴 때에도 그 군인은 여전히 자동 조종 장치로 제 역할을 수행할 수 있을 것이다.

1 ④　▶ 내용파악
① 용기 있는 행동은 반복적인 행동 훈련에 의해 가능하므로 용기 있는 사람들은 만들어지는 것이다. ② 위험한 상황에서 편도선이 의사결정을 방해하는 신호를 보낸다고 해서 안전한 때에는 의사결정을 원활히 하는 신호를 보낸다고 볼 수는 없다. ③ 용기 있는 사람들의 용기 있는 행동은 반복 훈련으로 인해 뇌의 바깥피질이 아니라 기저핵이 자극에 반응하게 되었을 때 가능한 것이지, 경고신호를 기저핵으로 보낼 때 가능한 것이 아니다. 마지막 문장에서 강한 공포가 일어나면 편도선이 보내는 신호로 전전두엽이 마비되고 이때 용기 있는 사람들은 자동 조종 장치로 제 역할을 수행할 수 있을 것이라 했는데, '자동 조종 장치로'라는 말은 '근육기억에 의해'라는 말과 같다. 따라서 ④가 사실이다.

---

primal a. 최초의, 원시의
hub n. 중추
prefrontal cortex 전전두엽
amygdala n. 편도선
interfere with 방해하다
paralyze v. 마비시키다
succumb to ~에 굴복하다
muscle memory 근육기억(반복 행동에 의해 몸이 기억하는 것)
basal ganglia 기저핵(대뇌반구의 중심부)
boot camp 신병훈련소
embed v. 묻다, 깊이 새겨두다
recruit n. 신병
shut down 폐쇄하다
autopilot n. 자동 조종 장치

2 ② **2 ②**　▶ **빈칸완성**
　　　　둘째 단락 둘째 문장에서 반복 훈련에 의해 행동수행 책무가 기저핵으로 내려간다고 했
　　　　으므로 빈칸에는 ② '혹독한 반복'이 적절하다. ① 정신단련 ③ 잠재학습 ④ 치열한 경쟁

3 ④　▶ **글의 어조**
　　　　이 글은 용기 있는 사람들이 위험한 상황에서도 그렇게 용기 있는 행동을 할 수 있는 생
　　　　물학적 메커니즘을 설명하여 알려주는 글이므로 '정보를 제공하는(informative)'이 글
　　　　의 논조로 적절하다. ① 고무적인 ② 논쟁적인 ③ 감탄하는

03

은유적으로 말하자면 자연 선택은 날마다 시간마다 전 세계에 걸쳐 가장 경미한 변화마저도 정밀 조사를 하고 있다; 나쁜 변화는 거부하고 좋은 모든 변화들을 보존하고 합치면서; 기회가 주어지는 언제든지 어디서든지 그것의 유기적이고 무기적인 생명의 조건과 관련하여 각각의 생명체의 향상을 위해 은밀히 눈에 띄지 않게 노력하면서. 우리는 오랜 세월이 경과되고 나서야 이러한 진화의 느린 변화들을 알 수 있게 되고, 우리의 오랜 과거의 지질학적 시대에 대한 지식이 너무 불완전하여 우리는 다만 생명의 형태가 지금은 그들의 과거 모습과는 다르다는 것을 알 뿐이다.

어떤 막대한 양의 변화가 하나의 종에 이루어지기 위해서는, 하나의 변종이, 일단 형성되고, 아마도 오랜 세월이 지난 후에, 전처럼 다시 한 번 동일한 유리한 속성의 개별적 차이를 변화시키거나 제시하여야 한다; 그리고 이러한 차이가 다시 한 번 보존되고, 단계적으로 그러한 과정이 계속되어야 한다. 동일한 종류의 개별적 차이가 영원히 반복되고 있으므로, 이것은 좀처럼 부당한 가정이라고 간주될 수는 없다. 그러나 그것이 사실이든 아니든, 우리는 오로지 어느 정도까지 그 가설이 자연의 일반적 상황들과 일치하는지 그리고 그것들을 설명해 내는지를 앎으로써만 판단을 내릴 수 있다. 반면에, 가능한 변화의 양은 엄격하게 제한적인 양이라는 일반적 믿음도 마찬가지로 하나의 단순한 가정이다.

1 ①　▶ **빈칸완성**
　　　　첫 문장의 "that" 이후의 내용인, "자연 선택은 날마다 시간마다 전 세계에 걸쳐 가장 경
　　　　미한 변화마저도 정밀 조사를 하고 있다; 나쁜 변화는 거부하고 좋은 모든 변화들을 합
　　　　치면서; 기회가 주어지는 언제든지 어디서든지 그것의 유기적이고 무기적인 생명의 조
　　　　건과 관련하여 각각의 생명체의 향상을 위해 은밀히 눈에 띄지 않게 노력하면서"라는
　　　　부분은 자연 선택이라는 생물학적 과정을 매우 꼼꼼하고 은밀한 사람이나 기계가 하는
　　　　일로 비유하고 있다. 이와 같이 상징을 통한 암시적 비유를 은유(metaphor)라 한다. ②
　　　　반어적으로 ③ 역설적으로 ④ 과학적으로 ⑤ 철학적으로

2 ②　▶ **내용추론**
　　　　"우리는 오랜 세월이 경과되고 나서야 이러한 진화의 느린 변화들을 알 수 있게 되고, 우
　　　　리의 오랜 과거의 지질학적 시대에 대한 지식이 너무 불완전하여 우리는 다만 생명의 형
　　　　태가 지금은 그들의 과거 모습과는 다르다는 것을 알 뿐이다."라는 진술을 통해 ②의 "우
　　　　리가 먼 지질학적 시대를 명확히 알 수 있다면, 우리는 어떻게 한 종이 진화를 통해 서서
　　　　히 변하는가를 알 수 있을 것이다."를 추론할 수 있다.

natural selection 자연 선택
organic a. 유기체의
lapse n. (시간의) 경과, 흐름, 추이
geological a. 지질학의
modification n. 수정, 변경, 변화
perpetually ad. 영구[영원]히, 끊임없이
recur v. 되풀이되다, 반복되다
unwarrantable a. 부당한

04

사실을 말하자면, 생명의 기원들에 대한 질문들은 과학이 지금까지 대면해온 문제들 가운데서 가장 성가신 문제다. 만일 당신이 무작위로 고른 백 명의 과학자들에게, 생명이 어떻게 시작되었는지에 대한 그들의 생각을 묻는다면, 당신은 십중팔구 백가지의 약간씩 다른 대답을 듣게 될 것이다. 문제를 더 복잡하게 만드는 것은, 기술이 계속해서 새로운 질문들이 쏟아져 나오는 새로운 문들을 열어젖히고 있다는 것이다. 그럼에도 불구하고 지난 반세기는 생명의 기원들이 기묘한 어떤 것이 아니라, 불가피한 어떤 것이었다는 점을 말해주고 있는 수많은 당혹스러운 발견들을 목격해왔다.

vexing a. 성가신, 골치 아픈, 짜증나는
bewildering a. 혼란스러운, 당혹스러운
spew v. 토하다, 내뿜다; 털어놓다
feedstock n. 공급원료
genomics n. 유전체학
proteomics n. 단백질 유전 정보학

해양의 깊은 곳에서 (생명의 탄생을 위한) 화학적 공급 원료를 분출하는 열역학 체계의 발견은 그러한 엄청난 과학적 발견의 한 가지 예다. 유전체학과 단백질 유전정보학에 있어서의 혁명적 발전은 지난 40억년 동안의 생명 기능과 진화와 관련된 핵심적인 정보들을 밝혀내면서 전체적으로 새로운 생명의 지도를 드러내 왔다. 그리고 물리학과 경제학을 아우르는 다양한 분야를 가로지르면서, 우리는 자발적으로 일어나는 질서, 과정, 행동의 출현을 보아왔는데, 그 자발적인 질서, 과정, 행동은 그것들이 분자들이건 새의 무리이건, 많은 더 단순한 작용자들의 상호작용으로부터 발생할 수 있다. 생명의 기원들에 대한 연구가 가지고 있는 가장 큰 좌절감을 주는 측면들 가운데 하나는 다음과 같다: 생명의 기원에 관한 흥미진진한 수수께끼들은 우리 주위에 넘쳐나고 있지만 우리는 여전히 그것들을 서로 잘 맞게 끼워 맞추지 못하고 있다는 것이다. 심지어 생명이 정말로 무엇인지를 정의 내리는 것도 만만치 않은 도전을 제기한다. '살아있음'에 대한 충분히 많은 양적인 척도가 없는 상황에서, 생명의 기원에 대해서 논의한다는 것은 실제로 어렵다. 이러한 난점은 불꽃이 살아 있는 것인지 아닌지, 여부를 놓고 토론을 벌이던 고대 그리스의 철학적 경연장으로 우리를 떨어트릴 위험을 내포하고 있다.

1 ③　　▶ 부분이해
　　　　생명의 기원에 대한 논의가 자칫 잘못하면 공허한 탁상공론이 될 수 있다는 것이 밑줄친 표현의 의미다.

2 ②　　▶ 내용파악
　　　　'~ one of the most frustrating aspects of the study of the origins of life; …'라는 단서로부터 정답을 추론할 수 있다.

juicy a. 수분이 많은; 흥미진진한; 유리한
mosh pit (무대 바로 앞부분의) 청중들이 춤추는 곳
bioethics n. 생명 윤리학

05

타감작용은 그리스어 단어 allelo(서로, 혹은 상호간의)와 pathy(고통)에서 온 것으로 한 식물이 다른 식물에 모종의 영향을 미치는 화학물질을 방출하는 것을 가리킨다. 이런 화학물질은 식물의 여러 다른 부위에 의해 방출될 수 있고 아니면 자연적인 분해를 통해 방출될 수도 있다. 타감작용은 씨앗 발아나 뿌리 발달이나 영양분 섭취를 억제함으로써 어떤 식물들로 하여금 근처의 식물들과 경쟁하고 종종 근처의 식물들을 죽이게 하는 생존 메커니즘이다. 박테리아, 바이러스, 곰팡이와 같은 다른 생물도 타감작용을 할 수 있다. 타감작용이라는 용어는 대개 그 영향이 해로울 때 사용되지만 이로운 영향에도 적용될 수 있다. 그리고 그 영향이 식물들에게는 해로울 때조차도 다른 면에서는 이로운 것일 수 있다. 옥수수 글루텐 가루가 어떻게 천연 제초제로 사용되는지 생각해보라. 많은 잔디 풀과 피복작물은 그들의 잡초 억제력을 향상시키는 타감적 특성을 갖고 있다. 아니면 곰팡이가 만드는 페니실린이 박테리아를 죽일 수 있는 방식은 또 어떠한가(마찬가지다). 당신은 아마도 검은 호두나무 가까이에 자라는 식물들이 경험하는 문제들에 대해 들었을 것이다. 검은 호두나무들은 모든 부위가 히드로주글론을 생산하는데 이것은 산소에 노출되면 알렐로톡신으로 바뀐다. 뿌리와 썩어가는 잎과 잔가지 모두가 주변 토양에 주글론을 방출하는데, 이 물질은 다른 많은 식물, 특히 토마토, 고추, 감자, 가지와 같은 가지 과(科) 식물의 성장을 억제한다. 진달래와 소나무와 사과나무 같은 나무와 관목도 주글론의 피해를 입기 쉽다. 다른 한편, 주글론에 잘 견디고 아무 악영향도 입지 않는 식물도 많이 있다.

1 ③　　▶ 빈칸완성
　　　　빈칸이 있는 문장의 corn gluten meal(옥수수 글루텐 가루)은 앞 문장의 예인데 그다음 문장에서 구체적으로 설명된다. 즉 이것에 의해 성장이 억제되는 잡초에게는 해가 되지만, 이것을 방출하는 잔디 풀과 피복작물에게는 이로운 것이다. 따라서 빈칸에는 잡초의 성장을 억제하는 ③의 '천연 제초제'가 적절하다. ① 성장촉진제 ② 유기농식품 ④ 인공생물연료

2 ④　　▶ 내용파악
　　　　① 둘째 문장의 natural decomposition(자연적인 분해)이 죽은 후의 부식을 의미한다. ② 셋째 문장에서 생존 메커니즘이라 했다. ③ 다섯째 문장이 단서다. 빈칸이 있는 문장 다음 다음 문장에서 '아니면 곰팡이가 만드는 페니실린이 박테리아를 죽일 수 있는 방식은 또 어떠한가'라고 한 것은 마찬가지라는 의미이다. 따라서 발견된 최초의 항생물질, 즉

allelopathy n. 타감작용(한 식물이 다른 식물의 생장에 영향을 미치는 것)
give off 방출하다
decomposition n. 분해, 부패
inhibit v. 억제하다, 방해하다
sprouting n. 발아
meal n. 거친 가루
herbicide n. 제초제
turf n. 잔디
black walnut 검은 호두
allelotoxin n. 알렐로톡신(주변 식물을 죽이는 물질)
Solanaceae family 가지 과(科)
azalea n. 진달래

페니실린이 병원균을 죽이는 것도 타감작용이라 할 수 있으므로 contradicts라고 한 ④는 사실이 아니다.

3 ②　　▶ **내용파악**

마지막 부분에서 주글론은 특히 토마토, 고추, 감자, 가지와 같은 가지 과(科) 식물의 성장을 억제한다고 했으므로 ②가 주글론을 방출하는 검은 호두나무 가까이에서 잘 재배될 수 없는 것이다.

06

대략 20년 전에, 생화학자들이 (세포에서) 분리할 수 있는 성분인, 디옥시리보핵산(일명 DNA)이 세포의 단백질 합성 구조를 유도하는 것 같다는 사실을 발견했다. DNA의 내부구조는 단백질 합성 유형을 지시하는 일련의 암호화된 명령을 나타내는 것으로 보였다. 몇몇 실험을 통해 적절한 효소가 있을 경우에, 각각의 DNA 분자는 새로운 DNA 분자를 복제할 수 있으며, 이 복제된 분자는 원래 DNA 분자에 들어있던 특정한 유도 메시지를 포함한다고 했다. 이런 생각은 세포의 유전과정에 대해 이미 알려진 것(특히 DNA는 염색체에 집중되어 있다는 지식)에 더해져서 분자에 기반을 둔 유전 이론을 확립하는 것처럼 보였다.

DNA는 '자기복제' 분자이며 또한 그 자체로 생물학적 유전을 결정하는 암호를 가지고 있다는 이론을 주장하는 사람들은 "중심이론"이라는 용어를 과학문헌에 도입해서 DNA의 지배적인 역할을 설명하는 이론을 기술하려고 했다. 그러나 이 중심이론은 처음부터 공인받지 못한 가설(이론)을 포함하고 있었다. 즉 핵산은 다른 핵산의 합성과 단백질의 합성을 유도할 수는 있지만, 그 반대 효과는 불가능하다는 것이다. 다시 말해서, 단백질은 핵산의 합성을 유도할 수 없다는 것이다. 그러나 본격적인 실험관찰을 통해 이런 가정의 후반부의 중요한 부분이 반박당하고 있다. 다른 시험관 실험들은 DNA 이외의 요인들이 지배적인 영향을 미치고 있다는 것을 제시한다. 어떤 종류의 단백질이 합성되느냐는 필요한 효소를 얻을 수 있는 개별 유기체에 달려 있다. 그것은 또한 시험관의 온도, 산도의 정도 및 존재하는 금속염이 얼마인가에도 달려있다.

1 ③　　▶ **글의 목적**

본문에서 작가가 의도하는 바는 생화학자들이 처음에 규정했던 정설과, 나중에 밝혀진 실험결과 내용과의 불일치하는 점을 밝히려는 것이므로 ③이 정답이다.

2 ③　　▶ **내용파악**

본문에서 작가는 처음에 발표된 DNA의 지배적 역할에 대한 정설에 대해 새로운 실험결과를 증거로 제시해서 그 차이를 설명하고 있다.

constituent n. 구성 성분
internal a. 내부의
coded a. 암호화된
enzyme n. 효소
replica n. 복제품, 모형
chromosome n. 염색체
inheritance n. 유산; 유전되는 것
proponent n. 지지자
scientific literature 과학서적
dogma n. 이론, 정설(定說)
admittedly ad. 널리 인정되고 있는 것처럼, 확실히, 명백히
unproven a. 증명되지 않은
synthesis n. 합성, 통합
reverse a. 정반대의
experimental a. 실험의
crucial a. 중대한, 결정적인
agent n. 대리인; 중요한 작용을 하는 동인; 물질

07

과학자들과 연구원들은 여러 이유로 쥐들에 의존한다. 한 가지는 편리함 때문이다: 설치 동물은 작고, 쉽게 키우고 간수할 수 있으며, 새로운 환경에 잘 적응한다. 그들은 또한 빠르게 번식하며 2~3년의 짧은 수명을 갖고 있어서 다양한 세대의 쥐들을 비교적 짧은 기간에 관찰할 수 있다. 의학실험에 이용되는 대부분의 쥐들은 근친교배되기 때문에, 성별의 차이를 제외하고는 유전적으로 거의 동일하다. 이점은 임상실험의 결과가 조금 더 균일하게 되도록 하는 데 도움이 된다.

설치 동물이 의학실험의 모델로 이용되는 또 다른 이유는 그것들의 유전학적, 생물학적 그리고 행동적 특징들이 인간의 특징들과 매우 닮았으며, 인간 질병의 많은 증상들이 쥐들을 통해 모사될 수 있기 때문이다. 지난 20년간, 이러한 유사성은 더욱 뚜렷해졌다. 과학자들은 이제 인간의 질병들을 야기하는 것과 유사한 유전자들을 지닌 '형질 전환 쥐'라 불리는 유전적으로 변형된 쥐들을 만들어 낼 수 있다. 마찬가지로, 암을 유발하는 화학물질(발암 물질)들의 영향에 대해 검토하고 약품의 안전도를 평가하는 데 이용될 수 있는 '특정 유전자가 제거된 쥐'를 만들어 내면서 선별 유전자들을 없애거나 활동하지 않게 할 수 있다.

쥐들은 잠재적으로 약물 중독을 끝낼 수 있는 갈망 억제 약물의 실험뿐 아니라 행동, 감각, 노화, 영양 그리고 유전학 연구에도 이용된다.

1 ③ ▶ **내용파악**
③ 잠재적 유전적 변이성은 실험용 쥐들의 특성과 반대되는 특징이다.

2 ① ▶ **글의 제목**
첫 문장에서 과학자들과 연구원들은 여러 이유로 쥐들에 의존한다 했으며 왜 그러한지를 임상실험용 동물로서 쥐들이 갖는 여러 장점에 대해 나열하며 설명해주고 있으므로 ①이 적절한 제목이다.

3 ② ▶ **내용일치**
① 형질 전환 쥐들은 마지막 단락에 제시된 것처럼 여러 분야(갈망 억제 약물치료, 행동, 감각, 노화, 영양, 유전학의 연구)에 활용할 수는 있지만 만병통치약을 만드는 것을 가능하게 했는지 알 수 없다. ③ 형질 전환 쥐의 장기가 인간에게 이식이 가능하다는 내용은 본문에 언급되어 있지 않다. ④ 설치 동물인 쥐의 신뢰도와 관련한 의혹이 제기된 적이 없었는지 이 글을 통해 알 수 없다. '특정 유전자가 제거된 쥐'를 만들어 내면서 선별된 특정 유전자들을 없애거나 활동하지 않도록 만들 수 있다고 했으므로 ②가 정답이다.

rodent n. (쥐·다람쥐 등의) 설치 동물
inbred a. 동종(同種) 번식의, 근친 교배의
lifespan n. 수명
condition n. <병리> (몸의) 이상, 병, 질환
replicate v. 사본을 뜨다, 모사[복제]하다
breed v. (새 품종을) 만들어 내다, 품종개량하다
transgenic a. 이식 유전자의, 유전자가 변형된
select a. 고른, 가려낸, 추려낸
knockout mouse 특정 유전자가 결여되게 한 쥐
carcinogen n. 발암(發癌)(성) 물질
anatomy n. 해부학적 구조
physiology n. 생리학
craving n. 갈망, 열망

08

일단 중합체가 형성되고 난 다음, 지구상의 생명체가 형성되는 과정에 있어서 다음 단계는 분자 집합체와 원시 '세포'가 형성되는 과정이었을 것이다. 여기서 '세포'라는 용어는 아주 대략적인 의미로 사용된다. 폴리펩티드나 폴리뉴클레오티드가 용액 속에서 결합될 때, 두 가지의 복잡한 단위들 중 하나를 형성하게 된다. 하나는 오파린(Oparin)이 코아세르베이트 방울이라고 불렀던 것이고, 다른 하나는 스탠리 폭스(Stanley Fox)가 프로테이노이드 마이크로스페어라고 불렀던 것이다. 코아세르베이트 방울들은 물 분자 껍질에 둘러싸여져 있는 고분자인데, 이 물 분자들은 '막'을 형성하는 고분자를 향해 단단히 정향되어 있다. 코아세르베이트 방울들은 서로를 흡수하고, 주변 환경으로부터 화학물질들을 흡수한다. 코아세르베이트 방울들은 복잡해질 수 있고, 더 많은 물질들이 막을 통과하여 코아세르베이트 방울들 속으로 통합됨에 따라 내부 구조가 점점 더 뚜렷해지는 것이 목격된다.

프로테이노이드 마이크로스페어는 뜨거운 폴리펩티드 수성 용액이 차가워질 때 형성된다. 프로테이노이드 마이크로스페어는 코아세르베이트 방울보다 훨씬 더 안정적이고, 원시적 생식에 해당하는 다음의 특징들을 가지고 있다. 염분농도가 높은 용액에서는 팽창하고, 염분농도가 낮은 용액에서는 수축되며, 이중으로 된 외벽을 갖추고 있는데 이는 세포막과 상당히 유사하고, 세포질 유동과 유사한 내부의 움직임을 보이며, 크기와 복잡성 면에서 성장하며, 표면적으로는 효모균의 생식과 유사한 방식으로 싹이 트며, 외벽을 가로질러 전기적인 잠재적 차이를 지니고 있는데 이는 세포막이 ATP를 발생시키는 데 필수적이며, 덩어리 모양으로 모인다. 어느 경우에나 (코아세르베이트

polymer n. 중합체(重合體)
aggregate n. 집합(체)
polypeptide n. 폴리펩티드
polynucleotide n. 폴리뉴클레오티드(DNA 또는 RNA 상의 뉴클레오티드의 배열)
solution n. 용액; 용해
coacervate n. 코아세르베이트(두 종류의 균질 수용액이 혼합되어 있을 때 생기는 균질하지 않은 다수의 액체 방울)
droplet n. 작은 물방울
proteinoid microsphere 프로테이노이드 마이크로스페어(최초로 실험실에서 합성해내는 데 성공한 단백질과 비슷한 물질)
macromolecule n. 고분자
membrane n. 막; 세포막
pronounced a. 확연한; 단호한, 천명된

방울이건 프로테이노이드 마이크로스페어이건 간에) 이 '원시 유기체'들은 구조적으로 복잡하며 그 주변 환경과 선명히 구별되어 있어서 주변 환경 속에서는 일어날 수 없는 화학적 반응들이 이 '원시 유기체'들 속에서는 일어날 수 있는 상황을 만들어낸다.

1 ②　　▶ **빈칸완성**

빈칸 Ⓐ 다음 콜론(:) 이하에서, "프로테이노이드 마이크로스페어를 관찰해보면 살아 있는 세포의 번식(생식 또는 복제)과 유사한 화학적 현상들이 일어난다."라는 것을 말하고 있다.

2 ④　　▶ **내용추론**

본문에 의하면 프로테이노이드 마이크로스페어는 뜨거운 폴리펩티드 수성 용액이 차가워질 때 형성된다. 폴리펩티드는 일종의 중합체다. 따라서 ④가 정답이다.

reproduction n. 생식, 번식; 복제, 복사	
cytoplasm n. 세포질	
streaming n. 유동	
superficially ad. 표면적으로, 피상적으로	
yeast n. 이스트, 효모균	
aggregate v. 모이다	
cluster n. 덩어리; 집단	
sharply ad. 날카롭게; 신랄하게; 선명하게	
medium n. 매개, 매체; (생물 등의) 환경	
prebiont n. 원시 유기체	

09

당신은 아마도 사람들이 스스로를 엄격하게 "우뇌지향적인" 혹은 "좌뇌지향적인"이라고 묘사하는 말을 들어왔을 것이다. 좌뇌지향적인 사람들은 대개 그들의 수학적인 재능을 자랑하고 우뇌지향적인 사람들은 그들의 창조성을 크게 선전한다. 그것은 뇌가 각각의 절반이 명백하게 구별되는 일련의 작업들을 수행하는 두 개의 반구로 나누어져 있기 때문이다. 로저 스페리(Roger Sperry)에 따르면, 인간의 뇌의 반구들은 서로가 서로에 대해 독립적이면서도 협력적인 방식으로 작동한다고 한다. 두 반구들은 그들을 이어주는 두툼한 뇌량을 통해서 감각기관에 의한 관찰 같은 정보를 서로 교환한다. 뇌의 오른쪽 반구가 몸의 왼쪽 부분의 근육을 통제하는 데 반해, 뇌의 왼쪽 반구는 인간 몸의 오른쪽에 있는 근육을 통제한다.

일반적으로 좌반구는 언어를 관장한다. 당신이 듣는 모든 것을 처리하고 말하는 임무의 대부분을 다룬다. 좌반구는 또한 논리와 정확한 수학적 계산도 책임지고 있다. 당신이 어떤 사실을 생각해낼 때, 당신의 좌뇌가 그 생각을 기억으로부터 끄집어낸다. 우반구는 주로 공간지각 능력, 얼굴 인식, 음악의 처리 등을 책임지고 있다. 우반구도 수학을 수행한다. 그러나 그 수행은 단지 대략적인 추측과 비교에 한정된다. 우뇌는 또한 시각적인 이미지리를 이해하고 우리가 본 것을 인식하는 데 도움을 준다. 우뇌는 또한 특히 문맥과 어떤 사람의 말의 톤을 해석하는 것을 통해 언어 작용에도 일정 정도 역할을 수행한다.

어떤 한 사람이 우뇌지향적인지 아니면 좌뇌지향적인지 여부는 물론이고 심지어 오른손잡이인지 혹은 왼손잡이인지 여부와 관련해서, 뇌의 양쪽 부분의 사용과 선호는 단순한 좌 대 우 대칭보다 훨씬 더 복잡하다. 예를 들어, 어떤 사람들은 공은 오른손으로 던지지만 글은 왼손으로 쓴다. "뇌의 불균형은 적절한 뇌의 기능을 위해 중요합니다."라고 유니버시티 칼리지 런던(University College London)의 교수인 스티븐 윌슨(Stephen Wilson)은 라이브사이언스(Live Science)와의 인터뷰에서 말했다. "뇌의 불균형은 뇌의 양반구에 전문성을 부여하는데, 이를 통해 뇌는 처리능력을 향상시키고 뇌의 양반구가 책임을 떠맡고자 시도하는 과정에서 발생하는 갈등 상황을 피하게 해줍니다."

1 ②　　▶ **빈칸완성**

빈칸 Ⓐ는 'than just a simple left vs. right equation'라는 단서로부터 정답을 추론할 수 있다. 빈칸 Ⓑ는 뇌의 두 영역이 저마다 특화된 기능을 가지고 있다는 진술로부터 정답을 유추할 수 있다. ① 간단한 ― 균형 ③ 흥미를 자아내는; 음모를 꾸미는 ― 구조 ④ 본래의 ― 출현

2 ③　　▶ **글의 목적**

이 글은 좌뇌와 우뇌의 기능을 비교분석하는 것을 통해서 뇌의 구조를 살펴보고 있다. 따라서 ③이 정답이다.

brag v. 자랑하다	
tout v. 크게 선전하다	
in concert with 협력하여	
corpus callosum 뇌량	
in charge of 책임이 있는, 담당하는	
computation n. 계산	
retrieve v. 회수하다; 생각해내다	
spatial a. 공간의; 공간적인	
rough a. 대강의, 대략적인	
comprehend v. 이해하다	
make sense of ~을 이해하다	

10

생태학자들은 열대우림의 매우 높은 생물다양성의 유래에 대해 오랫동안 논의해오고 있으며 지금까지는 만족스러운 설명을 내놓지 못했다. 무엇이 이 큰 다양성의 원인인지는 끈질기게 남아서 아직도 수수께끼인 문제다. 처음에는 많은 강우량과 높은 기온으로 인한 높은 생산성이 많은 다양성을 촉진시킬 것으로 여겨졌다. 그러나 생태학자들이 이런 생각을 면밀히 조사해보았을 때 그것은 사실이 아닌 것으로 드러났다. 사실, 더 큰 생산성이 실제로는 훨씬 더 낮은 다양성을 낳을 수도 있다는 설득력 있는 주장들이 있다. 단위 시간당 얼마나 많은 물질이 실제로 생산되느냐 하는 관점에서 보면, 세계에서 가장 생산성이 큰 생태계는 오늘날의 옥수수 밭이다. <다른 생태학자들은 대 빙하기들 동안 많은 온대지역을 뒤덮은 얼음장이 열대지방에는 없는 기간이 길어진 것이 더 많은 다양한 종류의 생물이 진화하도록 허용했다는 뜻의 말을 해왔다.> 그러나 여기에도 또한 반론이 있으며 이 "시간 가설"은 여전히 기껏해야 논란이 되는 정도다. 우리는 다양한 다른 설명들을 계속 논의할 수도 있겠지만 그 설명들 각각에서 전개되는 이야기는 마찬가지다. 뉴턴은 중력 법칙을 설명할 수 있었고 다윈은 생물들이 어떻게 진화했는가를 설명했지만, 왜 (열대지방 같은) 일부 지역에는 그렇게도 많은 종들이 있는 반면에 (북극지방 같은) 또 다른 지역에는 그렇게도 적은 종들이 있는지에 대해서는 이에 견줄만한 설명이 아직 존재하지 않는다.

1 ②　▶ **빈칸완성**
뒤의 and 다음에 '여전히 수수께끼인' 문제라 했으므로 ⓐ에는 persistent(끈질기게 남아있는)나 long-lasting(오래 지속되는)이 적절하고, 앞 문장에서 '높은 생산성이 많은 다양성을 촉진시킬 것이라는 생각이 사실이 아닌 것으로 드러났다'고 했으므로 ⓑ에는 lower가 적절하다. ① 통찰력 있는 — 더 높은 ③ 오래 지속되는 — 더 높은 ④ 명백한 — 더 낮은

2 ④　▶ **내용추론**
마지막 문장은 생물다양성의 원인에 대해서는 뉴턴의 중력 법칙이나 다윈의 진화론처럼 확실한 설명이 아직은 없다는 뜻이므로 ④가 추론할 수 없는 진술이다.

3 ③　▶ **문장삽입**
제시문이 Other ecologists로 시작되므로 처음 제시된 설명인 고온다습한 기후로 인한 높은 생산성이 많은 생물다양성의 원인이라고 하는 것과 그것이 성립될 수 없음을 언급한 다음인 ⓒ에 들어가는 것이 적절하다. 그러면 그다음 문장의 '시간 가설'이 이를 가리킨다.

biodiversity n. 생물다양성
come up with (답을) 찾아내다, 생각해내다
persistent a. 끈질기게 지속되는
enigmatic a. 수수께끼 같은
cornfield n. 옥수수 밭
duration n. 지속시간
the tropics 열대지방
hypothesis n. 가설
controversial a. 논란이 되는
gravity n. 중력
comparable a. 비교할만한, 견줄만한

11

충양돌기라고도 알려져 있는 사람의 충수는 대장과 소장이 연결되는 부분 근처에 위치한 신체기관이다. 보통 이 기관은 몸의 오른쪽 복부 아래, 다리 위쪽 부분에 위치하고 있다. 길이가 1~2인치에 불과한 충수는 대략 손가락 하나 크기다. 인간 이외의 다른 많은 포유동물들도 충수를 갖고 있다. 이런 사실에도 불구하고, 과학자들은 충수의 기능이 정확히 무엇인지에 대해 의견의 일치를 보지 못하고 있다. 일부 생물학자들은 충수는 몸이 질병을 이겨낼 수 있게 도와주는 면역체계의 일부라고 주장하기도 한다. 하지만, 이 이론에는 몇 가지 결함이 있다.
사람의 충수가 신체 건강 유지를 돕는다는 가설은 토끼의 충수 연구에 근거한 것이다. 토끼의 경우에는 이 기관이 면역반응과 연관된 특정 중요 세포조직들이 몰려있는 곳이므로, 충수가 없는 토끼는 병에 걸리는 경우가 많다. 하지만, 토끼의 충수로 사람의 충수 기능을 미루어 짐작할 수 있을지는 분명하지 않다. 양자를 서로 비교해보면 의문이 드는 것이, 토끼의 충수는 사람의 충수와 모양도 다를 뿐만 아니라 크기도 비교적 더 크다. 더욱이, 이 두 기관들이 수렴 진화로 형성되었다고 보는 생물학자들이 많다. 수렴 진화란 생물체들이 독립적으로 서로 비슷한 특성을 발전시키는 경우를 말한다. 예를 들어, 오리와 꿀벌은 모두 날개가 있지만, 이들은 서로 따로따로 진화했으며, 공통의 조상으로부터 날개를 물려받은 것도 아니다. 이 사실이 중요한 이유는 수렴 진화를 통해 얻게 된 기관들은 서로 비슷해 보이지만, 이들이 반드시 동일한 목적이나 기능을 가지고 있지는 않기 때문이다.

appendix n. 충수, 맹장
vermiform appendix 충양돌기
intestine n. 장(腸)
mammal n. 포유동물, 포유류
immune system 면역체계
flaw n. 결점, 결함
hypothesis n. 가설, 가정
comparison n. 비교, 대조; 유사
relatively ad. 비교적; 상대적으로
convergent a. 한 점으로 향하는, 수렴하는
attribute n. 속성, 특성, 특질
inherit v. 상속하다; 물려받다, 유전하다

1 ① ▶ 내용파악

사람의 충수는 대장과 소장이 연결되는 부분 근처, 몸의 오른쪽 복부 아래, 다리 위쪽 부분에 위치한다고 했다. 따라서 위와 대장 및 소장 사이에 위치한다고 언급한 ①은 사실이 아니다.

2 ③ ▶ 내용파악

토끼의 충수와 인간의 충수에 대한 비교가 문제가 있다는 이유로 ①, ②, ④는 본문에 언급되어 있다. 하지만 ③ "인간의 충수가 면역체계의 일부인 독특한 조직을 가지고 있다."라는 언급은 없으며, 면역반응과 연관된 특정 중요 세포들이 몰려있는 곳은 토끼의 충수라고 했으므로 인간과 토끼의 충수에 대한 비교의 이유로 적절치 않다.

3 ④ ▶ 내용파악

글쓴이가 수렴 진화를 설명하기 위해 언급한 내용으로 ① 오리와 벌의 날개를 비교하며 예를 들었으며, ② 수렴 진화를 통해 얻게 된 기관들이 반드시 동일한 목적을 가지고 있지 않다고 했으며, ③ 수렴 진화란 생물체들이 독립적으로 서로 비슷한 특성을 발전시키는 경우를 말한다고 했으므로 ①, ②, ③은 모두 맞게 언급되었지만, ④ 오리와 벌을 예로 들며 수렴 진화가 공통의 조상으로부터 유전 받은 것은 아니라고 했으므로 ④가 정답이다.

12

요컨대 단백질은 복잡한 실체다. 헤모글로빈은 겨우 146개의 아미노산 길이로서 단백질 기준에서 보자면 보잘것없는 존재지만 이것조차도 10190개의 아미노산 결합이 가능하다. 바로 이 점 때문에 케임브리지 대학의 화학자 맥스 퍼루츠(Max Perutz)가 23년의 경력 대부분 동안 그 비밀을 풀려고 하고 있다. 우연히 단 하나의 단백질이 만들어지는 것도 엄청날 만큼 불가능해 보인다. 그것은 마치 고물 야적장에 회오리바람이 불고 났더니 완전한 형태의 점보제트기가 조립될 가능성에 해당한다고 천문학자 프레드 호일(Fred Hoyle)은 흥미진진한 비유를 하였다.

그러나 우리는 지금 각각 고유하면서, 우리가 아는 한 당신의 건강과 행복을 유지하는 데 결정적인 수십만 가지 유형의, 아마도 약 백만 개에 달하는 단백질의 유형에 대해 이야기하고 있다. 그리고 그것은 그곳에서부터 계속된다. 단백질이 유용하려면, 올바른 순서에 따라 아미노산이 조립되는 것뿐만 아니라 일종의 화학적 종이접기가 있어야 하고, 아주 구체적인 형태로 접혀야 한다. 이런 구조적 복잡성을 성취했다 하더라도 만약 그것이 자가 복제를 할 수 없으면 당신에게 쓸모없는데, 단백질은 자가 복제를 할 수 없다. 그렇기 때문에 당신에게는 DNA가 필요하다. DNA는 복제의 달인이다. 그것은 몇 초 안에 스스로를 복제할 수 있지만 다른 것은 사실상 전혀 할 수 없다. 그래서 우리는 역설적인 상황에 처한다. 단백질은 DNA 없이 존재할 수 없고, DNA는 단백질이 없다면 소용이 없다. 그렇다면 이들은 서로를 지탱하기 위한 목적을 갖고 동시에 발생했다고 가정해야 하는 것인가? 만약 그렇다면, 이는 아주 놀라운 일이 아닐 수 없다.

그리고 그뿐만이 아니다. DNA와 단백질, 그리고 생명의 다른 구성요소들은 그들을 담아줄 세포막이 없다면 번영할 수 없다. 원자나 분자만으로 생명체가 이루어진 적은 한 번도 없다. 만약 당신의 몸에서 어떤 원자를 떼어낸다면, 그것은 모래알과 마찬가지로 살아 있지 못한다. 오로지 세포라는 양육하는 안전구역 안에 있을 때에만 이들 다양한 물질들은 우리가 생명이라 부르는 놀라운 춤에 참여할 수 있다. 세포가 없다면 이들은 그냥 흥미로운 화학물질에 불과하다. 그러나 이 화학물질들이 없다면 세포도 아무 소용이 없다. 물리학자 폴 데이비스(Paul Davies)가 표현하듯이 "만약 모든 것이 모든 것을 필요로 한다면, 애초에 분자들의 공동체는 어떻게 생겨날 수 있었을까?"

이것은 마치 당신의 부엌에 있던 모든 요리재료들이 어찌해서 한데 뭉쳐지고 스스로 구워져서 하나의 케이크가 된 것과 같다. 그뿐만 아니라 그 케이크는 필요하다면 더 많은 케이크들이 만들어질 수 있을 만큼 분할이 가능하다는 것이다. 우리가 이것을 생명의 기적이라고 불러도 과언이 아닐 것이다. 이제 겨우 우리가 그것을 이해하기 시작했다는 것도 그리 놀라운 것은 아니다.

1 ④ ▶ 글의 제목

DNA가 단백질을 필요로 하고, 단백질은 DNA를 필요로 하며 홀로 있어서는 의미가 없다고 한다. 이것은 말 그대로 생명은 생명이기 위해 존재한다는 것이고, 그렇기 때문에 필자는 이것을 생명의 기적이라고 불렀다. 이러한 취지를 가장 잘 담아낸 제목은 ④의

---

entity n. 실체, 본체

runt n. (한배에서 태어난 새끼들 중) 제일 작고 약한 녀석; 왜소한[보잘것없는] 사람

unravel v. (수수께끼 등을) 풀다

stunning a. 깜짝 놀랄

whirlwind n. 선풍, 돌개바람

junkyard n. 고물 야적장, 고물 집적소

simile n. 직유

origami n. 종이접기

whiz n. 달인, 명수, 수완가

replicate v. 복제하다

membrane n. 세포막

pluck v. 뽑다, 뜯다

nurture v. 보살피다, 육성하다

ingredient n. 성분, 재료

'생명은 생명에서 유래한다'이다.

2 ③ ▶ **내용일치**
"만약 당신의 몸에서 어떤 원자를 떼어낸다면, 그것은 모래알과 마찬가지로 살아 있지
못하다."라는 진술을 고려하면 ③은 틀린 진술이다.

13

인간의 모유에는 당 성분인 젖당이 들어있다. 우리가 아기들에 대해 알고 있는 것은 아기들이 태어
날 때부터 단맛을 선호한다는 것이다. 불과 2백 년 전만 해도 당신이 어머니나 유모에게서 젖을 먹
지 못했다면 생존할 확률이 거의 없었다. 쓴맛이 나는 음식을 싫어하는 것 또한 선천적인 것이며,
생존 가치와 관련되어 있다. 이것은(쓴맛이 나는 음식을 싫어하는 것)은 우리가 독소를 섭취하는 것
을 피하도록 도와주는데 식물은 인간을 포함하여 먹히지 않기 위해 진화하면서 독소를 가지게 되
었다.
음식인가 독인가? 척추동물은 바다에서 5억 년도 더 전에 생겨났으며 미각은 주로 그런 문제(음식
과 독을 구분하는 문제)를 해결하는 방법으로 진화해 왔다. 모든 척추동물들이 반드시 같은 곳에
미각 수용기를 갖고 있는 것은 아니지만 인간과 비슷한 미각 수용기가 있다. 큰 메기의 수염에는
수십 명의 사람의 혀에 있는 미각 수용기보다 더 많은 미각 수용기가 있다.
인간 발달의 가장 원시적이고 오래된 뇌간 이외에는 실질적으로 뇌가 없이 태어난 무뇌증의 유아
들은 외견상 기뻐하는 표정으로 단맛에 반응한다. 브로콜리에 대해 얼굴을 찡그리는 것 또한 원시
적이다. 실제로 우리의 혀는 단맛을 느끼는 수용체가 한두 개밖에 되지 않지만, 쓴 맛을 느끼는 수
용체는 적어도 24개가 된다. 이것은 독소를 피하는 것이 우리 조상들에게 얼마나 중요했는지를 보
여주는 증거다. 오늘날 우리 대부분이 겪고 있는 문제는 이와 다르다. 우리가 음식을 통해 얻는 즐
거움이 우리를 곤란에 빠트리게 한다. <현대의 음식 환경은 엄청난 즐거움의 원천이며 우리의 조
상들이 진화해온 즐거움의 원천보다 훨씬 더 풍부한 원천이다. 그리고 우리가 그들에게서 물려받
은 음식 선호도는 종종 우리가 좋아하는 것을 우리에게 파는 데 점점 능숙해진 음식 산업과 함께
우리가 건강에 안 좋은 습관을 갖게 한다.>
음식에 대한 집착은 미각 연구에 붐을 일으켰다. 그것은 매우 복잡한 감각으로 시각보다 더 복잡한
것으로 드러났다. 과학자들은 최근에 미각 수용기와 그것들을 부호화하는 유전자를 식별하는 데
상당한 진전을 이뤘지만, 그들은 우리의 음식에 대한 경험을 만들어 내는 감각 기관을 제대로 이해
하고 있지 못하다.

1 ④ ▶ **내용일치**
뇌간 이외에는 실질적으로 뇌가 없이 태어난 무뇌증의 유아들 또한 단맛에 반응한다고
했으므로, 쓴맛을 제외하고 다른 맛에는 반응할 수 없다고 한 ④는 이 글의 내용과 일치
하지 않는다.

2 ③ ▶ **문장삽입**
제시문은 즐거움의 원천인 음식이 과거보다 더 풍부해져 우리가 건강에 안 좋은 습관을
갖게 한다고 했으므로 그 앞 내용에는 인간이 음식을 통해 느끼는 즐거움이 우리를 곤란
하게 한다는 부정적인 내용이 와야 한다. 따라서 제시문은 ⓒ에 삽입되어야 한다.

3 ① ▶ **부분이해**
두 번째 단락에서 "음식인가 독인가?"라고 물으며 이 문제를 해결하는 방법으로 진화해
왔다고 했으므로 ⓐ settling that issue는 ① '음식과 독을 구분하는 것'을 의미한다고
볼 수 있다.

---

lactose n. 젖당, 락토오스

wet nurse 유모

aversion n. 혐오, 반감

inborn a. 선천성의

ingest v. 섭취하다

vertebrate n. 척추동물

taste receptor 미각 수용기

whisker n. (고양이·범·메기 따위의) 수염

anencephalic a. 무뇌증(anencephaly)의

brain stem 뇌간

grimace n. 얼굴을 찡그림

preoccupation n. 정신이 팔려 있음, (~에의) 몰두

14

영화 "쥐라기 공원(Jurassic Park)"의 중심이 되는 생각인 복원된 DNA를 이용하여 멸종된 종을 "유전적으로 부활시키는" 것은 북극 툰드라 지대에서 마지막 남은 거대한 동물이 사라지고 수천 년이 지난 후 털로 덮인 매머드를 되살리는 것을 목표로 하는 새로운 회사의 설립과 함께 점점 현실에 더 가까워지고 있을지도 모른다.

1,500만 달러의 아낌없는 자금을 받은 하버드 대학교의 유전학 교수인 조지 처치(George Church)는 유전자 염기서열 및 유전자 접합에 대한 선구적인 연구로 유명한데, 그는 보도 자료에서 대담한 말로 그 회사는 매머드가 "다시 북극 툰드라를 걸을 수 있는" 시대를 열 수 있기를 희망한다고 했다. 확실히 처치의 회사인 콜로설(Colossal)이 제안하고 있는 것은 (유전자 가위인) 크리스퍼(CRISPR-Cas9)로 알려진 유전자 편집 도구를 사용하여 냉동되어 있는 매머드 표본에서 발견된 DNA 조각의 일부를 매머드의 가장 가까운 살아있는 친척인 아시아 코끼리의 DNA와 접합하여 만들어진 잡종이 될 것이다. "매머펀트"로 알려진 실험 결과로 만들어질 동물은 털로 덮인 매머드와 모습이 흡사하게 보이고 아마도 비슷하게 행동할 것이다.

그러나 확실하지 않은 일이지만 콜로설의 연구원들이 매머드를 되살릴 수 있다 하더라도, 분명한 문제는 그들이 그렇게 해야 하는가?이다. 위스콘신 주의 메나샤(Menasha)에 위치한 바이스 지구 과학박물관의 관장이자 척추동물 고생물학자인 조셉 프레데릭슨(Joseph Frederickson)은 어린 시절 영화 쥐라기 공원에서 영감을 받았다. 하지만 그 마저 더 중요한 목표는 매머드를 되살리는 것보다는 멸종을 막는 것이라고 생각한다. 만약 당신이 매머드를 만들 수 있거나 시베리아에서 살아남을 수 있는 매머드와 유사한 복제 동물처럼 보이는 코끼리를 적어도 만들 수 있다면, 흰 코뿔소나 자이언트 팬더를 (보호하기) 위해 꽤 많은 것을 할 수 있을 것이다. 특히 "감소하는 유전적 다양성"을 가진 동물의 경우, 화석 기록에서 얻어진 오래된 유전자나 완전히 새로운 유전자를 더하는 것은 그 개체군의 건강을 증진시킬 수 있다고 프레데릭슨은 말한다. 2015년 NPR과의 인터뷰에서 산타크루즈 캘리포니아 대학의 고생물학자이자 『매머드를 복제하는 방법: 멸종 생물 복원의 과학(How to Clone a Mammoth: The Science of De-Extinction)』의 저자인 베스 샤피로(Beth Shapiro)는 "저는 매머드가 다시 살아 돌아오는 것을 보고 싶지 않습니다."라고 단호히 말했다. "100% 같은 종을 만드는 것은 절대 가능하지 않을 것입니다. 하지만 이 기술을 매머드를 되살리는 데 사용하는 것이 아니라 코끼리를 구하는 데 사용할 수 있으면 어떨까요?"라고 그녀는 말했다.

1 ① ▶ **빈칸완성**
빈칸 Ⓐ 다음에 처치의 회사인 콜로설이 복원하게 될 매머드에 대해 설명하고 있는데, 크리스퍼라는 유전자 편집 도구를 사용하여 매머드의 DNA와 아시아 코끼리의 DNA를 접합하여 "매머펀트"를 만들게 될 것이라고 했다. 이는 서로 다른 종이 유전적으로 접합하여 만들어진 것이므로 빈칸 Ⓐ에는 hybrid(잡종)가 적절하다. ② 태아 ③ 배아 ④ 순종

2 ② ▶ **내용추론**
두 번째 단락에서 유전자 기술을 이용해 복원될 매머펀트는 매머드와 흡사하게 보이고 아마도 비슷하게 행동할 것이라고 했으므로, 코끼리의 특징도 아울러 가진 털이 많은 매머드가 될 것이다. 따라서 ②가 정답이다.

3 ③ ▶ **글의 요지**
세 번째 단락에서는 유전 기술을 사용하여 매머드를 되살리는 것보다 멸종 위기에 처한 동물을 위해 사용하는 것이 더 좋겠다는 두 학자의 의견을 설명하고 있다. 따라서 세 번째 단락의 요지로 ③이 적절하다.

---

resurrect v. 부활시키다

extinct species 멸종된 종

bring back ~을 되살리다

woolly a. 털로 덮인

flush a. (~을) 아낌없이 쓰는

infusion n. 투입

bold a. 대담한

news release 공식 발표[성명], 보도 자료

splice v. 접합하다, (변형시킨 유전자 등을) 삽입하다

vertebrate n. 척추동물

paleontologist n. 고생물학자

reverse v. 뒤집다, 역전시키다

emphatically ad. 강조하여, 단호히

15

Ⓐ 면역체계는 복잡한 구조로서 환경적 조건에 반응하여 한 사람의 평생에 걸쳐 형성된다. 바이러스와 박테리아를 표적으로 삼아 공격하는 단백질인 항체는 과거의 침입자들을 "기억하여" 백혈구들이 이후의 감염 동안 신속히 대응하도록 한다. 유럽의 아메리카 정착민들은 가축들과 가까이 접촉했기 때문에 천연두, 홍역, 독감에 상당히 노출되었던 것처럼, 다른 집단의 사람들은 다른 질병들에 노출되기 때문에 그들에게 생기는 항체도 다르다. 그러나 면역체계 이면의 유전자들은 어떨까? 유전자들 역시 특정 질병에 대한 취약성을 변화시키게 될까?

Ⓑ 이를 알아보기 위해 어배너 소재 일리노이 대학의 인류학자 리판 말리(Ripan Malhi)가 이끄는 한 연구팀은 캐나다 브리티시컬럼비아 주의 프린스루퍼트 항구 지역의 캐나다 원주민의 일족인 침샨(Tsimshian)족의 양해를 구하여 이 지역에서 500~6000년 전에 살았던 사람들 25명의 유골로부터 DNA를 조사할 수 있었다. 이 고대의 원주민들 중 상당수가 현대 침샨족의 조상이 되었고, 그들은 1700년대 초에 유럽인들과 처음으로 접촉했던 해양 부족이었다.

Ⓒ 전체 진유전체 염기서열결정법이라고 알려진 기법을 이용하여 연구자들은 DNA를 꼼꼼하게 살펴서 면역반응과 관련된 유전자들을 추려내었다. 그리고 그들은 오늘날 프린스루퍼트 항구 주변에 살고 있는 침샨인 25명의 DNA 샘플들의 염기서열을 확인하였다. 두 집단의 유전자들을 비교한 결과, 연구진은 면역과 관련된 특정 유전자들의 변형체가 현대 침샨인들에게는 드물다는 사실을 발견하였다. 예를 들어, 'HLA-DQA1'이라고 알려진 유전자의 변형체는 침입하는 바이러스와 박테리아로부터 건강한 세포들을 갈라놓는 단백질을 생성하는 정보를 가지고 있는데, 이 변형체가 고대의 원주민들에게는 거의 100% 발견되었던 반면, 현대 침샨인들의 경우 36%만 발견되었다.

Ⓓ 이러한 결과는 고대 침샨인들의 면역 관련 유전자들은 현지의 질병들에는 잘 적응되어 있었지만 천연두나 홍역과 같은 새로운 전염병에는 그렇지 않았음을 시사한다고 연구팀은 오늘 『네이처 커뮤니케이션즈(Nature Communications)』지에 보고하였다. 유럽인들이 가지고 온 전염병이 질병의 지형을 바꾸어놓았기 때문에 생존자들이 새로운 질병에 대처하는 능력이 떨어지는 'HLA-DQA1'과 같은 변형체들을 지니고 있을 가능성이 낮아진 것이었다. "그러한 고대의 유전적 변형체들은 한때는 적응적이었을 지라도 유럽인들과의 접촉 이후에는 더 이상 적응적일 수 없었습니다."라고 말리는 말한다.

Ⓔ 고대의 DNA와 현대의 DNA 사이의 차이를 측정하면서 말리와 그의 동료들은 유전적 변화가 일어난 대략적 시기를 계산해보았는데, 대략 175년 전의 일이었다. 당시 천연두 전염병은 프린스루퍼트 항구를 비롯하여 아메리카 전역에 걸쳐 급속히 번졌다. 가장 취약한 면역체계 유전자를 가진 이들은 죽었다. 새로운 연구결과와 역사적 기록물들을 통해 유럽인들과 최초로 접촉한 지 수십 년 내에 원주민들의 대략 80%가 사망하였다고 연구진은 밝혔다.

1 ③ ▶ 글의 제목
"원주민 인구 감소가 유전적 원인으로 인한 것이다."는 의미를 가지고 있는 ②는 적절하지 않다. 이 글의 요지는 "과거 유럽인들과 함께 들어온 전염병으로 인해 원주민들에게 유전적 변화가 나타났다."는 것이다.

2 ⑤ ▶ 내용일치
Ⓐ 단락의 내용만 놓고 본다면, 항체 형성을 위해 부호화된 유전자가 모든 사람에게 같다는 말은 없으므로 ⑤는 사실이 아니다.

3 ② ▶ 내용일치
세 번째 단락에서 "HLA-DQA1이라고 알려진 유전자의 변형체는 침입하는 바이러스와 박테리아로부터 건강한 세포들을 갈라놓는(선별하는) 단백질을 생성하는 정보를 가지고 있다."고 하였으므로 ②의 진술은 일치한다. "원주민들의 면역체계가 완전히 파괴되었다."고 하는 ④의 진술은 과도하다.

4 ① ▶ 빈칸완성
선조들에게 유익했던 HLA-DQA1이라는 유전적 변형체는 유럽인들과의 접촉으로 인해 새로운 병균이 등장함으로써 더 이상 도움이 되지 않았기에 그러한 특징이 후대에 오면서 눈에 띄게 줄어든 것이다.

5 ④ ▶ 내용추론
맨 마지막 문장의 '역사적 기록물들을 통해'를 고려할 때 ①은 타당한 추론으로 볼 수 있다. 고대 원주민들의 면역체계와 유럽인들의 면역체계를 직접적으로 비교한 내용이나 그러한 내용을 추론할 수 있는 진술은 본문에 없으므로 ④가 정답이다.

immune a. 면역의

antibody n. 항체

tag v. 꼬리표를 붙이다

white blood cell 백혈구

subsequent a. 그다음의, 차후의

infection n. 감염

smallpox n. 천연두

measles n. 홍역

influenza n. 독감

vulnerability n. 취약성

anthropologist n. 인류학자

First Nations 캐나다 원주민(이뉴잇(Inuit)과 메티스(Metis)는 포함하지 않음)

Tsimshian n. 침샨족(族)(캐나다 브리티시컬럼비아 주의 해안 지대에 사는 아메리카 인디언)

skeletal remain 유골

indigenous a. 원산의, 토착의

seafaring a. 항해의; 선원의

exome n. 진유전체

sequencing n. 염기서열결정법

sift through ~을 꼼꼼하게 살펴 추려내다

gene variant 유전자 변형체

infection n. 감염; 전염병

variant n. 변종, 변이, 변형체

rage n. 격렬한 분노 v. 맹위를 떨치다; 급속히 번지다

massacre n. 대학살

01

인도네시아 말레오의 유난히 긴 타원형의 알은 감자와 아주 비슷한 모양으로 보일지도 모르지만, 이 새는 아주 재빠르다. 이런 모루 모양의 머리를 한 새들의 새끼가 부화할 때, 이 새끼들은 거의 즉시(태어나자마자) 날 수 있다. 수년간 과학자들은 왜 조류가 서로 다른 알 모양을 가지고 있는지 궁금하게 여겼다. 일부 과학자들은 형태(모양)가 알이 깨지는 것을 보호하거나 알이 둥지에 꼭 맞게 있을 수 있도록 한다는 이론을 세웠다. 아리스토텔레스(Aristotle)는 심지어 길고 끝이 뾰족한 알은 암컷이지만 둥근 알은 수컷이라는 (잘못된) 주장을 했다. 그러나 이런 생각을 실험하기 위한 종합적인 연구가 이제껏 실시된 적이 없었으며, 이에 대해 메리 스토다드(Mary Stoddard)와 그의 동료들은 회의적인 태도를 가졌다. "새들이 꽤 다양한 형태 — 구모양을 가진 올빼미 알부터 끝이 뾰족한 도요새의 알에 이르기까지 — 로 진화해왔다는 것을 눈치 채지 못하고 지나간 적은 없었습니다."라고 프린스턴 대학교의 생태학자인 스토다드는 말했다. 한 새로운 연구에서 그 연구팀은 놀라운 사실을 밝혔다. 알의 모양은 새들이 더 나은 비행을 위해 진화하면서 변화했다는 것이다.

그 결과는 더 높은 손-날개 지수(hand-wing index)를 가지고 있는 새들 — 가장 효율적이고 이에 따라 가장 잘 나는 새들 — 은 비대칭의 타원형 알을 가진 새들이었다는 것을 보여주었다. "우리는 다양한 알의 모양에 대한 가장 적합한 설명 중 하나가 비행 능력이었다는 것을 알고서 놀랐습니다. 이것은 알의 다양한 모양에 대한 가설에서 많은 주목을 받지 못했던 것입니다."라고 스토다드는 말한다.

1 ② ▶ **내용일치**

가장 효율적이고 잘 나는 새들은 비대칭의 타원형 알을 가진 새라고 했으므로 새들이 나는 능력은 알의 모양에 결정적인 요인이라고 볼 수 있다. 따라서 ②가 정답이다.

2 ④ ▶ **빈칸완성**

빈칸은 알의 모양과 관련하여 연구자들이 밝힌 새로운 연구 결과가 적절한데, 두 번째 단락에서 가장 잘 나는 새들은 비대칭의 타원형 알을 가지고 있다고 했으므로 알의 모양은 나는 능력과 관련이 있다고 설명한 ④가 빈칸에 적절하다.

be no slouch ~에 아주 능하다, 재빠르다	
chick n. 병아리, 새끼 새	
anvil n. 모루	
hatch v. 부화하다	
theorize v. 이론을 제시하다[세우다]	
shatter v. 산산이 부서지다	
snugly ad. 아늑하게, 포근하게; 꼭 맞게	
pointy a. 끝이 뾰족한	
skeptical a. 회의적인, 회의를 나타내는	
spherical a. 구 모양의, 구체의	
sandpiper n. 도요새의 일종	
asymmetric a. 비대칭의	
elliptical a. 타원형의	
airtime n. 방송 시간	

02

지난 8천만년 정도에 걸쳐 약 25,000종의 난초들이 여섯 대륙과 생각할 수 있는 거의 모든 지구상의 서식지에서 살게 되었는데, 서부 호주의 사막에서 중미의 운무림에 이르기까지, 숲의 임관(林冠)에서 지하에 이르기까지, 그리고 먼 지중해의 산꼭대기에서 전 세계의 거실, 사무실, 식당에 이르기까지 다양하게 서식한다.

그들의 성공 비결이 무엇이냐고 묻는다면 그것은 한 마디로 말해 속이기이다. 일부 난초는 그들의 꽃가루를 식물에서 식물로 날라다주는 곤충과 새에게 통상적(通常的)인 먹이보상을 제공하지만, 전체 난초 종의 약 3분의 1은 오래 전에 한 가지를, 물론 무의식적으로, 알아내었는데, 그것은 시각적 계략이든, 향기를 이용한 계략이든, 촉각적 계략이든, 아니면 셋 모두를 한꺼번에 이용한 계략이든, 영리한 속임수를 진화시켜서 꿀을 내주지 않고도 번식의 가능성을 높일 수 있다는 것이었다. 일부 난초는 꿀을 만드는 꽃의 외양을 모방하여 먹이(꿀)를 주겠다고 약속하며 벌을 유혹하는 반면, 다른 난초들은 드라큘라 난초의 경우처럼 곰팡이와 썩은 고기에서 고양이 오줌과 아기 기저귀에 이르는 여러 가지 고약한 냄새를 풍겨서 각다귀를 끌어들인다. 일부 난초는 곤충의 은신처나 알을 품는 방을 닮은 꽃 형태를 펼쳐 보이며 거처를 주겠다고 약속한다. 다른 난초들은 영역 싸움을 유발하여 결국 꽃가루받이가 이루어지게 되길 바라면서 날아다니는 수컷 벌을 흉내 낸다.

orchid n. 난초	
colonize v. 식민지로 만들다; 이식하다	
habitat n. 서식지	
cloud forest 운무림(雲霧林: 열대의 구름과 안개에 덮인 숲)	
forest canopy 산림덮개, 임관(林冠)	
Mediterranean a. 지중해의	
dupery n. 속이기, 사기	
conventional a. 관례적인, 통상적인	
pollen n. 꽃가루	
expense n. 지출, 비용	
nectar n. 화밀(花蜜), 꽃의 꿀	
odds n. 가능성, 확률	
deceit n. 속임수, 책략	

1 ③ ▶ **빈칸완성**

둘째 단락 둘째 문장에서 난초가 번성하게 된 성공 비결이 dupery(속이기)라 했으므로 빈칸에는 ③이 적절하다. ① 천적을 이용하여 ② 주변 환경에 숨어서 ④ 감각을 날카롭게 하여

2 ② ▶ **내용추론**

난초가 서식한지 8천만년 정도 되었으므로 오래전에 생겨난(of ancient origin) 것이라 할 수 있고, 지구상에 거의 모든 지역에 서식하므로 거의 어디에나 있다(ubiquitous)고 할 수 있으므로 ②가 추론할 수 있는 것이다. ① 여러 가지 악취를 내기도 한다. ③ 거의 모든 지역에서 산다는 것은 사막이나 극지방 같은 극한의 기후 지역에서도 산다는 말이 된다. ④ 전체 난초 종의 약 3분의 1은 꿀을 내주지 않고 속임수로 번식(꽃가루받이)을 한다.

3 ④ ▶ **글의 목적**

이 글은 속임수(dupery)라는 난초의 번식(꽃가루받이) 전략을 여러 예를 들어 세부적으로 설명한 글이므로 ④가 글의 목적으로 적절하다.

ruse n. 책략, 계략
aromatic a. 향기로운
tactile a. 촉각의
lure v. 유혹하다
mimic v. 모방하다, 흉내 내다
gnat n. 각다귀(피를 빨아먹는 작은 곤충)
an array of 여러 가지의
nasty a. 고약한
scent n. 냄새
fungus n. 곰팡이
urine n. 오줌
diaper n. 기저귀
deploy v. 전개하다, 배치하다
floral a. 꽃의
burrow n. 굴, 은신처
brood a. 알을 품는, 알을 까기 위한
incite v. 부추기다, 유발하다

03

기공이라 불리는 식물의 숨구멍들은 생명 유지에 필수적이다. 약 4억 년 전 기공이 진화함으로써 식물은 지상을 정복할 수 있었다. 식물들은 기공을 통해 이산화탄소를 흡수하고 산소와 수증기를 방출함으로써 지구의 탄소 및 물 순환의 일부가 되고 있다. 기공은 호흡 능력을 극대화시키기 위해 균등한 간격으로 배치될 필요가 있다. 그러나 식물의 성장기 동안 어떻게 일정한 공간적 패턴을 유지할 수 있는가 하는 것은 그동안 수수께끼였다.

『사이언스(Science)』지에 발표된 논문에서 JIC 과학자들은 세포 분열 후 세포의 기공 형성 능력은 매 분열 후 생기는 두 개의 딸세포 가운데 오직 하나에만 국한된다는 것을 밝혔다. 줄기세포 특성이라고도 알려진 이러한 패턴은 피부나 뼈를 형성할 때 특정 동물 세포에서도 발견되는 현상이다. 기공의 경우 줄기세포의 특성은 SPEECHLESS(SPCH)라고 불리는 단백질에 의존하는데, 이 단백질은 단 하나의 딸세포에서만 활성화된다. 매번 분열에서 세포들의 양극성이 바뀌는 일종의 분자적 춤을 거치며 딸세포는 다른 친족 세포들의 한 가운데 위치하게 된다. 여기서 딸세포는 기공을 만들지 않는 친족 세포들에게 둘러싸인 채 기공을 만들게 되는데 그 결과 기공들의 간격이 일정하게 떨어져 있을 수 있게 된다.

"이런 기제를 풀어낼 수 있었던 것은 오로지 생체 영상 기술과 컴퓨터 모델링 기술의 발전 덕분이었습니다."라고 JIC의 엔리코 코언(Enrico Coen) 교수는 말했다. 과학자들이 애기장대에서 실험적으로 입증할 수 있었던 규칙들을 컴퓨터 모델링 기술은 예측했었다. 그들은 성장 중인 잎 속에서 만들어지는 패턴들을 확인하기 위해 형광성 단백질과 같은 다양한 표지들을 추적하였다. 이번 연구 결과는 과학자들이 서로 다른 환경에 맞추어 기공의 숫자와 배치를 조절하는 데 도움을 줄 수 있을 것이다. 그렇게 된다면 식물들이 이산화탄소를 흡수하거나 수증기를 방출하는 효율성을 조절할 수 있을 것이다.

stoma n. 기공 (pl. stomata)
even a. 균등한
spatial a. 공간의
polarity n. 양극성
ensure v. 반드시 ~이게 하다
unravel v. (수수께끼 등을) 풀다
validate v. 입증하다
Arabidopsis n. <식물> 애기장대
marker n. 표지
fluorescent a. 형광성의
tailor v. (특정한 목적에) 맞추다, 조정하다
diffuse v. 발산하다

1 ④ ▶ **빈칸완성**

첫째 단락에서 "식물들은 기공을 통해 이산화탄소를 흡수하고 산소와 수증기를 방출한다."고 하였으므로 '기공의 숫자와 배치를 조절할 수 있게 되면 이산화탄소 흡수와 수증기 방출의 속도(효율성)를 조절할' 수 있을 것이다.

2 ③ ▶ **내용일치**

셋째 단락에서 "과학자들이 애기장대에서 실험적으로 입증할 수 있었던 규칙들을 컴퓨터 모델링 기술은 예측했었다."고 하였으므로 실험 결과와 예측 결과가 일치함을 알 수 있다.

04

동물의 지능을 테스트하는 보편적인 방법 중 한 가지는 동물이 거울에 비친 자신의 모습에 어떻게 반응하는가를 관찰하는 것이다. 사실, 침팬지나 돌고래를 포함하는 극소수의 종들만이 그 이미지의 실체를 인식하는 것 같다. 포획한 코끼리들을 대상으로 한 다양한 실험에서, 과학자들은 코끼리도 거울에 비친 모습이 자신의 모습이라는 것을 인식하는 행동에 주목했다. 가장 뚜렷한 단서는, 어떤 코끼리도 두 코끼리가 만날 때 흔히 하는 일종의 사교적인 인사 행위를 거울 속 모습을 향해서는 하지 않는다는 점이다. 더욱이 거울을 들여다보는 코끼리들은 사람과 매우 유사한 행동을 보인다. 몸이 더러우면 거울에 비친 자신의 모습을 보면서 닦으려고 한다. 코끼리들이 거울에 비친 모습의 실체를 인식할 수 있다는 사실은 과학자들의 관심을 끌었다. 왜냐하면 이것은 코끼리들이 분명히 많은 다른 동물들에게 없는 자의식을 갖고 있다는 의미이기 때문이다. 이런 자의식은 진정한 의식적 지능의 기본적인 특징의 하나로 여겨진다.

코끼리가 고도의 지능을 갖고 있다는 것을 보여주는 또 하나의 눈에 띄는 행동은 그들이 죽음을 인식하는 것처럼 보인다는 점이다. 코끼리들은 인간과 동일한 여러 방식으로 죽음에 대한 반응을 보인다. 무리의 한 구성원이 죽으면 나머지 구성원들이 시체 주변으로 모여들어 자신의 코로 그 코끼리를 쓰다듬거나 건드린다. 이런 행동은 코끼리가 죽음을 의식적 개념으로 이해할 수 있다는 것을 의미한다.

1 ② ▶ **내용추론**
이 글은 동물의 지능 테스트 방법인 거울 실험에 대해 설명하고 있다. 침팬지나 돌고래 같은 몇몇 종은 그 실체를 인식한다고 했으므로 돌고래가 고도의 지능을 가지고 있다는 ②는 추론할 수 있다. ①, ③, ④의 단서가 될 만한 내용은 나오지 않는다.

2 ③ ▶ **내용파악**
코끼리가 거울에 비친 자신의 모습에 대해 표출하는 여러 행동을 설명하고 있다. 하지만 ③ "코끼리가 만나서 인사할 때 반사된 모습에 코를 비비려고 한다."는 지문의 내용과 부합하지 않는다.

3 ① ▶ **내용파악**
두 번째 단락에서 코끼리들은 죽음에 대해 인간과 유사한 반응을 보이는데, 두드러진 특징이 무리의 동료가 죽으면 시체 주변으로 모여든다고 했으므로 ①은 코끼리들이 죽음의 개념을 갖고 있음을 보여주는 한 지표다.

reflection n. 반사; (거울에 비친) 이미지
captive a. 사로잡힌, 포획된
self-image n. 자신의 모습
telling a. 두드러진, 뚜렷한
clue n. 단서, 실마리
social greeting behavior 사교상의 인사 행동
sentient a. 지각의, 의식의
striking a. 현저한, 두드러진
seeming a. 외관상의, 겉으로 보이는
perish v. 죽다, 소멸하다
corpse n. 시체
stroke v. 쓰다듬다
trunk n. 코끼리의 코

05

백상아리(Carcharodon carcharias)는 가장 쉽게 알아볼 수 있는 상어 중 하나이지만, 백상아리에 대해 알려진 것은 거의 없다. 백상아리의 몸의 길이는 6m가 넘고 몸무게가 2,000kg 이상 나갈 수 있다는 점을 고려해보면 이는 실제로 놀라운 일이다. 그러나 백상아리는 주로 몸의 색깔 때문에 몸을 숨기는 게 매우 능숙하며 이로 인해 (수면) 위와 아래에서 알아보기 어렵다. 그리고 백상아리는 거의 추적이 불가능한 매우 깊은 바다에 틀어박혀 사는 것으로도 잘 알려져 있다.

백상아리의 행동 역시 예측하기 어려운데, 이는 이들이 겉보기에 무작위의 경로로 바다를 가로지르기 때문이다. 이 경로는 수컷, 암컷, 새끼들이 서로 다르다. 어떤 상어는 해안에서 접근해서 다니며, 어떤 상어는 일관성 없이 더 넓은 바다에 머무르는 것을 택한다. 결과적으로 과학자들은 백상아리가 몇 마리나 존재하는지조차 확신하지 못하지만, 백상아리의 수가 줄어들고 있는 취약한 종이라는 데에는 동의한다.

놀랍게도 백상아리가 짝짓기를 하거나 새끼를 낳는 것이 기록된 적이 없지만, 백상아리는 태평양의 깊은 바다에서 짝짓기를 하는 것으로 여겨진다. 백상아리의 임신 기간은 약 12개월로 추정되며 암컷이 새끼를 어디서 낳는지 거의 알려져 있지 않다. 심해의 거대한 동물인 백상아리는 자신의 비밀을 잘 지킨다!

great white shark 백상아리
recognizable a. (쉽게) 알[알아볼] 수 있는
remarkable a. 놀랄 만한, 주목할 만한
be adept at ~에 능숙하다
retreat v. 물러가다; 은거하다
track v. 추적하다, 뒤쫓다
seemingly ad. 외관상으로, 겉보기에는
juvenile n. 청소년, 아동; 어린 생물
hug v. ~에 접근해서 지나가다
gestation n. 임신[잉태] (기간)
deliver v. 분만[해산]하다, 낳다

1 ①   ▶ **글의 제목**

백상아리는 쉽게 알아볼 수 있는 종이지만, 종의 특성상 거의 알려진 게 없다고 했으므로 ① '백상아리의 수수께끼'가 제목으로 적절하다.

2 ②   ▶ **빈칸완성**

첫 단락에서 백상아리가 가진 신체적인 특성으로 사람들은 쉽게 백상아리를 알아볼 수 있지만 이들에 대해 알려진 것은 거의 없다고 했으므로 빈칸에는 '거의 없는, 부족한'의 의미인 ② scant가 적절하다. ① 강건한, 튼튼한 ③ 매혹적인 ④ 상세한

3 ②   ▶ **내용파악**

백상아리는 추적이 불가능한 깊은 바다에서도 살며, 어떤 상어는 해안에 접근해서 다니며, 어떤 상어는 더 넓은 바다에 머무른다고 했다. 따라서 백상아리가 대부분의 시간을 얕은 해안 가까이에서 보낸다고 볼 수 없으므로 ②가 정답이다.

06

중국 북동부 작은 마을 근처의 말라버린 호수 밑바닥 퇴적층에서 캐낸 동양 연꽃 씨앗이 1,200년 이상의 잠에서 깨어나 싹이 텄다. 이 씨앗은 지금까지 발견된 살아 있는 씨앗 가운데 가장 오래된 것으로 추정되고 있다.

이 연꽃 씨앗은 용케도 세월의 공격을 잘 막아냈다. 꽉 막힌 씨앗껍질 속에 있으면서 산소가 부족한 진흙 속에 빠져 있었기 때문에, 이 씨앗은 껍질을 쪼개어 열어 물속에 담가두자 온전히 보존된 유전계와 효소계가 다시 활동했던 것이다. (효소는 세포 속에서 화학 반응을 가속화시키는 단백질이다.) 손상된 단백질을 회복시키는 주요 효소가 발아과정 동안 있었는데, 이 효소는 오늘날의 연꽃 씨앗에도 비슷한 양으로 발견되었다. 회복 효소는 손상된 아미노산을 자연 상태에서 존재하는 기능적 형태로 전환시키는 역할을 한다. 이것은 세포막의 단백질을 '회복시키는' 데 있어 특히 중요하다. 온전한 막이 없으면 세포는 제 기능을 할 수 없고 그러한 손상은 세포의 죽음을, 그리고 결국에는 유기체의 죽음을 초래할 것이다.

의심할 여지없이 그 열매의 구조가 이 씨앗의 장수에 핵심적인 역할을 한다. 연꽃 열매는 원형이거나 타원형으로 길이가 10~13cm, 지름이 8~10cm이며, 열매 한 개마다 하나의 씨앗만이 들어 있다. 열매껍질, 즉 과피(果皮)는 물이 들어가지 않고 공기도 들어가지 않으며, 처음에는 초록색이다가 건조해지고 특히 단단해지면 자줏빛을 띤 갈색으로 변한다. 열매껍질이 단단하고 공기가 들어가지 않는다는 것은 이 씨앗의 특별한 장수에 기여하는 구조적 특징들 중에서도 가장 중요하다.

1 ①   ▶ **빈칸완성**

첫 번째 단락에서 씨앗이 1,200년의 잠에서 깨어났다고 했으므로 1,200년이라는 세월의 공격을 막아낸 것이다. ② 날씨 변화를 알다 ③ 때마침 나타나다 ④ 좋은 기회를 이용하다

2 ③   ▶ **글의 제목**

1,200년간 진흙 속에 묻혀 있다가 다시 소생한 연꽃 씨앗에 대한 이야기이므로 ③이 제목으로 가장 적절하다.

3 ④   ▶ **내용파악**

①, ②는 두 번째 단락 두 번째 문장에서, ③은 마지막 단락 첫 번째 문장에서 씨앗의 장수에 유리하게 작용한 요인임을 알 수 있다. 그러나 ④의 '열매의 크기와 모양'은 아무 관계가 없다.

Sacred Lotus 연꽃

sediment n. 퇴적물

germinate v. 싹트다, 발아하다

ward off 막다, 피하다

ravage n. 황폐, 침해

impenetrable a. 꿰뚫을 수 없는

seed coat 씨앗껍질, 종피(種皮)

mire n. 늪 v. 늪에 빠뜨리다

enzymatic a. 효소의

repair enzyme 회복 효소, 복구 효소

membrane n. 얇은 막; 양피지

architecture n. 구조, 구성; 건축

oblong a. 직사각형의, 타원형의

pericarp n. 과피(果皮)

impervious a. (물·공기가) 통하지 않는

purplish a. 자줏빛을 띤

07

동물의 몸은 무한정으로 작을 수 없다. (몸의 크기에 대한) 많은 제약은 그 어떤 주어진 형태에서나 몸의 크기가 작아짐에 따라 몸의 부피에 대한 표면적의 비율이 커진다는 사실에서 비롯된다. 이것은 온혈동물인 조류와 포유류에게는 중대한 문제인데, 이들은 크기가 작아질수록 열을 더 빨리 잃고, 이를 보충하기 위해 열을 더 빨리 발생시켜야 하기 때문이다. 작은 조류와 포유류는 몸의 신진대사를 절대한계까지(최대한으로) 실행한다. 크기에 대한 이런 한계의 전형적인 증거는 가장 작은 뾰족뒤쥐들에게 있는데, 이들은 피부를 통해 급속히 잃고 있는 에너지를 보충하기 위해 끊임없이 먹고 있다. 바로 이런 이유로 해서, 기록된 가장 작은 조류로 길이가 30mm인 쿠바의 벌새와 알려진 가장 작은 포유류로 유럽, 북아프리카, 동남아시아 전역에서 발견되는 40mm 길이의 에트루리아 피그미 뒤쥐는 알려진 가장 작은 파충류로 주둥이에서 항문까지의 길이가 단 14mm인 카리브해의 드와프 게코보다 훨씬 더 크다. 그러나 냉혈동물에게 열손실은 문제가 되지 않지만 수분손실은 문제가 된다. 이것은 양서류에게 특별한 문제다. 만일 작은 개구리가 건조한 대기 속으로 나가면 금방 말라버릴 수 있다. 어류는 상황이 더 쉬워 보일 것이다. 냉혈동물인데다가 수상생활을 하니 열손실과 탈수는 문제가 아니다. 그러나 그런 동물의 크기에 작용하는 또 다른 제약이 있다. 몸 여기저기에 뼈가 몇 개 없어져도 아주 작은 동물에게는 그다지 차이가 없을 지도 모르지만, 그래도 모든 신체부위들은 제 기능을 해야 한다. 그리고 신체기관의 크기를 어느 정도로까지 작아지게 할 수 있는가 하는 것에는 근본적인 한계가 있다. 한 가지 한계는 신체기관은 세포로 만들어져 있는데 뇌와 눈 같은 복잡한 기관을 만드는 데는 일정 수의 세포가 필요하다는 것이다. 결국, 작은 동물의 기관이 큰 동물의 기관보다 몸 크기에 비해 상대적으로 더 큰 셈이다.

1 ② ▶ **빈칸완성**
마지막 문장의 upshot이 '결과, 결론'의 뜻이므로 빈칸은 앞의 내용을 결론짓도록 채워져야 한다. 앞 문장은 몸 크기를 아무리 작게 해도 신체기관은 일정 수의 세포가 필요하니 더 이상 작게 할 수 없다는 말이다. 따라서 작은 동물의 기관은 큰 동물의 기관보다 절대적으로는 더 작겠지만 몸 크기에 비해 상대적으로는 더 클 것이다. ① 상대적으로 더 작은 ③ ~에 관계없이 더 작은 ④ ~에 관계없이 더 큰

2 ① ▶ **내용파악**
① '하루 중 활동하는 시간'은 주행성(diurnal)이냐 야행성(nocturnal)이냐 하는 문제로 몸 크기와는 무관하다. ② 체온조절 능력(온혈동물이냐 냉혈동물이냐) ③ 동물이 속한 부류(조류, 포유류, 파충류, 양서류, 어류) ④ 신체기관에 필요한 세포의 수

3 ③ ▶ **내용추론**
끝에서 아홉 번째 문장과 여덟 번째 문장에서 ③의 '개구리는 양서류에 속하는 냉혈동물임'을 추론할 수 있다. ① 부피(크기)가 같을 경우, 긴 동물이 표면적이 커서 체열을 더 빨리 잃는다. 구(球)의 표면적이 가장 작다(추울 때 몸을 웅크리는 이유). ② 작을수록 체열을 더 빨리 잃고 그러면 열을 보충하기 위한 신진대사는 더 빨라야 할 것이다. ④ 뇌와 눈 같은 복잡한 기관을 만드는 데 일정 수의 세포가 필요하다고 했을 뿐 뇌와 눈의 세포 수가 같다는 말은 아니다.

4 ④ ▶ **글의 어조**
이 글은 동물의 몸이 왜 무한정으로 작아질 수는 없는지를 주관적인 생각이나 주장을 배제하고 객관적인 사실과 정보를 기초로 하여 설명한 글이므로 ④의 descriptive(설명적인)가 적절하다. ① 훈계조의 ② 자기성찰(내면분석)의 ③ 감탄조의

constraint n. 제약
ratio n. 비율
compensate v. 보충하다
metabolism n. 신진대사
shrew n. 뾰족뒤쥐
renew v. 갱신하다, 보충하다
hummingbird n. 벌새
reptile n. 파충류
snout n. 주둥이
anus n. 항문
amphibian n. 양서류
in a matter of minutes 곧, 금방
have things easier 일이[사정이] 더 쉽다, 더 수월하다
desiccation n. 건조, 탈수
kick in 효과가 나타나다, 작용하다(= work)
scale down 축소하다
upshot n. 결과, 결말, 결론

08

약 800종의 성게가 이 세상에 존재한다. 그것들은 극지방에서 적도까지, 얕은 후미에서 수심 5천 미터 이상의 심해저까지 거의 모든 주요 해양 서식지에서 발견된다. 모든 성게에는 반드시 맛있지는 않지만 먹을 수 있는 알이 있다. 성게는 수백 개의 점착성 관족을 갖고 있으며 한가한 걸음으로 바다 밑바닥을 이동해 간다. 가시로 덮인 외각인 껍데기가 기본적으로 먹고 번식하는 기계인 이 동물을 보호한다. 성게의 골격은 오렌지 조각들처럼 위에서 아래로 나있는 여러 조각들로 나누어져 있다. 몸 안에는 때때로 혀라고 불리는 알집이 다섯 개 있다. <껍데기 아랫면에는 하나의 근육계와 돌도 어적어적 씹을 수 있게 해주는 탄산칼슘으로 된 스스로 연마하는 치아 다섯 개가 있다.> 이 씹는 기관은 아리스토텔레스의 등(燈)이라고 알려져 있는데, 이것은 그 그리스 철학자 겸 자연주의자의 『동물지(Historia Animalium)』에 나오는 설명에서 비롯된 말이다. (학자들은 그가 실제로는 고대 그리스의 청동 등을 닮은 성게의 껍데기를 가리키고 있었다는 의견을 최근에 내놓았다.)

허약하기도 하고 파괴적이기도 한 성게는 환경면에서 바다라는 큰 잔 속의 폭풍 같은 것이다. 지구의 모든 지역에 성게가 너무 적게 있거나 아니면 너무 많이 있거나 한 것 같다. 프랑스인들과 아일랜드인들은 그들 지역에 사는 성게를 여러 해 전에 고갈시켰다. 미국의 메인 주와 캐나다의 노바스코샤 주와 일본에서는 성게의 개체 수가 남획과 질병으로 현저히 감소되었다. 다른 한편, 미국의 캘리포니아 주와 호주의 태즈메이니아 주에서는 그 동물(성게)의 자연 포식자들(천적들)에 대한 남획과 기후변화의 결과로 믿어지는 해류 순환의 대대적인 변화로 인해 광대한 해저 지대가 달 표면을 연상시키는 "성게 황무지"로 변해버렸다. 성게들이 증식하고 갈조류를 씹어 먹고 해양 생태계를 황폐화시키고 있는 것이다.

1 ③ ▶ **문장삽입**
제시문에서 '돌도 어적어적 씹을 수 있게 해주는 치아'라 했으므로 '이 씹는 기관'으로 시작되는 문장 앞인 ⓒ에 들어가는 것이 적절하다.

2 ① ▶ **빈칸완성**
빈칸 앞에서는 성게가 고갈되거나 수가 격감된 지역에 대해 설명하고 빈칸 뒤에서는 성게가 과다하게 증식하는 지역을 설명하므로 빈칸에는 '그 사이에, 다른 한편'의 의미인 ①이 적절하다. ② 마찬가지로 ③ 그렇지 않다면 ④ 그럼에도 불구하고

3 ③ ▶ **내용파악**
아리스토텔레스가 랜턴 같이 생겼다고 설명한 것은 성게가 아니라 성게의 씹는 기관이나 성게의 껍데기였으므로 ③이 사실이 아니다. ④ 성게의 남획에 성게는 희생되기도 하고 성게의 포식자(천적)의 남획으로 성게가 걷잡을 수 없이 증식하기도 한다.

4 ④ ▶ **내용파악**
"성게 황무지"는 거칠고 하얀 달 표면과 마지막 문장에서 짐작할 수 있듯이 성게가 갈조류를 모두 먹어치워 흰색으로 변한 암반 지역을 말하며 백화현상이라고도 한다. 따라서 ④가 적절하다.

---

urchin n. 성게

inlet n. 후미, 작은 만

roe n. 곤이, 어란(魚卵)

edible a. 식용의

palatable a. 맛있는, 풍미 좋은

adhesive a. 점착성의, 들러붙는

tube feet 관족(管足)

test n. 껍데기, 외각(= shell)

spiny a. 가시로 덮인, 가시투성이인

breed v. 번식하다

coral n. 산호, (새우·게의) 알집

hone v. 갈다, 연마하다

calcium carbonate 탄산칼슘

chomp v. 깨물다, 어적어적 씹다

apparatus n. 장치, 기구; (몸의) 기관

lantern n. 랜턴, 초롱, 등(燈)

naturalist n. 박물학자, 자연주의자

tempest n. 폭풍

exhaust v. 고갈시키다

resident a. 거주하는, 상주하는

stock n. 군체(= colony); 자원

drastically ad. 과감하게, 철저히, 현저히

overfishing n. 남획

moonscape n. (망원경으로 보는) 달 표면

kelp n. 해초, 갈조류

09

꿀벌은 만능해결사다. 국제꿀벌연구협회에 따르면, 우리가 먹는 음식의 3분의 1이 꽃이 피는 농작물로부터 얻는 것이고 꿀벌은 이것 중 약 80퍼센트의 수분(受粉)을 책임지고 있다. 꿀벌은 상업적으로 재배되고 있는 적어도 90가지의 식량 생산에 있어 필수적이다. 꿀벌에 의해 수분되는 자주개자리와 토끼풀과 같은 가축용 사료 작물은 고기, 우유, 치즈를 제공해주는 동물들을 먹이기 위해서도 사용된다. 당신이 채식주의자인지 육식주의자인지는 상관없다. 워싱턴 소재의 미(美) 국립 연구위원회의 한 보고서는 정곡을 찔렀다. "꽃가루 매개자의 감소는 지상계의 모습을 실질적으로 바꿀 수 있는 엄청난 잠재력을 가진 지구 변화의 한 형태다." 꽃가루 매개자, 특히 꿀벌들은 전체 먹이 그물의 중심에 있는 핵심종(種)이다. 그 주춧돌을 제거하면 건물 전체가 무너진다.

설상가상으로, 토종벌과 나방, 나비, 박쥐, 벌새와 같은 다른 꽃가루 매개자들 또한 급격히 감소하고 있다는 증거가 늘어나고 있다. 질병은 북미 꿀벌 감소의 주된 요인으로 의심된다. 토론토 소재 요크(York) 대학의 야생벌 분야의 세계적인 전문가인 로렌스 패커(Laurence Packer) 박사는 미국의 온실재배자들이 가장 유력한 범인이라고 믿고 있다. 땅벌은 토마토와 후추 같은 온실재배 농작물의 '수분'에 널리 이용되고 있다. 1980년대에 온실재배자들은 육종기술을 개량하기 위해 꿀벌들을 유럽으로 보냈다. 그 꿀벌들은 동남아시아에서 처음으로 나타났던 단세포 원생동물인 노제마 세라네에 감염되어 돌아왔는데, 이것은 그 벌의 소화관을 파괴한다. 곧, 그 질병은 야생 땅벌에게로 퍼져나갔다.

꿀벌을 이용한 산업의 세계화는 진드기, 박테리아, 진균류, 기생충 그리고 온갖 치명적인 바이러스들과 같은 병원균들이 전 세계로 퍼져나가는 것을 촉진했다. 그러나 과학자들 사이에서는 서식지 감소, 농업 집약화, 화학비료의 일상적인 사용 또한 꿀벌 개체 수를 파괴하고 있으며 질병에 노출시키고 있다는 데 의견이 일치하고 있다. 꿀벌이 번성하기 위해서는 먹을 것이 다채로워야 한다. 그 어떤 꽃가루에도 좋은 영양 상태를 유지하기 위해 필요한 비타민, 단백질, 미네랄, 지방이 모두 들어 있지는 않다.

1 ② ▶ 내용일치

마지막 문단의 "꿀벌이 번성하기 위해서는 먹을 것이 다채로워야 한다. 그 어떤 꽃가루에도 좋은 영양 상태를 유지하기 위해 필요한 비타민, 단백질, 미네랄, 지방이 모두 들어 있지는 않다."라는 내용을 통해, 꽃가루 매개자인 꿀벌에게 충분하고 다양한 꽃가루가 필수적임을 확인할 수 있다.

2 ③ ▶ 부분이해

'hit the nail on the head'는 '바로 맞히다, 요점을 찌르다, 핵심을 찔러 말하다'라는 의미다. ① 기대에 어긋나다 ② 남의 공적을 가로채다 ④ 잘못된 추측을 하고 잘못된 것을 탓하다

3 ④ ▶ 글의 어조

첫 번째 단락의 마지막 문장에 꽃가루 매개자의 감소에 대한 우려가 잘 나타나 있다. 따라서 ④의 anxious and concerned가 적절하다. ① 공정한 ② 분개하고 퉁명스러운 ③ 자기비하적인

4 ② ▶ 빈칸완성

빈칸 ⑧ 앞에서는 꿀벌의 감소에 대해 언급하고 있고, 바로 뒤에서는 꿀벌 이외의 다른 꽃가루 매개자의 감소에 대해 설명하고 있다. 따라서 빈칸 ⑧에는 complicate 혹은 deteriorate처럼 '상황을 악화시키다'라는 의미의 단어가 필요하며, 빈칸 ⓒ에는 주어 globalization과 일맥상통할 수 있도록 around the world와 짝을 이룰 수 있는 spread가 적절하다. ① 간단하게 하다 ─ 전하다 ③ 조명하다, 비추다 ─ 흩뿌리다 ④ 악화시키다 ─ 근절하다.

---

generalist n. 종합 의사, 일반 의사; 다방면의 지식을 가진 사람

pollinate v. (꽃에) 수분시키다

terrestrial a. 지구의, 현세의, 속세의

keystone n. 핵심, 주축, 중추

edifice n. 건축물, 구성물; 체계

suspect n. 용의자, 요주의 인물

culprit n. 범인, 장본인

the digestive tract 소화관

pathogen n. 병원균, 병원체

a host of 수많은

deadly a. 치명적인

intensification n. 강화, 극화, 증대

agrochemical n. 화학비료

play havoc with ~을 파괴하다, 파멸시키다

10

Ⓐ 수십 년 동안 과학자들은 나무들이 지하의 곰팡이 네트워크를 통해 서로 의사소통한다는 사실을 알고 있었다. 이 곰팡이 네트워크를 통해 나무들은 심지어 영양분을 주고받을 수도 있다. 이 놀라운 발견을 처음으로 한 사람은 수전 시마드(Suzanne Simard)라는 생태학자로, 이미 20년도 더 전에 박사학위 논문을 준비하던 중 이 사실을 알게 되었다. 그녀는 다양한 식물 사이에서 매우 복잡한 사회적 관계가 존재하는 것을 발견했다. 놀라운 하나의 예를 들자면, '허브 나무' 혹은 '엄마 나무'라고 부를 만한 나무. 이 나무는 숲에서 가장 큰 나무로 보통 땅속 곰팡이 네트워크의 중앙 허브 역할을 한다. 엄마 나무들은 숲의 나머지 나무들이 잘 자랄 수 있도록 영양분을 공급해 준다. 마찬가지 방식으로 나이 든 나무들은 이제 막 자라기 시작한 어린 나무들에게 영양분을 공급해 준다.

Ⓑ 몇몇 경우 병들고 건강하지 못한 나무들은 이웃 나무들의 영양분을 지원받는다. 거꾸로, 만일 어떤 나무가 죽겠다고 작심을 하면, 그 나무는 자신이 가진 모든 영양분을 빼내어, 이웃들에게 나누어 줘서 낭비되지 않도록 한다.

Ⓒ 나무들이 필연적으로 마주칠 수밖에 없는 모진 환경에서도 살아남을 수 있는 것은 바로 이러한 과정 때문이다. 나이 든 나무들이 아직은 여린 어린 나무들을 키울 수 있는 것도 이 과정 덕분이다.

Ⓓ 아주 드물게 나무들이 서로 의사소통하기 위해 사용하는 곰팡이 네트워크가 이기적인 나무들에 의해 전유되는 경우도 있다. 이 나무들은 네트워크를 이용하여 주변 나무들을 희생시켜가며 자신만 영양분을 섭취한다. 하지만 이런 행동 유형을 보여주는 것은 몇몇 특별한 종에 불과하다. 일반적으로 나무들은 이타적이며, 영양분을 기꺼이 나누어준다는 사실을 연구자들은 발견하였다.

Ⓔ 이 놀라운 체제는 식물이 지구상에서 몇 백 년에 걸쳐 억세게도 잘 살아온 이유를 설명해 주고 있다. 우리 주변의 나무들은 환경 속 생명 없는 고정물이 아니다. 인간관계보다 더 복잡하다고까지는 말하지 못하겠지만, 그만큼은 복잡한 관계로 가득 찬, 살아 숨 쉬고 있는 생태계다.

1 ② ▶ 내용파악
허브 나무가 엄마 나무라고도 불리는 이유는 엄마처럼 다른 나무를 돌보기 때문이다. 따라서 '~를 돌보다'는 의미의 ② care for가 정답이다. ① 반대하다 ③ 잠깐 들르다 ④ 수술받다 ⑤ ~으로 가득 차다

2 ① ▶ 부분이해
이 과정은 결국 지하의 곰팡이 네트워크를 이용해 영양분을 주고받는 과정을 말하므로 ①이 정답이다. ③은 '남아돈다'는 의미의 redundant가 어색하다. 나무는 generous하다고 했으므로, 남아도는 영양분만 주지 않을 것이라고 추측되기 때문이다.

3 ⑤ ▶ 빈칸완성
자신만 살겠다고 영양분을 '훔치고, 빼앗는다'는 의미가 필요하다. ① 대신하다 ② 우회하다 ③ 양육하다 ④ 개선하다

4 ④ ▶ 내용일치
마지막 문장에 대한 재진술이 ④이다. ② 성장 저하는 이 글의 내용과 반대된다.

---

fungus n. 곰팡이

nutrient n. 영양분

incredible a. 믿기 힘든

ecologist n. 생태학자

boost n. 힘, 부양

conversely ad. 거꾸로

go to waste 낭비되다

harsh a. 모진, 가혹한

nurture v. 양육하다

vulnerable a. 연약한

appropriate v. 빼앗아가다, 전유하다

at the cost of ~을 희생하여

resilient a. 강인한

inanimate a. 죽은, 생명 없는

fixture n. 고정물

MEMO

MEMO

MEMO

MEMO

MEMO